1997

MORAL
DEVELOPMENT

A Compendium

Series Editor
BILL PUKA
Rensselaer Institute

A GARLAND SERIES

SERIES CONTENTS

VOLUME

5

NEW RESEARCH IN MORAL DEVELOPMENT

Edited with introductions by

BILL PUKA

GARLAND PUBLISHING, Inc.
New York & London
1994

Library of Congress Cataloging-in-Publication Data

Moral development : a compendium / edited with introductions by Bill
Puka.
    p.   cm.
    Includes bibliographical references.
    Contents: v. 1. Defining perspectives in moral development — v.
2. Fundamental research in moral development — v. 3. Kohlberg's
original study of moral development — v. 4. The great justice
debate — v. 5. New research in moral development — v. 6. Caring
voices and women's moral frames — v. 7. Reaching out.
    ISBN 0–8153–1552–X (v. 5 : alk. paper).
    1. Moral development.   I. Puka, Bill.
BF723.M54M66   1994
155.2'5—dc20   94–462
                                                CIP

Printed on acid-free, 250-year-life paper
Manufactured in the United States of America

Contents

SERIES INTRODUCTION

Moral development is an interdisciplinary field that researches moral common sense and interpersonal know-how. It investigates how children evolve a sense of right and wrong, good and bad, and how adults hone their abilities to handle ethical issues in daily life. This includes resolving value conflicts, fermenting trusting, cooperative, and tolerant relationships, and setting ethical goals. It focuses most on how we think about these ethical issues (using our cognitive competences) and how we act as a result.

These seven volumes are designed to function as a standard, comprehensive sourcebook. They focus on central concerns and controversies in moral development, such as the relation between moral socialization and development, moral judgment and action, and the effects of culture, class, or gender on moral orientation. They also focus on central research programs in the field, such as the enduring Kohlberg research on moral stages, Gilligan research on ethical caring and women's development, and related prosocial research on altruism.

The studies contained here were compiled from the "wish lists" of researchers and educators in the field. These are the publications cited as most important (and, often, least available) for effective teaching and research training and for conveying the field to others. Unfortunately, the most crucial studies and essays in moral development are widely scattered across hard-to-find (sometimes out-of-print) volumes. Compiling them for a course is difficult and costly. This compendium eases these problems by gathering needed sources in one place, for a single charge. Regrettably, rising reprint fees frustrated plans to include *all* needed resources here, halving the original contents of these volumes and requiring torturous excising decisions. Even so, compared to other collections, this series approaches a true "handbook" of moral development, providing key sources on central issues rather than "further essays" on specialized topics.

A major aim of this series is to represent moral development accurately to related fields. Controversies in moral development have sparked lively interest in the disciplines of philosophy, education, sociology and anthropology, literary criticism, political science, gender and cultural studies, critical legal studies, criminology and corrections, and peace studies. Unfortunately, members of these fields were often introduced to moral development through the highly theoretical musings of Lawrence Kohlberg, Carol Gilligan, or Jean Piaget—or by highly theoretical commentaries on them. Jumping into the fray over gender or culture bias in stage theory, theorists in the humanities show virtually no familiarity with the empirical research that gave rise to it. Indeed, many commentators seem unaware that these controversies arise in a distinct research field and are context-dependent.

This compendium displays moral development as a social science, generating research findings in cognitive developmental, and social psychology. (Students are invited to recognize and approach the field as such.) Theory is heavily involved in this research—helping define the fundamental notions of "moral" and "development," for example. But even when philosophically or ethically cast, it remains psychological or social scientific theory. It utilizes but does not engage in moral philosophy per se. Otherwise, it is not moral development theory, but meta-theory. (Several extensively criticized Kohlberg articles on justice are meta-theory.) The confusion of these types and levels of theory has been a source of pervasive confusion in the field. The mistaken assessment of psychological theory by moral-philosophical standards has generated extremely damaging and misguided controversy in moral development. Other types of theory (moral, social, interpretive, anthropological) should be directed at moral development science, focusing on empirical research methods and their empirical interpretation. It should be theory of data, that is, not meta-theoretical reflection on the "amateur" philosophizing and hermeneutics interpolations of psychological researchers. (Likewise, social scientific research should not focus on the empirical generalizations of philosophers when trying to probe social reality or seek guidance in doing so from this theoretical discipline.) The bulk of entries in this compendium present the proper, empirically raw material for such "outside" theoretical enterprise.

To researchers, theorists, and students in related fields, this series extends an invitation to share our interest in the fascinating phenomena of moral development, and to share our findings thus far. Your help is welcomed also in refining our treacherously qualitative research methods and theories. In my dual disciplines of psychology and philosophy, I have found no more inspiring area of study. Alongside its somewhat dispassionate research orientation, this field carries on the ancient "cause" of its pre-scientific past. This is to show that human nature is naturally good—that the human psyche spontaneously unfolds in good will, cleaving toward fair-mindedness, compassion, and cooperative concern.

The first volume, *Defining Perspectives*, presents the major approaches to moral development and socialization in the words of chief proponents: Kohlberg, Bandura, Aronfreed, Mischel, Eysenck, and Perry. (Piaget is discussed in detail.) This first volume is required reading for those needing to orient to this field or regain orientation. It is crucial for clarifying the relations and differences between moral development and socialization that define research.

The second volume, *Fundamental Research*, compiles the classic research studies on moral levels and stages of development. These studies expose the crucial relation of role-taking and social perspective to moral judgment and of moral judgment to action. They also divine the important role of moral self-identity (viewing oneself as morally interested) in moral motivation.

The third volume contains *Kohlberg's Original Study*, his massive doctoral research project. The study, which has never before been published, sets the parameters for moral development research, theory, and controversy. (Major critical alternatives to Kohlberg's approach share far more in common with it than they diverge.) Here the reader sees "how it all started," glimpsing the sweep of Kohlberg's aspiration: to uncover the chief adaptation of humankind, the evolving systems of reasoning and meaning-making that, even in children, guide effective choice and action. Most major Kohlberg critiques fault features of this original study, especially in the all-male, all-white, all-American cast of his research sample. (Why look here for traits that characterize all humans in all cultures through all time?) It is worth checking these criticisms against the text, in context, as depictions of unpublished work often blur into hearsay. It is also worth viewing this study through the massive reanalysis of its data (Colby, Kohlberg, et al.) and the full mass of Kohlberg research that shaped stage theory. Both are liberally sampled in Volume Five.

The Great Justice Debate, the fourth volume, gathers the broad range of criticisms leveled at moral stage theory. It takes up the range of "bias charges" in developmental research—bias by gender, social class, culture, political ideology, and partisan intellectual persuasion. Chief among these reputed biases is the equation of moral competence and development with justice and rights. Here key features of compassion and benevolence seem overlooked or underrated. Here a seemingly male standard of ethical preference downplays women's sensibilities and skills. Responses to these charges appear here as well.

Volume Five, *New Research*, focuses on cross-cultural re-search in moral development. Studies in India, Turkey, Israel, Korea, Poland, and China are included. While interesting in itself, such research also supports the generalizability of moral stages, challenged above. Indeed, Volume Five attempts to reconceive or re-start the central research program of moral development from the inception of its matured research methods and statistically well-validated findings. From this point research is more data-based than theory-driven. It can address criticism with hard evidence. Regarding controversy in moral development, Volumes Four and Five go together as challenge and retort.

Volume Six, *Caring Voices*, is devoted to the popular "different voice" hypothesis. This hypothesis posits a distinct ethical orienta-tion of caring relationship, naturally preferred by women, that complements justice. Compiled here is the main record of Gilligan's (and colleagues') research, including recent experiments with "narrative" research method. The significant critical literature on care is well-represented as well, with responses. While Gilligan's empirical research program is more formative than Kohlberg's, her interpretive observations have influenced several fields, espe-cially in feminist studies. Few research sources have more common-sense significance and "consciousness-raising" potential. The stu-dent reader may find Gilligan's approach the most personally relevant and useful in moral development.

Reaching Out, the final volume, extends moral development concerns to "prosocial" research on altruism. Altruistic helping behavior bears close relation to caring and to certain ideals of liberal justice. This volume emphasizes the role of emotions in helping (and not helping), focusing on empathic distress, forgive-ness, and guilt. It also looks at early friendship and family influ-ences. Moral emotions are related to ethical virtues here, which are considered alongside the "vices" of apathy and learned help-lessness. Leading researchers are included such as Hoffman, Eisenberg, Batson, and Staub.

INTRODUCTION

This volume provides the most empirically based and validated account of moral (stage) development, also focusing on cross-cultural findings. If the first published report of moral development research were *A Longitudinal Study of Moral Judgment* (or *The Measurement of Moral Development*), most criticism plaguing the field would have been avoided. Indeed, little criticism has occurred since this publication, detailing Colby and Kohlberg's fully developed research and scoring methods and statistical re-analysis of data.

Volume Five showcases the "new beginning" of moral development's central research program. It allows readers to see moral development science as it is fit to be seen—with its data properly in the lead. Standard Issue Scoring methods for deriving data from moral judgment interviews are explained and validated. The entire moral-stage research program is empirically reconstructed; with major theoretical claims reformulated to reflect the data base. This reconstruction also preserves the developmental past of this research. So does the Kohlberg, Levine, Hewer reply to critics and accounts of stage-theory applications to educational (Higgins and Power) and prison settings (Kohlberg, Scharf, and Hickey). Higgins and Power also rebut Gilligan criticism. Gibbs' essay updating the crucial "development versus socialization" issue rounds out this material.

Cross-cultural research in this volume helps identify the kind of universality being claimed for moral stages. It also clarifies differences between moral reasoning, orientation, and ideology. Individual studies from China, Korea, India, Poland, Israel, and Turkey, plus reviews of the cross-cultural literature, basically support this unlikely claim. Groups with radically different world views, life experience, and socialization ford the same moral stages, in sequence. But many subtle differences in moral perception and interpretation are found that shift the meaning of otherwise similar moral judgments. A careful reader may come to share the view of many cultural anthropologists: probing ethical relativity among cultures reveals underlying commonalities until subtler probings reveal relativizing influences on those commonalities, and so forth. One sees the need to relate as well as distinguish the developmental and socialization factors of moral cognition.

I. INTRODUCTION

This *Monograph* presents the results of a 20-year longitudinal study of moral development. The study represents an attempt to document the basic assumptions of Kohlberg's cognitive-developmental account of moral judgment. According to this account, moral judgment is said to develop through a sequence of six stages. Kohlberg (1969, 1976) followed Piaget (1965) in defining stages according to the following criteria:

1. Stages imply distinct or qualitative differences in children's modes of thinking or of solving the same problem at different ages.
2. These different modes of thought form an invariant sequence, order, or succession in individual development.
3. Each of these different and sequential modes of thought forms a "structured whole." A given stage response . . . represents an underlying thought organization which determines responses to tasks which are not manifestly similar.
4. Cognitive stages are hierarchical integrations. Stages form an order of increasingly differentiated and integrated structures to fulfill a common function. [Kohlberg 1969, pp. 352–53]

In line with this notion of stages, the cognitive-developmental approach to moral judgment focuses on the qualitative form of the child's moral reasoning and on developmental changes in that reasoning. Kohlberg has attempted to describe general organizational or structural features of moral judgment that can be shown to develop in a regular sequence of stages. The concept of structure implies that a consistent logic or form of reasoning can be abstracted from the content of an individual's responses to a variety of situations. It implies that moral development may be defined in terms of the qualitive reorganization of the individual's pattern of thought rather than the learning of new content. Each new reorganization integrates within a broader perspective the insights that were achieved at lower stages. The developing child becomes better able to understand and integrate diverse points of view on a moral conflict situation and to take more of the relevant

1

situational factors into account. In this sense, each stage presupposes the understanding gained at previous stages. As a result, each stage provides a more adequate way of making and justifying moral judgments. The order in which the stages develop is said to be the same in each individual, not because the stages are innate, but because of the underlying logic of the sequence. (See table 1 for a summary of the stages.)

Kohlberg has hypothesized that the developmental levels that he has described are stages in a strict Piagetian sense. To test this hypothesis, longitudinal data are required following subjects over a relatively long span of time. First, the stage concept implies that under normal environmental conditions the direction of moral change will always be upward. Second, it implies that there will be no stage skipping. The individual must pass through each stage in order to reach the next stage in the sequence. Third, the stage concept implies that an individual's thinking will be at a single dominant stage across varying content, though use of the adjacent stage may also be expected. Previous research has supported the general notion of an age developmental order of qualitative responses and a hierarchy of preference and comprehension in these levels. Such an order has been shown by cross-sectional age studies in a variety of cultures (see Edwards 1981). It has also been shown by a number of training studies which support the assumption that change after exposure to moral judgments at other stages is always to the next stage up. For example, Blatt and Kohlberg (1975), Colby, Kohlberg, et al. (1977), and Lockwood (1977) found that exposure to group moral discussions in which a range of stages was presented in general led to movement to the next stage up. Rest (1973) found that there was a Guttman scale hierarchy in comprehension of the stages, that is, individuals comprehended all stages lower than their own dominant stage, they comprehended the next stage up if they exhibited on the pretest some (15%) usage of that stage, but they did not comprehend stages more than one above their own dominant stage.

In addition to data supporting the general idea of a developmental hierarchy in Kohlberg's levels, a large number of studies reviewed by Blasi (1980) have generally found significant associations between moral judgment level and moral conduct. Reviews of the extant published literature on research in the development of moral judgment based on the Kohlberg levels generally support the cognitive-developmental assumptions about the antecedents and correlates of moral judgment development (see Rest 1983).

The data we have just cited as supporting the developmental level hypothesis have usually compared group means. The results of these studies have not directly supported the strong stage claim, as critics like Kurtines and Greif (1974) have pointed out. In part, the ambiguity in some of these

2

TABLE 1

SIX STAGES OF MORAL JUDGMENT

	Content of Stage		
Level and Stage	What Is Right	Reasons for Doing Right	Sociomoral Perspective of Stage
Level 1: Preconventional: Stage 1. Heteronomous morality	To avoid breaking rules backed by punishment, obedience for its own sake, and avoiding physical damage to persons and property.	Avoidance of punishment and the superior power of authorities.	Egocentric point of view. Doesn't consider the interests of others or recognize that they differ from the actor's; doesn't relate two points of view. Actions are considered physically rather than in terms of psychological interests of others. Confusion of authority's perspective with one's own.
Stage 2. Individualism, instrumental purpose, and exchange	Following rules only when it is to someone's immediate interest; acting to meet one's own interests and needs and letting others do the same. Right is also what's fair, what's an equal exchange, a deal, an agreement.	To serve one's own needs or interests in a world where you have to recognize that other people have their interests, too.	Concrete individualistic perspective. Aware that everybody has his own interests to pursue and these conflict, so that right is relative (in the concrete individualistic sense)
Level 2: Conventional: Stage 3. Mutual interpersonal expectations, relationships, and interpersonal conformity	Living up to what is expected by people close to you or what people generally expect of people in your role as son, brother, friend, etc. "Being good" is important and means having good motives, showing concern about others. It also means keeping mutual relationships, such as trust, loyalty, respect, and gratitude.	The need to be a good person in your own eyes and those of others. Your caring for others. Belief in the Golden Rule. Desire to maintain rules and authority which support stereotypical good behavior.	Perspective of the individual in relationships with other individuals. Aware of shared feelings, agreements, and expectations which take primacy over individual interests. Relates points of view through the concrete Golden Rule, putting yourself in the other guy's shoes. Does not yet consider generalized system perspective.
Stage 4. Social system and conscience	Fulfilling the actual duties to which you have agreed. Laws are to be upheld except in extreme cases where they conflict with other fixed social duties. Right is also contributing to society, the group, or institution.	To keep the institution going as a whole, to avoid the breakdown in the system "if everyone did it," or the imperative of conscience to meet one's defined obligations.	Differentiates societal point of view from interpersonal agreement or motives. Takes the point of view of the system that defines roles and rules. Considers individual relations in terms of place in the system.

SOURCE.—Reprinted from Kohlberg (1976).

3

TABLE 1 (*Continued*)

Level and Stage	Content of Stage		Sociomoral Perspective of Stage
	What Is Right	Reasons for Doing Right	
Level 3: Postconventional, or principled: Stage 5. Social contract or utility and individual rights	Being aware that people hold a variety of values and opinions, that most values and rules are relative to your group. These relative rules should usually be upheld, however, in the interest of impartiality and because they are the social contract. Some nonrelative values and rights like life and liberty, however, must be upheld in any society and regardless of majority opinion.	A sense of obligation to law because of one's social contract to make and abide by laws for the welfare of all and for the protection of all people's rights. A feeling of contractual commitment, freely entered upon, to family, friendship, trust and work obligations. Concern that laws and duties be based on rational calculation of overall utility, "the greatest good for the greatest number."	Prior-to-society perspective. Perspective of a rational individual aware of values and rights prior to social attachments and contracts. Integrates perspectives by formal mechanisms of agreement, contract, objective impartiality, and due process. Considers moral and legal points of view; recognizes that they sometimes conflict and finds it difficult to integrate them.
Stage 6. Universal ethical principles	Following self-chosen ethical principles. Particular laws or social agreements are usually valid because they rest on such principles. When laws violate these principles, one acts in accordance with the principle. Principles are universal principles of justice: the equality of human rights and respect for the dignity of human beings as individual persons.	The belief as a rational person in the validity of universal moral principles, and a sense of personal commitment to them.	Perspective of a moral point of view from which social arrangements derive. Perspective is that of any rational individual recognizing the nature of morality or the fact that persons are ends in themselves and must be treated as such.

SOURCE.—Reprinted from Kohlberg (1976).

findings has been due to the limited reliability of Kohlberg's 1958 method of interviewing and scoring moral stage. The longitudinal data published by Holstein (1976), Kuhn (1976), and White et al. (1978) have shown some anomalies in stage sequence. It has not been clear whether these anomalies represent a failure of fit of the strict stage model to moral judgment development or whether they have represented confusions in the conceptual definitions of the stages or problems in the reliability or validity of the measure. In an early report of his own longitudinal data over 10 years, Kohlberg (Kohlberg & Kramer 1969), while reporting some measurement problems leading to anomalies, stressed a genuine failure of the stage sequence hypothesis in the college years leading to so-called sophomore retrogression in development. In 1973, Kohlberg reinterpreted the anomalies as resulting not from retrogression but from incorrect conceptualization of stages as they appear in development after high school. He reported some clinical analyses of cases suggesting that college retrogressors were exhibiting a stage "$4\frac{1}{2}$" (having moved out of conventional morality but not yet into principled moral judgment) and proposed revised conceptual definitions of the fourth and fifth stages. In fact, such revision accounted for only a few of the anomalies reported by Kohlberg and Kramer. This implied that there were general problems in the reliability and validity of the stage criteria and scoring method.

The present *Monograph* attempts to address the validity of the stage model as applied to longitudinal data and the associated problems of stage definition and measurement which this task has required.

It reports a reanalysis of 1956–68 longitudinal data along with analysis of the subsequent data collected from the same subjects from 1968 through 1976. The current analysis involved the application of a new scoring method, Standard Issue Scoring (Colby, Kolhberg, Gibbs, et al., in press), based on a substantially revised account of the stages. One particularly noteworthy change in moral judgment stage scoring is the omission of stage 6 from the current manual. Stage 6 was omitted partly because none of the interviews in the longitudinal sample seemed intuitively to be stage 6, partly because the standard dilemmas are not ideal for differentiating between stages 5 and 6. The question of whether stage 6 should be included as a natural psychological stage in the moral development sequence will remain unresolved until research (using more appropriate moral dilemmas and interviewing techniques) is conducted with a special sample of people likely to have developed beyond stage 5.

Because the scoring method is critical to the validity of our study, we will include a fairly extensive description of Standard Issue Scoring before proceeding to the Methods chapter.

DEVELOPMENT OF THE STANDARD ISSUE MORAL JUDGMENT INTERVIEW AND SCORING SYSTEM[1]

In the early 1970s Kohlberg and his colleagues began to redefine the central features of the moral judgment stages and to construct a more adequate assessment instrument. Seven of Kohlberg's longitudinal cases were used as the data base for this endeavor. It was expected that this process would yield a more precise and accurate picture of moral judgment development. For example, it was expected that when Kohlberg's remaining longitudinal cases were analyzed using the revised stage criteria, the data would fit the core assumptions of cognitive-developmental theory more closely than they did in Kramer's original analysis. Because the longitudinal interviews used to validate the reformulations were kept entirely separate from those used to generate them, this revision process avoids circularity by allowing a test of prediction to data other than those used to generate the scoring system.[2]

The early (Kohlberg 1958) scoring systems, Sentence Rating and Global Story Rating, were based on what was essentially a content analysis. That is, both systems focused on what concerns a subject brought to bear in resolving a dilemma (e.g., a concern for love between a husband and wife, the importance of obeying the law, a fear of punishment) and treated those concerns as indicators of developmental stage. These scoring systems yielded enough sequence anomalies in the 1968 analysis of the longitudinal data to warrant substantial revision of the stage definitions. This revision process resulted in a clearer differentiation of moral judgment structure from content. That is, more formal or abstract features of moral judgment were identified and formed the core of the new stage conceptions.

The basic developmental concept underlying the revised stage sequence is level of sociomoral perspective, the characteristic point of view from which the individual formulates moral judgments. In discussing level of sociomoral perspective, let us begin by saying that we believe the perspective taking underlying the moral stages is intrinsically moral in nature rather than a logical or social-cognitive structure applied to the moral domain. In this interpretation we follow Damon (1983) and Turiel (1979) in their contention that there are many types of perspective taking, each of which develops separately as a result of experience in a particular domain. In this view, spatial, social, and moral perspective taking are fundamentally different processes rather than applications of a single general structure to different content areas. That is, the form of spatial perspective taking is intrinsically

[1] The research reported here was supported by National Institute of Child Health and Human Development grants HD02469-01 and 5R01HD04128-09.

[2] We will briefly address the issue of circularity later in this paper. For a fuller discussion of that issue and of the theoretical and methodological changes referred to here, see Colby (1978).

6

spatial, not moral or social, and the form of moral perspective taking is intrinsically moral, not spatial or social.

According to Kohlberg (1976), stages of social perspective taking, as portrayed by Selman (1980) both generally and specifically in descriptive concepts of friendship, peer group, and parent-child relations, are parallel to stages of moral perspective taking.

As distinct from descriptive and strategic social perspective taking, Kohlberg (1976, 1981) defines moral perspective taking as being a deontic or prescriptive judgment of obligations and corresponding rights. He defines the domain of moral judgment stages as the domain of justice reasoning and describes the following four moral orientations used by respondents to his dilemmas of conflicting rights: (1) general or impartial following of rules and normative roles; (2) utilitarian maximizing of the welfare of each person; (3) perfectionistic seeking of harmony or integrity of the self and the social group; and (4) fairness, balancing of perspectives, maintaining equity, and social contract.

While an emphasis on justice is most obvious in the fairness orientation, "just," impartial, or consistent and general rule maintenance is also central to the normative order orientation. The utilitarian orientation considers justice as the operation of quantitatively maximizing social welfare consequences. In the perfectionist orientation, the central element is treating the self, the other, and the self's relations to others as ends, not as means. Implicit in this orientation is fairness or avoidance of exploitation of others and the need to benefit them. Kohlberg (1981) claims that justice is the most "structural" or "operational" domain of moral or evaluative thought. For Kohlberg, as for Piaget, justice structures are operations of social interaction parallel to the operations of logico-mathematical thought. Justice "operations" of reciprocity and equality parallel operations of reciprocity and equality in the logico-mathematical domain. These operations are basic to the idea of fairness as a balancing or weighing of conflicting claims through operations of reciprocity, equity, desert, and prescriptive role taking (putting oneself in the place of the other, or the Golden Rule). Each stage uses these operations at its own level of moral perspective. For example, at stage 2 the Golden Rule is integrated as concrete reciprocity, "return favor for favor and blow for blow." At stage 3, the Golden Rule is interpreted as imagining how the self would feel in the other's place before deciding how to act.

The stage 3 moral perspective, then, differs from the stage 2 moral perspective in engaging in ideal role taking in dyadic or group relations. Comparable differentiations between any two of the five stages can be made using the five levels of moral perspective.

These levels of moral perspective, briefly described in table 1, provide a general organization of moral judgment and serve to inform and unite

7

other more specific moral concepts (moral norms and elements to be defined later) such as the nature of the morally right or good, the nature of moral reciprocity or moral rules, of rights, of obligation or duty, of fairness, of welfare consequences, and of moral values such as obedience to authority, preservation of human life, and maintenance of contracts and affectional relations. Within each of these specific moral concepts (norms and elements), the form of developmental change is to some extent specific to the nature of the particular concept in question. However, the general moral perspective can be seen to underlie its more specific manifestations.

The change in stage conceptions meant that the moral concerns which had been considered indicative of stage in the early systems became content in relation to the newly identified structures. This reformulation of core structure implied a need to redefine the unit of analysis in scoring such that the concerns that were confused with stage in the 1958 systems became the units of content for stage analysis in the 1971 Structural Issue Scoring System (Kohlberg 1971). In the latter system, stage was assigned to material within each content unit on the basis of level of perspective.

Structural Issue Scoring proved to be a substantial advance over earlier systems. The new stage definitions focusing on level of sociomoral perspective not only yielded more orderly data, they also made possible a more convincing rationale for the internal logic of the moral judgment stage sequence.

There were a number of problems with this approach, however. The need to determine level of perspective in stage scoring an interview implied that the scoring unit must be large and that scoring criteria must be very general and abstract. This meant that scoring decisions were subjective and often unreliable. Moreover, the reliance of this scoring system on very general features of stage structure meant that findings of invariant longitudinal sequence and stage consistency across issues could be attributed to consistency in or a universal sequence of the general features rather than providing evidence for consistency or sequentiality of the detailed conceptual differentiations included in more specific moral stage definitions.

The aim of Standard Issue Scoring was to overcome these limitations of Structural Issue Scoring—to achieve greater objectivity and reliability in scoring by specifying clear and concrete stage criteria and to define the developmental sequences of the specific "moral concepts" within each stage as well as the sequence of the global or general stage structures. The redefinition of the scoring unit was the key to achieving these aims. An understanding of the general framework of the Standard Issue Scoring System and of the procedures used to construct it is essential to an explanation of its validity. Let us turn, therefore, to a description of Standard Issue Scoring.

The procedure for construction of the Standard Issue Scoring System was designed to avoid the problem of circularity (theoretical verification as a self-fulfilling prophecy). With this in mind, seven cases were selected from

8

Kohlberg's longitudinal sample.[3] These "construction cases," chosen at random from among those tested at all six times, were assigned global stage scores based on intensive discussion and analysis using concepts from Structural Issue Scoring. The responses to each dilemma were then classified into clearly defined scoring units, or "interview judgments." Each of these interview judgments formed the basis for a "criterion judgment" to be entered in the scoring manual. The stage score of each criterion judgment was assigned on the basis of the global score of the interview from which it was derived and a conceptual analysis of the idea it embodied. The criterion judgments generated by these seven construction cases were later used to score the remaining interviews in the longitudinal study through a process of matching interview material to criterion judgments in the manual. Those cases not in the construction sample comprised a blind sample which was not used at all until the scoring manual had been completed.

MORAL JUDGMENT INTERVIEW

Three forms of moral judgment interview were constructed. Each form consists of three hypothetical moral dilemmas, and each dilemma is followed by 9–12 standardized probe questions designed to elicit justifications, elaborations, and clarifications of the subject's moral judgments. For each dilemma these questions focus on the two moral issues that were chosen to represent the central value conflict in that dilemma. For example, the familiar "Heinz dilemma" (Should Heinz steal a drug to save his dying wife if the only druggist able to provide the drug insists on a high price that Heinz cannot afford to pay?) is represented in Standard Scoring as a conflict between the value of preserving life and the value of upholding the law. Life and law are the two standard issues for this dilemma, and the probing questions are designed to elicit information on the subjects' conceptions of these two issues. Of course, the dilemma can also be seen to involve other value conflicts, for example, between the husband's love for his wife (affiliation) and the druggist's property rights (property). In order to standardize the set of issues scored for each interview, the central issues for each dilemma were predefined. This preidentification of standard issues not only allows the sampling of moral judgments about the same six issues (per interview) for each subject, it also allowed the construction of three parallel forms of the moral judgment interview. Thus, the first dilemma in interview forms A and B focuses on the same two issues, life and law. The second dilemmas of the two forms concern the conflict between morality/conscience (whether to be lenient toward someone who has broken the law out of conscience) and punishment (whether to punish someone who has broken the law). The

[3] Each case included four to six interviews with the same subject collected at 4-year intervals.

third dilemmas involve a conflict between authority (e.g., obeying one's parent) and contract (abiding by or holding someone to an agreement). Form C involves the same six issues but in somewhat different pairs than in forms A and B. (See App. A for interview forms.)

The first step in Standard Issue Scoring involves the classification of the subject's responses to a dilemma into the two standard issue categories. This is a fairly simple procedure. In the Heinz dilemma, for example, all responses arguing *for* stealing the drug are classified as upholding the life issue; all those arguing *against* stealing the drug are classified as upholding the law issue. In the follow-up dilemma (Should Heinz be punished if he does steal the drug?) all responses arguing for leniency are classified as morality/conscience; all those arguing for punishment are classified as punishment.

The first step in scoring responses to a dilemma, then, is to separate material into the two issue categories. Since the issue units are large and often contain a great deal of material, Standard Issue Scoring involves two further subdivisions (by norm and by element, see table 2) before stage

TABLE 2

CATEGORIES OF MORAL CONTENT

A. THE ELEMENTS

Upholding normative order:
1. Obeying/consulting persons or deity. Should obey, get consent (should consult, persuade).
2. Blaming/approving. Should be blamed for, disapproved (should be approved).
3. Retributing/exonerating. Should retribute against (should exonerate).
4. Having a right/having no right.
5. Having a duty/having no duty.

Egoistic consequences:
6. Good reputation/bad reputation.
7. Seeking reward/avoiding punishment.

Utilitarian consequences:
8. Good individual consequences/bad individual consequences.
9. Good group consequences/bad group consequences.

Ideal or harmony-serving consequences:
10. Upholding character.
11. Upholding self-respect.
12. Serving social ideal or harmony.
13. Serving human dignity and autonomy.

Fairness:
14. Balancing perspectives or role taking.
15. Reciprocity or positive desert.
16. Maintaining equity and procedural fairness.
17. Maintaining social contract or freely agreeing.

B. THE NORMS		
1. Life	4. Affiliation	(9. Civil rights)
a) Preservation	(5. Erotic love and sex)	(10. Religion)
b) Quality/quantity	6. Authority	11. Conscience
2. Property	7. Law	12. Punishment
3. Truth	8. Contract	

10

scoring begins. This results in a fairly small unit of analysis. The Standard Scoring unit, the criterion judgment, is defined by the intersection of dilemma × issue × norm × element. Classification of responses by issue involves determining which choice in the dilemma is being supported or which of the two conflicting issues is being upheld. Classification by norm is a further subdivision of the interview material by its value content. The norm represents the moral value or object of concern that is used by the individual to justify his or her choice in the dilemma. For example, one might argue that Heinz should steal the drug to save his wife's life (life issue) because of the importance of their loving relationship (affiliation norm). The elements represent the different ways in which the significance of a norm may be construed. They are the reasons for endowing the norms with value. To continue the above example, Heinz's love for his wife (affiliation norm) might be considered an important reason to save her (life issue) because that is a husband's proper role (duty element) because of his gratitude toward her (reciprocity element), or for a number of other reasons. Each of these is treated by Standard Issue Scoring as a discrete moral idea, and each represents a separate unit of material. The procedural complications of subdivision by norm and element were found to be necessary in order to define a unit that was narrow enough to be homogeneous, to capture what seems to be a single, discrete moral concept or idea, yet broad enough to represent the idea's full conceptual or structural significance for the subject. That is, the system provides a way for the scorer to categorize interview material in a nonarbitrary way into manageable, conceptually coherent units (interview judgments) which can then be stage scored by matching them to very specific and concrete criteria in the scoring manual (criterion judgments). (See App. B for illustration of norms and elements.)

This system of content classification provides for a meaningful definition of the scoring unit which, in addition to being essential to those preparing the scoring manual, is also necessary for each scorer in the process of analyzing an interview. In effect, material in the interview transcript is classified according to three types of content category before it is classified by stage or structure.

In addition to resolving the unit problem, this approach is useful in preventing some of the content-structure confusions which have been problems for earlier moral judgment scoring systems. For example, stage 3 reasoning often focuses on love or the affiliative relationship as a reason for Heinz to steal the drug in Dilemma III. That is, the content of affiliation is likely to occur in the context of a stage 3 (interpersonal concordance) structure. Earlier scoring systems, which failed to clearly differentiate content and structure, tended to misscore as stage 3 reasoning that was in fact structurally more advanced but that focused on affiliative content. (For example, "Heinz should steal the drug for his wife because of his deep commitment to her and to the marriage and the responsibility that results from that commitment.") By first categorizing according to content and then addressing the questions of structure or stage, Standard Scoring procedures involve explicit differentiation of form and content and, in effect, remind the rater that identification of a particular content has not answered the stage scoring question.

THE EXPLICATED CRITERION JUDGMENT

A structural or theoretical explication has been provided for each criterion judgment in the manual. Each explication includes a statement of the underlying stage structure reflected in the criterion judgment (Stage Structure), detailed criteria for defining a match to the criterion judgment (Critical Indicators), explanations of distinctions among criterion judgments a scorer is likely to confuse, and several examples of interview material which can be considered to match the criterion judgment. (See App. C for illustration of explicated criterion judgment.)

This criterion judgment format was an important advance over earlier scoring systems. The subjectivity of scoring decisions is minimized by the concrete and explicit specification of exactly what constitutes a match between interview material and a criterion judgment in the scoring manual.

STANDARD ISSUE SCORING RULES

As we have said, Standard Issue Scoring involves first classifying the responses to each dilemma into two broad categories—the standard moral issues for that dilemma. Within each issue a stage score is entered for each match between a criterion judgment in the manual and a moral judgment in the interview. Usually, somewhere between one and five such matches are assigned for the issue. Although in practice these matches tend to cluster at a single stage or at two adjacent stages, there is no restriction in the scoring rules that requires such consistency. The rules allow scores to be assigned at all five stages if matches are found at those stages.

In calculating an overall score for a three-dilemma interview form, one assigns a summary score for each of the six issues. As many as three stages may be represented in the issue summary score. The six issue scores are then combined to yield a global interview score and a continuous "moral maturity" score (weighted average) for the interview. (See App. D for further discussion of scoring rules.)

SUMMARY

In summary, Kohlberg has postulated six stages in the development of moral judgment and has described these stages as characterized by holistic internal organization or internal consistency of structure across differing content and by the invariant sequence through which individuals proceed through the stages. In Kohlberg's early work these stages were assessed using an interview based on hypothetical moral dilemmas and two systems for scoring responses to those interviews: Sentence Rating and Global Story Rating. Some 12 years later, a new scoring system, Structural Issue Scoring, was introduced. From a psychometric point of view, there were serious problems with these scoring systems. The early systems lacked validity as measures of structural-developmental stages since they involved what was essentially a content analysis of interview responses. The later system achieved increased validity when used by very experienced raters but was subjective, difficult to use, and unreliable, particularly when used by those who had not had extensive training and who had not studied with Kohlberg. Data will be presented here to show that the current system, Standard Issue Scoring, provides for reliable and valid assessment of moral judgment stage. This was achieved through redefining the unit of analysis and the relation between moral judgment content and structure and through specifying more precisely the process of inference from interview material to stage scores. We will also argue that this improved method of analysis, when applied to Kohlberg's longitudinal data, provides a more adequate test of the stage hypothesis in moral judgment development than has been possible to date.

II. METHOD

DESIGN

The design of the original cross-sectional study, which was later followed up longitudinally, was determined by a number of theoretical concerns. Three variables were included in the design: age, socioeconomic status, and sociometric status. Socioeconomic status was expected to be positively associated with moral judgment development in part because it was assumed to be an indicator of sense of participation in the society as a whole. Kohlberg, drawing on G. H. Mead (1934), considered this sense of participation to be an important determinant of moral development. Sociometric status was intended to be an indicator of peer group participation, which Piaget (1965) argued was crucial to moral development. The age variable was intended to establish the age developmental characteristics of types of response to the moral dilemmas. These originally cross-sectional subjects, stratified by three levels of age and two levels of social class and sociometric status, were followed longitudinally at regular 3–4-year intervals for 20 years.

At each testing time subjects were interviewed on the nine hypothetical moral dilemmas making up the three forms of Kohlberg's moral judgment interview: forms A, B, and C. At some testings subjects also responded to additional instruments not reported in this *Monograph*, including interviews concerning attitudes toward social and occupational roles and attitudes toward sex, the Thematic Apperception Test, Loevinger's Sentence Completion Test, Piagetian cognitive measures, and Selman's role-taking interview.[4]

SUBJECTS

The basic sample consisted originally of 84 boys filling the following $2 \times 2 \times 3$ factorial design (see table 3).[5]

[4] All of the data from Kohlberg's longitudinal study are archived at the Henry A. Murray Research Center of Radcliffe College where they are available to interested researchers for further analysis.

[5] Girls were not included in Kohlberg's original sample because adding gender as a fourth variable would have required doubling the sample. Given the laboriousness of the

14

TABLE 3

DESIGN OF STUDY

| | LOWER SES | | HIGHER SES | | |
	Integrates	Isolates	Integrates	Isolates	TOTALS
10 years....	6 (6)	4 (6)	6 (6)	5 (6)	21
13 years....	4 (6)	3 (6)	5 (6)	5 (6)	17
16 years....	6 (6)	2 (6)	3 (6)	4 (6)	14
Totals....	16	9	14	14	
		25		28	
			53		

NOTE.—Figures not in parentheses indicate number of cross-sectional subjects who were followed up longitudinally. Figures in parentheses indicate number of subjects in the original cross-sectional sample. As noted in text, five additional working-class subjects, age 19 at time 3, were added in 1964, at time 3.

The population had the following characteristics:

(a) *Age.*—Subjects were 10, 13, and 16 years old at time 1.

(b) *Class.*—To facilitate filling the design, two suburban Chicago school systems were selected, one predominantly upper middle class, the other predominantly lower middle and working class. Fourth-, seventh-, and tenth-grade classes formed the basis for selection. A dichotomous judgment of a boy's socioeconomic status was based on his parents' occupation and education, as reported in the school folder. In spite of efforts to obtain discrete groups, it was necessary to take children along a fairly broad continuum with a rather arbitrary, though conventional, dividing point. The fathers of boys in the lower- and lower-middle-class group included unskilled, semiskilled, and skilled laborers and white-collar workers without a college education. The fathers of boys in the upper-middle-class group included small businessmen, accountants, and salesmen with a college education, semiprofessionals, executives, and professionals.

(c) *Sociometric status.*—When entering a given classroom the investigator described the procedures to be followed, including a "revealed differences" discussion among three boys. The boys were then asked to write the names of three other boys with whom they would like to have the discussion. The sociometric test was informally discussed with the teacher and compared with notes in the school folder before a final selection was made, in order to somewhat reduce determinants of school and athletic achievement and temporary fluctuations of popularity. The teachers were asked to comment on the boys' social connectedness, not on their moral characters or reputations.

As in the case of socioeconomic status, there were not enough subjects available to obtain only extreme groups, so that the dichotomy tends to divide a continuum. Boys who were never chosen or who were chosen once

interviewing and scoring procedures, such a large sample was not feasible. In retrospect, however, the omission of girls is regrettable.

15

or twice but never by someone they had themselves chosen were designated sociometric isolates. Boys with at least two reciprocal choices or who were chosen at least three times, at least once reciprocally, were designated as integrates.

(d) *Intelligence.*—IQ scores were taken from school records at time 1 and were based on various group tests routinely administered in the various schools (e.g., the Otis and the Thurstone PMA). An attempt was made to equalize intelligence for the social class and sociometric groups. Those whose IQs were above 120 or below 100 were excluded from the study. Although complete equalization was not achieved, the IQ differences were small and nonsignificant. Mean IQ for middle-class boys was 109.7; for lower-class boys it was 105.9. Mean IQ for integrates was 111.2, for isolates 104.4.

(e) *Religion and ethnic.*—The ethnic and religious composition of our sample is presented in table 4.

LONGITUDINAL FOLLOW-UP AND SAMPLE ATTRITION

The study included six testing times—the original interview and five follow-up interviews. Because not every subject could be reached at each time, the number of interviews per subject ranged from one to six. Only those subjects with at least two interviews were included in our current analysis. This condition was met by 58 of the subjects. As shown in table 5, the most typical number of interviews completed for a single subject was four. All but three subjects were interviewed at least three times. Age, sociometric status, and socioeconomic status of origin of these 58 longitudinal subjects are presented in table 3.

There was no attempt to locate for later longitudinal follow-up those boys who were unavailable for follow-up at time 2. As shown in table 3, the initial dropout from the cross-sectional sample was not evenly divided by age and social class. Whereas 12 working-class boys dropped out, only 8 upper-middle-class boys did so. Ten of the time 1 16-year-olds dropped out, while only 3 of the 10-year-olds did so. To compensate for the attrition of

TABLE 4

RELIGIOUS COMPOSITION OF CROSS-SECTIONAL SAMPLE

Group	N
Working-class group:	
Catholic	14
Protestant	22
Upper-middle-class group:	
Catholic	3
Jewish	2
Protestant	31

16

working-class subjects, in 1964 (testing time 3) we added 5 working-class 19-year-olds to the sample. Because IQ and sociometric status data are missing for these subjects (subjects 91–96), they are not included in our analyses of social class, education, IQ, and sociometric status in relation to moral judgment. However, because they were each interviewed three or four times, they were included in our analyses of longitudinal sequence and internal consistency of moral judgment. Thus the final longitudinal sample was skewed somewhat toward the younger cohort but was balanced in terms of socioeconomic status. The cohort bias should not affect the basic findings of the study, however, because orderliness of longitudinal sequence and internal consistency of responses to the interview were not related to age cohort.

To determine whether the subset of subjects who dropped out after time 3 were higher or lower in their moral judgment than the sample as a whole, we compared time 1 moral maturity scores of the whole sample, subdivided by age group, with time 1 moral maturity scores of the dropouts, again subdivided by age group. As shown in table 6, the dropout means were almost identical to the total sample means, and there was no tendency for subjects who dropped out earlier in the study to show lower

TABLE 5

FREQUENCY OF LONGITUDINAL FOLLOW-UP

Number of Interviews Completed and Scored	N
2	3
3	8
4	25
5	12
6	10
Total	58

NOTE.—Because interviews from seven of these subjects were used to construct the scoring manual, the blind sample used for data analysis included only 51 subjects.

TABLE 6

TIME 1 MORAL MATURITY SCORES FOR DROPOUTS FROM SAMPLE

	AGE AT TIME 1 (Years)		
	10	13	16
Mean MMS at time 1 of subjects:			
Dropping out after time 2	203 (2)	. . .	. . .
Dropping out after time 3	. . .	. . .	. . .
Dropping out after time 4	176 (4)	240 (2)	260 (5)
Dropping out after time 5	191 (5)	227 (2)	249 (5)
Mean MMS at time 1 of dropouts	190 (11)	234 (4)	255 (10)
Mean MMS at time 1 of total sample	189 (21)	236 (17)	262 (14)

scores at time 1 than those who dropped out later. Thus, mean increase in moral maturity scores over time cannot be attributed to lower stage subjects dropping out of the longitudinal sample.

MORAL JUDGMENT INTERVIEWS

Subjects were interviewed first in 1955–56 and at 3–4-year intervals thereafter. The last set of interviews (including 35 subjects) was completed in 1976–77. Although the probe questions differed slightly from one testing time to another, the same nine dilemmas were used each time. These dilemmas were later used in constructing the Standard Issue Interviews and represent in effect the use of all three Standard Forms (A, B, and C) at each testing time for each subject. All interviews were conducted individually and were tape recorded and transcribed.

MORAL JUDGMENT SCORING

Interviews were scored according to the Standard Issue Scoring Manual (in press) forms, A, B, and C. (See App. D for a discussion of scoring rules.) Because the number of interviews to be scored was very large, a different rater scored each of the three forms A, B, and C. All three raters were highly experienced, and reliability among them fell within the limits discussed in the reliability section (Chap. III below) of this *Monograph*. None of the interviewers participated in coding the interviews. Scoring of all interviews was done blind. That is, raters coded the responses to each dilemma at each time without knowing the subject's age, identity, responses to (or scores on) other dilemmas at the same testing time, or responses to (or scores on) any of the dilemmas at other testing times.

III. RELIABILITY AND VALIDITY OF STANDARD ISSUE SCORING

RELIABILITY

Reliability data of several types were compiled for the Standard Issue instrument. As the following results indicate, the instrument has proven to be highly reliable.

Test-retest reliability.—Test-retest moral judgment interviews were conducted with 43 subjects using form A, 31 subjects using form B, and 10 subjects using both A and B. No test-retest data have been collected for form C as yet. The same forms were used at times 1 and 2 with conditions of testing held constant and intervals between time 1 and time 2 ranging from 3 to 6 weeks. Subjects were chosen from among volunteers in several Boston area elementary and high schools, colleges, and graduate schools. The college and graduate school students were paid for their time. Subjects ranged in age from 8 to 28 years and approximately half were male and half female.

Interviews were scored blind by two raters using the Standard Issue Scoring Manual (in press).

Test-retest reliability figures are summarized in table 7. As shown in that table, correlations between time 1 and time 2 for forms A and B are both in the high nineties. Since the correlations could be very high without much absolute agreement between scores at time 1 and time 2, we have also presented percent agreement figures. For almost all subjects, the scores on times 1 and 2 were within 1/3 stage of each other (one step—from 1 to 1[2] or 1[2] to 2[1] or 2[1] to 2, and so on). If we look at global scores based on a nine-point scale—the five stages and the four transition points between stages—we find between 70% and 80% complete agreement. We also calculated percent agreement using a more differentiated system of global scores with 13 categories. This system includes two transition points between each stage, distinguishing, for example, between an interview that is primarily stage 2 with some stage 3 and an interview that is primarily stage 3 with

TABLE 7

TEST-RETEST RELIABILITY

	Form A	Form B	Form A and B
Percent agreement:			
Within one-third stage................	93	94	100
Using pure and mixed stage scores[a] (N's = 43, 31, and 10).....................	70 (rater 1) 77 (rater 2)	75 (rater 2)	80 (rater 2)
Using major/minor stage differentiations[b]	59 (rater 1) 70 (rater 2)	62 (rater 2)	70 (rater 2)
Correlation $T_1 - T_2$.....................	.96 (rater 1) .99 (rater 2)	.97 (rater 2)	...

[a] Nine categories: 1, 1/2, 2, 2/3, 3, 3/4, 4, 4/5, 5.
[b] Thirteen categories: 1, 1/2, 2/1, 2, 2/3, 3/2, 3, 3/4, 4/3, 4, 4/5, 5/4, 5.

some stage 2. The agreement levels for this system were in the sixties for the separate forms, 70% for the two forms combined.

Overall, then, it appears that, on two interviews conducted about a month apart, almost all subjects receive scores within one-third stage of each other. About three-quarters receive identical scores on the two interviews when a nine-point scale is used, and between one-half and two-thirds receive identical scores with the most finely differentiated 13-point scale. When scores do change from time 1 to time 2, the change is as likely to be negative as positive, so it cannot be attributed to practice effect. There were no age or sex differences in test-retest stability.

Interrater reliability.—Test-retest interviews described above were also used for assessing interrater reliability. Twenty form A interviews were scored independently by five raters. Ten form B interviews were scored by four raters. In addition, 20 form C longitudinal interviews were scored independently by two raters.

Percent agreement figures for interrater reliability on form A ranged from 88% to 100% for agreement within a third of a stage, from 75% to 88% for complete agreement based on the nine-point scale and from 53% to 63% for complete agreement using the most finely differentiated 13-point scale. The correlation for raters 1 and 2 on the form A test-retest interviews was .98. Interrater figures for forms B and C are about the same as those for form A (see table 8).

Raters who scored these reliability data varied in degree of experience using the manual. Of the five form A raters, two were familiar with Structural Issue Scoring as well as Standard Issue Scoring and in fact were the authors of Standard Issue forms A and B (Colby and Gibbs). The third rater was also highly experienced but was not an author of the manual. The other two less experienced raters had learned to score within the prior 6–8 months using the manual. They consulted with more experienced raters as

TABLE 8

INTERRATER RELIABILITY

	AGREEMENT (%)		
	Agreement within 1/3 Stage	Complete Agreement (9 Categories)	Complete Agreement (13 Categories)
Form A:			
Rater pair 1.......	100	88	53
Rater pair 2.......	100	88	63
Rater pair 3.......	100	75	63
Rater pair 4.......	88	88	63
Rater pair 5.......	88	88	63
Form B:			
Rater pair 6.......	100	78	78
Rater pair 7.......	100	88	63
Form C:			
Rater pair 8.......	91	76	52

NOTE.—Correlation: raters 1 and 2, form A test-retest interviews = .98; form B = .96; form C = .92.

they learned to use the manual to score a separate set of practice cases, but this consultation was no more extensive than would be provided at the week-long training workshop held at Harvard each year. Interrater reliability figures between the two "new scorers" and between each of them and an experienced scorer were at least as high as reliability among the experienced scorers. The same was true for form B interrater reliability, which involved two experienced and two new scorers. Thus it seems warranted to conclude that the Standard Issue Manual can be reliably mastered by relatively inexperienced users.

This conclusion is further supported by interrater reliability achieved between an experienced rater (Colby) and a group of research assistants from another university who had participated in a 4-day seminar on Standard Issue Scoring. On 10 of the interviews from a study being conducted by Norma Haan at the University of California, Berkeley, percent agreement between Colby and the Berkeley raters was comparable to reliability figures achieved among Harvard raters. All pairs of scores were within one-third stage of each other; 83% agreed perfectly when a nine-point scale was used.

In general, then, the figures for interrater reliability look roughly comparable to the test-retest figures—almost all interviews were scored within one-third stage of each other by any two raters, and on about one-half to two-thirds of the interviews the two raters assigned identical scores even when using the 13-point scale.

Alternate form reliability.—Alternate form data between forms A and B are based on those 10 test-retest subjects who received both forms A and B and on the 233 longitudinal interviews that included both forms. A single rater independently scored both forms of the 20 test-retest sample interviews. Percent agreement between forms A and B for this sample was comparable to test-retest and interrater reliability: 100% of the interviews were given scores within one-third stage of each other for the two forms, 75% received identical scores for A and B using the nine-category system, and 67% received identical scores for the two forms using the 13-category system. The correlation between moral maturity scores for forms A and B in this sample was .95.

The level of agreement across forms for the longitudinal data is not as high (see table 9). This is to be expected since form A was scored by rater 1 and form B by rater 2. That is, the reliability figures confound form and rater differences. The correlation between forms A and B for the longitudinal sample is .84.

Alternate form reliability figures between form C and forms A and B also represent conservative reliability estimates since they too confound form and rater effects. The correlation is .82 for forms A and C, .84 for forms B and C. That is, form C is as highly correlated with each of the other two forms as they are with each other. Percent agreement figures are also comparable across all two-form comparisons.

Since essentially unrelated developmental variables may be correlated if a wide age range is included, we have also computed alternate form correlations with age partialed out. The partial correlations are .78 for forms A and B, .76 for forms A and C, and .78 for forms B and C. Correlations between alternate forms were also computed within each age group. As shown in table 10, the correlations are low, .37–.56 (probably due to restricted range), before age 16, but at age 16 and above they are in the .60's and .70's. In view of the relatively small sample sizes, the fairly restricted moral maturity score range even at the later ages, and the fact that each form was scored by a different rater, these correlations among the alternate forms can be considered psychometrically adequate.

TABLE 9

ALTERNATE FORM RELIABILITY

Longitudinal sample (N = 193):
   Correlation form A × form B = .84
      (Rater 1 for Form A, Rater 2 for Form B)
   85% agreement within 1/2 stage
      (other % agreement figures not available)
Test-retest sample (rater 2 for both forms):
   Correlation form A × form B = .95
   % agreement (9 categories) = 75%
   % agreement (13 categories) = 67%
   % within 1/3 stage = 100%

22

TABLE 10

ALTERNATE FORM CORRELATIONS WITHIN AGE GROUPS

	AGE (Years)						
	10	13–14	16–18	20–22	24–25	28–30	32–33
Form A × form B:							
r...............	.37	.39	.73	.65	.78	.78	.68
N...............	19	35	43	29	22	35	22
Form A × form C:							
r...............	.37	.40	.67	.59	.83	.70	.47
N...............	19	35	42	31	21	26	11
Form B × form C:							
r...............	.56	.46	.62	.67	.77	.55	.61
N...............	21	35	43	30	21	26	11

EQUIVALENCE OF FORMS A, B, AND C

It has been demonstrated that there are high correlations among the three forms using the continuous moral maturity scores and a high correspondence between the qualitative global stage scores. However, there are small absolute differences between the forms. These differences affect the results of intervention studies with a pre- and posttesting design where one form is used as the pretest and the other as a posttest.

Table 11 reports the stage usage and moral maturity scores on each of the three forms at various ages. It can be seen that each form gives slightly different estimates of moral maturity than the others, and has slightly different pulls for certain stages, for example, for stage 1 and for stage 5.

Because of the slight difference in "pull" between the forms, it is appropriate to provide a conversion formula or scale score which would equalize the three forms. Such a conversion formula adds a constant to the score on each form and a weighting factor for each form based on its correlations with the scores for the forms combined. This formula allows estimation of an absolute change value, given the use of one form for pretest and another for posttest.

Regression analyses were performed to create scale scores based on the overall moral maturity score and using the score on each form as a single predictor variable.

For the sample of 199 interviews with all three forms used, table 12 shows the coefficients and the proportion of variance accounted for by each form in predicting the overall score.

Regression was also performed on each age group, but the number of subjects ranged only from 20 to 40 and the results were highly unstable. In pretest-posttest designs, it is recommended that every individual should be randomly assigned to one interview form for the pretest and receive

23

TABLE 11

STAGE DISTRIBUTIONS OF SCORES WITHIN AGE GROUPS FOR FORMS A, B, AND C
(% of Subjects at Each Stage)

AGE (Years) AND FORM	STAGE								MEAN MMS
	1	1/2	2	2/3	3	3/4	4	4/5	
10:									
A........	5.3	26.3	42.1	15.8	10.5	.0	.0	.0	204
B........	.0	52.4	33.3	9.5	4.8	.0	.0	.0	184
C........	4.8	57.1	19.0	19.0	.0	.0	.0	.0	181
13–14:									
A........	.0	11.1	8.3	58.3	16.7	2.8	.0	.0	249
B........	2.8	5.6	33.3	36.1	11.1	8.3	.0	.0	235
C........	.0	11.1	16.7	55.6	13.9	2.8	.0	.0	246
16–18:									
A........	.0	2.3	4.5	22.7	31.8	36.4	.0	.0	299
B........	.0	4.5	9.1	27.3	16.4	20.5	.0	.0	280
C........	2.3	9.1	22.7	36.4	27.3	.0	.0	.0	288
20–22:									
A........	.0	.0	.0	6.5	25.8	54.8	9.7	3.2	335
B........	.0	.0	3.3	12.2	40.0	26.7	13.3	3.3	319
C........	.0	.0	.0	18.2	27.3	45.5	9.1	.0	325
24–26:									
A........	.0	.0	.0	4.3	17.4	43.5	21.7	13.0	365
B........	.0	.0	4.2	4.2	25.0	37.5	16.7	8.3	354
C........	.0	.0	.0	4.5	22.7	50.0	18.2	4.5	350
28–30:									
A........	.0	.0	.0	.0	21.6	48.6	16.2	13.5	362
B........	2.8	.0	.0	.0	13.9	52.8	16.7	13.9	366
C........	.0	.0	.0	.0	33.3	59.3	7.4	.0	338
32–33:									
A........	.0	.0	.0	.0	4.5	68.2	18.2	9.1	366
B........	.0	.0	.0	4.3	8.7	43.5	26.1	13.0	363
C........	.0	.0	.0	.0	9.1	81.8	9.1	.0	351
36:									
A........	.0	.0	.0	.0	.0	77.8	11.1	11.1	375
B........	.0	.0	.0	.0	12.5	37.5	50.0	.0	369
C........	.0	.0	.0	.0	.0	.0	100.0	.0	400

NOTE.—Rows indicate percentage of scores assigned at each stage on a given interview form at a given age.

TABLE 12

REGRESSION COEFFICIENTS AND R^2 FOR
EACH INTERVIEW FORM

Form	Constant	Coefficient (SE)	R^2
A......	18.618	.913 (.024)	.880
B......	55.400	.833 (.020)	.895
C......	29.152	.909 (.024)	.876

24

a different form as a posttest. Raw scores should be converted to scale scores using the linear transformations (table 12) before analysis and interpretation of the data.

INTERNAL CONSISTENCY

Cronbach's α was computed for each of the three interview forms, using issue scores as items. The results were as follows: form A, .92; form B, .96; and form C, .94. These figures indicate that the measure meets the psychometric criterion of internal consistency of a test. That is, they provide strong evidence that the moral judgment interview is measuring a single construct. Recall in this regard that each of the three dilemmas within each form was scored independently.

CONCLUSIONS—RELIABILITY OF STANDARD ISSUE SCORING

A review of the correlational reliability data for Standard Issue Scoring indicates that the instrument is well within the limits of acceptable reliability. A comparison with related measures may be helpful here. Loevinger and Wessler (1978) report interrater reliability correlations for their Sentence Completion Test of ego development in the mid .80's (using total protocol scores) as compared to our .98. Rest (1979) reports test-retest reliability of .68–.92 and internal consistency reliability of .77 and .79 for the Defining Issues Test of moral development. Recall that test-retest reliability for standard scoring ranged from .96 to .99 and that internal consistency ranged from .92 to .96.

The qualitative analyses emphasized in many studies of moral development require more than high correlational reliability, however. Percent of absolute agreement between global scores is also important. In this regard the Standard Issue System again compares favorably with Loevinger's Sentence Completion Test. Interrater agreement on total protocol Sentence Completion scores using a 10-point scale is reported to range from 50% to 80% (median 61%). This is substantially lower than the 75%–88% for the nine-point Standard Scoring scale and is, in fact, lower than even the 53%–78% agreement on our 13-point scale. Loevinger and Wessler find most protocols to receive scores within a half-stage step of one another (88%–100%, median 94%) while we find most protocols to be scored within one-third stage of each other (88%–100%). Rest (1979) does not report percent agreement figures since his instrument does not yield stage typology scores.

In addition to test-retest, interrater, and alternate form reliability, we have also calculated the standard error of measurement for the moral judgment measure. With the standard error of measurement defined as $\sigma_{meas} = \sigma\sqrt{(1 - e_{xx})}$ (Nunnally 1978), we have entered the standard deviation of the total longitudinal sample (69.87) as σ and .95 as e_{xx}, the reliability estimate of the measure. The standard error of measurement of the instrument based on these figures is 15.62 "moral maturity points."

VALIDITY OF THE STANDARD FORM

As we have argued elsewhere (Colby 1978; Kohlberg 1980), the appropriate validity concept for a developmental measure such as the Standard Issue system is construct validity, not prediction to an external criterion. For a measure of moral judgment stage, the two most critical empirical criteria of construct validity correspond to the two most central theoretical assumptions of the stage construct. They are invariance of stage sequence and "structural wholeness" or internal consistency (generality of stage usage across moral issues or dilemmas). As noted in the following description of our longitudinal data, the results confirm both invariant sequence and internal consistency. Among other things, we interpret "construct validity" to mean the fit of the data obtained by means of the test to primary components of its theoretical definition. The primary theoretical definition of structural moral development is that of an organization passing through an invariant developmental sequence. In other words, positive results of the longitudinal analysis support not only the theoretical assumptions but also the validity of the measure. Negative results, of course, could be due to an incorrect theory, an invalid test, or both. Furthermore, validity and reliability of a test are closely related notions since both refer to the generalizability of performance on a test, or a set of test items, to performance in other situations including the performance on other forms of the test or at other times of testing. In the case of structural stage, construct validity demands high generalizability or test-retest and alternate-form reliability. If a stage is a structural whole, the individual should be consistent over various stimuli and occasions of testing. Our reliability data fit this demand rather well.

In regard to the instrument's validity, one might also wonder whether Standard Issue Scores on responses to hypothetical dilemmas predict to moral judgment in real life. One should not expect, however, to find an exact correspondence between developmental stage of hypothetical and real moral judgments. As Damon (1977) has shown, the relation between moral judgments made by children in real and hypothetical versions of the same distributive justice situation is mediated by a number of factors including the individual's developmental level on the hypothetical judgments. Moreover, the most salient features of real-life dilemmas are not always unambiguously moral. Many of the issues dealt with in attempts to resolve such dilemmas may be practical or factual rather than moral. To the extent that such situations do elicit moral reasoning, the scores on individual's responses to hypothetical dilemmas should be predictive of, although not identical to, the scores on the real-life moral judgments. Of course, evaluation of this aspect of construct validity is limited by the absence of techniques for scoring real-life moral judgments.

One study which has reported data on the relation between Standard Issue Scores and scores on real-life situations is Gilligan and Belenky's (1980) longitudinal study of women deciding whether or not to have an abortion. Gilligan and Belenky (1980) reported that rank-order correlations on the relation between scores on the hypothetical abortion dilemma and on the standard dilemmas at time 1 and time 2 were .83 and .92, respectively. They present percent agreement figures but not correlations between scores on the real and hypothetical abortion dilemmas: 59% were scored at the same stage, all but one of the remainder were scored within one-half stage of one another. Gilligan and Belenky do not, however, interpret the discrepancies between actual and hypothetical abortion dilemma scores as measurement error. Rather, they argue that the discrepancies are important psychological phenomena that have significant implications for the future development and mental health of these women facing unwanted pregnancies. Like Selman and Jacquette (1978), they find that when individuals are unable to bring to bear their cognitive capacities (as measured in the hypothetical interview) in thinking about the real-life situation, they are more likely to exhibit emotional disturbance both at the time of the initial interview and in longitudinal follow-up 1 year later. Gilligan and Belenky also report that changes in moral judgment scores on the standard dilemmas in the year following the abortion were strong predictors of psychological adjustment at the time of the follow-up interview.

27

IV. RESULTS

INVARIANT STAGE SEQUENCE

According to our theoretical assumptions, the developmental sequence should be identical in every individual studied. Except under extreme circumstances, there should be no deviations from perfect sequentiality. That is, there should be no stage skipping and no downward stage movement. Let us first consider downward stage movement. Theoretically, our data should never yield a lower score at time $n + 1$ than at time n. Since we have not constructed an error-free measure, however, some discrepant scores must be expected to result from measurement error. A reasonable estimate of the number of such deviations attributable to measurement error can be derived from analysis of test-retest reliability data. That is, we can assume that virtually none of our subjects will have changed in stage of moral judgment within the short test-retest interval. Any differences between scores at times 1 and 2 can be attributed to measurement error. Therefore, the analysis of longitudinal sequence involved a comparison of the frequency of sequence reversals (downward stage movement) in the longitudinal data with the frequency of negative time 1–time 2 changes in our test-retest data. (Of course, this comparison depends upon a psychometrically adequate level of test-retest reliability.) If sequence reversals exceed test-retest instability, we cannot consider our data to support the invariant sequence assumption. Table 13 presents global stage scores for the three interview forms A and B and C separately and combined. The sequence reversals are noted with a *c*. In form A these sequence reversals (downward changes) occurred in only 7% of the adjacent times using even our most differentiated 13-point scale of global interview scores. The reversals were 6% in form B, 6% in form C, and 5% in forms A, B, and C combined. A comparison with downward stage change in test-retest data for forms A and B is presented in table 14. Since in every case the test-retest reversals are well over twice as great as the longitudinal reversals, it seems reasonable to attribute the violations of longitudinal sequence to measurement error.

A second type of sequence analysis involves comparing the proportion

28

TABLE 13

MORAL JUDGMENT STAGE SCORES

SUBJECT AND TESTING TIME	STANDARD GLOBAL SCORE			STANDARD GLOBAL SCORE (A, B, and C Combined)	KRAMER SCORES	STRUCTURAL ISSUE SCORES
	Form A	Form B	Form C			
1-1......	1[b]	2	2	1/2	...	...
1-2......	1/2	2	2/3	2	...	...
1-3......	2/3	2[b]	2/3	2/3	...	...
1-4......	2/3	3	2/3	3	...	...
1-6......	3/4	3/4	...	3/4	...	...
2-1[a].....	1/2	1/2	1/2	1/2	2/4	1/3
2-2......	3	3	3/4	3	...	3/4
2-3......	3/4	3/4	3/4	3/4	3/4	4/5
2-4......	3[c]	2/3[c]	3/4	3[c]	2/3	5
2-5......	4/5	4/5	4/5	4/5	...	...
2-6......	4/5	4/5	...	4/5	...	...
3-1......	1/2	2	1/2	2	1/2	2
3-2......	2/3	2/3	2/3	2/3	...	2/3
3-3......	3/4	3	3/4	3/4	3/4	3
3-4......	3/4	3/4	3[c]	3/4	...	3/4
3-5......	3/4	3/4	...	3/4	...	4
3-6......	3/4	4	3/4	3/4	...	...
4-1......	2/3	2	2	2	2/3	2
4-2......	3	2/3	2/3	2/3	...	2
4-3......	3/4	2/3	3/4	3	3/4	3/4
4-4......	3/4	2/3[b]	3[c]	3	3/4	3/4
4-5......	3/4	3/4	3/4	3/4	...	3/4
5-1......	2	1/2	1/2	1/2	1/2	1
5-2......	2/3	2	1/2	2/3	...	2
5-3......	2/3	1/2[c]	1[c]	1/2[c]	...	2
5-4......	3	2	2/3	2/3	...	2/3
5-5......	2/3[c]	2	3	2/3	...	2/3
6-1......	...	1/2	1/2	1/2	...	1/2
6-2......	...	2/3[b]	2/3	2/3	...	2
6-3......	...	3	3	3	...	2/3
6-4......	...	3	2/3[c]	2/3[c]	...	2/3
6-5......	...	2/3[bc]	2/3	2/3	...	3/4
8-1......	2	1/2	1	1/2	...	1/2
8-2......	2	1[c]	2	2	...	1/2
8-4......	3/4	3	3	3	...	3
9-1[a].....	1/2	1/2	1/2	1/2	1/2	1/2
9-2......	2/3	2/3	1/2	2/3	1/2	2
9-3......	2/3	3	3	3	3/4	3
9-4......	3	3	3/4	3	...	3/4
9-5......	3/4	3/4	3/4	3/4	...	3/4
9-6......	4	3/4[b]	...	4	...	...
11-1....	1/2	2	1/2	1/2	...	...
11-2....	2/3	2[b]	2/3	2/3	...	...

[a] "Construction case" used to develop scoring criteria.
[b] Guess score.
[c] Sequence inversion.

TABLE 13 (*Continued*)

SUBJECT AND TESTING TIME	STANDARD GLOBAL SCORE Form A	STANDARD GLOBAL SCORE Form B	Form C	STANDARD GLOBAL SCORE (A, B, and C Combined)	KRAMER SCORES	STRUCTURAL ISSUE SCORES
12-1.....	2	1/2	1/2	1/2	1/2	1/2
12-2.....	3	2	3	2/3	...	2
12-3.....	3/4	3/4	3	3/4	4	3
12-4.....	3/4	3ᶜ	3/4	3/4	3/4	3
13-1.....	1/2	2	1/2	2	...	...
13-2.....	2	2	2	2	...	...
13-3.....	3	3	3	3	...	...
14-1.....	2/3	2	2/3	2/3	...	1/2
14-2.....	2/3/4	2/3	3	2/3	...	2/3
14-4.....	4	4	4	4	...	4
14-5.....	...	4/5	...	4/5	...	4
15-1.....	2/3	2/3	2/3	2/3	...	...
15-2.....	2/3	3	2/3	2/3	...	...
16-1.....	2/3	2/3	2	2/3	...	1/2
16-2.....	3/4	3	2	2/3	...	2/3
16-3.....	3/4	3/4	3	3/4	...	3/4
16-4.....	4	4	3/4	4	...	4
16-6.....	4	4	...	4	...	...
17-1ᵃ.....	...	2	1/2	1/2	2/3	1/2
17-2.....	2/3	2/3	2/3	2/3	2/3	3/4
17-3.....	3/4	3	3/4	3	3/4	3
17-4.....	3/4	3	3/4	3/4	...	4
17-5.....	4	4	3/4	4	...	4
17-6.....	4/5	4/5	...	4/5	...	...
18-1.....	3	3	2/3	3	...	2
18-2.....	2/3ᶜ	3	2/3	2/3ᶜ	...	3
18-4.....	3/4	3/4	3/4	3/4	...	4
18-5.....	3/4	3/4ᵇ	4	3/4	...	4/5
18-6.....	4	4	...	4	...	...
19-1.....	2	1/2	2/3	2/3	...	2
19-2.....	2/3	3/4	3	3	...	2/3
19-3.....	...	...	3/4	3/4	...	...
19-4.....	3	3/4	3/4	3/4	...	2/3
19-5.....	3/4	3/4	...	3/4	...	2/3
19-6.....	3/4	4	...	4	...	...
21-1.....	2	1/2	1/2	1/2	...	2
21-2.....	2/3	2	2	2/3	...	...
21-3.....	3	2/3	2/3	2/3	...	2/3
21-4.....	2/3ᶜ	3	3	3	...	2/3
22-1.....	2	1/2	2	2	1/2	2
22-2.....	1/2ᶜ	2/3	1/2ᶜ	2/3	...	3
22-3.....	3/4	3/4	3/4	3/4	2/4	3
22-4.....	3/4	4	3/4	3/4	...	4
22-5.....	3/4	...	3/4	3/4	...	...
22-6.....	4	4/5	...	4	...	...

ᵃ "Construction case" used to develop scoring criteria.

ᵇ Guess score.

ᶜ Sequence inversion.

TABLE 13 (*Continued*)

Subject and Testing Time	Standard Global Score Form A	Standard Global Score Form B	Form C	Standard Global Score (A, B, and C Combined)	Kramer Scores	Structural Issue Scores
23-1[a].....	2	1/2	1/2	1/2	...	1/2
23-2.....	2/3	3/4	...	3/4	...	...
23-3.....	3/4	3/4	3/4	3/4	...	4
23-4.....	3/4	4/5	3/4	3/4	...	...
23-5.....	4/5	5	4	4/5	...	4/5
23-6.....	4/5	...	...	4/5	...	...
24-1.....	3	1/2	1/2	1/2	1/3	1/2
24-2.....	3	2/3	2/3	2/3	...	2/3
24-3.....	3/4	3	2/3	3	2/3	3
24-4.....	3/4	3/4	3/4	3/4	2/4	3/4
25-1.....	2/3	1/2	2/3	2/3	...	2/3
25-2.....	3/4	3	2/3	3	...	2/3
25-5.....	3/4	3/4	3/4	3/4	...	4/5
25-6.....	3/4	4	...	4	...	...
26-1.....	2	2	2/3	2	2/4	2
26-2.....	3	2/3[b]	3/4	3	3/4	3
26-4.....	3	3	3[c]	3	...	3
26-5.....	3	3/4[b]	3/4	3	...	3
26-6.....	3/4	3/4	...	3/4	...	...
27-1.....	2/3	1/3	2/3	2/3	3/4	3
27-2.....	3/4	3	3	3	3/4	3
27-4.....	3/4	3	3/4	3/4	...	3
27-5.....	3/4	3/4	3/4	3/4	...	3
29-1.....	2/3	2/3	2/3	2/3	3/4	...
29-2.....	3	3	3	3	2/4	...
29-4.....	3/4	3	3	3/4	...	...
29-5.....	4	3/4	3/4	3/4	...	...
31-1.....	1/2/3	2	2/3	2/3	...	...
31-2.....	3	2/3	3/4	3	...	...
31-5.....	3/4	3/4	3/4	3/4	...	...
32-1.....	1/2	2	2/3	2	...	...
32-2.....	2/3	2	2/3	2/3	...	...
32-5.....	3	3/4	3	3	...	...
32-6.....	3/4	3/4	...	3/4	...	...
36-1.....	2/3	1/2	1/2	1/2	1/2	...
36-2.....	1/2/2[c]	2	1/2	1/2	1/2	...
36-5.....	3/4	3	3/4	3/4	...	...
36-6.....	3/4	3/4	...	3/4	...	...
37-1.....	3	2/3	3	3	3/4	3
37-2.....	3/4	3/4	3	3/4	3/5	3/4
37-3.....	3/4[b]	3/4	3	3/4	3/4	3/4
37-4.....	4	4[b]	3/4	4	3/4	3/4
37-5.....	4/5	4/5	...	4/5	...	5
37-6.....	...	4/5	...	4/5	...	...

31

TABLE 13 (*Continued*)

Subject and Testing Time	Standard Global Score Form A	Form B	Form C	Standard Global Score (A, B, and C Combined)	Kramer Scores	Structural Issue Scores
38-1.....	2/3	2	2/3	2/3	2/4	...
38-2.....	3/4	3/4	3	3	3/4	...
38-5.....	3/4	4	3/4	3/4	...	...
38-6.....	3/4	3/4[b]	...	3/4	...	...
39-1.....	2/3	2/3	2/3	2/3	3/4	2/3
39-2.....	3/4	3	3/4	3/4	4/5	3/4
39-3.....	3/4	3	3/4	3/4	2/3	4
39-4.....	4	3/4	3/4	3/4	4/5	4/5
41-1.....	2/3	2	2	2	2/4	2
41-2.....	2/3	2/3	3	3	3/4	3
41-3.....	3	3	3/4	3	3/5	3/4
41-4.....	3	3	3/4	3	3/4	3/4
41-5.....	3	3	3/4	3	...	4
41-6.....	3/4	4	...	4	...	...
42-1[a].....	2/3	2/3	3	2/3	2/4	2
42-2.....	3	3	3/4	3/4	3/4	3
42-3.....	...	...	4	4	3/5	3/4
42-4.....	4/5	4	4	4	3/4	3/4
42-5.....	4/5	4/5	4	4/5	...	4
42-6.....	4/5	4/5	...	4/5	...	...
43-1.....	3[b]	2/3	2/3	2/3	3	...
43-2.....	3/4	3/4	3	3/4	3/5	...
43-3.....	3/4	3/4	3	3/4	3/4	...
43-4.....	3/4	3/4	3/4	3/4	3/5	...
44-1.....	3/4	3/4	3/4	3/4	4/5	...
44-3.....	4/5	3/4	4	4	4/5	...
44-4.....	4[c]	4/5	3/4[c]	4	4/5	...
44-5.....	4/5	4/5	...	4/5	...	...
44-6.....	4/5	4/5	...	4/5	...	...
45-1.....	2/3	2	2	2/3	2/4	2/3
45-2.....	3	2/3	2/3	2/3	3/4	2/3
45-4.....	4	3/4	3/4	3/4	3/4	3
45-5.....	4	4	4	4	...	4/5
45-6.....	4	4	...	4	...	...
47-1.....	2/3	3/4	2/3	2/3	2/3	...
47-2.....	2/3	3/4	3	3	2/4	2/3
47-3.....	3	...	2/3[c]	3	3/4	2/3
47-4.....	3	3/4	3	3/4	3/4	2/3
47-5.....	3/4	3/4	3	3/4	...	2/3
47-6.....	3/4	2/4[c]	...	4	...	...
48-1.....	2/3	...	2/3	...	...	...
48-2.....	3/4	2/3	3	3	...	2/3
48-4.....	3/4	3	4	3/4	...	3/4
48-5.....	3/4	3/4	3/4[c]	3/4	...	...
48-6.....	3/4	4	...	4	...	...

[a] "Construction case" used to develop scoring criteria.

[b] Guess score.

[c] Sequence inversion.

TABLE 13 (*Continued*)

Subject and Testing Time	Standard Global Score Form A	Standard Global Score Form B	Form C	Standard Global Score (A, B, and C Combined)	Kramer Scores	Structural Issue Scores
49-1.....	3/4	3	3/4	3	...	...
49-4.....	3/4	3/4	3/4	3/4	...	...
49-5.....	3/4	3c	3/4	3/4	...	...
49-6.....	3/4	3/4	...	3/4	...	...
50-1.....	3	2/3	2	2/3	...	...
50-4.....	3/4	3	3	3	...	...
50-5.....	3/4	4	3/4	4	...	...
50-6.....	3/4	4	...	4	...	...
51-1.....	2	2	...	2	...	...
51-4.....	3/4	3/4	3	3/4	...	...
51-5.....	3/4	4	3/4	3/4	...	...
51-6.....	3/4	3/4c	...	3/4	...	...
53-1.....	3	1/2/3b	2	2/3	...	...
53-2.....	3/4	3/4/5b	2/3	3/4	...	...
53-4.....	3c	3/4	3/4	3/4	...	...
54-1.....	2/3	2/3	2	2/3	...	...
54-5.....	4	3/4	3/4	3/4	...	...
56-1.....	2	...	...	2	...	...
56-4.....	3	...	...	3	...	...
56-6.....	3/4	...	...	3/4	...	...
59-1.....	2/3	1/2	2/3	2/3	...	...
59-2.....	3	2/3	3	2/3	...	...
59-4.....	3	3	3	3	...	...
59-5.....	3/4	2/3c	3/4	3	...	...
62-1.....	2/3	3	3	3	...	...
62-2.....	3/4	4	3/4	3/4	...	...
62-4.....	3c	3bc	3/4	3c	...	...
62-6.....	3/4	4	...	4	...	...
64-1.....	3	2/3	3	3	...	...
64-4.....	3	3/4	3	3/4	...	...
64-5.....	3/4	3/4	3/4	3/4	...	...
65-1a.....	3	3	3	3	4/5	...
65-2.....	4	...	2/3c	2/3/4c	2/4	...
65-4.....	3/4c	3/4	3/4	3/4	...	...
65-5.....	3/4	3/4	4	3/4	...	...
65-6.....	3/4	4	...	4	...	...
67-1a.....	3	2/3	2/3	2/3	3/4	...
67-2.....	3	3	3/4	3	3/5	...
67-3.....	...	...	...	...	4/5	...
67-4.....	3/4	3/4	3/4	3/4	...	...
67-5.....	4/5	3/4	3/4	4	...	...
67-6.....	4/5	3/4	...	4/5	...	...

33

TABLE 13 (*Continued*)

SUBJECT AND TESTING TIME	STANDARD GLOBAL SCORE			STANDARD GLOBAL SCORE (A, B, and C Combined)	KRAMER SCORES	STRUC- TURAL ISSUE SCORES
	Form A	Form B	Form C			
68-1.....	3	3	2	2/3	. . .	. . .
68-2.....	3/4	3	3	3/4	. . .	. . .
68-4.....	3/4	3/4	3	3/4	. . .	. . .
68-5.....	4	3/4[b]	3/4	3/4	. . .	. . .
68-6.....	4	3[c]	. . .	3/4	. . .	. . .
70-1.....	2/3	2/3	2/3	2/3	. . .	. . .
70-2.....	3/4	3/4	3/4	3/4	. . .	. . .
70-4.....	3/4	3/4	3[c]	3/4	. . .	. . .
70-5.....	4	3/4	3/4	3/4	. . .	. . .
70-6.....	3/4[c]	4	4	4	. . .	. . .
71-1.....	3	3	2/3	2/3	. . .	. . .
71-2.....	3/4	3	3	3	. . .	. . .
71-4.....	3/4	3/4	3	3/4	. . .	. . .
71-5.....	3/4	3[c]	3	3/4	. . .	. . .
81-1.....	3	1/2	2/3	2/3	. . .	. . .
81-2.....	3	2/3	3	3	. . .	. . .
81-5.....	3/4	3/4	3/4	3/4	. . .	. . .
91-3.....	3	3/4	3	3/4	. . .	. . .
91-4.....	2/3[c]	3[c]	3	3[c]	. . .	. . .
91-5.....	3/4	3	3/4	3	. . .	. . .
91-6.....	4	4	. . .	4	. . .	. . .
92-3.....	2/3	3	3/4	3	. . .	. . .
92-4.....	3/4	3/4	3/4	3/4	. . .	. . .
92-5.....	3[c]	3/4[b]	3/4	3/4	. . .	. . .
93-3.....	3/4	3	3	3	. . .	. . .
93-4.....	3/4	3	3	3	. . .	. . .
93-5.....	3/4	3/4	3	3/4	. . .	. . .
93-6.....	3/4	4	. . .	4	. . .	. . .
95-3.....	3	2/3	3	3	. . .	. . .
95-4.....	3/4	. . .	3	3/4	. . .	. . .
95-5.....	3/4	3	3/4	3[c]	. . .	. . .
95-6.....	. . .	3	. . .	3	. . .	. . .
96-3.....	3/4	3	2/3	3	. . .	. . .
96-4.....	3[c]	3	3	3	. . .	. . .
96-5.....	3/4	3/4	3/4	3/4	. . .	. . .
96-6.....	3/4	3[c]	. . .	3[c]	. . .	. . .

[a] "Construction case" used to develop scoring criteria.

[b] Guess score.

[c] Sequence inversion.

TABLE 14

Comparison of Downward Stage Change: Longitudinal and Test-Retest

Longitudinal	Form A (Rater 1)	Form B (Rater 2)	Form C	Forms A, B, and C Combined
	Pure and Mixed Stage Scores (9-Point Scale)			
$Tn \rightarrow Tn + 1$............	5%	6%	4%	3%
Test-retest T1 $\rightarrow$ T2.........	19%	23%	No data	No data
	Major/Minor and Pure Stage Scores (13-Point Scale)			
$Tn \rightarrow Tn + 1$............	7%	6%	6%	5%
Test-retest T1 $\rightarrow$ T2.........	19%	33%	No data	No data

Note.—Only the longitudinal interviews which were scored blind are included in this analysis.

of positive to negative stage change rather than focusing on negative change alone. Such a comparison is important because the invariant sequence assumption implies both that individuals will move upward through the developmental sequence and that they will not move downward. Data showing infrequent downward movement would be interpreted very differently if upward movement was equally infrequent. Although it is somewhat difficult to know what would constitute an adequate preponderance of upward stage change, Rest (1979) reports a ratio of 9.4:1 for positive to negative change on longitudinal data from the DIT. If we define change as one step of movement along our nine-point scale, the ratio of positive to negative change in our study is 14.75:1.

In addition to predicting that at no time will a subject move downward in the developmental sequence, cognitive-developmental theory holds that each stage is a prerequisite for those that follow it. That is, the concept of invariant stage sequence implies that no stage will be omitted as development proceeds. Since within a 4-year interval a subject might enter and leave a stage, we could not necessarily expect our data to corroborate this aspect of sequentiality. Fortunately, however, the interval seems to have been short enough in relation to our subjects' rate of development to capture each stage in the sequence for each subject. In fact, table 13 shows that in no case on any form did a subject reach a stage in the sequence without having gone through each preceding stage. For the most part, changes across the 4-year intervals were less than a full stage. In forms A and B only 3% changed more than a full stage in 4 years. In form C only 2% changed more than a full stage in 4 years. Scores combined across all three forms show only half a percent changing more than a full stage.

INTERNAL CONSISTENCY

According to our theoretical assumptions, the logic of each stage forms a "structured whole." In line with this assumption, one would expect to find

35

a high degree of internal consistency in stage scores assigned, at least within those units that are conceptually and psychologically coherent. The data support this assumption as clearly as they do that of invariant sequence.

One indication of degree of internal consistency in moral judgment is provided by distributions for each subject of proportion of reasoning scored at each of the five stages. Our analysis of these distributions showed that most interviews received all of their scores either at a single stage or at two adjacent stages. The mean percentage of reasoning at the individual's modal stage was 68% for form A, 72% for form B, 69% for form C, and 67% for forms A, B, and C combined. The mean percentage of reasoning at the subject's two most frequently used stages (always adjacent) was 98% for form A, 97% for form B, 99% for form C, and 99% for forms A, B, and C combined. (Remember that there are three dilemmas per form and each dilemma was scored without knowledge of responses to the other dilemmas, so these figures cannot be an artifact of scorer bias.) The high correlations among alternate forms and high Cronbach's α figures reported in the section on reliability provide further support for the consistency of subjects' stage of reasoning across differing content.

Some interviews, however, received scores at three stages. In order to determine the number of interviews that did exhibit reasoning at three stages, it was necessary to establish a boundary below which the entry would be treated as error and above which it would be treated as real. For example, if an interview received 80% of its scores at stage 1, 19% at stage 2, and 1% at stage 3, we would probably want to treat the 1% at stage 3 as error and consider the interview to exhibit only two stages of moral judgment. We established the error boundary at 10% with entries of 10% and below treated as error, entries above 10% treated as real. Our choice of the 10% figure can be justified as follows. The 10% boundary derives from the relation between the number of criterion judgment (CJ) matches assigned to an interview at a stage and the percentage of reasoning at that stage in the interview's distribution of stage scores. Through a comparison of distribution of stage use for each interview with a record of each individual CJ match score assigned, we determined that using a cutoff point of 10% would assure that in every case where the interview received one full criterion judgment match at a stage, the percentage use of that stage would fall above the cutoff and thus be treated as real. That is, any stage represented in the distribution at a level of 10% or below reflected less than one full criterion judgment match at that stage across the entire interview. For example, the existence of 8% stage 2 in a distribution of scores for an interview might reflect the assignment of a transitional CJ score at stage 2/3 in a predominantly stage 3/4 interview. Proportions of reasoning greater than 10% often reflected less than a full CJ on the score sheet, but proportions less than 10% never reflected a full CJ or more. Therefore our error boundary

36

is conservative. Using the assessment of one full CJ as an indication of stage presence would have allowed us to treat many more entries as error. That is, our 10% boundary errs in the direction of treating as real some entries that are in fact error rather than in treating as error entries that are real. Even so, we find that only 9% of our longitudinal interviews show a third stage of reasoning greater than 10%. Using a less conservative cutoff, we find that only 1% of our interviews show a third stage of reasoning greater than 20%.

It is safe to say, then, that very few interviews show any use of three stages of moral judgment. Where three stages do appear, they are always adjacent stages. It is unclear, however, whether the instances where a third stage is used should be interpreted as cases of measurement error not caught by our conservative error boundary or as real but unusual cases of stage heterogeneity in the subject's thinking. In at least two cases, to be discussed in more detail later, we interpret the lack of consistency as a real phenomenon. These two cases—subject 2, time 4, and subject 65, time 2—were the two that Kohlberg (1973) identified as representing a relativistic, transitional type of thinking that he called "Stage $4\frac{1}{2}$." Note that both of these cases represent sequence anomalies in our analysis as well as the absence of "structured wholeness."

FACTOR ANALYSES

Theoretical expectations lead us to believe that moral judgment development is a single general domain cutting across verbal dilemmas and issues. To examine this hypothesis, we factor analyzed the correlations among stage scores on each of the issues across the dilemmas.

Correlation matrices for the whole population and for the 16–17-year age group are given in tables 15 and 16. The correlations are all positive and moderately high, consistent with our expectations. Table 16 indicates that the correlations among moral issues are not due simply to their common correlation with age since the correlations remain positive and moderately high even within a single age group. The 16–18-year age group was used for this analysis because it is the group in which the number of subjects is largest.

Table 17 shows the results of the principal components analysis. The first row of each age group shows the highest and second highest eigenvalue and corresponding percentage of variance accounted for. The succeeding eigenvalues were much smaller (21) and therefore were not reported. The next three rows give the highest and second highest eigenvalues for each of the three forms. With all subjects pooled, the second eigenvalue is less than one and therefore, by convention, is disregarded. Within the different age

37

TABLE 15

CORRELATIONS AMONG 18 MORAL ISSUES FOR TOTAL SAMPLE (N's in Parentheses)

	Life (A1)	Law (A2)	Morality and Con- science (A3)	Punish- ment (A4)	Contract (A5)	Au- thority (A6)
Law (A2)...................	.74 (204)	1.00 (0)	.67 (149)	.76 (154)	.66 (200)	.63 (193)
Morality and conscience (A3)..	.73 (165)	.67 (149)	1.00 (0)	.68 (115)	.61 (166)	.61 (159)
Punishment (A4)............	.69 (156)	.76 (154)	.68 (115)	1.00 (0)	.65 (156)	.59 (154)
Contract (A5)...............	.70 (219)	.66 (200)	.61 (166)	.65 (156)	1.00 (0)	.66 (212)
Authority (A6)..............	.67 (290)	.63 (193)	.61 (159)	.59 (154)	.66 (212)	1.00 (0)

	Life (B1)	Law (B2)	Morality and Con- science (B3)	Punish- ment (B4)	Contract (B5)	Au- thority (B6)
Law (A2)...................	.74 (174)	.66 (167)	.74 (161)	.69 (170)	.67 (165)	.76 (139)
Morality and conscience (A3)..	.74 (144)	.70 (138)	.73 (135)	.66 (140)	.52 (136)	.70 (113)
Punishment (A4)............	.69 (136)	.65 (128)	.68 (121)	.69 (135)	.61 (131)	.77 (103)
Contract (A5)...............	.68 (187)	.69 (179)	.71 (171)	.64 (180)	.62 (182)	.67 (149)
Authority (A6)..............	.64 (178)	.65 (175)	.64 (170)	.64 (171)	.59 (175)	.66 (144)

	Life (Quality) (C1)	Life (Quan- tity) (C2)	Morality and Con- science (C3)	Punish- ment (C4)	Contract (C5)	Law (C6)
Law (A2)...................	.65 (115)	.70 (77)	.71 (152)	.74 (132)	.70 (161)	.68 (159)
Morality and conscience (A3)..	.57 (97)	.55 (68)	.60 (119)	.67 (100)	.60 (127)	.62 (125)
Punishment (A4)............	.64 (87)	.75 (58)	.67 (113)	.79 (104)	.66 (121)	.66 (117)
Contract (A5)...............	.62 (131)	.60 (93)	.55 (165)	.61 (144)	.62 (177)	.62 (174)
Authority (A6)..............	.57 (129)	.66 (86)	.57 (160)	.57 (141)	.53 (172)	.60 (167)

NOTE.—All correlations are significant at $p < .001$.

38

TABLE 15 (*Continued*)

	Life (A1)	Law (A2)	Morality and Conscience (A3)	Punishment (A4)	Contract (A5)	Authority (A6)
Life (B1)	.69 (188)	.74 (174)	.74 (144)	.69 (136)	.68 (187)	.64 (178)
Law (B2)	.60 (179)	.66 (167)	.70 (138)	.65 (128)	.69 (179)	.65 (175)
Morality and conscience (B3)	.71 (176)	.74 (161)	.73 (135)	.68 (121)	.71 (171)	.64 (170)
Punishment (B4)	.61 (178)	.69 (170)	.66 (140)	.69 (135)	.64 (180)	.63 (171)
Contract (B5)	.50 (180)	.67 (165)	.52 (136)	.61 (131)	.62 (182)	.59 (175)
Authority (B6)	.66 (148)	.76 (139)	.70 (113)	.77 (103)	.67 (149)	.66 (144)

	Life (B1)	Law (B2)	Morality and Conscience (B3)	Punishment (B4)	Contract (B5)	Authority (B6)
Life (B1)	1.00 (0)	.86 (161)	.88 (163)	.81 (159)	.71 (164)	.74 (143)
Law (B2)	.86 (161)	1.00 (0)	.83 (152)	.83 (161)	.66 (157)	.78 (131)
Morality and conscience (B3)	.88 (163)	.83 (152)	1.00 (0)	.79 (148)	.66 (156)	.74 (135)
Punishment (B4)	.81 (159)	.83 (161)	.79 (148)	1.00 (0)	.66 (158)	.72 (128)
Contract (B5)	.71 (164)	.66 (157)	.66 (156)	.66 (158)	1.00 (0)	.83 (133)
Authority (B6)	.74 (143)	.78 (131)	.74 (135)	.72 (128)	.83 (133)	1.00 (0)

	Life (Quality) (C1)	Life (Quantity) (C2)	Morality and Conscience (C3)	Punishment (C4)	Contract (C5)	Law (C6)
Life (B1)	.66 (116)	.66 (83)	.68 (149)	.70 (133)	.63 (155)	.70 (153)
Law (B2)	.62 (110)	.56 (76)	.67 (142)	.67 (127)	.62 (152)	.62 (144)
Morality and conscience (B3)	.68 (116)	.64 (78)	.66 (145)	.75 (130)	.64 (152)	.67 (150)
Punishment (B4)	.72 (111)	.69 (74)	.64 (138)	.74 (125)	.61 (142)	.66 (140)
Contract (B5)	.56 (118)	.49 (86)	.60 (149)	.64 (132)	.52 (161)	.58 (159)
Authority (B6)	.62 (102)	.55 (74)	.73 (119)	.77 (108)	.63 (127)	.64 (130)

TABLE 15 (*Continued*)

	Life (A1)	Law (A2)	Morality and Conscience (A3)	Punishment (A4)	Contract (A5)	Authority (A6)
Life (quality) (C1)...........	.65 (130)	.65 (115)	.57 (97)	.64 (87)	.62 (131)	.57 (129)
Life (quantity) (C2)..........	.62 (91)	.70 (77)	.55 (68)	.75 (58)	.60 (93)	.66 (86)
Morality and conscience (C3)..	.62 (168)	.71 (152)	.60 (119)	.67 (113)	.55 (165)	.57 (160)
Punishment (C4).............	.67 (147)	.74 (132)	.67 (100)	.79 (104)	.61 (144)	.57 (141)
Contract (C5)...............	.59 (177)	.70 (161)	.60 (127)	.66 (121)	.62 (177)	.53 (172)
Law (C6)..................	.62 (175)	.68 (159)	.62 (125)	.66 (117)	.62 (174)	.60 (167)

	Life (B1)	Law (B2)	Morality and Conscience (B3)	Punishment (B4)	Contract (B5)	Authority (B6)
Life (quality) (C1)...........	.66 (116)	.62 (110)	.68 (116)	.72 (111)	.56 (118)	.62 (102)
Life (quantity) (C2)..........	.66 (83)	.56 (76)	.64 (78)	.69 (75)	.49 (86)	.55 (74)
Morality and conscience (C3)..	.68 (149)	.67 (142)	.66 (145)	.64 (138)	.60 (149)	.73 (119)
Punishment (C4).............	.70 (133)	.67 (127)	.75 (130)	.74 (125)	.64 (132)	.77 (108)
Contract (C5)...............	.63 (155)	.62 (152)	.64 (152)	.61 (142)	.52 (161)	.63 (127)
Law (C6)..................	.70 (153)	.62 (144)	.67 (150)	.66 (140)	.58 (159)	.64 (130)

	Life (Quality) (C1)	Life (Quantity) (C2)	Morality and Conscience (C3)	Punishment (C4)	Contract (C5)	Law (C6)
Life (quality) (C1)...........	1.00 (0)	.83 (75)	.65 (120)	.70 (101)	.58 (129)	.63 (127)
Life (quantity) (C2)..........	.83 (75)	1.00 (0)	.57 (86)	.64 (71)	.59 (89)	.66 (91)
Morality and conscience (C3)..	.65 (120)	.57 (86)	1.00 (0)	.89 (146)	.62 (167)	.68 (164)
Punishment (C4).............	.70 (101)	.64 (71)	.89 (146)	1.00 (0)	.69 (146)	.75 (146)
Contract (C5)...............	.58 (129)	.59 (89)	.62 (167)	.69 (146)	1.00 (0)	.82 (182)
Law (C6)..................	.63 (127)	.66 (91)	.68 (164)	.75 (146)	.82 (182)	1.00 (0)

NOTE.—All correlations are significant at $p < .001$.

TABLE 16

CORRELATIONS AMONG 18 MORAL ISSUES FOR 16–17-YEAR-OLD AGE GROUP
(*N*'s in Parentheses)

	Life (A1)	Law (A2)	Morality and Conscience (A3)	Punishment (A4)	Contract (A5)	Authority (A6)
Life (A1)	1.00 (0)	.59 (37)	.41* (26)	.77 (29)	.49 (42)	.47** (37)
Law (A2)	.58 (37)	1.00 (0)	.22*** (23)	.68 (27)	.30* (37)	.29*** (33)
Morality and conscience (A3)	.41* (26)	.22*** (23)	1.00 (0)	.11*** (19)	.11*** (26)	.25*** (24)
Punishment (A4)	.77 (29)	.68 (27)	.11*** (19)	1.00 (0)	.52* (29)	.21*** (28)
Contract (A5)	.49 (42)	.30* (37)	.11*** (26)	.52** (29)	1.00 (0)	.41** (38)
Authority (A6)	.47 (37)	.29*** (33)	.25*** (24)	.21*** (28)	.41** (38)	1.00 (0)

	Life (B1)	Law (B2)	Morality and Conscience (B3)	Punishment (B4)	Contract (B5)	Authority (B6)
Life (A1)	.49** (37)	.45** (34)	.64 (30)	.38* (30)	.28* (36)	.44* (28)
Law (A2)	.57 (33)	.47** (30)	.50** (27)	.70 (29)	.46** (32)	.71 (25)
Morality and conscience (A3)	.13*** (24)	.46* (25)	.27*** (19)	.22*** (20)	.05*** (24)	.51* (19)
Punishment (A4)	.64 (29)	.35* (24)	.57** (21)	.61 (23)	.37* (27)	.49* (19)
Contract (A5)	.42* (37)	.53** (34)	.48 (29)	.44** (30)	.37* (37)	.33* (29)
Authority (A6)	.26*** (33)	.46** (32)	.59 (28)	.36* (28)	.10*** (35)	.22*** (26)

	Life (Quality) (C1)	Life (Quantity) (C2)	Morality and Conscience (C3)	Punishment (C4)	Contract (C5)	Law (C6)
Life (A1)	.24*** (28)	.18*** (19)	.45** (33)	.60 (28)	.27*** (37)	.29* (36)
Law (A2)	.41* (25)	.46* (17)	.59 (28)	.57** (25)	.54** (33)	.50** (32)
Morality and conscience (A3)	.29*** (21)	−.07*** (14)	.19*** (21)	.33*** (16)	.07*** (24)	.19*** (23)
Punishment (A4)	.07*** (19)	.35*** (13)	.41* (22)	.71 (22)	.61 (26)	.50** (24)
Contract (A5)	.21*** (29)	.31*** (20)	.17*** (32)	.37* (27)	.47** (38)	.49** (37)
Authority (A6)	.27*** (27)	.17*** (19)	.20*** (29)	.42* (25)	.09*** (34)	.29*** (33)

NOTE.—All correlations not asterisked are significant at $p < .001$.
* $p < .05$.
** $p < .01$.
*** Not significant.

41

TABLE 16 (*Continued*)

	Life (A1)	Law (A2)	Morality and Con- science (A3)	Punish- ment (A4)	Contract (A5)	Authority (A6)
Life (B1)............	.49** (37)	.57 (33)	.13*** (24)	.64 (29)	.42* (37)	.26*** (33)
Law (B2)............	.45** (34)	.47** (30)	.46* (25)	.35* (24)	.53** (34)	.46** (32)
Morality and conscience (B3).....	.64 (30)	.50** (27)	.27*** (19)	.57** (21)	.48** (29)	.59 (28)
Punishment (B4)......	.38* (30)	.70 (29)	.22*** (20)	.61** (23)	.44** (30)	.36* (28)
Contract (B5)........	.28* (36)	.46** (32)	.05*** (24)	.37* (27)	.37* (37)	.10*** (35)
Authority (B6)........	.44* (28)	.71 (25)	.51** (19)	.49* (19)	.33* (29)	.22*** (26)

	Life (B1)	Law (B2)	Morality and Con- science (B3)	Punish- ment (B4)	Contract (B5)	Authority (B6)
Life (B1)............	1.00 (0)	.67 (32)	.74 (28)	.78 (27)	.45** (34)	.41* (26)
Law (B2)............	.67 (32)	1.00 (0)	.56** (26)	.63 (26)	.38* (32)	.24*** (25)
Morality and conscience (B3).....	.74 (28)	.56* (26)	1.00 (0)	.77 (21)	.14*** (28)	.39*** (19)
Punishment (B4)......	.78 (27)	.63 (26)	.77 (21)	1.00 (0)	.69 (27)	.50* (20)
Contract (B5)........	.45** (34)	.38 (31)	.14 (28)	.69 (27)	1.00 (0)	.55 (25)
Authority (B6)........	.41* (26)	.24*** (25)	.39*** (19)	.50* (20)	.55** (25)	1.00 (0)

	Life (Quality) (C1)	Life (Quan- tity) (C2)	Morality and Con- science (C3)	Punish- ment (C4)	Contract (C5)	Law (C6)
Life (B1)............	.29*** (25)	.57** (19)	.31* (30)	.54** (27)	.43** (34)	.52** (33)
Law (B2)............	.23*** (26)	.35*** (18)	.34* (28)	.36* (24)	.26*** (33)	.55** (31)
Morality and conscience (B3).....	.55** (21)	.57* (14)	.38* (25)	.50** (23)	.21*** (27)	.46** (27)
Punishment (B4)......	.49* (22)	.68** (16)	.43* (26)	.68 (21)	.48** (27)	.62 (26)
Contract (B5)........	.18*** (26)	.24*** (20)	.18*** (28)	.23*** (25)	.21*** (35)	.38* (33)
Authority (B6)........	.03*** (23)	− .05*** (16)	.40* (22)	.55** (19)	.38* (27)	.37* (27)

NOTE.—All correlations not asterisked are significant at $p < .001$.

* $p < .05$.

** $p < .01$.

*** Not significant.

TABLE 16 (*Continued*)

	Life (A1)	Law (A2)	Morality and Conscience (A3)	Punishment (A4)	Contract (A5)	Authority (A6)
Life (quality) (C1)....	.24***	.41*	.29***	.07***	.21***	.27***
	(28)	(25)	(21)	(19)	(29)	(27)
Life (quantity) (C2)...	.18***	.46*	−.06***	.35***	.31***	.17***
	(19)	(17)	(14)	(13)	(20)	(19)
Morality and conscience (C3).....	.45**	.59	.19***	.41*	.17***	.20***
	(33)	(28)	(21)	(22)	(32)	(29)
Punishment (C4)......	.60	.57	.33***	.71	.37*	.42***
	(28)	(25)	(16)	(22)	(27)	(25)
Contract (C5).........	.27***	.54**	.07***	.61	.47**	.09***
	(37)	(33)	(24)	(26)	(38)	(34)
Law (C6).............	.29*	.50**	.19***	.50**	.49	.29***
	(36)	(32)	(23)	(24)	(37)	(33)

	Life (B1)	Law (B2)	Morality and Conscience (B3)	Punishment (B4)	Contract (B5)	Authority (B6)
Life (quality) (C1)....	.29***	.23***	.55**	.49*	.18***	.10***
	(25)	(26)	(21)	(22)	(26)	(23)
Life (quantity) (C2)...	.57**	.35***	.57*	.68**	.24***	−.05***
	(19)	(18)	(14)	(16)	(20)	(16)
Morality and conscience (C3).....	.31*	.34*	.38*	.43*	.18***	.40*
	(30)	(28)	(25)	(26)	(28)	(22)
Punishment (C4)......	.54**	.36*	.50**	.68	.23***	.55**
	(27)	(24)	(23)	(21)	(25)	(19)
Contract (C5).........	.43**	.26***	.21***	.48**	.21***	.38*
	(34)	(33)	(27)	(27)	(35)	(27)
Law (C6).............	.52**	.56**	.46**	.62	.38*	.37*
	(33)	(31)	(27)	(26)	(33)	(27)

	Life (Quality) (C1)	Life (Quantity) (C2)	Morality and Conscience (C3)	Punishment (C4)	Contract (C5)	Law (C6)
Life (quality) (C1)....	1.00	.75	.43*	.01***	.28***	.22***
	(0)	(17)	(25)	(19)	(28)	(29)
Life (quantity) (C2)...	.75	1.00	.47*	.34***	.67**	.60**
	(17)	(0)	(17)	(12)	(18)	(19)
Morality and conscience (C3).....	.43*	.47*	1.00	.87	.49**	.58
	(25)	(17)	(0)	(26)	(31)	(30)
Punishment (C4)......	.01***	.34***	.87	1.00	.59**	.69
	(19)	(12)	(26)	(0)	(27)	(27)
Contract (C5).........	.28***	.67**	.49**	.59**	1.00	.77
	(28)	(18)	(31)	(27)	(0)	(37)
Law (C6).............	.22***	.60**	.58	.69	.77	1.00
	(29)	(19)	(30)	(27)	(37)	(0)

43

TABLE 17

EIGENVALUES AND ASSOCIATED % OF VARIANCE FOR 18 ISSUES AND FOR
EACH FORM IN THE TOTAL SAMPLE AND THREE AGE GROUPS

Groups and Issues	First Eigenvalue	Variance (%)	Second Eigenvalue	Variance (%)
All subjects ($N = 190$):				
18 issues..............	12.35	68.6	.84	4.7
6 issues A............	4.35	72.5	.47	7.8
6 issues B............	4.83	80.6	.49	8.3
6 issues C............	4.43	73.8	.63	10.4
16–18 years ($N = 40$):				
18 issues..............	8.27	46.0	1.87	10.4
6 issues A............	3.06	50.9	1.30	17.1
6 issues B............	3.69	61.4	1.05	17.5
6 issues C............	3.63	60.6	1.29	21.5
20–22 years ($N = 29$):				
18 issues..............	7.91	43.9	2.05	11.4
6 issues A............	2.57	42.8	1.16	19.4
6 issues B............	3.90	65.0	.99	16.5
6 issues C............	3.26	54.3	1.12	18.6
28–30 years ($N = 30$):				
18 issues..............	8.62	47.9	2.46	13.7
6 issues A............	3.50	58.4	.86	14.4
6 issues B............	4.30	71.7	.74	12.3
6 issues C............	2.68	44.6	1.64	27.4

groups the second eigenvalue barely exceeds one and adds very little to the percentage of variance contributed by the first factor.

Table 18 gives the unrotated first factor loading, for the entire sample on all 18 issues and for each separate form. The loadings of each issue varied from one dilemma to another, so that no single issue is the best representative of a general moral judgment level.

In spite of the marginal contribution of succeeding factors in the age group with the largest number of subjects, we extracted all factors with eigenvalues greater than one. The unrotated loadings for that age group (16–18 years) are given in table 19. After the first general factor, the loadings on the specific factors are greatly diminished and reveal no consistent patterns that could be interpreted. Similar factor matrices resulted from the other age groupings.

In attempting to determine the existence and nature of a multifactorial solution, the factors were rotated using both orthogonal and oblique methods. Here, too, no clear interpretation is evident upon inspection across the five factors. In summary, then, for several age groups and for the sample as a whole, no more than one interpretable factor emerged even when the multiple factors were subjected to orthogonal and oblique rotations. In all cases, the eigenvalue and corresponding proportion of variance accounted for by the first factor far exceeded those of succeeding factors. Therefore we conclude that moral judgment, as measured by the Interview Forms A, B, and

TABLE 18

First Factor Loadings
(N = 190)

	18 × 18	6 × 6
Form A (alone):		
Life	.80	.87
Law	.86	.86
Morality and conscience	.79	.80
Punishment	.84	.82
Contract	.78	.79
Authority	.75	.76
Form B (alone):		
Life	.89	.92
Law	.84	.91
Morality and conscience	.88	.90
Punishment	.85	.87
Contract	.75	.79
Authority	.86	.86
Form C (alone):		
Life	.79	.81
Law	.77	.78
Morality and conscience	.80	.83
Punishment	.87	.90
Contract	.78	.79
Authority	.81	.86

TABLE 19

Unrotated Loadings for Five Factors in the 16–18 Age Group

	1	2	3	4	5
Life	.68	.34	.24	.19	−.14
Law	.79	.09	−.10	−.04	.26
Morality and conscience	.33	.29	.29	.24	.29
Punishment	.76	.24	−.17	−.09	−.27
Contract	.58	.05	.11	−.16	−.28
Authority	.46	.08	.41	.20	−.16
Life	.77	−.08	.12	−.26	−.15
Law	.65	.01	.30	−.11	−.09
Morality and conscience	.77	−.12	.46	.12	−.16
Punishment	.88	−.15	.08	−.28	.12
Contract	.51	.10	−.03	−.59	.28
Authority	.61	.54	−.07	−.12	.38
Life	.46	−.60	.30	.20	.38
Law	.64	−.75	−.12	.01	−.03
Morality and conscience	.66	−.03	−.32	.48	.22
Punishment	.80	.29	−.31	.33	−.12
Contract	.65	−.18	−.53	.01	−.10
Authority	.74	−.12	−.29	−.01	−.11
Eigenvalues	8.27	1.87	1.65	1.34	1.19
Variance (%)	46.00	10.40	9.20	7.20	6.60

45

C and scored using the Standard Form Scoring Manual, is a single, general domain.

RELATION OF MORAL JUDGMENT STAGE TO AGE

As one would expect of a developmental variable, our data show a clear relationship between age and moral judgment stage. The correlation between age and MMS was .78. As shown in table 20, mean moral maturity score increases monotonically from 188 (stage 2) at age 10 to 375 (stage 4[3]) at age 36. As shown in figure 1, the frequency of usage of stages 1 and 2 decreases from age 10 on, stage 3 increases up to age 16–18 and then decreases, and stage 4 begins at zero and rises monotonically to 62% at age 36. Stage 5

TABLE 20

PERCENTAGE OF SUBJECTS OF EACH AGE GROUP AT EACH STAGE

	AGE (Years)							
GLOBAL STAGE	10	13–14	16–18	20–22	24–26	28–30	32–33	36
1/2............	47.6	8.1	2.2	0	0	0	0	0
2...............	33.3	16.2	11.1	0	0	0	0	0
2/3............	14.3	56.8	17.8	9.4	8.0	0	0	0
3...............	4.8	16.2	44.4	31.3	12.0	16.2	8.7	0
3/4............	0	2.7	24.4	40.6	48.0	51.4	47.8	44.4
4...............	0	0	0	18.8	16.0	18.9	30.4	44.4
4/5............	0	0	0	0	16.0	13.5	13.0	11.1
Mean MMS......	189	246	290	327	357	361	369	375
S.D. MMS.......	31.4	37.7	43.7	36.1	49.1	42.3	41.5	25.6
N...............	21	37	46	33	25	38	23	9

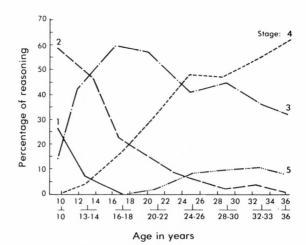

FIGURE 1.—Mean percentage of moral reasoning at each stage for each age group

46

also increases monotonically after its entry at age 20–22 but never rises above 10% of the reasoning in the sample as a whole.

Table 20 presents the data in terms of global as well as moral maturity scores. As that table indicates, the proportion of subjects at stage 1/2 in the sample decreases from a high of 47% at age 10 to 2% (one subject) at age 16–18. No subject is below stage 2 after that. Subjects at stage 2 decrease from about one-third of the 10-year-olds to 11% of the late adolescents (age 16–18). No one beyond age 18 was scored as stage 2. Very few subjects at age 20 or beyond were scored at stage 2/3. Most of our 2/3 subjects were in the 13–14-year age group. The proportion of stage 3 subjects increases up to age 18, then decreases to zero at our oldest age (36). The transition to stage 4 does not seem to begin before late adolescence—we found only one stage 3/4 subject before the 16–18-year age group. The proportion of 3/4 subjects in the sample increases through the early twenties and then levels off to a little less than half the sample. Consolidated stage 4 did not occur in our sample before age 20, and the proportion of stage 4's continued to increase through the oldest age in the study (age 36). The transition to stage 5 occurs even later, with no stage 4/5 subjects occurring before the mid-twenties. The proportion of subjects reaching stage 4/5 remains low (11%–16%) throughout the age range in which it appears, from the mid-twenties through the mid-thirties.

Looked at from the point of view of age norms in our sample, the interviews of most 10-year-olds were scored at stage 1/2 or 2, a few were scored at 2/3. Most early adolescents (13–14) were 2/3, though some were stage 2 or 3. Almost half of the late adolescents were scored as stage 3, about one-fourth had begun the transition to stage 4, and a little less than one-fifth were still in transition from stage 2 to stage 3. Youths in their early twenties were most likely to be in transition between stages 3 and 4 or to be still solidly at stage 3. About one-fifth of these subjects had completed the transition to stage 4. Most subjects from the mid-twenties through the mid-thirties were scored as stage 3/4 mixtures (or transitionals) with decreasing numbers at stage 3 and increasing numbers at consolidated stage 4. Subjects scored as postconventional (4/5 or 5) represent about one-sixth to one-eighth of the sample from the mid-twenties on.

Curves of mean stage usage for a group do not necessarily represent curves of growth for any of the individuals in the group. Accordingly, we present figures of changes in stage usage over time from four representative individuals (figs. 2–5). These subjects were randomly chosen from among those who were tested at all six times, and they can be considered typical of our data. Subject 3, for example, never shows reasoning at more than two adjacent stages.[6] His reasoning at age 10 is scored at stages 1 and 2. At age

[6] Note that we treat reasoning that represents less than 10% of the subject's total as error. For example, the 4% of stage 3 at age 10 reflects less than one full CJ across all dilemmas scored and thus should not be considered to be true use of stage 3 reasoning.

47

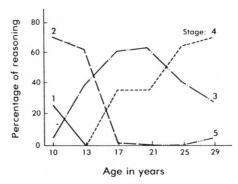

FIGURE 2.—Percentage of moral reasoning at each stage for each age: subject 3 (10 years old at time 1).

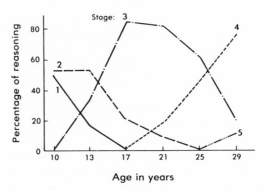

FIGURE 3.—Percentage of moral reasoning at each stage for each age: subject 9 (10 years old at time 1).

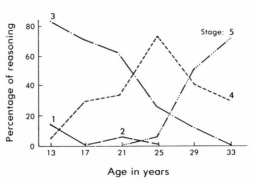

FIGURE 4.—Percentage of moral reasoning at each stage for each age: subject 37 (13 years old at time 1).

48

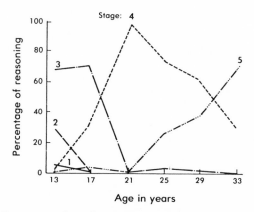

FIGURE 5.—Percentage of moral reasoning at each stage for each age: subject 42 (13 years old at time 1).

13, his moral judgment remained dominantly stage 2, but the stage 1 has dropped out and has been replaced by substantial use of stage 3. At age 14 the stage 3 has become dominant and stage 4 has entered as a second stage. This pattern remains stable between ages 17 and 21, but as he reaches young adulthood stage 4 begins to predominate over stage 3. Between ages 21 and 25 this trend continues, with the proportion of stage 4 usage increasing and the proportion of stage 3 decreasing. Perhaps most noteworthy is the orderliness and regularity of the developmental curves, with earlier stages dropping out as later stages enter such that the subject seems to be always in transition from one stage to the next. Also noteworthy is the fact that development continues throughout the age range sampled, never reaching a final plateau. The figure for subject 9 shows a similar pattern, except that some use of stage 1 seems to linger even after the entry of stage 3 at age 13. (This may be due to the fact that scoring errors confusing stages 1 and 3 are common when responses are ambiguous or poorly probed.) The rate of development for subject 9 is slower than that for subject 3, with stage 2 still in evidence at age 17 and stage 4 barely above the error boundary at age 21. Development between ages 25 and 29 is particularly striking in this subject, however, and at age 20 he is scored globally as consolidated stage 4, while subject 3 remains globally at stage 4(3) at that age. Subjects 37 and 42 also show the regular pattern of movement through the stages. These figures are of particular interest in that they show substantial development occurring into young adulthood—between ages 29 and 33. Stage change with age in all four subjects seems to alternate between periods of fairly rapid development and periods of slower development or consolidation. The curves for subject 3, for example, are especially steep between ages 13 and 17, plateau to some degree between 17 and 21, and become steep

49

again, indicating a second growth period between ages 21 and 25. Further-more, in all four cases a fairly saltatory model of development appears justified. That is, the absence at each time of three-stage mixture not only supports the assumption that reasoning at a given time forms a structured whole, it also bears on the process of development. The point here is that for the most part stage 1 has dropped out by the time use of stage 3 has begun, stage 2 has dropped out by the time use of stage 4 has begun, and so on. The holistic character of the developmental change is evident across the entire age range in our study.

COHORT EFFECT

Our sample can be considered to be composed of subjects from three cohorts—those who were 10 years old at time 1, those who were 13 at time 1, and those who were 16 at time 1. When data from these three groups are analyzed separately, we find that they all show the same moral judgment patterns. That is, subjects from all three groups demonstrate "structured wholeness" and invariant stage sequence in their moral judgment. As is shown in figure 6, the mean moral maturity scores for the three groups differed somewhat, particularly in that the means for the time 1 16-year-olds were lower at each testing time than were the means for the time 1 10-year-olds. The difference is not significant, however, and is most likely due to sampling procedures. The 10- and 13-year-olds were chosen from an ele-mentary school, while the 16-year-olds were chosen from a high school in the same community. Although each cohort was composed of half working-class and half middle-class subjects, there was a tendency for the high school subsample to come from somewhat lower socioeconomic origins within the broader working-class and middle-class categories than was

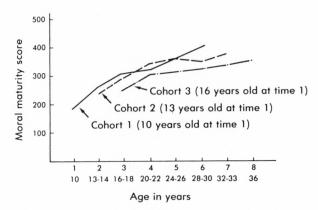

FIGURE 6.—Mean moral maturity scores at each age for each cohort

true for the younger subjects. That is, the high school tended to draw the lower end of both the working-class ("lower" rather than "upper lower" class) and the middle-class (lower middle and middle rather than upper middle class) categories. This may have resulted in the consistent though nonsignificant tendency for the time 1 16-year-olds to score a little lower than the others at each testing time. Based on the information available to us, there is little reason to believe that the slight group mean differences represent a historical cohort effect. Neither do we interpret the data as indicating a practice effect on the moral judgment interview since in our test-retest analysis we found no such practice effect.

STABILITY OF INDIVIDUAL DIFFERENCES

Our data bear on the question of whether there are stable individual differences in rate of moral judgment development. The issue here is whether scores at one age predict to scores at a later age. As table 21 shows, the correlations between moral maturity scores at age 10 and scores at ages 13, 17, and 21 are positive and significant but not very high. The age 10 scores do not predict adulthood scores at all. In contrast, moral judgment scores at age 13 are much more highly correlated with later scores, even with scores at age 32–33. Though the *highest* correlation between scores at age 10 and those from a later testing was .47, the *lowest* correlation between scores at age 13 and later ones was .46 and the correlations ranged up to .70. Scores at age 16 do not seem to predict later scores any better than do

TABLE 21

Correlations among Moral Maturity Scores at Different Ages
(*N*'s in Parentheses)

	Age (Years)							
Age (Years)	10	13–14	16–18	20–22	24–26	28–30	32–33	36
10............		.395* (21)	.456* (15)	.473* (18)	.198 (13)	−.249 (10)		
13–14.........	.395* (21)		.699* (30)	.464* (24)	.696* (23)	.668* (23)	.571* (10)	
16–18.........	.456* (15)	.699* (30)		.682* (31)	.732* (36)	.685* (23)	.448* (23)	.164 (10)
20–22.........	.473* (18)	.464* (24)	.683* (31)		.710* (19)	.481 (23)	.764* (12)	−.119 (6)
24–26.........	.198 (13)	.696* (23)	.732* (21)	.710* (19)		.905* (16)	.862* (7)	
28–30.........	−.249 (10)	.668* (23)	.685* (36)	.481 (23)	.905* (16)		.809* (21)	.083 (10)
32–33.........		.571* (10)	.448* (23)	.764* (12)	.862* (7)	.809* (21)		.880* (8)
36............			.164 (10)	−.119 (6)		.083 (10)	.880* (8)	

* $p < .05$.

51

the scores at age 13, but at age 20 the scores again seem to increase in stability to some degree.[7] (By stability we mean maintenance of relative rank order rather than a decrease in developmental change within individuals.) It seems, then, that there are two periods during which stabilization in this sense occurs. The first occurs between ages 10 and 13, that is, as the subjects enter adolescence. The second period of stabilization occurs between the ages of about 17 and 21, that is, as the subjects enter early adulthood. This does not necessarily imply that these are periods of particularly rapid development in moral judgment. In fact, the mean increase for the group as a whole was not much greater between ages 10 and 13 than between ages 13–14 and 16–18, nor was it greater between 16–18 and 20–22 than between 13–14 and 16–18. As was shown in table 20, the increase in mean MMS with age is gradual and quite even across the age range studied. Rather, these periods of stabilization reflect a tendency for subjects to shift their positions in relation to each others' moral judgment scores as they enter adolescence and again as they enter adulthood.

THE RELATIONSHIP OF MORAL JUDGMENT STAGE TO OTHER VARIABLES

Given the existence of fairly stable individual differences in moral judgment stage, the question arises as to what determines these differences. Our study provides data on a number of variables that might be expected to be related to moral judgment stage. These variables include socioeconomic status of origin, sociometric status (as measured at time 1), IQ (group test scores taken from school records at time 1), and educational level attained.

Socioeconomic status.—As table 22 indicates, correlations between par-

TABLE 22

CORRELATIONS BETWEEN MORAL JUDGMENT AND SOCIAL CLASS, SOCIOMETRIC STATUS, IQ, AND EDUCATION

	AGE (Years)							
	10 (N = 21)	13–14 (N = 36)	16–18 (N = 46)	20–22 (N = 34)	24–26 (N = 24)	28–30 (N = 38)	32–33 (N = 23)	36 (N = 10)
$r_{\text{MMS, SES}}$	.60*	.42*	.38*	.54*	.36*	.22*	.41*	.57*
$r_{\text{MMS, SMS}}$	−.36	−.12	−.17	−.04	−.17	−.22	−.18	−.35
$r_{\text{IQ, MMS}}$	.19	.25	.17	.27	.37*	.51*	.60*	.37
$r_{\text{education, MMS}}$	...	...	...	...	.69*	.54*	.59*	.77*

* $p < .05$.

[7] Recall that the test-retest correlations were in the high nineties. This indicates that the unexplained variance in predicting from earlier to later ages cannot be attributed to measurement error.

52

ents' SES and subjects' moral judgment scores were moderate at every age. They ranged from .32 to .62, and all but one were above .40. There was no tendency for the relationship to either strengthen or attenuate with age, and the fluctuations of correlations across age showed no clear pattern.

Perhaps more enlightening is a comparison of working-class and middle-class subsamples on mean percentage of each stage used at each age. As shown in figure 7, the distributions are quite different for the two subsamples. Both stages 3 and 4 exceed the 10% error cutoff level at earlier ages in the middle-class group. Stage 3 is present at age 10 for middle-class subjects but not until age 13 for working-class subjects. Stage 4 appears at age 16 in the middle-class group but not until age 20 in the lower-SES group.

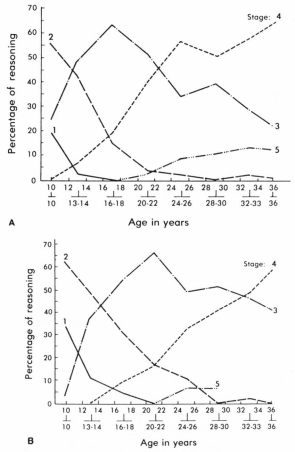

FIGURE 7.—Mean percentage of moral reasoning at each stage for each age group. a, High-SES subject. b, Low-SES subject.

53

Furthermore, stage 2 remains above the 10% cutoff somewhat longer for lower-SES subjects. Whereas stage 5 use exceeds 10% at age 28 in the upper-SES group, it never exceeds the error cutoff in the lower-SES group.[8]

Sociometric status.—Correlations between moral maturity score and sociometric status were substantially lower than correlations between moral judgment scores and SES. Except at age 10 they did not achieve significance. Again no clear pattern emerged in fluctuation of SMS/MMS correlations across time (see table 22).

A comparison of stage × age figures (fig. 8a, 8b) for sociometric integrates and isolates reveals that stage 3 exceeds the 10% cutoff at age 10 in the integrated group but does not do so among the isolates until age 13. In addition, the isolates at age 10 show substantially more stage 1 use than do 10-year-old sociometric integrates. Stage 1 drops below 10% at age 13 for integrates but not until age 16 for isolates. As the correlations show, differences in sociometric groups beyond age 13 are minimal. Overall, then, the data show that at the time that sociometric status was evaluated, integrates tended to show more stage 3 and less stage 1 than sociometric isolates. However, the difference between groups is not maintained over time.

A multiple regression analysis indicates that age accounts for 60% of the variance in moral maturity scores. Adding SES raises the proportion of variance accounted for to 67%, and adding sociometric status adds very little, raising the proportion of variance accounted for to 68%. Because SES was not reassigned for adult subjects who may have changed in social class and because sociometric status was assessed only at time 1, these figures on the relative importance of age, SES, and SMS should be interpreted cautiously.

Intelligence.—Correlations between moral maturity score and IQ were nonsignificant and ranged from .17 to .27 in childhood and adolescence for our sample but become substantially higher at age 24 and above (.37–.60) (see table 22). Except at age 36 (an analysis which included only 10 subjects), the correlations increase steadily from age 24 on and are significant at the three age levels between 24 and 33. This occurs in spite of the fact that IQ was assessed only at time 1. It appears, then, that while rate of moral development in childhood and adolescence is only slightly related to IQ, the final level achieved in adulthood is more closely related to intellectual capacity, perhaps partly via differential educational experiences that are related to intelligence.

Educational level attained.—Correlations between adult moral maturity

[8] The stage 5 present in the low-SES group is due to one subject (case 2) reaching stage 4/5 at age 24. Since he was age 10 at time 1 and age 28 at time 6, he was not interviewed at age 32 or 36. That is, the decrease in mean percentage of stage 5 does not reflect a decrease in stage 5 use in any one subject, but rather the absence of the one stage 4/5 subject at the last two ages.

54

score and educational level attained ranged from .54 to .69 ($p < .05$), with no clear relationship between strength of correlation and age (see table 22). (Only ages 23, 27, and 31 are reported because formal education for many subjects was not completed before age 23 and the N at age 36 is small.) Note that these correlations are somewhat higher than the correlations between moral judgment and either social class or IQ.

Partial correlations substantiate the interpretation that moral judgment stage is related to educational experience itself rather than to educational level as a reflection of IQ and SES differences. The correlation between MMS and subject's education with IQ partialed out is .36 ($p < .05$) at age

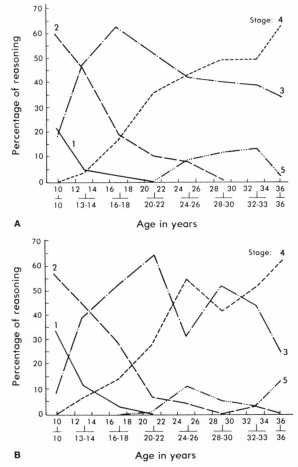

FIGURE 8.—Mean percentage of moral reasoning at each stage for each age group. *a*, Sociometric integrates. *b*, Sociometric isolates.

55

TABLE 23

RELATION BETWEEN EDUCATION AND MORAL JUDGMENT DIVIDED BY SOCIAL CLASS

STAGE	Finished High School Only	Some College	Four Years College and/or B.A.	Graduate School, M.A. and/or Ph.D.
	EDUCATION (%)			
	Working Class			
4/5......	...	...	...	33 (N=1)
4.......	...	17 (N=1)	33 (N=1)	33 (N=1)
3/4.....	75 (N=3)	83 (N=5)	67 (N=2)	33 (N=1)
3.......	25 (N=1)			
	Middle Class			
4/5......	...	...	14 (N=1)	50 (N=5)
4.......	...	33 (N=1)	57 (N=4)	50 (N=5)
3/4.....	50 (N=2)	67 (N=2)	29 (N=2)	...
3.......	50 (N=2)	...	...	...

NOTE.—Data taken from age groups 28–36.

28, the only age at which the N was large enough to make a partial correlation feasible. The correlation between MMS and subject's education with parents' SES partialed out is slightly higher, $r = .45$ ($p < .05$) at age 28. The correlation between MMS and education with both IQ and SES partialed out was somewhat lower but still significant, $r = .26$, $p < .05$. It appears, then, that educational experience per se is related to moral judgment maturity beyond the association of education to SES and IQ.

Table 23 presents the moral judgment $\times$ education data in a way that is perhaps more revealing than a correlational analysis. The table indicates that no subjects from either working-class or middle-class origins achieved consolidated stage 4 moral judgment without attending at least some college and no subject from either social class achieved stage 4/5 without having completed college. (Recall in this regard that no one reached stage 4 before age 20 and no one reached stage 4/5 before age 24.) Whereas more middle-class than working-class subjects reached stages 4 and 4/5, both of these moral judgment levels were attainable by subjects of working-class origins who had attended college. (No statistical analysis was performed on these data because expected values in the tables' cells were less than 5.)

V. DISCUSSION

STANDARD SCORING RELIABILITY AND VALIDITY

Taken together, the data presented here indicate that Standard Issue Scoring has succeeded in addressing the central methodological concerns raised in critiques such as the widely cited paper by Kurtines and Grief (1974). The criticisms of Kohlberg's method presented by Kurtines and Grief fall into three general categories: (1) nonstandardization of the interview and coding scheme; (2) questionable reliability of the coding schemes, especially important given their complexity and "subjectivity"; and (3) questionable validity of the coding schemes, particularly a failure to present clear evidence of invariant stage sequence.

As its name indicates, the Standard Issue Moral Judgment Interview and Scoring System represent an attempt to standardize the assessment of moral judgment stage. The nine hypothetical dilemmas constitute three parallel interview forms, the probing questions are specified, and the scoring system is no longer undergoing revision.[9] Although the system remains complex, it can be mastered by individuals who are relatively inexperienced as indicated by the interrater reliability figures presented here. Test-retest and alternate form reliability are also high, as is internal consistency of scores assigned an interview. This should both assure reliable scoring within each study that uses the measure and provide enough standardization to allow comparison of results across studies by different investigators. This increase in reliability and objectivity in scoring was achieved by the creation of a small but conceptually, rather than arbitrarily, defined unit of analysis, by the elaboration of clear rules for classification of material and for defining a match between manual and interview judgments, and by the construction of specific and detailed stage criteria, the critical indicators, which specify exactly what is required in the interview in order for a stage

[9] The scoring manual itself is currently in press with Cambridge University Press. Consistent use of the published manual should make possible greater comparability across independently conducted studies.

score to be assigned. On the other side of the reliability/validity balance, structural explications of each manual item were provided in order to minimize loss of validity due to overly literal interpretation of the manual.

With regard to validity, we have argued that prediction to an external criterion such as action taken in a moral conflict situation is not an appropriate indicator of the instrument's validity. The appropriate question is whether the interview and scoring system provides a valid assessment of moral judgment stage, not of moral character as a whole. If validity is understood in this way, the present longitudinal study can be considered to provide substantial support for the validity of Standard Issue Scoring. That is, when Standard Issue Scoring was used to score longitudinal interviews not used to construct the measure, it yielded scores that agreed very closely with the theoretical predictions of invariant sequence and internal consistency.

In order to establish fully the validity of Standard Issue Scoring, there is a need for further research on discriminant and construct validity, particularly longitudinal studies of populations differing from that described here. Four such longitudinal studies using Standard Issue Scoring have been reported: one with American girls and young women (Erickson 1980), one with American male and female college students (Gilligan & Murphy 1979), one with Turkish boys and young men (Nisan & Kohlberg 1982), and one with Israeli boys and girls (Snarey 1982).

The studies conducted in the United States are difficult to interpret because of design problems. Both Erickson's and Gilligan and Murphy's samples participated between times 1 and 2 in courses intended to promote moral development. Particularly problematic is the fact that these courses included direct study and discussion of Kohlberg's theory. Furthermore, these studies used different forms of the moral judgment interview at different testing times rather than maintaining a consistent set of dilemmas across all waves of data collection. Since scores on different dilemmas may differ somewhat, the unsystematic variation in dilemmas used may introduce error into the data. A further limitation of these studies is the fact that Erickson's subjects at each testing time and Gilligan and Murphy's at time 1 and time 2 filled out a written version of the moral judgment interview rather than participating in individually administered taped interviews. Since responses to written interviews are less well elaborated than responses to oral interviews, misscoring of the former is more likely to occur.

Possibly as a result of these methodological problems, both Erickson and Gilligan and Murphy report somewhat more frequent sequence reversals than were found in the present study. Over three 3–8-year intervals, the Gilligan and Murphy data show 12%–15% downward stage movement as compared to our 3%. Over a 4-year interval (between time 1 and time 5), the Erickson data show 9% downward stage movement. Calculated over all

58

1-year testing intervals, Erickson finds 13% downward stage movement. It should be noted that in spite of indicating somewhat more frequent stage reversal, all of these figures fall within the limits of measurement error as represented by our test-retest data.

The difference between Erickson's 1-year and 4-year interval data is consistent with earlier findings (Kuhn 1976; White, Bushnell, & Regnemer 1978) that the longer the time interval between subsequent testings, the more likely a subject was to have advanced rather than regressed. These results have been interpreted as evidence that short-term fluctuations in moral judgment occur in the context of long-term progression. Whether it is most appropriate to treat the short-term fluctuations as measurement error or as actual stage change is impossible to determine with certainty. Of course, the present study does not allow us to compare short-term fluctuation with long-term progression within the same individuals since all interviews were conducted 3–4 years apart. However, we have seen that downward changes from time 1 to time 2 in our test-retest sample are substantially more frequent than from time n to time $n + 1$ in our longitudinal sample.

We interpret the differences between time 1 and time 2 in the test-retest sample as measurement error rather than as true developmental fluctuation, primarily because the percent agreement and correlation coefficients are essentially the same for test-retest, interrater, and alternate form reliability. That is, there seems to be slippage or error of about 1/3 stage in the system. When this confidence interval is superimposed on negligible developmental progress, as in the case of testings 1 year apart, the result will be relatively more frequent occurrence of lower scores at time $n + 1$ than at time n. When the measurement error is superimposed on developmental progress, as in the case of testings 3 years apart, the occurrence of a score 1/3 stage below the individual's "true stage" would result in either no change from time n to time $n + 1$ or a smaller positive change than would otherwise appear. If most individuals move forward at least 1/3 stage in 4 years, this interval will not yield many cases of apparent regression.

The two cross-cultural longitudinal studies that used Standard Issue Scoring more closely parallel the present study in design. Subjects did not participate in programs of moral education, dilemmas used were held constant across all waves of data collection, and interviews were individually administered. In both these studies, the stage sequence data were as clear-cut as in the present American longitudinal study. Nisan and Kohlberg (1982) report the results of data collected over a 12-year period in Turkey. Subjects were 23 boys ranging in age from 10 to 17 at time 1. Interviewing took place in 1964, 1966, 1970, and 1976 in three locations in Turkey: a rural village, a seaport provincial capital, and the national capital. Stages 1–4 were present in this sample. There was no stage skipping and only one instance (3%) of downward stage movement. Snarey (1982) reports 10-year

59

longitudinal data on 92 boys and girls from Israeli cities and kibbutzim. Snarey found that the Standard Issue Scoring System yielded reliability data on Israeli interviews comparable to the reliability data reported here for our American sample. Stages 2 through 4/5 were present in this sample. With regard to invariant sequence, he found that downward stage change occurred in only 5% of the adjacent times.

To sum up, there have been four reported longitudinal studies of moral judgment using Standard Issue Scoring in addition to the present study. In two of these studies there were methodological problems which might be expected to increase measurement error. The stage sequence data are in fact somewhat less orderly in these two studies than in the others. However, the frequency of sequence anomalies even in these studies is quite low, substantially lower than the frequency of downward stage change in our test-retest data. In the two cross-cultural studies, the sequence data are essentially identical to those reported in the present study. Of these four studies, only one, Snarey, presents internal consistency data. The results of Snarey's Israeli study regarding internal consistency of moral judgment are essentially identical to our own results. That is, in a factor analysis only one general factor emerged, and very few subjects showed reasoning at more than two adjacent stages.

In light of criticisms of Kohlberg's theory by Holstein (1976), Gilligan (1977), and others, one might wonder whether subjects in the studies that report more orderly sequence data are more predominantly male and subjects in the studies with less orderly data are more predominantly female. The fact that Erickson's subjects were all female and Nisan and Kohlberg's subjects as well as those in the present study were all male may seem to support this interpretation. However, the subjects in Gilligan and Murphy's and Snarey's studies were approximately half male and half female. The issue of sex differences in orderliness of stage sequence may be addressed by calculating separately the percentage of reversals among males and females in the Gilligan and Murphy and Snarey studies. In fact, there do not appear to be significant sex differences in either of these studies in either developmental stage or in orderliness of stage sequence.

Overall, these four studies using Standard Issue Scoring are consistent in yielding more orderly sequence data than have been reported by investigators using earlier scoring systems. We have already referred to Kramer's analysis of Kohlberg's data and we shall discuss it further in the next section.

Holstein (1976) has reported 3-year longitudinal data on Kohlberg's moral judgment interview with 52 13-year-old boys and girls and their parents. Using Structural Issue Scoring on interviews that were primarily written, she found that a substantial number of subjects skipped stages or reverted from a higher to a lower stage between time 1 and time 2. Holstein found both age and sex differences in the frequency of stage skipping. While

21% of the adolescents skipped at least one stage between time 1 and time 2, only 7% of the adults did so. Stage skipping in males tended to be from stage 1 or 2 to stage 4, in females from stage 3 to stage 5. Holstein also reported a substantial amount of regression from time 1 to time 2 along with a dramatic difference in frequency of regression for lower-stage (1–3) subjects and for higher-stage (4–6) subjects. While virtually none of the lower-stage subjects regressed, many (20%–33%) of the higher-stage subjects did revert to a lower stage at time 2. Without rescoring Holstein's interviews, it is impossible to determine whether the differences between her results and those presented here are due to scoring differences, sampling differences, or some other feature that differs across the two studies. Holstein interprets the high rate of regression among higher-stage subjects as an indication that Kohlberg's stages 4 through 6 do not represent an invariant developmental sequence but rather are alternative and equally mature forms of moral judgment. An alternative interpretation is the higher stages were inadequately defined in scoring systems prior to Standard Issue Scoring. Perhaps the strongest evidence for the validity of this interpretation is the fact that Kramer's (1968) analysis of Kohlberg's longitudinal data showed patterns of regression and stage skipping that were almost identical to those Holstein found. On rescoring using Standard Issue Scoring, virtually all of the anomalies in Kohlberg's data disappeared. That is, in the study reported here, stages 4 and 5 do appear to be developmentally ordered. The relation between stages 5 and 6 cannot be addressed, of course, since stage 6 has been dropped from the system. Among the other longitudinal studies that used Standard Issue Scoring, only two traced the stage sequence up to stage 5. The results with regard to sequence in these two studies are inconclusive. While Snarey (1982) finds virtually no downward stage change at either low stage or high stage levels, Gilligan and Murphy (1979) do report a tendency for subjects to regress from stage 5 to transitional level 4/5. This difference may be an artifact resulting from the fact that the latter subjects had studied Kohlberg's theory while the former subjects had not. On the other hand, it might indicate some remaining unresolved inadequacy in the differentiation of stage 5 from transitional level 4/5.

White, Bushnell, and Regnemer (1978) present longitudinal data collected on the island Eleuthera in the Bahamas. Their data include a 3–7-year longitudinal sample and a series of 2–7-year longitudinal samples. Like Holstein, they used Structural Issue Scoring. Although the findings indicate a general pattern of upward stage change over time, some respondents in all subsamples did regress. Since the authors report analyses of variance rather than frequency of regression, we cannot directly compare their results with those from the other studies discussed here. White et al. point out that in their data, the longer the time interval between subsequent testings, the more likely a subject was to have advanced rather than regressed. They

MONOGRAPHS

argue that their findings suggest that moral judgment stages develop sequentially, but short-term fluctuations either up or down may often take place in the context of long-term progression. This is the same pattern that Erickson (1980) found using Standard Issue Scoring. We have argued above that the pattern is probably an indication of measurement error superimposed on steady developmental progression.

Another instance of this pattern has been reported by Kuhn (1976) in a 1-year longitudinal study of 50 5–8-year-old children. Kuhn used simplified versions of the dilemmas from Standard Form A and used global story scoring to analyze the responses. The children were interviewed three times—at time 1, 6 months after time 1, and 1 year after time 1. Kuhn found that at 6-month intervals the data showed a considerable amount of downward as well as upward stage movement. In fact, between time 1 and time 2, and between time 2 and time 3, subjects were not significantly more likely to move upward than downward. The pattern of change from time 1 to time 3 was drastically different, however. While there was a substantial amount of upward stage change, only one subject out of 50 (2%) showed any downward movement (using our nine-point scale). There were no occasions of stage skipping. It is worth noting that at this age level 1 year is a long enough interval to show steady progression, while at older ages 1-year intervals show the kind of short-term fluctuation that Kuhn found in her 6-month intervals. This is no doubt due to age differences in rate of development.

Also noteworthy is the fact that the sequence in Kuhn's 1-year data is as orderly as it is in our data despite the fact that she used an earlier scoring system. This further illustrates the point made earlier that in Standard Issue Scoring the higher stages were more radically redefined than were the lower stages.

Turning to our own longitudinal data, we see a dramatic improvement over Kohlberg and Kramer's earlier analysis in the fit between theory and data in relation to both structured wholeness and invariant sequence. Before considering the details of that improvement, we must raise again the question of circularity. Is the improvement simply the result of post hoc manipulations that ensure our obtaining the desired results (i.e., it could not have been otherwise)? We think not. As indicated earlier, Standard Issue Scoring rules do not force consistency of stage scores assigned an interview. According to the rules, scores could have been scattered across three or four stages for an individual subject, yet they were not. Our design could not prevent the halo effect of a scorer bias toward consistency *within* dilemmas but did prevent such an effect *across* dilemmas by requiring that each of the nine dilemmas for each subject be scored independently of one another. Furthermore, the interviews from which sequence and internal consistency data were derived were not used at all in reformulating the stages or creating

62

the scoring manual. If there were no clear sequence in moral judgment development, it should not have been possible to derive a system from seven "construction cases" that would yield such clear sequence for the 51 blind cases. The fact that the raters were required to use specific, objective criteria in assigning scores makes the sequence and internal consistency findings even more convincing. The records kept on each subject document in exactly what sense the subject was judged to have developed (or remained the same) from one time to the next and in exactly what sense that subject's responses can be considered structurally consistent from one dilemma to the next at the same testing time.

Let us look, then, at the improvement of theory/data fit by comparing our results with those of Kramer (1968) using the early scoring systems of Sentence and Story Rating. Figure 9 presents the average distribution of stage use for Kramer's analysis and our own. There is clearly a much greater spread of scores for Kramer's subjects across nonadjacent stages. While Kramer reports an average of 16% of a subject's scores are assigned at stages two steps removed from his modal stage, in our sample only 1% of scores were assigned to those stages. Whereas none of our subjects used reasoning three steps removed from the modal stage, Kramer did find 5% of such use. (Recall that according to our scoring rules such an occurrence is perfectly permissible but, nevertheless, empirically it did not occur.) We also see an improvement in the sequence data. While Kramer's scores show 19% downward stage change using the nine-point scale, we find only 4%.

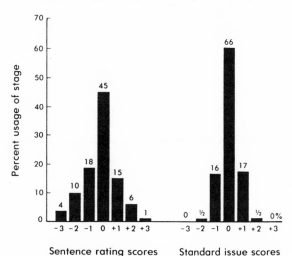

FIGURE 9.—Distributions of stage usage in relation to modal stage: sentence rating and standard scores.

What accounts for this improvement? One factor is surely the increased reliability of Standard Issue Scoring. If scores are unstable due to unreliability, there will be greater heterogeneity across dilemmas and more frequent sequence anomalies due to measurement error. But we have argued that Standard Scoring is more valid than earlier systems as well as more reliable in that it more adequately differentiates moral judgment content from the organization or structure of moral judgment. If content associated with structure is used as a scoring criterion, the data may yield appropriate trends, but exact sequence will not be found, as was true of Kramer's scores. Because content is only probabilistically related to structure, a subject may begin to use the content associated with a higher stage before he has used the content usually associated with a lower stage. Whereas a structurally accurate evaluation might show an increase in the sophistication of this individual's reasoning, a content analysis would show regression. Also, in terms of internal consistency, if scores are not assigned on the basis of the truly developmental features of the judgments, then those scores may or may not be equivalent across dilemmas or issues.

THEORETICAL EVOLUTION

The method we have used in responding to early theory/data discrepancies is not strictly hypothetico-deductive. In other discussions we have called this method "bootstrapping" (Colby 1978; Kohlberg 1980; see also Loevinger 1976). By "bootstrapping" we mean the notion of an evolving research program in which data feed back into theory and method to improve the account of development we offer. This process is not unique to our efforts. In fact, it could be argued that it is the model used in all scientific endeavors.

In justifying the legitimacy of this model, we shall consider and respond to a critique of Kohlberg's theory by Nicolayev and Phillips (1979). (See Puka [1979] for a more complete reply to Nicolayev and Phillips.) These authors have attempted to evaluate Kohlberg's theory in relation to criteria set forth by Lakatos (1976). As Nicolayev and Phillips point out, Lakatos distinguishes between a theory's "hard core" assumptions (those elements of theory that cannot be changed without abandoning the theory) and its "protective belt" (those aspects of the theory that are subject to change in light of experience). A progressive research program includes "a partially articulated set of suggestions or hints on how to change, develop the 'refutable variants' of the research programme, how to modify, sophisticate, the 'refutable' protective belt." The resulting modification of the protective belt must anticipate new facts or be "content-increasing" rather than simply be means to explain away discrepant findings.

Though we agree with Nicolayev and Phillips in identifying the structural wholeness and invariant sequence of stages as defining the hard core,[10] we are led to conclusions very different from theirs. Our point here is not to argue that the data support these assumptions (as they clearly do) but rather to defend the theoretical revision process as progressive rather than "a readjustment of scoring procedures to give the results required by the theoretical assumptions" (p. 241). We have already pointed out that the procedure for revising the stage descriptions, constructing the manual, and scoring the data did not in any sense guarantee the results that were obtained. The theoretical and methodological evolution did not consist in generating new scoring rules that would force internal consistency or postulation of new stages to explain sequence regression. In fact, the two interviews identified by Kohlberg (1973) as "Stage $4\frac{1}{2}$" are still counted as violations of sequence in the current analysis. Instead the evolution entailed a sweeping revision of the entire stage sequence and a radical redefinition of the basic structures in moral judgment development.

These revisions have not only permitted the generation of new and testable hypotheses (e.g., the predictive value of moral judgment substage for moral conduct; see Kohlberg and Candee [1981]). They also constitute theoretical advances in ways that go beyond the fact that they yield improved reliability, internal consistency, and sequence data. One example is of particular interest in light of Nicolayev and Phillips's argument that there is no "logical necessity" to the order of the moral judgment stages. Although we shall not take up here the critics' confusion about what Kohlberg means by logical necessity (see Puka [1979] for this), we can provide an illustration of the sense in which the current stage descriptions allow a clearer rationale for the invariance of the sequence than did the early, more content-based stage descriptions. If stage 3 is considered the "interpersonal concordance orientation" and stage 4 is defined as the "law and order orientation," there is no discernible reason for stage 4 to develop only after one has passed through stage 3. Neither is there any clear justification for the greater adequacy of law-and-order thinking. In fact, to most liberal social scientists this claim must seem counterintuitive, even objectionable. Fortunately, the more formal stage criteria of the current system provide a solution to this problem. Development in level of perspective is one important contributor to the increasing cognitive adequacy of each stage. To oversimplify a bit, development through the stages yields ever better understanding of and ability to integrate several points of view about a moral conflict situation along with a greater ability to distinguish morally relevant situational factors and to take them into account.

[10] One need not accept Phillips's and Nicolayev's statement that "the assumption that moral development occurs in fixed stages . . . could not be given up, for then nothing of the program would remain." Although we consider the stage concept to be central, others, such as Rest (1979), do not.

With regard to the question of each stage presupposing the understanding achieved at lower stages, the level of perspective notion again provides a convincing rationale. The claim is simply that one cannot take a prior-to-society perspective without the capacity to think in terms of a social system; one cannot take a social system perspective without the capacity to think in terms of shared norms and expectations of a group or mutually oriented dyadic relationships; one cannot respond in terms of coordinated individual perspectives until one can differentiate individual perspectives; and so on. In addition to this very general sense in which each stage presupposes development through the previous stages, Standard Scoring clarifies the increasing sophistication, differentiation, and integration of specific moral concepts such as promise keeping or the importance of intentionality in assigning punishment. Consider, for example, the following items from the form A manual. These are responses to the question, Should the judge punish Heinz if he does steal the drug?

Stage 2:   The judge should be lenient because Heinz wanted to keep his wife alive.

Stage 3:   The judge should be lenient because Heinz acted unselfishly in stealing the drug for his wife.

Stage 4:   The judge should be lenient because (s)he should recognize the extenuating or mitigating circumstances and be lenient within the parameters of the law.

Stage 4/5: The judge should be lenient because (s)he can find a precedent or develop a rule of law that reflects what is right.

These examples illustrate a developmental progression in the understanding of intentionality in relation to punishment. At stage 2 the argument for leniency is that Heinz had a good reason for stealing the drug. That is, it is assumed that there is no need to punish transgressions that make pragmatic sense. At stage 3, the argument expands to include a concern for good motives. It is no longer enough for the reason to be pragmatically sensible. At stage 3 the intention must be prosocial and its significance derives from its implications for the actor's underlying good character. That is, it is assumed that one ought not to punish someone who is good, well intentioned, unselfish, and so on. Whereas at stage 2 the excusing conditions (reasons) are transitory and situational, at stage 3 they are relatively stable or permanent, referring to character. Although the individual who reasons at stage 4 appreciates that Heinz had a good reason to steal and was well intentioned, having good intentions is no longer seen as sufficient to justify leniency toward a lawbreaker. The stage 4 judgment reflects an understanding of a systematic, formalized way to take intention into account within the established legal framework. That is, leniency is justified on the basis of a judge's discretion within a framework that assumes the value of maintaining legal consistency. The level 4/5 judgment goes beyond the stage 4 conception of *maintaining* legal precedent toward a recognition of the legitimacy of creating precedent through interpretation of the law. It should be apparent that each stage involves an awareness of the considerations of previous stages and some recognition of the legitimacy of those considerations. As a new stage is entered, however, the argument from the previous stage is no longer seen as sufficient. At the new stage the argument is qualified and placed within a more complex framework which transforms its meaning.

AGE NORMS

An important aspect of the change in moral judgment scoring criteria is that the current system stresses more heavily the need for the rater to look beyond the subject's superficial verbal responses to the conceptual significance of those responses for the individual. This is achieved methodologically through intensive probing of statements made in the interviews (e.g., What do you mean by that? Why is that important?) and by requiring each interview/manual match to undergo a structural evaluation based on the stage structure paragraph provided with each criterion judgment. One result of this shift is that people are less likely to be "given credit" for cliches and language that resemble those of higher stages if they do not exhibit the appropriate conceptual underpinning. This means that stage criteria are in general more stringent than in earlier scoring systems. The result is a fairly radical change in age norms.

Figure 10 presents percentage of stage usage for the middle-class longitudinal subjects aged 10 through 24 using Sentence Rating scores (fig. 10a) and Standard Issue scores (fig. 10b).[11] The distributions are clearly very different. One noteworthy difference is that the Sentence Rating scores show spread across a wider range of stages for each age. This no doubt reflects a tendency for the early scoring system to treat content differences as developmentally significant both within and across subjects.

Along with the greater variance in the Sentence Rating scores, we see a tendency for Sentence Rating scores to be higher than those using the Standard Issue System. In the early analysis, stage 4 is in evidence at age 10 and is relatively heavily used at ages 13 and 16. In our analysis there is no use of stage 4 at age 10, less than 10% at age 13, and less than 20% use of stage 4 even at age 16. The difference in use of stage 5 is even more dramatic. Sentence Rating assigns some stage 5 scores to subjects as young as age 13 and shows stage 5 as the group's most frequently used stage at age 16. We show no use of stage 5 until age 24.

As subjects move from age 16 to age 20, stages 4 and 5 reverse in the

[11] Only the middle-class subsample is used because a comparable figure for the total sample based on Sentence Rating scores was not available.

early analysis. That is, at age 16 stage 5 predominates over stage 4 while at age 20 stage 4 predominates over stage 5. This reversal indicates the presence of sequence anomalies in the early data such that a number of subjects scored at stage 5 at age 16 were scored as stage 4 at age 20. The Standard Issue data show no such reversal. Between ages 16 and 20 stage 4 use increases steadily and stage 3 use decreases. There is no evidence of stage 5 until age 24 and stage 5 use does not decrease once it has occurred. This results in a very different picture of stage use in late adolescence and early adulthood than had been assumed previously. According to Standard Issue

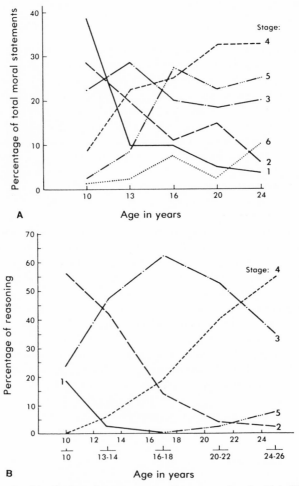

FIGURE 10.—Distribution of stage usage. a, Sentence rating for high-SES subjects. b, Standard scoring for high-SES subjects.

Scoring, moral judgment at age 20 is essentially completely conventional, whereas using the 1958 system subjects show substantial representations of stages 4, 5, 3, and 2.

In summary, both within and across subjects, Standard Issue scores show greater homogeneity than scores reported in earlier analyses of these data. The range of moral judgment stages used by middle-class American boys at a given age seems to be fairly limited. From our current perspective it is clear that Sentence Rating profiles were reflecting a range of content emphases or orientations rather than a range of qualitatively different structures. Superficial differences which in the earlier system were treated as structurally significant are no longer represented by different stage scores.

One important issue raised by the difference in the two analyses is the question of adulthood stages. In light of the emergence of stages 5 and 6 in adolescence, Kohlberg and Kramer (1969) concluded that "there was no new way of thinking about the moral situations that was found in adulthood and not found in adolescence" (p. 105).[12] Our interpretation of this finding is that the early scoring systems could not discriminate properly among superficially similar moral judgments at stages 3, 4, and 5. This meant that when "true Stage 5" began to emerge in early adulthood, it was not recognized as a qualitatively new form of reasoning. We can now discriminate principled reasoning from superficially similar conventional reasoning, and we no longer see stage 5 being used in junior high or high school. This means that there *is* a new stage in adulthood and that many of our subjects continued to develop in their twenties and thirties, rather than reaching a ceiling in mid-adolescence. This result is intuitively appealing since 30-year-olds often do seem to be more sophisticated in their moral judgment than 16-year-olds. However, it does raise the question of whether stage 5 is a "naturally developing" stage in the strict Piagetian sense (see Gibbs 1979).

Along with the age shift in onset of stage 5, we also see a reduction in the prevalence of principled moral judgment once it begins to appear. In our analysis, stage 5 scores do not rise above 15% even at age 36, whereas Kramer (1968) shows almost 30% stage 5 use at age 16. According to Standard Issue Scoring, the percentage of individuals who reach at least the 4/5 transition in adulthood is only 16%. Kramer reports that about 30% of the subjects in his analysis have at some point shown substantial usage of stage 5.

INDIVIDUAL DIFFERENCES

Our results support the assumption that relative maturity of moral judgment is a fairly enduring characteristic of individuals throughout their

[12] Kohlberg and Kramer analyzed interviews of some longitudinal subjects as old as age 24 as well as the moral judgment interviews of their fathers.

69

development and becomes even more stable in adulthood. That is, if an adolescent is advanced in his moral judgment relative to his age peers, he is likely to be advanced in adulthood as well. However, the correlations are not so high as to preclude some changes in relative position for many subjects. Bloom (1964) has suggested that shifts in stability of individual differences in intelligence are useful in defining open periods for educational intervention. There are a number of problems in taking this idea literally in the domain of intelligence (Kohlberg 1968) and in moral judgment. However, the fairly dramatic increase in correlation with adult scores that occurs between the ages of 10 ($r = .20$) and 13 ($r = .70$) suggests that the period before 13 years may be particularly fruitful for educational stimulation or intervention. This implication of the findings is discussed at length elsewhere (Kohlberg 1970).

SOCIAL ROLE AND STATUS VARIABLES AND MORAL DEVELOPMENT

The variable of sociometric status was included in the original design in order to illuminate Piaget's (1965) argument that peer group participation is an important determinant of moral judgment maturity. Our data provide some very limited support for this hypothesis in that our sociometric integrates used more stage 3 and less stage 1 than the sociometric isolates. Of course, there is no way of knowing whether these results are due to stage 3 children being more popular or whether more active peer group involvement and social interaction facilitate the transitions out of stage 1 and into stage 3. Both are theoretically possible, and both may have occurred. In any case, the effect of sociometric status in childhood, at least as measured here, does not seem to extend beyond the transition to stage 3.

Differences in socioeconomic status, on the other hand, seem to be associated with moral judgment differences across the entire stage range. Whereas peer group participation may be especially important for the onset of stage 3, social class seems to be related to the development of stages 4 and 5 as well as 3. Many more middle-class than working-class subjects reached both consolidated stage 4 and the postconventional 4/5 level, although stages 4 and 4/5 do seem to be accessible to college-educated subjects with working-class origins. In previous writing, Kohlberg (1969) has interpreted social class differences in rate and terminus of development as reflecting differential participation in and identification with the society and its secondary institutions. It is argued that this differential participation creates differential role-taking opportunities for middle-class and working-class children which allow those from the middle class to experience, for example, being integral participants in the society and thus to develop the social system perspective that characterizes stage 4. Since the design controlled for IQ, the relation between moral judgment and SES cannot be accounted for by IQ differences between working-class and middle-class subjects.

Educational attainment is, however, confounded with social class. Formal education is itself a very important experience that is more often available to middle-class individuals and may mediate at least to some degree the relation between moral maturity and social class. Whereas only 37% of our working-class sample completed college, 71% of our middle-class sample did so. However, when the variables of social class and educational attainment are separated, as in table 23, it appears that social class is related to moral judgment stage even with educational level held constant. Although the small N's preclude any definite conclusions, the table indicates that, except for the "high school only" group, the scores are higher for middle-class than working-class subjects within each of the three education levels—some college, completed college, and graduate school. This suggests that the differential experiences of middle-class and working-class children include but go beyond differential opportunities for formal education.

FORMAL EDUCATION AND MORAL DEVELOPMENT

The finding of a moderate relationship ($r = .54$) between moral judgment stage and education is not surprising given the cognitive-developmental nature of the moral judgment stages. As noted earlier, we found that none of our subjects reached stage 4 without having attended some college, and none reached the 4/5 level without having completed college. This does not imply that college study is always necessary for development of consolidated stage 4 or movement to stage 5. In an era or a culture with less emphasis on formal education or less accessibility to college, one might find many self-educated people at stage 4 or 5. However, the relationship does suggest that development to the higher stages is facilitated by educational experience. Using Rest's Defining Issues Test (DIT), G. Rest (1977) found a comparable moderate correlation ($r = .45$) between education and moral judgment in adults.[13]

IQ AND MORAL DEVELOPMENT

The cognitive basis of Kohlberg's stages is also reflected in moderate correlations between IQ and moral judgment. Although the positive correlations point to the cognitive component in moral development, the modest size of the correlations (.37–.59 for our sample) indicates that moral judg-

[13] Rest's Defining Issues Test involves the presentation of hypothetical moral dilemmas along with a set of stage-keyed ideas, issues, or considerations relevant to resolution of each dilemma. The subject is asked to rate and rank the importance of these considerations in his thinking about the dilemma. Scores are based on the relative importance for the subject of considerations at the six moral judgment stages.

ment is not reducible to intelligence. As in the case of educational experience, correlations between IQ and moral judgment as measured by the DIT are comparable to those between IQ and moral judgment in our sample. Rest (1979) reports that most studies have found IQ × DIT correlations in the .20–.50 range. (Recall that ours range from .37 to .59 between ages 19 and 36.)

COLLEGE RELATIVISM AND "REGRESSION" IN THE LONGITUDINAL SAMPLE

Readers familiar with the work that was generated in response to Kramer's (1968) finding of sequence anomalies may wonder what happened to "Stage $4\frac{1}{2}$." This phenomenon—an apparent regression from stage 5 to stage 2 or 3 in late adolescence—was first interpreted (Kohlberg & Kramer 1969) as a "functional regression in the service of the ego." Kohlberg (1973) later reinterpreted the phenomenon as a structural progression characterizing the transition from conventional to principled moral judgment for some subjects.

In fact, only one of the anomalous cases in the original analysis can be attributed to the phenomenon Kohlberg called stage $4\frac{1}{2}$. As table 13 indicates, Standard Issue scores for case 2 went from a 3/4 score at the end of high school to college-period scores of stage 3 on form A, stage 2/3 on form B, and stage 3/4 on form C. This scatter and regression in moral judgment scores coincided with nonscorable metaethical views of ethical relativism and ethical egoism. On follow-up 4 years later, case 2 had moved to a postconventional score of 4/5, as table 13 indicates. Case 2 was one of the cases discussed in the Kohlberg (1973) account of college transitional relativism.

A second case discussed as "Stage $4\frac{1}{2}$" in Kohlberg (1973) was case 65. Table 13 indicates that case 65 was scored as stage 3 (Standard Issue Scoring) at the end of high school. In college his scores were stage 4 on form A, stage 2 on form B, and stage 2/3 on form C. Like case 2, case 65 gave evidence of moral cynicism and relativism in spontaneous college interview material. Unlike those of case 2, however, case 65's scattered college scores, including stage 2 judgments, did not represent a transition from conventional to principled or postconventional reasoning. Before his college moral "crisis," case 65 had reasoned primarily at stage 3. After this crisis, his reasoning was successively stage 3/4 and stage 4.

Our current interpretation of the phenomenon of "college-age relativism" is that it does not necessarily represent a transitional period between stages 4 and 5. Instead, moral relativism appears to be a metaethical position that can be taken at a number of different developmental stages. Whereas the level of sophistication of the relativistic metaethic may differ developmentally, the effect of this stance on normative judgments appears to be very much the same whether the subject is moving from stage 4 to stage 5 or shifting within the conventional level. The increased stage scatter in these interviews can be interpreted as reflecting a breakdown of faith in the currently held moral frame of reference with no substitution of a more adequate system. Subjects in this position sometimes refuse to make moral judgments. When they do make moral judgments they seem to rely on whatever has some lingering validity for them even if these intuitions from stages 2, 3, and 4 fail to represent a coherent whole.

THE STAGE MODEL

Let us turn now to the more usual pattern of moral judgment development. Our data seem to provide strong support for the strict Piagetian stage model of development. With regard to the criterion of "structured wholeness" or internal consistency, we found that the great majority of our interviews were scored at only one moral judgment stage or at most two adjacent stages. Only 9% showed evidence of a third stage. On the average, across nine independently scored dilemmas, two-thirds of all scores were assigned at the subject's modal stage and almost all the remaining scores (32%) were assigned to a single stage adjacent to the modal stage. The structured wholeness assumption was also supported by the high degree of alternate form and test-retest reliability, the high Cronbach's α, and the results of factor analyses of issue and dilemma scores.

The factor analyses indicate that there was a single factor of general moral level across the domain of dilemmas and issues. The absence of issue or dilemma factors along with the absence of scatter across more than two adjacent stages indicates that we have succeeded in defining a coherent moral domain united by a single underlying organizational structure. This position contrasts with that taken by Damon (1977) who argues that, at least in young children, the moral domain is broken down into a number of issues or dimensions each with its own unique structure. The two moral issues on which Damon has focused are authority and distributive justice. Although Damon's research does not use Kohlberg's hypothetical dilemmas, it is clear that Kohlberg dilemmas do involve both authority and distributive justice. If Damon's interpretation of the moral issues as independently organized were true at the age level addressed by our study, the factor analysis should have indicated multiple factors rather than a single general factor of moral stage that cuts across the content of the dilemmas.

This high degree of structural coherence within each interview leads to a relatively saltatory picture of development if we compare interviews across time for any single individual. Developmental change in any given 3-year period seems to involve predominantly an increase in the next higher stage of reasoning along with a simultaneous decrease in the lower stage. This means that the subject is most often in transition between two adjacent stages, has given up using all earlier stages, and uses no reasoning more than one stage above his modal stage. This contrasts with a model in which the distribution of a subject's reasoning extends across all five stages and in which development involves the gradual increase in use of the higher stages along with decrease (but not decrease to zero) in use of lower stages. Kohlberg's early results based on the Sentence Rating method may have appeared to support this latter model but we now interpret those results as artifactual (i.e., due to inappropriate definition of the scoring unit and a confusion between moral judgment content and structure).

Our results also support the Piagetian stage model's assumption of invariant developmental sequence. With a few exceptions which can be attributed to scoring error, each of our subjects proceeded through the stages in the prescribed order, neither skipping stages nor regressing to an earlier level once a later stage had been attained.

This stage model of development has recently been criticized—in the cognitive domain by Flavell (1971) and, most directly, in the moral judgment domain by Rest (1979). Rest agrees with Kohlberg that qualitatively different forms of moral judgment can be identified and that development involves the increasing use of more advanced or sophisticated types and the decreasing use of less sophisticated types. He disagrees, however, with Kohlberg's claim that development proceeds through a stepwise sequence of internally consistent stages. He holds instead that individuals simultaneously use reasoning of many types and that an adequate description of an individual's moral judgment must include a quantitative account of the proportion of each type rather than a global designation for the individual. He interprets our finding of internal consistency as a methodological artifact and points to his own results with the DIT as consistent with a more complex model of development.

One interpretation of the discrepancy between Rest's results and ours derives from the fact that the DIT is measuring comprehension and preference of moral judgments made by others while the Standard Issue System is measuring an individual's spontaneous production of moral judgments in response to very open-ended questions. We suggest that the development of moral judgment as a whole (including comprehension and preference as well as spontaneous production) may be too broad a scope for what Rest calls the "simple stage model." Development of moral judgment comprehension and preference may not follow a stagelike pattern even though spontaneous production appears to do so when assessment conditions pull for the subject's competence.

This would mean that the developing individual has one basic framework for resolving moral dilemmas and justifying those resolutions. This

74

framework has some coherence for the individual and undergoes developmental transformation, hierarchically integrates the insights from lower levels, and so on. On the other hand, other aspects of moral development such as the comprehension of judgments made by others may not be stagelike in this sense. In fact, given Kohlberg's assumptions, there is little reason to expect that subjects will comprehend statements at only one stage (or at two adjacent stages). Rather, they can be expected to comprehend all stages below their own as well as possibly a stage or two above their own. Thus we would not characterize the development of moral judgment comprehension as following a stagelike sequence. Preference for moral judgments made by others is somewhat more problematic, however. According to a simple stage model, how would one explain the endorsement of judgments that represent stages below one's own level of spontaneous production? One possible explanation derives from the Piagetian assumption of hierarchical integration. That is, while the stage as a whole may undergo transformation as the individual develops, many of the insights achieved at the lower stages remain valid from the higher-stage perspective though they are now embedded in a more complex and sophisticated position. For example, the stage 3 judgment that "you ought to keep a promise because the person you promised trusts you" would be endorsed or agreed to by individuals who reason predominantly at stages 4 and 5 as well as stage 3. The difference is that at the higher stages one's conception of trust and reasons for its importance have developed beyond what is available at stage 3.

Another consideration with regard to Rest's preference data is methodological. When subjects endorse an item on the DIT, it is not clear how they understand the item. The Standard Issue Moral Judgment Interview involves probing for elaboration and clarification and pooling all responses to the dilemma which refer to a single idea (as defined by norm and element). This system will naturally lead to greater internal consistency than assigning a score for each unelaborated statement the subject judges to have some validity. We do not interpret our finding as an artifact. It is true, as Rest points out, that according to Standard Issue Scoring rules an interview cannot receive more than one stage (or stage transition) score for a single norm/element intersection. However, scores at all five stages may be assigned to a single issue, dilemma, or interview if interview/manual matches at those stages occur. In fact, such variance does not occur in our data even though the nine dilemmas were scored independently and by three different raters. We agree with Rest that moral judgment comprehension and preference are important aspects of moral development that are separable from spontaneous moral judgment production and that a full developmental account of an individual's moral judgment requires scores on all those aspects (that is, the information from the various sources is not redundant). However, we feel that a careful look at our methods and data should convince the reader of the validity of the Piagetian stage model for describing the development of spontaneous moral judgment at least within the limits of our instrument and sample.

In general, then, we interpret the results of this study as consistent with cognitive-developmental theory, in particular as consistent with a stage model of development. The results in relation to moral judgment compare favorably with longitudinal studies of the stage model in purely cognitive development (Kohn 1969). Our subjects did seem to use a coherent structural orientation in thinking about a variety of moral dilemmas. Their thinking developed in a regular way up the stage sequence, neither skipping stages nor reverting to use of a prior stage. Our results also serve to validate the moral judgment stages as operationally defined in Standard Issue Scoring and to indicate that the Standard Issue system is a reliable and valid measure of moral judgment.

APPENDIX A

DILEMMA III: In Europe, a woman was near death from a special kind of cancer. There was one drug that the doctors thought might save her. It was a form of radium that a druggist in the same town had recently discovered. The drug was expensive to make, but the druggist was charging 10 times what the drug cost him to make. He paid $200 for the radium and charged $2,000 for a small dose of the drug. The sick woman's husband, Heinz, went to everyone he knew to borrow the money, but he could only get together about $1,000, which is half of what it cost. He told the druggist that his wife was dying and asked him to sell it cheaper or let him pay later. But the druggist said, "No, I discovered the drug and I'm going to make money from it." So Heinz gets desperate and considers breaking into the man's store to steal the drug for his wife.

1. Should Heinz steal the drug?
1a. Why or why not?
2. If Heinz doesn't love his wife, should he steal the drug for her?
2a. Why or why not?
3. Suppose the person dying is not his wife but a stranger. Should Heinz steal the drug for the stranger?
3a. Why or why not?
4. [If you favor stealing the drug for a stranger] Suppose it's a pet animal he loves. Should Heinz steal to save the pet animal?
4a. Why or why not?
5. Is it important for people to do everything they can to save another's life?
5a. Why or why not?
6. It is against the law for Heinz to steal. Does that make it morally wrong?
6a. Why or why not?
7. Should people try to do everything they can to obey the law?
7a. Why or why not?
7b. How does this apply to what Heinz should do?

DILEMMA III': Heinz did break into the store. He stole the drug and gave it to his wife. In the newspapers the next day, there was an account of the robbery. Mr. Brown, a police officer who knew Heinz, read the account. He remembered seeing Heinz running away from the store and realized that it was Heinz who stole the drug. Mr. Brown wonders whether he should report that Heinz was the robber.

1. Should Officer Brown report Heinz for stealing?
1a. Why or why not?
2. Officer Brown finds and arrests Heinz. Heinz is brought to court, and a jury is selected. The jury's job is to find whether a person is innocent or guilty of committing a crime. The jury finds Heinz guilty. It is up to the judge to determine the sentence. Should the judge give Heinz some sentence, or should he suspend the sentence and let Heinz go free?
2a. Why?
3. Thinking in terms of society, should people who break the law be punished?
3a. Why or why not?
3b. How does this apply to how the judge should decide?
4. Heinz was doing what his conscience told him when he stole the drug. Should a lawbreaker be punished if he is acting out of conscience?
4a. Why or why not?
    [Questions 5–10 are designed to elicit the subject's theory of ethics and should be considered optional.]
5. What does the word conscience mean to you, anyhow? If you were Heinz, how would your conscience enter into the decision?
6. Heinz has to make a moral decision. Should a moral decision be based on one's feelings or on one's thinking and reasoning about right and wrong?
7. Is Heinz's problem a moral problem? Why or why not?
7a. In general, what makes something a moral problem or what does the word moral mean to you?
8. If Heinz is going to decide what to do by thinking about what's really right, there must be some answer, some right solution. Is there really some correct solution to moral problems like Heinz's? When people disagree, is everybody's opinion equally right? Why?
9. How do you know when you've come up with a good moral decision? Is there a way of thinking or method by which one can reach a good or adequate decision?
10. Most people believe that thinking and reasoning in science can lead to a correct answer. Is the same thing true in moral decisions or are they different?

DILEMMA I: Joe is a 14-year-old boy who wanted to go to camp very much. His father promised him he could go if he saved up the money for it himself. So Joe worked hard at his paper route and saved up the $40.00 it cost to go to camp and a little more besides. But just before camp was going to start, his father changed his mind. Some of his friends decided to go on a special fishing trip, and Joe's father was short of the money it would cost. So he told Joe to give him the money he had saved from the paper route. Joe didn't want to give up going to camp, so he thinks of refusing to give his father the money.

1. Should Joe refuse to give his father the money?
1a. Why or why not?
2. Is the fact that Joe earned the money himself the most important thing in the situation?
2a. Why or why not?
3. The father promised Joe he could go to camp if he earned the money. Is the fact that the father promised the most important thing in the situation?
3a. Why or why not?
4. Is it important to keep a promise?
4a. Why or why not?
5. Is it important to keep a promise to someone you don't know well and probably won't see again?
5a. Why or why not?
6. What do you think is the most important thing a son should be concerned about in his relationship to his father?
6a. Why is that the most important thing?
7. What do you think is the most important thing a father should be concerned about in his relationship to his son?
7a. Why is that the most important thing?

FORM B

DILEMMA IV: There was a woman who had very bad cancer, and there was no treatment known to medicine that would save her. Her doctor, Dr. Jefferson, knew that she had only about 6 months to live. She was in terrible pain, but she was so weak that a good dose of a pain-killer like ether or morphine would make her die sooner. She was delirious and almost crazy with pain, and in her calm periods she would ask Dr. Jefferson to give her enough ether to kill her. She said she couldn't stand the pain and she was going to die in a few months anyway. Although he knows that mercy killing is against the law, the doctor thinks about granting her request.

79

1. Should Dr. Jefferson give her the drug that would make her die?
1a. Why or why not?
2. Should the woman have the right to make the final decision?
2a. Why or why not?
3. The woman is married. Should her husband have anything to do with the decision?
3a. Why or why not?
4. Is there any way a person has a duty or obligation to live when he or she does not want to, when the person wants to commit suicide?
4a. Why or why not?
5. It is against the law for the doctor to give the woman the drug. Does that make it morally wrong?
5a. Why or why not?
6. Should people try to do everything they can to obey the law?
6a. Why or why not?
6b. How does this apply to what Dr. Jefferson should do?

DILEMMA IV': Dr. Jefferson did perform the mercy killing by giving the woman the drug. Passing by at the time was another doctor, Dr. Rogers, who knew the situation Dr. Jefferson was in. Dr. Rogers thought of trying to stop Dr. Jefferson, but the drug was already administered. Dr. Rogers wonders whether he should report Dr. Jefferson.

1. Should Dr. Rogers report Dr. Jefferson?
1a. Why or why not?
2. The doctor does report Dr. Jefferson. Dr. Jefferson is brought to court and a jury is selected. The jury's job is to find whether a person is innocent or guilty of committing a crime. The jury finds Dr. Jefferson guilty. It is up to the judge to determine the sentence. Should the judge give Dr. Jefferson some sentence, or should he suspend the sentence and let Dr. Jefferson go free?
2a. Why?
3. Thinking in terms of society, should people who break the law be punished?
3a. Why or why not?
3b. How does this apply to how the Judge should decide?
4. The jury finds Dr. Jefferson legally guilty of murder. Would it be wrong or right for the judge to give him the death sentence (a legally possible punishment)? Why?
5. Is it ever right to give the death sentence? Why or why not? What are the conditions when the death sentence should be given (if ever) in your opinion?
5a. Why are these conditions important?

6. Dr. Jefferson was doing what his conscience told him when he gave the woman the drug. Should a lawbreaker be punished if he is acting out of conscience?

6a. Why or why not?

[Questions 7–12 are designed to elicit the subjects' theory of ethics and should be considered optional.]

7. What does the word conscience mean to you, anyhow? If you were Dr. Jefferson, how would your conscience enter into the decision?

8. Dr. Jefferson has to make a moral decision. Should a moral decision be based on one's feelings or on one's thinking and reasoning about right and wrong?

9. Is Dr. Jefferson's problem a moral problem? Why or why not?

9a. In general, what makes something a moral problem or what does the word morality mean to you?

10. If Dr. Jefferson is going to decide what to do by thinking about what's really right, there must be some answer, some right solution. Is there really some correct solution to moral problems like Dr. Jefferson's, or when people disagree is everybody's opinion equally right? Why?

11. How do you know when you've come up with a good moral decision? Is there a way of thinking or method by which one can reach a good or adequate decision?

12. Most people believe that thinking and reasoning in science can lead to a correct answer. Is the same thing true in moral decisions or are they different?

DILEMMA II: Judy was a 12-year-old girl. Her mother promised her that she could go to a special rock concert coming to their town if she saved up from babysitting and lunch money for a long time so she would have enough money to buy a ticket to the concert. She managed to save up the $15.00 the ticket cost plus another $3.00. But then her mother changed her mind and told Judy that she had to spend the money on new clothes for school. Judy was disappointed and decided to go to the concert anyway. She bought a ticket and told her mother that she had only been able to save $3.00. That Saturday she went to the performance and told her mother that she was spending the day with a friend. A week passed without her mother finding out. Judy then told her older sister, Louise, that she had gone to the performance and had lied to her mother about it. Louise wonders whether to tell their mother what Judy did.

1. Should Louise, the older sister, tell their mother that Judy had lied about the money or should she keep quiet?

1a. Why?

2. In wondering whether to tell, Louise thinks of the fact that Judy is her sister. Should that make a difference in Louise's decision?

3. Is the fact that Judy earned the money herself the most important thing in this situation?

3a. Why or why not?

4. The mother promised Judy she could go to the concert if she earned the money. Is the fact that the mother promised the most important thing in the situation?

4a. Why or why not?

5. Why in general should a promise be kept?

6. Is it important to keep a promise to someone you don't know well and probably won't see again?

6a. Why or why not?

7. What do you think is the most important thing a daughter should be concerned about in her relationship to her mother?

7a. Why is that the most important thing?

8. What do you think is the most important thing a mother should be concerned about in her relationship to her daughter?

8a. Why is that the most important thing?

FORM C

DILEMMA V: In Korea, a company of Marines was greatly outnumbered and was retreating before the enemy. The company had crossed a bridge over a river, but the enemy were mostly still on the other side. If someone went back to the bridge and blew it up, with the head start the rest of the men in the company would have, they could probably then escape. But the man who stayed back to blow up the bridge would probably not be able to escape alive; there would be about a 4:1 chance he would be killed. The captain himself is the man who knows best how to lead the retreat. He asks for volunteers, but no one will volunteer. If he goes himself, the men will probably not get back safely and he is the only one who knows how to lead the retreat.

1. Should the captain order a man to go on this very dangerous mission or should he go himself? Why?

2. What is the best justification for saying it is right to send someone besides himself?

2a. Why or how do you say it is right to save more lives in this case, when it means ordering someone to his death?

3. What is the best, or most important reason for saying it is wrong to send someone else, when ordering someone else will save more lives?

4. Does the captain have the right or the authority to order a man if he thinks it best to? Why?

5. Would a man have the right to refuse such an order? Why?

6. The captain has a family, the men do not. Should that enter into his decision? How?

6*a.* If he is going to pick someone to go, how should he pick someone? Why?

7. There is some conflict between fairness and survival here. Which is more important, or how can he deal with both here? What does fairness mean anyhow, and why is it important?

DILEMMA VIII: In a country in Europe, a poor man named Valjean could find no work, nor could his sister and brother. Without money, he stole food and medicine that they needed. He was captured and sentenced to prison for 6 years. After a couple of years, he escaped from the prison and went to live in another part of the country under a new name. He saved money and slowly built up a big factory. He gave his workers the highest wages and used most of his profits to build a hospital for people who couldn't afford good medical care. Twenty years had passed when a tailor recognized the factory owner as being Valjean, the escaped convict whom the police had been looking for back in his home town.

1. Should the tailor report Valjean to the police? Would it be right or wrong to keep it quiet? Why?
2. What would be the best or most important reason for reporting this?
3. What would be the best or most important reason for keeping quiet?
4. If Valjean were reported and brought before the judge, should the judge send him back to jail? Why?
5. Would it be unfair or unjust to send him back to jail or would it still be just? Why?
6. Suppose that Valjean had escaped from jail and lived an ordinary life instead of building a hospital to help other sick people. Should the tailor report him in that case? Should he be sent to jail? Why?
7. Does a citizen have a duty or obligation to report an escaped convict?
8. According to the law, a citizen is required to report an escaped convict. Is it morally right to fail to report him in that case? Why?
9. Suppose Valjean was a close friend of the tailor. Does that make a difference in what he should do? Why?

DILEMMA VII: Two young men, brothers, had gotten into serious trouble. They were secretly leaving town in a hurry and needed money. Alexander, the older one, broke into a store and stole $500. Joe, the younger one, went to a retired old man who was known to help people in town. Joe told the man that he was very sick and he needed $500 to pay for the operation. Really he wasn't sick at all, and he had no intention of paying the man back. Although the man didn't know Joe very well, he loaned him the money. So Joe and Alex skipped town, each with $500.

1. If you had to say who did worse, would you say Alex did worse to break in the store and steal the $500 or Joe did worse to borrow the $500 with no intention of paying it back? Why?
2. Which would you rather do, which would make you feel worse, stealing like Alex or cheating like Joe?
3. When people say their conscience bothers them, what do they mean?
3a. What does someone do when his conscience bothers him?
3b. Do some people have more conscience than others?
3c. Where do you fit in there?
3d. Do you think your conscience should be the basis of making a decision, or should you think of other things?
4. What was the worst thing about what Alex did in stealing? Why?
5. What was the worst thing about what Joe did in cheating the man? Why?
6. Does that enter into deciding which was worse? Why?
7. Why shouldn't someone steal from a store or steal anyhow?
8. Joe deceived the old man and agreed to do something he didn't. Why shouldn't someone do that anyhow?
9. Does the law enter into your decision in this case?
10. Both men are caught and brought before the judge. Should one be given more punishment than the other? Why?

ILLUSTRATIONS OF MORAL NORMS AND ELEMENTS

The following examples illustrate judgments which exhibit similar content (issue, norm, and element) but different stage structures.

STAGE: 3 NORM: Affiliation ELEMENT: Having a duty	(1) (Heinz should steal the drug or it is Heinz's duty to steal the drug) because he should care about her or love her; *OR* because he is supposed to stick close to her; etc. (2) (Heinz should steal the drug even if he doesn't love his wife) because he must have loved her at one time or should still care about her; *OR* because he is still her husband; etc.
STAGE: 4 NORM: Affiliation ELEMENT: Having a duty	(Heinz should steal the drug) because he is obligated by his marital responsibility, wedding vows, covenant of marriage; etc.
STAGE: 4/5 NORM: Affiliation ELEMENT: Having a duty	(Heinz should steal the drug) because he freely accepted an explicit responsibility or commitment in marriage and is now obligated to honor it.

Each moral judgment can be seen as an argument for one of the two conflicting issues in the dilemma. In justifying his or her argument for that issue choice, the subject appeals to a moral value which we have called a norm and construes the importance or meaning of that norm in terms of a third kind of value, an element. For example, the following statement argues that Heinz should steal the drug (life issue) because of the value of love or affiliation (the norm) and interprets the value of love in terms of the element of role duties.

85

Norm: Affiliation   (1) (Heinz should steal the drug or it is Heinz's
Element: Duty   duty to steal the drug) because he should care about
her or love her; *OR* because he is supposed to stick
close to her; etc.
(2) (Heinz should steal the drug even if he doesn't
love his wife) because he must have loved her at one
time or should still care about her; *OR* because he
he is still her husband; etc.

In contrast, the following judgment argues that Heinz should steal the
drug (life issue) because of the same value or norm—love or affiliation—but
interprets the importance of that value in terms of the element of reciprocity
or positive deservingness.

Norm: Affiliation   (1) (Heinz should steal the drug even if he doesn't
Element: Reciprocity love his wife) out of gratitude or appreciation; *OR*
because she has shared her life with him, and the
least he can do is to save her; etc.

Both judgments represent the same *stage* of moral judgment (stage 3),
but they are conceptually distinguishable from one another and can be
considered two different "ideas."

APPENDIX C

ILLUSTRATION OF THE EXPLICATED CRITERION JUDGMENT
CRITERION JUDGMENT (FORM B)

DILEMMA: IV
ISSUE: Law
NORM: Law
ELEMENT: Seeking reward (avoiding punishment)
STAGE: 2

Criterion Judgment

(The doctor should not give the woman the drug) because he would risk losing his job or going to jail.
(Note: Do not match score this point if it is a response to the general question "Why is it important to obey the law?" unless the response refers to the doctor in this mercy-killing situation.)

Stage Structure

Not killing the woman is justified because it involves a risk (rather than certainty) of punishment. Punishment is seen as something to be instrumentally avoided. The risk of punishment overrides the recognition of the pragmatic reasonableness from the woman's point of view of giving her the drug.

Critical Indicators

One of the following must be used as the central justification for not killing the woman: (*a*) punishment as possible or probable, a risk to be weighed in the decision; or (*b*) other possible disadvantageous consequences to the doctor (he might lose his job, etc.).

Distinctions—Other Stages

This stage 2 treatment of sanctions as a factor to be included among one's pragmatic or instrumental considerations should be distinguished from the stage 1 view of sanction as automatically defining the wrongness of an act and from the stage 1/2 focus on the *likelihood* of punishment as a reason not to mercy kill. In stage 1/2 judgments, it is ambiguous as to whether punishment automatically defines the act as wrong or whether it is seen as pragmatic consideration. At stage 2, the pragmatic quality of the concern is clear.

Do not score as matches the statements that it is unfair of the woman to expect the doctor to risk punishment, that the doctor is not *obligated* to kill her if he will be risking punishment or loss of license, that he has the right to consider consequences to himself, or that he should not do it if it will mean loss of the right to practice medicine, destruction of his career, etc.

Match Examples

1. SHOULD THE DOCTOR GIVE HER THE DRUG THAT WOULD MAKE HER DIE? WHY?

   No, the doctor could be charged with killing her. He should give something to calm her. (WHY?) He would lose his career and go to prison. He should protect himself first and not kill her.

The following euthanasia dilemma responses from two different interviews both seem to approximate the criterion judgment presented here. In each case, one must decide whether or not the response can be said to embody the concept specified in the criterion judgment. Without the critical indicators this decision is very difficult to make, and the interrater reliability for such decisions is not likely to be high. In most cases, the critical indicators resolve such questions fairly unambiguously.

Example 1

SHOULD THE DOCTOR GIVE HER THE DRUG THAT WOULD MAKE HER DIE? WHY?

No. He would be blamed for killing her. She could take her own overdose. If he did, he could lose his license and be out of a job.

Example 2

SHOULD THE DOCTOR DO WHAT SHE ASKS AND GIVE HER THE DRUG?

No, I don't think so. I think it's asking too much of a doctor for one thing, that she should ask this even though she is in great pain. A doctor isn't supposed to do this. WHY? I believe it's in their code that you shouldn't give a drug to any person to help them die sooner or to put them to death right away. *If he were found out to have given her this drug, he'd probably be kicked out of his profession and he might not be able to get into something else.* (case 41-B)

88

This (Form B) dilemma involves the question of whether a mercy killing should be performed for a woman who is terminally ill, in great pain, and asking to be killed. At first glance these two responses both seem to warrant a score of stage 2 on the basis of this criterion judgment. However, only the first qualifies as a match based on the critical indicators.

The second example refers to the likelihood that the doctor will lose his job as required by critical indicator b, but the risk of undesirable consequences is not used as the central argument against mercy killing as the critical indicators specify. The requirement that the risk of losing his job be used as a central justification reflects the fact that at higher stages a pragmatic concern such as this maintains some validity (the stages are "hierarchically integrated") but is no longer seen as a sufficient justification from the moral point of view. In fact, longitudinal case 41 (time B) was scored globally at stage 3.

Scoring for more detailed, concrete, and narrowly defined concepts rather than for the stage structures in their more general form has also made it possible to gather evidence for sequentiality and consistency in all aspects of the more detailed stage descriptions. That is, the smaller scoring unit has made it possible to describe the developmental distinctions among parallel "moral ideas" across the stages. For example, in the punishment follow-up to the Heinz dilemma, the idea of deterrence as an argument for punishment is used at seven points in the sequence, beginning at transitional level 1/2 and proceeding through stages 2, 2/3, 3, 3/4, 4, and 4/5. The criterion judgments specify exactly what the conception of deterrence is at each point, and the "Distinctions" paragraphs explain the differences among the seven interpretations.

STANDARD ISSUE SCORING RULES

As discussed in Chapter I, Standard Issue Scoring involves classifying responses to a dilemma into the two standard issue categories and then assigning a stage score for each match between a manual criterion judgment and a moral judgment in the interview.

The only exception to this occurs when a higher stage match constitutes the elaboration of an idea represented in a lower stage match. In this case, only the higher stage score is assigned. A subject might, for example, argue that if Heinz steals the drug the judge should punish him because "when someone has broken the law a judge is expected to or supposed to give a sentence." Such a statement matches a stage 3 punishment issue criterion judgment. The subject might then go on to elaborate his or her conception of the judge's role in stage 4 terms (the judge should punish because he has accepted a responsibility to uphold the laws of society). In such a case only a stage 4 score would be assigned. If, however, the subject made the stage 3 statement referred to above along with a stage 4 statement that did not constitute an elaboration of the stage 3 idea (e.g., the judge should punish Heinz in order to promote respect for property rights), then two scores would be assigned—one at stage 3 and one at stage 4.

Sometimes an idiosyncratic or poorly probed interview will not yield even a single match for the issue being scored. In such cases, if moral judgment material is found corresponding to the issue in question, the material is assigned a "guess score" which represents the rater's intuitive evaluation of the stage of that material.

In calculating an overall stage score for a three-dilemma interview, one begins by assigning a score for each of the six issues based on the criterion judgment match scores (or guess scores) assigned for material on each issue. As many as three different stages may be represented in the issue total. In our data we have never encountered an interview with matches at more than three stages for a single issue. Even the case of three stages on a single issue almost never occurs. The six issue scores are then combined (with guess-issue scores given half the weight of issue scores based on matches) to yield a global score and a "moral maturity" score for the interview. The global score consists of a major stage (the subject's modal level) and one or more minor stages (any stage that has received at least 25% of the total points assigned the interview). A global score of stage 3, for example, indicates that most of the scores assigned the interview were stage 3 and that no stage other than stage 3 reached the 25% cutoff point. A global score of stage 3(2) indicates that the subject's modal stage was stage 3 and that he or she also received at least 25% of his or her (weighted) scores at stage 2. The moral maturity score represents a weighted average of the issue scores and ranges from 100 (stage 1) to 500 (stage 5).

COMPUTATION INSTRUCTIONS FOR GLOBAL SCORES AND MMS

Computing Issue Scores

1. A three-class scale is used for issue scores. That is, an individual issue score can be either a pure stage score, a major-minor score, or a transitional score, for example, 2, 2(3), 2/3, 3(2), or 3.

2. Where only one stage is represented in the criterion judgment scores for an issue or where only one stage exceeds 25% of the total criterion judgment scores, that stage score is the issue score. That is, a pure stage score is given for the issue.

3. If two or more stages are represented each by 25% or more of the issue's criterion judgment scores, all are registered in the issue total with the one used most frequently being the major stage, the ones used less frequently the minor stages. (They should appear in order of frequency.) If the frequency of the two (or three) is exactly equal, a transitional score with no major-minor designation is assigned. Scores for chosen issues should be circled unless they are guess scores. Guess scores are not circled.

Global and MMS

In computing global and moral maturity scores, use the following weights: 3 = chosen issue (based on match scores); 2 = nonchosen issue (based on match scores); 1 = guess score (whether on chosen or nonchosen issues). When an issue score is a pure stage, assign 3 points to the stage if it's a nonchosen issue (match), and one if it's a guess.

When the score for a chosen issue involves a major and a minor stage (e.g., 3[2]), assign two of the three points to the major stage, one point to the minor stage. When the score for a chosen issue is a transitional stage (e.g., 2/3), assign one and a half points to each stage.

When a nonchosen issue involves a major and a minor stage, assign one point for the major and one point for the minor stage. That is, treat major/minor scores on nonchosen issues as if they were transitional type scores.

When a guess score involves two stages, for example, G2(3) or G2/3, assign one half point for each stage.

Begin by listing the stages which appear in the issue totals. For example: 3 = life; 2(1) = morality and conscience; G3 = contract; 2(3) = law; G2/3 = punishment; 2/3 = authority. This interview involves the use of three stages, 1, 2, and 3: stage 1 = 1; stage 2 = 5; stage 3 = 7; total = 13.

Stage 1 is assigned only one point because it occurs only once, as the minor stage of a chosen issue score, 2(1). The major stage of this issue, stage 2, receives 2 points. Stage 2 also receives one point for the law issue (half of the 2 points given to a nonchosen match based score), $\frac{1}{2}$ point for the punishment issue (half of the one point given for a guess issue score), and $1\frac{1}{2}$ points for the authority issue (half of the 3 points for this chosen issue). The total for stage 2 is 5 points. Stage 3 receives 3 points for life (chosen issue), 1 point for law, $\frac{1}{2}$ point for punishment, 1 point for contract, and $1\frac{1}{2}$ points for authority for a total of 7 points. The total number of points assigned for the interview is 12.

Global stage is assigned as follows: The stage with the largest proportion of points is the major stage. If a second stage has received at least 25% of the total assigned points, it is entered as a minor stage. If two stages exceed 25% of the total, two minor stages are listed in order of proportion of points assigned the stages. If two stages (or three) are assigned an exactly equal number of points, the highest stage is the major stage. For example, an interview with 50% at stage 2 and 50% at stage 3 would be assigned a global score of 3(2).

Clearly in our example, stage 3 is the major stage for the interview since it received the most points. Stage 2 is entered as a minor stage since it exceeds 25% of the total (5/13 = 38%). Stage 1 is not entered since it received less than 25% of the total (1/13).

Moral Maturity Score

In order to calculate MMS, multiply each stage by the number of points at that stage: $1 \times 1 = 1$; $2 \times 5 = 10$; $3 \times 7 = 21$; total products = 32.

Divide the sum of the products (32) by the total number of points assigned (13) and then multiply by 100, to yield 246.

ACKNOWLEDGMENTS

We wish to acknowledge our debt to Dan Candee, Ros Hewer, Clark Power, and Betsy Speicher-Dubin for their years of arduous and careful labor in refining the moral stage definitions, creating the Standard Issue Scoring System, and scoring hundreds of moral judgment interviews. Ann Higgins, Kelsey Kauffman, and Laura Rogers also contributed in important ways to the development of the stage definitions and scoring system. We acknowledge also the patient efforts of Dan Candee, Bill Jennings, and Steve Ries in tracking down and interviewing our subjects. We would like to thank Bill Damon, Ed De Vos, Jane Loevinger, Bill Puka, and Jim Rest for reading earlier drafts of the manuscript and offering insightful comments and suggestions which helped to shape the *Monograph* in its final form. We are indebted to the National Institute of Child Health and Human Development for generous funding of this research. Finally, we are most grateful to the 58 men who contributed their time and thoughtful responses to this project over a 20-year segment of their lives. Without these men, our research subjects, the project would, indeed, have been impossible.

93

REFERENCES

Blasi, A. Bridging moral cognition and moral action: a critical review of the literature. *Psychological Bulletin*, 1980, **88,** 1, 1–45.

Blatt, M., & Kohlberg, L. The effects of classroom moral discussion upon children's level of moral judgment. *Journal of Moral Education*, 1975, **4,** 129–163.

Bloom, B. *Stability and change in human characteristics*. New York: Wiley, 1964.

Colby, A. Evolution of a moral-developmental theory. In W. Damon (Ed.), *New directions for child development: moral development*. Vol. 2. San Francisco: Jossey-Bass, 1978.

Colby, A.; Kohlberg, L.; Gibbs, J.; Candee, D.; Hewer, A.; Power, C.; & Speicher-Dubin, B. *Measurement of moral judgment: standard issue scoring manual*. New York: Cambridge University Press, in press.

Colby, A.; Kohlberg, L.; Fenton, E.; Speicher-Dubin, B.; & Lieberman, M. Secondary school moral discussion programmes led by social studies teachers. *Journal of Moral Education*, 1977, **6,** 2.

Damon, W. *The social world of the child*. San Francisco: Jossey-Bass, 1977.

Damon, W. *Social development from childhood through adolescence*. New York: Norton, 1983.

Edwards, C. P. The comparative study of the development of moral judgment and reasoning. In R H. Munroe, R. L. Munroe, & B. Whiting (Eds.), *Handbook of cross-cultural human development*. New York: Garland, 1981.

Erickson, V. L. The case study method in the evaluation of developmental programs. In L. Kuhmerker, M. Mentkowski, & L. V. Erickson (Eds.), *Evaluating moral development*. New York: Character Research Press, 1980.

Flavell, J. J. Stage-related properties of cognitive development. *Cognitive Psychology*, 1971, **2,** 521–543.

Gibbs, J. Kohlberg's moral stage theory: a Piagetian revision. *Human Development*, 1979, **22,** 89–112.

Gilligan, C. In a different voice. *Harvard Educational Review*, 1977, **47**(3), 365–378.

Gilligan, C., & Belenky, M. A naturalistic study of abortion decisions. In R. Selman & R. Yando (Eds.), *Clinical-developmental psychology*. No. 7. San Francisco: Jossey-Bass, 1980.

Gilligan, C., & Murphy, J. M. Development from adolescence to adulthood: the philosopher and the dilemma of the fact. In D. Kuhn (Ed.), *Intellectual development beyond childhood*. No. 5. San Francisco: Jossey-Bass, 1979.

Holstein, C. Irreversible, stepwise sequence in the development of moral judgment: a longitudinal study of males and females. *Child Development*, 1976, **47,** 51–61.

Kohlberg, L. The development of modes of moral thinking and choice in the years ten to sixteen. Unpublished doctoral dissertation, University of Chicago, 1958.

94

Kohlberg, L. Early education: a cognitive-developmental approach. *Child Development*, 1968, **39**, 1013–1062.

Kohlberg, L. Stage and sequence: the cognitive-developmental approach to socialization. In D. A. Goslin (Ed.), *Handbook of socialization theory and research*. Chicago: Rand-McNally, 1969.

Kohlberg, L. The moral atmosphere of the school. In N. Overley (Ed.), *The unstudied curriculum*. Monograph of the Association for Supervision and Curriculum Development. Washington, D.C., 1970.

Kohlberg, L. Structural Issue Scoring Manual. Unpublished manuscript, Harvard University, 1971.

Kohlberg, L. Continuities in childhood and adult moral development revisited. In P. Baltes & K. W. Schaie (Eds.), *Life span developmental psychology*. New York: Academic Press, 1973.

Kohlberg, L. Moral stages and moralization: the cognitive-developmental approach. In T. Lickona (Ed.), *Moral development and behavior*. New York: Holt, Rinehart & Winston, 1976.

Kohlberg, L. *The meaning and measurement of moral development*. Worcester, Mass.: Clark University Press, 1980.

Kohlberg, L. *Essays on moral development*. Vol. 1. *The philosophy of moral development*. New York: Harper & Row, 1981.

Kohlberg, L., & Candee, D. The relation between moral judgment and moral action. Paper presented at the International Conference on Morality and Moral Development, Florida International University, Miami, December 1981.

Kohlberg, L., & Kramer, R. Continuities and discontinuities in childhood and adult moral development. *Human Development*, 1969, **12**, 93–120.

Kohn, N. Performance of negro children of varying social class background on Piagetian tasks. Unpublished doctoral dissertation, University of Chicago, 1969.

Kramer, R. Moral development in young adulthood. Unpublished doctoral dissertation, University of Chicago, 1968.

Kuhn, D. Short-term longitudinal evidence for the sequentiality of Kohlberg's early stages of moral judgment. *Developmental Psychology*, 1976, **12**(2), 162–166.

Kurtines, W., & Greif, E. The development of moral thought: review and evaluation of Kohlberg's approach. *Psychological Bulletin*, 1974, **81**(8), 453–470.

Lakatos, I. Falsification and methodology of scientific research programmes. In I. Lakatos & A. Musgrave (Eds.), *Criticism and the growth of knowledge*. Cambridge: Cambridge University Press, 1976.

Lockwood, A. L. The effects of values clarification and moral development curriculum on school-age subjects: a critical view of recent research. Unpublished manuscript, University of Wisconsin, 1977.

Loevinger, J. *Ego development*. San Francisco: Jossey-Bass, 1976.

Loevinger, J., & Wessler, R. *Measuring ego development*. San Francisco: Jossey-Bass, 1978.

Mead, G. H. *Mind, self, and society*. Chicago: University of Chicago Press, 1934.

Nicolayev, J., & Phillips, D. C. On assessing Kohlberg's stage theory of moral development. In D. Cochrane, C. Hamm, & A. Kazepides (Eds.), *The domain of moral education*. New York: Paulist, 1979.

Nisan, M., & Kohlberg, L. Universality and variation in moral judgment—a longitudinal and cross-sectional study in Turkey. *Child Development*, 1982, **53**, 865–876.

Nunnally, J. C. *Psychometric theory* (2d ed.). New York: McGraw-Hill, 1978.

Piaget, J. *The moral judgment of the child*. New York: Free Press, 1965. (Originally published in English, London: Kegan Paul, 1932.)

95

Puka, B. A Kohlbergian reply. In D. Cochrane, C. Hamm, & A. Kazepides (Eds.), *The domain of moral education*. New York: Paulist, 1979.

Rest, G. Voting preference in the 1976 Presidential Election and the influences of moral reasoning. Unpublished manuscript, University of Michigan, 1977.

Rest, J. The hierarchical nature of moral judgment: a study of patterns of comprehension and preference of moral stages. *Journal of Personality*, 1973, **41,** 86–109.

Rest, J. *Development in judging moral issues*. Minneapolis: University of Minnesota Press, 1979.

Rest, J. Morality. In J. H. Flavell & C. Markman (Eds.), *Carmichael's manual of child psychology*. 4th ed., 1983.

Selman, R. *The growth of interpersonal understanding*. New York: Academic Press, 1980.

Selman, R., & Jaquette, D. Stability and oscillation in interpersonal awareness: a clinical-developmental analysis. In C. B. Keasey (Ed.), *Twenty-fifth Nebraska Symposium on Motivation*. Lincoln: University of Nebraska Press, 1978.

Snarey, J. The moral development of Kibbutz founders and sabras: a cross-sectional and ten year longitudinal cross-cultural study. Unpublished doctoral dissertation, Harvard University, 1982.

Turiel, E. Social-cognitive development: domains and categories. Paper prepared for a plenary session of the Ninth Annual Symposium of the Jean Piaget Society, Philadelphia, 1979.

White, C. B.; Bushnell, N.; & Regnemer, J. L. Moral development in Bahamian school children: a three-year examination of Kohlberg's stages of moral development. *Developmental Psychology*, 1978, **14,** 58–65.

COMMENTARY

ILLUMINATING THE PROCESSES OF
MORAL DEVELOPMENT

BY KURT W. FISCHER

Twenty-five years ago Kohlberg (1958) proposed a new theory of the development of moral judgment. Generating an unusual degree of excitement, the model changed many scholars' ways of thinking about social development and helped to place morality in the center of developmental science as one of the most important topics for scholarly inquiry.

There were, however, lingering doubts, arising in part from problems in methodology and statistics (e.g., Holstein 1976; Kurtines & Greif 1974) and in part from fundamental questions about the nature of developmental process (e.g., Damon 1977; Fischer 1980). Happily, the current *Monograph* has dealt with a large number of these problems and questions, thus making a substantial contribution to the study of moral development. The new methods and statistics used provide clear-cut, interpretable results that not only support the existence of Kohlberg's stages but also illuminate the nature of the processes of moral development.

Particularly clear answers are provided to three questions: Do Kohlberg's stages form a developmental sequence? Do individuals show consistent reasoning at one stage? What is the course of development of each stage? The answers to these questions in turn shed light on the processes producing the stages, suggesting a model that differs in important ways from the Piagetian approach usually associated with Kohlberg's theory.

The stages clearly do form a developmental sequence, and individuals show moderate consistency of responding at their modal stage. But substantial inconsistency in moral stage remains, and the consistency that does obtain is shown by this study to take a remarkably long time to develop. This lengthy developmental course suggests that the type of reasoning at

I would like to thank Wayne Carr, Marilyn Pelot, Sandra Pipp, William Sobesky, and Gwendolyn Sorell for their contributions.

97

each stage must move through a slow and gradual process of generalization and consolidation, in which environmental factors seem to play a major role.

Resolving Important Methodological Problems

In the research reported here Kohlberg's basic testing situation has been kept virtually intact, but the scoring system has been changed drastically. The stages have been redefined in terms of "sociomoral perspective." The scoring criteria have been altered to focus on large pieces of the respondent's answers for each dilemma, which seems sensible given the complexity of the reasoning involved in the moral stages. These large pieces are scored in terms of standard issues that serve as prototypes for each stage.

All of Kohlberg's original interviews have been rescored with the new system, and in addition extensive new data are reported. The result is a large body of new data analyses, including a 20-year longitudinal study, test-retest and interrater reliabilities, and factor analyses. Consequently, a relatively complete portrait of the measurement properties of the Moral Judgment Interview is presented.

The results are impressive. Not only does the new scoring method seem to be much easier to use than the previous methods, but it appears to produce better data. Interrater reliability was very high, and test-retest reliability was adequate. The patterns of results were simple and clear-cut: The sequentiality of the stages was firmly supported, and individuals showed substantial consistency in stage of reasoning.

The sequentiality of the stages is of course central to Kohlberg's theory, especially since he has made strong claims about the universal invariance of the sequence (e.g., Kohlberg 1971). The authors have shown convincingly that short-term violations of sequentiality in these data arise from problems of test-retest reliability. When the data were corrected for the occasional unreliability of the measure, sequentiality held consistently and powerfully for stages 1 through 5.

A set of methodological changes have thus led to an important conceptual advance. It now seems that Kohlberg's first five stages can be accepted as a legitimate description of the development of moral judgment in this sample of white lower- and middle-class males. Other research indicates that the results are likely to generalize more broadly, at least to other males in groups influenced by Western culture and ideology and probably to a wide range of cultures (Edwards 1981; Harkness, Edwards, & Super 1981), although Kohlberg's scheme clearly does not capture everything important about moral judgment in all individuals or cultures.

Internal Consistency and Structured Wholes

Now that the sequentiality of Kohlberg's moral stages has been convincingly demonstrated, one of the central issues that demands investigation

98

seems to be the breadth of behavior the stages encompass. The results of the moral judgment study demonstrate moderate consistency within the Moral Judgment Interview. Yet considerable inconsistency in behavior remains, both within the interview and across a wider range of situations. This inconsistency seems to require reconceptualization of the processes underlying development of the stages of moral judgment.

The authors argue that their data support Piaget's (1957) concept of the structured whole (*structure d'ensemble*), a logical scheme so powerful that it pervades the mind and changes thinking to a more advanced stage. By hypothesis, for each new stage a structured whole emerges that acts as a powerful catalyst of the mind, spreading quickly throughout a person's schemes and transforming them. A strong pattern of data is therefore required to demonstrate the emergence of a structured whole as originally hypothesized: the predicted sequence of stages, relatively sudden emergence of performance at each new stage, and consistent performance at each stage after it has emerged (Fischer & Bullock 1981; Rest 1979).

The empirical criteria that the authors specify for structured wholeness, however, reflect a much weaker version of the structured-whole hypothesis. They require only sequentiality and moderate internal consistency in stage usage. That is, besides sequentiality, the data need only demonstrate a moderate degree of consistency of responding at individuals' modal stage. The authors require neither the high degree of consistency that Piaget originally hypothesized nor the sudden emergence of each new stage.

Following the authors' criteria, the moral judgment study did show moderately high internal consistency, with 66% of the responses at the individuals' modal stage. Such consistency or developmental synchrony is impressive when compared with other cognitive- and social-developmental research. Repeatedly in tests for synchrony, developmental unevenness or horizontal décalage (Piaget 1941) has proven to be the rule (Biggs & Collis 1982; Fischer 1980; Flavell 1971). Indeed, the consistency in this study is more substantial than anything Piaget himself ever reported in his research.

Nevertheless, this consistency does not demonstrate the sort of pervasive transformation of mind required by Piaget's original structured-whole hypothesis. On the Moral Judgment Interview itself, one-third of the responses fell at stages other than the individuals' modal stage, so that most individuals showed a range of at least two or three stages. Moreover, many other patterns in the data highlighted the pervasiveness of unevenness and the contributions of various environmental influences to stage of performance. Different dilemmas produced different modal stage assignments for many subjects, and alternate forms of the interview produced different stages as well. Among the 36-year-olds, for example, 11.1% of the responses on Form A were placed at the highest stage obtained (stage 4/5) while none of the responses on Forms B and C were placed at that stage.

99

This substantial variability occurred despite the fact that the Moral Judgment Interview involves a limited sample of behavior in a highly restricted context scored with a system designed to highlight consistency (Rest 1979). The procedure and format are similar for all the dilemmas, and the dilemmas themselves all follow a common plan—the presentation of two opposite justifiable actions in a complex situation set in a Western cultural context. These important similarities increase the degree of consistency found in individual behavior.

When the set of domains is widened beyond the Moral Judgment Interview, the inconsistency in stage becomes still more prominent, even when the domains are restricted to those involving the authors' definition of morality (social-moral perspective dealing with justice). The stages seem to apply to moral judgments but not to moral comprehension or preference, according to the authors. Even comprehension/preference tasks that are specifically designed to reflect Kohlberg's stages, such as Rest's Defining Issues Test, demonstrate wide variability in stage within individuals (Rest 1976; Sobesky, in press). Likewise, the authors indicate that the stages of moral judgment do not show any one-to-one relationship with moral action, even when the issue of justice is salient. Yet if the stages of moral development are indeed general, then they should apply to moral behavior in general, not merely to a restricted set of moral dilemmas presented in a highly structured interview.

The moral judgment study, then, does *not* allow the conclusion that moral development demonstrates a strong form of the structured-whole hypothesis. With substantial variations in task and context, moral behavior seems instead to fit what is becoming the standard empirically based portrait of cognitive and social-cognitive development. Considerable variability in stage within an individual is the norm (Flavell 1971; Martarano 1977; Piaget 1972; Rest 1979).

Consistency in Stage With and Without Environmental Support

The degree of individual consistency may be insufficient for the strong form of the structured-whole hypothesis, but it is nevertheless notable. On a nine-point scale (stages 1, 1/2, 2, 2/3, etc.), individuals over a wide age range showed an average of two-thirds of their responses at their modal stage. For measurement conditions that provide little environmental support for optimal performance like those in the moral judgment study, this degree of consistency seems to be near the limit obtainable. Even replications of exactly the same task under such conditions frequently show less consistency. For a sample of tasks that includes significant variations in content, two-thirds consistency is impressive. The authors appear to have developed a notably effective method for detecting consistency under conditions of low environmental support.

Although evidence seems to be scanty on the highest degree of consistency obtainable, we did investigate this question systematically in one study in our laboratory, testing how consistency at a single cognitive-developmental level varied with differences in the degree of environmental support for optimal performance (Fischer, Hand, & Russell, in press; Kenny & Fischer, in preparation). Subjects carried out a series of different tasks involving the concepts of addition or subtraction and all designed to test the same level. Under low-support conditions like those in most research, performance showed little consistency until a very late age. Although the first successful performance on some of the tasks appeared at 10 years, overall success did not reach 50% until the age of 17.

Why is perfect or near-perfect consistency so difficult to obtain? The best hypothesis at this point seems to be that high consistency is common only when environmental support is provided to optimize performance. Vygotsky (1978) pointed out that different environments provide different degrees of support for particular behaviors and that individuals will therefore demonstrate variations in developmental level depending upon the degree of support. Research has confirmed this argument, showing that small changes in context that decrease support for high-level performance can have enormous effects on the stage of virtually every individual (Hand 1981; Watson & Fischer 1980). An extension of this hypothesis is that individuals will be able to demonstrate higher consistency or synchrony across tasks if the context provides support for their best possible performance in the tasks (Fischer & Bullock 1981).

In the arithmetic study, when procedures were designed to optimize performance, the pattern of development fit the support hypothesis. Successful performance on the arithmetic tasks rose abruptly from near zero at 9 years to approximately 40% at 10 years and over 60% at 11 years. Thus an increase in consistency that had taken 8 years without environmental support occurred in 2 years with support. Even under these procedures, however, perfect consistency (100%) was not attained until age 16. Although very few investigators have examined the effects of environmental support on developmental change, a similar pattern has been found in a few other studies (e.g., Tabor & Kendler 1981).

The moral judgment study did not use procedures designed to provide environmental support for optimal performance and therefore obtained only moderate consistency. In order to understand variations in the degree of consistency, it seems that the authors will need to introduce assessments of the effects of context on stage of moral judgment.

High Consistency Develops Slowly

The original structured-whole hypothesis requires not only that individuals show a high degree of consistency but also that the consistency

101

develop quickly, since the logical structured whole is supposed to catalyze change rapidly throughout the mind. The moral judgment study provides clear evidence about the speed with which consistency developed: It took an enormously long time. Indeed, the pattern of data is similar to that in the arithmetic study for performance with low environmental support.

The results for stage 4 are probably the most instructive because they show what seems to be the entire developmental course for high consistency. At the youngest age, 10 years, there was virtually no stage 4 reasoning. The first substantial usage of stage 4 (approximately 5%) appeared at 13 years, as shown in figure 1 in the current *Monograph*. The percentage of stage 4 usage then increased slowly over the entire remaining age range. It did not pass 50% until age 32–33, and only at the last assessment at age 36 did it approach two-thirds. Individual profiles were similar, not showing consistent stage 4 judgments until subjects reached their twenties and thirties (with one exception).

Plainly, consistent stage 4 reasoning did not emerge suddenly but took 10–25 years to develop. The strong structured-whole hypothesis is therefore clearly not supported. If high stage 4 consistency without environmental support could be shown to emerge in a few years, it might be argued that the change was sudden enough to fit Piaget's original hypothesis, but the development of high consistency required what amounted to half or more of the life span of the individual to date.

The data for the other stages appear to reflect the same pattern—a long period of increase, followed in some cases by a long period of decrease as later stages replaced the earlier ones. At the beginning of the study (age 10), stage 1 seemed to have already passed its peak and stage 2 seemed to be at or near its peak. Both of them decreased systematically as the sample grew older. At age 10, stage 3 seemed to be in the midst of rising to its peak, which occurred 7 years later at approximately 60% of judgments. During early adulthood, stage 3 showed a gradual, slow decline. Stage 5 first emerged at the 20–22-year assessment and increased gradually over the remaining 15 years of the study, never surpassing a mean of roughly 10% of the responses.

For none of the stages, then, is there evidence of sudden development of high consistency without environmental support. To the contrary, it seems to require a remarkably long time to develop.

A Process of Emergence and Gradual Generalization

The original structured-whole hypothesis requires rapid development of high consistency, which did not obtain. The weak structured-whole hypothesis put forward by the authors may fit the data post hoc, but it is not obvious how it could predict the exceedingly slow development of consistency. What sort of alternative model can account for the pattern of slow development that did occur? One model that has been suggested recently by a number of theorists fits the data remarkably well—a process of emergence and gradual generalization (Biggs & Collis 1982; Fischer 1980; Flavell 1971).

When a type of reasoning emerges initially, it can be applied in only a few situations. To be applied more generally without environmental support, it has to be elaborated in a wide variety of situations, which takes a very long time. That is, at some point in development, people develop the minimum capacity needed for a certain "stage" of reasoning, and they begin to use the reasoning spontaneously in a few situations. To be able to use the reasoning across many situations, however, they must work out how it applies in each of a long series of different contexts—a process that is slow and gradual. At the end of this process, people have developed skills that allow them to apply the reasoning broadly, but there always remain many situations where they have still not learned to apply it.

This model seems to match the data for all the moral-judgment stages. With stage 4, for instance, a number of studies indicate that the minimal abilities necessary to produce a stage 4 response emerge at 10–13 years, when children develop formal operations and begin to understand concepts like law and society (e.g., Adelson 1972; Arlin 1975; Broughton 1978; Lee 1971). Indeed, the results reported for the new scoring system indicate that stage 4 responses first appeared at this age (figs. 1, 10b in the current *Monograph*), and even the results using the earlier scoring system showed a sharp spurt in stage 4 judgments then (fig. 10a).

The minimum capacities for stages 1, 2, and 3 all seem to develop before 10 years. Based on other studies, a reasonable estimate would be that stages 1 and 2 first emerge during the preschool years, and stage 3 at 6 or 7 years (Fischer 1980; Kitchener, in press; Kuhn 1976; Lee 1971). Stage 5 first emerges in the moral judgment study in the early twenties (figs. 1, 10b), an age at which recent research shows a number of major cognitive advances (Broughton 1978; Commons, Richards, & Kuhn, in press; Fischer et al., in press; Kitchener & King 1981). Thus, each of the five stages seems to emerge at a specific age period.

After the early emergence of a stage, important developmental changes in the nature of the reasoning may still occur. A plausible hypothesis is that later advances in cognitive capacity will produce important changes in the stage, at the least promoting consolidation and generalization of the type of reasoning (see Flavell 1971).

With emergence of the minimum capacity for each stage, then, the type of judgment is shown in only a few situations. Generalization and consolidation of each stage seem to take a very long time, as the data from the moral judgment study indicate. Apparently, individuals must extend and strengthen their skills over many years in order to be able to apply a given type of reasoning to a wide range of situations without environmental support.

103

Environmental Influences and Individual Differences

The data from the moral judgment study demonstrate, then, that for a limited range of situations an individual can gradually develop the ability to apply a single type of reasoning. For a wider array of situations, however, that individual still seems to show developmental unevenness—different stages in different contexts.

The next obvious step for elaboration of Kohlberg's theory of moral development is to begin to investigate these variations. The authors have acknowledged that environmental factors are relevant to moral stage, but specification of how they are relevant would strengthen their theory immeasurably. What environmental factors produce variations in stage, and what are the patterns of variation? What kinds of individual differences are there in the use of the stages? What kinds of other types of reasoning do people use in dealing with moral questions? Are there particular patterns of individual behaviors that tend to promote more rapid development of consistent reasoning at a particular stage? What variables lead to the relatively high consistency found for the Moral Judgment Interview?

One starting point is to devise procedures that provide environmental support for optimal moral performance, similar to those discussed earlier in connection with the arithmetic study. With such support, consistency in moral reasoning should appear within a short time after the stage first emerges. For example, after stage 4 reasoning emerges at approximately 12 years of age, high consistency should be evident within 2 or 3 years, and virtually perfect consistency might be obtainable within 5 or 6 years.

Such research would improve the understanding of the course of moral development enormously, both because it would demonstrate that moral consistency can develop relatively quickly under certain circumstances and because it would begin to explain how environmental factors contribute to moral development. The recent development of a new group test of moral judgment may facilitate this type of research (Gibbs, Widaman, & Colby 1982).

The investigation of environment factors will also lead naturally to analysis of variations in developmental paths for moral judgment and behavior (Feldman 1980). When a person is presented with a set of tasks designed to assess a particular developmental sequence, there is an important sense in which the assessment method is an intervention that elicits the stages in the person's behavior (Fischer & Corrigan 1981; Watson & Fischer 1980). Surely, if the tasks or the stages are grossly invalid, the person's behavior will not support the sequence. But even when the behavior fits the predicted stages, the stages may not accurately represent the person's naturally occurring behavior. For example, many people may approach moral questions from a perspective different from that required for Kohl-

104

berg's stages, such as a more conciliatory, group-oriented viewpoint (Gilligan 1982), yet if only Kohlberg's stages are used to analyze these people's behavior, this alternative orientation will never be evident.

To test for individual differences in developmental paths, researchers can introduce multiple assessments. For instance, the combination of measures for detecting a hypothesized sequence with measures of more spontaneous behavior can determine how accurately the sequence represents naturally occurring behavior (Hand 1981). The simultaneous assessment of multiple 'pathways can also be useful; for example, could an individual's behavior fit Kohlberg's sequence while at the same time following another manifestly different sequence of stages (e.g., of Macchiavellian reasoning)? Surely people might develop along multiple pathways, even apparently contradictory ones, and it is time for developmentalists to begin investigating such individual differences.

It seems, then, that not only have Colby and her colleagues illuminated many of the important issues about Kohlberg's stages, but their results also have pointed the way to the major questions to be asked next. How does high consistency in stage gradually develop, and under what circumstances will it develop quickly? How do some contexts evoke high consistency and others low consistency? More generally, how do environmental factors contribute to moral development, and what sorts of individual differences are there in developmental pathways?

References

Adelson, J. The political imagination of the adolescent. In J. Kagan & R. Coles (Eds.), *Twelve to sixteen: early adolescence*. New York: Norton, 1972.

Arlin, P. K. Cognitive development in adulthood: a fifth stage? *Developmental Psychology*, 1975, **11**, 602–606.

Biggs, J., & Collis, K. *A system for evaluating learning outcomes: the SOLO taxonomy*. New York: Academic Press, 1982.

Broughton, J. Development of concepts of self, mind, reality, and knowledge. In W. Damon (Ed.), *Social cognition*. New Directions for Child Development, no. 1. San Francisco: Jossey-Bass, 1978.

Commons, M.; Richards, F.; & Kuhn, D. Metasystematic reasoning. In M. Commons, F. Richards, & C. Armon (Eds.), *Beyond formal operations*. New York: Praeger Scientific, in press.

Damon, W. *The social world of the child*. San Francisco: Jossey-Bass, 1977.

Edwards, C. P. The comparative study of the development of moral judgment and reasoning. In R. H. Munroe, R. L. Munroe, & B. Whiting (Eds.), *Handbook of cross-cultural human development*. New York: Garland, 1981.

Feldman, D. H. *Beyond universals in cognitive development*. Norwood, N.J.: Ablex, 1980.

Fischer, K. W. A theory of cognitive development: the control and construction of hierarchies of skills. *Psychological Review*, 1980, **87**, 477–531.

Fischer, K. W., & Bullock, D. Patterns of data: sequence, synchrony, and constraint in cognitive development. In K. W. Fischer (Ed.), *Cognitive development*. New Directions for Child Development, no. 12. San Francisco: Jossey-Bass, 1981.

105

Fischer, K. W., & Corrigan, R. A skill approach to language development. In R. E. Stark (Ed.), *Language behavior in infancy and early childhood.* Amsterdam: Elsevier–North Holland, 1981.

Fischer, K. W.; Hand, H. H.; & Russell, S. The development of abstractions in adolescence and adulthood. In M. Commons, F. Richards, & C. Armon (Eds.), *Beyond formal operations.* New York: Praeger Scientific, in press.

Flavell, J. H. Stage-related properties of cognitive development. *Cognitive Psychology,* 1971, **2,** 421–453.

Gibbs, J. C.; Widaman, K. F.; & Colby, A. Construction and validation of a simplified, group-administerable equivalent to the moral judgment interview. *Child Development,* 1982, **53,** 895–910.

Gilligan, C. *In a different voice.* Cambridge, Mass.: Harvard University Press, 1982.

Hand, H. H. The relation between developmental level and spontaneous behavior: the importance of sampling contexts. In K. W. Fischer (Ed.), *Cognitive development.* New Directions for Child Development, no. 12. San Francisco: Jossey-Bass, 1981.

Harkness, S.; Edwards, C. P.; & Super, C. M. Social rules and moral reasoning: a case study in a rural African community. *Developmental Psychology,* 1981, **17,** 595–603.

Holstein, C. Irreversible, stepwise sequence in the development of moral judgment: a longitudinal study of males and females. *Child Development,* 1976, **47,** 51–61.

Kitchener, K. S. Human development and the college campus: sequences and tasks. In G. Hanon (Ed.), *Assessing student development.* New Directions for Student Services. San Francisco: Jossey-Bass, in press.

Kitchener, K. S., & King, P. M. Reflective judgment: concepts of justification and their relation to age and education. *Journal of Applied Developmental Psychology,* 1981, **2,** 89–116.

Kohlberg, L. The development of modes of moral thinking and choice in the years ten to sixteen. Unpublished doctoral dissertation, University of Chicago, 1958.

Kohlberg, L. From is to ought: how to commit the naturalistic fallacy and get away with it in the study of moral development. In T. Mischel (Ed.), *Cognitive development and epistemology.* New York: Academic Press, 1971.

Kuhn, D. Short-term longitudinal evidence for the sequentiality of Kohlberg's early stages of moral judgment. *Developmental Psychology,* 1976, **12,** 162–166.

Kurtines, W., & Greif, W. The development of moral thought: review and evaluation of Kohlberg's approach. *Psychological Bulletin,* 1974, **81,** 453–470.

Lee, L. C. The concomitant development of cognitive and moral modes of thought: a test of selected deductions from Piaget's theory. *Genetic Psychology Monographs,* 1971, **83,** 93–146.

Martarano, S. C. A developmental analysis of performance on Piaget's formal operations tasks. *Developmental Psychology,* 1977, **13,** 666–672.

Piaget, J. Le mécanisme du développement mental et les lois du groupement des opérations. *Archives de Psychologie, Genève,* 1941, **28,** 215–285.

Piaget, J. Logique et équilibre dans les comportements du sujet. *Etudes d'epistémologie génétique,* 1957, **2,** 27–118.

Piaget, J. Intellectual evolution from adolescence to adulthood. *Human Development,* 1972, **15,** 1–12.

Rest, J. R. New approaches in the assessment of moral judgment. In T. Lickona (Ed.), *Moral development and behavior.* New York: Holt, Rinehart & Winston, 1976.

Rest, J. R. *Development in judging moral issues.* Minneapolis: University of Minnesota Press, 1979.

Sobesky, W. E. Effects of severity of consequences on moral judgments. *Child Development,* in press.

106

Tabor, L. E., & Kendler, T. S. Testing for developmental continuity or discontinuity: class inclusion and reversal shifts. *Developmental Review*. 1981, 1, 330–343.

Vygotsky, L. *Mind in society* (M. Cole, V. John-Steiner, S. Scribner, & E. Souberman, Eds.). Cambridge, Mass.: Harvard University Press. 1978.

Watson, M. W., & Fischer, K. W. Development of social roles in elicited and spontaneous behavior during the preschool years. *Developmental Psychology*, 1980, 16, 483–494.

[**Kurt W. Fischer** (Ph.D., Harvard University, developmental psychology, 1971) is associate professor of psychology at the University of Denver. His research focuses on processes of change in the organization of behavior, as evidenced in cognitive, social, and emotional development. His recent publications include "A Theory of Cognitive Development: The Control and Construction of Hierarchies of Skills," *Psychological Review*, 87 (1980): 477–531, and he was the editor for number 12 of the New Directions for Child Development series, *Cognitive development* (San Francisco: Jossey-Bass, 1981).]

107

COMMENTARY

CRITICAL ISSUES IN KOHLBERG'S THEORY OF MORAL REASONING

BY HERBERT D. SALTZSTEIN

Kohlberg's theory of moral development has aroused considerable controversy about its theoretical assumptions, empirical claims, and social implications (e.g., Baumrind 1978; Kurtines & Greif 1974; Simpson 1974; Sullivan 1977). Indeed, for a presumably "cool" theory of morality, it has generated an unusual degree of heat. It seems appropriate, therefore, to begin with a general appreciation of what I believe to be Kohlberg's most important contribution to the study of moral and social development. Next, some controversies about the approach will be discussed, including the core issues addressed in the present *Monograph* and other issues more peripheral to the study. This will lead into a discussion of some limitations of the approach and possible future lines of development.

General Contributions

Kohlberg and his colleagues have made at least three general contributions to the field of moral development. First, they have taken the thinking of young children about moral dilemmas seriously and respectfully but not at face value. With the notable exception of Piaget, much previous research on the moral development of children had either reduced children's thought to overly simplified indices or ignored it, as if what the child says has no value but is at best an epiphenomenon or reducible to nonrational processes (e.g., Aronfreed 1968).[1]

Second, Kohlberg and his co-workers have attempted to extract from moral judgments the form or structure of the thought in contrast to its con-

I wish to thank Alan Weiner for critically reading an earlier version of this paper and for making a number of helpful comments.

[1] Indeed, I am struck with the parallel in method (despite the differences in content) between this style of interviewing and the clinical interviewing of children.

tent. The latter is viewed as labile and therefore of peripheral interest, and the former as invariant and of central interest. It is also upon this form-content distinction that the Kohlberg group and many, though not all, of its critics (e.g., Kurtines & Greif 1974) have had the most trouble communicating.

Kohlberg's third general contribution to the study of moral development in particular, and social development in general, is the idea of *constructivism*, which he also adapted from Piaget (1970). This has offered a viable alternative to biological determinism and to learning theories, either of the conditioning (e.g., Aronfreed 1969) or the more eclectic and cognitive type (e.g., Whitehurst & Zimmerman 1979), as well as internalization theories, Freudian or neo-Freudian (e.g., Sears, Rau, & Alpert 1965). The constructivist view is that the child/adolescent/adult constructs his or her own moral structures to make sense out of the observed rights, duties, claims, etc., in society, especially as they appear to conflict. A theoretical implication of this view which has sometimes been overlooked, however, is that the reasoning by which the child constructs the rules and principles from his observations must not be restricted to induction but also allow for generative modes of reasoning. That is, if the only mode of learning is inductive, there is no way to account for the emergence of *novel* modes of thought, such as post-conventional reasoning. To attribute unconventional thought to the "norm" of the particular subgroup (e.g., that the individual learned or "identified" with a particular minority group, be it Bahai, political radicals, or 80-and-over-year-olds) only pushes the question back a step; it does not solve it.

Core Propositions

As Colby and her colleagues state at the beginning of this *Monograph*, the core propositions motivating the study are: that the stages represent distinct or qualitatively different modes of thought which may be reliably identified, that they form an invariant sequence for the individual, and that each form of thought imposes similar responses over tasks which are manifestly different in content. Further, these moral-cognitive stages are assumed to be hierarchically organized, such that each succeeding stage includes the preceding ones in reorganized and better equilibrated form. This last implies that regression is not a normal part of development but represents the exception. As the authors note, these criteria are adopted from Piaget (e.g., Piaget 1970). They imply the present enterprise will yield the following results:

1. Distinct forms of reasoning are reliably distinguishable and consistent within the individual across disparate content (e.g., stories).

2. Change in stage (form) of reasoning is gradual (thus, high test-retest reliability), orderly (with little stage skipping), and progressive (little or no stage regression).

109

3. Similar patterns of results are to be found in different populations (e.g., working and middle class) though the rate and actual modal endpoint of development may vary with the social and cultural characteristics of the sample. In general, rate of development should be more closely related to intellectual development—for example, intelligence scores and education—than to other nonintellectual social indices such as income or ethnicity. This follows from the primarily cognitive character of the stages.

The present study supports these central propositions quite well, with some reservations.

First, the various forms of thought are found, and they appear to characterize an individual subject's responses to different stories. To reduce "halo" effects, coding was by story, not by subject. There is an inevitable potential halo effect built into coding the individual's response to a particular story since coding cannot be done without detailed knowledge of the theory and often has involved strong commitment to it. However, the danger of over-generalization of coding is reduced across stories and testings by the procedures used in the study.

And yet it is with regard to the "structured whole" assumption that the reader may be less than fully satisfied. The central contribution of Kohlberg's approach, the attempt to distinguish structure (form) from content, is also the hardest to evaluate unless one is able to immerse oneself in the data, not available to most readers, no matter how eager they may be to take the plunge. What really constitute the differences between the stages? These differences are primarily structural in nature, and much is made of this point by the authors. Yet these structural differences are not always fully explicated, though in all fairness it must be recognized that this is a research report, not a theoretical exposition. Nonetheless, it would help to know what the authors mean by "moral" role taking as distinct from "social" role taking. Clearly they are correct in pointing to the need for something in addition to role taking (or perspective taking) since, as most writers have noted (e.g., Selman 1976), role taking is a necessary but not sufficient condition for moral development. Further, clinical phenomena—in particular, sociopathy (or, to use the more current term, antisocial personality)—point up the need to go beyond cognitive skills. Sociopathic individuals are capable of perspective taking; indeed, they may be particularly good at it, but they are incapable and/or unwilling to translate that ability into moral reactions such as a sense of responsibility. What is missing? The answer may lie in distinguishing between moral and social perspective taking—or in introducing other concepts (below).

In any case, an analysis of the structure of the thought, like that which Selman (e.g., 1976) has partially provided for the earlier stages, would be most helpful. Stage 3 is an example of particular ambiguity. It has been designated as "approval-seeking," "good boy/girl morality," etc. However,

110

these designations imply content categories emphasizing motivational or value orientations, not cognitive structure. What emergent structure or structures characterize this development? Is it the development of the ability for recursive role taking (which is a new organization of role taking) (Kuhn, Langer, Kohlberg, & Haan 1977) or perhaps development of the concept of personality (or character) as a new level of object permanence and as an entity to be evaluated? The latter might be further related to the development of causal attributions by the child (Sedlak & Kurtz 1981). It is to be hoped that these and related questions will be answered when the second volume of Professor Kohlberg's projected three-volume series is published (Kohlberg, in press). Such clarification will help avoid the many misunderstandings of the theory, including some of those writers cited, and render the method more accessible to others. Such theoretical clarification may help resolve one controversy about the approach: that it is arcane, unwieldly, requires theoretical commitment beyond that needed for the use of other research tools, and is therefore even "cultish." There has always been the danger that Kohlberg's approach might evolve into a cult or movement, as the psychoanalytic enterprise did to some extent. Kohlberg's approach is also similar to psychoanalysis in that the method may be so tied to the theory that perhaps the former cannot be used to evaluate the latter. The danger lies not only in the opposition engendered but in the confusion such a development would create between social and intellectual commitments. The theory and method should not be relegated to "true believers," and it is good to see that the authors appear to recognize this danger. They acknowledge that use of the technique requires training, as is the case with any complicated research tool (e.g., microelectrode recording, projective tests, individual intelligence testing, EEG), but they claim that such skills can be developed in a relatively brief time, allowing for adequate research on the theory by independent and even unsympathetic groups. Further, theoretical clarification in characterizing the stages will help.

Second, testing the sequential and progressive nature of the stages was one of the major purposes of the study. Here, too, there has also been a major controversy about Kohlberg's theory, especially as it applies to the higher three stages (4, 5, and 6).

For example, some researchers, notably Holstein (1976) and later Murphy and Gilligan (1980), found substantial evidence of stage regression, either between stages and within levels or at the higher stages. Colby et al. attribute these deviations to the fact that the method used involved written questionnaires rather than individual interviews. Furthermore, as they point out, Murphy and Gilligan's data were collected in a class devoted to a study of moral issues and to an examination of Kohlberg's theory. In contrast, Kuhn (1976) and White, Bushnell, and Regnemer (1978) used an individual interview method of assessment and found little evidence of a stage regression at the three lower stages. From this one might conclude that the different results might reasonably be traced to the different methods employed, but it is also true that Kuhn and White et al. studied younger children, while Holstein studied older children or adolescents and Murphy and Gilligan studied adults. Thus, the discrepancy may also be due to the different age (and stage) ranges under investigation. Some have concluded that Kohlberg is half or two-thirds right, that perhaps the first three or four stages form an invariant sequence but that the latter two or three stages do not. Kohlberg himself has recently abandoned the claim that stage 6 is a "natural" stage, and Gibbs (1977), a close collaborator of Kohlberg and coauthor of the *Monograph*, has suggested that the last three stages are "existential," not "natural." In the past, Kohlberg (1981) has argued vigorously that at least the distinction between stages 4 and 5 is developmental, and the present study seems to bear his assertion out. The so-called sophomoric regression was found to be infrequent. It is now explained in two ways: partly as miscoding due to failure of the previous structural coding system to distinguish clearly enough between content and structure, and partly as a (nonstructural?) metaethic state that may occur between any two stages.

Third, the stage 5 mode of thinking proved to be rare, constituting less than 15% of responses. This lack of universality has also suggested to some critics that the higher stages are not developmentally "real" (e.g., Kurtines & Greif 1974). It seems to me that universality is not an appropriate criterion. Kohlberg's theory is not maturational, as some continue to imply (e.g., Liebert 1979). The higher stages constitute potential, not necessarily actual, development. Certainly the relevance of the stages is not to be decided by their popularity! The theory is constructionist in that each stage is presumed to resolve certain kinds of conflicts among claims or perspectives in society. The nature and range of these conflicting perspectives determine the complexity of the form of reasoning needed. In a traditional society with a homogeneous population and *relatively* little differentiation of roles and authority, there may be fewer or less severe conflicts and therefore less need to move beyond the stage 3 conception of right, based on consensus and social relatedness (Baumrind 1978). This does not mean that these societies are inferior or primitive, simply less highly differentiated. With more consensus and communality, there may be less need for a societal perspective (e.g., as in the stage 4 concept of legal precedence) and with less conflicting moral codes, less need for a stage 5 metatheory for evaluating and choosing between moral systems.

What does follow from Kohlberg's constructivist theory is that (*a*) *if* such stages do appear, they will appear in the prescribed order and maintain themselves in that order. (*b*) Further, the advanced stages would appear as society, or one's participation in it, exposes one to greater conflict among perspectives. Only modest support for this is to be found in the present study, which was not designed to test this proposition. However, the present world scene, with traditional societies changing into modern ones, seems to offer much opportunity to test the relationship between moral thought and societal complexity and structure. Yet relatively little published work on this problem has appeared.

A notable exception is the study by White et al. (1978) already cited. These investigators employed a longitudinal cohort design in a study of the Eleuthera Islands in the Carribean. They largely confirmed the stage character of the reasoning, with little evidence of stage skipping or (gross) regression but also little evidence of reasoning above stage 3, even in adults. However, they estimated time-of-testing effects three times the size of the age effects. Unfortunately, they used the structural coding scheme, which Colby and her colleagues report to be unreliable. It would be well worth reanalyzing those data with the more reliable and valid standard scoring system or repeating the study in another developing society to reevaluate the relative contribution of age and social conditions. White and his colleagues attributed the strong time-of-testing effects to changes in the school system that followed independence, but they acknowledge that this is only an educated guess, which needs documentation and proof.

In summary, the present study musters strong data in support of some of the core propositions of the theory, especially (a) the existence of qualitatively different modes of thought, which appear to be structurally discernible (reliably so), stable, and applicable across somewhat different tasks (content); and (b) the sequentiality and nonregressive nature of the change. The study was not primarily designed to test other central propositions, in particular, the hierarchical nature of the stages, a precise structural characterization of the stages, and the universality of the stage system. Without question, however, this is the strongest study in method and empirical results to come out from the Kohlberg group.

Other Controversial Issues

Other controversial issues not directly empirically addressed in the present studies include the relationship to be expected between thought and action. Some of the criticisms directed to Kohlberg's approach on this issue rest on a profound misunderstanding of the nature of the stage concept. For example, Kurtines and Greif (1974) write of the stages as a moral development "scale." This assumption that the stages represent the "amount" or "degree" of morality leads them astray, for example, to expect monotonic relationships between moral thought and moral action. For example, research of ours (Saltzstein, Diamond, & Belenky 1972) is cited as possible counterevidence because we found a curvilinear relationship between stage and conformity. They also point out that sometimes a stage is associated with

113

"moral" and sometimes with "immoral" behaviors. They seem to miss the point, which is that the stages represent organizations of thought, with different factors considered relevant and organized in different super- and subordinate relationships at each stage. Therefore, the appropriate judgment-action prediction is not directly between stage and action. What is to be expected is a relationship between the subject's moral reasoning stage and his or her reasons for making the moral action decision *in that situation*. Subjects at different stages should make their decision—whatever it is—for different reasons, that is, based on separate factors, organized in different ways. For example, a stage 2 subject might decide to obey or not to obey in the celebrated Milgram situation because of the opportunities for concrete reciprocity (quid pro quo) that may exist in the situation, while stage 3 subjects might decide on the basis of concern for social consensus, impact on individual social relationships, relative sympathy for the various actors, and maintaining goodness of character. At other stages, other considerations would be paramount (e.g., concern for maintenance of and loyalty to the group or society). The point is that the stage does *not* determine the action decision but the *reasons* for deciding. Translated into design terms, this means either that the subjects are asked why they took the particular course of action or, better still, the researcher varies the settings of the action in ways that will help reveal the reason for the decision. This second research strategy involves interaction designs and predictions of the general type: moral stage $\times$ situation $=$ action. Very few of these studies (e.g., Malinowski 1979; Saltzstein et al. 1972) have been attempted and even fewer have been successful in creating the conditions for testing interaction.

Another controversy has concerned how the results of experimental change studies reflect on theoretical controversies. What kind of a paradigm/finding would constitute a critical test between the social constructivist and environmental views of acquisition? It seems to me that often the central point has been overlooked. Most of the experimental studies designed to test the sequentiality hypothesis experimentally, both those emanating from cognitive structuralists (e.g., Turiel 1966) and others (e.g., Bandura & McDonald 1963), have not put the theory to its most critical test. They have for the most part *not* excluded opportunities for modeling. Therefore, while they have made a contribution in demonstrating that developmental direction (progressive or retrogressive) or developmental distance (in stages) does or does not make a difference in the degree, generalizability, or stability of the modeling effects, they have not demonstrated moral reasoning as an *emergent* phenomenon. Studies are needed which under some conditions *exclude* opportunities for modeling the response to be acquired (moral stage) but provide the conflict or disequilibration among elements of the structure such that a new form of thought is required. Among studies of cognitive development, the work of Inhelder, Sinclair, and Bovet (1974) may provide

114

an example. Only two unpublished studies (Gunsburg 1973; Saltzstein & Handelman 1978) appear to take this approach by attempting to induce change, direct and indirect (transfer), by promoting conflict among perspectives (the elements within the structure) *without* opportunities for modeling. At least one other study (Walker, in press) has opposed two opinions at the subject's own stage and tested for emergence of the *next* stage of thought. (However, a limit of the study is that opinions are not structural elements.) More such studies are needed. Such research will, however, require a careful delineation of the structure of the stages in order to create theoretically meaningful change conditions.

Finally, three interrelated issues have been raised with regard to Kohlberg's theory and method: that the moral dilemmas are all hypothetical and mostly far removed from the life experiences of the child, adolescent, or even adult; that Kohlberg's sample is male and that the findings may therefore only hold for males; and, most important, that affect plays little or no role in the theory. It seems to me that these are valid points that must be addressed and that are, in my opinion, interrelated.

The weakness of Kohlberg's method is the obverse side of its strength. The subject's attention is largely directed to hypothetical, indeed often strange, situations about which the respondent knows little. By thus reducing the subject's emotional involvement, specific knowledge, and action commitment, subjects approach the task with perhaps fewer preconceptions and certainly greater opportunity for reflection. Such "simplification" of the task does *not* invalidate its results but may limit their generalizability. For example, Colby et al. acknowledge slightly different pulls of different stories for different stages of moral thought, and Haan (1975) has noted something similar in comparing responses to the standard hypothetical stories and to the Berkeley political situation, as have Gilligan (1977) and Murphy and Gilligan (1980). Often practical moral thought lags behind hypothetical moral thought. In contrast, Piaget (1932) asserted that children's judgments about practical and personally relevant situations preceded their development of judgments about hypothetical situations. Let me try to make the point clear. I am *not* asserting that moral thought has to relate directly to, or represent, moral action. As indicated earlier, following Piaget (1932) and Kohlberg (e.g., in the present report), moral thought stands on its own and needs no external validation. But moral thought about hypothetical situations may not adequately reflect moral thought about practical situations.

The issue of sex differences has been discussed elsewhere (e.g., Gilligan 1977; Holstein 1976). It seems to me that findings of modal sex differences in stages (e.g., Holstein 1976; Saltzstein et al. 1972) are not an embarrassment for the theory, but Gilligan's finding that different *categories* apply is or at least poses a problem which eventually must be addressed. Both of these issues, practical versus hypothetical moral reasoning and sex differences,

115

may devolve onto the third issue, the relationship between cognition and affect, which is often taken to mean the relationship between rationality and irrationality. The importance of affect, and its relationship to cognition has only recently regained attention in developmental psychology (e.g., Hoffman 1981; Sroufe 1979) and general psychology (e.g., Mandler 1975).

As indicated earlier, Kohlberg's theory is "cool" in the sense that affect plays no important role. Some writers (e.g., Shweder 1981) has cast the conflict as between those who believe in the primacy of cognition (rationality) and those who believe affect (irrationality) is prepotent. It seems to me that this is not the correct way to put the question. It is not cognition *or* affect, but cognition *and* affect in interaction.

One view, which seems to be held by some who stress cognition, is that affect either is a performance factor which impairs or degrades competence or it simply parallels cognitive structures.[2] Another view is that affect may facilitate performance. For example, Piaget suggested, and Keasey (1977) later confirmed, that children may show "higher level" responses (based on intentions and motives) in judging self than in judging others.[3] If we assume that practical or realistic situations, especially those involving self, engage affect more than hypothetical situations not directly involving self, this assertion may mean that affective involvement facilitates the development of moral cognition. Here, we have two views of how affect might influence moral judgment: by degrading it, or by maximizing its potential. Other possibilities exist, of course. For example, in their study of causal attributions by children, Kun, Murray, and Sredl (1980) suggest that which of two kinds of (nondevelopmentally ordered) causal attribution schemas is used might be determined by the affective involvement of the reasoner in the situation and the need to reduce ambiguity. The general point is that without considering the role of affect (commitment, involvement, etc.) we have only a limited side of the child's, adolescent's, and adult's moral thought and that several models of how cognition and affect interact are possible.

It is perhaps here that Gilligan in her study of woman's decisions on abortion (1977) and Murphy and Gilligan (1980) have posed a major challenge to Kohlberg's theory as it concerns postconventional moral thought. They note that the reasoning of late adolescents and adults may be less "abstract" "principled," and "absolute" (one might say, Kantian) and more sensitive to "context" and "personalistic" considerations. In the abortion study, Gilligan appears to attribute this to the fact that her subjects

[2] Many years ago I had the pleasure of meeting regularly with Professor Kohlberg and others interested in moral development. During those meetings he and I had a long but friendly argument on whether the concept of guilt was useful at all in understanding normal development.

[3] Alan Weiner and I (Saltzstein & Weiner 1982) have suggested that this may be in part due to the kinds of causal attributions made, which is itself related to affect.

116

were female, and she may be right. (Gilligan's findings may be seen as consistent with, though not reducible to, Freud's [1961/1925] well-known comment that women's superego is never "so inexorable, so impersonal, so independent of its emotional origins" as that of men.) What is also possible, however, is that her findings of more context-sensitive, less absolute, and more functional thinking at the postconventional level may have less to do with the sex of her subjects and more to do with the "hot" issue the subjects (whether they be male or female) are facing.[4]

The conclusions of Murphy and Gilligan are intuitively appealing to me, in part because they fit my experience (and I suspect that of other presumably postconventional reasoners) that even one's thinking about what is right or wrong (let alone one's action) is more contextual and personal than suggested by the universal purity of Kohlberg's stages 5 and 6 as described. In any case, we need more studies of moral judgment and reasoning about real-life and affectively involving situations. This might be done by careful choice of situations for judging, on-the-spot observations and interviews, role playing, etc. The purpose would not be to disprove Kohlberg's theory. His contribution stands. Rather, the aim would be to understand how "cool" and "hot" (or "hotter") reasoning converge and diverge. In doing so, we can hope to learn something important about morality and about the general relationship between the cognitive and affective sides of life and development.

This discussion does not do justice (if I may use the word) to Kohlberg's contribution to developmental psychology. Despite the limitations described above, Kohlberg, following Piaget, has made a seminal contribution to understanding children's social thought and development. All of us who are interested in how children think and develop are in his debt.

References

Aronfreed, J. *Conduct and conscience: the socialization of internalized control over behavior.* New York: Academic Press, 1968.

Bandura, A., & McDonald, F. J. The influence of social reinforcement and the behavior of models in shaping children's moral judgments. *Journal of Abnormal and Social Psychology*, 1963, **67**, 274–281.

Baumrind, D. A dialectical materialist's perspective on knowing social reality. In W. Damon (Ed.), *Moral development.* San Francisco: Jossey-Bass, 1978.

Freud, S. Some psychical consequences of the anatomical distinction between the sexes. In J. Strachey (Ed.), *The standard edition of the complete psychological works of Sigmund Freud.* Vol. 19. London: Hogarth, 1961. (Originally published, 1925.)

Gibbs, J. C. Kohlberg's stages of moral judgment: a constructive critique. *Harvard Educational Review*, 1977, **47**, 43–61.

Gilligan, C. In a different voice: women's conception of the self and of morality. *Harvard Educational Review*, 1977, **47**, 481–517.

[4] I wish to thank Margo Morse, a student in developmental psychology at CUNY, for making this observation.

Gunsburg, L. Conflict training and the development of moral judgment in children. Unpublished Ph.D. dissertation, Yeshiva University, 1973.

Haan, N. Hypothetical and actual moral reasoning in a situation of civil disobedience. *Journal of Personality and Social Psychology*, 1975, **32**, 255–270.

Hoffman, M. L. Perspectives on the differences between understanding people and understanding things: the role of affect. In J. H. Flavell & L. Ross (Eds.), *Social cognitive development*. Cambridge: Cambridge University Press, 1981. Pp. 67–81.

Holstein, C. Development of moral judgment: a longitudinal study of males and females. *Child Development*, 1976, **47**, 51–61.

Inhelder, B.; Sinclair, H.; & Bovet, M. *Learning and the development of cognition*. Cambridge, Mass.: Harvard University Press, 1974.

Keasey, C. B. Young children's attributions of intentionality to themselves and others. *Child Development*, 1977, **48**, 261–264.

Kohlberg, L. *Essays on moral development*. Vol. 1. *The philosophy of moral development: moral stages and the idea of justice*. New York: Harper & Row, 1981.

Kohlberg, L. *Essays on moral development*. Vol. 2. *The psychology of moral development: moral stages and the life cycle*. New York: Harper & Row, in press.

Kuhn, D. Short-term longitudinal evidence for the sequentiality of Kohlberg's early stages of moral judgment. *Development Psychology*, 1976, **12**, 162–166.

Kuhn, D.; Kohlberg, L.; Langer, J.; & Haan, N. The development of formal operations in logical and moral judgment. *Genetic Psychology Monographs*, 1977, **95**, 97–188.

Kun, A.; Murray, J.; & Sredl, K. Misuses of the multiple sufficient causal scheme as a model of naive attributions: a case of mistaken identity. *Developmental Psychology*, 1980, **16**, 13–22.

Kurtines, W., & Greif, E. B. The development of moral thought: review and evaluation of Kohlberg's approach. *Psychological Bulletin*, 1974, **81**, 453–470.

Liebert, R. M. Moral development: a theoretical and empirical analysis. In G. J. Whitehurst & B. J. Zimmerman (Eds.), *The functions of language and cognition*. New York: Academic Press, 1979.

Malinowski, C. Cheating as a function of moral judgment and selected personality and situational factors. Unpublished Ph.D. dissertation, City University of New York, 1979.

Mandler, G. *Mind and emotion*. New York: Wiley, 1975.

Murphy, J. M., & Gilligan, C. Moral development in late adolescence and adulthood: a critique and reconstruction of Kohlberg's theory. *Human Development*, 1980, **23**, 77–104.

Piaget, J. *The moral judgment of the child*. London: Kegan Paul, 1932.

Piaget, J. Piaget's theory. In P. H. Mussen (Ed.), *Carmichael's Manual of Child Psychology*. Vol. 1. New York: Wiley, 1970.

Saltzstein, H. D.; Diamond, R. M.; & Belenky, M. Moral judgment level and conformity behavior. *Developmental Psychology*, 1972, **7**, 327–336.

Sears, R. R.; Rau, L.; & Alpert, R. *Identification and child rearing*. Stanford, Calif.: Stanford University Press, 1965.

Sedlak, A. J., & Kurtz, S. T. A review of children's use of causal inference principles. *Child Development*, 1981, **52**, 759–784.

Saltzstein, H. D., & Handelman, M. Inducing change in moral reasoning by training in perspective taking. Unpublished manuscript, 1978.

Saltzstein, H. D., & Weiner, A. Moral intentionality: a review and theoretical reformulation. Unpublished manuscript, 1982.

Selman, R. L. Social-cognitive understanding: a guide to educational and clinical practice. In T. Lickona (Ed.), *Moral development and behavior: theory, research, and social issues*. New York: Holt, Rinehart & Winston, 1976.

Shweder, R. A. Discussion: what's there to negotiate? Some questions for Youniss. *Merrill-Palmer Quarterly*, 1981, **27**, 405–412.

Simpson, E. L. Moral development research: a case study of scientific cultural bias. *Human Development*, 1974, **17**, 81–106.

Sroufe, L. A. Socioemotional development. In J. D. Osofsky (Ed.), *Handbook of infant development*. New York: Wiley, 1979.

Sullivan, E. A study of Kohlberg's structural theory of moral development: a critique of liberal social science ideology. *Human Development*, 1977, **20**, 325–376.

Turiel, E. An experimental test of the sequentiality of developmental stages in the child's moral judgments. *Journal of Personality and Social Psychology*, 1966, **3**, 611–618.

Walker, L. J. Sources of cognitive conflict for stage transition in moral development. *Developmental Psychology*, in press.

White, C. B.; Bushnell, N.; & Regnemer, J. L. Moral development in Bahamian school children: a 3-year examination of Kohlberg's stages of moral development. *Developmental Psychology*, 1978, **14**, 58–65.

Whitehurst, G. J., & Zimmerman, B. J. (Eds.), *The functions of language and cognition*. New York: Academic Press, 1979.

[**Herbert D. Saltzstein** (Ph.D. 1961, University of Michigan) is professor of psychology at Lehman College and executive officer of the doctoral program in psychology at the Graduate Center of the City University of New York. His general research interests are in the development of moral and social thought in normal and atypical populations. Recently his research has been on children's and adolescents' representations of adult moral judgments and on the relationship between moral judgment and causal attribution.]

119

REPLY

REPLY TO FISCHER AND SALTZSTEIN
BY LAWRENCE KOHLBERG AND ANNE COLBY

We wish to begin by expressing our appreciation of the thoughtfulness and understanding of both commentators. In this response we shall attempt to clarify our position on several issues raised in the commentaries and to refer to some other publications in which these issues are discussed.

Let us first take up the question of intrapersonal consistency of moral reasoning raised by Kurt Fischer. It is important to point out in this regard that we do not hold the extreme version of the structured whole hypothesis that Fischer attributes to us and would agree with his proposal that a new form of reasoning emerges first in some areas of an individual's thinking and rather gradually generalizes across the moral domain. In saying that stages of moral judgment are "structured wholes" we mean that under conditions that support expression of the individual's most mature thinking, his or her reasoning will form a coherent system best described by one of Kohlberg's five stages or by a mixture of at most two adjacent stages. Our position is more appropriately termed a "dominant stage model" than a "simple stage model." This issue is discussed in detail by Puka (1982). This model does not imply that development from one stage to the next will be rapid, nor does it imply that the individual will use under all circumstances the highest stage available to him or her. On the other hand, our position does imply and our data do indicate more internal consistency and somewhat less gradual development than Fischer grants. His statement that "most individuals showed a range of at least two or three stages" is misleading. In fact, very few of our subjects showed reasoning at more than two adjacent stages. Since our subjects are developing through adolescence into early adulthood, it is logical that they should be a mixture of two stages, that which they are leaving and that into which they are developing. As Fischer

We wish to express our gratitude to Alexandra Hewer for aiding and advising in the writing of this response.

points out, there is through early adulthood a continuing consolidation of stage 4. The process shown in individual curves is less gradual, however, than that suggested by the group average trends cited by Fischer. The change is not saltatory, but it is less gradual than Fischer suggests. Furthermore, there is a rather striking regularity in the slight "horizontal décalage" that pertains across moral issues or dilemmas. We interpret this to mean that the ease with which an individual applies a new form of thinking to the various issues within the moral domain appears to be a function of the relation between the characteristics of the emerging stage and the characteristics of each content area to which the reasoning is being applied (cf. Lieberman 1970).

Fischer also raises the question of consistency among judgments made in response to the standard hypothetical dilemmas, moral judgments made in other contexts, and moral action. In doing so, he appears to be confusing three quite separate issues: (1) stage consistency across different content areas under standard conditions designed to optimize the individual's expression of his or her highest stage; (2) consistency between hypothetical moral judgments and moral judgments made under the complex changing conditions of real life; and (3) consistency between hypothetical moral judgments and moral action. We have already addressed the first of these issues. In regard to the second, we would agree with Fischer that the processes involved in making "real-life moral judgments" have only begun to be explored and are an important direction for further research. It is already clear, however, that hypothetical moral judgment stage is one powerful predictor of the moral thinking used to resolve actual moral dilemmas in one's life (cf. Belenky 1978; Gilligan & Belenky 1980).

As Herbert Saltzstein points out, the relation of moral judgment to moral action is a difficult theoretical issue that cannot be treated as a question of stage consistency. This point was also discussed by Broughton (1978) in his reply to Kurtines and Greif (1974). Our latest thinking on the relation of moral judgment to action is reflected in papers by Kohlberg and Candee (1981) and Higgins, Power, and Kohlberg (1981). In the first paper, a distinction is made between deontic judgments of rightness or justice (e.g., it would be *morally right* for me to steal the drug) and aretaic judgments of responsibility (e.g., it is *my responsibility* to steal the drug; I am accountable if I do not steal the drug). In the paper, data are presented that indicate that judgments of responsibility serve to mediate between deontic judgments of moral correctness and action taken in a real situation. Moreover, these judgments of responsibility themselves appear to be related to moral stage of responses to the hypothetical dilemmas. It should also be noted that the normal pattern of relation of hypothetical moral judgment stage to moral choice and moral action is monotonic, not curvilinear (Kohlberg & Candee 1981). Saltzstein's report of a curvilinear finding in the Asch situation may

121

reflect the fact that the Asch situation is not a true moral justice dilemma but rather a test of ego autonomy or conformity. The Higgins et al. (1981) paper hypothesizes what Fischer suggests, that consistency depends partly on situational factors, factors we term the moral atmosphere of the group or institutional context in which action takes place.

Turning to Saltzstein's commentary, let us consider first the question he raises about the distinctly moral nature of Kohlberg's stages. As discussed in the *Monograph*, we distinguish between the descriptive social perspective taking described by Selman (1980) and the prescriptive perspective taking used in making and justifying moral decisions. Our method is limited to scoring prescriptive judgments, a criterion used by Durkheim (1925/1961), Hare (1963), Kant (1949), and Piaget (1932) to define the moral domain. Obligation or prescriptive judgment is in turn related to rights. Our dilemmas tap structures for adjudicating conflicting rights or justice claims. For example, the Heinz dilemma (Dilemma III, Form A) opposes the rights of the druggist to his property to the wife's right to life. The Joe and the father dilemma (Dilemma I, Form A) opposes the right of the son to have a contract or promise maintained to the right of the father to exercise his authority. That is, our dilemmas oppose one basic moral norm, value, or right (e.g., life) against another basic norm, value, or right (e.g., law). The stage of the subject's response is defined by the justice principle used to adjudicate between conflicting rights or norms. As we outline in the *Monograph*, the "principles" used by each stage to adjudicate these conflicts are social interactional operations parallel to but not simple applications of the operations Piaget describes as characterizing logical mathematical reasoning (e.g., the operations of reciprocity, equality, maximization, and so on). Saltzstein is correct in noting that the specific nature of these operations and their developmental transformation has not yet been fully explicated. The formal properties of each stage must be abstracted from the criterion judgments that serve to define the stages in the scoring manual. This is an important next step in the future development of Kohlberg's theory. Progress on this issue to date is presented in Colby, Kohlberg, Gibbs, Candee, Speicher-Dubin, Kauffman, Hewer, & Power (1982).

A second issue Saltzstein raises is related to Fischer's concern about consistency of stage usage across varying contexts. Saltzstein argues that one important difference between hypothetical and real-life moral judgments is that real situations engage one's affect more powerfully than do hypothetical dilemmas. He points to the need for further research on the role of affect in moral thought and action. Although we agree that further research on this issue would help to illuminate the complex process of actual moral decision making, we must disagree with Saltzstein's characterization of Kohlberg's theory as one in which "affect plays no important role." Kohlberg (1969) has held that as cognitive components of moral judgment

122

develop, there is a parallel restructuring of moral affect. With moral judgment development from the preconventional level (stages 1 and 2) to the conventional level (stages 3 and 4), negative moral affect shifts from denial and fear of punishment to guilt. This was found using a variety of measures of guilt in delinquent youths (Ruma & Mosher 1967).

Just as guilt is a moral emotion developing with cognitive moral change, so is the emotion of a sense of justice or moral indignation regarding injustice. As Peters (1981) notes, morality includes "rational passions," and the development of these passions is closely related to the development of moral judgment.

Saltzstein's commentary serves to place our study within the broader context of issues that go beyond the scope of this particular study. Rather than to present here our perspective on the many controversies discussed by Saltzstein, we shall instead direct the reader to an extensive treatment of these issues presented elsewhere (Kohlberg, Levine, & Hewer 1983).

References

Belenky, M. Conflict and development: a longitudinal study of the impact of abortion decisions on moral judgments of adolescent and adult women. Unpublished doctoral dissertation, Harvard University, 1978.

Broughton, J. The cognitive-developmental approach to morality. *Journal of Moral Education*, 1978, 1(2), 81–96.

Colby, A.; Kohlberg, L.; Gibbs, J.; Candee, D.; Speicher-Dubin, B.; Kauffman, K.; Hewer, A.; & Power, C. *The measurement of moral judgment: a manual and its results*. New York: Cambridge University Press, 1982.

Durkheim, E. *Moral education: a study in the theory and application of the sociology of education*. New York: Free Press, 1961. (Originally published, 1925.)

Gilligan, C., & Belenky, M. A naturalistic study of abortion decisions. In R. Selman & R. Yando (Eds.), *Clinical developmental psychology*. San Francisco: Jossey Bass, 1980.

Hare, R. M. *Freedom and reason*. New York: Oxford University Press, 1963.

Higgins, A.; Power, C.; & Kohlberg, L. Student judgments of responsibility and the moral atmosphere of high schools: a comparative study. Paper presented at Florida International University Conference on Morality and Moral Development, Miami Beach, December 1981. To appear in W. Kurtines & J. L. Gewirtz (Eds.), *Morality, moral behavior and moral development: basic issues in theory and research*. New York: Wiley Interscience, 1983.

Kant, I. [*Foundations of the metaphysics of morals*.] (L. Beck, trans.). Indianapolis: Bobbs-Merrill, 1959. (Originally published, 1785.)

Kohlberg, L. Stage and sequence: the cognitive-developmental approach to socialization. In D. A. Goslin (Ed.), *Handbook of socialization theory and research*. Chicago: Rand McNally, 1969.

Kohlberg, L., & Candee, D. The relation of moral judgment to moral action. Paper presented at Florida International University Conference on Morality and Moral Development, Miami Beach, December 1981. To appear in W. Kurtines & J. L. Gewirtz (Eds.), *Morality, moral behavior and moral development: basic issues in theory and research*. New York: Wiley Interscience, 1983.

Kohlberg, L.; Levine, C.; & Hewer, A. An update of the theory and response to critics. In T. Meacham (Ed.), *Human development monograph series.* New York: Karger, in press.

Kurtines, W., & Grief, E. B. The development of moral thought: review and evaluation of Kohlberg's approach. *Psychological Bulletin,* 1974, **81,** 453–470.

Lieberman, M. Estimation of the moral judgment level using items whose alternatives form a graded scale. Unpublished doctoral dissertation, Chicago University, December 1970.

Peters, R. S. Concrete principles and the rational passions. In *Moral development and moral education.* London: Allen & Unwin, 1981.

Piaget, J. *The moral judgment of the child.* London: Kegan Paul, 1932.

Puka, B. An interdisciplinary treatment of Kohlberg. *Ethics,* 1982, **92,** 3, 486–491.

Ruma, E., & Mosher, R. The relationship between moral judgment and guilt in delinquent boys. *Journal of Abnormal Psychology,* 1967, **72,** 122–127.

Selman, R. *The growth of interpersonal understanding.* New York: Academic Press, 1981.

3. Synopses of Criticisms and a Reply

In the course of our synopses and replies to criticism we shall divide critics into two groups: first, those who critique the theory and its accompanying method as fundamentally flawed or biased; second, those who suggest some revisions in the formulation and use of the theory and paradigm. In the first group are Schweder [1982], Simpson [1974], Sullivan [1977], Gilligan [1977, 1982], Gilligan and Murphy [1979], and Murphy and Gilligan [1980]. In the second group are Levine [1979], Gibbs [1979], and Habermas [1979].

Schweder, R.:
Review of Lawrence Kohlberg's Essays in Moral Development, Vol. I.
The Philosophy of Moral Development.
Contemporary Psychology June, 1982: *421–424*

Synopsis
Schweder's critique is expressed in the subtitle of his review, 'Liberalism as Destiny'. He begins by stating:

'Kohlberg believes that reason is on the side of those who oppose capital punishment, hierarchy, tribalism and divine authority (pp. 21, 30, 176, 289). Moved by the spirit of developmentalism (pp. 87, 134, 136, 137), he holds out secular humanism, egalitarianism, and the Bill of Rights as rational ideals or objective endpoints for the evolution of moral ideas (pp. 164, 165, 215). For Kohlberg, the history of the world (p. 227) and the history of childhood (in all societies) (p. 25) is the story of the progressive discovery of the principles of the American Revolution (pp. 8, 38, 154, 237). Hegel's Prussian state has been replaced by Western liberal democracy. Liberalism has become destiny (pp. 227, 253).'

Schweder, an anthropologist, is fundamentally critical of Kohlberg's claim that what is moral is not historically and culturally relativistic. He states:

'The dominant theme in Kohlberg's essays is that what is moral is not a matter of taste or opinion. Kohlberg abhors relativism. He shudders at the idea that the moral codes of man might be like the languages and foods of man; different but equal. Kohlberg's project in these essays is to establish that there is an objective morality which reason can reveal; to define that objective morality in terms of justice, equity, equal respect for all persons and the 'natural' rights of man; and to defend that formulation against relativists, behaviorists, romantics, emotivists, psychoanalysts and advocates of capital punishment and character education. What Kohlberg seeks is a conceptualization of what is moral derived from premises which no rational person could possibly deny, by means of which no rational person could possibly avoid – preferably deductive logic (pp. 226, 293).'

Philosophically, Schweder draws primarily upon *After Virtue,* a recently-written book by the historically relativistic philosopher MacIntyre [1982]. This book presents a critique of modern liberal moral philosophy from Locke, Hume, and Kant to what Schweder calls two recent great books: Rawls' [1971] *Theory of Justice* and Gewirth's [1978] *Reason and Morality.* He considers MacIntyre's critique of these other two books itself a third great book; a book which fundamentally reveals the lack of viability of modern (post-medieval) philosophy, Rawls and Gewirth being recent 'liberal' examples. He states:

'MacIntyre persuasively argues that every notable attempt since the Enlightenment (including Rawls and Gewirth) to construct a rational foundation for an objective morality has been built out of non-rational premises, premises which any rational person might reasonably deny... Kohlberg quite properly criticizes "emotivist" theories about the meaning of moral terms, and instead defines moral concepts by their impersonality and their implication that as a person with reason you are obligated to behave in such-and-such a way. That is what we mean when we say "that's good" (or "bad"), but, if MacIntyre is right, we have no rational warrant for meaning it. We speak to each other (or at least to those with whom we are still on speaking terms) as though our moral choice had a rational foundation. Upon examination, that rational foundation turns out to be the soft sand of preferred (and often shared) assumptions. At its limit, moral discourse becomes ideology, a deceptive form of "mock rationality".'

Schweder claims that we are unsuccessful in both our effort to separate form and content and to hold that at the higher postconventional stages there is a formal similarity of moral judgment and reasoning across both culture and particular moral theories. He holds that Kohlberg has confused a postconventional or principled form of moral judgment with the content of liberal ideology. He continues: 'To decide how particular people are to be treated as alike or different is to introduce non-rational assumptions; for example, that to be just is to treat everyone as though they had the same natural and inalienable rights. That quite substantive idea of justice is faithfully endorsed by secular humanists but is not required by fact or reason.' Schweder concludes that Kohlberg runs into both empirical and conceptual difficulties in his 'quest for a rationally dictated objective morality'.

Besides believing that a rational and non-relativistic morality is an impossible quest, Schweder finds Kohlberg's book to be full of conceptual contradictions and inconsistency. As is argued in the reply to follow, a number of these inconsistencies seem to be *distinctions* made by Kohlberg's theory rather than contradictions.

Schweder also holds that the data base of the theory is weak. He believes that available research data do not support the idea that principled or Stage 5 and 6 reasoning is to be found in non-Western cultures. He also argues that the empirical data do not support the Piagetian assumption of invariant stage sequence and structural wholeness. In Schweder's words: 'Finally, the world of cognitive-developmental psychology has changed over the last ten years. The idea of general stages has taken a beating. It is no longer 1970. In 1981 the waning of the orthodox Piagetian paradigm cannot be ignored. Kohlberg's silence on the issue is deafening.'

Reply

As reply to Schweder's review, we reprint below Kohlberg's [1982b] response which appeared in *Contemporary Psychology,* December, 1982. It is titled: 'Moral Development Does Not Mean Liberalism as Destiny: a Reply to Schweder[14].'

'Rick Schweder's [1982] recent review of my book, *Essays on Moral Development,* consists of two parts; an exposition of the argument of the book and a critical reply to the argument. As an anthropologist Schweder wishes to uphold cultural, historical and ethical relativism and relies upon Alisdair MacIntyre's historically relativistic critique of modern moral philosophy to do so. My major purpose in writing this reply is not to deal with this complex issue but to point out that (1) Schweder's statement of the theory expounded in the book is an inaccurate caricature of its thesis; (2) his claims that I contradict myself in various parts of the book are usually incorrect; and (3) his assertion that I have no data base for my basic stage claim is inaccurate. Schweder uses the paraphernalia of scholarship, i.e., reference to specific pages in his exposition, but the reader who actually refers to the pages cited will usually not find what Schweder claims I say. Schweder's title, "Liberalism as Destiny", as the supposed theme of the book is stated in the opening of his review. He says: "Kohlberg believes that reason is on the side of those who oppose capital punishment, hierarchy, tribalism, and divine authority (pp. 21, 30, 176, 289). Moved by the spirit of

[14] Copyright 1982 by the American Psychological Association. Reprinted by permission of the author and publisher.

developmentalism (pp. 87, 134, 136, 137), he holds out secular humanism, egalitarianism, and the Bill of Rights as rational ideals or objective endpoints for the evolution of moral ideas (pp. 164, 165, 215). For Kohlberg, the history of the world (p. 227) and the history of childhood (in all societies) (p. 25) is the story of the progressive discovery of the principles of the American Revolution (pp. 8, 38, 154, 237). Hegel's Prussian state has been replaced by Western liberal democracy. Liberalism has become destiny (pp. 227, 253)."

If one turns to page 227, however, one finds instead a statement that liberalism as an ideology which has dominated the West is in trouble and, to be viable, requires some reconstruction or further development. My book, however, is not about the history of ideologies; rather, it is about the ontogenesis of forms of reasoning about justice in various cultures based on longitudinal studies done in Turkey [Nisan and Kohlberg, 1982], Israel [Snarey, 1982], and the United States [Colby et al., 1983b]. In these longitudinal studies we find universal stages defined by *forms* of reasoning. As Chapter 7 elaborates, *sometimes* the form of Stage 5 or 6 moral reasoning is associated with the content of a moral or political view like "liberal" opposition to capital punishment. While moral-political liberal ideological *content* is sometimes found to be associated with a stage or *form* of moral reasoning, the book represents a theory about the ontogenetic growth of forms of moral reasoning, not a theory about the growth of societies toward an ideology of liberalism. In the sections listed by Schweder, I do report a generational advance in the usage of principled or Stage 5 reasoning in our longitudinal sample, now adults, compared to their parents. I note that in constitutional democracies like the United States there is a trend toward a growing extension of rights to disenfranchised persons and groups if one takes a 200-year perspective. Finally, I note that in 1906 Hobhouse's *Morals in Evolution* reported studies using cross-cultural and historical data which found a correlation between technological and sociopolitical complexity and "stages" of juridical practices, laws, and moral customs from society to society. Hobhouse described his "stages" in ways greatly similar to my own. The burden of my point in the section on page 227 is that increased sociopolitical complexity poses new problems for members of a society which give an impetus to the growth of a new stage to cope with these problems. But principled reasoning was also used by Socrates 2,500 years ago; it is not a modern development.

While my book is a presentation and defense of what might be called "liberal thought", a tradition including thinkers from Locke and Kant to Rawls, Dewey, and Piaget, my argument is not based on a claim for liberalism as destiny or as a necessary movement to a present or future ideology.

If Schweder's page citations do not lead to the statements he claims I make, neither do these citations document the basic inconsistencies in my book which he claims to find. It is true that the book is a collection of essays written over a period of ten years; it is not a presentation of tight systematic moral theory like Rawls' *A Theory of Justice*. But most of the "inconsistencies" Schweder reports reflect distinctions made by the theory which Schweder fails to note or understand.

As a single example, Schweder finds it inconsistent to say that "there may be long range trends toward a sociomoral evolution (p. 227)" and to say that moral principles (or stages) "are not scales for evaluating collective entities (p. 111)". My theoretical claim that a higher stage of justice reasoning is a more adequate stage is a claim about deontic judgments and reasons (judgments of rightness or obligation about an action or practice). As textbooks on ethics (like that of Frankena) note, a deontic judgment is one thing and an aretaic judgment of the moral worthiness of persons or cultures is another. I explicitly state that my stage theory is not a theory claiming to aretaically grade individuals or cultures on some scale of moral worthiness.

The same distinction between deontic and aretaic judgment is used by Schweder to make another charge of inconsistency against me. He says: "We are told that stage 6 ethics cannot tell us what is virtuous or worthy of praise or blame (p. 172). Then Kohlberg states the opposite (pp. 192, 272)." I do not state the opposite on pp. 192 and 272. I say there that deontic judgments of rightness are more adequate and more likely to lead to consensus at Stage 5 or 6 but this does not mean that I assume that a morally conscientious and consistent actor using Stage 4 deontic reasoning to guide actions is to be assigned lesser moral worth on some aretaic scale I explicitly say I do not have.

Besides inconsistency, Schweder charges me with the failure to have a data base. Piagetian stages, he tells us, are out. Our own previously-cited longitudinal studies in the United States, Turkey, and Israel, however, indicated 5% or less of subjects studied violated the invariant progressive sequence criteria of stage growth, a percentage lower than that observed within acceptable levels of test-retest error. Subjects use, at most, two adjacent stages in their reasoning and tend to have one predominant stage, a finding consistent with Piaget's claim that "stages are structured wholes". Finally, Schweder's claim that principled thinking is "Western" confuses a principled form of thinking with the Western liberal content of reasoning. In India, Turkey, Taiwan, Zambia, and other non-Western societies, Stage 5 reasoning has been found by various researchers.

In critiquing my work Schweder draws on MacIntyre's *After Virtue*. MacIntyre defines modern moral philosophy as the "Enlightenment project" begun in the seventeenth and eighteenth centuries. This project marked the collapse of the Aristotelian approach to science which held that all things had an aim or telos and that man's virtue and happiness could be defined in terms of a telos for human nature living in a political community. Modern moral philosophy, "the Enlightenment project", replaced this view. It began with Hume and the British school of utilitarianism and with the continental deontological school headed by Kant. It held that morality consisted of those laws and principles which an autonomous and rational moral agent would consent to as ordering his or her society or any other. From MacIntyre's point of view this project or theoretical program has failed despite the vigorous recent involvement and contributions of Rawls, Gewirth, Peters, Hare and others. MacIntyre says that these scholars have failed because as a social scientist he finds educated Western thinkers to be relativists and emotivists, unconvinced of the validity of the rational principles outlined by "the Enlightenment project". He also says the project has failed because there is a lack of consensus among these liberal theorists both in their normative ethical theories and in their resolution of substantive dilemmas of moral life, such as abortion and principles for the distribution of wealth.

I would like to point out that all these modern theorists can be characterized as postconventional in their form of reasoning despite their divergence on the substance or content of the theories that come out of this form of reasoning. In this sense there are formal similarities among these thinkers, despite content divergencies. However, there is also considerable agreement on substantive moral questions among both philosophers and lay adults in several cultures that we have studied. For example, the right thing for Heinz to do in our story is to steal the drug to save his wife's life, rather than follow that law that upholds the druggist's property rights and let his wife die. Whether someone is a Kantian deontologist or a utilitarian, they agree that it is right for Heinz to steal the drug, if they use postconventional reasoning. While there is vigorous disagreement among philosophers about theory formulation, these disagreements exist within what could be called a common paradigm. In this paradigm of modern moral philosophy, basic assumptions are shared as to rigorous methods of argument. Similarly there is a common paradigm shared by modern psychology which harbors large areas of agreement about assumptions and method of argument despite diversity of theoretical view point. This at least would be my answer to Schweder's opinion that "what we mean when we say 'that's good' is something we have no rational warrant for meaning. We speak to each other as though our moral choices had a rational foundation. Upon examination that rational foundation turns out to be the soft sand of preferred assumption."

Whether my argument is correct or not, Schweder does not present my fundamental standpoint as a moral psychologist which is to create a theory which is a rational recon-struction of ontogenesis, drawing jointly on philosophy and psychological data. As Haber-mas [1982] has pointed out, empirical theorizing about moral development *presupposes* some standard of adequacy defining the direction of development; such theorizing cannot be value neutral. Even value-neutrality, implying relativism, has its own underlying moral assumptions. My own effort to rationally reconstruct the ontogenesis of moral reasoning makes use of what MacIntyre has called the "Enlightenment project", the project of con-structing arguments and theories which would lead rational people to agree on principles of justice to define an endpoint of ontogenetic development. The validity of my assumption of such a standard of adequacy in describing the moral development of individuals can only be assessed by the extent to which it provides order to empirical data and by the intelligibility of the order it defines. Like the "Enlightenment project" itself, a psychology of moral development based on it should be an open and growing enterprise. It thrives on disagreement, including some of Schweder's disagreements, but it does require a fair expo-sition of what it tries to say.'

Simpson, E.L.: Moral Development Research.
Human Development 17: 81–106 (1974)

Synopsis

At the core of Simpson's critique is the argument that Kohlberg's stages need not be and actually are not culturally universal. She argues that our claims of universality have no validity because Kohlberg has not studied a sufficient number of cultures to substantiate such claims. In addition, Simpson asserts that the fact that we have not found postconventional rea-soning (Stages 5 and 6) in all the cultures we have studied also undermines our universality claim. She goes on to claim that if postconventional rea-soning is found more prevalently in urban cultures that are Western influenced, then it follows that Kohlberg's stage scheme or definition of higher stages is ethnocentric or culturally biased.

Simpson objects to the idea of a culturally universal sequence of stages on two types of grounds; empirical and philosophical. On empirical grounds she claims: (a) that the validity of the stage sequence is contradicted by findings reported in some cross-cultural studies (i.e., in some cultures reasoning beyond Stages 3 and 4 is not found); (b) that in some cultures reversal in developmental sequence has been found [p. 99]; and (c) that lagging in or absence of postconventional reasoning in some cultures may not reflect differences in moral judgment *competence* but simply reflect differences that arise due to researchers' insensitivity to conditions of *performance* from one culture to another. To make this last point, Simpson uses three illustrations: (i) that rating a subject as postconventional may not reflect the presence of underlying structure but may simply reflect linguistic sophistication [p. 94]; (ii) that the test situation or context in which competence is tested may not be a familiar one for certain subjects; and (iii) that insensitivity to cultural meaning on the part of the researcher may lead to the down-scoring of responses from unfamiliar cultures.

On philosophical grounds Simpson claims: (a) that a research-based scale of development cannot be applied universally or objectively because it is the product of a researcher or theorist who has a particular cultural identity and background. Thus, Kohlberg's search for universal principles must therefore be recognized as necessarily biased and limited by its genesis in modern Western society and ideology [pp. 85, 86]; and (b) that our claims to universality are objectionable because they imply a scale for grading some cultures as 'morally superior' to others [p. 91].

Reply

We will first address the empirical criticism raised by Simpson. First, we claim that the sequence hypothesis of Kohlberg's stage model is not invalidated by the current empirical finding that all human beings in all cultures do not arrive at the postconventional stages of reasoning. We have observed in our own studies the low frequency of Stage 5 reasoning in Western as well as in non-Western cultures. Nevertheless, while low in frequency in non-Western cultures, Stage 5 reasoning has been found in a fairly large number of such cultures [Parikh, 1980; Lei and Cheng, 1982; Nisan and Kohlberg, 1982; Grimley, 1973; Edwards, 1975]. The researchers in these studies have expressed their open-mindedness to the possibility of finding alternative forms of Stage 5 reasoning in response to those typified dilemmas used by us. The following example from Israel illustrates the existence of Stage 5 reasoning that uses norms not included in our standard manual norm list (see table VII above). This example is from Snarey's [1982] work and is a kibbutznik's response to the Heinz dilemma:

'It (stealing) will be illegal not against the formal law but against the moral law. If we were in a Utopian society my hierarchy of values and those of others would be actualized through consensus. (What are those values?) Socialism, but don't ask me to explain it. In the Utopia there will be all the things I believe in, everyone will be equal. In this society the value of life is perfectly held. I believe everyone has the right to self-growth and happiness. People are not born equally genetically and it is not fair that one physically or mentally stronger should reach happiness at the expense of someone weaker because the right to happiness is a basic right of everyone and equal to all.'

This respondent's concern with norms of equality and socialism is different from the typical value of equal opportunity expressed by Stage 5 American respondents. However, this response nevertheless demonstrates Stage 5 prior-to-society perspective-taking combined with Stage 5 equity operations. Thus, while our manual was constructed on the basis of responses of American subjects it can still be used to identify Stage 5 reasoning used in conjunction with different cultural norms and values not identified in our manual. Other examples of cross-culturally observed Stage 5 reasoning are given by Lei and Cheng [1982] and Parikh [1980].

For us, the fact that postconventional reasoning occurs with low frequency has no logical bearing on the claim that Stage 5 exists as a structure. In this context, the pertinent question for us becomes one of identifying those socio-environmental conditions that impede or facilitate the emergence of principled reasoning.

Simpson's concern with how Kohlberg's theory can handle 'regression' will not be dealt with since longitudinal and cross-cultural data, scored with a scoring system developed since Simpson's article, do not show reversal and regression. However, to some extent we take up this issue later in the context of a competence-performance distinction discussed with reference to Levine's [1979] criticism.

With regard to the fact that Stage 4 and Stage 5 reasoning is comparatively rare, Simpson argues that our moral judgment interview techniques and our scoring system may be incapable of asking the type of questions and coding those responses that would elicit and document higher stage reasoning in other cultures. In response, we agree.

We agree that it is important to be sensitive to this type of criticism and indeed we have attempted to frame our dilemmas in ways that are meaningful, that do produce conflict, in the populations we have studied (e.g., in the Turkish and Indian studies). Insofar as the dilemmas used did produce conflict and did elicit responses that were scorable, they seem to have been meaningful in these other cultures as well as in our own. Since longitudinal and cross-cultural study has validated the stage sequence we hypothesized and has provided examples of postconventional reasoning, we retain confidence in our measuring instrument. Also, we have no reason to think that the dilemma interviews we use are only particularly suited to or partial to American populations, since we have found postconventional reasoning in only a minority of our American longitudinal subjects as well. However, it is true that in some cross-cultural research, minor features of the interview dilemmas were altered to make them more meaningful (e.g., Heinz needs food, not a drug, for Taiwanese, Mexican, and Turkish respondents). Thus, we accept Simpson's general point that one has to be sensitive to such methodological issues in cross-cultural research, and we believe we have been.

Part of Simpson's general argument is that our method may not tap competence in cultures other than our own because it is a method which is linguistically dependent. Studies conducted in the United States, however, indicate that there is a low to moderate correlation ($r = 0.30$–0.40) between verbal fluency or complexity and moral stage [Colby et al., 1983b]. This finding suggests that assessment of high stage reasoning is not dependent on verbal sophistication. There are, of course, multiple problems in the interpretation of moral concepts defined in different cultures. Thus, being sensitive to problems of translation has been an important and usually stressed focus of those researchers conducting cross-cultural studies. Furthermore, we are in agreement with Simpson's general point that we must be very careful about assuming that our methodology allows us to translate differences in performance on our instrument into cultural differences in competence. Kohlberg's longitudinal study within the United States, showing validation of the moral stage sequence, does not lead us to assume that our test is methodologically adequate as a test of competence in all cultures. The fact that Stages 3 and 4 appear more slowly in a Turkish village than in an American city may reflect a difference in competence but it also may reflect different performance factors in Turkish and American subjects. The fact that the developmental *sequence* of stages is the same in both cultures, however, indicates that our methodology is adequate to capture competence as defined by the logic of developmental theory.

Since Simpson's paper was published, some longitudinal cross-cultural studies have been completed in Turkey [Nisan and Kohlberg, 1982] and in an Israeli kibbutz [Snarey, 1982]. These studies indicate that the *sequence* of movement through Stage 4 into Stage 5 is invariant in the urban settings of these cultures, among their college educated subjects. In the small-scale village samples of the above studies, Stage 5 reasoning and sometimes Stage 4 reasoning was not found, nor has it been found in other studies of small-scale societies [Edwards, 1981, 1982]. Given the urban findings, however, it seems fair to conclude that the fact that Stage 4 or 5 reasoning is not found in small-scale villages is not because these stages simply express Western values. Rather, it seems more likely that such stages have not been observed in these villages because of their relatively simple degree of social-structural complexity and because their populations have little or no formal education. In all societies, including the United States, we have found that Stage 5 is a relatively infrequent form of reasoning and, again, this finding suggests that the occurrence of Stage 5 is not a reflection of Western ideological content biasing our definitions of moral stages.

We now turn to the non-empirical criticisms made by Simpson. At the heart of her claim that our theory and method is culturally biased is her objection to rating one culture as having more moral worth than another. We share Simpson's concern here. We do not believe that the comparison of one culture to another in terms of moral development is a theoretically useful strategy for the growth of scientific knowledge. However, it is useful to compare the conditions leading to development in one culture with the conditions leading to development in another culture and to establish relations between environmental conditions and moral stage growth that are universal across cultures. An example of such work is the study by Parikh [1980] which replicated in India the relations between parental values and adolescent moral reasoning found in America by Holstein [1972]. However, such studies do not employ direct comparisons of mean moral stage scores between cultures; such comparisons appear to have no scientific justification or value since they would imply that it makes sense to speak of one culture having more moral worth than another. It is difficult to understand what a valid concept of 'comparative moral worth of culture' might be, but in any case such a concept could not be established on the basis of a comparison of means on our moral judgment assessment scale. There is no direct way in which group averages can be translated into statements of the relative moral worth of groups.

Like most anthropologists, we would agree that cultures should be treated evaluatively as unique configurations of norms and institutions which help social organizations to adapt to local conditions as well as to universal normative problems. In this sense anthropological cultural relativism is compatible with our philosophic assumption of the universal validity of moral principles. However, our agreement with relativism in this sense does not require us as moral agents to adopt an ethically relativistic position and so claim, for example, that Aztec human sacrifice is right. While it is true that the principles compatible with postconventional reasoning would lead one not to endorse the Aztec practice of human sacrifice, such a judgment constitutes a moral evaluation of a specific cultural practice, not of a culture per se. In a similar view, Kohlberg's [1981b] argument against the morality of capital punishment is not a moral evaluation of the American culture as a whole, for the complexity of cultural institutions and norms precludes overall cultural assessment. We do not understand how a 'moral ranking' of cultures could either be done or be scientifically useful.

Just as there is nothing in Kohlberg's theory that justifies using the moral judgment scale to compare the moral worth of cultures, so too there is nothing in Kohlberg's theory which justifies the use of the justice reasoning scale to rank or evaluate the relative moral worth of individuals. In our opinion, what is to be morally evaluated about individual persons are their specific moral actions. It is true that the stage of reasoning associated with a specific action may help determine the moral quality or value of the action. However, the claim that Stage 5 reasoning is more adequate to resolve more moral problems than is Stage 3 reasoning is not a claim that an individual scored as a Stage 5 reasoner has more moral worth than a person scored at Stage 3. There is a difference between the moral adequacy of a process of thought and the moral worth of persons that use it. Principled moral reasoning awards equal moral worth to all persons even though it recognizes that specific moral *actions* may be more or less moral.

In other words, the fact that our theory and related instruments are not morally neutral, that they are designed to provide a rational reconstruction of moral ontogenesis, does not mean that the instrument is a measure of the moral worth of individuals. It does not tell us how to judge the moral worth of people. It does not imply that it is morally fair to preferentially treat someone scored Stage 5. The assumed desirability of Stage 5 reasoning is quite a different matter from the differential judgment and treatment of Stage 5 and Stage 2 reasoners.

The final philosophical issue we wish to respond to is Simpson's claim that our theory and instrument are biased because of the historic and cultural location of Kohlberg and his theory. Simpson states [pp. 85, 86]: 'Like each of us, Kohlberg himself, his interest in cognitive development and moral reasoning, his choice of a Kantian or Deweyian infrastructure for this theory and his predilection for abstractions of such principles as justice, equality, and reciprocity are all, in a sense, accidents of time and place and the interaction of his personality with a specifiable social environment and the norms of the subgroups within that environment.'

The above statement expresses a truism that we accept; i.e., that the environment a theoretician is socialized in is likely to have an influence on his theory. However, to go on to infer from this that the validity of the theory is ipso facto suspect is to commit an instance of the genetic fallacy. This is a fallacy, like the naturalistic fallacy, of drawing conclusions about the validity or truth of a theory by reference to its genetic origins.

Simpson's implicit assumption is that the only way to avoid the bias inherent in a theory because of historical and biographical circumstance is to be self-consciously a relativist about one's own views. In response, we believe that the way to avoid bias in the development of a theory is to subject its development and validation to the scientific method and critical appraisal. The intent of Kohlberg's theory is that it be used, verified, or revised by people other than himself; by people of different social origins, cultures, and classes. The scientific method as we understand it is a product of modern Western history. However, we claim that it represents the most adequate cross-culturally understood method available for avoiding the type of bias that Simpson is concerned about and that it constitutes the best available method for assessing the truth value of claims to objective knowledge. Like our theory, the scientific method is primarily a product of modern Western thought, but it, like our theory, cannot be dismissed as therefore biased because of its genetic origins.

Sullivan, E. V.:
A Study of Kohlberg's Structural Theory of Moral Development.
A Critique of Liberal Social Science Ideology.
Human Development 20: 352–376 (1977)

Synopsis
Sullivan evaluates Kohlberg's theory as a 'style of thinking' and suggests that as a style of thought it is rooted in certain socio-historical circumstances and therefore reflects the interests of those who live(d) within those circumstances. In other words, Sullivan's article is an exercise in the 'sociology of psychological knowledge' and his purpose is to argue that theories in social science, including Kohlberg's, are 'tied to the infrastructure of a society or socially defined groups'.

With this conceptual posture, Sullivan correctly identifies Kohlberg's theory as an example of liberal ideology. It is a 'style of thought' developing from the period of the French revolution and thus reflects many of those ideas articulated by the Philosophes; i.e., notions of social contract; an emphasis on the rights of individuals; and a view of persons as ideally rational. Kohlberg's theory, Sullivan claims, has both the content and methodology of the style of thinking he calls 'natural-law thought'.

With the above introduction, Sullivan directs himself to a critique of Kohlberg's conception of Stage 6 justice reasoning. Given its Enlightenment roots, he argues that Kohlberg's notion of Stage 6 reasoning constructs a parochial rather than universally accurate model of 'moral man' [p. 360]; that 'Kohlberg sees his Stage 6 structure as synonymous with the Rawlsian conception of justice...' [p. 358]; and that this Stage 6 model of man is both impersonal and ahistorical, recognizing only an 'atomistic' social agent in man and thus ignoring the moral significance of his ties with community. For Sullivan, Kohlberg's conception of 'Stage 6 man' is based on an intellectual posture of abstract formalism, a posture which results in a 'falsely conscious' understanding of moral development. Sullivan draws from the writings of Marx, Engels, and Lukacs to critique Kohlberg's position of 'abstract formalism'. He writes that 'abstract formalism was the organizing principle structuring social relations of production within Western capitalism...(and that)...abstract formalism implies...(a)...universality that...(in actuality only)...masks middle-class ideology' [p. 360]. Sullivan argues that Rawls' 'original position', because it is a hypothetical perspective for seeing how one might contract into society, based on principles of justice, serves in fact, the vested interests of powerful social groups. Presumably, this is the case because the hypothetical nature of the original position requires the assumption of a just society a priori and thus fails to address itself to real injustices in our present society. In diverting our attention away from actual injustice in the here and now, the method of reasoning implied by adopting the original position therefore functions as conservative ideology in support of the status quo. Thus, for Sullivan, the abstractly formal, impersonal, and ahistorical nature of Rawls' and Kohlberg's views constitutes an unconscious 'defense of exploitation' while standing in theory for human freedom [p. 362].

In addition to the above 'problems' with Kohlberg's perspective, Sullivan perceives others which he attributes to Kohlberg's structuralist bias. Like other structuralists, Sullivan reasons that Kohlberg dichotomizes thought and action, form and content, and in so doing, incorrectly equates the more abstract with the more moral. Not only does Kohlberg's theory fail to grasp what is, in reality, the dialectical tension between reflection and action, it also ignores those factors that one must attend to if one's goal is to develop an adequate theory of moral commitment. In this context, Sullivan points to Kohlberg's failure to integrate into his theory an account of 'moral sensitivity', emotion, and moral imagination.

In sum, Sullivan is arguing that the ideological and structuralist basis of Kohlberg's perspective has produced a 'morally blind' understanding of man. It is a theory which expresses an alienated view of the moral being because it uses what are essentially false dichotomies to describe him or her. For Sullivan, a theory of moral development must be more than a structuralist account of the ontogenesis of justice reasoning.

Reply

In our view, Sullivan's article raises the following three points of criticism: (a) that Kohlberg's theory is biased because of its liberal intellectual roots; (b) that it is biased because of its structuralist orientation; and, finally, (c) that it is insufficient as a theory of moral development because it ignores such factors as emotion and moral imagination. Our reply to Sullivan is relatively brief and selective since our replies to Simpson [1974] and Gilligan [1982], as well as our review of Habermas's work (see below), contain material which would make a lengthy reply to Sullivan redundant.

(a) Kohlberg's Liberal Bias. In our opinion, Sullivan's description of Kohlberg's intellectual roots is an accurate one. It is accurate in a socio-historical sense and it is accurate in the sense that it depicts Kohlberg's concern with developing a formalist account of morally adequate procedures for adjudicating moral conflicts. What we disagree with is Sullivan's contention that these intellectual roots and interests have produced: (i) a theory that articulates a parochial rather than universally valid view of Stage 6 and of the development of structures of justice reasoning, and (ii) a theory that can only function as a false-conscious justification of the exploitive practices endemic to Western capitalist societies.[15]

In response to the above, we believe, in the first place, that whether Kohlberg's theory articulates a parochial or universalistically valid *descrip-*

---

[15] With these assertions, Sullivan appears to have committed the genetic fallacy in two ways. The reader will recall that the genetic fallacy is the tendency to evaluate a theory, not on its own merits, but on the basis of either the interests or biographical characteristics of its author or its socio-historical underpinnings.

tion of justice reasoning and its development is a question to be answered on the basis of empirical test. In our opinion, this is not a question that can be answered a priori, through an analysis of the ideological and intellectual foundations of Kohlberg's theory.

In the context of the discussion of revisions to Kohlberg's theory we have stated in general terms our reply to Sullivan's charge of parochialism regarding Stage 6 per se (chapter 2, sections 1, 9, and 10, part ix). In that discussion we stated that we no longer claim to have empirically verified the existence of Stage 6 reasoning. However, given our posture of a rationally reconstructive perspective, we maintain and, in a normative ethical sense, defend our conception of Stage 6 as the endpoint of the ontogenesis of justice reasoning. We noted earlier that our conception of Stage 6 is open to philosophical debate and that a researcher need not accept our normative ethical views as his or her own in order to carry out research in the area of justice reasoning. From our perspective, we defend our notion of Stage 6 because it represents for us a structure of justice reasoning which is fully reversible. While Habermas [1979] has questioned this claim, we believe that we successfully defend our perspective against his critique. (Our discussion of Habermas completes this chapter.) However, Sullivan does not critique our conception of Stage 6 in this way. Instead, he raises questions regarding both Stage 6 and our general theory, arguing that they constitute a false-conscious defense of the status quo and misrepresent the domain of the moral due to our reliance on the perspective of structuralism.

We disagree with Sullivan's contention that Kohlberg's theory can only function as a false-conscious justification of the status quo. Sullivan may be correct in believing that the spirit of the Enlightenment is dead, that throughout the last three hundred years liberal ideals have been espoused dishonestly and used to disguise the vested interests of some powerful groups. However, just because Kohlberg's theory of justice reasoning grows out of the liberal tradition does not mean that it will or can only be used in similar fashion. Hammers can be used to drive nails or bludgeon people and which of these uses hammers are put to cannot be predicted on the basis of an understanding of the technological, cultural, or socio-historical factors which led to their creation.

We are not claiming that because it can be used for various purposes that Kohlberg's theory is therefore 'value-free', for we have acknowledged that it is not independent of various normative-ethical assumptions which we hold. In this context, we are simply claiming that how Kohlberg's theory is used cannot be predicted on the basis of a consideration of its intellectual roots. Kohlberg's theory could be and perhaps has been used to preoccupy minds with 'moral' rationalizations for immoral acts. However, it can be more easily used, and hopefully will be more frequently used, to occupy minds with moral reasons for moral acts. If the principles articulated by Stage 6 reasoning can be used by a Machiavellian as 'moral slogans' to disguise exploitive realities, it is also true that they can be used as moral justifications for denouncing such realities.

(b) Kohlberg's Structuralist Bias. It will be recalled that Sullivan perceives a formalistic and structuralistic bias in Kohlberg's work that prevents him from coming to grips with concrete moral reality. Instead of developing a theory that acknowledges the 'dialectical tension' between 'thought and action' and 'form and content', Sullivan argues that Kohlberg is preoccupied with 'thought' and 'form' and ignores their dialectical complements. Sullivan assumes that 'Kohlberg sees his Stage 6 structure as synonymous with the Rawlsian conception of justice' [p. 358]. This assumption allows Sullivan to rely upon his perception of the hypothetical nature of Rawls' 'original position' to bolster his critique of Kohlberg's work as being too abstract.

While our task is not to defend Rawls, we should point out that the procedure of 'assuming the original position under a veil of ignorance' need not be interpreted as a strategy which avoids dealing with the real world. Rather, we understand it as a procedure that has the potential to allow one to reflect upon the world in a just manner because it requires one to control, not forget, the bias of vested interest when adjudicating moral conflicts. However, even if one questions the legislative potential of Rawls' work, even if one sees it simply as a hypothetical moral exercise for constructing hypothetical moral communities, we still see it as an excellent example of justice reasoning at a postconventional level.

More to the point, however, is the fact that we do not interpret Rawls' notions as synonymous with Kohlberg's conception of Stage 6 reasoning. We understand Stage 6 prescriptive role-taking as a procedure which requires one to avoid the biasing impact of vested interests by evaluating their worth as legitimate moral claims, not by ignoring them. The fact of the matter is that prescriptive role-taking is a procedure for resolving moral conflicts that *requires* one to focus on the stated claims and interests of real persons in real situations. This fact should not be confused with another; i.e., that Kohlberg derived, in part, the procedure of prescriptive role-taking through the use of fictitious actors involved in hypothetical dilemmas.

141

We believe, more generally, that the nature of theorizing often requires one to buy abstraction and generality at the expense of concreteness. Kohlberg, like many theorists, has paid this price. However, Kohlberg has not *ignored* action and content. Instead, he has *emphasized* thought instead of action, and form instead of content with the intent of defining what thought and form are. Kohlberg's work should not be construed as denying the 'dialectical tension' between thought and action, for he has involved himself more recently in the study of this relationship with Candee [Kohlberg and Candee, 1983; Candee and Kohlberg, 1983a, b]. Thus, we believe that his work should be understood as a necessary contribution to what will hopefully become our greater appreciation of the complexities of the dialectical tensions to which Sullivan has referred.

(c) Kohlberg's Failure to Deal with the Issue of Moral Commitment. In calling for a more complete theory of moral development, Sullivan correctly understands that Kohlberg has not addressed to a sufficient extent the role played by such factors as moral sensitivity and moral imagination. Of course, we understand Sullivan's comments in this context as constructive rather than critical.

Kohlberg's theory of moral development is a theory that focusses on moral decision-making processes and the cognitive-moral structures assumed to give rise to these processes. We have acknowledged earlier that we understand our theory of justice reasoning to be necessary but not sufficient for defining the full domain of what is meant by moral development. Thus, we welcome any constructive attempt to enlarge our appreciation of this domain.

However, in conclusion, we wish to emphasize one point which for us is obvious; i.e., that a cognitive approach to the study of justice reasoning is, by definition, a perspective which studies the development and use of cognitive-moral processes. As we define and study them, moral judgments are 'reasoned' judgments. We agree that their construction most probably is influenced by their relationship with emotion, imagination, and moral sensitivity and we encourage anyone who is interested in doing so to investigate these relationships. However, we believe that the study of moral reasoning is valuable in its own right.

To embellish his argument about the importance of moral imagery and imagination in fostering a sense of moral commitment, Sullivan quotes at length from one of Martin Luther King's most memorable speeches. It is true that the moral imagery and imagination used by Martin Luther King to foster commitment to action in the service of civil rights is ample evidence justifying Sullivan's concerns. We also believe that it is probable, however, that if one could ask Mr. King *why* it was important to 'Let Freedom ring from the hilltops of New Hampshire and from the mighty mountains of New York', he would have articulated for us a Stage 6 moral *reason.*

Gilligan, C.: In a Different Voice.
Psychological Theory and Women's Development
(Harvard University Press, Cambridge, Mass. 1982)

Synopsis
In 1982 Gilligan published a book collecting and integrating her essays on the subject of women's development and morality, entitled *In a Different Voice.* In our synopsis of the position of this book we will try to define positions which she adopts that we agree with, positions she takes which we disagree with, and ignore a number of interesting statements in the book which are not directly relevant to moral development.

The general thesis of this book, with which we are in partial agreement, is that the influential theories of personality development for the most part have been created by males and reflect greater insight or understanding into male personality development than into female personality development.

With regard to morality, Gilligan points to the fact that the two greatest theorists of personality development, Freud and Piaget, both identified morality with justice. In addition, both theorists noted that their observations of females suggested to them that either females were less developed in their sense of justice than males or that the nature and development of women's morality could not be fully explained by their theories. Freud saw morality and justice as a function of the superego, that heir of the Oedipus Complex which stemmed from identification with paternal authority. In addition he saw superego formation as a more clearly defined phenomenon in male than in female development. In a similar vein Piaget related early morality to heteronomous respect for the parents, especially the father. This heteronomous respect was a sui generis mixture of fear and affection which defined the young child's moral attitude toward others as well as rules. Observing the games of children, Piaget noted a much greater interest in the codification of rules on the part of boys than girls. This interest developed in a context of peer interaction, a factor which was instrumental in leading to Piaget's second stage of morality based on peer cooperation.

Gilligan suggests that morality really includes two moral orientations; first, the morality of justice as stressed by Freud and Piaget and second, an ethic of care and response which is more central to understanding female moral judgment and action than it is to the understanding of judgment and action in males. Gilligan correctly notes that Kohlberg's [1958] original work began with an acceptance of Piaget's conception of morality as justice and of moral development as a movement toward autonomy. In addition to Piaget's work, Kohlberg also focussed on the work of Freud and Mead. To investigate Piaget's theory of peer interaction as the source of moral autonomy, Kohlberg compared the moral orientations of peer group sociometric 'stars' with peer group sociometric 'isolates'. To test the effects of Mead's notion of 'generalized-other' role-taking, he compared the moral orientations of working and middle-class males. To investigate several psychodynamic hypotheses he constructed a measure of father identification for boys. After controlling for IQ and other variables in making these comparisons, Kohlberg decided not to add the complicating issue of sex differences to his study and, thus, did not include girls in his doctoral thesis sample. Thus, the major part of Kohlberg's work on the development of moral judgment has been based upon the longitudinal analysis of the follow-up data from his original cross-sectional male samples. He did not collect longitudinal data on females until he began a longitudinal study of kibbutz males and females in 1969. Thus, Gilligan points to the possibility of sex bias in Kohlberg's theory and measures, a bias presumably shared by his predecessors, Freud and Piaget. Unlike Freud and Piaget, however, Kohlberg has never directly stated that males have a more developed sense of justice than do females. In several publications [Kohlberg, 1969; Kohlberg and Kramer, 1969] Kohlberg did suggest that youthful and adult females might be less developed in his justice stage sequence than males for the same reasons that working-class males were less developed than middle-class males. He suggested that if women were not provided with the experience of participation in society's complex, secondary institutions through education and complex work responsibility, then they were not likely to acquire those societal role-taking abilities necessary for the development of Stage 4 and 5 justice reasoning.

What Gilligan postulates is a second moral orientation different from a justice orientation; an orientation which is neither adequately elicited by our justice dilemmas nor adequately identified by our 1983 Standard Issue Scoring Manual for assessing moral stage on our dilemmas. In our chapter on the current status of Kohlberg's moral theory, we have largely agreed with Gilligan that the acknowledgement of an orientation of care and response usefully enlarges the moral domain. Philosophers, such as Frankena [1973], have agreed with Gilligan in stating that there are two distinct principles or moral orientations, one of beneficence and care, the other of justice, and that both must be accounted for by a moral theory. Gilligan asserts, and Lyons [1982] documents, that it is these two different moral orientations that are reflected in sex differences in spontaneous ways of framing personal moral dilemmas. While Lyons notes that most males and most females frame moral dilemmas by using both orientations, she reports that females are likely to use the orientation of care and response as their predominant mode and males are more likely to use justice as theirs.

Gilligan's book does not cite quantitative findings. However, in collaboration with Lyons she is in the process of reporting quantitative findings on sex differences in the use of the ethic of care and the ethic of justice. These differences are reported in Gilligan et al. [1982].

In these pilot findings Gilligan et al. found in the personal constructions of real-life dilemmas in a sample of 16 women and 14 men that both orientations were used by both sexes. They also calculated whether each subject had a preponderant use of one orientation over the other, with preponderance defined as more than 50% of responses scored in one orientation to the dilemmas. They found that 75% of the females used predominantly the response orientation and only 25% used predominantly a rights or justice orientation. The balance was reversed among males where 79% used predominantly the rights orientation and 14% the response orientation. Seven percent of male responses were equally distributed in both orientations.

In an appendix to the Gilligan et al. study, the authors report on responses from a larger sample of subjects. This larger sample responded not only to the personal moral dilemmas studied by Lyons, but also to Kohlberg's justice dilemmas. This cross-sectional sample consisted of 144 males and females. Their responses were scored by graduate students trained by Kohlberg.

The adult males and females of this sample were largely matched, all being high in education, and all being involved in professional work. Among children and adolescents, the authors report no difference in average stage between women and men in justice reasoning. In the adult sample of 64 (32 females and 32 males) however, they report a difference in mean moral maturity score with the mean for males being 413 and that for females being 400. Parametric tests of this difference failed to attain significance. Given this, they used a nonparametric test to assess this sex difference. Their dependent measure was the frequency of postconventional 'points' used by respondents with a 'point' defined as one interview judgment. The chi-square test calculated indicated that the difference between male and female response means was significant at the 0.02 level.

In reference to the statistical significance of the point system we may note that for us the creation and use of a dichotomous variable (i.e., the use of some postconventional 'points' versus the use of none) raises two problems. First, it is difficult for us to evaluate the importance of the Gilligan et al. study's findings because there are no inter-judge or test-retest reliability data available on a 'point' matching scoring technique. Second, the act of classifying subjects on the basis of whether they did or did not utter a single postconventional 'point' is of unknown significance to us since the validity and reliability of the Kohlberg scale has been established by assigning individuals to a global or mixed stage score with the intent being to uncover longitudinal progression in such scores. In other words, for us a 'point' scoring technique cannot capture the conceptual integrity of a person's moral development.

In terms of psychological significance, we should note that the field does not regard a difference of fifteen points in moral maturity scores between groups (and Gilligan et al. report a difference of only thirteen points) to be a psychologically meaningful difference. A fifteen point difference is well within the limits of test-retest error variance found in various studies [Colby et al., 1983a, b].

Gilligan et al. [1982, p. 36] draw the following conclusion from the above analysis:

'Thus, in replicating under well-controlled conditions the previously reported sex difference favouring men in Kohlberg's standard of moral maturity, the current research supports critics of Kohlberg's theory who claim that particularly at the postconventional level, that theory reflects a limited Western male perspective and may therefore be biased against women and other groups whose moral perspectives are somewhat different.'

We totally disagree with this conclusion and in our reply we will discuss in depth the evidence for our disagreement with their conclusion based on a review of the field of research in general. Gilligan hypothesizes that to solve problems of interpersonal conflict and relationship, males are more likely to use Piagetian balancing operations of reciprocity and equality. In contrast, she hypothesizes that females are more likely to construe a moral problem as lying within the boundaries of unquestioned relatedness and to use altruism or self-sacrifice as the solution to interpersonal problems.

In her book and in the above cited research with her colleagues Gilligan makes a leap to a conclusion of test bias with which we do not agree. We do agree that our justice dilemmas do not pull for the care and response orientation and we do agree that our scoring manual does not lead to a full assessment of this aspect of moral thinking. We do not agree, however, that the justice reasoning dilemmas and stages lead to an unfair biased downscoring of girls' and women's reasoning as Holstein suggests because it measures them using a stage sequence and scoring manual developed on a sample of males.

This charge of sex bias in the test may have been partially true of the original Kohlberg [1958] method for stage scoring. At that time a respondent's concern with norms of caring and affiliation tended to be scored Stage 3 and a concern with norms of law tended to be scored Stage 4. We now see such concerns as content characteristics of reasoning. The 1983 Standard Issue Scoring System now holds such normative content constant and assesses formal differences in the use of socio-moral perspective and justice operations to define justice stage. The justice stage methodology is intended to be an assessment of competence rather than of preference and spontaneous performance. Therefore, even though some females may spontaneously prefer thinking within the care and response orientation, our standard methodology which pulls for optimal competence in justice reasoning is, we believe, still a fair measure of that very basic aspect of moral judgment development. In our reply to follow we will cite a variety of sex-difference studies whose findings are pertinent to the issues we have been discussing.

Of more theoretical interest than the charge of test bias is another claim, made by Gilligan's colleague Lyons [1982], with which we disagree. Lyons says [p. 14]: 'This thesis offers the empirical confirmation of two explicit hypotheses generated by Gilligan's observations and speculations: (1) That there are two modes of thinking about moral conflict – justice and care; and (2) That these two modes of moral judgment – although not confined to an individual by virtue of gender – are gender related.'

The implication of this statement seems to be that justice and care define two separate or distinct tracks of moral development. We shall indicate in our reply that considerations of care and considerations of justice are interwoven in working out resolutions to moral dilemmas. This is not necessarily inconsistent with Lyons' [1982] findings and conclusions. We do not think that the experiences that lead to development on the justice side of moral judgment are distinctly different from those experiences which lead to the development of the caring side of morality. The educational approach of our colleagues to stimulating moral judgment development is called the 'just community' approach. Their work indicates that experiences of democratically resolving issues of conflicting rights are interwoven with considerations of community and considerations of caring and responsibility for the group and for each of its members. In our philosophic endpoint of moral reasoning, the hypothetical sixth stage, there occurs, we believe, an integration of justice and care which forms a single moral principle. We shall attempt to describe this idea in our reply.

We should note that implicit in Gilligan's [1982] book is a second set of issues pertaining to the appropriateness of justice principles when placed in conjunction with an awareness of contextual relativity. These issues we shall discuss separately in our synopsis and response to two articles not included in Gilligan's book, articles by Murphy and Gilligan [1980] and Gilligan and Murphy [1979].

Before we move to a detailed reply, however, let us summarize what appears to be the essence of Gilligan's perspective. Gilligan believes that there is a different moral orientation characteristic of females in comparison with males. Females employ a care and response orientation whereas men are primarily concerned with justice. This difference in orientation, Gilligan implies, leads to a sex-biased assessment of the moral judgment development of females since the Kohlberg instrument, she argues, misrepresents the caring orientation as Stage 3 justice reasoning. Thus, it is asserted that women have been inappropriately down-scored. While Gilligan has not defined structural stages in the caring orientation, she does distinguish among three levels in this orientation: a preconventional level which is primarily egocentric; a conventional level which is primarily concerned with caring for others; and, finally, a postconventional level which balances care for self and care for others.

Reply

In chapter 2, section 2, on the enlargement of the moral domain, we discussed at length Gilligan's view that there is a caring orientation distinct from a justice orientation, and assumed that this is Gilligan's most important thesis. However, the claim by Gilligan which has received the most popular attention, and which is the most critical of the Kohlberg theory and method, is the claim that the standard moral dilemmas and scoring system have a built-in sex bias and downgrade female responses.

To deal with this issue we shall briefly summarize the studies on sex differences in justice reasoning on our standard dilemmas. Two issues are involved here. The first issue with which we will deal is whether there are mean sex differences between males and females on our justice reasoning dilemmas. The second issue is whether women's responses to the dilemmas can be scored in terms of the justice stages and yield the same results of invariant sequence and structured wholeness which the longitudinal studies of Colby et al. [1983b] have found for males.

(1) Sex Differences in Mean Scores. With regard to the issue of mean sex differences in moral judgment stages, we shall quote from an extensive literature review by Walker [1982] of 54 studies using Kohlberg's moral judgment interview and 24 studies using Rest's [1979] Defining Issues Test (DIT) measure of moral judgment. Walker starts by noting:

'A theory could warrant the charge of sex bias for either of the following reasons. First, a theory could advocate or popularize a poorly founded claim that the sexes are fundamentally different in rate and endpoint of moral development. For example, Freud [1927] asserted that women lack moral maturity because of deficiencies in same-sex parental identification. Second, a theory might offer no such opinion, but entail various measurement or scoring procedures which inadvertently favor one sex or the other, and thus create a false impression that real differences in moral maturity do exist. The allegations of sex bias against Kohlberg's theory have been primarily based on the latter reason.

If there is sex bias in Kohlberg's approach, how could it have arisen? A trite response is that because Kohlberg is a man, he has taken a masculine point of view in theorizing about moral development. An equally trite rejoinder would be to point out that Kohlberg has had a number of female colleagues and that the senior author of the recent editions of the scoring manual is a woman, Anne Colby. A second and much more important possible source of bias is that the stage sequence has been constructed from the longitudinal data provided by an exclusively male sample [Colby et al., 1983b]. While this lack of representativeness is a real threat to the generalizability of the model and could easily be a source of sex bias, the stage sequence has now been corroborated by both longitudinal [Holstein, 1976] and experimental intervention studies [Walker, in press] using both males and females. Nonetheless, it is impossible to determine whether the same stages and sequence would have been derived if females had originally been studied. A third potential source of bias is the predominance of male protagonists in the moral dilemmas used as stimulus materials in eliciting reasoning. Females may have difficulty relating to these male protagonists and thus exhibit artifactually lower levels of moral reasoning. Three studies have examined the effect of protagonist's sex theory; one found more advanced reasoning with same-sex protagonists, while another found more advanced reasoning with opposite-sex protagonists, and the third found no evidence of differential responding when protagonist sex was varied. Thus, the data are equivocal regarding this potential source of bias.

To summarize, it is possible that sex bias exists in Kohlberg's theory, in particular due to his reliance on an exclusively male sample, but this remains to be determined.

In order to summarize the research concisely, the studies are presented in three tables which divide the lifespan into the somewhat arbitrary periods of (a) childhood and early adolescence, (b) late adolescence and youth, and (c) adulthood.

Studies which examined sex differences in moral reasoning in childhood and early adolescence are first summarized. There are 27 such studies involving a total of 2,430 subjects who range in age from about 5 years to 17 years. The overall pattern revealed by these studies is that sex differences in moral reasoning in childhood and early adolescence are infrequent; for the 34 samples, only 4 significant differences were reported.'

Next, 34 studies of sex differences in adolescence and youth are summarized. Of those studies not employing methodological variation or artifacts, only nine report sex differences.

'Five findings indicate significant sex differences remain after removing methodological artifacts. Two of these were reported by Bar-Yam et al. [1980] in a study of Israeli high school students. In both the Moslem-Arab and Youth-Aliyah samples, boys were found to have higher levels of moral reasoning than girls (296 vs. 249, and 376 vs. 350, respectively). Both samples were drawn from ethnic groups where the status of women has traditionally been low, with few opportunities for decision-making within the family and society and with typically low levels of education. (Youth Aliyah were recent immigrants who were typically from North Africa or the Middle East.) It is interesting to note that no differences were found in the kibbutz and Christian samples in which attitudes would be more egalitarian.'

Eleven studies examined sex differences in moral reasoning in adulthood.

'These studies involve a total of 1,131 subjects who range in age from 21 years to over 65 years. Sex differences in moral reasoning in adulthood are slightly more frequent than earlier in the lifespan; or alternately, sex differences are more frequent in this generation than in later generations. (It is impossible to separate developmental and cohort differences with these data.) Of the 19 samples considered, 4 significant differences were reported, all favoring men.

Unlike the studies discussed in previous sections which involved rather homogenous samples of school and university students, it is apparent in these studies revealing differences in moral reasoning, that sex was grossly confounded with education and/or occupational differences. Haan et al. [1976] found that men scored higher in both the 21- to 30-year-old sample and the 47- to 50-year-old sample (parents of the younger group). The older women in this study were mostly housewives [according to Haan, 1977].

In the two remaining studies that revealed differences, sex was similarly confounded with occupational differences. Holstein [1976] found differences on her first test favoring men (409 vs. 366), but none on the retest. In her upper-middle-class sample, nearly all the men had careers in business, management, or the professions, whereas only 6% of the women were employed. Similarly, Parikh [1980] found that the men in her Indian sample scored higher than women (326 vs. 280). The men were all self-employed professionals, whereas most of the women were housewives.

To summarize, it is apparent that sex differences in moral reasoning in adulthood are revealed only in a minority of studies, and then when sex differences are confounded with differences in level of education and occupation. There is no evidence of sex differences in dominant stage of moral reasoning in adulthood.

In Rest's [1979] review of sex difference in DIT research, he found that only 2 of 21 samples yielded sex differences. In both samples, females evidenced higher scores. Since that review, a few additional studies have yielded sex differences, all with females evidencing higher moral development [Cistone, 1980; Garwood et al., 1980; Leahy, 1981]. An additional, and particularly relevant, finding reported by Garwood et al. [1980] was that males exhibited greater preference for Stage 3 statements than did females.'

To elaborate on Walker's review, the only studies showing fairly frequent sex differences are those of adults, usually of spouse housewives. Many of the studies comparing adult males and females without controlling for education and job status, as defined by the Hollingshead index or some similar measure, do report sex differences in favor of males. These include Holstein [1976], Kuhn et al. [1977], Haan et al. [1976], and Parikh [1980]. Two studies comparing middle-class husbands and wives have been conducted using the new Colby et al. [1983a] Standard Issue Scoring Instrument. These studies are by Speicher-Dubin [1982] and Powers [1982]. Both studies report sex differences in favor of males. However, both studies report that these sex differences disappear when the variables of higher education and job status are statistically controlled for by step-down multiple regression techniques.

The need to control for higher education and job status in examining sex difference is documented by the Colby et al. [1983a] longitudinal study of males. In this study, movement to Stages 4 and 5 after high school was found to be systematically related to higher education and to job satisfaction and responsibility. Given these results as well as Kohlberg's general contention that moral Stages 4 and 5 depend upon a sense of participation, responsibility, and role-taking in the secondary institutions of society such as work and government, then it appears necessary to control for such factors as education and employment when assessing sex differences in the use of advanced stages of justice reasoning.

Studies which match males and females on education, job status, and responsibility are better suited to testing for sex differences within an interactionist cognitive-developmental paradigm than are studies which employ techniques of control through step-down regression analysis. The single most clear-cut study of this sort is the longitudinal study by Snarey et al. [1982]. In this longitudinal study of kibbutz males and females aged 12 to

24, no significant mean sex-differences were found. On the kibbutz, both males and females were found scoring Stage 4, 4/5, and 5 even though not exposed to higher education. We explain this by the fact that in the egalitarian framework of the kibbutz, females' job responsibility and participation in the democratic governance of the kibbutz is formally equal to that of males. In line with Kohlberg's cognitive-developmental theory, then, no mean differences in justice reasoning stage would be expected and indeed none were found.

Another study controlling for education and occupational status was Weisbroth's [1970]. This study compared male and female graduate students, thus equalizing the sexes in higher education and in occupational aspiration. As cognitive-developmental theory would predict, no sex differences were found. In summary, studies comparing the sexes in justice reasoning stage either report no sex differences or report sex differences attributable to higher education and role-taking opportunity differences related to work.

(2) Female Data and the Invariant Sequence Hypothesis. A second hypothesis raised by Gilligan's theory is that our standard justice reasoning dilemmas and issue scoring system will not reproduce the findings of invariant sequence and structured wholeness for females that they have for males as reported in the Colby et al. [1983a] longitudinal study. This hypothesis would be anticipated if, as Gilligan claims, our justice scoring system is not applicable to females given that their preference is for a caring and response orientation. Again the Snarey et al. [1982] study provides the best data on this hypothesis. The same findings of invariant sequence and structured wholeness found in American males were found in this longitudinal study of both females and males. A second study showing upward movement and no stage skipping in females within the limits of test-retest reliability was the study by Erickson [1980]. In addition, clinical analysis of the Snarey et al. data suggests that many females, as well as some males, made some use of Gilligan's caring and response orientation in response to our standard justice dilemmas. This fact, however, did not lead to down-scoring on the Standard Issue Scoring Instrument which pulls for the justice orientation. In other words, while there may be sex differences in preferential orientation to framing moral dilemmas, as Gilligan suggests, this does not lead to the conclusion of bias or invalidity of the justice reasoning test as an assessment of competence in justice reasoning.

(3) Sex Differences in Orientation. A third implication of Gilligan's theory is the notion that women are more likely to spontaneously use the care and response orientation in their reasoning than are men. While Lyons [1982] found that both sexes use both justice and care considerations in construing personal dilemmas, she also noted that there was some preference by females for the caring and response orientation. These results stem from a scoring system which dichotomously classifies response as either rights-oriented or care-oriented. In our discussion about enlarging the moral domain, we suggested that these orientations were not bipolar or dichotomous, but rather that the care and response orientation was directed primarily to relations of special obligations to family, friends, and group members, relations which often included or presupposed general obligations of respect, fairness, and contract.

Our standard general moral dilemmas tend to be framed and probed in terms of justice. We believe that Lyons' study indicates not that women prefer care over justice in responding to such general justice dilemmas, but rather that they more often choose, as examples of personal dilemmas, dilemmas of special relationships to family or friends. As noted in chapter 2, section 2, however, many women do not define or select special relationships dilemmas as moral. We quoted a 31-year-old woman who said: 'Take my decision to divorce. I didn't view that as a moral problem. It wasn't. ... Because there weren't any moral issues involved really. The issue involved was whether it was the right thing for us. I don't really see that as a moral problem'. She continued: 'Usually where two principles that I consider valuable look as though they may be clashing, then it's very hard to make a decision about things. Fortunately, it hasn't come up that often. It's hard to say, but yeah, that would make it hard. That would be a moral problem for me.' This woman defined moral dilemmas, as we have done, as conflicts between two general legitimate norms or 'principles'. She does not see dilemmas of responsibility in special relationships as moral in the same sense.

The study by Higgins et al. [1983], summarized in chapter 2, section 8 of this volume, reported that both sexes used justice and care considerations in school dilemmas. The major differences in the use of the two orientations were attributable to (a) the type of dilemma asked and (b) the socio-moral atmosphere of the school situation. The dilemma about helping another student elicited caring considerations, while a dilemma about theft elicited justice concerns. The most striking differences, however, were neither dilemma differences nor sex-differences but were, rather, differences in the

153

nature of school environments. In the alternative democratic community schools the caring and response orientation was much more frequently used than in the high school counterpart. In summary, this study suggests that both considerations are used by both sexes and that preferential orientation is largely a function of the type of moral problem defined and of the socio-moral atmosphere of the environment in which the dilemma is located. Dilemmas located within a 'community' or 'family' context are likely to invoke caring and response considerations; so too do dilemmas of responsibility and caring that go beyond duty (i.e., supererogatory dilemmas and dilemmas of special obligation to friends and kin). In brief, choice of orientation seems to be primarily a function of setting and dilemma and not sex.

In our work we have also attempted to isolate a care and response orientation in our standard justice dilemmas, based on the description of this orientation given in chapter 2. To maximize the possibility of finding such an orientation we focussed on the females in the Israeli kibbutz sample, assuming that we were most likely to find the orientation being used by females and in a setting which, like our just community schools, would have strong ties of interpersonal caring and of caring for a special group or community.

Our tentative findings are: (a) that the use of such a global orientation was rare, even in the female sample; (b) that when found it was dilemma-specific rather than occurring in all dilemmas (Form A was used in this study); and (c) that when found it was stage-specific (i.e., it was most likely to be found at the age at which the subject was 'early conventional' or Stage 3, and would be replaced by a justice orientation at a later stage).

A female kibbutz case example illustrating the above points is Case 252. At age 14, when she is scored Stage 3, she answers the Heinz dilemma (Dilemma III, Form A) as follows:

'He's debating whether he should steal. He loves his wife, he doesn't want her to die, so he's doing the right thing. He didn't have any other way. (Is it a husband's duty?) It's a moral obligation. It depends on the person whether he loves his wife and is willing to steal for her. There might be another person who won't. She's so dear to him that he's willing to steal for her.'

Although scorable using our standard manual this response could be classified in the caring orientation. In Dilemma III' (Should Heinz be sentenced or shown leniency?) she more clearly uses the deontic and justice orientation. She says:

'It's a hard question. Yes he should send him to prison because a law is a law. He breaks the law and it doesn't matter for what reason. What would happen in the country if everyone would steal? It would be terrible.'

On Dilemma I (Joe and his father) she focusses on the special relationship between the two people. Again this response could be classified in the caring orientation. She states:

'If Joe thinks the reason his father is asking for the money is really important then yes, but if not he shouldn't give him the money. I think if it was my father I'd give him the money. I really want to go to camp but I understand, it's worth helping him.'

At age 21, when case 252 is scored Stage 4 (3), her responses were classified as being primarily in the deontic orientation, though considerations of caring were integrated into this orientation. On the Heinz dilemma (Form A, Dilemma III) she says:

'Absolutely, because when human life is at stake and the only way to save it is getting money, life is more important than money. The ends justify the means in this case. Especially when his wife's life is at stake and it is not a stranger. That enhances the obligation. I think that human life is such an important thing and has great value. (What if Heinz doesn't love his wife?) Yes, because as a moral and humane person he should do everything he can to save another human life. If he didn't have enough courage to do it, he is not guilty because it was his inner obligation to do it and no one has the right to force him to do it.'

Her response to Dilemma III' (i.e., whether Heinz should be sentenced to jail) was again scored primarily in the justice orientation. However, elements of care were integrated in her response. She states:

'The judge should suspend the sentence because Heinz is not a criminal. Heinz is not stealing for his own benefit and the judge should recognize that fact. He has to take into account the special circumstances that led Heinz to the crime. From the moral perspective, he is acting from his own morality. He is breaking the law for morality. From the moral point of view, it was not a crime. Yet a suspended sentence is also a sentence since I don't think he is innocent in that he did commit a crime and that should be recognized. The law is to protect society, otherwise the condition of society would break down. If a person would behave only according to his conscience, there would be chaos, but if Heinz's conscience is identical with society's conscience or morality then he should not get a severe punishment: both society and Heinz feel life is important.'

In response to Dilemma I (Joe and his father) she says:

'Joe shouldn't give his father the money because he had promised and Joe is working very hard. It's unfair to break a promise, it's kind of exploitation by the father of the son. (Is the promise the most important consideration?) Yes, it is a principle that has its own value, a promise is creating a trust and breaking a promise is like a betrayal. (How about to someone you don't know?) Yes, if you disappoint your son or a stranger, it makes no difference. In both cases the other side expects you to keep your promise and has placed confidence in you.'

Related to our questioning of the dichotomy between the justice and care orientations and linked to the dichotomy of gender, is our general view that many moral situations or dilemmas do not pose a choice between one or the other orientation, but rather call out a response which integrates both orientations. As an example of this observation, consider the fact that for most individuals the Heinz dilemma is not a dilemma of caring and response for Heinz's wife as opposed to a concern for justice considered vis-à-vis the druggist's property rights. Rather, the wife's right to life is often linked to a caring concern for her welfare and the druggist's right to property is often related to concerns about the welfare to persons in general and to society as a whole (i.e., to a concern about the impact of theft on the social fabric). In other words, it would appear that the concerns for justice and care are often hard to distinguish.

A case-example illustrates the two points we have made: first, that males also have the capacity for caring and response considerations and, second, that caring and response considerations need not pose a tension or conflict between care and justice, but may be integrated into a response consistent with justice, especially at the postconventional level. The Stage 5 response of Kohlberg's longitudinal subject 42D to the Heinz dilemma follows with our analysis of its justice and caring components.

(Should Heinz have done that?)
'Well, I don't think there is enough here to indicate that he had tried every alternative before he did it, so it is not necessarily the case whether or not he should have done it but whether he had an alternative and it isn't in the facts here. But he might have approached other people or local authorities or doctors or something like that before getting desperate. On the other hand, the fact that he was desperate might have meant that he had already done that, so ... Presumably, if he was desperate, he had tried everything he knew of. Now it may not have been adequate. Getting right down to that choice of theft versus that chance of saving his wife's life, I think yes, he should steal it.'
(In what sense would it be worth it?)
'In the sense of the value of human life, because it is all well and good to talk about the sanctity of private property and property rights and so on, but I don't think they mean much in a society that doesn't value human life higher. I guess that is the sense in which I am thinking. In the sense that it is his wife and he has made some kind of commitment to her and so on, but basically because of the value of human life.'
(Was it actually wrong or right for Heinz to have done that?)

'Well, with all my conditions ... I guess it was right. I get entangled in the sense that sometimes I am not even sure if terms like right and wrong apply, but yes.'

(Is it a husband's duty to steal the drug for his wife? If he can get it no other way?)

'Yah, I think so.'

(Why?)

'Well, because of the commitment to the marriage, what it means to me. I guess that is why I respond that way. It is, I just am trying to think of what, it is – I think I know what I mean but I don't know how to say it. The commitment to another person is a total commitment and in a sense he is taking this action because she can't take it herself, in the sense of marriage being something in two bodies. And in that sense there is not much difference in terms of responsibility of her trying to do something for him. This is an ideal proposition.'

(You are sort of arguing from the position of marriage being the union of two persons ...)

'... that involves a commitment to each other and to some kind of form of life or something like that. And it's a commitment that means essentially that. I think I have said it already, that whatever that he would do for her, as much as he would do for himself. It is like an extension of yourself, yah, I guess that is what I am saying.'

(Would you say that that comes in under the idea of duty?)

'Yes, it's a part of the commitment that he made at the time they were married.'

(Suppose the person dying is a stranger?)

'Then he should.'

(Why?)

'Again, because I think the value of human life is higher than the material values that the druggist is after. I was working towards something about not feeling an obligation for someone you don't know, but that doesn't make any sense at all. I am baulking. I am groping. What I am thinking of is the parable that Jesus tells of the guy at the side of the road and the stranger who helped him. That was kind of preaching the value of human life whether it is the life of someone you know or not. *He felt human and that was enough of a bond.'*

To understand this case it is helpful to turn to table I of chapter 2, section 2, in which we elaborated characteristics of the caring and response orientation in a manner similar to the views of Gilligan [1982] and Lyons [1982]. The central feature of this adult male's caring orientation is his assumption of a connectedness or union between husband and wife. This sense of the connected self led to a feeling of psychological responsibility, necessity, or 'desperateness' about the obligation to take care of his wife. The bond is seen as intrinsically valuable. As noted in chapter 2, section 2, this subject is able at the same time to universalize this bond of caring in order to declare that Heinz would have a responsibility for stealing even to help a stranger. He does not come to this conclusion directly from the stranger's right to life (as would happen in the justice orientation) but from the Christian notion of the Good Samaritan, from caring; from a sense of agape for all human beings who are in relationship to one another. It will be recalled that he states: 'Jesus tells of the guy at the side of the road and the stranger who helped him. That was kind of preaching the value of human life whether it is the life of someone you know or not. He felt human and that was enough of a bond.'

In other words, the decision to help the stranger comes from a caring orientation to universal bonds, to the connectedness of all selves in the human community. We also note in case 42D's response a quality of cautious contextual relativism, uncertainty about deontic rightness, and a search for alternative means of dialogue and communication which Gilligan and Lyons suggest are part of the considerations of their caring and response orientation. However, while showing these signs of care and response, this subject also equally relies on justice considerations which support and define his response to the dilemma in terms of a hierarchy of rights; i.e., of the right to life over property.

This subject's justice orientation is indicated by the basic way in which he justifies the rightness of the husband stealing. He does this by establishing that societies in general must recognize the hierarchical value of the right to human life before property rights. He states: '(It would be worth stealing) in the sense of the value of human life, because it is all well and good to talk about the sanctity of ... property rights ... but I don't think they mean much in a society that doesn't value human life higher.' This statement expresses a Stage 5 justice criterion judgment in the Standard Scoring Manual (i.e., the Life *issue;* the Life *norm;* the *element* of serving human dignity or autonomy) which specifies a prior-to-society sense of a hierarchy of rights which forms the foundation of the social contract. In addition, we note that this respondent supports his caring responses regarding the husband-wife relationship with a contractual judgment of justice when he is asked the deontic question 'Is it a husband's duty to steal the drug for his wife?'. He replies: 'Yes, it's part of the commitment he made at the time of marriage.' Thus, this subject's sense of the responsibilities of caring is supported by and integrated with his deontic judgments of justice and duty.

We are more clearly able to score his responses in the justice orientation in terms of our justice stages than we are able to stage score his responses in the caring orientation. We leave to Gilligan and her colleagues the task of defining more fully and formally levels and stages within the caring orientation. For the purposes of this theoretical reply, however, we see the responses we have cited as *non-supportive* of any view that justice and caring are two different tracks of moral development which are either independent or in polar opposition to one another, a conclusion some researchers have drawn from the Gilligan [1982] and Lyons [1982] work.

We may note that at the postconventional stages there is typically an effort to integrate concerns of benevolence and care on the one hand with justice concerns on the other. At this level of moral reasoning, justice concerns lose their retributive and rule bound nature for the sake of treating persons as persons; i.e., as ends in themselves. This principle of persons as ends is common to both the ethic of care and the ethic of justice. The former ethic sees the other person in relationship to self and others; the latter sees persons as autonomous ends in themselves, relating to one another through agreement and mutual respect.

As an example of the above convergence of the justice and care orientations we just suggested two responses to the Heinz dilemma which focus on issues of rights and justice and yet center on issues of care as well. Another example of this convergence can be seen in responses to caring dilemmas used by Higgins et al. [1981] which asked whether Harry, a class mate, should volunteer to drive an unpopular student, Billy, to a college interview.

In order to demonstrate how both the caring and justice orientations come together at Kohlberg's postconventional level, we will answer the Higgins et al. dilemma with the logic of Stage 6 reasoning as described by Kohlberg [1981b] in *Justice as Reversibility*. Let the dilemma be called 'Harry's Dilemma'. The question to the respondent is as follows: 'Should Harry drive Bill to Bill's interview or should he sleep in?' Some adolescent high school students answer this question in terms of a potential relationship between Harry and Bill as classmates and friends. In this sense they are responding within Gilligan's caring orientation. Many students at the conventional moral stages, however, respond in terms of notions of fairness as captured by the Golden Rule; i.e., if they were in Bill's situation, they say, they would want someone to help them to get to the interview. This idea of the Golden Rule would be formulated with Kohlberg's conception of Stage 6 as the following question: 'If Harry did not know whether he was the needy student Bill, or himself with the car who could not sleep in if he drove Bill, he would choose the option to offer to drive Bill. He would make this choice reasoning that, not knowing his own identity, the loss of not attending the interview was far greater than not being able to sleep in for one morning'. This is an example of Stage 6 justice reasoning which resolves a dilemma which might normally be expected to elicit an ethic of care; and it should be noted, it resolves the dilemma in the same direction as a mature ethic of care would.

In the New Testament there are two alternative statements of the Golden Rule. The first can be seen in the fairness orientation as 'Do unto others as you would have them do unto you'. The second version is phrased in terms of the orientation of care as 'Love thy neighbour as thyself'. Like other statements of postconventional morality, the teachings of the New Testament often integrate considerations of care and justice presenting, as modern moral philosophy does, a view of justice which is beyond either strict contract, strict retribution, or strict obedience to rules. Rather, it is a view of justice which focusses on ideal role-taking, a principle which can be called, alternatively, respect for persons (i.e., justice) or caring for persons as ideal ends in themselves (i.e., the ethic of care).

In the parable of the vineyard, the vineyard owner gives the same wage to those who come late as he does to those whom he hires first and who, therefore, work longer. The vineyard owner, in making the last who come equal to the first, is acting out of a generosity which is not unfair to those who come first since he has kept his contract with them. In terms of justice as equity or distribution according to need, the last to come are as needy as the first. As outlined by Kohlberg [1981a], postconventional justice reasoning, particularly that reasoning called Stage 6, is blind to many of the considerations of merit and retribution which are the connotations of justice to many who reason at lower stages. Earlier stage reasoning often separates justice from an ethic of care. For the sake of a regard for respecting persons as ends in themselves, however, our Stage 6 vineyard owner's action represents not only justice but also the ethic of care.

Not only at the postconventional stages but at the conventional stages as well, we see persons responding to both real life and hypothetical dilemmas in ways which include and attempt to integrate concerns for both justice and care. Justice and care, we believe, do not represent different tracks of moral development. Piaget spoke of childhood morality as representing two moralities, not one; i.e., a morality of heteronomous respect and a morality of mutual respect. Our own work suggests that these differences represent different substages within the sequential growth through Kohlberg's stages of justice reasoning. Similar to our recognition of 'Piagetian' substages within a larger context of sequential stage growth, we partially accept Gilligan's differentiation of two orientations in moral judgment which may vary in stress from person to person and from situation to situation. We do not believe, however, that the growth of justice and the ethic of care represent two distinct tracks of moral stage (i.e. structural) development.

We may summarize the above discussion by stating that Gilligan's emphasis on the care and response orientation has broadened the moral domain beyond our focus on justice reasoning. However, we do not believe that there exist two distinct or polar orientations or two tracks in the ontogenesis of moral stage structures. In the chapter on revisions to Kohlberg's theory, we indicated why our focus on justice was more amenable to a formulation in terms of 'hard' Piagetian structural stages than would be some other focus on other elements of the moral, such as a focus on considerations of care. It remains for Gilligan and her colleagues to determine whether there are, in fact, 'hard' stages in the care orientation. If she wishes to claim that there are stages of caring in a Piagetian sense of the word stage, she will have to demonstrate the progressive movement, invariant sequence, structured wholeness, and the relationships of thought to action for her orientation in a manner similar to the way Kohlberg has demonstrated such ontogenetic characteristics for the justice orientation [see, for example, the presentation of the longitudinal data on justice reasoning in Colby et al., 1983b].

The questioning of the notion of two distinct moralities made in this reply is paralleled in a paper by Nunner-Winkler [1983] entitled *Two Moralities? A Critical Discussion of an Ethic of Care and Responsibility versus an Ethic of Rights and Justice.* Nunner-Winkler says that insofar as there are differences between the caring and justice approaches they are not differences in basic ethical position but differences in emphasis on two types of moral duty. Following Kant, Nunner-Winkler takes perfect duties to be negative duties of non-interference with the rights of others. Perfect or negative duties can be followed by everybody at any time and location and with regard to everybody. Imperfect duties, in contrast, are positive duties which do not prescribe specific acts but only formulate a maxim which is to guide action; e.g., the practice of care. She says:

'Such a maxim delineates a broad set of recommendable courses of action some of which the actor realizes by at the same time applying pragmatic rules and taking into account concrete conditions such as individual preferences or locations in space and history. Imperfect duties can never be observed completely; it is impossible to practice caring all the time and with regard to everybody. Positive maxims or principles do not specify which and how many good deeds have to be performed and whom they are to benefit so that the maxim can be said to have been followed. This orientation to imperfect duty, which Gilligan characterizes as an ethic of care, finds its most precise expression in the following quotation Gilligan [1977] cites: 'Is it right to spend money on a pair of shoes when I have a pair of shoes and other people are shoeless?'

The form this reflection takes, the questioning, is proof of its being derived from an imperfect duty, namely the principle of charity which does not define its own form of application, its own limits and the degree to which it is binding ... No one would deny that both kinds of duties are considered part of one's morality, the unity of which is constituted by adhering to some universalizing procedure which Kant would hold applies to both types of duties.'

From this point of view Nunner-Winkler interprets Gilligan's claim as meaning that females (a) feel more obliged to fulfill imperfect duties than do males and (b) in cases of conflict, are more likely to opt for the fulfillment of imperfect duties while males opt for the fulfillment of perfect duties.

Nunner-Winkler says that Gilligan's second claim, that females compared to males will more likely opt for imperfect duties over perfect duties, is implausible, since Gilligan ascribes to the ethic of care an orientation to contextual particularity. It is precisely this consideration of contextual particularity that Gilligan sees as lacking in the ethic of rights and justice. Gilligan's equation of an orientation to imperfect duties with contextual particularity, Nunner-Winkler says, holds true only for a very specific aspect of Kant's moral position which is hardly shared by anyone; namely, that perfect duties allow for no exceptions. Such a position is not held by Kohlberg, she says, '... even though he presents his construction of rights in such a misleading way that it does provoke the kind of criticism that Gilligan voices. ... Therefore one cannot very well hold context orientations to be a feature to constitute contrasting approaches to morality. Context orientation is a prerequisite for all actual moral judgments.'

Given the above, Nunner-Winkler then rephrases Gilligan's theory as implying that females feel more obliged to fulfill imperfect duties and males to fulfill perfect duties, though both apply to the field of morality. She presents both logical arguments for her case as well as empirical data from her study with adolescents in which she did not find sex-differences in orientation to imperfect as opposed to perfect duties. As an example, females are not more likely than males to endorse the 'caring' or 'imperfect' duty of relieving a terminally-ill person of her pain, where this is in contrast with the perfect duty of preserving the woman's life (Kohlberg's Form B Dilemma IV). Since Nunner-Winkler did not find these sex differences in moral judgment, in the strict sense of justice reasoning, she suggests that what Gilligan is really talking about are sex-differences in ideals of the good life. These ideals of the self and of the good life may be related to the image of the self as connected, but operate not through moral judgment but rather through specific ego interests. As an example, Nunner-Winkler quotes Gilligan's example of one male and one female six-year-old responding to the dilemma created when in playing with a friend they discover they want to play a different game. 'Gilligan cites as characteristic of the little girl "We don't have a real fight and we agree about what we will do", while the little boy says "I wanted to go outside, he wanted to stay in. I would do what I want, he would do what he wants."' Nunner-Winkler then states:

'As long as it is so described, however, this dilemma is not a moral dilemma but the inner conflict of an individual choosing among his own inner needs. Each child has two desires, the desire to play a specific game, and the desire to play with a specific friend. The little girl prefers foregoing the chance to play the preferred game for the chance to play with her friend. The little boy proves to be more interested in playing the preferred game, and be it alone, than to play with his friend. Thus far each child may have chosen among different needs which proved not to be simultaneously satisfiable. On the face of it there is nothing moral about this choice; it is well known that females are more interested in relationships and males more in things (objects). Neither one nor the other of these preferences is morally more recommendable.'

Nunner-Winkler's relating of an ethic care to an ego interest or an ideal of the good life, rather than to morality in its strictly more other-regarding and universalizable sense, coincides with our statement that many of the judgments in this orientation are personal rather than moral in the sense of a formal point of view. Further research should attend to differences in what may be considered either 'moral content' or 'moral style', but we believe it unlikely that such research will find divergent moral 'hard' stage sequences for justice and care.

Murphy, M. and Gilligan, C.: Moral Development in Late Adolescence and Adulthood. Human Development 23: 77–104 (1980)

Gilligan, C. and Murphy, M.: Development from Adolescence to Adulthood. The Philosopher and the Dilemma of the Fact; in Kuhn, Intellectual Development beyond Childhood (Jossey-Bass, San Francisco 1979)

Synopsis
In these two articles Murphy and Gilligan first claim that there is regression in prescriptive reasoning about justice on our 'classical' dilemmas in early adulthood. Second, and leaving aside the reported regression on classi-

cal dilemmas, they report continued progression on real-life dilemmas as measured with the Perry [1970] scale of epistemological and metaethical development. They interpret this finding in light of their own theorizing about a 'responsibility orientation' to moral judgment which they seem to consider as more context-relevant than Kohlberg's justice orientation.

In other words, these essays by Murphy and Gilligan [1980] and Gilligan and Murphy [1979] deal with Gilligan's contrast between the justice and responsibility orientations in terms of a different issue: i.e., Gilligan believes that postconventional reasoning in the responsibility orientation does not rest on 'abstract principles' but, rather, on contextually relative perceptions of the factual moral situation and its psychological implications. In some sense Gilligan and Murphy believe that the principled morality of justice which we have defined as Stage 5 and 6 represents an adolescent form of over-theoretical and over-abstract moral perception which in more mature adulthood is modified or develops into a more contextually relative form of moral perception. This relativism results from actual experiences of what adults take to be contradictions in conflicts between generalized principles and the factual complexities and ambiguities of real-life situations, situations to which late adolescents attempt to apply their justice principles.

In developing their notion of a post-adolescent movement to a moral methodology of contextual relativism, Gilligan and Murphy rely upon Perry's [1970] statement of intellectual and ethical development in the college years. Gilligan and Murphy make two quantitative empirical claims in this context. The first claim is that there is developmental advance on the Perry scale, moving toward responsibility in the context of relativism, detected in longitudinal data in the college and post-college years. The second claim they make is that there is some regression on the Kohlberg scale from principled (Stage 5) moral reasoning to transitional (4/5) moral reasoning. They assume that this retrogression is a *consequence* of the advance observed on the Perry scale. With the use of case material they interpret these quantitative findings as indicating the development of a mature awareness that questions the validity of general or universal principles and their application in the context of confronting concreté moral 'dilemmas of the fact'.

Gilligan and Murphy [1979] paraphrase Perry's important developmental work as follows, and we quote them at length:

'Empirical evidence for such a divergence in ethical orientations comes, instead, from the work of Perry who, like Kohlberg, followed intellectual and ethical development in the college years. However, where Kohlberg speaks of the order of reason and the conception of the moral ideal, Perry talks of the disorder of experience, the realization that life itself is unfair. How thought comes to account for experiences that demonstrate the limits of both knowledge and choice is the problem that Perry sets out to address. In doing so, he describes a revolution in thinking that leads to the perception of all knowledge as contextually relative, a radical "180° shift in orientation" that follows from the discovery that, in even its farthest reaches, reason alone will leave the thinker with several legitimate contexts and no way of choosing among them – no way, at least that he can justify through reason alone. If he then throws away reason entirely, he retreats to the irresponsible in Multiplicity (anyone has a right to his opinion). If he is still to honor reason, he must now also transcend it. Because the ultimate welding of epistemological and moral issues makes the act of knowing an act of commitment for which one bears personal responsibility, Perry centers the drama of late adolescent development on the theme of responsibility which enters first as a new figure on the familiar ground of logical justification. However, because the understanding of responsibility demands a contextual mode of thought, the concern with responsibility signifies a fundamental shift in ethical orientation that ushers in what Perry calls "the period of responsibility". Following this shift, judgment is always qualified by the nature of the context in which one stands back to observe, so that the interpretation of the moral problem determines the way in which it is judged and resolved. Thus principles once seen as absolute are reconsidered within a contextual interpretation. As a result, moral problems formerly seen in philosophical terms as problems of justification come to be considered in psychological terms as problems of commitment and choice.'

Reply

The Murphy and Gilligan findings are of particular interest because they stem from interviews with a *longitudinal* sample of Harvard students in the upper range of intellectual and moral sophistication. While Murphy and Gilligan claim to find regression in moral stage on our classical dilemmas, we hold that their findings do not support this conclusion. This is because a conclusion of regression in longitudinal data must make some allowance for measurement error, an allowance they did not appear to make. The test-retest reliability reported in Colby et al. [1983b] also indicated some 'regression' among subjects tested and retested over an interval of one month. We argue that Murphy and Gilligan cannot establish that the 'regression' they found is not just due to test factors, unreliability in scoring, etc. When Colby et al. tried to determine if regression actually did occur in Kohlberg's longitudinal data, they used a one month test-retest 'regression' score as an error margin. With this margin they found that on average only 4% of the longitudinal subjects dropped one half stage or more in a 3-year test interval as compared to 17% of the one-month retest sample. On this basis Colby et al. concluded that there were no determinable regression data in Kohlberg's longitudinal sample. If one applies this line of thinking, that corrects for measurement error, to the Gilligan and Murphy sample, one has to conclude that they too have no determinable regression data. If one counts only those cases which contain more than one dilemma (our 1980 Standard Issue Scoring Instrument requires a full protocol of three dilemmas), and if one assesses change as Colby et al. [1983b] do on the basis of a 9-point scale (e.g., 3, 3/4, 4, 4/5, etc.) then one finds only 4 cases of 'regression' in the Murphy and Gilligan data, 3 of which are a drop of half a stage and only one of which is a full stage drop. Out of all possible occasions for regression, there were only 15% observed (4/26). This is within the limit of 19% 'regression' due to test factors found in test-retest data by Colby et al. [1983b]. Thus, we cannot know whether Murphy and Gilligan's four cases are truly regressors.

While we have argued that the Murphy and Gilligan findings of regression are within the limits of measurement error, there is another aspect of their data which needs to be noted. The students in their study all participated in a course on ethical and political choice taught by Gilligan, Kohlberg, and other colleagues. The course focussed on discussion of hypothetical and real-life moral dilemmas as well as on the study of classical moral philosophers. An explicit goal of the course was the moral development of students and the formation of a principled moral orientation. Two assessments of moral reasoning were made in this class. There was about a quarter stage upward movement observed from Time 1 to Time 2, though the data are not reported by Murphy and Gilligan. This upward stage movement is the same in magnitude as that found in other experimental and intervention projects. Some of these studies [Blatt and Kohlberg, 1975] have also reported occasional regressions on follow-up testing, where higher stage reasoning had been only superficially assimilated and was more than one stage above the subject's pretested level. Thus, some of the questioning or partial rejection of principled reasoning, noted anecdotally in a few cases by Murphy and Gilligan, may reflect a later questioning of didactic content rather than a later rejection of an acquired natural stage of reasoning.

Another point made by Gilligan and Murphy is that despite apparent regression in their sample on the Kohlberg scale, their sample of subjects demonstrates continued development as measured by Perry's scale of ethical reasoning in adulthood. We agree with their view that there is a development in moral epistemology or metaethical reflection upon the validity of 'absolute' interpretations of morality in late adolescence and adulthood. We also believe that this development may occur after the attainment of principled stages of justice reasoning. However, we do not agree with their interpretation that this development leads to retrogression in justice reasoning or in the questioning of or abandonment of principles of justice when applied to real-life moral dilemmas.

In our discussion of revisions to our theory (chapter 2, section 3) we discussed the distinction between 'hard' Piagetian structural stages and 'soft' levels or stages of reflection upon the self, the social world, and the larger cosmos. We said that these 'soft' stages might characterize that adult development which is based on personal reflection; a development which 'hard' stages would fail to define. Perry's levels or stages, in our opinion, also represent forms of metaethical reflection on the validity of standards of truth and rightness, on the source of their authority, and on their limits in the face of disagreements between persons and authorities who hold them. Like the Fowler [1981] levels of faith, Perry's stages reflect adult metaethical or reflective development not captured by our 'hard' structural stages. In our discussion in chapter 2, section 10, part vii, we dealt with the nature of moral judgments as rule governed versus principled and we clarified that our interpretation of principles sees them as human constructions rather than as the application of absolute a prioris to moral conflicts. Unlike fixed and absolute moral rules, moral principles were characterized as methods or ways of seeing and of constructing responses to complex moral situations. Our own 'constructivistic' view of the nature, source, and validity of moral principles is itself a metaethical position based upon psychological research and moral-epistemological reflection. In this sense our position is not a normative statement of principles which would be captured by our justice stage descriptions but is, rather, characterizable by schemes of epistemological and metaethical development such as those of Perry [1970] and Broughton [1982]. In this sense, our own constructivistic position is consistent with Perry's notion of development in adulthood that goes beyond or implies more than the attainment of principled (Stage 5) justice reasoning.

Let us now turn to the example supplied by Gilligan and Murphy which they claim demonstrates simultaneous development on the Perry scale and abandonment of principled (Stage 5) moral reasoning on the Kohlberg scale. We will argue, instead, that their case material does not indicate that continuing development in 'contextual relativism' leads to the abandonment of Stage 5 principles, but rather that such development leads to a more contextual framing of these principles. We will be claiming that there is *not* a contradiction between a principled and contextually relativistic framing of moral conflict as Gilligan and Murphy imply. We will use as an example of the issue a case which Gilligan and Murphy report as Philosopher 2's 'dilemma of the fact'. They interpret Philosopher 2's integration of experience with this dilemma as representing a relativistic erosion of the formerly-held Stage 5 principles of justice. In contrast, we see this growth over time as a more contextualized search for the correct application of his principles to which he remains committed.

The dilemma facing Philosopher 2 (a respondent scored at Stage 5 on 'classic' hypothetical dilemmas) was that the husband of the woman with whom he was having an affair was uninformed of this fact. This lack of information raised for Philosopher 2 a question of moral obligation to see that the husband knew of the affair. He said: 'If I see some kind of ongoing, unjust situation, I have some kind of obligation to correct it in whatever way I see ... The husband should be told since otherwise he would not be getting the information he needed to judge what his best interests should be in the situation ...' 'I would have wanted to know the full truth. I think that truth is an ultimate thing.'

We would agree with Gilligan and Murphy's interpretation that Philosopher 2 orients to the dilemma in terms of justice or rights and in terms of some role-taking of the positions of the others in the situation. They interpret as a Stage 5 or 6 principle his idea that 'truth is an ultimate thing'. Reflecting later on his thinking about the dilemma he says: 'I was always aware of the kind of situation in which truth was not absolute. If a person comes up to me with a gun in his hand ... in that sense I never thought truth was ultimate.' Thus, he was aware, though not in a clear way, that truth telling, while a basic prima facie rule, was not a final decisional moral principle. Either a Stage 5 principle of justice or a Stage 5 principle of choosing the greatest welfare would dictate not telling the truth in situations in which other basic values, say the value of life, were at stake.

Philosopher 2's idea that justice to the husband dictated informing him was complicated by his taking the point of view of his lover and her needs and claims. Overwhelmed by other pressures, she was unable to face the additional stress of informing her husband of the affair at that time, and said that she would tell him at a more peaceful time. In the interim, the husband discovered the affair. 'So my dilemma was whether I should call the guy up and tell him what the situation was. I didn't, and the fact that I didn't has had a tremendous impact on my moral system. It did. It shook my belief and my justification of the belief that I couldn't resolve the dilemma of the fact that I felt that someone should tell him. I did feel there was some kind of truth issue involved here, higher than the issue of where the truth comes from. The kind of thing that no matter what happens the other person should have full knowledge of what is going on, is fair. And I didn't tell him.'

From our point of view, Philosopher 2's confrontation with the dilemma of the fact led him to a greater awareness of the inherent ambiguity of factual definitions of dilemmas like his; that is, an interpretation of the facts of a dilemma may be difficult to achieve or to get consensus on. He says: 'It led me to question whether somehow there is a sense in which truth is relative. Or is truth ever relative? That is an issue I have yet to resolve.' This growing relativism about factual interpretation is not in itself a questioning of the universality or validity of moral principles, like the principles of justice or human welfare, but it is a growing awareness of the difficulties encountered in getting clarity or consensus on their application to concrete situations. This experience has also lead Philosopher 2 to question further the absolute value of truth-telling in favor of some more contextual application of the principle of justice, a principle he does not yet feel he can define for himself. As Philosopher 2 states: 'With interpersonal situations that dealt with psychological realities and with psychological feelings, with emotions, I felt that the truth should win out in most situations. Then after that situation I became more relativistic about it. As you can tell, right now, I have not worked out a principle that is satisfactory to me that would resolve that issue if it happened again tomorrow. If I were the husband I would certainly want to know the truth, but if I were the wife would I see what I (Philosopher 2) wanted to do as being the right thing? And was her right to sanity which I think was being jeopardized, less important than his right to know? That is a good moral dilemma. Now you figure it out.'

In our interpretation, Philosopher 2 is struggling to formulate a principle of justice which would resolve the situation of conflict between the husband's right to truth and the wife's right to sanity. In trying to do this, he attempts to engage in a process of what we call ideal role-taking or 'moral musical chairs', a process at the heart of our hypothetical notion of a sixth stage of moral judgment [see *Justice as Reversibility,* in Kohlberg, 1981b]. He says, however, that he cannot find a principle which is morally valid or reversible, seeing the situation from all perspectives. If, following the ideal role-taking process we have referred to, and assuming the factual correctness that disclosure of the truth would risk the wife's sanity, then if Philosopher 2 would imaginatively continue the process and ask whether the husband's claim to truth would be valid if he placed himself in the wife's position, he would be likely to conclude that justice is better served by withholding the truth because if the husband puts himself in the wife's position he sees her right to sanity. In other words, in this case Philosopher 2 realizes that choosing sanity over truth-telling is a more reversible decision than the converse. In this sense it is not different from his earlier awareness that truth was not an absolute, but that choosing life over truth was a more just solution if 'someone came up to me with a gun in his hand ...' Philosopher 2's increased relativism arising from the conflict represented a growing awareness of the complexity of moral decisions in the interpersonal domain. His relativism is partly a relativism about the psychological complexity of defining 'facts' about a person's immediate and long-term feelings. However, it is also a growing awareness of the ambiguity of defining principles of justice or respect for the personhood of others in the interpersonal domain. In conclusion we would see Philosopher 2 as engaged in a search for the refinement and differentiation of his principles of justice; he is attempting to apply them in more complex situations, rather than either abandoning them in favor of a sceptical or nihilistic relativism or in favor of some orientation to moral decisions other than one of principles or justice.

How do Gilligan and Murphy interpret Philosopher 2's response? In the first place they assume that our Stage 5 orientation of principled justice implies a rule-based rigorism or fixity of application of a principle and a sense that such a principle is an immutable absolute defining choice. In fact, we use the term principle to mean a human construction which guides perceptions and responses to human claims in conflict situations (see our earlier discussion in chapter 2, section 10, part vii, on morality as principledness). Gilligan and Murphy seem to believe that Philosopher 2 has changed from an absolutistic Stage 5 moral orientation to a 'morality eroded by relativism'. They say: 'Thus, the relativism that has begun to erode his former claim to absolute knowledge to the "right thing to do" arises from his incipient awareness of the possible legitimacy of a different point of view.' In contrast, while we grant a growth in contextual relativism has occurred for Philosopher 2, we cannot see any inconsistency between this fact and his use of principled reasoning.

A more central thrust of Gilligan and Murphy's interpretation of the case is that it represents adult development away from a justice orientation to a more contextually relative responsibility and care orientation. We noted earlier that Gilligan defined this orientation partly in terms of sex-differences, as a preferential orientation of women. In the context of Philosopher 2, Gilligan and Murphy say that his response represents development in a male toward a greater awareness of the responsibility and care orientation, one which they see as being in conflict with a justice orientation to the same dilemma. They say: 'Thus, the question becomes one of definition as to what is included in the moral domain since the justice approach does not adequately address the responsibilities and obligations that come from life choices.' According to Gilligan and Murphy, for Philosopher 2 'a contextual morality of responsibility for the actual consequences of choice thus enters into a dialogue with the abstraction of rights, resulting in a judgment with contradictory normative statements scored as a mixture of Kohlberg's stages 4 and 5'. They go on to state:

'Our interpretation that Philosopher Two's apparent regression is an artifact of a new, more encompassing perspective is supported by his retrospective reflection at age 27 on the dilemma he had reported five years earlier. Now the moral discussion "about who tells the truth and who doesn't" appears to him in a "very different perspective"; as legitimate to "the justice approach" but ancillary to "the more fundamental issue" of the causes and consequences of infidelity. Focusing his discussion at age 27 on his understanding of why the situation arose in the first place and the problem of life choice its occurrence presented, he attributes his previous unawareness of these issues to "an incredible amount of immaturity on my part" which he sees reflected in his "justice approach".'

We would agree with Gilligan and Murphy that life experience in relationships has given Philosopher 2 a more complex perception of the factual realities of interpersonal relationships and of the personal values that enter into interpersonal choice. What we question is that this is a qualitative shift in moral orientation, from the justice to the responsibility orientation. Kohlberg has speculated that there are indeed dilemmas and conflicts of interpersonal responsibility and choice which are not fully resolved by principles of justice, but it is not clear to us that Philosopher 2's dilemma constitutes one of these instances. In references to his later interview at age 27 Gilligan and Murphy state: 'His revolution combines the absolute logic of a system of moral justification with a probabilistic contextual assessment of the likely consequences of choice.' Without the word 'absolute', we would agree that this statement by Gilligan and Murphy describes Philosopher 2's development. But we also believe that this statement, without the word 'absolute', describes the task of moral principles of justice, whether they be utilitarian principles of justice as the greatest welfare maximization, or Kantian principles of justice as respect for human personality or ideal role-taking.

For Gilligan and Murphy, Philosopher 2's judgment at age 27 occurs in 'two contexts that frame different aspects of the moral problem: the context

of justice in which he articulates the universal logic of fairness and reciprocity and the context of compassion in which he focuses instead on the particularity of consequences for the actual participants.' For us, both these
concerns enter into the hypothetical dilemmas of justice which define our
moral stages throughout the stage hierarchy. Whether the dilemma is one of
whether to convict an escaped but reformed convict of his previous crime,
or whether the dilemma is one of an air-raid captain leaving his assigned
post out of concern for the immediate welfare of his family, our stages of
justice attempt to define choices in which both fairness or reciprocity and
compassionate concern for consequences are enmeshed. We believe moral
stage development is the development of one morality, not of two, because
moral situations and choices always involve both issues of justice and compassion.

The work of Gilligan and her colleagues has added depth to the description of moral judgment focussed on responsibility and caring but we do not
believe that it defines an alternate morality confronted in adulthood by
Philosopher 2. More than justice is required for resolving many complex
moral dilemmas but justice is a necessary element of any morally adequate
resolution of these conflicts. Future work by Gilligan and her colleagues
may modify our general conclusions but we believe that this continuing
work will primarily clarify the reflective and metaethical 'soft' stage levels
through which adolescents and adults develop, rather than give us a different picture of the development of 'hard' structures of moral reasoning.

Levine, C.G.: Stage Acquisition and Stage Use.
Human Development 22: 145–164 (1979)

Synopsis

Three models of the structuralist assumption that moral stages constitute a hierarchy are presented and critically discussed by Levine. The most
radically structuralist model identified by Levine is Turiel's 'displacement'
model. The displacement model claims that when a new stage is acquired the
previous stage is totally reorganized and no longer exists as a structure; i.e.,
any empirical example of the use of the previous stage is conceptualized by
Turiel not as the use of structure but as the content of the subject's current
modal stage undergoing reconstruction. Turiel holds this view because he
argues that one must see instances of apparent lower stage use in this way in
order to be loyal to the requirements of transformation and non-regression

implied by a strictly structural stage model. Levine argues that Turiel's interpretation of stage transformation, based on a literal interpretation of displacement, is a view which cannot explain fluctuations in stage use predicted on the basis of the hypothesized effects of situational stimuli.

The next model discussed by Levine emerges from Rest's work and has been called by Turiel the 'layer cake' model, in contrast with his own. This model asserts that stages are acquired in an invariant sequence but postulates the continued availability of lower stages. Nevertheless, it is argued that there is a hierarchical preference to use the highest stage available. Levine calls this model a much less radical displacement model than Turiel's. It is only the assumption of hierarchical preference (not the assumption of sequential stage acquisition) that Levine finds problematic, because he feels that this assumption has biased inquiry against a systematic study of social conditions that can elicit the use of stages below the most advanced stage acquired.

The third model presented is Levine's 'non-displacement, additive-inclusive' model of stage development. He believes that this model remains consistent with the premises of structural developmental theory but more adequately justifies adopting a method which measures fluctuations in rates of moral stage use based on a concern for the effects of variation in dilemma and situational stimuli. At the basis of Levine's concern is his adherence to interactionist assumptions in order to understand performance rather than competence. While Levine believes that patterns of performance probably have a bearing on development, his major point seems to be that if this is so it ought to be investigated more than it has been, and must be investigated by any theory which claims to offer a complete explanation of the ontogenesis of justice reasoning in the real world.

Levine suggests that his concern for investigating performance is not in any way incompatible with the logic of Kohlberg's theory, but that it may not have been pursued too rigorously because of Kohlberg's primary concern with assessing patterns of development from a competence perspective. In developing his interactionist orientation, Levine is interested in demonstrating that a research perspective which defines competence as the highest stage of reasoning calculated over standardized dilemmas may not be a perspective which enables one to predict reasoning in other situations. Given studies by Rest [1973] and Turiel [1969], which demonstrate that hierarchical preference is a characteristic of moral stage use, as well as Kohlberg's theoretical emphasis on stage growth as movement towards principled reasoning, Levine thinks that a lag between competence and performance, if there is one, is likely to be greatest at the lower end of Kohlberg's stage hierarchy. Levine acknowledges that his thoughts stem from an earlier study [Levine, 1976] in which he demonstrated variation in rates of Stage 3 and 4 use as a function of varying the identity of actors in the dilemmas presented to respondents.

Reply

We do not see Levine's article as a criticism of Kohlberg's theory; rather, we understand it as suggesting that the theory be used for assessing research questions from a social interactionist perspective. We agree that we have focussed on attempts to assess optimal competence and not fluctuations in everyday performance, since our interest has been focussed on a theory of structures of moral development and not on a theory of the use of stages of moral reasoning. Levine's [1976] findings, however, while showing fluctuating proportions in the use of *adjacent* stages, do not violate the *performance* expectations we have from the point of view of our competence perspective.

The issues raised by Levine about interaction between stimulus situation and stage performance seem to lead into the study of performance in terms of moral action, a study which we have explored under the name of moral atmosphere [Kohlberg, 1981b; Kohlberg et al., 1981]. However, it is true that our concern with moral atmosphere does not amount to an extensive research program into performance questions. In sum, we see Levine's argument as an extension of social psychology theory compatible with the premises of our structural developmental theory. A good portion of Levine's [1979] article explores some of the implications of applying an interactionist approach to Kohlberg's theory. We see it as a useful article which specifies some of the research questions one might ask when attempting to explore patterns of stage use in conjunction with social environmental factors.

Gibbs, J.C.: Kohlberg's Moral Stage Theory. A Piagetian Revision. Human Development 22: 89–112 (1979)

Synopsis

Gibbs' interpretation of moral development is based on a two-phase model. Phase 1 is a Piagetian model of development which maps Kohlberg's Stages 1–4. Within Kohlberg's Stages 3 and 4 Gibbs sees the development of second-order thought which for him constitutes the basis for the construction of his existential phase of adult development; a developmental period which he calls his second phase. Gibbs claims that his second phase is not structural in the Piagetian sense but is, rather, developmental in a 'purely phenomenological and functional' sense [p. 106]. By this Gibbs means that his second phase cannot be described in hard structural stage terms since it explains the development of a search for meaning, identity, and commitment as described in writings by Erikson and Fromm.

The reason Gibbs develops this model is to compensate for what he considers to be a lack of evidence supporting Kohlberg's structural treatment of postconventional reasoning. The lack of evidence Gibbs refers to is both theoretical and empirical. Theoretically, Gibbs argues that Kohlberg's stages do not constitute operative structures (i.e., Piaget's notion of a 'system in action') and that they do not appear to be 'spontaneous' (i.e., they appear to be non-spontaneous utterances based on the education and understanding of intellectual traditions of a particular society). In addition, Gibbs [p. 97] claims that the cross-cultural empirical rarity of postconventional reasoning suggests that Kohlberg's postconventional stages are not Piagetian structural stages. If Kohlberg's moral stages are Piagetian structural stages they should, for Gibbs, empirically correlate with the use of similar structures in the cognitive domain. Gibbs [p. 108] charges that no relation has been found between Piaget's cognitive-logical stages of development and postconventional moral thinking.

Given the above, Gibbs concludes that Kohlberg's postconventional stages are not structural in Piaget's sense but are, rather, metaethical positions which adults develop in the course of their existential growth. Thus, Gibbs would say that Kohlberg's postconventional stages are different but are not more structurally advanced than Kohlberg's substages at Stage 3 or 4. Gibbs' model, then, uses Kohlberg's Stages 1–4 as a structural explanation of moral development and explains existential non-structural development with Kohlberg's Stages 3B, 4B, 5, and 6.

Reply
In our reply we start by accepting the usefulness of Gibbs' distinction between Piagetian structural stage development in adulthood and the development of non-structural levels of reflection upon existential issues in adulthood. Gibbs says that this latter type of development is more closely related to Erikson's [1963] and Fromm's [1947] notions of ego development than it is to an extension of Piaget's idea of stages.

As noted above, Gibbs has offered several reasons for questioning whether Stages 5 and 6 really define new moral stages. In the comments to follow, we deal primarily with Stage 5 because, as we have noted in our discussion of the current status of the theory, we do not have extensive or sufficient empirical data to substantiate any claims as to use of a sixth stage, even though we still maintain its usefulness as a theoretical construct (see chapter 2, section 9). The core of Gibbs' criticism is that Stage 5 moral reasoning is not a new operative structure or system-in-action. Thus, Stage 5 is not a new form of normative ethical judgment but is only a new set of theoretical reflections upon already given normative judgment structures; i.e., only a new position of metaethical reasoning associated with the normative ethical reasoning of Stages 3 and 4. (We refer the reader to our discussion of the basic distinctions between normative and metaethical reasoning in chapter 2, section 10.)

Gibbs wishes to call our postconventional stages 'existential' positions rather than new moral or normative ethical structures. Central to his conception of existential thinking is the notion that it is 'second order': e.g., 'the ability to adopt the detached, meta-perspective on not only logical physical problems, social relationships and social systems, (but also on) consciousness, ethics, reason and life itself' [p. 102]. It seems then, that second order thinking requires formal operational thought, i.e., the capacity to reflect on thought. Thus, in this context, what we have distinguished as metaethical reasoning, as opposed to normative ethical reasoning, is what Gibbs would call 'existential thinking'. What Gibbs calls 'existential thinking' at Stages 3B, 4B, and 5 we identify as the development of the ability to generate statements about what morality is, to identify the grounds for it in conceptions of human nature and metaphysics, and to justify its necessity. An example of such moral theorizing would be a generalized theoretical statement about the nature of a social contract, typical of Stage 5 thinking. Such a statement might identify the laws of a society and then provide a theoretical justification or criticism for them with the use of a prior-to-society perspective. While Stage 5 thinkers sometimes generate such moral theories (i.e., metaethical ones), it is their normative-ethical reasoning about particular dilemmas which we use in classifying them as Stage 5. This normative reasoning involves new justice operations in the sense in which justice operations were discussed in our earlier section on the primacy of justice. The fact that Stage 5 justice reasoning is not particularistic, 'existential' moral theorizing rooted in culturally-specific metaethical thinking is indicated by the fact that Stage 5 appears to be used by 'educated' persons in both Eastern countries as well as in the West [Nisan and Kohlberg, 1982; Parikh, 1980; Lei and Cheng, 1982; Snarey et al., 1982].

Another criterion of Piagetian or 'hard-stages' is their relationship to action. A variety of studies of judgment and action [Blasi, 1980; Kohlberg and Candee, 1983; Candee and Kohlberg, 1983a, b] indicate that Stage 5 judgment is more predictive of moral action than is any other lower stage. We introduce this evidence from the judgment-action research because it documents to us that our moral structures are, in fact, 'hard' structures and systems-in-action in the Piagetian sense.

Thus, while we do not agree with Gibbs' elimination of Stage 5 as a natural Piagetian hard stage, we do agree that moral development in adulthood beyond Stage 5 appears to be characterizable by metaethical and 'existential' reflection and theorizing, phenomena that can be studied with 'soft' stage models of epistemology [Perry, 1970], faith [Fowler, 1981], responsibility [Gilligan, 1982], and conceptions of 'the good life' [Erdynast et al., 1978].

As our discussion of the substage B construct indicates (see chapter 2, sections 6 and 10, part ix), thought content linked with the B-substage is not a matter of metaethics as moral theory but is firmly defined as a normative-ethical orientation to specific dilemmas. Finally, we note that Gibbs' argument that postconventional reasoning is rare and is therefore suspect as a natural Piagetian system-in-action, is a criticism we have already addressed in our reply to Simpson.

Habermas, J.: Moral Development and Ego Identity;
in Habermas, Communication and the Evolution of Society
(Beacon Press, Boston 1979)

Synopsis

In closing this reply to critics, we felt that a review of Habermas's [1979] article *Moral Development and Ego Identity* would be appropriate. While Habermas raises one criticism of Kohlberg's theory in this paper [i.e., that Kohlberg's theory is insufficient because it does not define a seventh stage) we understand his article, nevertheless, as a clarification and constructive extension of certain aspects of Kohlberg's work. Since this review of Habermas's article is selective, the reader is encouraged to read his book,

Communication and the Evolution of Society [1979], in order to gain a fuller appreciation of his important contribution to the moral development literature.

As was noted earlier, Habermas is a critical theorist who sees his task to be the theoretical reconstruction of social evolution at various levels of analysis; i.e., the interactive-communicative, the cognitive-affective, and the social-structural. For Habermas these levels of analysis reflect at an empirical level the three interacting and interpenetrating realities of communication, self, and society. Habermas investigates each of these levels of analysis by reconstructing what he perceives to be the developmental logic inherent in each. In other words, there are structures of communication, self, and society that can be ordered hierarchically from a developmental point of view. Habermas seems to use the words self and ego interchangeably and it is this unit of analysis with which the present review is primarily concerned. However, the reader should understand that invariably Habermas's perspective is both critical and social-psychological, and that for him any complete social inquiry must address the interaction between structures of communication, self, and society.

Moral Development and Ego Identity is an essay which describes and validates the logic of development Kohlberg employs to understand the ontogenesis of his moral stages. However, to understand how Habermas develops this justification of Kohlberg's perspective we must momentarily digress to a brief discussion of Habermas's theory of communication. (This discussion is based on his article *What Is Universal Pragmatics?*, to be found in *Communication and the Evolution of Society*, 1979.) Habermas's theory of communication is based on the assumption that the ontogenesis of the communicative competence necessary to engage in 'speech-acts' has universal and formal developmental characteristics. Specifically, Habermas argues that communicative competence evolves through three levels or structures of communicative action; i.e. incomplete interaction, complete interaction, and finally, communicative action and discourse. A fuller description of these structures will follow shortly. For the moment, it is important to understand the basic point; i.e., that communicative competence develops through these three stages of communicative action.

What is communicative competence? It is the ability to engage successfully in speech-acts, an ability acquired by an individual through the mastering of those rules of speech necessary to 'fulfill the conditions for a happy employment of sentences in utterances'.

For a speech-act to be competently performed, the speaker must utter his or her sentence in such a way that (a) its propositional content appears to fulfill the requirement of 'truth'; (b) its linguistic content expresses his or her intentions 'truthfully'; and (c) as an utterance, it is 'right' in the sense that it conforms to a recognized moral or normative context. In other words, communicative competence is manifested in the speaker's ability to 'embed a well-formed sentence in relation to reality' in a manner which is defined as acceptable by the hearer. The hearer must be able to share the speaker's knowledge, trust his or her expressions as sincere, and, finally, share the value-orientation implicated by the speech-act. Thus, speech-acts situate the speaker and hearer in an interpenetrating matrix composed of the following three 'reality domains': (a) '"The" world of external nature', about which we make statements of truth; (b) '"My" world of internal nature', about which we make truthful expressions of our needs and intentions; and (c) '"Our" world of society', about which we make statements implying rightness or legitimacy (and in so doing, normatively sanction interpersonal relationships). It is important to note that when situations arise that threaten to undermine consensus between speaker and hearer, then the former must articulate and successfully redeem assertions about truth, truthfulness, and rightness as explicitly raised validity claims.

In more simple terms, Habermas is stating (a) that communicative competence is the ability to articulate and, if necessary, argumentatively redeem claims of truth, truthfulness, and rightness through the medium of speech; and (b) that communicative competence is developmental in the sense that it is structured by three levels or stages of communicative action.

Before reviewing Habermas's perspective on moral reasoning we must first briefly comment on his conception of ego identity formation. For Habermas, the ideal endpoint of ego identity formation is a state of rational autonomy; i.e., a state of self-awareness and communicative competence which allows the individual to maintain and reinterpret his or her identity through 'communicative action'. Speech acts at the level of communicative action foster the autonomous realization of self through dependency on interaction with other individuals. The competence to engage in such speech action is based upon a post-sociocentric, 'postconventional' awareness of actions and motives of self and other and hence constructs and employs 'communally followed procedures' for redeeming validity claims of truth, truthfulness, and rightness. Ego identity as a state of rational autonomy is, in other words, a state in which both cognitive and affective components of self can be articulated and realized through a communicative process allowing

Table VIII.

General structures of communicative action					Qualifications of role behavior		
Cognitive presuppositions	Levels of interaction	Action levels	Action motivations	Actors	Perception of		
					Norms	Motives	Actors
I Preoperational thought	Incomplete interaction	Concrete actions and consequences of action	Generalized pleasure/pain	Natural identity	Understand and follow behavioral expectations	Express and fulfill action intentions (wishes)	Perceive concrete actions and actors
II Concrete operational thought	Complete interaction	Roles, systems of norms	Culturally interpreted needs	Role identity	Understand and follow reflexive behavioral expectations (norms)	Distinguish between 'ought' and 'want' (duty/inclination)	Distinguish between actions and norms, individual subjects and role bearers
III Formal-operational thought	Communicative action and discourse	Principles	Competing interpretations of needs	Ego identity	Understand and apply reflexive norms (principles)	Distinguish between heteronomy and autonomy	Distinguish between particular and general norms, individuality and ego in general

From Communication and the Evolution of Society, by Jürgen Habermas. Copyright 1979 by Beacon Press. Reprinted by permission of Beacon Press.

for 'discursive will formation'. Thus, for Habermas, ego identity is based on a notion of autonomy as dependent on interaction with others.

From the above discussion, it should be obvious that rather than being tangentially related to his theory of ego development, Habermas's theory of communication provides the conceptual basis for it. As we shall now see, this interpenetrating relationship associating communicative competence and ego development is displayed in Habermas's analysis of moral reasoning. For him, a moral judgment is a manifestation of the use of communicative skills to redeem a validity claim of rightness, which, in turn, is an interactive expression of ego identity formation.

It should now be noted, however, that when focussing on the topics of ego and moral development, Habermas speaks of interactive rather than communicative competence. Interactive competence is a concept which synthesizes the notion of communicative competence, developing within structures of communicative action, with (a) those cognitive stages whose existence must be assumed as prerequisites for communicative competence and (b) the ways in which social roles are perceived throughout the ontogenesis of communicative competence. This idea of interactive competence is represented in table VIII. The rows of table VIII represent the three levels of interactive competence (i.e., a synthesis of the competencies within 'General Structures of Communicative Action' with 'Qualifications of Role Behavior'). These levels of interactive competence are also depicted in the first two columns of table IX, where they are labelled 'Role Competence' by Habermas. It appears, from table VIII and IX, that Habermas considers levels of interactive competence as based in part upon transformations of an actor's perceptions of norms, motives, and other actors.

As we noted above, one of Habermas's major purposes in this paper is to validate the developmental logic underlying Kohlberg's stage hierarchy. Habermas accomplishes this task by deducing Kohlberg's stages of moral reasoning from his stages of interactive competence. For Habermas, moral reasoning can be appropriately seen as 'the ability to make use of interactive competence for consciously processing morally relevant conflicts of action' [p. 88]. Thus, moral reasoning can be understood as a facet of interactive competence, manifested in asserting a validity claim of rightness. As such, moral reasoning is, for Habermas, a manifestation of ego identity formation. Habermas [1979, p. 82] expresses his task of validating Kohlberg's stage hierarchy in the following manner[16]:

[16] From Communication and the Evolution of Society, by Jürgen Habermas. Copyright 1979 by Beacon Press. Reprinted by permission of Beacon Press.

Table IX.

Role competence			Stages of moral consciousness				
Age level	Level of communication	Reciprocity requirement	Stages of moral consciousness	Idea of the good life	Domain of validity	Philosophical reconstruction	Age level
I	Actions and consequences of action	Incomplete reciprocity	1	Maximization of pleasure – avoidance of pain through obedience	Natural and social environment		IIa
	Generalized pleasure/pain	Complete reciprocity	2	Maximization of pleasure – avoidance of pain through exchange of equivalents		Naive hedonism	
II	Roles	Incomplete reciprocity	3	Concrete morality of primary groups	Group of primary reference persons		IIb
	Culturally interpreted needs (Concrete duties)						
	Systems of norms		4	Concrete morality of secondary groups	Members of the political community	Concrete thought in terms of a specific order	
III	Principles	Complete reciprocity	5	Civil liberties, public welfare	All legal associates	Rational natural law	III
	Universalized pleasure/pain (utility)						
	Universalized duties		6	Moral freedom	All humans as private persons	Formalistic ethics	
	Universalized need interpretations		7	Moral and political freedom	All as members of a fictive world society	Universal ethics of speech	

From Communication and the Evolution of Society, by Jürgen Habermas. Copyright 1979 by Beacon Press. Reprinted by permission of Beacon Press.

'I should like to arrive at this goal through connecting moral consciousness with general qualifications for role behavior. The following steps serve this end: first I introduce structures of possible communicative action and, indeed, in the sequence in which the child grows into this sector of the symbolic universe. I then coordinate with these basic structures the cognitive abilities (or competencies) that the child must acquire in order to be able to move at the respective level of the social environment; that is, taking part first in incomplete interaction, then in complete interaction, and finally in communications that require passing from communicative action to discourse. Second I want to look at this sequence of general qualifications for role behavior (at least provisionally) from develop-mental-logical points of view in order, finally, to derive the stages of moral consciousness from these stages of interactive competence.'

Habermas derives Kohlberg's stages from his own stages of interactive competence through his emphasis on reciprocity as a fixed property of the structures of interaction possible at each level of communicative action.[17] As noted earlier, these structures of interaction are first incomplete interaction, then complete interaction, and, finally, communicative action and discourse (see column 2 of table VIII). With the assumption that reciprocity is not a norm per se but, rather, 'belongs eo ipso to the interactive knowledge of speaking and acting subjects', Habermas reasons that incomplete interaction, because of its egocentric nature, is compatible with either incomplete or complete reciprocity; that complete interaction is compatible only with incomplete reciprocity, and finally, that communicative action is compatible only with complete reciprocity (see column 3 of table IX). Based on this observation, Habermas [1979, pp. 89, 90] derives Kohlberg's stages. He states:

'Stages of moral consciousness can be derived by applying the requirement of reci-procity to the action structures that the growing child perceives at each of the different levels (table IX). At level 1, only concrete actions and action consequences (understood as gratifications or sanctions) can be morally relevant. If incomplete reciprocity is required here, we obtain Kohlberg's stage 1 (punishment obedience orientation); complete reciproc-ity yields stage 2 (instrumental hedonism). At level II the sector relevant to action is

[17] It is important to note that Habermas uses the concept of reciprocity to denote a property of interaction structures and, thus, this use of the concept should not be confused with our use of it to denote a justice operation. For Habermas, reciprocity as a fixed property of structures of interaction can be either complete or incomplete. (As a point of further clarification, this notion of complete or incomplete reciprocity should not be con-fused with Habermas's reference to complete or incomplete interaction.) For Habermas 'two persons stand in an incompletely reciprocal relation insofar as one may do or expect $\underline{x}$ only to the extent that the other may do or expect $\underline{y}$ (e.g., teacher/pupil, parent/child). Their relationship is completely reciprocal if both may do or expect the same thing in compara-ble situations $(\underline{x} = \underline{y})$'.

expanded; if we require incomplete reciprocity for concrete expectations bound to reference persons, we obtain Kohlberg's stage 3 (good boy orientation); the same requirement
for systems of norms yields stage 4 (law and order orientation). At level III principles
become the moral theme; for logical reasons complete reciprocity must be required. At this
level the stages of moral consciousness are differentiated according to the degree to which
action motives are symbolically structured. If the needs relevant to action are allowed to
remain outside the symbolic universe, then the admissible universalistic norms of action
have the character of rules for maximizing utility and general legal norms that give scope to
the strategic pursuit of private interests, under the condition that the egocentrism of the
second stage is literally raised to a principle; this corresponds to Kohlberg's stage 5 (contractual legalistic orientation). If needs are understood as culturally interpreted but
ascribed to individuals as natural properties, the admissible universalistic norms of action
have the character of general moral norms. Each individual is supposed to test monologically the generalizability of the norm in question. This corresponds to Kohlberg's stage 6
(conscience orientation). Only at the level of a universal ethics of speech (Sprachethik) can
need interpretations themselves – that is, what each individual thinks he should understand and represent as his "true" interests – also become the object of practical discourse.
Kohlberg does not differentiate this stage from stage 6 although there is a qualitative
difference: the principle of justification of norms is no longer the monologically applicable
principle of generalizability but the communally followed procedure of redeeming normative validity claims discursively. An unexpected result of our attempt to derive the stages of
moral consciousness from the stages of interactive competence is the demonstration that
Kohlberg's schema of stages is incomplete.'

Reply

The above review has emphasized Habermas's concern that we understand structures of moral reasoning as embedded within structures of communicative action. In understanding moral reasoning in this way, Habermas offers us a detailed analysis of what we believe Piaget [1932] meant
when he stated that 'apart from our relations to other people, there can be
no moral necessity'. What Habermas seems to be stating is that it is the
nature of our relations to other social actors, as defined by structures of
interactive competence and the property of reciprocity, that determines our
conceptions of moral necessity.

Before we address Habermas's claim that Kohlberg's stage hierarchy is
incomplete because it does not define a seventh stage, we wish to emphasize
the following point. In our view, Habermas's conceptualization of ego and
moral development does not define structures of justice reasoning per se. For
us, structures or 'hard' stages of justice reasoning include operations of
equality, equity, and reciprocity, operations which we understand as interpersonal interaction analogues of logical operations Piaget describes in the
cognitive domain. What Habermas's work appears to define are levels of
communicative and role competence which, together, seem to us to be anal-

ogous to Selman's social perspective-taking levels. If this interpretation is correct (and with it we certainly do not mean to imply that Habermas's article simply reflects Selman's work), then we understand Habermas's levels of interactive competence to have the same logical relationship to our structures of moral reasoning as do Selman's levels of social-perspective taking; i.e., we understand them as necessary but insufficient to define the structure of our moral stages. While the justice operations of our moral structures are transformed at each level of social perspective-taking, our structures are not conceptually reducible to social perspective-taking levels.

We will now address Habermas's claim to have discovered a seventh hard stage of moral reasoning. In this context, Habermas makes several observations which he sees as justifying his derivation of a seventh stage. As we implied above, he sees this seventh stage as both one of the manifestations of ego identity as well as one of the competencies contributing to the maintenance of ego identity. Ego identity is, from the perspective of Habermas's ideal speaker, an awareness of self and other as formative; i.e., as involved in a creative, on-going process of articulating and validating needs. This ideal endpoint of ego identity as an on-going process of discursive will-formation can only exist in an unfettered manner when its basis, interactive competence at the level of communicative action and discourse, is itself given free reign. In other words, speech, at the level of discourse, must be protected if ego identity is to emerge and be maintained. Thus, dialogue per se must be raised to the level of a principle.

In arguing for the principle of dialogue, for a 'communically-followed procedure for redeeming normative validity claims discursively', Habermas is defining and defending a universal speech ethic as the basis of an evolving, unconstrained, and autonomous ego. (One point of interest, which may have some bearing on certain aspects of Gilligan's critique (see above), is to be seen in Habermas's conception of ego autonomy. For him ego autonomy can only exist through dependency on others, since speech and interactive competence cannot exist otherwise. Thus Habermas's emphasis on the principle of dialogue denies the differentiation, which Gilligan makes, between separation and attachment and conceives of ego identity and a seventh stage of justice reasoning as dependent upon both.)

While Kohlberg's theory has not explicitly addressed the topics of ego identity or the development of communicative competence, we understand Habermas's treatment of these subjects as being consistent with our conception of human development generally, as well as with our conception of moral development specifically. We also appreciate the contribution Habermas's analysis is likely to have on subsequent research in the areas of ego and moral development. However, we believe that Habermas's derivation of a Stage 7 of justice reasoning is unnecessary since we understand our conception of Stage 6 as being consistent with his writing.

It appears that Habermas argues in favor of a seventh stage because he reasons that Kohlberg's conception of a sixth stage overlooks the principle of dialogue. However, in *Justice as Reversibility,* Kohlberg [1981b] attempted to include a process of dialogue in moral judgment-making via the introduction of his concept 'moral musical chairs' (i.e., ideal reversible role-taking). Though this process was primarily expressed in reference to a cognitive-moral structure we call Stage 6, it is based upon principles of respect for persons which are perfectly consistent with the notion of actually engaging in dialogue. Thus, we consider this aspect of Kohlberg's writings to be equivalent to Habermas's emphasis on the notion of 'discursive will-formation'.

Further evidence of the fact that we consider the principle of dialogue to be consistent with Kohlberg's Stage 6 descriptions can be seen in his work on moral education within 'just communities' [Kohlberg, 1982a]. In these intervention studies, Kohlberg employed actual dialogue over moral conflicts until a consensus was reached through the reciprocal modification of participants' understanding of their own needs.

It is probably because of the use of hypothetical dilemmas that the participatory and dialogic nature of the Stage 6 justice procedure has not been apparent. However, Kohlberg's position on the Stage 6 justice procedure is that in the 'moral musical chairs' activity of prescriptive role-taking one can only proceed so far intellectually. Kohlberg believes that his Stage 6 reasoning procedure logically requires dialogue in actual, real-life moral conflicts, otherwise its intention to achieve fairness could be easily subverted by an egocentric interpretation of the needs and perspectives of self and other. Thus, we disagree with Habermas's conception of Stage 6 as employing a 'monological' procedure. However, in closing this review, we may note that Habermas [1982] has come to agree with Kohlberg. He now understands monologic 'moral musical chairs' and dialogic discursive will-formation protected by a universal speech ethic as similar conceptions of a sixth stage of justice reasoning.

4. Summary and Conclusion

Kohlberg's last general statement of his theory of moral judgment development was published in 1976. The present volume represents a considerable amount of revision and expansion of the theory. While the 1976 statement has been fully supported by the longitudinal studies in America [Colby et al., 1983b], in Turkey [Nisan and Kohlberg, 1982], and in Israel [Snarey et al., 1982], both the work and the criticisms of other scholars such as Gilligan [1982], Habermas [1979], and Gibbs [1979] have led us (a) to enlarge the domain of moral development so as to include areas of 'soft stage' development as distinct from the development of our 'hard stages' of justice reasoning and (b) to develop some theoretical constructs basic for relating judgment to action, including our distinction between judgments of responsibility and judgments of justice, as well as our A-B substage distinction.

From a more philosophical view, we have softened our claims for having empirically defined and philosophically justified a final or sixth stage of moral reasoning. Along with this more tentative Stage 6 claim, we have distinguished the identity or isomorphism thesis between psychological theory and normative moral philosophic theory, postulated by Kohlberg [1971], from the complementarity thesis to which we now subscribe. We now argue that certain elements of our normative theory are assumed by our psychological theory and that empirical support for the latter gives some support to our normative claims. We hold that empirical evidence could nullify or undermine the plausibility of our normative claims but that it cannot positively 'prove' them. However, this weakening of our philosophic claims has not led us to abandon our theoretical construction of a sixth or highest stage, though the exact nature of this stage is in doubt both empirically and philosophically. We hold that the philosophic formulations of such writers as Rawls [1971], Habermas [1979], and Kohlberg [1973b] himself offer definitions of an endpoint of development which are necessary for defining stages as rational reconstructions of ontogenesis. We have pointed out, however, that even if psychologists do not choose to endorse our conception of a highest stage and our claims about the greater moral adequacy of each successive stage, they may find it useful, nevertheless, to accept the metaethical assumptions which we make in order to commence their scientific explorations in the field of moral development. Critics like Habermas, Gilligan, and Gibbs seem to accept our metaethical assumptions although they do question various aspects of our stage definitions, particularly our definitions of stages at the principled or postconventional level.

In this monograph we have tried to distinguish those issues about which we agree with our critics from those issues about which we disagree with them. In the instances of disagreement, we have tried to summarize both the logical considerations and the empirical findings which have led us to maintain our position. At this point, however, many of the issues we have raised are still open to debate; a debate which requires further empirical research as well as further philosophic reflection. One such issue for further research is the status of our hypothetical sixth stage. In this context we intend to use dilemmas central to our conception of a sixth stage instead of employing the standard dilemmas we have used in our longitudinal research. In addition, we also hold that this research will require the study of persons who have some recognized competence in making moral decisions in the adult social world; for example, judges, statesmen, etc.

In addition to the issue regarding Stage 6, we believe that much theoretical and empirical work remains to be done on the issue of understanding the relationship between moral judgment and action. Such work should yield information which will tell us more about the logical structure of our justice stages and about our claim that they form a hierarchy of increasing adequacy.

In conclusion, what we believe our critics have successfully accomplished with their writing is to highlight certain theoretical and methodological issues to which we must be sensitive. We do not believe that they have discovered that Kohlberg's work has been biased in any 'hard' sense of the word, but that his work and any other social scientific investigation can and would be biased if investigators do not take cognizance of the normative and metaethical assumptions they employ. In addition, we believe, in line with Weber [1949], Habermas [in press], and others, that objectivity is a 'moment' of scientific inquiry; that the essence or 'truth' value of objectivity does not reside in some reified, permanent, or factual quality inherent in the object of inquiry, but is, rather, to be found in and understood as a process of understanding which is the changing relationship between the investigator and what he or she observes. We believe that it is this theoretical and methodological orientation, aptly expressed in Habermas's notion of 'objective hermeneutics', that characterizes our work.

CHAPTER 5

The Relationship of Moral Atmosphere to Judgments of Responsibility

ANN HIGGINS, CLARK POWER, AND LAWRENCE KOHLBERG

Interventions in moral education based on a cognitive-developmental approach and on the structural-psychological theory of individual moral judgment development have been tried in prisons, halfway houses, and elementary and secondary schools since 1970. The core of these interventions were group moral discussion of hypothetical and practical dilemmas and democratic governance. The evaluations done usually reported individual moral-judgment-stage change. This is the first report of an evaluation of the moral atmosphere of three alternative democratic high schools and their three companion high schools. This chapter utilizes the distinction between hypothetical classical dilemmas and practical dilemmas introduced by Leming and the distinction between deontic or justice reasoning and responsibility reasoning introduced by Gilligan in the analysis of individual moral judgment. Second, this chapter describes and discusses the moral atmosphere of each school in terms of the existence and development of sociomoral collective norms and the valuing of community. Three student case studies and preliminary group results for four of the six schools are presented.

In the preceding chapter, Kohlberg and Candee hypothesized that between a deontic judgment of rightness or justice and a situational decision to act morally there is an intervening variable or process of judgment of responsibility on real-life decisions. Our discussion of judgments of rightness and responsibility is embedded in our discussion of the way in which each judgment is influenced by the moral atmosphere of a group or institution such as a school.

In Chapter 4, it is hypothesized that a judgment of responsibility is a mediating bridge from a deontic judgment of rightness and justice to moral action. In the Milgram experiment, for instance, it was found that higher-stage subjects quit shocking the stooge victim because of a judgment of responsibility, asserting that what was going on was their responsibility, not just that of the experimenter, despite the experimenter's assertion that he would take the responsibility for shocking the victim. Moral action usually takes place in a social or group context, and that context usually has a profound influence on the moral decision making of individuals. Individual moral decisions in real life are almost always made in the context of group norms or group decision-making processes. Moreover, individual moral action is often a function of these norms or processes. For example, in the massacre at My Lai during the Vietnam War, individual American soldiers murdered non-combatant women and children. They did so not primarily because, as individuals, their moral judgment that the action was morally right was immature, or because, as individuals, they were "sick" in some sense; they did so because they participated in what was essentially a group action taken on the basis of group norms. The moral choice made by each individual soldier who pulled the trigger was embedded in the larger institutional context of the army and its decision-making procedures. Their decisions were dependent in large part on a collectively shared definition of the situation and of what should be done about it. In short, the My Lai massacre was more a function of the group "moral atmosphere" that prevailed in that place at that time than of the stage of moral development of the individuals present. The realization of the important role that moral atmosphere or group norms play in individual moral action has led us to hypothesize that in many cases the best approach to moral education is one that attempts to reform the moral atmosphere in which individual decisions are made. This hypothesis has guided our interventions and research in the schools and prisons.

In the research reported here comparing judgments of responsibility and the moral atmosphere of democratic alternative high schools and traditionally governed high schools, we hypothesized that the democratic school students would both make more responsibility judgments and make them at a higher stage than would the regular school controls. There were two reasons we expected this. First, participatory democracy puts sociomoral decisions in the hands of the students, giving them a greater sense of responsibility for school-related actions. Second, participatory democracy, we believed, helps create a sense of the school as a caring community. Students would develop shared or collective norms of helping, of trust, and of active participation on behalf of the group, norms supported by a sense of community or of a valued sense of group solidarity and cohesion. Students' practical judgments of responsibility, we believed, would derive from their perception of the moral atmosphere of the school, that is, from their perception of the school's norms and the school's sense of itself as a community.

Having outlined our educational evaluation aims and hypothesis, we should add that our theoretical interest lay in developing concepts and measures that would bridge moral psychology and sociology. According to Durkheim's *Moral Education* (1925/1961), the classroom or school group creates collective norms and attachments to the group that are group phenomena *sui generis.* We believed him. We thought a Stage 3 collective norm is not the same thing as an average of individuals' stage judgments at Stage 3. In a school promoting moral development, collective norms would be formulated at a stage that was the leading edge for the group, and adapting to these norms would stimulate those students whose individual stage was lower to grow (Kohlberg, 1980, 1981; Power, 1979). Still more basically, we thought by building collective norms and ideas of community at a higher stage we would promote morally better student action.

In this chapter we discuss the moral judgment of groups of high school students about how they would act if certain prototypical high school dilemmas occurred in their school. One purpose of the research was that of formative educational evaluation, which had as its aim not only evaluating the effects of an intervention program but also providing categories of analysis that can be used conceptually to change and guide the ongoing intervention program. In our own work this means that the categories we use indicate the existence, sharedness, and strength of prosocial, moral norms and evidence of whether and how members of a school value it as a moral community.

1. PREVIOUS RESEARCH

Before presenting the method and results of our research on high schools, we need a brief review of previous work in the field on which we have tried to build. The three areas reviewed represent the three categories of variables used in our study: (1) the kinds of dilemmas, (2) the kinds of judgments, and (3) the influence of the moral atmosphere on moral reasoning.

A. Classical and Practical Moral Dilemmas: The Leming Study

The first scores in Table 5.3 are the stage scores of deontic judgment on standard dilemmas like the Heinz dilemma, which taps what we shall call *classical* moral judgments. The Standard Issue Scoring method used has proved to be useful for measuring individual longitudinal changes in a variety of cultures and subcultural settings. The very abstractness of the standard moral dilemma situations helps make them a standard test stimulus having similar meanings to individuals living in various cultural worlds. Their focus on what someone in general, Heinz, *should* do minimizes nonmoral personality and situational variations in responses that might be brought out by the question, What would you do? As a result, it yields a good picture of the student's moral judgment *general competence,* regardless of variations in personality and situation that might influence his or her specific moral judgment *performance.*

In addition to being abstract and hypothetical, and in addition to asking for *should* and not for *would* answers, the standard dilemmas are primarily dilemmas of justice. They pose a conflict between the rights of one person (Heinz's wife) and that of another (the druggist). Alternately stated, they oppose one social norm (respecting property) to another social norm (respecting life). The resolution of such justice conflicts requires reference to a principle, such as the utilitarian principle of the greater good or the justice principle of equal respect for each person. The rules or principles just cited are those found at Stage 5, but each stage has its characteristic rules or principles of choice.

In our study of democratic schools, we were less interested in students' general moral judgment competence about justice than we were interested in how students actually made real-life moral decisions in action. Research reviews by Blasi (1980) and by Kohlberg and Candee (Chap. 4) show that classical moral judgment correlates with, or predicts to, moral action in naturalistic and experimental situations. These correlations, however, tell us little about the process of moral decision making or about moral judgment in action.

Leming (1973, 1976) started exploration of a somewhat different method for studying moral judgment related to action, the method of studying "practical," as distinct from "classical," moral judgment. According to Leming, the standard dilemmas tap classical moral judgment for two reasons. First, it is classical because of the type of dilemma—abstract hypothetical dilemmas rather than dilemmas representative of the respondents' life space, that is, more "real-life" dilemmas. Second, it is classical because it asks for deontic or prescriptive moral judgment, and a deontic judgment alone. It asks, Should Heinz or anyone have stolen the drug, was he right or wrong? In contrast, says Leming, practical decision making is in the deliberative mode, What will or would you do if you were in Heinz's situation? This mode is future oriented, it is concrete (What would *you* do), and it is descriptive (What *would* you do), not simply prescriptive (What *should* you do?).

Real moral decision making is not only a prescription but also a description of facts of the situation and of the self's needs and motives and those of others in an integrated deliberative practical judgment. In calling the judgment elicited by the standard test prescriptive, we may elaborate and call them, in the terms of moral philosophy, deontic (Frankena, 1973) judgments of the right, or judgments of duty and obligation.

Our reasons for calling classical moral judgments deontic will become clearer after we report Leming's actual findings. Leming set up four cells to represent his basic practical-classical distinction. One cell involved classical dilemmas with prescriptive moral reasoning; one with classical dilemmas with deliberative reasoning; one with real dilemmas with prescriptive moral reasoning; and one with real dilemmas with deliberative reasoning. Leming interviewed 60 7th- and 12th-grade students, filling all four cells for each student. He used three classical (standard hypothetical) dilemmas and three practical (or more everyday real-life) dilemmas. The first practical dilemma centered on a choice involving deception of one's parents in order to go to a party. The second dilemma dealt with the issue of cheating on a school assignment, and the third with a peer group conflict. Leming's results were just what he and common sense might expect. First, Leming had little difficulty in stage scoring practical judgment, using the Kohlberg 1972 Clinical Issue Rating System. Even though the stage descriptions were meant to classify prescriptive reasoning about justice, Leming had little difficulty classifying pragmatic exchanges in the peer group or family as Stage 2, or concerns about hurting the feelings and expectations of others as Stage 3. Stage scores in classical moral judgment correlated well with other classical dilemmas ($r = 80$), less well with deliberative judgments on the classical dilemmas ($r = 70$), and least well with deliberative judgments on the real dilemmas ($r = 60$) (Leming, 1976). Of more importance, Leming found that practical judgment was systematically lower than classical judgment. Students scoring Stage 3 in classical moral judgment were often Stage 2 in practical moral judgment. This result corresponds to the commonsense expectation that classical moral judgment taps highest competence, the moral "high road," whereas more real-life practical judgment is more likely to take the "low road." It is plausible to believe that Leming's assessment of practical judgment is more likely to represent performance, that is, real-life moral decisions, than is assessment of classical moral judgment.

B. Responsibility and Deontic Reasoning on Practical Moral Dilemmas: The Gilligan and Belenky Studies

In 1976 Carol Gilligan and Mary Belenky reported in preliminary form the results of their clinical interviews with women in the process of making the decision as to whether to have an abortion. Not only were their interviews of Leming's practical-reasoning type but they also were not typically framed as deontic justice dilemmas. The framing was left to the subjects. The dilemma was typically not framed by the women subjects as a justice conflict between the fetus's right to life and the mother's rights violated by the existence of an unwanted child; rather, they were typically framed as conflicts of caring and responsibility. Gilligan and Belenky interpreted that these caring and responsibility judgments emerge directly from intrinsically valued relationships or connectedness of persons, not from balancing individual rights through reciprocity and contract. In addition to dilemmas of justice, our high school students also faced these dilemmas of caring or responsibility. Caring dilemmas, as studied by Gilligan (1977), Eisenberg-Berg (1976), and Mussen and Eisenberg-Berg (1977), put in conflict individual responsibility for the care of the self and social responsibility for the care and welfare of another person or a group. The intrinsically moral quality of relations *per se* suggested by Gilligan and Belenky and Eisenberg-Berg is somewhat like Durkheim's belief that the sheer existence of a solidary group creates moral responsibilities, obligations, and aspirations.

Gilligan (1977) builds partly on H. Richard Niebuhr's *The Responsible*

Self (1963), which suggests that in addition to a "civic" deontological rules and justice orientation and a teleological or utilitarian orientation, there is a third "responsibility" orientation, the responsiveness of a social self in a network of relations with other selves.

Drawing on Gilligan, we have in Table 5.1 outlined the elements of a responsibility orientation or a responsibility judgment. Lyons (1982) has developed a complex and reliable method for classifying orientations to personal moral dilemmas as either care oriented or rights oriented, or a mixture of both. She has found that males tend to respond more in the rights orientation and females more in the care orientation but that a majority of both males and females show use of both orientations.

The coding system developed by Lyons based on Gilligan's research was not available at the time we scored our school dilemmas, nor did the distinctions we wished to make exactly correspond to the Gilligan and Lyons notion of two independent moral orientations of rights and of care. Instead, we thought that deontic judgments of rightness were often embedded in judgments of responsibility but that judgments of responsibility went beyond deontic judgments in a number of ways.

In designing our school dilemmas, we enlarged the sphere from our classical dilemmas of justice to dilemmas of care, responsibility, and altruistic action. We also sensitized ourselves to listening to practical judgments made in the language of responsibility as well as in the deontic language of rightness and justice. Gilligan, Lyons, and Langdale (Note 1) have just begun exploring definitions of stages in the responsibility or care orientation. With the need to complete our project, we made up a rough scoring manual for Stages 2–4 for both deontic and responsibility judgments for school practical moral dilemmas. The criteria and rules that we used to define and score judgments of responsibility and a tabular summary of the responsibility stages on our practical school dilemmas are given in Table 5.1.

C. Moral Atmosphere: The Scharf and Hickey Studies

At the same time Leming conducted his study, Kohlberg, Scharf, and Hickey (1972) conducted a different study pointing in the same direction, although the interpretations at the time were different. The starting point of the Scharf (1973) study was observations in conducting moral discussion of real and hypothetical dilemmas in a group at the Cheshire Reformatory. Inmates' judgments and reasoning appeared to be higher concerning hypothetical dilemmas, both the standard test dilemmas and the hypothetical group discussion dilemmas, than were their judgments about real Cheshire Reformatory dilemmas. Furthermore, the way they judged prison dilemmas in the group discussions was different from the way they reported making decisions when they were out of the group and back on the cell block.

To test these observations, Scharf (1973) designed a set of real-life or practical prison dilemmas and gave them to both the discussion group mem-

TABLE 5.1. Criteria for Judgments of Responsibility and Stages of Responsibility Judgments

A. Judgments of responsibility go beyond deontic judgments in one of four ways:

    1. Judgments that consider the needs and welfare of the other as an individual where the other's welfare seems to be a matter of a right or claim the other has or where it is a matter of not harming the other's welfare is a deontic concern. Judgments that consider filling the other's need when it is not based on a right or claim or where it is a matter of enhancing his or her welfare, not just preventing harm, is a responsibility concern.

    2. Judgments of responsibility consciously consider the involvement and implication of the self in the action or in the welfare consequences to the other.

    3. Judgments of personal moral worth (aretaic) of the kind of self the actor wants to be (perfecting character) or would be if he or she failed to perform the action (judgments of blame, guilt, loss of integrity) are judgments of responsibility when explicitly used as a basis for action rather than rights or obligations.

    4. Judgments that use an intrinsic valuing of social relationships such as friendship or relationships of community as justification for performing a moral action are judgments of responsibility.

B. Stages of responsibility judgments:

Stage 1. Responsibility and obligation are seen as being the same. The person feels compelled to fulfill the commands of superiors or authority figures or the rules given by them.

Stage 2. Responsibility is differentiated from obligation from this stage onward. The person is responsible only to and for himself or herself and his or her welfare, property, and goals.

Stage 2/3. There is a recognition that everyone is responsible to and for themselves, their welfare, property, and goals. Persons who are irresponsible or careless lose some of the right to have themselves, their welfare, and so on, respected. For example, being careless mitigates the right to have one's property respected as well as justifying a lessened concern for the person's welfare.

Stage 3. Responsibility for the self is to do the "good" thing, to live up to generally known and accepted standards of a "good person." Responsibility to others is limited to those with whom one has a personal relationship and is defined as meeting their needs or promoting their welfare.

Stage 3/4. Responsibility is seen more as a process for maintaining and enhancing feelings of closeness and affection in personal relationships. Being irresponsible is defined as "hurting the other's feelings" within a relationship and is considered a valid basis for a lessened concern of the other's welfare.

Stage 4. Responsibility is seen as a mutually binding set of feelings and agreements among people in relationships, groups, or communities. Being responsible for the self means one must act out of dependability, trustworthiness, and loyalty regardless of fluctuating feelings among people. Irresponsibility on the part of those people within the same group does not mitigate concern for their welfare or rights by other group members.

80

bers and to control group prisoners involved in a larger study. Like the Leming practical dilemmas, the prison dilemmas elicited much "would" or deliberative judgments as well as eliciting some deontic rights and duty judgments. If Leming found Stage 3 classical moral judgments on the standard dilemmas giving way to more Stage 2 judgments on the practical dilemmas, Scharf found this effect in spades in the prison. He found that "none of the 34 inmates scored higher on the prison dilemmas than on the standard non-prison dilemmas. Of the 16 inmates characterized as Stage 3 on non-prison dilemmas, for example, 11 were rated as Stage 2 on the prison dilemmas. Inmates tended to see relationships with other inmates in Stage 2 instrumental terms. Inmates were seen as 'ripping' each other off, 'ratting' on their friends and 'punking' weaker inmates" (Kohlberg, Scharf, & Hickey, 1972, p. 6).

At the time these researchers did not think clearly of what their findings might mean for moral deliberation and action in general. Instead, they saw it as a statement of what they called the moral atmosphere of the prison. More generally, it indicated that practical moral judgment is not simply a product of a fixed property of the individual, his or her moral competence, but is a product of the interaction between his or her competence and the moral features of the situation, what we also term the "moral atmosphere" of the social situation in which he or she makes decisions.

In our view, the Stage 2 practical reasoning of the prisoners with Stage 3 competence in classical moral judgment was more a function of the prison environment than of the prisoners as personalities. We would characterize the real environment of prison guards and inmate peer groups as a Stage 2 environment or moral atmosphere, and inmates' Stage 2 practical judgments were a realistic adaptation to it. Again then, the Scharf study got closer to action or performance stage, but by tapping something that mixes the level of the environment with the level of individual moral judgment. The Scharf study addressed the moral atmosphere component of practical moral judgment but did not elaborate a systematic method for its study, a task taken up in the present research.

2. METHODOLOGY OF THE HIGH SCHOOL STUDY

A. Samples

The research project included samples of between 20 and 30 students from each of six high schools. The results reported in this chapter are preliminary, including about two-thirds of the students from only four schools.

Three of the six groups of students attended public alternative schools within the larger high school. The other three attended the regular high school counterparts of these alternative schools. The three alternative schools made and enforced rules and settled issues of fairness in a weekly community meeting based on participatory democracy—one person, one vote, whether teacher or student. The school-wide democratic meeting had 60–90 participants, depending on the size of the alternative school. It was preceded by a small group discussion of the moral issues in the decisions to be made, discussions with 10–20 students and a teacher leader.

We expected and found individual moral stage change on the standard hypothetical justice dilemmas in the alternative school students compared with controls in the regular high schools. The upward change in individual moral reasoning was about a quarter stage per year for the alternative school students in two of the three schools. This is the expected change from a good moral discussion program. Such change, however, was not the focus of our research interest. Our focus was on developing two related kinds of assessment: first, an assessment of the presence of and stage of judgments of responsibility on the real school dilemmas, and second, an assessment and comparison of the differences in the moral atmosphere between the alternative schools and their companion traditional high schools.

B. Types of Dilemmas

Table 5.2 presents the four school dilemmas used in the present study. All of the four dilemmas used in the current study we have classified as practical dilemmas as defined by Leming; that is, they ask about situations in the students' own school, and they ask how students think they would reason and act and how their peers would reason and act as well as how they should reason and act.

TABLE 5.2.   The Practical School Dilemmas

---

1. Caring Dilemma

The college Harry applied to had scheduled an interview with him for the coming Saturday at 9:00 A.M. As the college was 40 miles away from Harry's town and Harry had no way of getting there, his guidance counselor agreed to drive him. The Friday before the interview the guidance counselor told Harry that his car had broken down and was in the repair shop until Monday. He said he felt badly but there was no way he could drive him to his interview. He still wanted to help him out, so he went to Harry's homeroom and asked the students if there was anyone who could drive Harry to the college. No one volunteered to drive him. A lot of students in the class think Harry shows off and talks too much, and they do not like him. The homeroom teacher says he has to take his children to the dentist at that time. Some students say they cannot use the family car, others work, some do not have their licenses. One student, Billy, knows he can use his family car but wonders whether he should do something for Harry when the few students in class who know him best say they are busy or just cannot do it. Besides, he would have to get up really early on a Saturday morning, the only morning during the week he can sleep late.

1.   Should Billy volunteer to drive Harry to the college? Why or why not?

2. Restitution Dilemma

Tom took the money. When Mary returns to the classroom she looks into her pocketbook and notices the 20-dollar bill is missing. She goes to the teacher and reports what has happened. The teacher asks the person to return the money, but no one does. Zeke, a friend of Tom, saw Tom take the money.

1. Should Zeke persuade Tom to return the money? Why?
2. If Zeke tries to persuade Tom to restitute and Tom will not, should Zeke report Tom to the teacher?
3. If no one in the class admits to taking the money or knowing who did it, what should the teacher do? Why?
4. Would there be a general feeling or an expectation in your school that everyone should chip in? Are people supposed to chip in?
5. Would you expect all members of your school to chip in? Would you feel that any member of your school because he or she is a member of your school should chip in? Why?

3. Stealing Dilemma

When Mary arrived at her history class, she noticed that although the students were all there, the teacher had not arrived. She sat down for a few seconds but decided to chat with a few of her friends in the hall until the teacher came. She opened her pocketbook, pulled out a letter she wanted to show her friends, and ran out of the classroom, leaving her pocketbook unsnapped and lying on her desk. Tom, a student in the class, looks into Mary's pocketbook and sees a 20-dollar bill. He thinks about taking the 20-dollar bill from her pocketbook.

1. What do you think a student like Tom would do in a situation like this? Why?
2. Should Mary have been trusting like that in this situation, or should she have been more careful?

4. Drug Dilemma

Before the junior class trip the faculty told the students that the whole class had to agree not to bring or use alcohol or drugs on the trip. If students were found using drugs or alcohol, they would be sent home. The students knew that without faculty approval they would not be able to have their trip. The students said in a class meeting that they all agreed to these conditions. On the trip, several students ask Bob, a fellow student, to go on a hike with them to the lake. When they get to the lake, they light up a joint and pass it around.

1. Should Bob refuse to smoke? Why or why not?

The first two dilemmas we have labeled as prosocial discretionary, following the use of the concept "prosocial" put forth by Eisenberg-Berg (1976) for labeling hypothetical dilemmas given to school children. We call them discretionary because although the actions involved are usually considered to be good, the carrying out of these actions is not usually considered a duty or obligation. The first example is the caring dilemma.

The second example involves a class decision about whether collectively to restitute to a member of the class for the money stolen from her pocketbook by an unknown member of the class. This involves a prosocial and discretionary action by the other members of the class for the victim.

The third dilemma is a mandatory justice dilemma that asks whether anyone should or would steal money from a purse lying open and unattended in a classroom. Obviously, in a dilemma such as this there is consensual agreement by most students that it would be wrong for the protagonist to steal money for reasons of justice, that is, that it is a violation of the property rights of the victim. Even though a deontic justice judgment that it is mandatory not to steal is made, it is possible that a practical judgment to steal could be made by the self or for other students.

The fourth dilemma about the use of marijuana comes close to the type that Turiel (1980) has classified as conventional. In this dilemma the prescription of not smoking arises from a particular organizational school rule rather than from inherent moral justice considerations of violating the rights of other individuals. Our drug dilemma does not fit the strict definition of conventionality offered by Turiel, for laws have been made against it on the grounds that smoking marijuana is inherently harmful to the smoker. This inherent harmfulness, however, is questioned by many adolescents and adults today.

C. Variables of Individual Moral Judgments and Choices

There are six variables used to describe the individual's ways of moral reasoning. Variable 1 is the stage score (and moral maturity score) for the classical standard moral dilemmas (Forms A or B). The remaining five variables are all categories of responses to the four practical school dilemmas described in the previous section. Variable 2 is a stage score of deontic reasoning. Variable 3 is a stage score of responsibility reasoning. Both of these are "moral judgment" scores assigned to material determined to be in either the deontic or the responsibility orientations according to the criteria in Table 5.1. Each individual, then, can have three moral stage scores but will always have at least two, one based on responses to the standard dilemmas and one based on responses to the school dilemmas.

Variable 4 is the proportion of the use of responsibility judgments over all judgments made in the school dilemmas and is reported as a percentage.

Variables 5 and 6 are the frequencies (in percentages) of making the prosocial (should) moral choice for oneself (Variable 5) and of predicting that one would act in the prosocial way across the four school dilemmas (Variable 6).

These variables are listed in Table 5.3 in the same order as presented here. That table gives both case study and group results.

D. Variables of the Moral Atmosphere

There are seven variables we have constructed to describe and analyze the moral atmosphere of a school. In this chapter we define and describe them in terms of how they appear in individual school dilemma interview material. We should note here that five of these variables were first constructed using group community meeting transcripts as the data base. Only the first two variables are unique to the individual interview data.

Table 5.4 presents both the case study and group results of the perception of the moral atmosphere for the following seven variables in the order described herein.

TABLE 5.3. Summary of Results for Four Schools: Group Medians of Individual Moral Judgments and Choices

Variable	Brookline High School	(Jay)	School-Within-A-School	(Sarah)	Cambridge High School	(Rob)	Cluster School	(Betsy)
1. Median classical hypothetical moral judgment stage	3/4 (318 MMSᵃ)	(3/4) (317 MMS)	3/4 (330 MMS)	(3/4) (335 MMS)	3 (287 MMS)	(3/4) (321 MMS)	3 (305 MMS)	(3/4) (345 MMS)
2. Median practical school deontic stage	3	(3/4)	3/4	(3/4)	2/3	(2/3)	3	(3)
3. Median practical school responsibility stage	2/3	(2/3)	3/4	(3/4)	3	—	3/4	(3/4)
4. Proportion of all judgments that are responsibility judgments	12%	(75%)	55%	(66%)	3%	(0%)	46%	(75%)
5. Frequency of prosocial choice for self	75%	(50%)	86%	(75%)	66%	(50%)	83%	(100%)
6. Frequency of predicted prosocial behavior for self	61%	(50%)	77%	(75%)	63%	(50%)	74%	(75%)
Number of students	10		16		15		20	

ᵃ Moral maturity score.

201

TABLE 5.4. Summary of Results for Four Schools: The Moral Atmosphere

Variable	Brookline High School	(Jay)	School-Within-A-School	(Sarah)	Cambridge High School	(Rob)	Cluster School	(Betsy)
7. Frequency of perceived prosocial choice for others	34%	(0%)	81%	(75%)	45%	(50%)	84%	(100%)
8. Frequency of predicted prosocial behavior for others	26%	(0%)	67%	(50%)	34%	(25%)	58%	(75%)
9. Median degree of collectiveness of norms (1–15)	4	(2 and 5)	11	(12)	4	(1 and 6)	13	(14)
10. Stage of collective norm as represented at median degree or above of collectiveness	3	(2/3)	3/4	(3/4)	2/3	(2/3)	3/4	(3/4)
11. Modal phase of norms	0	(0)	4	(5)	0	(0)	4	(4)
12. Median degree of community valuing (1–4)	1	(0)	3	(3)	0	(1)	3	(4)
13. Median stage of community valuing	2	—	3/4	(3)	2/3	(2/3)	3	(3/4)

Variables 7 and 8 are the frequencies in percentages of students' perceptions of their peers' prosocial *should* choices and a prediction of whether their peers *would* actually act in the prosocial manner across the four school dilemmas.

Variables 9, 10, and 11 are three related ways of characterizing the prosocial moral norms highlighted in the four dilemmas. They are norms of caring or helping, of restituting collectively, of trusting and of upholding property rights, and of upholding the community's rules against drug use. Variable 9 is a measure of the degree to which a norm is collectively shared by members of a school *because* they are members of the school. The scheme for categorizing norms by degree of collectiveness is given in Table 5.5. Variable 10 is the stage of the norms as represented at the median degree of collectiveness or above. Our research assumes that a group norm can be perceived as being at a certain stage that is not necessarily the same as the average stage of individual judgments relevant to that norm. The last variable concerned with norms, Variable 11, is a measure of the strength of the expectations a group has that its norms will be upheld. We call this the phase of the norm. Because phase is the measure of the strength of group norms held in common, norms held only by individuals as personal values are given a phase score of 0. In terms of our scoring rules, this means that norms categorized between 1 and 6 on degree of collectiveness have no phase.

TABLE 5.5.   Degree of Collectiveness of Norms

1.	I—Rejection	No one can make a rule or agreement in this school that would be followed or taken seriously.
		Descriptive. I as an individual. No group constituency.
2.	I—Conscience	An action in accordance with the norm should not be expected or demanded by the group because it should be left to each individual's free choice.
		Prescriptive. Could be descriptive. I as an individual.
3.	I—No awareness	Does not perceive the existence of a shared norm concerning this issue and does not take a position pro or con about the group developing such a norm. Also does not have an individual norm concerning this issue.
		Descriptive. I as an individual. Group constituency.
4.	I—Individual	An action should be performed that is in accordance with the norm where this action is not defined or implied by membership in the group. There is no suggestion that the task of the group is or should be to develop or promote the norm.
		Prescriptive. I as an individual. Constituency is universal, applied to people in the group as much as to people outside the group.
5.	I—Individual ambiguous	An action should be performed that is in accordance with the norm where this action is implied by membership in the group.
		Prescriptive. I as an individual. Constituency is ambiguous but seems to apply to people in the group more than to those outside.

TABLE 5.5 **(Continued)**

6. Authority	An action should be performed because it is expected or demanded by the teacher or administrator whose authority derives from his or her status or the law that makes the teacher a superior member of the group.
	Prescriptive or Descriptive. Teacher as authority. Group constituency.
7. Authority—Acceptance	An action should be performed because it is expected by authority or law with the clear implication that the group accepts this authority and thinks promoting and upholding the norm is in the interest of the group's welfare.
	Prescriptive. Teacher as authority. Group constituency. The speaker perspective is the individual speaking as if he or she and others have internalized the norm.
8. They—Aggregate (I disagree)	They, the group or a substantial subgroup, have a tendency to act in accordance with a norm in a way that the individual speaker does not share or disagrees with.
	Prescriptive or Descriptive. I as a member of the group. Group constituency.
9. I and they—Aggregate	They and I have a tendency to act in the same way in accordance with a norm.
	Prescriptive or Descriptive. I and they as members of the group. Group constituency.
10. Limiting or Proposing I	The speaker thinks the group or all members of the group should follow or uphold this norm better or should have this new norm. (This category overlaps with Phase I—Proposing.)
	Prescriptive. I as a member of the group. Group constituency.
11. Spontaneous—Collective	They or they and I think that group members should act in accordance with the norm *because* they feel naturally motivated to do so due to the sense of belonging to the group.
	Descriptive. They and I as members of the group. Group constituency.
12. They—Limited collective	They think that group members should act in accordance with the norm without the speaker identifying himself or herself with that normative expectation. The speaker can differentiate his or her own normative perspective.
	Prescriptive. They as members of the group. Group constituency.
13. I and they—Limited collective	Both I and they, as members of the group, think that group members should act in accordance with the norm.
	Prescriptive. I and they as members of the group. Group constituency.
14. Implicit—We collective	The members of this group think that all of us should act in accordance with the norm.
	Prescriptive. Speaker perspective is group member qua group member.
15. Explicit—We Collective	We, the members of this group, think that we should act in accordance with the norm.
	Prescriptive. We (explicitly stated), members qua members. Group constituency.

The two remaining variables are Variable 12, the degree of community valuing, and Variable 13, the stage of community valuing. Degree of community valuing is a four-point scale roughly categorizing the extent to which members of a school value their school as a community for its own sake. This measure is described in Table 5.6. The stages of community valuing are given in Table 5.7.

3.   STUDENT CASE ILLUSTRATIONS OF THE METHOD

The following three cases are prototypical members of three of the schools studied. These students' Standard Form moral judgment scores are all the same and are close to the averages for their groups. We quote from these cases to illustrate how the practical school dilemmas are scored and the meaning of the variables listed in the preceding sections.

The students are from Brookline High School, Cambridge Rindge and Latin School, and the Cluster School of Cambridge, Massachusetts. Their individual scores appear in parentheses beside the scores for their groups in Tables 5.3 and 5.4. These tables also include the scores of a prototypical student from the Brookline alternative school, School-Within-A-School, although considerations of chapter length precluded discussion of that case.

A.   The Case of Jay

Jay is a 10th-grader in the regular Brookline High School, a school composed primarily of adolescents from middle and professional classes. Most of the students in this school are white and most are either Jewish or Irish-Catholic. Of the 10% black minority, most are bused to the high school.

TABLE 5.6.   Degree of Community Valuing

I.	Instrumental extrinsic	The school is valued as an institution that helps the individual to meet his or her own academic needs.
II.	"Esprit de corps" extrinsic	The school is valued as an institution that helps the individual and that the individual feels some loyalty toward as manifest in team spirit and support of teams or groups in school.
III.	Spontaneous community intrinsic	The school is valued as the kind of place in which members feel an inner motivation to help others in the group community and the community generates special feelings of closeness among members.
IV.	Normative communal intrinsic	The school as a community is valued for its own sake. Community can obligate its members in special ways, and members can expect special privileges or responsibilities from the group and other members.

TABLE 5.7.   Stages of the Sense of Community Valuing

Stage 2

There is no clear sense of community apart from exchanges among group members. Community denotes a collection of individuals who do favors for one another and rely on one another for protection. Community is valued insofar as it meets the concrete needs of its members.

Examples:

The community is like a "bank." Members meet to exchange favors, but you cannot take more than you give.

Stage 3

The sense of community refers to a set of relationships and sharings among group members. The group is valued for the friendliness of its members. The value of the group is equated with the value of its collective normative expectations.

Examples:

1.   The community is a family in which members care for one another.
2.   The community is honorable because it helps others.

Stage 4

The school is explicitly valued as an entity distinct from the relationships among its members. Group commitments and ideals are valued. The community is perceived as an organic whole composed of interrelated systems that carry on the functioning of the group.

Examples:

Stealing affects "the community more than the individual because that is what we are. We are not just a group of individuals."

On the classical hypothetical moral dilemmas Jay was Stage 3/4. This transitional stage was the median stage for the regular Brookline High School comparison sample.

In the classical dilemmas Jay demonstrates a sense of justice obligating him to keep contracts and trusts even to unrelated strangers based on golden rule reciprocity. His sense of obligation to help an unrelated stranger in the Heinz dilemma is very different from his response to the first practical school dilemma, the caring dilemma. In answering this dilemma, Jay equates obligation with responsibility and concludes that he is not responsible to or for a stranger. See Table 5.2 for the dilemma stories.

Should Billy volunteer to drive Harry to college?

I don't think he has any obligation. If I was in his place, and I didn't know the kid too well, if I wanted to sleep late, I don't feel that it is my responsibility to go drive somebody to their interview, it is up to them, they are responsible. If I were going there, if I had an interview there at the same time, sure I would. But if I had the opportunity to sleep late and didn't know the kid at all, I wouldn't.

Why is it not a responsibility?

It's not really that you are obligated to a person because you are more responsible to yourself and your actions. I know I have been through this year, a whole mess of garbage with my friends about driving around since I got my license. People seem to think as long as you have a car they have a ride, and in my opinion it doesn't operate that way. If I wanted to give him a ride, I will give him a ride, if I am going there and they want to go there. It is my car and I am the one who is driving, and I don't see why I should give him a ride.

You think you shouldn't give them a ride?

It doesn't mean I shouldn't give them a ride, but if I don't know them well enough, I think just out of protection for myself and my property, I wouldn't. I think people may say that being responsible to yourself is more important than other pople. I think there is an extent where you put yourself first. And when you believe in putting yourself first, like I do, or try to at least, I don't feel I should be obligated to do somebody else's work, especially if I don't know them, I don't think I should give them a ride.

Jay helps us to understand the relation between two kinds of judgment, deontic judgments of duty and judgments of responsibility.

We could say one has a responsibility to drive Harry without implying Harry has a right to be driven. *Responsibility* is sometimes a stronger word than *duty,* sometimes a weaker word. Responsibility is weaker in the caring dilemma in that one may have some responsibility to drive Harry even though prosocial caring for the other is supererogatory, driving is an altruistic act beyond the call of duty. *Responsibility* may be a stronger word than *duty* as in a justice dilemma. A stranger dying in the Heinz dilemma may have a right to live, and one may have a duty to maintain the right, but one would not ordinarily be said to have a responsibility for the stranger's life in the sense one does for one's spouse's life.

Jay's introduction of his idea of responsibility into the caring dilemma helps us make sense of the discrepancy between the moral stage or level of his response to that dilemma and his response to the Standard Form moral dilemmas.

In the caring dilemma Jay understands full well the Stage 3 niceness of helping Harry. But he makes a Stage 2/3 judgment of individualistic responsibility in making his decision. A judgment of responsibility, as Gilligan points out, depends on the positing of a social bond or relationship as necessary. Jay posits a relationship of friendship but defines it in Stage 2/3 reciprocity terms. He says, "I think it really depends on the relationship of a person to the person who needs a ride. If they are good friends I don't think he has an obligation. I think it would be nice and I know if it was my friend, if it was an important interview, he would do the same for me, then I would do it." As noted before, a brief summary of our definitions of stages in judgments of responsibility is given in Table 5.1.

We think that responsibility judgments are a species of practical judgment; they are not readily elicited by the standard justice dilemmas. Jay speedily falls into psychological or *would* language in explaining his idea of responsibility in the caring dilemma. Responsibility language is at the intersection between prescriptive moral structures and the descriptive language of an acting self.

The question remains, however, of whether Jay's Stage 2/3 response to the caring dilemma is due to his practical moral judgment being lower than his classical moral judgment or whether it is because his responsibility judgments are lower than his deontic judgments. In our opinion, it is the latter case. We hypothesized that the stage development of an orientation or judgment of responsibility lags behind development of deontic judgments if there is a discrepancy between the two. In the caring dilemma Jay makes only a judgment of responsibility. We find Jay is consistently at a lower stage in his judgments of responsibility than in deontic judgments as we move from a caring situation to a justice situation, stealing, in which he makes both types of judgment.

In responding to the practical school dilemma of stealing, the third dilemma, he says, "I would leave the money there because I respect people's property because I expect them to do that to my property. I know it is a big temptation but its her money, she earned it however way she did. Besides it being against the law, it's also respect of a person's property, and you don't have any right to take it just because you want it. Otherwise we would have a pretty sick society with no laws and with chaos." Jay's use of deontic justice reasoning in this response is indicated by his use of rights, of the golden rule, and of the need to maintain social order. We score this as deontic Stage 3/4 consistent with his standard moral judgment stage.

Jay's Stage 2/3 responsibility reasoning comes out in the stealing situation in his response to the restitution dilemma, asking about responsibility for restitution to Mary, the victim of the theft. In reply to the idea of the whole class chipping in to help Mary because the thief is unknown, he says, "No, because there are two reasons. One because it was Mary's fault or lack of responsibility by leaving her purse out. She was too trusting. The second thing is why should I pay for what somebody else did? Why should I get involved?" Jay also feels other students would not want to chip in. He says, "The same thing, why should they pay for what other people are doing, or other people's lack of responsibility that it got stolen."

Jay's lower-stage (2/3) judgments of responsibility compared with his higher-stage (3/4) judgments of justice are closely connected to his perception of the moral atmosphere of the high school. According to Jay, the high school lacks collective norms for caring and responsibility and lacks a sense of community. He is asked on the caring dilemma, "Should the school have some kind of agreement or understanding that someone should help out someone else?" In response he says, "I think this school really lacks that. It lacks in togetherness, I think. Nobody really takes pride in the school except a few who are good students or very good athletes. Where people don't take pride in something, go out of their way to help each other, the community doesn't really benefit. It doesn't promote the welfare of the school."

Jay thus tells us that there are no collective norms of helping and little sense of community in his school. He responds in a similar way on the stealing dilemma. Asked, "Would you express your disapproval and try to find out who took Mary's money?" Jay answers, "It depends. I wouldn't go much out of my way, again it's her responsibility . . . in this school people care too much for themselves, and they wouldn't really go out of their way to do something. We have a lot of things stolen from lockers. Nothing seems to get done about it. In that sense I guess nobody really cares. There is a lack of trust or caring about other people's property in this school."

Jay's sense of the nonexistence of collective norms of trust and helping and his sense of his fellow students' lack of feeling or valuing community are scored in our moral atmosphere manual as 1 on the scale of the degree of collectiveness of norms displayed in Table 5.5 and as 0 on the scale of degree of community valuing presented in Table 5.6.

To summarize, we have presented Jay to give some feeling for the differences between deontic and responsibility judgments and to highlight the way in which these different modes of judging usually appear on the practical school dilemmas.

To illustrate the constructs of moral atmosphere we will compare two students from Cambridge, Betsy, a student of the Cluster School, a just community alternative school, and Rob, a student at Cambridge Rindge and Latin, the regular high school.

B.   The Cases of Betsy and Rob

Betsy and Rob are both 10th-graders and both scored Stage 3/4 on the hypothetical classical moral dilemmas. These students are one-half stage higher on individual moral judgment than the median of their groups, which were Stage 3. Both Betsy and Rob are middle-class students in schools where at least half of the students are working class. Ethnically, Cambridge Rindge and Latin School was 25% black and 10% Hispanic and other minorities, and Cluster School was half black and half white in 1979, when these interviews were done.

In answer to why people in her school should help out on the caring dilemma, Betsy says: "Yes, they should because Cluster is a community. Because you have a responsibility to the kids in this school, even if you don't like them all that much, you are in school and you're with them every day, you know, you are supposed to think of them as part of the school and part of the community, so you should do it."

Betsy clearly expresses the value of community. We categorized her response as being at Degree 4, the normative communal level (see Table 5.6). We see this way of thinking about community in her idea that the school is a community that expects members to help one another because they are all members of the same group. This idea implies an awareness and valuing of community that creates moral obligations and norms. The interviewer asks: "What does it mean, it does sound kind of corny, because it sounds like a cliché when you say it, we are a community, so we are supposed to help each other?" Betsy says, "Because everyone is supposed to be one, it is our school, it is not a school that all these separate people go to that don't care about each other."

Betsy's response indicates three aspects of this level of community valuing. First is the idea that a community implies a strong degree of unity, a oneness or solidarity. Second, it expresses the idea of personal identification with the group and its objectives: "It is our school." Third is the feature that membership in the group means mutual caring about one another as group members.

On the caring dilemma she also clearly indicates the existence of a shared or collective norm of helping. She says, "Anyone who is in Cluster knows they should help out . . . there is a general feeling and everyone knows that."

Should someone help out?

Yes, they should because Cluster school is a community. Because you have a responsibility to the kids in this school. You are supposed to think of them as part of the school and part of the community, so you should do it.

Betsy's response depicts a group with a high degree of collective norm, Degree 14 (see Table 5.5). Her statement exemplifies the three aspects of the highest two levels of the collectiveness of the helping norm. When Betsy says, "you are supposed to," she is speaking as one member of a collective to other members of the collective, and she is representing the point of view of the group as a whole. This aspect of her response we call "speaker's perspective," a perspective ranging from speaking from the standpoint of oneself as an individual to speaking from the standpoint of *we,* the members of the group. At the highest level, speaking from the point of view of the group becomes explicit, taking the form of "we think we should . . ."

Betsy is Degree 14 because her command of "you have a responsibility to the kids in this school" does not come from her as an individual but is a statement from the perspective of the group representative of the collective norm. The speaker perspective defines the group *for* whom the subject is speaking or representing. The group constituency defines the group membership of the persons *to* whom the subject is speaking or prescribing a rule or action. In this example, it is clear to whom Betsy is speaking; she is prescribing to the members of the Cluster School. In our system, constituency is either individual or a specified group. Degrees 1–4 represent the individual as the constituent, and Degrees 5–15 specify a particular group as the constituency.

The third aspect is that the norm is stated prescriptively in terms of an obligation at the higher levels. We distinguish norms that are prescriptive from norms that are aggregate or stated as descriptive of the behavior of individuals or groups. Aggregate norms reflect a "statistical tendency" rather than a clearly shared idea of obligation.

In contrast with Betsy, Rob, a student of the regular Cambridge High School, does not see a shared valuing of community, but it is not clear whether he sees the school as a valued organization serving learning and other goals. He individually values the school but thinks that others do not: I don't consider this school a community. Too many people hold grudges against each other, because maybe they look different or act different. Or some kids come to school to be with their friends or to be stoned, and some kids come to do work. Like the kids who get stoned might stand around and see someone with a lot of books walk by and laugh. But they won't laugh when graduation comes. No, most people think of themselves, really.

How do you think thinking about the community would affect that?

If they did think about it, I don't really know, because I don't know if they ever did, like I said only people in committees and stuff would think about it and talk about it, and those would be a small minority.

In handling issues about respecting other people's property and trusting other people, do you think Cambridge Rindge and Latin School is really a community?

Well not really, because in a way like we own this school and a lot of kids mess it up. Like write on the walls, there is no need for that, there is paper to write on. I don't know, some people do and some people don't. I don't really know the percentage.

These comments indicate that Rob is Degree 1 in his thinking about the value of the school (see Table 5.6). He, as an individual, attaches some value to the school as an organization and says, "in a way like we own this school and a lot of kids mess it up." He feels some ownership of the school and finds vandalism or injury to it offensive. He also values its major function, academic learning, even though he sees that many other students do not. Thus, there is a contrast between his individual valuing of the school as an organization and his perception of the attitudes of most of the students in this regard. Moreover, Rob does not perceive any shared norm of helping. He believes that it would be a good thing to have a shared norm to help but does not believe that it exists. When asked if his school should have a shared agreement to help out, he says: "Yah, right. Like it is not a law, but everybody knows that it is good to help someone out. But people just don't care about anyobdy else." Going on the theme of a lack of a sense of community

211

and caring at the high school, he comments that "seventy-five percent of them wouldn't care."

Why?

They are worried about their own problems probably.

Rob himself as an individual holds a norm of helping, but he is conspicuously aware of the discrepancy between his individual norm of helping and the absence of any collective norm of helping.

What should the agreement be and why should it be such an agreement?

It's really—it should be an agreement with yourself, you know. It is like, I have strong feelings toward other people. I don't like to think bad things and I never say anything bad about anybody, and it is more of an agreement with yourself than with anybody, you couldn't make an agreement with somebody about something like this.

Not only is Rob aware of the discrepancy between his individual norm of helping and the lack of any collective norm, but also his response indicates that he thinks it is impossible to develop shared moral norms on issues such as helping. This is scored as Degree 1 on our scale, explicit rejection of the possibility of developing a shared norm (see Table 5.5).

The statements by Rob that "I just believe in helping people" and "it should be an agreement with yourself" demonstrate clearly that he is speaking only for himself rather than from a "we" perspective, as is involved in the higher levels. His responses indicate that his idea that one should help is not defined in terms of a specific group, like members of the school, who should follow the norm and be the persons toward whom help is directed. He sees that any "good person" would hold this norm for himself or herself. His norm does not define a group constituency, a bounded group of people where responsibilities are felt toward one another. For Rob, the idea of helping is not obligatory or prescriptive but is a positive value that is based on a concern or caring for others. When this concern is absent, he sees no possibility for expecting someone to help out another person. Accordingly, Rob's conception of the norm of helping is nonprescriptive.

Although Rob does not see a positive collective norm of helping, he does perceive a counternorm in this situation that makes helping an unpopular student disapproved of by the peer group.

What would you do?

I would wait till after class, I would keep it quiet so nobody might know about it, and then I could help the kid. Then nobody would say anything to me, because they would not know about it.

Rob's feeling that he would help but in a way so that others did not know about it indicates he is concerned about disapproval for helping, presumably because of the existence of a peer group norm making it "uncool" to associate with or aid an unpopular student.

For example, when Rob says he would be secretive about helping, he is responding to his daily observation that students do not help their unpopular classmates. The consistency of his observation shows both Rob and ourselves that there exists an *aggregate* counternorm (Degrees 8 and 9). This aggregate norm of helping influences Rob's behavior, but it is not obligatory in the same sense as Betsy's articulation of the norm of helping. Explicit shared agreements in a group have obligatory force, whereas the power of statistical or "average" behaviors do not. Aggregate norms arise out of a concern to fit into the average behavioral pattern of one's peers.

Assigning the degree of collectiveness or sharedness to the way Betsy and Rob perceive the norm of helping in each of their schools still does not tell us the extent to which the norm is upheld by either the students or his peers. Table 5.8 describes another dimension in the perception of school norms, the dimension of phase of commitment to upholding the norm. The phase of the norm came to be defined when we were observing Cluster School's community meetings in terms of the development of its norms over time.

In our observations of the development of collective norms from meeting to meeting and from year to year in the Cluster School, we identified a dimension of phase of commitment to and institutionalization of the norm that could be distinguished from the existence or degree of collectiveness of the norm itself. Our scheme describes the evolution of collective norms going through distinct phases from the time they are first proposed to the time they are expected and upheld.

We designed a set of questions about phase intended to form a Guttman scale. In a Guttman scale, saying yes to a question implies having said yes to all the lower items of questions in the scale. For example, the highest point in our Guttman scale of phase is expressed willingness publicly to sanction a member for violating a norm. The Guttman scale notion implies that anyone who says yes to this, for example, Phase 6 willingness publicly to express disapproval to a member for violating a norm says yes to all less extreme phases of commitment to the norm.

On the caring dilemma, Betsy says that the Cluster School holds its collective norm of helping at Phase 6. She says, "They would disapprove. . . . I think the kids would be very mad at him if he didn't do it. They would have said something [to Billy] . . . because of why it's important to do it [that is, to help] and why they would bitch at him for not doing it."

Comparing Rob's responses on the caring dilemma with Betsy's responses, we said that he perceives his school as having no shared expectation of helping. It is always the case that when a norm is perceived to be at a low degree of collectiveness (Degree 6 or below), the phase will be 0 or nonexistent. On the caring norm, Rob is Degree 1 and says, "You couldn't make an agree-

TABLE 5.8.   Phases of the Collective Norm

Phase 0:   No collective norm exists or is proposed.

Collective Norm Proposal

Phase 1:   Individuals propose collective norms for group acceptance.

Collective Norm Acceptance

Phase 2:   Collective norm is accepted as a group ideal but not agreed to. It is not an expectation for behavior.
   a.   some group members accept ideal
   b.   most group members accept ideal

Phase 3:   Collective norm is accepted and agreed to but is not (yet) an expectation for behavior.
   a.   some group members agree to collective norm
   b.   most group members agree to collective norm

Collective Norm Expectation

Phase 4:   Collective norm is accepted and expected. (Naive expectation)
   a.   some group members expect the collective norm to be followed
   b.   most group members expect the collective norm to be followed

Phase 5:   Collective norm is expected but not followed. (Disappointed expectation)
   a.   some group members are disappointed
   b.   most group members are disappointed

Collective Norm Enforcement

Phase 6:   Collective norm is expected and upheld through expected persuading of deviant to follow norm.
   a.   some group members persuade
   b.   most group members persuade

Phase 7:   Collective norm is expected and upheld through expected reporting of defiant to the group.
   a.   some group members report
   b.   most group members report

---

ment with somebody about something like that." When he was asked, "Should there be an agreement?" he said, "It wouldn't get followed anyway." These statements tell us three things: that there is not existing agreement in Cambridg Rindge and Latin to help (a Phase 3 idea); that there is no shared ideal of helping (a Phase 2 idea); and that Rob feels it would be unrealistic to propose such an agreement (a Phase 1 idea).

The remaining concepts in analyzing "moral atmosphere" using individual interview material are the stage of the representation of the collective norm and the stage of the representation of community valuing. We define the stage of representation of the collective norm as the stage the individual uses to explain how most people in the school understand the meaning of the particular norm. Betsy represents the stage of Cluster School's collective norm of caring as being 3/4. She says, "Because you have a responsibility to the kids in this school, even if you don't like them all that much, you are supposed to think of them as part of the school and part of the community, so you should do it." Furthermore, Betsy understands the school community in a transitional 3–4 sense, as being an entity separate from the individuals who compose it. Betsy's response illustrates that both the norm of caring and the value of community can be stage scored. The stages of the valuing of community are presented in Table 5.7. Although we distinguish for analytical purposes an individual's stage of the collective norm and the stage of community value, on any particular school dilemma these are almost always the same.

As we discussed earlier, speaker perspective is important in defining the degree of collectiveness of a group norm. It is equally important in determining what responses in an interview are stageable representations of the collective norm rather than simply the individual's own stage of reasoning. The speaker perspective defines *for* whom the subject is speaking or representing. Thus, it helps us identify the material representative of the collective norm. When a subject, like Betsy, speaks *to* the group on *behalf* of the group and does so prescriptively, we identify and use that material as indicative of the *collective* norm. Material isolated in this way, furthermore, generally has clear stageable characteristics. In other words, the way we assess the structure or stage of the collective reasoning is parallel to the way we assess the structure or stage of an individual's reasoning.

After Betsy prescribes that Cluster School members should uphold their own norms of caring, she then states an exception when she as an individual would not uphold this norm. She says, "The only way I would say he shouldn't help him is if he was a creep and he really did something rotten to him in the past, if he showed he didn't care about Billy or anyone else, then I wouldn't help him out." In this statement Betsy is prescribing only for herself; she is specifying for herself the conditions and reasons for which she would not uphold the norm under certain circumstances. Her individual reasoning in this case is Stage 3. She feels no obligation to help someone who has in the past violated the group's shared expectations of caring.

Contrasting Rob's interview with Betsy's, we know there is no collective stage of a norm of helping because, as Rob tells us, there is no such collective norm. He does this in two ways. First, in response to the question "Should there be an agreement about helping?" Rob says, "Yeh right . . . like it is not a law but everybody knows that it is good to help somebody out but people just don't care about anybody else; . . . it is more of an agreement with yourself than with anybody; you couldn't make an agreement with anybody about anything like this." In his response Rob denies the possibility of even establishing a collective norm in Cambridge Rindge and Latin and tells us that he can speak only for himself. Thus, there is no collective norm of caring to be staged. This material is, however, stageable; it reflects Rob's own Stage 3 reasoning that good people should try to help others, a stage score assigned to his individual norm of helping.

Remembering that Rob did report an aggregate counternorm in his school, however, one that said it is "uncool" to be seen helping an "unpopular" student, he represents it as being moderately collective (Degree 8) and at a very high phase (Phase 6). He believes people would actually say he should not help if they saw him doing it. Although assigning stage to counternorms is ambiguous because they are descriptions of behavior often given without any justification, frequently we feel we can assign guess stage scores. In this case Rob is representing a counternorm against helping that seems to be Stage 2 or 2/3. The important point is that we and Rob agree that it is clearly a lower stage than his own individual norm of care, which is Stage 3. Rob's representation of the stage of community valuing is also 2 or 2/3. He describes the school as an institution legitimately used by some for their own academic ends and abused by others for arbitrary and personal reasons.

Turning to Rob's and Betsy's responses on the school dilemma about collective restitution, we will quickly run through our assessment procedure. When Betsy is asked:

Would there be a general feeling or expectation in the class that everyone should pitch in 50¢?

Yes, because the reason why is it is just easier that way, first of all, and if something like that is going to happen at the school, the school should be responsible for it, the kids.

Why is that fair?

It is fair because if everyone gets away with stealing and no one cares here, then it just can't be a good place, first of all. If people think everything is everyone else's tough luck and it is too bad that happened, then this place would not be a very caring place. Stealing from someone in the community is just like stealing from the community.

Would that make it an unfair place?

Sure, it would make it a very unfair place.

Why?

Because some people have better luck than other people. Some people have more or less and some people are bigger and can get their way more and if that is the way it worked, then it would be very unfair.

If the teacher asks the kids to chip in and some kids say they will not, what should they do?

They should chip in. But if they won't, they are not really in a community, they don't care. You have to do what the majority wants to do, or else we would have no school and it would be very unorganized and nothing goes right.

From these responses, we say that there is an explicit shared norm of collective restitution at Degree 14. Betsy speaks prescriptively as a member of the community in explaining that the norm should be upheld in order to affirm the community qua community. Thus, the degree of community valuing is 4. The phase of this norm is not explicitly stated, but we know it is at least Phase 4, that Betsy expects people to act consistently with the majority vote to chip in. The norm of collective restitution and the degree of community valuing as represented by Betsy are both Stage 3/4. She argues that because individuals in the school may have differential advantages, the school must be equally responsible to all its members and the way to be responsible is to act according to the majority will.

Rob, on the other hand, has very little to say about collective restitution or even about what the teacher could do to help the victim of a classroom theft to get her money back. Moreover, although Rob has made the deontic judgment that it is wrong to steal, it does not help him decide whether he would report a friend who did steal:

Do you think Zeke should report Tom for the theft?

If he is his friend, he won't. I don't know.

No one in the class admits to taking the money or knowing who did, what should the teacher do?

He can't really do anything. There is nothing he can do.

If you were in Zeke's position, would you try to persuade your friend to return the money?

Definitely, because I don't just care about myself, I care about other people, probably the girl doesn't care about the money either, but just cares that somebody had the gall enough to take it right there in the room, you know. I'd persuade him to give her the money back for that sake, too.

If your friend refused to return the money, would you report him?

No.

Why not?

Because he did it, I don't know. I don't feel obliged to do it, I don't feel I should.

Should you report him?

I guess so, I'm not really sure, Zeke should I guess.

217

Why?

Because it [stealing] is against my conscience, it is against what I believe in.

Should the class all chip in to repay Mary her money?

No.

Why not?

Because the class didn't steal it, just one person did.

What would you do?

If I was in the class and it got stolen, I would just ask everybody, I wouldn't accuse anybody. There is nothing I could really do except for that.

Should a good member of your school be willing to chip in?

No.

If there was an agreement that students should do that, would most students chip in willingly?

No, not willingly.

Do you think this school should have an agreement that everyone should chip in in situations like this?

Nope.

Again Rob tells us there is no collective norm of restitution of any form in his school. He does reiterate his individual norm (Degree 4) of caring about other people, here scored as Stage 3. From Rob's responses, we learn that the moral atmosphere of the regular high school does not contain any ideas or norms of restitution. Thus, no degree of collectiveness, stage, phase, or degree of community valuing scores can be assigned for this dilemma. From Rob's answers on the stealing dilemma, we hear again about his individual norm against stealing, represented at Stage 3 and at Phase 5, an expression of personal disappointment that stealing occurs in his school.

When asked whether he should or would be trusting in his school, he says:

Would you be as trusting as Mary about your possessions?

I have been bringing a skateboard to school and I have really been thinking about leaving it in my locker, because I know someone in the voc ed school that I went to for a year, they used to break in the lockers all the time and I kind of never used a locker for that reason and I only use a locker for my books. I was—when nobody was looking, I put my skateboard in there, because I don't trust some people.

218

Do you think you should be trusting about leaving stuff in this school?

You should be, but you can't be.

Why can't you be?

Because there are people who do steal and people who will steal outside of school will do it in school, too, because I know people who have done it.

The norm of trust is scored as Degree 1 of collectiveness, an explicit rejection of the possibility of having a shared norm of trust. Therefore, the phase is 0. The degree of community valuing implicit in this passage is 0, no feeling that the school is valued even as an educational institution to foster individual academic achievement. The stage of reasoning Rob uses to describe his school and his own lack of trust we can loosely call Stage 1/2.

E. Summary Data for Brookline and Cambridge

Looking at Table 5.3 and 5.4, which report the median scores for each of four groups in the school dilemmas, we see that the differences between Jay and Betsy and Rob are prototypical of the difference between democratic alternative school students and regular high school students on responsibility reasoning and on the moral atmosphere for the four schools.

The downward stage discrepancy evident for the regular high school students illustrates the relevance of the distinction we have made between classical and practical reasoning (Table 5.3). These students did not use their highest or best moral reasoning when thinking about real-life dilemmas in the context of their own schools. We attribute this fi   g to the lack of democratic discussion and decision making, to the lack c   llective and relatively high stage group norms, and to the lack of valuing e schools as communities. We now turn to the comparative results on the variables that operationalize these components of the moral atmosphere.

Table 5.4, which gives summary results for the four schools and four average students, lists the proportion of students in each school that make the choice of social responsibility over the individual responsibility choice. In terms of the content of choice rather than the mode of judgment about it, there was a moderate tendency for the democratic schools to lead students to make the prosocial choice as opposed to the individual choice.

When we asked what each student should or would do, we considered that to be a part of the evaluation of individual judgments. When we then asked what they thought their peers should or would do, make the prosocial choice or not, we move to consideration and evaluation of the moral atmosphere of each school. In the democratic schools, over 80% of the responses of the students showed that they believed their peers felt they should act prosocially, whereas in regular high schools about 40% of the responses indicated that students believed their peers felt they should act prosocially.

In predicting their peers' behavior, about 60% of the democratic school students' responses indicated that they felt their peers would act consistently with their prosocial choice. In the regular high schools, about 30% of the responses showed that students believed their peers would act prosocially.

The disparity between answering for themselves and for others is interesting. Whereas the majority of regular high school students make the prosocial choice for themselves, less than half, or one-third, feel their peers would make the prosocial choice. This phenomenon seems to be an example of "pluralistic ignorance." In other words, most students in the regular high schools say they would help but do not believe many of their peers would help. Seeing their peers as different from themselves and in some sense as less responsible, we think, is in part a result of the school environment that provides few opportunities for discussing and creating explicitly shared norms.

In the democratic schools, most students report that they themselves would make the prosocial choice and act on it. They also report that most of their peers would do the same. This congruency between students' perceptions of others and their self-reports is evidence that pluralistic ignorance can be overcome through open democratic discussion. The relationship of judgments of responsibility to moral action as discussed by Kohlberg and Candee in Chapter 4 seems to us to be reflected in our own results. That there were equally high percentages of judgments of responsibility and predictions of prosocial moral action for others and themselves suggests that such judgments create a way of thinking that leads to moral action. Additionally, we feel that a positive moral atmosphere provides the context in which students feel it makes sense to think in terms of responsibility and to act morally toward their peers and teachers.

There are sharp differences between the democratic school students and the regular high school students in the frequency of use of responsibility judgments. Although half of the responses of alternative school students were in the responsibility mode, only 5–12% of responses made by regular high school students were classified in this mode.

Looking at the median stage scores for deontic and responsibility reasoning on the school dilemmas, we see that in both modes the regular high school students' reasoning was one-half to one stage lower than the stages used by democratic alternative school students (see lines 2 and 3, Table 5.3). This result is striking because the median classical moral judgment scores were the same within each pair.

For the degree of collectiveness of norms, Table 5.4 shows that neither regular high school has truly collective norms. The predominance of a score 4 indicates that the students held only individual norms about caring, trust, and so on. In contrast, students in both democratic schools articulated strongly shared norms at Degree 11 for School-Within-A-School and Degree 13 for Cluster School. Table 5.5 describes this difference. Most students in the former school felt norms should be upheld because of positive feelings and motivations that they saw as generated spontaneously by being in a close and caring community. Cluster School students saw the norms as morally prescriptive and as generated by a collective decision process.

The median stage of the Degree 4 individual norms is 3 for Brookline and 2/3 for Cambridge Rindge and Latin School, in both cases, one-half stage lower than the median stage for each sample on the classical hypothetical dilemmas. The stage of the collective norms for both democratic schools was 3/4; this is the same or higher than the median stages of both on the classical hypothetical dilemmas.

The results mean that when students reason individually about school norms, they tend to formulate them at a lower stage. In contrast, when students through explicit discussion formulate truly collective norms, they do so at a higher stage, sometimes a half stage above that of most students in the group.

Degree of community valuing and its median stage give parallel results for the four schools. Cambridge Rindge and Latin High School students indicated on the whole that they did not value their school even as an educational institution. The score is 0. Brookline High School students mostly valued their school as an educational institution, a place to go to meet their own academic needs. The score was 1. Both alternative schools were intrinsically valued as communities by their students, as is indicated by a score of 3 on degree of community valuing. The stage of community valuing scores reflect these differences. Brookline and Cambridge students' conceptions of their schools as Stage 2 and 2/3 places is consistent with not valuing or instrumentally valuing their schools. School-Within-A-School and Cluster students conceptualized their communities in Stage 3/4 and 3 terms, respectively. This also is consistent with the expressed valuing of their communities as enabling and promoting caring, trusting, and sharing relationships.

In summary, the democratic school students were higher than their regular high school controls in the content of their school dilemma choices, favoring prosocial responsibility; in their mode of judgment, making judgments of responsibility; and in their stage of judgment. We believe that these differences reflect real differences in moral action in the schools, a belief we support in a detailed history of the alternative schools that we are now writing. We interpret these differences in practical moral judgment as arising from the differential moral atmospheres of the democratic and comparison schools. The democratic schools have a high sense of collective prosocial norms and a strong sense of community. The methodology that we have described is useful for studying the moral atmosphere not only of the school but also of the work place and the family. Pilot extensions of the methodology for these other institutions are now underway.

REFERENCES

Blasi, A. Bridging moral cognition and moral action: A review of the literature. *Psychological Bulletin,* 1980, *88,* 1–45.

Durkheim, E. *Moral education: A study in the theory and application in the sociology of education.* New York: Free Press, 1961. (Originally published, 1925.)

Eisenberg-Berg, N. *The development of prosocial moral judgment and its correlates.* Unpublished doctoral dissertation, University of California, Berkeley, 1976.

Frankena, W. K. *Ethics* (2nd ed.). Englewood Cliffs, N.J.: Prentice-Hall, 1973.

Gilligan, C. In a different voice: Women's conceptions of self and morality. *Harvard Educational Review,* 1977, *47,* 481–517.

Gilligan, C., & Belenky, M. A naturalistic study of abortion decision. In R. Selman & R. Yando (Eds.), *Clinical-developmental psychology.* San Francisco: Jossey-Bass, 1980.

Kohlberg, L. Exploring the moral atmosphere of the school. In L. Kohlberg, *The meaning and measurement of moral development.* Worcester, Mass.: Clark University Press, 1980.

Kohlberg, L. *Essays on moral development* (Vol. 1): *The philosophy of moral development.* San Francisco: Harper & Row, 1981.

Kohlberg, L., Scharf, P., & Hickey, J. The justice structure of the prison: A theory and intervention. *Prison Journal,* 1972, *51,* 3–14.

Leming, J. S. *Adolescent moral judgment and deliberation on classical and practical moral dilemmas.* Unpublished doctoral dissertation, University of Wisconsin, 1973.

Leming, J. S. An exploratory inquiry into the multi-factor theory of moral behavior. *Journal of Moral Education,* 1976, *5*(2), 179–188.

Lyons, N. *Two orientations to morality; Rights and care: A coding manual.* Unpublished doctoral dissertation, Harvard University, 1982.

Mussen, P., & Eisenberg-Berg, N. *Roots of caring, sharing and helping.* New York: Freeman, 1977.

Niebuhr, H. R. *The responsible self.* New York: Harper & Row, 1963.

Power, F. C. *The moral atmosphere of a just community high school: A four-year longitudinal study.* Unpublished doctoral dissertation, Harvard University, 1979.

Scharf, P. *The moral atmosphere of the prison and an intervention to change it.* Unpublished doctoral dissertation, Harvard University, 1973.

Turiel, E. The development of social-conventional and moral concept. In M. Windmiller, N. Lambert, & E. Turiel (Eds.), *Moral development and socialization.* Boston: Allyn & Bacon, 1980.

REFERENCE NOTE

1. Gilligan, C., Lyons, N., & Langdale, S. Personal communication, 1982.

222

The Justice Structure of the Prison— A Theory and an Intervention

by

Lawrence Kohlberg, Peter Scharf, and Joseph Hickey*

OVER A PERIOD OF EIGHTEEN YEARS, the writers have formulated and empirically validated a conception of moral development based on movement through six stages of moral judgment: Stage 1, the punishment and obedience orientation; Stage 2, the instrumental exchange orientation; Stage 3, the interpersonal concordance or "good boy-nice girl" orientation; Stage 4, the "law and order" orientation; Stage 5, the social contract legalistic orientation; and Stage 6, the universal ethical principle orientation. These stages have been found to occur, and occur in the same age order, in every culture studied (Taiwan, Mexico, Turkey, U. S., Israel). They have been found to correspond to an invariant step-by-step movement in the longitudinal development of a group of fifty American males studied every three years from age ten to twenty-seven.

Further research has suggested that passage through these stages of moral development is facilitated by various processes. These processes can be summarized in terms of the following propositions:

1. Provision of enhanced opportunities for role-taking and social participation stimulates moral development.
2. Participation in group and institutional structures perceived as fair or just stimulates moral development.
3. Exposure to cognitive conflict, to contradictions in one's own moral views and in their relations to the views of others, stimulates moral development.
4. Exposure to moral reasoning one stage above one's own promotes moral development.

These propositions suggest strategies for moral intervention. At the same time, the existence of invariant developmental stages provides a philosophically and psychologically defensible approach to intervention in moral development, free of the charge of indoctrination with the relativistic values of the intervenor.

Initial attempts at moral intervention were conducted in high school classrooms with varying age, race, and social class compositions. These programs have led to one-stage upward movement in 33% to 50% of the students compared to 5% of the students in control popula-

---

* Department of Education and Social Psychology, Graduate School of Education, Harvard University.

3

tions (The theoretical and research work just described has been supported by an N.I.C.H.D. grant running from 1965 through 1973.)

Encouraged by these results, the writers decided to take steps towards elaborating moral development theory as a basis for an intervention program in corrections. A two-year grant from the Russell Sage Foundation, terminating June, 1972, supported a series of pilot studies designed to establish the feasibility of applying moral development theory to correctional innovations. Two of these studies are described here.

THE CHESHIRE EXPERIMENT

The writers began by posing two questions: a) could the justice structure of the prison be conceptualized in terms of moral stages, and b) did inmates agree in perceiving justice practices and moral obligation within the prison at the same moral stage regardless of the inmate's own stage of judgment on outside dilemmas.

Following Rawls (1971), the "justice structure" of the prison was defined as the "public principles which govern the assignment of rights and duties and define the proper distribution of the benefits and burdens of social cooperation." We hypothesized that prison justice structures could be understood in terms of five "ideal" types, loosely related to the moral stages:

1. Coercive Power Orientation:
    Use of arbitrary personal power by staff without regard to fixed rule standards (e.g., Cummins farm).
2. Instrumental Exchange Orientation:
    Exchanges between staff and inmate elites (e.g., "Big House" gangster orientation).
3. Informal Norm Agreement:
    Shared traditions, definitions and conventions between inmates and staff (e.g., McLeery's "Traditional" prison).
4. Structured Norm Agreement:
    Staff and inmates bound by fixed rule standards (e.g., Weberian bureaucratic prison).
5. Shared Principled Agreement:
    Contractual definitions of rights with impartial adjudication of conflicts (various experiments at self-government).

Observations were then made of prison justice practices at a reformatory in Cheshire, Connecticut. Using interviews and participant observation, we attempted to classify four "aspects" of the prison structure: 1) the system of civil rights, 2) social roles in relation to status and power, 3) rewards, and 4) punishments.

4

These observations indicated that inmates had no fixed civil rights. Liberties of political expression, freedom of movement, property rights and rights of assembly were all restricted by prison officials. "Privileges" granted by staff were subject to arbitrary revocation by staff. No "moral appeal" by inmates to demand that rights be honored was possible. Inmates, through their role definitions, were systematically excluded from power in decision-making.

In regard to rewards, some were "doled out" automatically by impersonal bureaucratic rules, e.g., job pay, work release and good time. Other rewards, such as admission to the honor block and job preferences, were "manipulated" by prison authorities as an exchange for cooperation among key (powerful) inmates.

Punishments were largely decided bureaucratically, sometimes for infractions of fairly innocuous rules, e.g., exchanging library books. Punishment often involved segregation in the "hole." The discipline board hearings involved little effort to ascertain inmate guilt or innocence and no attempt was made to explain the reasons for punishment to the inmate. Some episodes of punishment represented acts of personal retaliation by guards.

From these observations it was concluded that the Cheshire reformatory operated partly with Type 4 fixed rule standards (often bureaucratic), partly by Type 2 manipulations of rules by staff in order to create exchanges in matters of concern to them. Cooperative powerful inmates were given special privileges and, occasionally, "trouble makers" would be "gotten" by the discipline board. This pattern is similar to that of other traditional prisons as described by Sykes (1958) and others.

PERCEPTION OF MORAL ATMOSPHERE AT CHESHIRE

Given these sociological observations of the prison justice structure, it was desired to see if inmates perceived the prison structure as operating at a particular moral justice stage. To investigate this question, we utilized a standard set of non-prison moral dilemmas and we developed a parallel series of dilemmas which reflected conflicts experienced by guards and inmates in the prison context. We were aided by inmates who offered us examples of conflicts which troubled them. One dilemma asked if an inmate should aid a young boy from his own town who was shaken down for cigarettes by some older inmates. Others asked if guards should punish inmates for such offenses as "fighting" or "sniffing glue."

The prison dilemmas were scored in two ways. First they were scored for moral judgment stage, using a special scoring guide. This was done reliably (72% agreement between judges). In addition, inmate

5

responses were analyzed for their perception of moral atmosphere. The moral atmosphere was defined as the perceived level of justice of the prison. These perceptions were rated independently from the inmate's normative moral judgment. The moral judgments expressed what the inmate considered what one *should* do in a prison situation. The perceptions of moral atmosphere related to what the inmate believed *to be true* of justice practices in the institution.

Results indicated that inmates used lower modes of moral judgment on the prison dilemmas as compared with the standard non-prison dilemmas.[1] In effect, what one *should* do in the prison context was relegated to a lower moral order than what one *should* do in the outside community. These differences were paralleled by discrepancies between the inmates' moral judgments and their perception of how the institution actually operated. Inmates in the reformatory tended to perceive the prison largely in terms of Stage 1 and 2 categories. They generally saw the prison as operating at a level of coercive-punitive force, or alternatively, at a level of instrumental-exploitation. This seemed true independent of the inmate's own stage of moral development.

Inmates tended to see relationships with other inmates in Stage 2 instrumental terms. Inmates were seen as "ripping" each other off, "ratting" out their friends and "punking" weaker inmates. Relationships with other inmates were necessary for mutual protection; however, they were usually seen as marred by "fronting." "Fronting" was necessary to defend one's interests and to "con" the guards and other inmates. In this state inmates saw no generally agreed upon norms, nor were there fixed standards which actively regulated transaction among inmates.

If relationships among inmates were largely perceived in Stage 2 terms of instrumental exploitation, then the "justice" of the prison administrators was often perceived as the Stage 1 exertion of coercive power. As an example, rules were said to exist to "jam inmates," punishments were inflicted to "get" particular trouble-makers. One inmate, when asked if he had any rights, responded, "Yes, we can take orders."

It appeared, then, than an official social structure composed of mixed Type 4 bureaucratic rules and Type 2 instrumental exchange was perceived by inmates as defining a moral atmosphere of a mixed Stage 1 punishment and obedience and a Stage 2 instrumental egoistic order. Even the *S's* who might have had the capacity to perceive the Type 4

---

[1] Interestingly, none of the 34 inmates scored higher on the prison dilemmas than on the standard non-prison dilemmas. Of the 16 inmates characterized as Stage 3 on non-prison dilemmas, for example, 11 were rated at Stage 2 on the prison dilemmas. The overall difference in group means was significant at the .05 level.

6

bureaucratic-rule components of the institution as Stage 4, did not seem to perceive the institution as operating at that high a level.

The study of the moral atmosphere of the Cheshire reformatory brought us to a number of tentative conclusions:

—The justice structure of the prison, at least in theory, could be conceptualized in terms parallel to the moral stages; much work remains, however, before organizational justice structures can be "typed" with reliability or confidence.

—Inmates tended to reason at lower levels on dilemmas placed within the prison context. Even "conventionally reasoning inmates" (with Stage 3 or 4 thinking) reverted to Stage 2 instrumental thinking on dilemmas placed in the prison context.

—*Independent* of stage, inmates perceived justice practices of the institution in Stage 1 (punishment and obedience) or Stage 2 (instrumental exchange) terms.

—It was surmised that the prison justice process operating as a distant, alien authority tended to lead towards the inmate's perception of the institution as punitive and unjust. This obviously has implications for the inmate's development of moral reasoning; the inmate is given no basis for developing an understanding of the moral basis for law and society.

Completion of the Cheshire Intervention made certain realities quite evident. First, where it was possible to stimulate small changes in moral maturity through group discussions, the low stage "moral atmosphere" of the reformatory placed a "ceiling" on the increases in moral maturity one might expect. As the "rules" of the institution were largely perceived as illegitimate, it was difficult to get inmates to accept the validity of Stage 4 reasoning.

It was also found that the social structure of the institution placed inmates into judgment-action binds. Where an inmate might be made aware of Stage 3 or 4 modes of reasoning, the exploitative inmate peer culture encouraged behavior consistent with more primitive reasoning (often Stage 2). The authority system of the prison likewise encouraged Stage 1 compliance from inmates rather than moral behavior, even at the contract levels.

Finally, the bureaucratic authority system and the rigid structuring of social interactions blocked "role taking" and perspective taking among inmates. The types of experiences which might have stimulated personal and socio-moral growth among inmates were almost wholly absent in prison life.

7

Given these observations, we concluded that if we were to make a substantial input towards rehabilitating offenders, we would have to create a correctional community quite different from what we observed at Cheshire. We developed the following goals for such a correctional community:

1. It would be perceived as fair and legitimate by inmates (the justice structure would be understood as operating at the stage of the inmate's own level of moral maturity or above).

2. It would stimulate inmate moral thinking by creating a social situation in which dilemmas evolving from conflicts of claims could be resolved collectively by staff and inmates. It would provide a democratic constitutional process which would establish rules related to internal maintenance of the community.
   The line staff would engage in the community process and lead moral discussions in such a way as to generate a new and higher-stage role in the inmates' eyes.

THE NIANTIC INTERVENTION

Given these broad goals, we began to search for a suitable site for our intervention. In June, 1971, we began "training and orientation" meetings with staff at the Niantic State Farm for Women. For a number of reasons, the Niantic State Farm was suitable for our needs. Physically the farm was broken into small "cottage units" (20-30 women). Working in a minimum security facility meant that women could be given a relatively wide range of freedom in determining the rules of the cottage. The staff at the Farm seemed open to an experimental program.

The intervention began quite modestly. "Training sessions" were offered to line staff. We focused upon moral development theory, simple clinical practice and group discussion techniques. These training sessions also gave us a chance to present ourselves and to enable staff (line staff, administrators and treatment personnel) to "air" conflicts and tensions.

The issues and problems raised during these sessions became critical in determining the focus of the intervention; several binds in which line staff were placed seemed critical in terms of understanding the seeming malaise of the institution.

Line staff were placed under "bureaucratic" supervision of the "front street" administrators and were obliged to enforce a long list of minor regulations concerning custody. Few of the line staff conceived of their function strictly in custodial terms. They identified with "helping"

8

the inmates and with "treatment" but they had neither training nor role definitions compatible with this.

Beginning with the issues raised in the early sessions, we were able to transform the groups from "gripe" sessions to problem-solving groups. The involved staff members committed themselves to an intervention which, working from a moral development framework, would address the problems of the institution. A supervisor was selected and given training in moral development theory. A group of six line staff and a parole agent were selected (on the basis of interest, moral-stage criteria and personal style) and a mutual commitment was made to undertake a moral development intervention in a single cottage of twenty-two women, the "Model Cottage" program.

A first step was to clarify the administrative autonomy the cottage would enjoy in being able to determine the cottage rules. The role of line staff was redefined as being centrally involved in the treatment process through serving as counselors and as leaders of small-group discussions. Parole and release were to be coordinated from the cottage instead of from a central office. This would allow us to involve line staff in parole and work-release supervision. Our role in the program was to be largely one of consultation and training. While initially we were to take an active role in running small groups, it was decided that a goal of the program would be to have it become self-maintaining using Niantic personnel, within one to two years.

The next step in terms of developing the program involved establishing small training groups with inmates (ten inmates each). This enabled staff members to learn moral discussion group techniques. It also allowed us to use the groups as a "sounding board" in order to glean from inmates ideas concerning the projected cottage. Finally, the groups gave us a chance to learn about the differences between male and female inmates.

After, roughly, a month of these preliminary meetings, we invited inmates from throughout the institution to attend a "constitutional convention." Here staff, inmates, and administrators would meet to determine the rules, procedures and policies for the model cottage. We invited proposals from inmates for a "set of rules." Several "lists" of rules were soon forthcoming. The initial proposals were characterized by concreteness ("if a woman does not feel like going to dinner, she should not be made to") and a simple attempt to gain extra privileges ("inmates can eat whatever a visitor brings them to eat from the outside"). Most importantly, none of the rules offered initially represented a constitution, a basis for establishing a coherent community. It was necessary to go through many sessions in which staff and inmates argued as to the

9

possibility of a particular set of rules before inmates began to produce rule systems which might possibly maintain the planned community for any period of time.

During the convention, inmates and staff viewed each other suspiciously. Staff members would accuse inmates of being "unrealistic," opportunistic and manipulative. Inmates, on the other hand, accused staff of duplicity and refused, initially, to believe that staff would allow them any "real say" in the new cottage.

During these debates the Harvard staff attempted to establish itself in a mediating role. Inmates would approach us after group meetings and say, "See, you can't trust a pig." Staff, in their training sessions, would accuse us of being manipulated ("You can't trust these women"). In spite of the tensions involved, as well as the real conflicts of interests, a constitution emerged which was acceptable to almost all staff and inmates.

Shortly before the cottage opened, we made our final selections for the cottage. All inmates who applied for the cottage and had six months remaining were accepted providing they had attended the meetings. Initially there was, perhaps, an unrealistic aura of hopefulness among inmates and staff. Staff hoped that they could act simply in the role of counselors and achieve a rapport they had never had before with inmates. Inmates, on the other hand, believed that rehabilitation would be almost effortless once one had entered into the model cottage.

EARLY RESULTS

Perhaps the greatest accomplishment in the first months was the creation of a working self-governing structure. The entire discipline process of the cottage is handled through community meetings. In cases of severe breech of the rules, a "discipline board" may be called by the community meeting which determines the nature of the punishment. In these meetings members are free to say anything they like. Occasionally, staff are put on the spot as are inmates. The inmates generally make a great effort to explore all aspects of an incident (personalities, circumstances, etc.). A community meeting may be called at any time by any member of the community. In practice, 90% of the meetings have been called by inmates. Both staff and inmates have a single vote.

Initially, inmates felt it impossible or difficult to participate in discipline proceedings. One woman said bluntly in one of the first meetings, "Look, I'll do any thing you like, I'll be here, I'll talk in the meetings, but don't ask me to lock my sisters, or discipline them nohow." After an incident in which there was violence between inmates, this woman came to argue for a form of "positive discipline." "Look, it's not to punish her, it's to maintain the respect of the house." What

10

seems to have happened is that most of the inmates have come to believe that the model cottage is their political community. They have come to recognize that they must protect it and the people within it. For many of the women, the rules of the model cottage are the first social institutions with which they have identified and definitely are the first which they have actively maintained.

The small group meetings (two groups of ten inmates each) have been at least partially successful as well. These groups deal with personal issues and dilemmas, often upon the fears, hopes and plans of the women as they leave prison. Often the issues are introduced by the inmates, themselves, rather than the· staff leaders. Almost always the issues involved are generated from life issues of the women on the streets or in the cottage.

Roughly half of the line staff have developed skill approximating that of the trainers in running these discussions. Difficulties found in the staff's running of discussions include: a) transforming moral issues into management issues (for example, when there is a discussion about "clean up" it gets handled as a management issue "how do we get the place clean" rather than as a moral issue or a conflict of claims), b) differentiation of leadership from participant—argumentative roles (staff often see themselves as protagonists in an argument rather than as facilitators of discussion among inmates), c) difficulty in recognizing moral stages in a fluid discussion, d) difficulty in therapeutically or non-judgmentally responding to statements of personal problems. It is hoped that our continuing training program will make some progress in helping staff achieve these goals.

At this point in our writing we must be optimistic as well as realistic. We have accomplished much. We have created a fair self-governing community which operates within the constraints of a larger total institution and correctional system. Half the original women have been placed in either work release or parole programs. Most of them seem to be doing quite well. None have failed as of this writing. The work release and educational release programs, we hope, will involve most of the women in the cottage. At present, two women are doing well in a local community college and others, hopefully, will enroll. A group has been formed which will discuss the conflicts of the work or educational setting for inmates involved in the program. There is a functioning educational program which offers courses in the cottage on Women's Studies, Black Studies and Psychology.

JUSTICE AS TREATMENT

In sum, we are developing a rehabilitation program that contains

11

the components familiar to progressive correctional practice, yet our program is distinct in the following ways:

1. It stresses establishment of a community process in an institution at a level larger than the small group of 10-15.
2. It directly stresses moral justice as representing "treatment" rather than phrasing "treatment" in psychological or mental terms.

With regard to the first point, our theory holds that the moral development rehabilitation process requires participation in an organized community with "secondary institution" features. Rehabilitation implies that the individual can function as a citizen in secondary institutions of work and community, that he reaches the level of a Stage 4 law-maintaining morality which recognizes the need for formal rules and institutions. Our approach stresses a community self-government process with a formal constitution, quite distinct from the face-to-face treatment group.

In our view, the school, family and work settings of the offenders are often so poor in permitting participation and affiliation that the offender needs an experience of a genuinely just, participatory community before he can affiliate with more unjust and rejecting institutional settings. In other words, moral development is a precondition for institutional identification as well as a result of it. A major aim of our project is to stimulate the development of the offender's values and moral judgment to a higher level, and to stimulate correspondence of judgment and action. This aim is easier to achieve in an institution where a consistent moral atmosphere may be established than it is on the street.

With regard to our second point, our moral theory is distinctive. A moral framework is, of course, not itself new to correctional work. Traditional correctional procedures were always moralistic, in the sense that correctional procedures were viewed as retributive punishment, as "paying the price" for one's crime through suffering. Until the 19th century, criminals were primarily "corrected" by hanging, flogging and other forms of retribution rather than by incarceration. With the development of incarceration, goals of retribution and rehabilitation were combined in the notion that the aim of imprisonment was "reformation," i.e., a recognition of moral error and an improvement of moral character through psychological persuasion and/or treatment. In this older practice, moral reform was conceived of in terms of promoting a bag of virtues of honesty, self-control, respect, obedience. inculcated through sermonizing and punishment and reward.

Partly in reaction to the failure of this form of moralism and

12

partly on philosophic grounds, the newer approaches to corrections have usually been oriented to "non-moral" sociological or psychological objectives. As an example, two of the most successful innovative programs, Guided Group Interaction and the Community Treatment Project both use a terminology of understanding and solving personal problems. "Guided Group Interaction is based on psychological and sociological conceptions but psychological and sociological terms are not used in the sessions. Only two concepts are voiced by the boys. The first is that of 'problem.' What is my problem? How can I go about solving my problems? The second concept is that of 'progress.' Have I made progress in understanding and solving my problem?" (McCorkle, Elias and Bixby, 1958).

The writers would contend that even when such apparently morally neutral definition of the problem of corrections is adopted, morality enters by the back door. Even if the purpose of incarceration is said to be for "self-understanding," both inmates and staff continue to maintain moral definitions and evalutions of what is going on.

Put in slightly different terms, in our view, the major force for change in small-group rehabilitation programs is the *moral pressure of the group* on its members and the *moral evaluation* of the individual by the staff and other members of the group. This is quite explicit in self-help or inmate organized forms of treatment. As an example, the Daytop program prospectus says:

"honesty, a basic principle required in Daytop, is not only necessary for the emotional growth residents need, but is almost inevitable because of the identification between them, after entering Daytop a new resident finds himself being corrected every time he lies. Even the seemingly small variations from the truth, which have become a part of his character are now being pointed out to him. He is shown that he must be honest in order to do anything for himself. He is shown that he cannot manipulate the other residents as he did his doctors or jailers because these manipulations are transparent. At this point the new resident realizes how foolish it is for him to lie and begins to do his best to be honest.

When people enter Daytop they are projecting an image, an emotional and behavioral mask, designed to let others see only what the individual wants them to see.

When a new resident enters Daytop, his seductive manipulative attempts to prove himself are picked up immediately by the group. Again, he is embarrassed, ridiculed, scolded and laughed at in his new environment. His 'code of the streets'

13

values change. It is now a matter of honor to be open and honest. The Daytop law, being honest with yourself and others, takes hold. No secret, no matter how personal, has any immunity."

This statement, while using some psychological terminology, clearly states that moral pressures and moral evaluations by the group ("being corrected when he lies," "being embarrassed, ridiculed and scolded") are the primary forces for change and that the goals of change are equally moral ("being honest," "not manipulating others," "changing his 'code of the streets' values").

What the self-help groups indicate is that it is only the presence of "value-neutral" psychological or sociological theorists involved in the treatment process which inhibits or disguises the moral nature of rehabilitation groups. Our approach accepts this moral nature of the rehabilitation process but grounds a moral analysis on a psychological theory of moral development.

14

Moral Development "Versus" Socialization

A Critique

John C. Gibbs and Steven V. Schnell
The Ohio State University

ABSTRACT: Kohlberg's challenge to socialization theories of morality—and counterchallenges to Kohlberg's own moral stage theory—are critiqued. Moral developmental and socialization theories differ, respectively, in whether the individual and cognition or society and affect are emphasized in the account of morality. In the literature on the controversy, however, these emphases tend to be mistaken for outdated, simplistic positions. It is argued that contemporary moral developmental and socialization theories should be viewed as providing complementary and interdependent analyses of human social interaction and the affective–cognitive unity of psychological events. Through recognition of this complementarity may emerge a relatively comprehensive understanding of sociomoral development and behavior.

With his dissertation in 1958, Lawrence Kohlberg imported a European controversy to American psychology. Decades earlier, Piaget had challenged Emile Durkheim's (1925/1961) understanding of moral socialization as a cultural "impression" upon the child. Mature morality, Piaget (1932/1965) had asserted, is not a basically emotional value transmission from a particular society to its upcoming generation, but rather represents an understanding constructed through the conflicts of social interaction natural to growing up in any society. Similarly, Kohlberg disputed the sufficiency of traditional psychoanalytic and social learning accounts of morality, positing a sequence of stages in the development of moral reasoning that could be found in any culture.

Currently, more than 20 years after the start of his challenge, Kohlberg's developmental approach to morality seems to have been assimilated into mainstream psychology. Kohlberg has become one of the most frequently cited psychologists in the contemporary social and behavioral science literature (Endler, Rushton, & Roediger, 1978, p. 1074), as moral development has ascended from the status of an "odd" topic in the 1960s to a major theoretical and research area (Brown & Herrnstein, 1975, p. 307). The supportive results of Kohlberg's 20-year longitudinal study (Colby, Kohlberg, Gibbs, & Lieberman, 1983)

have now appeared in a prominent monograph series, and Kohlberg's theory has been accorded space in virtually every introductory psychology textbook—especially every introductory developmental psychology textbook—on the current market.

This apparent assimilation is surprising when one realizes that Kohlberg's challenge would seem to imply the rejection of two mainstream psychological theses about morality. The first is that morality is a matter of accommodation of the individual to the values and requirements of society, through conformity and internalization processes. This thesis was termed "societalism" by Spiro (1951), who related it to the assumption that "society is prior to the individual, both chronologically and morally. It is the source of all values, which are eventually reflected in the individual" (p. 20; cf. Kohlberg, 1971, p. 175). Yet putting society first, Kohlberg pointed out, can mean that the individual is misconstrued as a passive recipient in the socialization process. Where champions of societalism saw the values of social order and stability, Kohlberg saw the danger of social stagnation as well as the stunting and even oppression of the individual. Nor are Kohlbergians comfortable with seeing morality as a matter of internalization and adjustment to society, because "to identify morality with conformity is to be forced to take the position that a loyal Nazi was behaving morally" (Lickona, 1976, p. 3).

The second mainstream thesis about morality is that it is fundamentally a matter of feeling and that moral behavior owes its motive power to affective socialization processes. If societalism posits the primacy of society, this thesis posits the primacy of affect. When the affective-primacy thesis is associated with the relegation of moral judgment to the realm of attitudinal dispositions, it is termed emotivism (see Brandt, 1959, pp. 205–214). It is clear that the affective-primacy thesis fits well with the societalist thesis: Indeed, to say that morality emanates from society to the individual is usually taken to mean that the originally "external" sanctions motivating moral conduct are partially replaced by compelling "internal" feelings of right and wrong. What Durkheim described as the inculcation of respect for the group through "impression," Freud conceptualized as the establish-

Copyright 1985 by the American Psychological Association, Inc. 0003-066X/85/$00.75
Vol. 40, No. 10, 1071–1080

ment of the superego through identification, and social learning theorists such as Mowrer (1960) and Aronfreed (1968) have seen as cognitive self-control through affective conditioning. In any case, if the individual is left with no internal feelings and "pull" regarding the rightness of moral norms and conduct, socialization has not taken place.

According to Kohlberg's challenge, however, placing affect before mind results in a severely limited account of morality. Kohlberg (1971) claimed a distinct role in moral motivation for "a rational or cognitively mature belief" as opposed to that of "an irrational belief" (p. 231). Similarly, Blasi (1983) has suggested that despite the role in moral motivation of "the impulse to satisfy irrational needs and the resulting anxieties and fears," there is a "normative pull" in morality toward an equally fundamental *cognitive* motivation, defined as "the desire to grasp reality in its own terms and to be open and unbiased" (p. 195).

The fact that Kohlberg's theory challenges societalism and affective primacy—two fundamental theses of mainstream socialization theories—prompts us to take a second look at Kohlberg's ostensibly integral status within psychology's "establishment." Certainly Kohlberg has gained prominence and influence of international proportions, but the controversy surrounding his challenge has not abated; the vast annual literature referencing Kohlberg represents continuing controversy, not consensus. It is time to take stock of the controversy generated by Kohlberg's challenge.

Evaluating Kohlberg's Challenge: A Case Study of Socialization Theories

How strongly Kohlberg intended to challenge socialization theories is not clear. At some points he seemed to be denying any value to such theories, supplanting them with his own theory. At other points, he granted that the theories may provide "partial insight" (Kohlberg, 1971, p. 155) and seemed merely to be proposing a supplementation to compensate for their insufficiency. We will suggest, upon inspecting a contemporary socialization theory, that the latter, more moderate position is more valid.

One of the most sophisticated and comprehensive socialization theories on the contemporary scene is that of Martin Hoffman, whose "hybrid theory" (Rest, 1983, p. 566)—focusing on the internalization of prosocial norms—has incorporated numerous features of both organismic and mechanistic theoretical paradigms as found in psychoanalytic, social learning, and other socialization theories (see Hoffman, 1983, especially pp. 236–242, 266–267). In order to evaluate Kohlberg's challenge, we will consider Hoffman's theory in some detail as a case study of contemporary socialization theory. Can Hoffman's theory justifiably

be characterized as entailing societal and affective primacy? The answer is yes—but as emphases, not as simplistic positions.

It is because Hoffman made the societalist assumption that the source of prosocial morality is society (primarily, the child's parents) that he devoted theoretical attention to the resulting question: If moral norms are "initially external" (Hoffman, 1983, p. 236), how does the child come to experience morality as self-produced? Hoffman argued that the self-attribution involved in internalized morality is fostered by certain child-rearing practices that allow "parental pressure to be low in salience" (p. 255); thus, a "selective memory" (p. 254) takes place such that the content of the norm is retained but not its parental source (see pp. 254–259), and the norm, activated in an appropriate subsequent social situation, is self-attributed.

Hoffman also devoted theoretical attention to the motivational question of "what people who have internalized the norm of considering others do when the norm requirements of a situation conflict with their desires of the moment" (p. 245). To account for prosocial behavior Hoffman has focused on the discipline encounter, wherein conflicts between moral requirements and moral desires were first faced and negotiated. Hoffman's analysis of the discipline encounter is designed to account for research findings that

a moral orientation characterized by independence of external sanctions and by high guilt is associated with frequent use of induction. . . . Inductions . . . are discipline techniques that point up the effects of the child's behavior on others. . . . A moral orientation based on fear of external detection and punishment, on other hand, is associated with the frequent use of power-assertive discipline, that is, physical force, deprivation of possessions or privileges, direct commands, or threats.[1] . . . There appears to be no relationship

This article is based on a paper presented at the meeting of the Society for Research in Child Development, Toronto, April 26, 1985.

We thank Marvin Berkowitz, Valerie Viereck Gibbs, Martin Hoffman, Larry Kohlberg, Mary Mullaney Schnell, John Snarey, Felicisima Serafica, and Charles Wenar for their helpful comments on a draft of this article. We thank Phil Allen for his technical assistance.

Requests for reprints should be sent to John C. Gibbs, Psychology Department, The Ohio State University, 142 Townshend Hall/1885 Neil Avenue, Columbus, OH 43210.

[1] Hoffman also noted, however: "The occasional use of power assertion as a means of letting the child know that the parent feels strongly about a particular act or value, or as a means of controlling the behavior of a child who is acting in an openly defiant manner—by parents who usually employ inductions—may make a positive contribution to moral internalization . . ." (pp. 246–247). Aronfreed (1968), Burton (1984), and others (e.g., Eysenck, 1964) have offered conditioning interpretations of the partial contribution of power assertion in early socialization to subsequent moral behavior.

between moral internalization and love-withdrawal techniques in which the parent simply gives direct, but nonphysical, expression of anger or disapproval of the child for engaging in some undesirable behavior. (p. 247)

Hoffman pointed out that discipline techniques are usually "multidimensional," that is, they have power-assertive and love-withdrawal as well as inductive features; typically, however, one or another feature will be dominant, and its role in the disciplinary encounter can be analyzed. The inductive feature provides the cognitive content of the prosocial norm. Whether the child attends to and learns the induction, however, depends on "motive arousal":

Power-assertion and love-withdrawal together comprise what I call the motive-arousal component of the technique, which is hypothesized as necessary to motivate the child to change behavior, and, more important for present purposes, to pay attention to the parent. Having attended, the child may often be expected to be influenced cognitively and affectively by the information contained in the inductive component. . . . But it must be noted that too little arousal may prompt the child simply to ignore the parent. Too much arousal, that is, if the love-withdrawal/power assertion is salient, may provoke several reactions [e.g., anxiety, anger, fear] that may interfere with the processing of information in the inductive component. (p. 249)

When the motive arousal is optimal for eliciting attention, the child learns the induction. Discipline encounters featuring induction constitute precisely the child-rearing practice that fosters self-attribution of moral prescriptions, because the inductive focus "on the child's act and its consequences" allows the "source" of the communication—the parents—"to be low in salience" (p. 250; cf. Dienstber, D. Hillman, Lehnhoff, J. Hillman, & Valkenaar, 1975).

Affect is primary not only in whether the prosocial norm is learned but also in whether it acquires sufficient motive power. Because inductions "direct the child's attention to the victim's pain or distress," they tend to "enlist" a "motivational resource that exists in the child from an early age, namely, the child's capacity for empathy, defined as a vicarious affective response to others" (p. 252). Furthermore, because the child's causal role in the other's distress is also indicated in induction, feelings of guilt are elicited (resulting from "the combining of empathic distress and the awareness of being the causal agent," p. 252). The elicited empathy and empathy-based guilt "suffuse" the induction, rendering it "emotionally charged," or "hot" (p. 261). In the subsequent internalized morality, affects of empathy and anticipatory guilt enable the induction-guided behavior to have sufficient motive power to overcome egoistic motives. Socialization of behavior has taken place.

It is important to note that Hoffman tempered his use of societalist and emotivist theses. Societalism

sees the individual as a passive recipient of society's normative values (Asch, 1952, p. 243). Hoffman asserted, however, that, although children do receive society's norms, one cannot understand the socialization process unless one studies not only society and child-rearing practices but also the child, for example, the "cognitive and affective capabilities that young children bring to the disciplinary encounters" (p. 264). The crucial role played by the child's capacity for empathy and other affects has already been noted. Hoffman also wrote that the child brings to disciplinary encounters "simple, at first nonmoral, cognitive structures and causal schemas" (p. 265). He suggested (p. 246) that the child's cognitive developmental level influences the sophistication of the inductions that parents are likely to use (cf. Maccoby, 1980).

Even the effect of the child's empathic resources depends not only on the disciplinary induction but also "on the level at which [the child cognizes] others, and that process undergoes dramatic changes developmentally" (see Hoffman, 1978, p. 181). Generally, the appropriateness, subtlety, and scope of empathy-based behavior is enhanced with cognitive development (pp. 181–186). Cognitive mediation and interpretation can also, however, reduce empathic motivation through "empathy-inhibiting perceptual and cognitive strategies" (p. 188). Indeed, cognitive mediation may negate empathy by classifying the distressed other as a dissimilar outgroup member (Hoffman, 1978, p. 204) or may even partially transform empathic affect into derogation by attributing to the other causal responsibility for his or her (or their) distress (p. 186; cf. Bandura, 1978, pp. 354–355).

Hoffman in effect tempered the societalist thesis, then, by pointing out the active participation and influence of the developing child in socialization. Because the child's activity includes *cognitive* activity—and because extreme (emotivist) versions of affective primacy minimize the role of cognition—the affective-primacy thesis is also tempered. Hoffman's point that the overall development and interpretations of the child must be considered in their own right is consistent with contemporary views of socialization as a social interactive process (see Maccoby & Martin, 1983).

Nonetheless, Hoffman's theory is not reducible to those of the Kohlbergian ilk. His theory is still "societalist" in that it seeks to account for the acquisition of initially external moral norms—not for the "fully developed moral system" or moral judgment maturity of the individual (Hoffman, personal communication, September 14, 1984). Also, despite Hoffman's major use of cognitive processes and development, his theory still posits affective preconditions for moral learning and motivation.

Hoffman's socialization theory, with its societalist and affective-primacy emphases, remains incomplete

237

in several respects. As Maccoby (1983) pointed out, not only aversive experiences but also positive emotional states engendered in children's "playful and cooperative interactions with their parents" (p. 362) foster attention to the parents (thereby making possible socialization influences). More to the present point, Hoffman himself noted that his theory does not deal with moral cognition qua moral judgment structure in the Kohlbergian sense:

A . . . limitation may be revealed in situations involving moral judgments, especially when several behaviors must be compared or competing moral claims evaluated. To be objective in such situations may require recourse to moral principles that go beyond showing consideration for others. The developmental link between the simple moral motive discussed here and the complex cognitive processes involved in . . . establishing moral priorities is a worthy topic for research. (p. 271; cf. Hoffman, 1984, pp. 299–300; cf. Rest, 1983, p. 561)

Hence, Hoffman acknowledged that his theory does not address certain important facets of morality—namely, the cognitive structural facets addressed by Kohlberg.

By the same token, however, the processes Hoffman did study—processes not represented directly in Kohlberg's work—need to be recognized as providing, in Kohlberg's words, at least "partial insight" into the processes of sociomoral development and behavior. Contemporary socialization theories (at least as exemplified in Hoffman's work), then, withstand Kohlberg's challenge. But does Kohlberg's own theory withstand the counterchallenge it has provoked?

Evaluating the Counterchallenge

Kohlberg's challenge to socialization approaches has not gone unanswered; indeed it would seem that Kohlberg's two charges have been inverted and thrown back at him. Whereas Kohlberg charged socialization theories with societalist extremes, critics have charged Kohlberg's theory with extreme individualism; whereas Kohlberg charged emotivism, Kohlberg's critics have countercharged rationalism or cognitive primacy.

Individualism

As defined by Spiro (1951), individualism is the assertion of "the priority of the individual, both chronologically and morally. All values derive from the individual and finally find expression in society at large, society being but a combination of individuals" (p. 20). Some critics see Kohlberg's theory as positing the priority of an asocial individual; for example, Emler (1983; cf. Haney, 1983; Youniss, 1981) charged that Kohlberg's theory "retain[s] the individual as the exclusive and sole focus of analysis" (p. 54). In Kohlberg's theory, Emler alleged, "individuals act autonomously and independently. . . . They do not co-operate or inter-act" (p. 55).

In fact, however, "individualism" in Kohlberg's hands is a thoroughly social affair. Kohlberg (1969) has consistently asserted the symbolic–interactionist view that "the basic unit of the self is a bipolar self-other relationship" (p. 417), and that "the self is born out of the social or sharing process" (p. 416). Kohlberg (1969) even stated that "moral development is fundamentally a process of the restructuring of modes of role-taking," and that "the fundamental social inputs from family, peer group, workplace may be termed 'role-taking opportunities.' . . . Instead of participation in various groups causing conflicting developmental trends in morality, it appears that participation in various groups converges in stimulating the development of basic moral values" (pp. 399, 402; cf. Rest, 1983, pp. 617–618). In recent years, Kohlberg (1984) has made clear his view that moral decision making and action almost always take place in a social context, indeed, that "moral atmosphere in the form of collective norms and a sense of community can be very strong factors in determining moral behavior" (p. 267). Kohlbergians (Snarey, Kohlberg, & Noam, 1983, p. 329) do acknowledge, however, that despite the social–interaction frame of reference, an individualistic *emphasis,* specifically, a focus on the cognitive activity of the individual, does characterize much cognitive–structural research.

A more specific referent for the individualistic charge is Kohlberg's equating of sociomoral judgment maturity with a "postconventional level" (stages 5 and 6) wherein the person "has differentiated his self from the rules and expectations of others and defines his values in terms of self-chosen principles" (Kohlberg, 1976, p. 33; cf. Dewey & Tufts, 1908, pp. 38–39). In Kohlberg's (1973) refinement of his postconventional level, he defined it as based on a "theory-defining level of discourse," that is, "defining a moral theory and justifying basic moral terms or principles from a standpoint outside that of a member of a constituted society" (p. 192).

The message is clear, and it has not escaped critical attention. Hogan (1975; cf. Mischel & Mischel, 1976, p. 107; Sampson, 1977) saw this equating of "*post*conventional" and "individually differentiated" with "mature" as "ideological individualism," defined as "the obligation of the individual to ignore public standards in the name of his private vision of truth" (p. 535). Ideological individualism "may ultimately be . . . the ruin of us all," because there are "anarchistic implications" to the view that "uncritical compliance with social norms is a sign of arrested development, a tendency that maturity allows one to transcend" (p. 536). Similarly, Wallach and Wallach (1983) in their critique of Kohlberg's theory asserted: "It is difficult to see how the general good will be

238

furthered by one's always giving one's own principles precedence over the laws and agreements of one's group" (pp. 186–187).

In effect, Kohlbergian theory is construed in these critiques as placing at the summit of moral development the subjective—and possibly antisocietal—ethical philosophies of elite individuals who consider themselves "beyond" society. The subjectivist implication is ironic, because Kohlberg has consistently and emphatically claimed that the ethical enterprise at developmentally and philosophically adequate levels is *not* subjective, and indeed, can generate "right" answers in some nonrelative (if not absolutist) sense (Kohlberg, 1971, 1984). In education, Kohlberg and Mayer (1971) explicitly distinguished the interactionist position (cf. subsequent "just community" innovations) from that of "romanticism" with its subjectivist elaborations. By his reference to individuals "differentiated from society" with "self-chosen principles," Kohlberg did not intend to abandon his social context for moral development and maturity; on the contrary, it is for the sake of social reform or progress—not anarchy—that the "principled" individual takes a stand. As Maccoby (1980; cf. Rest, 1983, pp. 557, 609; Waterman, 1981) pointed out: "The person who goes to jail in defense of the right to exploit other people for personal gain is not considered a martyr or saint" (p. 300).

Nonetheless, although postconventional principles in Kohlberg's hands are not "subjective" and apply to social ideals, it remains true that they are far from common and require considerable intellectual sophistication. In this sense, Hogan's (1975) complaint that in Kohlberg's theory moral maturity is reserved for individuals who have "transcended" conventional society through philosophical ideology takes on a certain degree of validity. Other writers' positions (Dien, 1982; Kitwood, 1983; Shweder, 1982; Simpson, 1974; Sullivan, 1977) are consistent with Hogan's characterization of Kohlberg's "postconventional" principles as "ideological," in the sense of reflecting not structure but the content of Western individualistic philosophy.

Kohlberg seems to have partly accommodated to this aspect of individualistic criticism. Most notable was Kohlberg's (1984) announced "suspension" (p. 273) of claims for postconventional stage 6 "as a commonly identifiable form of moral reasoning" (p. 270). Kohlberg acknowledged that his "theoretical definition of a sixth stage came from the writings of a *small elite sample* [emphasis added]; elite in the sense of its *formal philosophical training* and in the sense of its ability for and commitment to moral leadership" (p. 270). Stage 5, however, is less rare and was firmly defended by Kohlberg as a "*form* of moral reasoning" that is only "sometimes" "associated with the content of a moral or political view, like 'liberal' opposition to capital punishment" (p. 323).

Others who have pondered the philosophical individualism at the highest reaches of Kohlberg's theory, however, have been moved to suggest the need for further revision. These constructive—or, rather, reconstructive—critics have questioned the appropriateness of even stage 5 as a cross-culturally valid end-state of moral development and have proposed revisions designed to enhance the validity of the moral maturity construct in Kohlberg's theory. Some writers have suggested that stage 5 is inappropriate as an end-state because it is at present incompletely described. Edwards (1981), noting the cross-cultural infrequency of stage 5, suggested research on "adults from societies that are as complex as the Western industrial nations but are guided by different political and economic ideologies (e.g., China)" (p. 523). In a recent review, Snarey (1985) cited reflective philosophical data from Taiwanese, Indian, and Israeli kibbutz adults suggestive of more "collective" (p. 226) postconventional principles; he concluded that stage 5 is based on the individualistic philosophies of "Kant, Rawls, and other Western philosophers" and hence is "incomplete" (p. 228).

Gibbs (1977, 1979a; Gibbs & Widaman, 1982, chapter 3; Gibbs et al., in press) has suggested that stage 5 is an inappropriate definer of sociomoral judgment maturity not because it is cross-culturally incomplete, but more basically because *any* "theory-defining discourse" (Kohlberg, 1973, p. 192), even in broadened form, generates a misrepresentation of moral judgment maturity as the exclusive province of the philosophically articulate. Gibbs (1979a, p. 108; Gibbs & Widaman, 1982, pp. 36–39) pointed out that Kohlberg and colleagues (e.g., Colby, 1978; Kohlberg, 1984, pp. 252–257, 652–653; Tappan, Kohlberg, Poley, & Higgins, in press) have discovered that considerable ethical ideality can be present even at stages 3 and 4; hence, the traditional Kohlbergian view of stages 3 and 4 as necessarily merely "conventional" and less than mature becomes harder to maintain. Ethical–philosophical thinking is seen as functionally helpful ("Merely the explicit formulation of principles about obligations should make us more sensitive to those obligations"; Brandt, 1959, p. 14), but not as representing moral judgment maturity per se.

Kohlbergian theory as currently constituted would indeed seem to be compromised by philosophical individualism with its ethnocentric and elitist ramifications and would appear to be in need of revision. Overall, however, the basic Kohlbergian emphasis on individualism per se—on the actively constructing and contributing individual—should invite complementation rather than criticism.

Cognitive Primacy

Kohlberg's challenge to socialization theory as emotivist has also not gone unanswered. Kohlberg's error in accounting for morality, according to these critics, is the inverse of putting affect before mind, that is, putting mind before affect. Critics see Kohlberg's emphasis on fair-minded rationality in morality as inappropriately "cold" (Maccoby, 1980, p. 325): as failing to encompass the "caring" entailed in the behavioral application of moral–cognitive maturity, or as reducing affectively intense, sometimes irrational "moral" interchanges to the dispassionate deliberations of an abstract thinker. Emler (1983) explicitly linked individualism to this "cold cognition" criticism of Kohlbergian morality by suggesting that individualism and rationalism originated in the 17th century Cartesian celebration of "solitary thought" (hence his claim that "rationalism constitutes an intellectual form of individualism," p. 49). Indeed, individualism and rationalism are closely linked in the literature: the individualistic criticism is that Kohlberg fallaciously located morality in the individual, but, specifically, moral maturity in the individual qua rational *thinker* (especially, Western philosophical thinker). Hogan and Busch (1984; cf. J. Gilligan, 1976; Haan, 1978) flatly declared as wrong Kohlberg's assumption that human moral motivation is largely rational; instead, they posited a nonrational (and even irrational) basis for morality in personality structure. (Historically, this view finds antecedents not only in Freudian skepticism regarding rationality, but also in the Hobbesian view of reason as "slave to the passions.") Sullivan (1977) argued that Kohlberg's cognitive–structural bias leaves the person lost in abstract thought, with no affective impetus for moral action and commitment. C. Gilligan (1982; cf. Puka, 1976) juxtaposed against Kohlberg's developmental morality of justice a developmental morality of responsible *caring,* thereby correcting what was perceived as a male chauvinism in Kohlberg's theory (but cf. Gibbs, Arnold, & Burkhart, 1984; and Walker, 1984).

Kohlberg has perhaps been influenced by these critics, because he struck a more conciliatory tone in his latest work (1984): "We admit . . . that this emphasis on the virtue of justice in my work does not fully reflect all that is recognized as being part of the moral domain" (p. 227). Hence, Kohlberg was concessionary to psychologists who "find our analysis of moral judgment too 'bloodless,' tied too much to cold reasoning, as not offering a sufficiently formative role in moral judgment to feelings of empathy, compassion, indignation, and so on" (p. 290).

Despite this conciliatory stance, however, Kohlberg defended against the counterchallenge his cognitive–primacy position that "role-taking"—through which sociomoral development is seen as taking place— is "*first of all* a cognitive act" that cannot be derived "from sentiments of empathy or sympathy" (Kohlberg, 1984, pp. 291–292, emphasis added). It is important to note that for Kohlberg, cognition does not refer to inert informational content but rather to intrinsically motivating *structure,* especially mental balances or equilibria—the forms of "reciprocity" or "justice" engendered by the often unconscious coordinating of role-taking opportunities. The sense of justice or injustice, as Rest (1983) noted, may have "a counterpart in people's sense of logical necessity derived from the application of basic logical schemes to phenomena" (p. 616).

Conclusion

If Kohlberg's critics were fully accurate, then Kohlberg would have to describe his theory as the reduction of morality to the abstruse, unmotivating cognitions of the isolated, subjective individual. Correspondingly, if Kohlberg's challenge were fully correct, then even contemporary socialization theorists such as Hoffman would have to describe their approach as the reduction of morality to mindless conformity by passive individuals, that is, the internalization of possibly stagnant, stultifying social traditions. Contemporary versions of the theories, however, are quite distinct from critics' representations (see Table 1). The possibility is intriguing that Kohlberg's challenge—and the subsequent counterchallenge—stimulated the many refinements in socialization and moral development that attenuate the contemporary applicability of those challenges (M. L. Hoffman, personal communication, December 28, 1984).

These reciprocal criticisms are helpful in specifying the respective dangers of the alternative emphases in sociomoral development and behavior (see Table 1). Although it is clearly incorrect to attribute to Kohlberg a claim that individuals autonomously construct morality in an asocial vacuum, it is fair to say that it is all too easy to neglect social interaction processes in the course of studying individuals' progressively mature structures of thought. Although Kohlberg did not claim that fair-minded rationality is all it takes for moral behavior (thus distancing himself from the Platonic dictum, "To know the good is to do the good"), one can overestimate the motivating power of ethical ideality relative to egoistic affectivity when the former is the focus of one's research. Correspondingly, the individual undergoing socialization is anything but "passive" in contemporary socialization theories; yet "malleable clay" or "empty vessel" metaphors are quite compatible with emphases on society as the primary locus of activity (for example, the sender of "transmissions" through modeling and discipline). Similarly, in the focus on affect as primary in the motivation of moral behavior and the expression of morality, the danger is in discounting altogether any role for cognitive motivation and in failing to see that moral cognition includes structure as well as content.

Table 1
Representations of Developmental and Socialization Approaches to Morality

Representation	Sociomoral development		Socialization	
	Morality primarily constructed by individual	Morality primarily cognitive	Morality primarily acquired from society	Morality primarily affective
Self-attributed	Progressive social equilibration, adequacy; fulfillment through liberty and justice; social reform credited to those with principled morality; universalist ideals	Basis in mature rationality (fairness, impartiality); "pull" toward cognitive motivation	Active acquisition of norms, self-control; security through identification with community; societal order, stability, tradition; theoretical respect for diversity of cultures	Affect (e.g., empathy) makes possible moral learning, motivates moral behavior
Attributed by theorists of alternative approach	Morality reduced to decrees of elite philosophers; subjectivism, anomie, disintegration of the social fabric; theoretical intolerance of "inferior" cultures	Morality reduced to unmotivating or ruthless abstract ideology; neglect of empathy and caring	Morality reduced to passive accommodation to constricting social group; possible stunting of the individual; societal stagnation; ethical paralysis from cultural relativism	Morality reduced to mindless, automatized behavior or even irrationality; ethical paralysis from emotivism

Interdependence of Society and the Individual

Individualism may go beyond celebrating the contribution of the individual to morality to ask: Is not reality to be found in the living, active individual? Are not "society" and "morality" mere abstractions owing their "reality" to the constructions of the individual (indeed, of the individual theorist)? Conversely, societalism may see particular individuals as usually ineffectual and replaceable vehicles of network-level cultural processes (Asch, 1952, pp. 242–244). Each thesis qua ontological doctrine can in fact claim an impressive intellectual history in social thought; for example, the individualism of Spencer, Frazier, and Homans; or alternatively, the "collectivism" of Comte, Durkheim, and Levi-Strauss (see Ekeh, 1974).

The potential for an integrative view of the societalism–individualism antitheses was suggested by Spiro (1951). Spiro argued that the individual–society dichotomy was essentially false in the first place and hence was not in need of "resolution." In his analysis, Spiro concluded that the developing individual (or "personality" representing a partially unique, individually created "culture") and society (or the ongoing cultural heritage contributing to individual personalities and to which individual personalities contribute) are *both* "part and parcel of the same process of [parent–child, peer, other human social] interaction" (p. 43; cf. Asch, 1952, pp. 257–272). Extending from this primary social interaction, Damon (1983; cf. Bandura, 1978; Snarey et al., 1983) saw a "dialectical interplay" or "creative tension" between cultural heritage and personality development (or in his terms between socialization and individuation), pointing out that "the individual can only construct the self in the context of relations with others, but at the same time, the individual must step beyond the confines of those relations and forge a unique destiny" (p. 5).[2]

---

[2] It is worth noting that Damon's (1983) depiction of a relational interplay between the individual and society resonates with the more general epistemological suggestions of transactional psychologists as well as of the cognitive psychologist Ulric Neisser (1976). Whereas Damon points out that "the individual can only construct the self in the context of relations with others" (p. 5), Neisser points out, more generally, that the individual can only

The occasionally antithetical yet fundamentally interdependent character of the relationship between the individual and society can be related to the relationship between two basic "directions" or "tendencies" in human nature. Angyal (1952; cf. Bakan, 1966; C. Gilligan, 1982) elucidated "two different vantage points" on human personality functioning: one perspective focusing on active self-determination, and the other focusing on "self-surrender" wherein "the person appears to seek a place for himself in a larger unit of which he strives to become a part" (p. 132). Angyal pointed out that without some self-surrender, self-determination degenerates into alienation and a self-centered approach to social relationships. Correspondingly, self-surrender without some self-assertive aspects "is in danger of deteriorating into helpless dependency" or vulnerability to exploitation (p. 136). Hence, both tendencies should be adequately developed in a mutually enriching relationship for healthy personality and behavior (p. 135).

Interdependence of Affect and Cognition

Just as "societalism" and "individualism" qua doctrines are founded upon a false dichotomy, so too are one-sided positions on affect and cognition. Although one can find in the literature arguments for both affective primacy and cognitive primacy (e.g., see Lazarus, 1984; Zajonc, 1984), the most broadly encompassing stance is Piagetian (Piaget, 1954/1981): affect and cognition are inseparable, that is, psychological events constitute affective–cognitive unities. In the Piagetian perspective, *affect* can be provisionally defined as "the intensity and valence of our experiences (the magnitude of our investment in moving toward or away), whereas what we call cognition refers to the specific content of our experience and to its underlying structural organization" (Cowan, 1982, p. 51). It should be clear that the constructs are not independent: Even the simplest "investment in moving" (e.g., fear) entails at least minimal cognitive involvement (e.g., recognition of perceptual stimuli), and even the "coldest" cognitive activity entails some affect or investment in its behavioral continuance (interest, "will") or discontinuance (boredom, fatigue). Moreover, injustice or social nonreciprocity as a cognitive event may be intrinsically motivating.

Despite their theoretical inseparability, *affect* and *cognition* may in many instances be helpful as distinct terms as long as the qualifiers are kept in mind. In contexts where the intensity of experience, need, or temperament is strong and impelling ("hot"), we can term the psychological event affective, reserving cognitive for generally less intense, more complex psychological events (e.g., rational hypotheses). Highly affective processes (e.g., severe anxiety) are disruptive and hence usually entail less complex rational or linear structuring of experience and guidance of behavior (although neurotic anxieties often entail quite complex "irrational" or primary-process meanings).

Socialization theories such as Hoffman's do focus upon the role of affective events (specifically, affective arousal) in the motivation of moral behavior, whereas Kohlberg's developmental theory does focus upon cognitive events (specifically, role-taking equilibration). Nonetheless, Hoffman (1983) explicitly preferred as "making the most sense" an interpretation of psychological events as entailing an "affective–cognitive unity" (p. 261). Also, Kohlberg (1969) has asserted "that the *development* of cognition and the *development* of affect have a common structural base" (p. 389). Thus, both kinds of theories are compatible with a recognition of affect (e.g., empathy) and cognition (e.g., justice) as integral aspects of psychological processes in morality. It is probable that *both* cognitive and affective sources of motivation are usually required for the accomplishment of good and fair behavior in the face of narrowly egoistic impulses. An action that is fair or that rectifies an injustice is especially likely to be completed if its cognitive motivation is enhanced by empathy or empathy-based guilt.

Comment

Strictly speaking, it is not accurate to describe Kohlberg's theory as exclusively individualistic and cognitive or to describe socialization theories as exclusively societalistic and affective. Contemporary versions of both approaches are social interactionist and posit an affective–cognitive unity to psychological events. Greater mutual recognition of this common foundation should engender understanding of the quotation marks in the moral development "versus" socialization controversy. We find no necessary dichotomy dividing the camps—only contrasting but complementary *emphases,* the proper referent for the individualistic–cognitive and societalistic–affective adjectives. Consider the observation that children usually come to know and feel the consequences of their actions for others and to engage in cooperative and unselfish behavior. Must we choose between attributions of this prosocial development and cooperative behavior to the affect–laden acquisition of a prosocial norm in specific inductive–discipline encounters "versus" its attribution to the cognitive con-

---

develop cognitive schemata and accurate perceptions of the world through the acquisition of information from the world. On the other hand, Damon's concern for active individuality relates to Neisser's alternative Kantian point that new information cannot be acquired "without some preexisting structure in the individual" (p. 43). Objective and subjective primacies (Gibbs, 1979b, 1980), respectively, distort our understanding of life and knowledge unless they are integrated into a larger transactional view: Knowledge (including sociomoral knowledge, cf. Damon, 1983) is generated through a progressive interplay not only between individual and society but more generically "between schema and situation" (Neisser, 1976, p. 43; cf. Piaget, 1977, pp. 30–31).

242

struction of sociomoral understanding through participation in diverse (family, peer, school) role-taking opportunities? The question is of course rhetorical. The psychological events of social interaction include not only the affectively aroused content learning of specific parent–child interchanges but also the structural equilibration of diverse role-taking experiences over extended time. Both camps are harmed when the lines of continuity are severed by misrepresentations of Kohlberg's theory as asocial, subjective rationalism or of contemporary socialization theories as passive, conformist emotivism.

In other words, there is an inextricable interdependence between moral developmental and socialization approaches. Neither approach by itself provides a sufficient account of sociomoral development and behavior, but together they provide complementary emphases within a relatively comprehensive representation of morality (cf. Kuhn, 1978; Moshman, 1982; Nisan, 1984; Peters, 1971; Rest, 1983). Theoretical disputes can be healthy to the development of both approaches, as long as proponents of both approaches understand the interdependence of their common labor in the study of human social and moral life.

REFERENCES

Angyal, A. (1952). A theoretical model for personality studies. In D. Krech & G. S. Klein (Eds.), *Theoretical models and personality theory* (pp. 131–142). Durham, NC: Duke University Press.

Aronfreed, J. (1968). *Conduct and conscience: The socialization of internalized control over behavior.* New York: Academic Press.

Asch, S. E. (1952). *Social psychology.* Englewood Cliffs, NJ: Prentice-Hall.

Bakan, D. (1966). *The duality of human existence.* Chicago: Rand McNally.

Bandura, A. (1978). The self system in reciprocal determinism. *American Psychologist, 33,* 344–358.

Blasi, A. (1983). Moral cognition and moral action: A theoretical perspective. *Developmental Review, 3,* 178–210.

Brandt, R. B. (1959). *Ethical theory: The problems of normative and critical ethics.* Englewood Cliffs, NJ: Prentice-Hall.

Brown, R., & Herrnstein, R. J. (1975). *Psychology.* Boston: Little, Brown.

Burton, R. V. (1984). A paradox in theories and research in moral development. In W. M. Kurtines & J. L. Gewirtz (Eds.), *Morality, moral behavior, and moral development* (pp. 193–207). New York: Wiley–Interscience.

Colby, A. (1978). Evolution of a moral developmental theory. In W. Damon (Ed.), *Moral development: New directions for child development* (No. 2, pp. 89–104). San Francisco: Jossey-Bass.

Colby, A., Kohlberg, L., Gibbs, J. C., & Lieberman, M. (1983). A longitudinal study of moral judgment. *Monographs of the Society for Research in Child Development. 48*(1–2, Serial No. 200).

Cowan, P. A. (1982). The relationship between emotional and cognitive development. In D. Cicchetti & P. Hesse (Eds.), *Emotional development: New directions for child development* (Monograph No. 16, 49–82). San Francisco: Jossey-Bass.

Damon, W. (1983). *Social and personality development: Infancy through adolescence.* New York: Norton.

Dewey, J., & Tufts, J. H. (1908). *Ethics.* New York: Holt.

Dien, D. S. F. (1982). A Chinese perspective on Kohlberg's theory of moral development. *Developmental Review, 2,* 331–341.

Dienstber, R., Hillman, D., Lehnhoff, J., Hillman, J., & Valkenaar, M. C. (1975). An emotion-attribution approach to moral behavior: Interfacing cognitive and avoidance theories of moral development. *Psychological Review, 82,* 299–315.

Durkheim, E. (1961). *Moral education: A study in the theory and application of the sociology of moral education* (E. K. Wilson & H. Schnurer, Trans.). New York: Free Press. (Original work published 1925)

Edwards, C. P. (1981). The comparative study of the development of moral judgment and reasoning. In R. L. Munroe, R. Munroe, & B. B. Whiting (Eds.), *Handbook of cross-cultural human development* (pp. 501–526). New York: Garland.

Ekeh, P. P. (1974). *Social exchange theory: The two traditions.* Cambridge, MA: Harvard University Press.

Emler, N. (1983). Morality and politics: The ideological dimensions of the theory of moral development. In H. Weinreich-Haste & D. Locke (Eds.), *Morality in the making: Thought, affect, and the social context.* Chichester, England: Wiley.

Endler, N. S., Rushton, J. P., & Roediger, H. L. (1978). Productivity and scholarly impact. *American Psychologist, 33,* 1064–1082.

Eysenck, H. J. (1964). *Crime and personality.* London: Routledge & Kegan Paul.

Gibbs, J. C. (1977). Kohlberg's stages of moral judgment: A constructive critique. *Harvard Educational Review, 47,* 43–61.

Gibbs, J. C. (1979a). Kohlberg's moral stage theory: A Piagetian revision. *Human Development, 22,* 89–112.

Gibbs, J. C. (1979b). The meaning of ecologically oriented inquiry in contemporary psychology. *American Psychologist, 34,* 127–140.

Gibbs, J. C. (1980). Psychology and epistemology: Reply to Rosenberg. *American Psychologist, 35,* 672–673.

Gibbs, J. C., Arnold, K. D., & Burkhart, J. E. (1984). Sex differences in the expression of moral judgment. *Child Development, 55,* 1040–1043.

Gibbs, J. C., Clark, P. M., Joseph, J. A., Green, J. L., Goodrick, T. S., & Makowsky, D. (in press). Relations between moral judgment, moral courage, and field independence. *Child Development.*

Gibbs, J. C., & Widaman, K. F. (1982). *Social intelligence: Measuring the development of sociomoral reflection.* Englewood Cliffs, NJ: Prentice-Hall.

Gilligan, C. (1982). *In a different voice: Psychological theory and women's development.* Cambridge, MA: Harvard University Press.

Gilligan, J. (1976). Beyond morality: Psychoanalytic reflections on shame, guilt, and development of altruistic motives. In T. Lickona (Ed.), *Moral development and behavior: Theory, research, and social issues* (pp. 144–158). New York: Holt, Rinehart, & Winston.

Haan, N. (1978). Two moralities in action contexts. *Journal of Personality and Social Psychology, 36,* 286–305.

Haney, C. W. (1983). The good, the bad, and the lawful: An essay on psychological injustice. In W. S. Laufer & J. M. Dauy (Eds.), *Personality theory, moral development, and criminal behavior* (pp. 107–118). Lexington, MA: Lexington Books.

Hoffman, M. L. (1978). Empathy, its development and prosocial implications In C. B. Keasey (Ed.), *Nebraska Symposium on Motivation* (Vol. 25, pp. 169–217). Lincoln: University of Nebraska Press.

Hoffman, M. L. (1983). Affective and cognitive processes in moral internalization. In E. T. Higgins, D. N. Ruble, & W. W. Hartup (Eds.), *Social cognition and social development: A sociocultural perspective* (pp. 236–274). Cambridge, England: Cambridge University Press.

Hoffman, M. L. (1984). Empathy, its limitations, and its role in a comprehensive moral theory. In W. M. Kurtines & J. L. Gewirtz (Eds.), *Morality, moral behavior, and moral development* (pp. 283–302). New York: Wiley–Interscience.

Hogan, R. (1975). Theoretical egocentrism and the problem of compliance. *American Psychologist, 30,* 533–540.

Hogan, R., & Busch, C. (1984). Moral action as autointerpretation. In W. M. Kurtines & J. L. Gewirtz (Eds.), *Morality, moral be-*

havior, and moral development (pp. 227–240). New York: Wiley–Interscience.

Kitwood, T. (1983). "Personal identity" and personal integrity. In E. Weinreich-Haste & D. Locke (Eds.), Morality in the making: Thought, action and the social context (pp. 213–230). Chichester, England: Wiley.

Kohlberg, L. (1958). The development of modes of moral thinking and choice in the years ten to sixteen. Unpublished doctoral dissertation, University of Chicago, Chicago.

Kohlberg, L. (1969). Stage and sequence: The cognitive–developmental approach to socialization. In D. A. Goslin (Ed.), Handbook of socialization theory and research (pp. 347–480). Chicago: Rand McNally.

Kohlberg, L. (1971). From is to ought: How to commit the naturalistic fallacy and get away with it in the study of moral development. In T. Mischel (Ed.), Cognitive development and epistemology (pp. 151–235). New York: Academic Press.

Kohlberg, L. (1973). Continuities in childhood and adult moral development revisited. In P. B. Baltes & L. R. Goulet (Eds.), Lifespan developmental psychology (2nd ed., pp. 179–204). New York: Academic Press.

Kohlberg, L. (1976). Moral stage and moralization: The cognitive-developmental approach. In T. Lickona (Ed.), Moral development and behavior: Theory, research, and social issues (pp. 31–53). New York: Holt, Rinehart & Winston.

Kohlberg, L. (1984). The psychology of moral development: Essays on moral development (Vol. 2). San Francisco: Harper & Row.

Kohlberg, L., & Mayer, R. (1971). Development as the aim of education. Harvard Educational Review, 42, 449–496.

Kuhn, D. (1978). Mechanisms of cognitive and social development: One psychology or two? Human Development, 21, 92–118.

Lazarus, R. S. (1984). On the primacy of cognition. American Psychologist, 39, 124–129.

Lickona, T. (1976). Critical issues in the study of moral development and behavior. In T. Lickona (Ed.), Moral development: Theory, research, and social issues (pp. 3–27). New York: Holt, Rinehart & Winston.

Maccoby, E. E. (1980). Social development: Psychological growth and the parent–child relationship. New York: Harcourt Brace Jovanovich.

Maccoby, E. E. (1983). Let's not overattribute to the attribution process: Comments on social cognition and behavior. In E. T. Higgins, D. N. Ruble, & W. W. Hartup (Eds.), Social cognition and social development: A sociocultural perspective (pp. 356–370). Cambridge, England: Cambridge University Press.

Maccoby, E. E., & Martin, J. A. (1983). Socialization in the context of the family: Parent–child interaction. In E. M. Hetherington (Ed.), Handbook of child psychology (4th ed., Vol. 4, pp. 1–101). New York: Wiley.

Mischel, W., & Mischel, H. N. (1976). A cognitive social-learning approach to morality and self-regulation. In T. Lickona (Ed.), Moral development and behavior: Theory, research, and social issues (pp. 84–107). New York: Holt, Rinehart & Winston.

Moshman, D. (1982). Exogenous, endogenous, and dialectical constructivism. Developmental Review, 2, 371–384.

Mowrer, O. H. (1960). Learning theory and the symbolic processes. New York: Wiley.

Neisser, U. (1976). Cognition and reality: Principles and implications of cognitive psychology. San Francisco: Freeman.

Nisan, M. (1984). Content and structure in moral judgment: An integrative view. In W. M. Kurtines & J. L. Gewirtz (Eds.), Morality, moral behavior, and moral development (pp. 208–224). New York: Wiley.

Peters, R. S. (1971). Moral development: A plea for pluralism. In T. Mischel (Ed.), Cognitive development and epistemology (pp. 237–267). New York: Academic Press.

Piaget, J. (1965). The moral judgment of the child (M. Gabain, Trans.). New York: Free Press. (Original work published 1932)

Piaget, J. (1977). The role of action in the development of thinking (H. Furth, Trans.). In W. F. Overton & J. M. Gallagher (Eds.), Knowledge and development: Vol. 1. Advances in research and theory (pp. 17–42). New York: Plenum Press.

Piaget, J. (1981). Intelligence and affectivity: Their relationship during child development. (T. A. Brown & C. E. Kaegi, Eds. & Trans.). Palo Alto, CA: Annual Reviews. (Original work published 1954)

Puka, B. (1976). Moral education and its cure. In J. R. Meyer (Ed.), Reflections on values education (pp. 47–87). Waterloo, Canada: Laurier University Press.

Rest, J. R. (1983). Morality. In J. H. Flavell & E. M. Markman (Eds.), Handbook of child psychology (4th ed., Vol. 3, pp. 556–629). New York: Wiley.

Sampson, E. E. (1977). Psychology and the American ideal. Personality and Social Psychology, 35, 767–782.

Shweder, R. A. (1982). Liberalism as destiny. Contemporary Psychology, 27, 421–424.

Simpson, E. L. (1974). Moral development research: A case study of scientific cultural bias. Human Development, 17, 81–106.

Snarey, J. (1985). The cross-cultural universality of social–moral development: A critical review of Kohlbergian research. Psychological Bulletin, 97, 202–232.

Snarey, J., Kohlberg, J., & Noam, G. (1983). Ego development in perspective: Structural stage, functional phase, and cultural age-period models. Developmental Review, 3, 303–338.

Spiro, M. (1951). Culture and personality: The natural history of a false dichotomy. Psychiatry, 14, 19–46.

Sullivan, E. V. (1977). A study of Kohlberg's structural theory of moral development: A critique of scientific cultural bias. Human Development, 17, 81–106.

Tappan, M. B., Kohlberg, L., Poley, D., & Higgins, A. (in press). Heteronomy and autonomy in moral development: Two types of moral judgments. In A. Colby & L. Kohlberg (Eds.), The measurement of moral judgment (Vol. 1). New York: Cambridge University Press.

Wallach, M. A., & Wallach, L. (1983). Psychology's sanction for selfishness: The error of egoism in theory and therapy. San Francisco: Freeman.

Walker, L. J. (1984). Sex differences in the development of moral reasoning: A critical review. Child Development, 55, 677–691.

Waterman, A. S. (1981). Individualism and interdependence. American Psychologist, 36, 762–773.

Youniss, J. (1981). Moral development through a theory of social construction: An analysis. Merrill-Palmer Quarterly, 27, 385–403.

Zajonc, R. B. (1984). On the primacy of affect. American Psychologist, 39, 117–123.

244

Universality and Variation in Moral Judgment: A Longitudinal and Cross-sectional Study in Turkey

Mordecai Nisan and Lawrence Kohlberg

Harvard University

NISAN, MORDECAI, and KOHLBERG, LAWRENCE. *Universality and Variation in Moral Judgment: A Longitudinal and Cross-sectional Study in Turkey.* CHILD DEVELOPMENT, 1982, **53**, 865–876. A longitudinal and cross-sectional study of moral judgment development in Turkey is described. Rural and city subjects aged 10 through 28 were individually interviewed on Kohlberg's moral dilemmas. The responses were analyzed using a new manual, which calls for matching responses to criteria judgments. The results support the claim for structural universality in moral judgment: the Turkish responses fitted the moral judgment stages and exhibited the claimed sequence in both the longitudinal and the cross-sectional studies. The study also showed several aspects of variation in moral judgment. Village subjects showed a slower rate of development than city subjects. Beyond the age of 16 all the village subjects showed some conventional judgment; however, they seemed to stabilize at stage 3. Independent of stage level, the village subjects tended to justify their moral decisions mainly in the norm-following and utilitarian modes, while city subjects (in the older group) showed a tendency to use deontological and perfectionistic justifications.

Basic assumptions of cognitive-developmental approaches lead to the proposition that both stages and sequence in the development of moral reasoning are universal, or culturally invariant. According to cognitive-developmental theorists (Kohlberg 1969; Piaget 1948), moral judgment represents underlying thought organization rather than specific responses; its development results from a process of interaction between organismic structuring tendencies and universal features of social experience, rather than from "transmission" through genetics or direct shaping; and the direction of development is toward greater equilibration in the organism-environment interaction and reciprocity between the self and other (Kohlberg, Colby, Gibbs, Speicher-Dubin, & Powers 1978). These features of the development of moral judgment lead to a culturally invariant sequence of stages, or hierarchical organizations, each more differentiated and integrated, and thus more equilibrated, than its predecessor (Kohlberg 1971).

While the specific content of moral judgment may vary among cultures, the basic structures are said to be universal. Kohlberg's description of the stages (Kohlberg et al. 1978) is an attempt to expose such structures.

The hierarchical organization attributed to the stages implies that the individual should proceed through them in an invariant order. Evidence for this claim is provided by cross-sectional (Kohlberg 1963; Rest, Davison, & Robbins 1978), longitudinal (Kohlberg 1973; Kuhn 1976; Rest et al. 1978), and experimental (Rest, Turiel, & Kohlberg 1969; Turiel 1966) studies with U.S. subjects. Cross-sectional studies in Kenya (Edwards 1975), Honduras (Gorsuch & Barnes 1973), the Bahamas (White 1975), India (Parikh, Note 1), and New Zealand (Moir 1974) provide support for the universality claim. However, universality is properly tested by longitudinal studies of individuals in different cultures. In one such short-term

The affiliation of the first author is with the School of Education, Hebrew University of Jerusalem. This paper was prepared while the first author was a research associate in the Center for Moral Development and Education, Harvard University. The authors express their appreciation to Sumru Erkut for her invaluable help in collection, translation, and interpretation of the data. We are grateful to Betsy Speicher-Dubin and Clark Powers for assistance in scoring the interviews. Requests for reprints should be sent to Mordecai Nisan, School of Education, The Hebrew University of Jerusalem, Israel.

[*Child Development*, 1982, **53**, 865–876. © 1982 by the Society for Research in Child Development, Inc. All rights reserved. 0009-3920/82/5304-0018$01.00]

longitudinal study, White, Bushnell, and Reg-nemer (1978) assessed the level of moral judgment in Bahamian pupils over 2 or 3 consecutive years. Their results support the hypothesis that moral judgment advances with age (at least through the first three stages). However, their analysis is limited to group means. They do not examine whether all observed individuals do indeed develop in the sequence delineated by the theory. Turiel, Edwards, and Kohlberg (1978) did examine this point. Theirs was a longitudinal and cross-sectional analysis of moral judgment among village and city subjects in Turkey. The sequential advance of each individual anticipated by Kohlberg's theory was indeed found in this sample. The results also indicated that the rate of development was slower among village than among city subjects.

The first aim of the present study is to examine further the universality claim by broadening and elaborating the study of Turiel et al. Included are data collected in 1976, providing more longitudinal data on more subjects. We now have subjects who were interviewed four times, into their twenties. More subjects were also added to the cross-sectional study in the oldest age group. The invariant sequence hypothesis can thus be examined more adequately and for more mature subjects. The broadening of age range is of special interest in light of results from the United States which show that moral development continues into the third decade of life. We would like to see whether this holds true for the Turkish subjects, and also whether there is a ceiling in moral development not passed by our oldest village subjects, as is the case in at least one traditional society (Edwards 1975).

Furthermore, all the material used in this study (i.e., both earlier and recent interviews) was scored according to the new scoring manual (Kohlberg et al. 1978). This manual was constructed from a reanalysis of a great deal of empirical data and presents a more refined definition of the stages as well as a more reliable scoring system (Colby 1978). By requiring the scorer to match subjects' statements with detailed criterion judgments, the new scoring system would appear to reduce the subjectivity of the scoring process. This scoring method seems especially valuable in a cross-cultural study, where interpretations of the material are more prone to personal bias.

The second aim of this article is to present some data relating to cultural variation in moral judgment. Because such variation is so preva-lent and recognized (indeed, it is probably the basis for perceptions of moral relativity), any claim of universality in moral judgment should carry with it a distinction between the universal and cultural aspects. The Turkish study offers an interesting opportunity for such a distinction. The subjects of this study were all citizens of one country, speakers of one language, and followers of one religion (Islam), yet they seemed to represent two culturally distinct groups—traditional village and modern city (Lerner 1958). Comparison of these two groups reveals two facets of cultural variance in moral judgment. One relates to the mode of the subject's moral justifications and the second relates to the level of moral judgment across different issues. Clearly, these facets do not exhaust the types of cultural differences in moral judgment, but they show possible sources of variation. They also demonstrate the compatibility of the universality claim with the observations of variation. We shall comment on each of these aspects in turn.

1. An individual's moral justifications can be classified into four modes (Kohlberg et al. 1978): (1) the norm-following mode, a justification in terms of existing rules (e.g., "You shouldn't steal the drug because one should not steal"); (2) the utilitarian mode, a justification in terms of the material consequences of the decision; (3) the perfectionistic mode, a justification in terms of achieving a proper intrapersonal or interpersonal harmony (e.g., avoiding guilt); and (4) the deontological mode, justification in terms of justice, equality, and the value of life. Each of these four modes may be used in any of the five stages included in the manual.

Justifications in the first and second modes are situation-bound and closely related to the norms and circumstances given in the dilemma. They are classified as substage A. In a traditional society with common and stable norms, one can expect such substage A reasoning to suffice as justification for the decision in a moral dilemma. Justifications of the third and fourth modes, classified as substage B, represent principles operating in a more interpretive and general manner. In a modern society where norms change and their validity is questioned, one may expect such substage B justifications to be more frequent. We thus hypothesized that our village subjects would tend to use substage A justifications more than our city subjects.

2. Level of moral judgment may vary across different issues because of differential ex-

perience, involvement, etc. Cultural differences in social conventions, norms, and habits may thus result in cultural variation in the pattern of moral judgment level across different issues. We shall clarify and operationalize the term "issue," and then explain this suggestion.

Each of the moral dilemmas presented by Kohlberg first requires a choice between competing values and then stimulates judgment about related rules and institutions. The response to a dilemma is thus focused on the confrontation of two moral values or issues, and can be divided into arguments in regard to these two issues. For example, Dilemma III of the Moral Judgment Interview (Kohlberg et al. 1978) deals with stealing a drug in order to save life and elicits judgments about the value of upholding the law (arguments for not stealing the drug) versus the value of preserving life (arguments for stealing the drug). (A more detailed treatment of this subject can be found in Kohlberg et al. 1978.)

When scored with the new manual, individual responses are classified according to issues so that the level of judgment in each issue can be evaluated separately. Six issues are assessed: life and law (e.g., in response to the dilemma of whether it is right to disobey law— to steal—in order to save life); punishment and morality-conscience (e.g., in response to the dilemma of whether punishment should be exacted when a transgression is performed for appropriate reasons, i.e., stealing in order to save life); and contract and authority (e.g., in response to the dilemma of whether a son should obey his father when he does not fulfill the conditions of his contract, as when the father demands money the child has earned and saved for summer camp).

The comparison between levels of judgment on different issues is stimulated by findings suggesting that the level of cognitive functioning in a certain domain (with regard to a certain content) may be affected by the individual's familiarity with and experience in this domain (Flavell 1977; Piaget 1972). This leads to the hypothesis that when dealing with issues which are closer to their everyday experience, subjects might argue on a higher level than when reasoning about dilemmas which are far from their experience. This may introduce cultural variance in the level of moral judgment across different issues, due to differences in life conditions and environmental demands (Berry 1971).

Ethnographic material suggested that the issues of law and punishment (by law) are farther from our subjects' experience than those of (a father's) authority, contract (keeping promises), and life. We thus hypothesized that the level of moral judgment would be lower for the former issues than for the latter ones. We also expected that this trend would be accentuated in the village sample which supposedly had less opportunity to have explicit or implicit experience with law and punishment by law.

Method[1]

Subjects

Data were collected from male subjects in three locations in Turkey: a rural village (population 1,580 in 1960); a seaport provincial capital (population 520,000); and the national capital (population over 1 million). Subjects from the village were boys attending the local school, young workers, and young men who had recently returned from serving in the Turkish army. These subjects represent a fairly traditional society according to the criteria used by Lerner (1958) in dealing with Turkish society. Subjects from the cities were elementary school, high school, and college students or young workers. All city subjects analyzed in the present study were middle-class (judged by parental occupation).

Interviewing took place in 1964, 1966, 1970, and 1976. In 1964, 23 village subjects, aged 10–17 years, were tested. In 1966, 15 of these subjects were retested and 10 village subjects and 26 urban subjects were added to the sample. In 1970, six of the village subjects were retested and 15 college students aged 18–25 were interviewed. In 1976, nine of the village subjects and five of the city subjects were retested. Thus some of the subjects were interviewed only once, while others were interviewed two, three, or four times. All the subjects are included in the cross-sectional study; only those interviewed two or more times are included in the longitudinal study. The number of subjects in the longitudinal and cross-sectional studies, by age and social group, is presented in tables 1 and 2. A complete picture of the longitudinal sample is given in table 4.

Moral Judgment Interview and Scoring

Each subject was given an individual oral interview, including (each year) the same six hypothetical moral dilemmas and a standard set of probing questions. These dilemmas were

[1] Parts of this section are taken from Turiel et al. (1978). See that source for more details.

revised versions of Kohlberg's (Note 2) standard stories adapted to make them more suitable for the Turkish setting. An example of one such dilemma is presented in table 3. In 1964 and 1966, the interviews were administered through an interpreter. In 1970 and 1976, the interviews were given by the same Turkish-speaking graduate student attending a university in the United States, who had been trained in the technique of moral judgment interviewing.

For the purpose of this study, all the interviews were organized by dilemmas, randomized by subjects and year, and then scored using the new Standard Form Scoring Manual (Kohlberg et al. 1978), which entails a matching of interview judgments to stage-oriented moral judgment criteria organized by moral issue (two issues per dilemma). Scoring was done by dilemma, not by protocol. Thus, one dilemma was scored for all subjects, then a second dilemma, etc. Scorers were blind to the identity, age, and social group of respondents. In addition to moral stage, the criteria judgment also indicates the mode of moral justification. For each subject, percent usage of each of five stages of moral judgment was then computed as a function of all scored judgments. The subject then received a stage score (SS), which could be a single stage (if only one stage had more than 20% of his judgments) or a mixed stage, indicating his dominant stage and secondary stage (when more than 20% of his judgments fell in this stage).[2] Each subject was also given a substage score, which indicated whether 50% or more of his scored judgments were justified in norm-

TABLE 1

NUMBER OF SUBJECTS IN THE LONGITUDINAL STUDY BY YEAR AND AGE AT TESTING

YEAR OF TEST-ING	AGE AT TESTING				
	10–12 Years	13–15 Years	16–18 Years	19–23 Years	24–28 Years
1964....	7	5	3	...	...
1966....	7	9	6	2	...
1970....	...	...	3	3	...
1976....	...	...	...	9	5

TABLE 2

NUMBER OF SUBJECTS IN THE CROSS-SECTIONAL STUDY BY AGE AND SOCIAL GROUP

SOCIAL GROUP	AGE				TOTAL
	10–12 Years	13–15 Years	16–18 Years	19–28 Years	
Village..	17	14	16	16	63
City....	11	9	6	20	46

NOTE.—Longitudinal subjects are represented more than once.

TABLE 3

AN EXAMPLE OF A DILEMMA USED IN THE STUDY

DILEMMA III. Equivalent to Kohlberg's (1958) "Heinz and the Drug"
A man and wife have just migrated from the high mountains. They started to farm, but there was no rain and no crops grew. No one had enough food. The wife became sick from having little food and could only sleep. Finally, she was close to dying from having no food. The husband could not get any work and the wife could not move to another town. There was only one grocery store in the village, and the storekeeper charged a very high price for the food because there was no other store and people had no place else to go to buy food. The husband asked the storekeeper for some food for his wife, and said he would pay for it later. The storekeeper said, "No, I won't give you any food unless you pay first." The husband went to all the people in the village to ask for food, but no one had food to spare. So he got desperate and broke into the store to steal food for his wife.
1. Should the husband have done that? Why?
2. Is it a husband's duty to steal the food for his wife if he can get it no other way?
3. Did the storekeeper have the right to charge that much?
3a. (If the subject thought he should steal the food:)
    Why is it alright to steal if it is to save a life?
4. If the husband does not feel very close or affectionate to his wife, should he still steal the food?
4a. (If the subject thought the husband should not steal the food:)
    Would you steal the food to save your wife's life?
5. Suppose it wasn't his wife who was starving but it was his best friend. His friend didn't have any money and there was no one in his family willing to steal the food. Should he steal the food for his friend in that case? Why?
5a. If you were dying of starvation but were strong enough to steal, would you steal the food to save your own life?
6. (Everyone:)
    The husband broke into the store and stole the food and gave it to his wife. He was caught and brought befoer the judge. Should the judge send him to jail for stealing or should he let him go free?

[2] Thus, in principle one could obtain a score indicating a mixture of more than two stages, and these could be far apart, e.g., 1(3)(5). This never happened in the present sample, where all subjects were either in one stage or in a mixture of two adjacent stages.

following or utilitarian modes (substage A) or in idealizing and deontological (fairness and balancing) modes (substage B). In addition, a moral maturity score (MMS) was calculated, where the MMS is the weighted sum of percent usage of each stage multiplied by the number of that stage (Kohlberg et al. 1978). The MMS can range from a low of 100 (pure stage 1) to a high of 500 (pure stage 5). Stage score and MMS were calculated for each issue as well as across all issues.

Thirty protocols, randomly selected, were scored by another trained scorer. For 23 protocols (78%) there was complete agreement for the stage score, while for seven protocols there was a discrepancy in a half stage (e.g., 2[3] and 3[2]). In no case was there a larger discrepancy. For all the protocols there was an agreement for the substage. The correlation between the MMS given by the two scorers was .83. Internal consistency was calculated over the scores received by the individual on the six dilemmas. The obtained Cronbach α figure was .72.

Results

Stage of Moral Judgment

Table 4 presents the stages and MMS of subjects in the longitudinal study at each testing point. Each row presents one subject. The table allows us to follow the development of an individual's moral judgment at two, three, or four points in time, where the range of ages represented is 10–28 years. The table shows a clear sequence of advance in moral judgment: out of 35 changes, only four, or 11.4%, go against our prediction, a distribution whose chance probability is only .001 (by sign test, Siegel 1956). In no case do we find the skipping of a stage.

Table 5 presents the distribution of subjects in the cross-sectional study according to stage, by age and social group. Subjects with a mixed score (i.e., those who had more than 20% of their responses in each of two stages) were combined into one mixed-stage category, which does not distinguish between dominant and secondary stages (i.e., stages 2[3] and 3[2] appear under the same category of 2-3). Table 6 presents means and standard deviations of MMS according to age and social group. The MMS data were subjected to analysis of variance by age (four groups) and social group. The analysis showed a strong effect of age, $F(3,101) = 48.1$, and of social group, $F(1,101) = 26.7$, both significant at .001 level, and no significant interaction. Further analysis (post hoc t tests) revealed that all age-group differ-

ences in each social group were significant at the .05 level.

An examination of tables 5 and 6 suggests the following points: (1) In both village and city groups, the findings of the cross-sectional study are consistent with those of the longitudinal study. The results show a sequential advance with age through the stages of moral judgment. The correlation between MMS and age is .71 ($N = 109$). In no case do we find a regression in MMS mean of a group with advancing age. (2) The data show that the development of moral judgment continues after the age of 18 in both village and city subjects. This result is similar to findings in the United States, which show that moral development continues at least into the third decade of life (Kohlberg 1973). This result is of special interest for the village population in light of the following points. (3) We find that the rate of moral judgment development is slower in the village than in the city, and that this is also true for our oldest subjects. The differences between village and city subjects are statistically significant for each of the four age groups (significance is at the .01 level by post hoc t test in all four cases). (4) We find no subject older than 15 in the city or 18 in the village within a pure preconventional stage (i.e., stages 1 and 2), although even in the oldest age group sampled we do find subjects in a mixed stage 2-3. (5) Among the village subjects there is an indication of stabilization at stage 3. Only 2 out of 16 (12.5%) in the oldest age group show any sign of stage 4 development, as compared to 9 out of 20 (45%) city subjects of this age. The impression that village subjects stabilized at stage 3 is strengthened by the tendency noted in point 6. (6) Table 4 shows that, in general, subjects tend to show a mixed rather than a pure stage. However, this tendency is weaker after the age of 18, especially for our village subjects. Up to the age of 18, only 13 out of 73 (17.8%) are in a pure stage (where a pure stage indicates that only one stage gets more than 20% of the scored responses of the subject), while after this age we find 9 out of 16 (56.3%) village subjects and 7 out of 20 (35%) city subjects showing pure stage 3 responses. The difference between percentage of subjects of pure stage in the 10–18-year-old group and in the older age group is statistically significant, $\chi^2 = 7.18$, $p < .01$. The consistency in the moral reasoning of the older subjects, especially those from the village, suggests a tendency to stabilize, at least temporarily, at this stage of reasoning. Is it then the case that the village people tend to remain in stage 3, as do Edwards's (1975) Kenyan sub-

TABLE 4

MORAL STAGE, MORAL MATURITY SCORE (MMS), AND SUBSTAGE (SS) FOR LONGITUDINAL SUBJECTS

	AGE GROUPS														
	10–11 Years			12–13 Years			14–15 Years			16–17 Years			18–19 Years		
SUBJECT	Stage	MMS	SS	Stage	MMS	SS	Stage	MMS	SS	Stage	MMS	SS	Stage	MMS	SS
1	1	118	A	1(3)	186	A									
2	2(1)	150	A	2(3)	224	A				2(3)	239	B			
3	1(2)	133	A	2	178	A				3(1)	229	A			
4				1(2)	158	A									
5				2(1)	192	A	2(1)	177	A				3(2)	263	B
6							2(3)	198	A				3(2)	247	A
7							2(3)	207	A	2(3)	208	A	2(3)	243	A
8										3(2)	216	A	2	196	A
9	1(2)	124	A	2	200	A				2	192	A			
10	1(2)	146	A	2	209	A									
11				1(2)	160	A	2	203	A						
12				2(1)	176	A	2(3)	247	A						
13				2(1)	188	A	1(2)	150	A						
14				2	216	A	2(3)	207	A						
15										2	217	A	2(1)	198	A
16	1(2)	153	A												
17	1(2)	172	A												
18	2	183	A												
19		191													
20															
21				3(2)	259	A				2(3)	230	A			
22				3(2)	277	A									
23															

TABLE 4—Continued

	20-21 Years			22-23 Years			24-25 Years			26-28 Years		
	Stage	MMS	SS	Stage	MMS	SS	Stage	MMS	SS	Stage	MMS	SS
1				2(3)	218	A						
2				3	281	A						
3				3	296	A						
4							3	294	A			
5												
6										3(2)	283	A
7				3	311	B				4(3)	365	A
8										3	261	A
9												
10												
11												
12												
13												
14												
15												
16	4(3)	340	B									
17	4(3)	347	A									
18	2(3)	231	A									
19	4(3)	353	B	4(5)	434	B						
20				3(4)	367	B						
21												
22										2(3)	241	A
23	3(2)	218	A	3	296	A						

TABLE 5

Number of Subjects in Various Stages by Age and Social Group

Age and Social Group	1	1/2	2	2/3	3	3/4	4	4/5	Total
10–12 years:									
Village.........	1	12	3	1	...	...	...	...	17
City...........	...	4	2	4	1	...	...	...	11
13–15 years:									
Village.........	...	5	3	6	...	...	...	...	14
City...........	...	1	...	8	...	...	...	...	9
16–18 years:									
Village.........	...	2	2	12	...	...	...	...	16
City...........	...	...	...	4	1	1	...	...	6
19+ years:									
Village.........	...	...	...	5	9	2	...	...	16
City...........	...	...	...	4	7	8	...	1	20

TABLE 6

Means and Standard Deviation for MMS by Age and Group

Social Group	Age			
	10–12 Years	13–15 Years	16–18 Years	19+ Years
Village:				
M....	167.05	202.6	228.7	279.3
SD...	31.19	31.4	27.7	39.9
City:				
M....	206.7	243.3	274.8	312.6
SD...	51.4	32.9	34.3	41.0
t value..	2.549*	2.979*	3.266*	2.457*

* p < .01.

jects? No decisive answer is possible here without further follow-up of the village subjects.

Stage Level across Different Issues

Table 7 presents the MMS in six issues represented in three dilemmas: life and law in Dilemma III; morality-and-conscience and punishment in Dilemma III'; and contract and authority in Dilemma I. (These same issues are represented in the other dilemmas, for which the material is less complete and scorable data are available for fewer subjects. The results for the issue scores in the other dilemmas are similar to those presented here.) The means are presented for ages 10–15 in one group, 16 and above in another group.

An examination of the data reveals that in the younger group the level of moral judgment is higher in the life issue (i.e., when justifying

stealing a drug in order to save life) than in the counterissue of this story, the law issue, $t(27)$ for repeated measures = 3.66, $p < .001$, and higher in the morality-conscience issue (i.e., for those justifying no punishment or slight punishment for stealing the drug) than in the counterissue for this story (i.e., the punishment issue), $t(44) = 5.9$, $p < .001$.[3] However, the difference in levels of judgment in the two issues dissipates in the older age group, where the difference in MMS between two related issues fails to reach statistical significance in any case. These differences fit our expectation, based on the assumption that the issues differ in their degree of relevance to the subjects' experience. However, analysis of variance for each issue by age and social group reveals that our village subjects are significantly ($p < .01$) lower in their moral judgment than the city subjects, not only on the issues of law, $F(1,80) = 13.6$, and punishment, $F(1,58) = 10.3$, with which they assuredly have little experience, but also —in contrast with our expectation—on life, $F(1,86) = 13.8$, contract, $F(1,98) = 10.9$, and authority, $F(1,95) = 2.9$ ($p < .05$ in this case), issues, with which their experience is presumably similar to that of city subjects. As expected, for every issue the older age group had higher scores than the lower age group ($p < .001$ on every issue). In no case did the interaction between age and social group approach significance.

Substages (Modes of Moral Judgment)

Table 8 presents the number and percentage of subjects who were classified as being of

[3] Twenty-eight subjects had scores for both the life issue and the law issue; these are compared in a repeated-measures test. Only one subject had a score on both the morality-conscience issue and the punishment issue; his data are deleted and the scores on these issues are compared across independent samples.

substage A and substage B, according to age and social group. The table shows that in young age groups, up to the age of 15, all subjects except one in the city belong to substage A, that is, they justify their decisions using the norm-following or utilitarian modes. After the age of 15 we find a significant difference between city and village subjects. Almost all village subjects continue to be in substage A, while most of the city subjects belong to substage B, that is, they now tend to justify their positions by using the perfectionist mode or by relating their positions to principles of justice and equality, $\chi^2 = 8.036$, $p < .001$, for the difference between village and city in the older age group.

Discussion

Universality in Development of Moral Judgment

The first aim of this study was to examine whether the claim of universal structures in moral reasoning, which grew mainly out of research in the United States, would find support in a different culture. Our Turkish village subjects represent a traditional culture quite distinct from the Western urban culture which characterized the subjects of Kohlberg's longitudinal study. Two aspects of the claim of universality are that moral responses of individuals in any culture fit the structures suggested by Kohlberg (i.e., are classifiable in one of his stages) and that the stage sequence is constant

TABLE 7

MEANS AND STANDARD DEVIATIONS IN MORAL MATURITY SCORES IN SIX ISSUES BY AGE AND SOCIAL GROUP

ISSUE AND AGE GROUP	Village N	Village M	Village SD	City N	City M	City SD
Life:						
10–15 years	19	216	39.9	19	248	51.0
16–28 years	27	274	43.8	25	316	46.3
Law:						
10–15 years	26	154	49.9	15	207	62.9
16–28 years	27	252	86.6	16	322	84.7
Morality and conscience:						
10–15 years	8	206	52.7	15	247	49.9
16–28 years	20	268	57.6	22	311	54.2
Punishment:						
10–15 years	19	124	57.1	5	160	49.0
16–28 years	17	244	63.9	20	298	71.5
Contract:						
10–15 years	29	200	52.4	20	243	55.4
16–28 years	29	274	46.6	24	308	44.9
Authority:						
10–15 years	26	210	48.1	16	222	66.1
16–28 years	31	273	47.2	24	310	55.9

TABLE 8

DISTRIBUTION OF SUBJECTS IN SUBSTAGES BY AGE AND SOCIAL GROUP

AGE	Village Substage A N	Village Substage A %	Village Substage B N	Village Substage B %	City Substage A N	City Substage A %	City Substage B N	City Substage B %
10–12 years	17	100	0	0	11	100	0	0
13–15 years	14	100	0	0	8	88.9	1	11.1
16–18 years	14	87.5	2	12.5	4	67	2	33
19–25 years	14	87.5	2	12.5	7	35	13	65
Total	59	93.7	4	6.3	30	65.2	16	34.8

across cultures. A longitudinal study is essential in examining this second element.

The present study has found support for both aspects of the claim, support which should be seen as only a single step in a necessarily much larger body of research in different cultures. The longitudinal study presents a consistent picture of sequential advance in the stages of moral development up to stage 4, as well as in the quantitative score of MMS. This picture was supported in the cross-sectional study both in the village and in the city. It should be mentioned, however, that the sequence observed in this study is limited to the first four stages in Kohlberg's scheme.

Turning to the fitting of Kohlberg's stages to the Turkish data, it seems quite remarkable that the scorers had no difficulty and achieved satisfactory agreement analyzing the Turkish responses according to Kohlberg's stages, using a manual which requires a matching of responses. There were differences between Turkish and American responses, as well as between city and village. However, these differences did not interfere with the identification of basic structures which framed the responses. The scorers generally felt the match between actual responses and criterial judgments in the manual to be satisfactory and not forced.

One may argue that this apparent ease in scoring the Turkish data results from an inevitable overlaying of preconceptions on the data, leading to biased interpretation of the responses. This argument is somewhat weakened both by the relatively high reliability between judges and by the observed sequence in development. However, a more important—although far from conclusive—test of this argument would be the judgment of a sensitive and open person who is aware of the possibility of bias (Piaget 1929). The scorer in this study was aware of the possibility of bias, and sought for cross-cultural variance in addition to searching for universality. Our analysis rests, not on one standard and mechanical response, but on a multitude of judgments generated by several moral dilemmas, each possessing a number of questions. This seems to add to the credibility of the scoring. Yet there is no doubt that more research with maximal openness to the possibility of bias is needed (Price-Williams 1975).

A related issue concerns the representativeness of our data. Do the dilemmas presented to the subjects constitute true moral issues in their lives? Do their responses to these dilemmas represent genuine thinking in these do-mains rather than "playing the researcher's game"? The best we can do in regard to these basic problems of cross-cultural research is to examine the dilemmas and the responses from this viewpoint, using relevant ethnographic material (Cole, Gay, Glick, & Sharp 1971). Our impression is that the dilemmas are representative. The least we can say is that the Turkish responses were given with an appropriate sense of reality and involvement. Again, more research and further examination of these issues are clearly needed.

The universality claim may have another ramification to which this study does not relate. A strong claim of universality would imply that the structures described by Kohlberg exhaust more or less the whole domain of morality in every culture. Even if one assumes a degree of success in representing the moral domain of his own culture, such an assumption does not seem as simple for other cultures. It is possible that in other cultures, principles are held which are distinct from ours, and moral reasoning is used that does not fit the structures described by Kohlberg. This is likely in regard to higher stages of moral development. Gibbs (1977) has suggested that only the first four stages described by Kohlberg meet the criteria for a naturalistic developmental sequence, while the higher stages, which are almost absent in our interviews, appear to be formalized extensions of earlier stages. Such extensions seem to be culture-dependent, and may take forms which are hard for "outsiders" to identify. Examination of this argument would require—in addition to an agreed-upon definition of the moral domain—the study of a broader sample of moral dilemmas, composed through cooperation with expert and sensitive informants from other cultures.

The Rate of Development and Cultural Variation

The universality claim allows for the possibility of differences in the rate and endpoint of development. Such differences are indeed revealed in our study. The rate of development is slower among village than among city subjects. Our findings do indicate that after the age of 16, all village subjects develop beyond the preconventional level and show stage 3 judgment (or a mixture of stages 2 and 3). At the same time, they show scarcely any sign of development beyond stage 3. Clearly, the data cannot show whether village subjects will adopt stage 4 judgment in the future. However, the high frequency of a pure stage 3 and the almost complete lack of stage 4 among the oldest subjects indicate that stage 3 may be the stage in which the judgment of village subjects is stabilized, later development being mainly in a further decline of stage 2 judgments. This coincides with the finding of stage 3 as the final point of development in the traditional culture studied by Edwards (1975) and supports her suggestion that stage 3 is a necessary and sufficient level of functioning in societies having a social order based on face-to-face relationships and a high level of normative consensus. These conditions do not necessitate differentiation and integration beyond stage 3. Thus we have here an equivalent—in the moral domain—of what Berry (1971) has called ecological functionalism.

The analysis of the issues sheds further light on this subject, for it reveals that the level of reasoning across the issues was indeed different. In the youngest age group, the level of judgment was lower for the issues of law and punishment than for the other issues (life, contract, authority, and morality and conscience). These issues are less available to the experience of the child and allow him fewer opportunities for role taking. In the oldest age group, where experience with the law may be assumed, there is no significant difference between the scores for the different issues. This is true for both city and village subjects. These findings suggest that individuals tend to use a higher level of judgment in issues which are closer to their experience. This agrees with Piaget's (1972) argument that the differential achievement of formal operations accords with the amount of experience in a specific domain.

The analysis of the issues also shows that across all ages the village subjects use lower-level reasoning on all the issues, including two which stem from Story I (dealing with a father/son conflict), which seem close to their own experience. This suggests that the slower rate of development in the village stems less from a lack of experience with the moral issues than from a more general factor also acting in more familiar situations. One possible factor suggested by our analysis is that of a strong normative consensus in the traditional village, and hence a strong adherence to the normative system in general. In the absence of external stimulation to question the normative system, and in the presence of high pressure to adhere to it, one would expect less accommodation of moral concepts, and hence less differentiation and integration of moral reasoning. Indeed, as suggested earlier, stage 3 reasoning seems a sufficient or satisfactory level in the moral functioning of traditional communities (Edwards 1975).

The social ecology of the small village does not seem to call for the broader, generalized system perspective which is the hallmark of stage 4. A strong adherence to the normative system may be seen as part of a more generalized characteristic of a traditional (as opposed to scientific) society, which is described as not having awareness of alternatives to an established system of beliefs (Horton 1967).

This explanation is supported by the results of the analysis of substages. It will be remembered that the substage score is independent of the stage (one can be at stage 3A or 3B). Almost all the village subjects were found to belong to substage A (i.e., their moral justifications were in the norm-following or the concrete utilitarian mode). Justifications of this kind indicate that acceptance of the norm is so clear that one has no reason to look for other explanations. Among the older city subjects, we find a predominance of substage B (i.e., justifications in terms of justice and perfectionism), an indication that the norm itself or the immediate consequences of behavior are not perceived as sufficient group for justifying moral decisions. The large variation in norms within the city and the resulting questioning of norms seem to require reference to other types of justification.

The strong hold of norms and the tendency to use a norm as a first response to a moral dilemma is evident in an unexpected observation made during our analysis of the material. We looked at 40 protocols to see whether a moral decision (whether the husband should steal the drug in order to save his wife) changed during the course of the interview. In 20 of these protocols the first decision was not to steal. Only in eight protocols did we find a change in decision, and in all these cases the change was from an initial decision in terms of the norm (not to steal) toward a decision to steal. In no case was the change the other way around. Thus it seems as if the norm provided a ready-made initial response to the dilemma. Only after the interviewer's questions encouraged them to give it more thought could the subjects free themselves from the initial response and seek other justifications.

Reference Notes

1. Parikh, B. Moral judgment and development and its relation to family environmental factors in Indian and American upper-middle class families. Unpublished doctoral dissertation, Boston University, 1975.

2. Kohlberg, L. The development of modes of moral thinking and choice in years ten to sixteen. Unpublished doctoral dissertation, University of Chicago, 1958.

References

Berry, J. Ecological and cultural factors in spatial perceptual development. *Canadian Journal of Behavioral Science*, 1971, **3**, 324–336.

Colby, A. Evolution of a moral-developmental theory. In W. Damon (Ed.), *Moral development*. San Francisco: Jossey-Bass, 1978.

Cole, M.; Gay, J.; Glick, J.; & Sharp, D. *The cultural context of learning and thinking*. New York: Basic, 1971.

Edwards, C. P. Society complexity and moral development: a Kenyan study. *Ethos*, 1975, **3**, 505–527.

Flavell, J. H. *Cognitive development*. Englewood Cliffs, N.J.: Prentice-Hall, 1977.

Gibbs, J. C. Kohlberg's stages of moral judgment: a constructive critique. *Harvard Educational Review*, 1977, **47**, 43–61.

Gorsuch, R. L., & Barnes, M. L. Stages of ethical reasoning and moral norms of Carib youths. *Journal of Cross-cultural Psychology*, 1973, **4**, 283–301.

Horton, R. African traditional thought and Western science. *Africa*, 1967, **37**, 50–71, 155–187.

Kohlberg, L. The development of children's orientations toward a moral order: I. Sequence in the development of moral thought. *Vita Humana*, 1963, **6**, 11–33.

Kohlberg, L. Stage and sequence: the cognitive-developmental approach to socialization. In D. Goslin (Ed.), *Handbook of socialization theory and research*. Chicago: Rand McNally, 1969.

Kohlberg, L. From is to ought: how to commit the naturalistic fallacy and get away with it in the study of moral development. In T. Mischel (Ed.), *Cognitive development and epistemology*. New York: Academic Press, 1971.

Kohlberg, L. Continuities in childhood and adult moral development revisited. In P. B. Baltes & K. W. Schaie (Eds.), *Life-span developmental psychology: personality and socialization*. New York: Academic Press, 1973.

Kohlberg, L.; Colby, A.; Gibbs, J.; Speicher-Dubin, B.; & Powers, C. *Assessing moral development stages: a manual*. Cambridge, Mass.: Center for Moral Education, 1978.

Kuhn, D. Short-term longitudinal evidence for the sequentiality of Kohlberg's early stages of moral judgment. *Developmental Psychology*, 1976, **12**, 162–166.

Lerner, D. *The passing of traditional society*. Glencoe, Ill.: Free Press, 1958.

Moir, J. Egocentrism and the emergence of conventional morality in preadolescent girls. *Child Development*, 1974, **45**, 299–304.

Piaget, J. *The child's conception of the world*. London: Routledge & Kegan Paul, 1929.

Piaget, J. *The moral judgment of the child*. Glencoe, Ill.: Free Press, 1948.

Piaget, J. Intellectual evolution from adolescence to adulthood. *Human Development*, 1972, **15**, 1–12.

Price-Williams, D. R. *Explorations in cross-cultural psychology*. San Francisco: Chandler & Sharp, 1975.

Rest, J.; Davison, M. L.; & Robbins, S. Age trends in judging moral issues: a review of cross-sectional, longitudinal and sequential studies of the defining issues test. *Child Development*, 1978, **49**, 263–279.

Rest, J.; Turiel, E.; & Kohlberg, L. Level of moral development as a determinant of preference and comprehension of moral judgments made by others. *Journal of Personality*, 1969, **37**, 225–252.

Siegel, S. *Nonparametric statistics*. New York: McGraw-Hill, 1956.

Turiel, E. An experimental test of the sequentiality of developmental stages in the child's moral judgment. *Journal of Personality and Social Psychology*, 1966, **3**, 611–618.

Turiel, E.; Edwards, C. P.; & Kohlberg, L. Moral development in Turkish children, adolescents and young adults. *Journal of Cross-cultural Psychology*, 1978, **9**, 75–85.

White, C. B. Moral development in Bahamian school children: a cultural examination of Kohlberg's stages of moral reasoning. *Developmental Psychology*, 1975, **11**, 535–536.

White, C. B.; Bushnell, N.; & Regnemer, J. L. Moral development in Bahamian school children: a 3-year examination of Kohlberg's stages of moral development. *Developmental Psychology*, 1978, **14**, 58–65.

Development of Moral Judgment and Its Relation to Family Environmental Factors in Indian and American Families

Bindu Parikh

London

PARIKH, BINDU. *Development of Moral Judgment and Its Relation to Family Environmental Factors in Indian and American Families.* CHILD DEVELOPMENT, 1980, **51**, 1030–1039. The present research is a study of (*a*) the rate of development of moral judgment in a sample of urban upper-middle-class Indian children, adolescents, and parents; and (*b*) the relationship of family environmental factors to moral judgment development. The results are compared with similar studies of American families. The assumptions underlying the study are based on Kohlberg's theory of moral judgment development. The results of the study support Kohlberg's claim of cross-cultural universality of sequences and stages. Some differences in the rate of development of Indian and American parents are observed, although the size of the sample and possible variation in the scoring methods do not allow for final conclusions. Family influences favorable for the American samples are also found to be so for the Indian sample in the 15–16-year age group but not for the 12–13-year age group, which nonetheless indicates that reciprocity in parent-child relationships is a favorable condition for the moral judgment development of the children of urban upper-middle-class families in both cultures.

This research is a study of the sequence of the development of moral judgment and the role of family environmental factors, namely, role-taking opportunities in the family, among a sample of Indian upper-middle-class urban children of different age and sex groups. This study also investigates (*a*) to what extent the development of moral judgment occurs in the same stages and the same sequential order among Indian children and American children and (*b*) whether the positive relationship found between the family factors determining the role-taking opportunities and moral judgment development in the American studies will be the same for the Indian families.

The assumptions underlying the problem are based on Kohlberg's theory of the development of moral judgment (1969). Moral judgments are assumed to occur in different stages, which are sequential, universal, and approximately related to age. Environmental factors speed up, slow down, or stop the development, but they do not change the sequence of development, nor can they create struc-

tures. Stages in the development of moral judgment reflect fundamentally the restructuring of the modes of role taking (such as the awareness that the "other" is in some way like the "self" and that the "other" knows or is responsible to the "self" in the system of complementary expectations).

Cross-sectional studies in Kenya (Edwards 1975), Honduras (Gorsuch & Barnes 1973), New Zealand (Moir 1974), and the Bahamas (White 1975) provide support for the claim of universality in the sense that the data obtained in those countries were scorable using Kohlberg's systems and the same sequential order in the stages of moral development was found.

Two studies—Holstein's (Note 1) and Shoffeitt's (Note 2)—have looked at the relation of parents' behavior to children's moral judgment development. They have identified the following factors as determining the role-taking possibilities in the family and the moral judgment development of the child: (*a*) the level of moral judgment development of the

This research was done as a partial fulfillment of the requirements for a doctoral degree at the Department of Special Education, Boston University. The fieldwork in India was supported by the Indian Council of Social Science Research, New Delhi. I sincerely thank them for the financial help. I would like to express appreciation to Lawrence Kohlberg, Caroline Fish, and Esther Hill for invaluable help. I would also like to thank Betsy Speicher-Dubin for scoring the interviews and Bharat Pathak for rating the family discussions. Author's address: 67 Sutherland Road, London N9 7QL, England.

[*Child Development*, 1980, **51**, 1030–1039. © 1980 by the Society for Research in Child Development, Inc. 0009-3920/80/5104-0007$01.00]

parents, (b) the extent of encouragement used by the parents, and (c) the parents' use of reasoning and discussion while interacting with the child.

Shoffeitt (Note 2) studied the relationship of child-rearing techniques identified by Hoffman and Saltzstein (1967) to the development of moral judgment in children. These are (a) use of power assertion (physical punishment and material deprivation), (b) withdrawal of love (direct but nonphysical expression of love), and (c) induction (where the parent uses explanations and reasons for requiring the child to change). Shoffeitt's sample included 60 boys ranging from 11 to 16 years of age (model age, 13) and their parents. The families came from Tennessee and Alabama and were middle class. His results showed, first, that regardless of whose report of maternal discipline was viewed, the use of power assertion and love withdrawal was found to correlate insignificantly and/or negatively with each of the various indicators representing boys' moral development (e.g., moral stages from 1 to 6 and moral stage type—preconventional, conventional, and principle). However, the use of induction correlated significantly and positively with all these indicators of moral development. The same relationships were found between fathers' use of power assertion, love withdrawal, and induction and the childrens' moral judgment development. Second, the boys' stage of moral judgment was found to correlate positively with the moral judgment stage presented by their mothers. Finally, the stage of moral reasoning that parents reported presenting to their sons correlated positively with induction and negatively with power assertion and love withdrawal.

A study of Holstein (Note 1) indicates that parental provision of role-taking opportunities in moral discussion is a powerful predictor of moral judgment at ages 12–13. Holstein took a sample of 53 suburban middle-class families from the San Francisco Bay area and tested three major hypotheses. Advanced judgment in young adolescents is encouraged when parents themselves operate at more advanced stages of moral judgment, when they stimulate the child's own cognitive resources by encouraging his participation in decision making, and when they encourage greater exploration of structural properties of moral problems by allocating time for this purpose. One major finding was that the parents who encouraged their children to participate in the discussion (i.e., who were rated as taking the child's opinion seriously and discussing it) tended to have children with more advanced moral judgment. Holstein's results also showed that the relationship between the developmental levels of moral judgment in parents and children was stronger for mothers than for fathers.

With regard to the cross-cultural universality of the findings on the relationship of family factors to the development of moral judgment in the child, it may be noted that the family influences favorable to moral development are largely those typical of "rational democratic" society. This is hardly surprising in the American culture where a democratic relationship between parents and children is typical. Whether similar findings would be obtained given a different family structure "ideal" is uncertain.

It is characteristic of Indian families that there is a hierarchy in family roles, especially in terms of age and sex; the extent of shared activities among the family members is large (larger in Indian families than in Western families), but the use of explanations and the number of opportunities to participate in decision making are less for Indian children. Furthermore, Indian families are joint families. In a classic joint family the child's parents, his uncles, aunts, and their children, plus the grandparents live under one roof, with common kitchen and purse (Khatri 1970). The question is, Given that there is a hierarchy in family roles and/or when a joint family is providing multimodels, will the Indian parents have the same effect on the child's moral development as Western parents?

Method

Subjects

Fifteen hundred eighth- and tenth-grade children from four schools in Ahmedabad, India, filled out a form that included questions about their family structure and their socioeconomic and religious background. Forty families satisfied the criteria for inclusion in the sample. Except for one, all the families agreed to participate in the study. From each family three members were included: one child and both the parents. As the sample size was small, it was considered essential to keep it as homogeneous as possible. Participants in the study belonged to an upper middle socioeconomic group and were Jains and Hindus by religion. All the fathers were self-employed professionals (doctors, lawyers, chartered accountants, engineers, architects, and professors), and the mothers had a minimum of a high school education. There were two to five children in each family; 20 families had a child 12–13 years of age (eighth graders) and 19 had a child 15–16 years old (tenth graders). Of these 20 families 10 were extended and 10 were nuclear families. In each of the nuclear as well as the extended (joint) family groups there were five families with a male child and five with a female child.

Limitations of the sample.—The majority of the joint families in the present study were not classic joint families. An attempt was made to obtain ideal joint families, but from the total of 1,500 children it was possible to obtain only two such families among the families of the professionals.

Measures

Moral judgment.—Four moral dilemmas (Kohlberg's situations I, III, VI, and VII) were adapted to Indian society and presented to the subjects. The moral judgment development protocols were scored by the researcher and an experienced coder at Kohlberg's center. There were two measures assessing the level of development: the global stage score and the moral maturity score. Scores for both these measures were obtained considering the subjects' responses to situations I and III. The subjects' responses to situations VI and VII were not scored because a number of subjects did not take a stand, finding the dilemmas too hypothetical for them. The global stage score defines the moral stage acquired by a particular subject. For the global stage score a subject could get only a major stage score (such as 2, 3, etc.) or could receive scores for both major and minor stages: a subject obtains a minor stage score along with a major stage score when the majority of the subject's responses are at a particular stage and 25% of the responses are at some other stage. The moral maturity score is obtained in the following manner. The relative proportion of responses for each stage is obtained in terms of percentages. The percentages are multiplied by the corresponding stage (e.g., if 40% of the responses fall into stage 2, then $40 \times 2 = 80$). These computed numbers are totaled to give the moral maturity score.

The intercoder reliability for the assignment of moral judgment stage score was computed, which is .87. The computation of the intercoder reliability is based on 50 randomly selected protocols.

Induction.—For the measure of induction, Shoffeitt's (Note 2) adaptation of the child-rearing practice scale developed by Hoffman and Saltzstein (1967) was used. After a score for extent of use of induction was obtained for each parent separately, the total group was divided into low and high induction groups. Those scoring above the median are high scorers and belong to the high induction group; those scoring below the median are low scorers and belong to the low induction group.

Extent of encouragement.—Extent of encouragement refers to the amount of opportunity provided by the parents for the child to participate in the discussion of moral dilemmas. The discussion is taped. Two coders (the researcher and a blind coder in the field of social work who was familiar with Indian society) rated the taped discussion independently. Parents get a score of either high or low encouragement. Intercoder reliability was .97.

Holstein defined low encouragement in her study as comprising three categories ranked in order of extent of encouragement: (1) the child is silent or is simply expected to agree with adults, (2) the child is expected to agree with adults but is given some reasons why their position is right, (3) the child's expression of his/her opinion is tolerated but not related to the adults' decision making. High encouragement was defined as category 4, in which the child's opinion is taken seriously and is related to decision making.

Holstein included rank 3 in low encouragement, but in the present study it was included in high encouragement for the following reasons. While rating the group discussions, the researcher as well as the second rater realized that, in regard to the attitudes toward their children, the parents who had obtained rank 3 were closer to those of the parents obtaining rank 4 than to those of the parents obtaining ranks 1 and 2. In the discussions ranked as 3, although the parents eventually make their own decision, the child is a part of that decision making, feels free enough to express his opinions, and is taken seriously. Later, for certain analyses comparing these data with Holstein's, rank 3 was considered low encouragement.

Procedure

The data were collected in two meetings, which took place at the homes of the subjects.

In the first meeting the father, the mother, and the child were interviewed individually by the researcher using moral dilemmas. The interviews were taped and the order of presentation of moral dilemmas was the same for all the subjects. This was followed by a group discussion among the three. The issues on which there was a partial or complete disagreement in the responses of the father, the mother, and the child were selected for discussion. The instruction prior to the group discussion was: "On most issues the three of you agree but there are also some issues on which you do not agree, of which I have selected two. Please discuss them and try to reach an agreement if possible." The researcher turned on the tape recorder and left the room, and returned when the discussion was finished.

In the second meeting the questionnaires on child-rearing practice were explained and individually given to the father, the mother, and the child to be completed without mutual consultation. The researcher was available whenever help was needed.

Interviews were conducted in Gujarati, the mother tongue of the subjects as well as

of the researcher. They were transcribed and translated into English by the researcher herself. The first 10 translations were checked by a professor of English and a native of Gujarat. A list was made of those words for which it was difficult to get equivalents in English and this list was then discussed with a professor of Gujarati and another of English.

The researcher and the expert American scorer read the interviews together in English translation and then scored them independently.

Results

Age-Stage Relationships

The results from both measures of moral judgment development indicate that 12–13-year-old children, as expected, score at a lower level in their development of moral judgment than do older children (tables 1 and 2). Significantly fewer 12–13-year-old children (50%) than 15–16-year-old children (78%) reach the conventional stage in moral development, $\chi^2(1)$

TABLE 1

COMPARISON OF LEVEL OF MORAL JUDGMENT DEVELOPMENT ASSESSED ON THE BASIS OF MORAL MATURITY SCORE BETWEEN CHILDREN OF DIFFERENT AGE AND SEX GROUPS, BETWEEN CHILDREN AND PARENTS, AND AMONG THE PARENTS

	MORAL MATURITY SCORE			
	M	SD	t	N
13-year-olds	245.15	38.19		20
			2.316*	
16-year-olds	272.78	34.17		19
Boys	253.05	39.92		20
			.585	
Girls	262.32	37.10		19
Mothers of 13-year-olds	283.95	28.40		20
			3.102*	
13-year-olds	245.15	38.19		20
Mothers of 16-year-olds	277.21	40.70		19
			.367	
16-year-olds	272.78	34.17		19
Mothers of total group	279.58	34.93		39
			2.48*	
Children of total group	258.58	38.74		39
Fathers of 13-year-olds	321.30	48.64		20
			4.945**	
13-year-olds	245.15	38.19		20
Fathers of 16-year-olds	331.84	31.84		19
			5.471**	
16-year-olds	272.78	34.17		19
Fathers of total group	326.43	45.63		39
			6.186**	
Children of total group	258.58	38.74		39
Mothers of total group	279.58	34.93		39
			5.20**	
Fathers of total group	326.43	45.63		39

* $p < .05$.
** $p < .01$.

TABLE 2

DISTRIBUTION OF STAGES IN MORAL JUDGMENT DEVELOPMENT FOR PARENTS AND CHILDREN

	STAGES IN MORAL JUDGMENT DEVELOPMENT							
	2	2(3)	3(2)	3	3(4)	4(3)	4(5)	5 or 5(4)
Fathers.........	0	1 (2.5)	4 (10.25)	11 (28.23)	14 (36)	7 (18)	1 (2.5)	1 (2.5)
Mothers.........	1 (2.5)	7 (18)	8 (20)	19 (49)	3 (8)	1 (2.5)	0	0
13-year-olds......	6 (30)	4 (20)	6 (30)	3 (20)	0	0	0	0
16-year-olds......	2 (10.5)	2 (10.5)	5 (26)	9 (48)	1 (5)	0	0	0
Boys............	6 (30)	2 (10)	5 (25)	6 (30)	1 (5)	0	0	0
Girls............	2 (10.5)	4 (21)	6 (31.5)	7 (37)	0	0	0	0

NOTE.—Numbers in parentheses are percentages. Preconventional stages = 2, 2(3); conventional stages = 3(2), 3, 3(4), 4(3), 4, 4(5); principle stages = 5, 5(4).

= 3.548, $p < .01$. There is also a significant difference in the mean moral maturity score for the two age groups of children (table 1).

When 12–13-year-olds and 15–16-year-olds are compared with the mothers' group, the level of moral judgment development of mothers is significantly higher than that of the 12–13-year-old children. When the 12–13-year-old children and their mothers are compared in terms of number of conventional and preconventional subjects, there is a significant difference, $\chi^2(1) = 7.61$, $p < .01$. There is also a significant difference in the mean moral maturity score of 12–13-year-old children (245) and of their mothers (283), $t(38) = 3.10$, $p < .01$. There is no difference between the mothers and 15–16-year-old children in their level of moral judgment development (tables 1 and 2). When the fathers' level of moral judgment development is compared with that of the children, the fathers' score is significantly higher than that of the children of both age groups: for the 12–13-year age group, $\chi^2(1) = 10.156$, $p < .01$; for the 15–16-year age group, $\chi^2(1) = 4.25$, $p < .05$. When the fathers' level of moral development is compared with the children's level by comparing the mean moral maturity score, the results are the same (table 2). When the fathers' level is compared with that of the mothers (table 1 and 2), the mothers are at a significantly lower level in their moral reasoning. The mean moral maturity score for the mothers was 279, for the fathers 326, $t(76) = 5.20$, $p < .001$. The difference in the distribution of the mothers' and fathers' levels also shows that the mothers are nearly at a significantly lower level than

the fathers, $\chi^2(1) = 3.548$, $p < .10$. Compared with the fathers more mothers are at the preconventional stage, and very few scored above stage 3. The differences in the level of moral judgment development between the mothers and the fathers suggests a possible sex difference, but the results do not show any significant difference between the boys and the girls (tables 1 and 2).

Family Structure and Moral Judgment Development

The results show that there is no statistically significant difference in the development of moral judgment between the children of nuclear and joint families in the present study.

Family Factors and Moral Judgment Development

Relationship between the parent's and child's moral development.—The results show that the mothers at the advanced stage (i.e., at the conventional stage of morality) have the majority (74%) of children at the higher stage of moral judgment development. For the preconventional stage mothers the majority of the children (75%) are at the preconventional stage. The positive relationship between the child's stage and the mother's stage is statistically significant, $\chi^2(1) = 6.68$, $p < .01$. It is not possible to make any conclusive statement with regard to the relationship between the children's and fathers' stages, as there are not enough preconventional stage fathers in this sample.

In the group of mothers at the preconventional stage, there are two cases in which the child's stage is higher than that of the mother. In both these cases, the father's stage of moral development is higher than that of the child; that is, at least one parent is available who is at a higher stage than the child. Additionally, both the children are 16 years old and the educational level of their mothers is low (secondary school level).

The relationship between the stages of the child and of each of his parents is weaker and nonsignificant for the 12–13-year-old group but significant for the 15–16-year-olds, $\chi^2(1) = 10.97$, $p < .001$. In the 15–16-year age group all the children of the conventional stage mothers are also at the conventional stage of morality. Among the 12–13-year-olds, however, only half (56%) of the children of conventional stage mothers are at the conventional stage, the other half (44%) being at the preconventional stage. In other words, if a child is 16 years old, he tends to be at the conventional stage regardless of his parent's level. But if the child is 13, he will not necessarily be at the conventional stage. These findings support the assumption underlying cognitive developmental theory that the child's moral judgment level is not a simple reflection of his parent's level, but it occurs as a result of interaction between environmental and organismic factors.

Relationship between encouragement given and moral development.—The results show that the higher stage parents are more likely to be high encouragers than the lower stage parents. The mean moral maturity score (296) for the mothers using high encouragement is significantly higher than that (258) for the mothers using low encouragement, $t(37) = 3.785$, $p < .001$. A similar trend is observed in the case of fathers, although the difference on the mean moral maturity score is not significant. Still, the relationship is in the expected direction. The moral stage score also gives similar findings (table 3). Further examination of the results shows that all the mothers ($N = 8$, 100%) and fathers ($N = 1$) with preconventional stage morality use low encouragement. When the higher or conventional stage mothers and fathers are analyzed separately as well as jointly, it is found that the majority of conventional stage fathers (60%) as well as mothers (70%) use high encouragement.

The present findings are that all the parents who use high encouragement in a group discussion are at least at the conventional stage morality. But all the parents who are at a conventional level of morality are not necessarily high encouragers. In addition to the parents' stages, the child's age is a factor which seems to be related to the extent to which a parent will or will not use encouragement. Table 3 reveals that all the mothers who are at the conventional stage use high encouragement when the child is 16 years old, whereas only 50% of the conventional stage mothers use high encouragement when children are 13 years old. This is also true for the fathers.

The results on both the measures of moral judgment development show that when a child

TABLE 3

RELATIONSHIP BETWEEN CHILD'S STAGE IN MORAL JUDGMENT DEVELOPMENT AND EXTENT OF ENCOURAGEMENT USED BY MOTHERS AND BY FATHERS CONTROLLING FOR MOTHER'S STAGE AND FOR FATHER'S STAGE IN MORAL JUDGMENT DEVELOPMENT

	CHILD'S STAGE OF MORAL JUDGMENT DEVELOPMENT					
	13-Year-Olds		16-Year-Olds		Total Group	
	Precon-ventional	Conven-tional	Precon-ventional	Conven-tional	Precon-ventional	Conven-tional
Preconventional mothers:						
Low encouragement.....	2	0	4	2	6	2
High encouragement.....	0	0	0	0	0	0
Conventional mothers:						
Low encouragement.....	5	4	0	0	5	4
High encouragement.....	3	6	0	13	3	19
χ^2.....................	.900		4.98*		5.861*	
Conventional fathers:						
Low encouragement.....	6	4	3	1	9	6
High encouragement.....	4	6	1	13	3	19
χ^2.....................	.800		6.193*		6.153*	

* $p < .05$.

is 15–16 years old the chances of his being at the conventional stage are significantly greater when the parents use high as opposed to low encouragement, but when the child is 12–13 years of age this relationship remains insignificant.

The results in table 3 show that for the 15–16-year age group or for the total group level, two thirds of the preconventional stage children have mothers as well as fathers who use low encouragement. For the majority of the conventional stage children, the mothers as well as the fathers use high encouragement. In the 13-year age group, in spite of mothers being at the conventional stage and using high encouragement, three children have remained at the preconventional stage.

The mean moral maturity score of the children of the mothers using high encouragement is significantly higher than the mean moral maturity score of the children whose mothers use low encouragement. This is true for the children of the total group and for the 15–16-year group but not for the 12–13-year-old children. Similar results are found for the fathers.

Relationship between the use of induction and moral development.—The results show that there is a positive relationship between the extent of induction used by the mother and the child's level of moral judgment development when the mother's use of induction is assessed on the basis of her answers; there is also a positive trend in the relationship when induction is assessed on the basis of the child's answers. At the total group level, when the mother's inductive behavior is assessed on the basis of her views, the mean moral maturity score for the high-induction children is 275, which is significantly higher than the mean moral maturity score for the low-induction children, 241, $t(37) = 2.95$, $p < .01$. Similarly, at the total age group level the proportion of the high moral stage children (78%) in the high-induction group is also significantly higher than the proportion of high moral stage children (50%) in the low-induction group, $\chi^2(1) = 4.50$, $p < .05$. When the total group is divided in terms of age groups this relationship remains significant for the 15–16-year-old children, $\chi^2(1) = 5.629$, $p < .02$, but not for the 12–13-year age group. All the measures show that the extent of induction used by the fathers has no relationship to the child's moral judgment development.

In the case where the mother's use of induction is assessed on the basis of the child's report as well as of her own report, the extent of induction used by the mother differentiates the mothers with high and low levels of development in moral judgment. The mean moral maturity score of mothers using high induction is significantly higher than that of the mothers using low induction: when the mother's use of induction is assessed on the basis of the child's report, $t(37) = 2.07$, $p < .05$; when the mother's use of induction is assessed on the basis of mother's report, $t(37) = 3.19$, $p < .01$. Similarly, the proportion of high moral stage (i.e., conventional stage) mothers is significantly higher for the high-inductive group than for the low-inductive group: induction assessed on the basis of the child's report, $\chi^2(1) = 9.55$, $p < .01$; induction assessed on the basis of the mother's report, $\chi^2(1) = 10.59$, $p < .01$. The results also show that all the mothers of preconventional stage used low induction, and none of the mothers using high induction are at the preconventional stage.

Discussion

Claims of universality for the sequential order in the developmental stages of moral judgment development were tested by taking a cross-sectional sample of children of different ages. The results do show that stages appear in the prescribed order and that age is an important factor determining the level of moral judgment development. On the other hand, the results show that the mothers and the 16-year-old children are at the same level of development. The mothers are at a lower level than the fathers in spite of the fact that they are more or less the same age.

It is likely that moral judgment development does not continue indefinitely. According to cognitive developmental theory a person moves from one stage to another only when there is a disequilibrium between his level of development and his experiences. The majority of the Indian mothers in the present sample are at stage 3 and the fathers at stage 4. Differences in the level of moral judgment development of the mothers and the fathers are probably related to their roles in life. Most of the mothers in the present sample are housewives. By contrast, all the fathers are working men and, therefore, have more opportunity to interact with the society. The four mothers who have obtained scores above pure stage 3 (stage 3[4]) are presently working or have worked in the past.

Relative rate of moral judgment development.—It is not possible to compare the present data with Shoffeitt's findings, as he does not break his group down in terms of age. But Holstein's study (1976) can be used for age comparisons. In a longitudinal study, Holstein interviewed families of 13-year-olds (after 3 years) from her 1969 study, which also gives data on 16-year-olds. Moreover, she has rescored her earlier data using the issue scoring method (Kohlberg, Note 3) also used in the present study.

Holstein's results indicate that American children in the 13- and 16-year age groups have reached a higher stage in moral judgment development than Indian children from the same age groups and socioeconomic class. In the 13-year age group 17% of Holstein's children have reached stage 4, and the proportion of preconventional children in her sample is 30% as against 50% in the Indian sample. Similarly, in the 16-year age group of the present study, 21% are at the preconventional level or at stage 2, and 74% are at stage 3 as against the 40% in Holstein's sample who are at stage 3. Of her 16 year olds, 57% are above stage 3, 44% at stage 4, and 13% at stage 5.

In Holstein's study (1976) quite a few American fathers and mothers have obtained the score of stage 5, while none of the Indian mothers and one father are at stage 5. In the Indian sample 28% of the fathers are at stage 3, while none of the American fathers in Holstein's sample are at a stage lower than 4. Proportionately more American mothers (52%) are at stage 4 compared with Indian mothers who are at stage 3(4) or 4(3) (10.5%). None of the mothers in Holstein's sample is at the preconventional stage, while 8 (20.5%) Indian mothers are at this stage.

It would be wrong to conclude on the basis of the above data that Indian children develop at a slower rate than American children and that American parents have reached a higher stage than Indian parents. The above comparisons are based on fairly small and not perfectly matched samples. Even though both the studies have used the issue scoring method, it seems likely that Holstein was more liberal in scoring and may therefore have obtained higher scores for her subjects. Holstein's result shows that some of her 16-year-olds have reached stage 5, but according to Kohlberg

and Kramer (1969) stage 5 is found among only a few older adolescents.

The question of relative rate of moral development among Indian and American children and parents could only be answered if the same researcher were to conduct studies on closely matched Indian and American samples and use the same method of scoring. And even if the methodological factors are properly controlled, the question remains, Are different principles of morality operating in Indian society? It is not possible to examine this question here, as almost all the subjects in the present sample are at the conventional or preconventional stage. The answer to this question requires a study of Indian subjects who are at the principle stage. For instance, a study of a sample of nonwesternized Hindu philosophers may help. Nonetheless, the present research does provide some support to the claim that stages of moral development are universal, because the qualitative analysis shows that the majority of responses which are used in the assessment are scorable using Kohlberg's system and that they show the expected age trends.

Family Factors and Their Relation to Moral Judgment Development

Why should the parents' level of moral judgment development, their use of encouragement, and their use of induction as a technique to bring up children be positively related to children's development of moral judgment?

Parents who are advanced in moral reasoning provide more advanced ideas and reasoning than parents who are less matured. The development of a child's moral judgment is affected by the extent to which the parents elicit and consider the child's point of view. Thus it is not sufficient that moral ideas be available within the family: they must also be actively shared. The child's movement from one stage to another can best be facilitated by encouraging the child's active participation. In addition, the parents' use of induction appears to be a factor indicating the level of moral maturity in their interaction with the child. Use of induction as a technique to bring up children implies that a parent is nonauthoritarian and nonarbitrary, that he resorts to reasoning.

The present results show that the relationship between the child's and mother's moral stage is stronger than the relationship between the father's stage and the child's stage. A possible explanation is that a child spends more time with the mother. In the present sample, most of the fathers were working professionals, and most of the mothers spent much of their time at home; in such a situation the children might have more chance of learning from their mothers than from their fathers. This is further indicated by the following findings. There is a close correspondence between the mothers' use of induction and the way mothers look at their own behavior. There is, however, a discrepancy between the way the children and fathers view the fathers' use of induction.

Parents' attainment of conventional stage morality is linked to their use of high encouragement and high induction. Perhaps, since the preconventional stage is that of the egoistic, instrumental, and authoritative orientation, the tendency of stage 2 parents toward their children would be to say, "We do things for you, so you should do things for us" or "We are older so you must obey us." Furthermore, preconventional stage parents perhaps cannot see the child as a responsible decision maker, and, as a result, they use low encouragement. On the other hand, conventional level parents have high cognitive potential or conceptual tools available to them, and, as a result, may be more likely to resort to reasoning while disciplining children.

The family factors which were found to be favorable for the moral judgment development of children among American samples (Holstein, Note 1; Shoffeitt, Note 2) are also found to be so among the Indian upper-middle-class sample. This in a way suggests that the meaning of family factors influencing role-taking opportunities is the same for the two cultures despite different values and ideals for family relationships. Holstein (Note 1) has found that parents' use of encouragement is positively related to parents' and children's levels of moral judgment development. She also found that children's and parents' levels of moral judgment development are positively related. Shoffeitt (Note 2) studied the relationship of use of induction and moral judgment development in parents and children, where he also finds a positive relationship.

However, there are some significant differences in the findings of the American studies and the present study of Indian families. In the American studies the relationship of family environmental factors to children's development of moral judgment is significantly positive, while in the present study the relationship is significant only for the older age group; there is a positive trend in the relationship for the younger age group, but it is not statistically significant. In Indian society the age of the child seems to be an important factor in determining the hierarchical interaction pattern in the family.

There is some suggestion that the interaction patterns in American families are more democratic than those of Indian families of comparable socioeconomic background. In Holstein's sample the percentage of parents using high encouragement (71%) is greater than that of Indian parents in the present sample (42%). Moreover, Shoffeitt found that the father's use of induction is positively correlated with moral judgment development of the child, while in the present study no significant relationship is found between the father's use of induction and the child's moral judgment development. Though the samples in these two cases come from two distinct societies, there are considerable resemblances. Both samples are from an industrialized urban population with similar educational levels and more or less the same relative position in the society. Boys and girls from upper-middle-class families in present-day industrialized society in India get similar opportunities for education and social interaction as children get in America. These facts may explain the similarity in the pattern of relationships observed in specific subsets of Indian and American societies. This, though, does not indicate that similarity would also be observed in a rural nonindustrialized population of the two societies, or if the subjects were chosen from other socioeconomic strata, especially from poor sections of the population.

Reference Notes

1. Holstein, C. B. The relation of children's moral judgment level to that of their parents and to communication patterns in the family. Paper presented at the biennial meeting of the Society for Research in Child Development, Santa Monica, Calif., 1969.

2. Shoffeitt, P. G. The moral development of children as a function of parental moral judgments and child-rearing practices. Unpublished doctoral dissertation, George Peabody College for Teachers, 1971.

3. Kohlberg, L. Issue scoring guide. Unpublished manuscript, Harvard University, 1972.

References

Edwards, C. P. Societal complexity and moral development: a Kenyan study. *Ethos,* 1975, **3,** 505–527.

Gorsuch, R. L., & Barnes, M. L. Stages of ethical reasoning and moral norms of Carib youths. *Journal of Cross-Cultural Psychology,* 1973, **4,** 283–301.

Hoffman, M. L., & Saltzstein, H. D. Parent discipline and child's moral development. *Journal of Personality and Social Psychology,* 1967, **5,** 45–47.

Holstein, C. B. Irreversible, stepwise sequence in the development of moral judgment: a longitudinal study of males and females. *Child Development,* 1976, **47,** 51–61.

Khatri, A. *Manual of the scale of measure joint-ness of families in India.* Ahmedabad: B.M. Institute, 1970.

Kohlberg, L. Stage and sequence: the cognitive developmental approach to socialization. In D. Goslin (Ed.), *Handbook of socialization theory and research.* Chicago: Rand-McNally, 1969.

Kohlberg, L., & Kramer, R. Continuities and discontinuities in childhood and adult moral development. *Human Development,* 1969, **12,** 93–120.

Moir, J. Egocentrism and the emergence of conventional morality in preadolescent girls. *Child Development,* 1974, **45,** 299–344.

White, C. B. Moral development in Bahamian school children: a cross-cultural examination of Kohlberg's stages of moral reasoning. *Developmental Psychology,* 1975, **11,** 535–536.

Psychological Bulletin
1985, Vol. 97, No. 2, 202–232

Cross-Cultural Universality of Social–Moral Development: A Critical Review of Kohlbergian Research

John R. Snarey
Laboratory of Human Development
Harvard University

Over the past 15 years, children and adults around the world have been asked if Heinz should steal a drug to save his dying wife, if Njoroge should disobey the rules to help a lost child, or some other similar moral dilemma. These cross-cultural studies have been undertaken to test Lawrence Kohlberg's theory, which posits a universal model of moral development. This review identifies the major empirical assumptions underlying Kohlberg's claim for cross-cultural universality, including culturally diverse samplings, universal moral questions, invariant stage sequence, full range of stages, and general applicability of the stages. It then reviews the cross-cultural research literature, much of which has not been previously published, and evaluates the support for each assumption. In addition to providing striking support for the underlying assumptions, the 45 studies examined here also identify some major caveats regarding the range and general applicability of the stages across cultures. In particular, biases in favor of complex urban societies and middle-class populations are identified. Based on these findings, the conclusion presents an alternative to Kohlberg's perspective on the relation between culture and moral development.

Lawrence Kohlberg's stage model of moral development, briefly summarized in Table 1, has attracted a great deal of positive attention from psychologists and educators. Not surprisingly, however, his work has also inspired considerable criticism and revisionism (cf. Gibbs, 1977; Gilligan, 1982; Kurtines & Grief, 1974; Rest, 1983). The aspect of Kohlberg's theory that has been most difficult for many social scientists to accept is the claim that the development of moral reasoning about the social environment follows a universal invariant sequence, toward the same universal ethical principles, in all cultural settings (cf. Bloom, 1977; Buck-Morss, 1975; Edwards, 1975, 1982; Guidon, 1978; Shweder, 1982a, 1982b; Simpson, 1974; Sullivan, 1977). This article identifies the primary empirical assumptions underlying Kohlberg's claim of cross-cultural universality and clarifies the appropriate evidence necessary to judge the claim. It then presents a comprehensive examination of the available empirical evidence that has accumulated over the last 15 years and evaluates the support or lack of support indicated. The assumptions are discussed in evaluative order, from those that receive the most support to those that receive the least support.

Assumptions and Hypotheses

Kohlberg (1971) stated his claim for the cross-cultural universality of moral development as follows: "All individuals in all cultures use the same thirty basic moral categories, concepts, or principles, and all individuals in all cultures go through the same order or sequence of gross stage development, though they vary in rate and terminal point of development" (1971, p. 175). I believe that Kohlberg's claim implies at least five empirical assumptions, each of which may be understood as a testable hypothesis.

The first assumption is that moral devel-

Preparation of this review was supported in part by National Institute of Mental Health Grant MH14088. I gratefully thank Agusto Blasi, John Broughton, John Gibbs, Lawrence Kohlberg, Stuart Hauser, Betty J. House, Harry Lasker, Robert LeVine, Joseph Reimer, Richard Shweder, and Carol Snarey for their helpful comments on a preliminary draft of this article. Special thanks to Carolyn Edwards for her extensive and careful comments.

Requests for reprints should be sent to John Snarey, Laboratory of Human Development, Harvard University, Larsen Hall 300, Appian Way, Cambridge, Massachusetts 02138.

Table 1

Stages of Moral Development According to Kohlberg (1981)

Stage	What is considered to be right
Stage 1: Obedience and punishment orientation	To avoid breaking rules backed by punishment, obedience for its own sake, avoiding physical damage to persons and property
Stage 2: Instrumental purpose and exchange	Following rules only when it is to someone's immediate personal interest; acting to meet one's own interests and letting others do the same; right is an equal exchange, a good deal
Stage 3: Interpersonal accord and conformity	Living up to what is expected by people close to you or what people generally expect of people in your role; being good is important
Stage 4: Social accord and system maintenance	Fulfilling the actual duties to which you have agreed; laws are always to be upheld except in extreme cases where they conflict with other fixed social duties; right is also contributing to society, the group, or institution
Stage 5: Social contract, utility, individual rights	Being aware that people hold a variety of values and opinions, that most values and rules are relative to your group but should usually be upheld because they are the social contract; some nonrelative values and rights like life and liberty, however, must be upheld in any society regardless of the majority opinion
Stage 6: Universal ethical principles	Following self-chosen ethical principles; particular laws or social agreements are usually valid because they rest on such principles; when laws violate these principles, one acts in accordance with the principle; principles are universal principles of justice: the equality of human rights and respect for the dignity of human beings as individual persons; the reason for doing right is the belief, as a rational person, in the validity of universal moral principles and a sense of personal commitment to them

Note. Stages 5 and 6 are not distinguished for research purposes; there is also a transition stage (e.g., 2/3) between each of the stages.

opment research has been conducted in a sufficiently wide range of sociocultural settings to jeopardize adequately the claim. It is not possible to conduct research in all cultures, of course, and one does not need to test all possible cultures to accept the claim as solidly based. How many cultures need to be studied to arrive at a reasonable degree of certainty is not easy to decide; the usual criteria of chance error may be misleading in this case. More important than number are the type and variety of cultural settings that are studied. The minimal requirement might be that research must be done in several non-Western and nonindustrialized traditional cultural groups in addition to Western European countries. Ideally, the cultural groups should be historically independent if each society is to serve as an independent unit of analysis (cf. Naroll & D'Andrade, 1963; Whiting, 1968). Further, the samples ideally should be internally diverse: They should include children, adolescents, and mature adults—both males and females—and all major levels of social stratification.

The second assumption is that all persons in all cultures inquire about the moral domain and, in doing so, ask the same basic kinds of questions or resort to the same basic issues. Kohlberg's model of moral development was constructed by presenting people with specific moral dilemmas and by asking specific moral questions. Do Kohlberg's dilemmas and the accompanying questions adequately sample the universe of moral dilemmas and questions? Do they reflect the general moral issues that people universally tend to set for themselves? Because the dilemmas and questions included in Kohlberg's interview obviously were not randomly selected, but reflect a prior understanding of moral issues, it is not obvious that these questions are universally shared.

The empirical data relevant to this second assumption include individual researchers' attempts to adapt the interview dilemmas and questions into a culturally or functionally equivalent form. This includes the relative success of adapted versus nonadapted dilemmas, such as an interviewer's reported observations regarding the salience for subjects of the general issues contained within a particular dilemma. Further, because each dilemma essentially requires subjects to make a choice between two competing issues (e.g., life vs. law), culturally defined patterns in issue choices are important criteria for evaluating the degree to which Kohlbergian dilemmas adapt themselves to cultures that stress different issues. To the extent that the way the dilemmas and questions are understood parallels the stages of moral development, however, this proposition is closely related to the next assumption.

The third assumption is that stage development among individuals is found to be upwardly invariant in sequence and without significant regressions, regardless of cultural settings. In other words, all individuals in all cultures will follow the same stage sequence in a step-wise order, provided that their moral reasoning undergoes change. This particular assumption concerns only the order of appearance of the stages in individual development and not the presence of any one of the stages other than the first (cf. Kohlberg & Kramer, 1969). It does not state, for instance, that Stage 5 or any other stage will be achieved by every individual sooner or later, nor does it state that it will be found in every culture.

The hypothesis of a universal sequence would be supported if longitudinal testing reveals the same sequence, regardless of the cultural setting. Stage regressions and stage skipping would be evidence against the hypothesis. However, these empirical requirements cannot be understood as an absolute requirement, even for longitudinal studies. One reason is that Kohlberg has not constructed an error-free instrument, and regressions could be accounted for by measurement error if the frequency of regression is less than measurement error. Second, the time interval required for moving from one stage to the next varies between individuals, and probably between cultural groups and stages. Thus, data that suggest a skipped stage may in fact hide stage change if the interval between interview times was long enough to encompass two stage changes. Kuhn and Angeleu (1976) showed that 1 year was the minimum interval for observing clear changes in moral reasoning in a sample of children in the United States. In contrast, intervals of 3 years or less have also shown stage skipping to be extremely rare for adolescents and adults in the United States (Colby, Kohlberg, Gibbs, & Lieberman, 1983).

Cross-sectional testing can also provide valuable, although not conclusive, evidence if a properly selected sample is used (e.g., moderately large samples of age groups at approximately 3-year age intervals). Evidence in support of the proposition would be finding that all stages below the highest stage observed are also found in a particular cultural group and that, in each cultural group, higher stages correspond to older age groups. Evidence against this proposition would include nonordered or nonsequential relations between stage and age or the complete absence of a stage between the lowest and highest stages represented in the sample.

The fourth assumption is one to which Kohlberg himself is reluctant to assent, that the full range of moral stages, including the highest, should be found in all types of cultures. To be part of an empirical claim, all stages including the postconventional need to be present somewhere at some time. If this condition is met, however, Kohlberg and some of his developmentalist colleagues would claim that the overall stage model would be affirmed to be universal, and that only the rate and terminal point of development is culturally defined (cf. Broughton, 1978; Kohlberg, 1971; Lickona, 1969, 1976). Cross-cultural researchers, however, more often claim that the consistent absence of some stages in some types of cultures would indicate that the missing stages are culturally relative, the opposite of universal (Edwards, 1981; Simpson, 1974). Can one logically require that all cultural groups demonstrate all levels of moral reasoning in Kohlberg's model to establish its universality? The claim here is not that every individual should reach the highest stage, and it is not even that the highest stage should be found in every society studied. Rather, this proposition requires that all types of cultural groups (e.g., Western versus non-Western, urban versus folk) must demonstrate all levels of moral reasoning in Kohlberg's model to establish its universality. The failure to find a particular stage in all studies of a particular type of cultural group could indicate that the stage is culture specific, not universal. Of course, studies that include only adults cannot be required to find examples of the earliest stages, just as studies that include only children cannot be required to find the most mature stages present. One of the best test cases for the postconventional stages would be samples of adult subjects from non-Western, nonurban populations chosen because the other adult members of their society deemed them to be examples of unusual moral maturity. If the postconventional stages were absent among this last type of sample, then there would be grounds for doubting the universality of the full range of stages as they are presently defined.

The fifth assumption is that all instances of genuine moral reasoning in all cultures will correspond to one of the modes or stages of moral reasoning described by Kohlberg. This final proposition extends Kohlberg's set of stages to the most general applicability. Whereas some moral statements may fit more than one type, because later stages hierarchically incorporate earlier ones, no moral reasoning should be found for which none of the available stages or stage transitions is pertinent, because Kohlberg originally claimed that all individuals use the same basic concepts or principles. In other words, there is no wastebasket category. It is, of course, possible that moral statements may be found for which either the subject gives no explanation or the explanation is vague and brief. In this case, the available categories cannot be applied, not because they are inadequate as a set but because there is no clear or genuine moral judgment that can be interpreted. It is necessary, however, that clear criteria be provided to determine if the information given is inadequate or whether the available stage categories are insufficient. Otherwise, the meaning of *vague* or *incomplete* may be interpreted in such a way that Kohlberg's set of categories could never be proven false.

With this preface, the above proposition can be considered to be supported empirically if all moral judgments of a sample—regardless of culture (e.g., Western or non-Western) or of subculture (e.g., age, sex, and social-class subgroups)—are classifiable in one of the nine stages or stage transitions. In other words, all genuine moral responses given to Kohlberg's moral judgment interview can be scored according to the standardized scoring manual. Counterevidence to the hypothesis would be reports of moral judgments that are unscorable. If examples are reported from different studies, patterns in the various researchers'

observations would be helpful in precisely defining areas of inadequacy in Kohlberg's theory. If the interview material in a particular study was usually readily scorable, however, the evidence of some unscorable material would necessarily jeopardize only this particular assumption. Any general theory can be valid and solidly supported and, at the same time, incomplete and open to modifications and additions.

Review Method

To evaluate the empirical support for the primary empirical assumptions underlying Kohlberg's claim, all available cross-cultural studies of moral reasoning that had used Kohlberg's model and method were systematically reviewed. Many of these studies are as yet unpublished, and thus a debt of gratitude is owed to their authors for granting access to their findings. Because of the considerable variation in the research methods and reporting formats used by various researchers, I first attempted to make the studies as comparable as possible over four problem areas: scoring system, scoring algorithm, stage range, and stage scale.

The scoring system has evolved over the years, as Anne Colby described (1978). The earliest studies used the Sentence and Story Scoring method (Kohlberg, 1958) or the Global Rating Guide (Kohlberg, 1968), both of which were subjective and often unreliable content-analysis approaches that inflated the presence of the higher stages. These approaches evolved into the *Structural Issue Scoring Manual* (Kohlberg, 1972), a substantial advance over earlier systems but one that was overly abstract and more susceptible to ideological and cultural bias. The current *Standardized Scoring Manual* (Colby et al., 1978) has achieved greater objectivity and reliability in scoring by specifying clear and concrete stage criteria, defining the developmental sequences of specific moral concepts and the general structures of each stage, and focusing on operative moral judgments rather than on ethical assumptions. Most important, the 10 longitudinal cases used to construct the standardized manual included 3 Turkish subjects and 2 working-class subjects in addition to 5 upper middle-class subjects.

Along with the more stringent scoring criteria provided by each successive system, there has been a marked increase in scoring reliability. It is thus necessary to consider the different scoring systems used when evaluating cross-cultural research. To handle this problem, the studies were coded as follows: *A* or acceptable scoring for studies that used the 1978 standardized manual, *B* or borderline acceptability for studies that used the 1972 structural issue approach, and *C* or caution for studies that used the earlier 1958 and 1968 content-analysis approach.

A second source of variation between the studies is the method of calculating and reporting global stage scores, which has become standardized in recent years. It was originally common to report only the percentage of a group of subjects' reasoning at all stages, with no cutoff to control for scoring error, or to report only mean scores. The current approach is to report individual scores as well as group means and to use a more refined scoring algorithm. The current method of calculating an interview's global stage score requires that 25% of a person's reasoning be at a particular stage for that stage to be included in the subject's global stage score. Thus, if a subject's reasoning was 50% at Stage 3, 45% at Stage 4, and 5% at Stage 5, the interview will now be given a global stage score of 3/4 rather than 3/4/5. This change also affects the range of stages reported to be present in a sample because, in the past, if one subject out of the entire sample used Stage 4 reasoning only 5% of the time, then Stage 4 would be reported as present in the population even if all other subjects used only Stage 1 to 3 reasoning. This proved to be an unreliable scoring method, and it also made it difficult to interpret the finding meaningfully without having access to the raw data. For those studies that did not use the current scoring algorithm, the scores were reestimated, on the basis of the data that were published or made available to me, so that the stage range that is reported here for the study is more comparable with the other studies that have used the standardized algorithm. The stage range could still be somewhat distorted, however, if a less reliable *C* scoring manual was used.

A third change that contributes to the unevenness of the research data is that the range of stages has been reduced. The current scoring manual does not score for Stage 6;

rather, Stages 5 and 6 are not distinguished for scoring purposes, and potential Stage 6 responses are now scored as Stage 5 to establish acceptable scoring reliability. Although Stage 6 apparently remains as a philosophical claim, its quiet disappearance from the scoring system has removed it from the status of an empirical claim. To handle this change, when studies reported Stage 6 interviews, they were recoded as Stage 5. This procedure of rolling in the end of the distribution is not perfectly adequate, because the Stage 6 scores might also be rescored even lower by the current standardized scoring manual. Thus, when appropriate, the analyses are also presented for only those studies that used standardized scoring.

A final area of diversity is in the stage scale that researchers use to report their findings. The current convention is to use a 9-point scale (e.g., 1, ½, 2 . . .), whereas studies in the past have sometimes used a 5-point scale (1, 2, . . .), a 13-point scale, for example, 1, 1(2), 2(1), 2, and so on, or some idiosyncratic scale. An obvious problem with the 5-point scale is that it was not able to handle cases of transition between stages. The 13-point scale made overly fine distinctions between types of transition stages and lowered scoring reliability. Thus, for studies that used the 13-point scale, I recalculated the scores on a 9-point scale, for example, 2(3) and 3(2) were both recoded as Stage 2/3. For studies that used the 5-point scale, I recalculated the scores when it was possible to obtain the raw data necessary to make this transformation. Otherwise, the 5-point scale is reported.

Although the preceding standardization procedures make it possible to compare meaningfully the various studies, these methodological caveats must also be kept in mind in the following examination of the correspondence between the empirical findings and the assumptions underlying Kohlberg's claim of cross-cultural universality.

Findings and Discussion

Culturally Diverse Samples

Elizabeth Simpson was one of the first to point out a lack of cross-cultural diversity in moral development research:

In his prolific writing [Kohlberg] does not make clear the empirical sources of his claims to universality in the empirical realm. . . . The evidence is suggestive but hardly conclusive enough for the use of those firm dogmatic "all's." Not that much work has been done. In one article, work in five cultures is referred to; in later work, still only twelve cultures are given as the basis for generalizing to mankind as a whole (1974, pp. 83, 86).

Kohlberg based his original claim of universality on the empirical findings of his research among children in five cultural settings—the United States, Taiwan, Turkey, urban Mexico, and a Yucatan village in Mexico. Although he presented graphs of the cross-sectional age trends from his research (1969), the details regarding sample size, interview translation procedure, or the means and range of scores have not been published prior to this present review. This free-wheeling approach to cross-cultural research thus, understandably, made it difficult for the claim to be evaluated or accepted.

The number of studies, however, has grown considerably. At present, 44 studies have been completed in 26 cultural areas (45 studies in 27 cultural areas if one includes, for comparative purposes, Kohlberg's original United States research). Longitudinal research has been carried out in the following countries: Bahamas, Canada (French), India, Indonesia, Israel (kibbutz), Turkey, and the United States. The remaining 20 cultural areas are represented only by cross-sectional studies: Alaska (Eskimos), England, Finland, Germany, Guatemala, Honduras, Hong Kong, Iran, Japan, Kenya, Mexico, New Zealand, Nigeria, New Guinea, Pakistan, Puerto Rico, Taiwan, Thailand, Yucatan, and Zambia. All 45 studies are listed in Table 2.

Not surprisingly, the types of samples represented and the research methodology used within each study vary considerably. The 27 cultural areas vary in the degree to which they represent non-Western cultures: Approximately 22% of the cultural areas represent primarily Western European populations (e.g., Finland, Germany, New Zealand), 44% are non-European populations that have been influenced by the West (e.g., India, Japan, Taiwan), and 33% include tribal or village folk populations (e.g., Ladakh Indians, rural Guatemalan Indians, Kalskagamuit Eskimos, rural Kenyan Kipsigis). The age groups studied also vary considerably: Approximately 30% of the 27 cultural areas included children, adolescents, and adults in the research, 18%

included children and adolescents or adolescents and adults, and 52% included only children or adolescents or adults. Approximately 56% of the 27 cultural areas included both male and female subjects in at least one of the samples studied in that country.

If this research were begun from scratch, one might have selected 27 somewhat different countries to obtain a larger representation of non-Western traditional folk societies, including hunter–gatherer groups, and of non-capitalist societies, including Eastern European countries. The samples also do not necessarily represent societies that are historically independent (e.g., there is no longer a society that has not been influenced by the West to some degree). One also would prefer larger sample sizes, broader age ranges, and more uniformity in the scoring systems. Nevertheless, this being an imperfect world where cultural diversity is infinite and research time and money are finite, it seems reasonable to conclude that the diversity and number of cultures in which Kohlberg's model and measure have been applied are sufficient to evaluate the claim of cultural universality. The array generally compares favorably with cross-cultural research on other developmental theories, such as those of Erik Erikson, Jane Loevinger, and Jean Piaget (cf. Ashton, 1975; Dasen, 1972; Snarey & Blasi, 1980; Snarey, Kohlberg, & Noam, 1983).

Universal Moral Questions

Do Kohlberg's moral dilemmas and the accompanying questions adequately sample the universe of moral dilemmas or are they so culture-bound that they do not elicit a subject's best performance when the subject is from another culture? Do the moral issues contained in the dilemmas reflect the general issues that people, universally, tend to see as ethically relevant? Kohlberg argued that because the dilemmas focus on universal issues such as life, property, authority, and trust, they will represent real moral conflicts to anyone anywhere if suitable modifications are made in the content details of the dilemmas. Researchers have addressed this question on a number of levels to ensure that the interviews were culturally fair.

First, Kohlberg himself created three alternative forms of the standard interview. Each (*text continues on page 213*)

Table 2
Cross-Cultural Studies of Moral Development

Study	Sample, design, & procedure	Scoring system & interrater reliability	n	Age (years)	Moral stage scores Mode	Moral stage scores Range
		Alaskan Eskimos				
Saxe (1970)	Kalskagamuit Eskimos; cross sectional[a]	C, r = NR	8[b]	8–10	1	1–2[c]
			7[b]	11–15	2	1–2
			7	16–20	2	1–3
			7	21–25	2	1–4
		Bahamas				
White (1975, 1983); White, Bushnell, & Regnemer (1978)	Bahamian rural school children on the Island of Eleuthera; 2-year longitudinal[d]	A, r = .89	182	7–8	1/2	1–1/2
			252	9–10	1/2	1/2–2
			170	11–12	1/2	1/2–2/3
			44	13–14	2	1/2–2/3
			8	15–16	2	1/2–2/3
White (1977, 1983)	Elderly adults on the Island of Eleuthera; cross sectional[d]	A, r = .90	19	57–95	2	1–2/3
		Canada				
Sullivan, McCullough, & Stager (1970)	School children; cross sectional[e]	C, r = NR	40	12	2/3	1/2–3/4
			40	14	3	2–4/5
			40	17	4	3–4/5
Sullivan & Quarter (1972)	Male university students in a study of student activists; cross sectional[e]	C, r = NR	208	Adult	5	3–5
Sullivan & Beck (1975); Sullivan, Beck, Joy, & Pagliuso (1975)	School children; 2-year longitudinal[e]	C, r = NR	51	9–10	1	1–3
			45	10–11	3	1–4
			41	11–12	3	1–4
Marchand-Jodoin & Samson (1982); Samson (1983)	French Canadian adolescents; 2-year longitudinal[e]	B, r = .68	39	12–14	3	1–4[c]
			75	15–16	3	2–4
			60	17–18	4	2–5
Saadatmand (1972)	Rural Canadian Hutterites; cross sectional[d]	C, r = .70	13	9–12	4	3–4
			22	13–16	4	3–4
			26	Adult	4	3–4
		England				
Simpson & Graham (1971)	Working-class male and female students; cross sectional[e]	C, r = .86	75[b]	11	2	1–4[c]
			75[b]	14	2	1–4
	Middle-class male and female students; cross sectional		75[b]	11	3	1–4
			75[b]	14	3	1–5
Weinreich-Haste (1977)	School boys in Sussex; cross sectional[d]	C, r = NR	30	10	3	1–4[c]
			30	13	3	2–4
			30	15	4	2–5
Grimley (1973, 1974)	Lower, middle, and upper class males; cross sectional[e]	B, r = .87	19	19+	3/4	2/3–5
		Finland				
Helkama (1981)	Male and female students Helsinki University; cross sectional[d]	NR, r = .86[b]	110	Adult	3/4	3–5

274

Table 2 (*continued*)

Study	Sample, design, & procedure	Scoring system & interrater reliability	n	Age (years)	Moral stage scores	
					Mode	Range
		Germany				
Gielen (1982)	West German radical and nonradical male and female students at the University of Cologne; cross sectional[e]	B, r = .85	91	21–28[b]	4	2/3–5
Villenave-Cremer & Eckensberger (1983; cf. Eckensberger, 1983)	German mothers; cross sectional[e]	B, r = NR	16	Adult	3	2–3
		Guatemala				
Saadatmand (1972)	Rural Guatemalan Indian boys, girls, and adults; cross sectional[d]	C, r = .53	9	9–10	3	1–4
			5	11–12	4	2–4
			4	13–14	4	3–4
			6	15–16	4	3–4
			40	Adult	3	2–4
		Honduras				
Gorsuch & Barnes (1973)	Black Caribbean boys from villages and from town of Punta Gorda; cross sectional[f]	C, r = .48[b]	19	10–11	1	1–2[c]
			34	12–14	1/2	1–2
			18	15–16	2	1–2/3
		Hong Kong				
Grimley (1973, 1974)	College students; cross sectional[f]	B, r = .87	12	19+	4	3–5
		India				
Parikh (1975, 1980)	Jain and Hindu upper middle-class families in Ahmedabad; cross sectional[d]	B, r = .87	20	12–13	2/3	2–3
			19	15–16	3	2–3/4
			78	26–50	3	2–4/5
Vasudev (1981, 1983)	Hindu, Jain, and Sikh upper middle-class children and adults; cross sectional[f]	A, r = NR	16	11–13	2/3	1/2–3
			16	15–17	3	2/3–3/4
			16	21–23	3/4	3–4/5
			16	24–28	3/4	3–5
			16	30–35	3	3–5
			14	40–45	3/4	3–5
			18	50+	4	3–5
Gielen & Kelly (1983)	Children, adults, and Buddhist monks from Tibetan Ladakh, India; cross sectional[e]	A, r = NR	9	10–12	1	1
			10	14–16	1	1–2/3
			10	Adult	3	2–3
			10	Monks	1	1–3
Saraswathi (1977)	Middle-class children; cross sectional[d]	B, r = NR	20	8	2	1–2
			20	9	2	1–3
			20	10	2	2–3
			20	11	2	1–3
			20	12	2	2–3
Saraswathi & Sundaresan (1982)	Upper middle-class Indian boys; 1-year longitudinal[d]	B, r = .88	28	10–13	2/3	1/2–2/3
			28	12–15	2/3	1/2–3/4

(*table continued*)

Table 2 (*continued*)

Study	Sample, design, & procedure	Scoring system & interrater reliability	n	Age (years)	Moral stage scores Mode	Moral stage scores Range
		India (*continued*)				
	Working-class Indian boys; 1-year longitudinal		27	10–13	1/2	1/2–2/3
			27	12–15	2	1/2–2/3
		Indonesia				
Setiono (1982)	Indonesian university students; 1-year longitudinal[a]	NR, r = NR	160	Adult	3	2–4
			160	Adult	4	2–4
		Iran				
Saadatmand (1972)	Middle-class Muslim families; cross sectional[d]	C, r = .85	30	9–10	4	2–4[c]
			16	11–12	4	2–4
			21	13–14	4	2–5
			22	15–16	4	2–5
			64	Adult	4	2–5
		Israel				
Snarey, Reimer, & Kohlberg (in press); Snarey (1982); Reimer (1977); Kohlberg & Bar-Yam (1971)	Kibbutz born and educated male and female adolescents; 5- to 9-year longitudinal[d]	A, r = .89	20	12–14	3	2/3–3/4
			16	15–17	3	2/3–3/4
			24	18–26	3/4	3/4–4/5
	City-born but kibbutz-educated Middle Eastern lower class males and females; 5- to 9-year longitudinal		45	12–14	2/3	2–3/4
			29	15–17	3	2/3–3/4
			35	18–26	3/4	2/3–4/5
	City-born and city-educated upper middle-class Israeli youth; cross-sectional		9	15–17	3	2/3–3/4
	City-born and city-educated Middle Eastern youth; cross sectional		10	15–17	2/3	2/3–3/4
Snarey (1982)	Kibbutz founders, senior male and female residents of Israel; cross sectional[e]	A, r = .92	39	51–55	4	3–5
Bar-Yam & Abrahami (1982)	Adult kibbutz residents, male and female adult members, and senior founders; cross sectional[e]	A, r = .88	12	20–30	4/5	3/4–5
			12	45–56	4/5	3/4–5
		Japan				
Grimley (1973, 1974)	College students; cross sectional[f]	B, r = .87	26	19+	3/4	3–4

Table 2 (*continued*)

Study	Sample, design, & procedure	Scoring system & interrater reliability	n	Age (years)	Moral stage scores	
					Mode	Range
		Kenya				
Edwards (1974, 1975)	Secondary school and Nairobi Univ. students; adult community leaders; cross sectional[d]	B, $r = .84$	25[b]	17–27	2/3	1/2–4
			52	19–31	2/3	2–4/5
			36	23–75	2/3	2–3/4
Edwards (1978)	Kikuyu secondary school students; cross sectional[a]	B, $r = .86$	40	16–21	2/3	1/2–3/4
Harkness et al. (1981)	Kipsigis adults from rural Kotwet; cross sectional[d]	A, $r = .77$	12	28–74	2/3	2/3–3/4
		Mexico				
Kohlberg (1969)	Middle-class boys in Merida; cross sectional[d]	C, $r =$ NR	6	10	1	1–4[c]
			6	13	3	1–4
			6	16	3	1–5
	Lower class Mayan boys in Merida; cross sectional		6	10	1	1–4[c]
			6	13	1	1–4
			6	16	1	1–4
		New Guinea				
Tietjen & Walker (1984)	Male leaders and nonleaders in the Maisin villages of Ulakuand and Ganjiga, Papua New Guinea; cross sectional[d]	A, $r = .75$	22	40–70[b]	2/3	1/2–3
		New Zealand				
Moir (1974)	Middle-class elementary school girls; cross sectional[e]	C, $r = .82$	40	11	2	1–4[c]
		Nigeria				
Maqsud (1976, 1977a, 1977b, 1979)	Middle-class Muslim Hausa and Yoruba boys in Kano City; cross sectional[d]	C, $r = .94, .87$	60	12–13	4[b]	1–4[c]
			135	12–14	4	1–4
			210	12–14	4	1–5
			60	14–15	4	2–4
		Pakistan				
Maqsud (1977b)	Punjabi Pakistani Muslim boys residing in Nigeria; cross sectional[d]	C, $r = .93$	30	12–13	4	1–5[c]
		Puerto Rico				
Pacheco-Maldonado (1972)	Puerto Rican male and female children in San Juan; cross sectional[d]	C, $r = .93$[b]	20	10–12	1/2	1/2–2/3[c]
			20	13–15	3/4	2/3–4
			20	16–18	4/5	3/4–5

(*table continued*)

Table 2 (*continued*)

Study	Sample, design, & procedure	Scoring system & interrater reliability	n	Age (years)	Moral stage scores	
					Mode	Range
		Taiwan				
Lei (1980, 1981);	Elementary, junior	A, r = .91	30	7	2	1–2/3
Lei & Cheng	high, senior high,		30	9	2/3	1/2–3
(1984)	college, and graduate		30	12	3	2/3–3/4
	students in Taipei;		40	14	3	1/2–3/4
	cross sectional[d]		29	18	3/4	3–4/5
			43	23	3/4	3–4/5
			10	Adult	4/5	3/4–4/5
Kohlberg (1969)	Lower class boys; cross	C, r = NR	4	10	1	1–4[c]
	sectional[d]		3	13	3	1–5
			3	16	3	1–5
	Middle-class boys;		4	10	1	1–4
	cross sectional		4	13	3	1–5
			3	16	3	1–5
Chern (1978)	Chinese school	C, r = NR	NR	8–9	2	1–3
	students; N = 490;		NR	11–12	3	1–3
	cross sectional[e]		NR	13–14	3	1–4
			NR	16	3	1–4
		Thailand				
Batt (1974, 1975)	Lower class adults; cross sectional[f]	C, r = NR	28	26–65	3	2–4
	Middle-class adults; cross sectional		56	26–65	3	2–5
		Turkey				
Turiel, Edwards, &	Village males; 10-year	A, r = .83	17	10–12	1/2	1–2/3
Kohlberg (1978);	longitudinal and		14	13–15	2/3	1/2–2/3
Nisan &	cross sectional[d]		16	16–18	2/3	1/2–2/3
Kohlberg (1982)			16	19–28	3	2/3–3/4
	City males, middle and		11	10–12	2	1/2–3
	working class; 10-		9	13–15	2/3	1/2–2/3
	year longitudinal		6	16–18	2/3	2/3–3/4
	and cross-sectional		20	19–28	3/4	2/3–4/5
		United States				
Kohlberg (1958);	Working-class males;	A, r = .98	10	10	1/2	1–2/3
Colby et al.	20-year longitudinal		17	13–14	2/3	1/2–3
(1983)			22	16–18	3	1/2–3/4
			22	20–22	3/4	2/3–3/4
			20	24–26	3/4	2/3–4/5
			16	28–36	3/4	3–4/5
	Upper middle-class		11	10	2	1/2–3
	males; 20-year		21	13–14	2/3	1/2–3/4
	longitudinal		25	16–18	3/4	2/3–3/4
			30	20–22	3/4	2/3–4
			21	24–26	3/4	3–4/5
			24	28–36	4	3–4/5
		Yucatan				
Kohlberg (1969)	Village boys in	C, r = NR	6	10	1	1–3[c]
	Pustunich; cross		6	13	1	1–4
	sectional[d]		5	16	2	1–4

Table 2 (*continued*)

Study	Sample, design, & procedure	Scoring system & interrater reliability	*n*	Age (years)	Moral stage scores	
					Mode	Range
		Zambia				
Grimley (1973, 1974)	Lower, middle, and upper class males; cross sectional[f]	B, *r* = .87	22	13	3	1/2–3/4
			24	15	3	2/3–3/4
			23	17	3	2/3–5

Note. A indicates that the more acceptable standardized scoring manual was used (Colby et al., 1978). B indicates that the borderline scoring manual was used (Kohlberg, 1972). C indicates that a cautionary scoring manual was used (Kohlberg, 1958, 1968). NR = information not reported. The stage range and modal stage, rather than the actual age × stage frequency distribution, are presented because virtually none of the early studies reported this information. This information is presented in a later table, however, for those recent studies that used the standardized scoring manual and reported the age × stage frequency distribution.
[a] Used a culturally adapted interview, but did not report that the interviews were conducted in native language.
[b] Figure given is an approximation.
[c] Stage scores were recalculated by converting to a 9-point scale, recoding Stage 6 to Stage 5, or by using the current scoring algorithm.
[d] Used a culturally adapted interview and interviewed in native language if appropriate.
[e] Conducted interview in native language, but did not report that a culturally adapted interview was used.
[f] Did not report that interview was adapted and did not report that subjects were interviewed in their native language.

of the three forms contains three dilemmas. In each form, the first dilemma is based on the issues of life versus law, the second is based on the issues of conscience versus punishment, and the third dilemma is based on the issues of contract versus authority. The alternate interview reliability is quite high, and thus a researcher can choose which of the three different dilemmas for each of the three sets of moral issues will be included in a complete protocol. Although many researchers have simply used the three best-known dilemmas in the Form A interview, others have taken advantage of the alternative forms to select dilemmas that seemed to be the most relevant or most easily adapted to the culture in which they were conducting research.

As Table 2 indicates, most researchers have also adapted the interview by translating it into the native language rather than attempting to interview subjects in English. Only six of the 45 studies clearly failed to make this minimal level of cultural adjustment (cf. Awa, 1979; Berry & Dasen, 1974; Cole & Scribner, 1974). Beyond literal translation, the majority of the studies also attempted to adapt the dilemmas so that the content was culturally relevant and the moral conflict was felt to be real. For instance, the names of the actors in

the dilemmas have been changed to indigenous ones, the problem of stealing a drug to save a life has been changed to the problem of stealing food, and numerous other functional-equivalent translations have been undertaken (cf. Bredemeier, 1955; Mayers, 1974). Rachel Okonkuo (1983), for instance, found it necessary to adapt Dilemma III involving a father who unfairly asks his son for his savings so that the father can go on a fishing trip. Okonkuo's Nigerian subjects did not understand a fishing trip as a form of recreation but rather as a form of work by which to support one's family. Table 3 presents three different versions of the same dilemma to illustrate this adaptation process. With the exception of 9 of the 45 studies, all researchers made this type of cultural adaptation when appropriate. Although researchers do not commonly comment on the perceived effectiveness of this adaptation process, they have been consistently positive when they do. Gorsuch and Barnes (1973) stated that "Carib children appeared to experience no more difficulty in formulating answers to most of the stories than did U.S. children of a similar age" (1973, p. 287). Vasudev (1983) similarly observed that "although the Heinz dilemma is posed as a hypothetical dilemma, for many Indians it is an immediate and real dilemma.

Heinz's predicament parallels mass deprivation, poverty and social injustice suffered by
an overwhelming number of individuals" in
India (1983, p. 5). Because of the open-ended
or semiclinical nature of the interview, researchers also did not report that they encountered the typical problems found when
administering a structured task or test to
people who were not accustomed to interviews
or tests.

Another area of possible testing bias involves the moral issues contained within each
dilemma. Even if one selects the three seemingly most culturally relevant dilemmas from
Kohlberg's set of nine, and even if one carefully translates and adapts the dilemmas to
the culture, the underlying moral issues on
which the dilemmas are based remain the
same. This is both a weakness and a strength
of Kohlberg's approach. On the one hand, as
Simpson suggested, rather than constructing
dilemmas "according to a series of issues

which have been selected because they are
deemed to have universal applicability" (1974,
p. 96), the issues should grow more spontaneously out of the culture under study to
ensure that they are truly salient issues in
that particular society. On the other hand, a
subject's score is not based on the issue
chosen (e.g., life: "Steal the drug," or law:
"Don't steal the drug"), but rather on the
reasons given for why a choice is preferable.
This allows subjects in a society that stresses
the law issue more commonly to choose that
issue without their stage score being penalized,
whereas subjects from a society that stresses
the life issue have the same freedom from
penalty.

Studies that have examined the actual issue
choices made by their subjects have often
found that the choices are culturally patterned. Lei, for instance, found that his Taiwanese subjects chose the punishment issue
twice as often as the conscience issue (Lei,

Table 3
Three Versions of the Classic "Heinz and the Drug" Dilemma

Original United States Version (Kohlberg, 1969)
    In Europe, a woman was near death from a special kind of cancer. There was one drug that the doctors thought
might save her. It was a form of radium that a druggist in the same town had recently discovered. The drug was
expensive to make, but the druggist was charging 10 times what the drug cost him to make. He paid $200 for the
radium and charged $2,000 for a small dose of the drug. The sick woman's husband, Heinz, went to everyone he
knew to borrow the money, but he could only get together about $1,000, which is half of what it cost. He told the
druggist that his wife was dying, and asked him to sell it cheaper or let him pay later. But the druggist said, "No, I
discovered the drug and I'm going to make money from it." So Heinz got desperate and broke into the man's store
to steal the drug for his wife.
    Should Heinz have done that? Why or why not?

Adapted Kenyan Version (Edwards, 1974)
    In a rural area of Kenya, a woman was near death from a special kind of heart disease. There was one kind of
medicine that the doctors at the government hospital thought might save her. It was a form of medicine that a
chemist in Nairobi had recently invented. The drug was expensive to make, but the chemist was charging 10 times
what the drug cost him to make. He paid 80 shillings for the drug, and then charged 800 shillings for a small dose
of the drug. The sick woman's husband, Joseph, went to everyone he knew to borrow the money, but he could only
get together 400 shillings, which was half of what it cost. He told the chemist that his wife was dying, and asked
him to sell it cheaper or let him pay the rest later. But the chemist said, "No, I'm the one who invented this
medicine, and I'm going to make money from it." So Joseph got desperate and broke into the store to steal the
drug for his wife.
    Should Joseph have done that, broken into the store to take the drug? Why or why not?

Adapted Turkish Version (Turiel, et al., 1978)
    A man and wife have just migrated from the high mountains. They started to farm, but there was no rain and
no crops grew. No one had enough food. The wife became sick from having little food and could only sleep.
Finally, she was close to dying from having no food. The husband could not get any work and the wife could not
move to another town. There was only one grocery store in the village, and the storekeeper charged a very high
price for the food because there was no other store and people had no place else to go to buy food. The husband
asked the storekeeper for some food for his wife, and said he would pay for it later. The storekeeper said, "No, I
won't give you any food unless you pay first." The husband went to all the people in the village to ask for food, but
no one had food to spare. So he got desperate and broke into the store to steal food for his wife.
    Should the husband have done that? Why or why not?

1980, p. 8). I found that kibbutz youth nearly always chose the life rather than the law issue in the husband–wife dilemma compared with a more even distribution in the United States, and that the kibbutz-born youth nearly always made the contract rather than the law choice in the father–son dilemma compared with Middle Eastern youths, who usually chose the authority issue and argued that the son should give his father the money (Snarey, 1982, pp. 288–316). Harkness similarly reported that the elders in a rural Kipsigis community in Kenya invariably responded to the father–son story by stating that the boy should give up the money to his father (Harkness, Edwards, & Super, 1981, p. 599). Nisan and Kohlberg (1982) also found that Turkish city subjects were more likely than Turkish village subjects to decide that one should not steal even if it was to save a human life. In each case, the differences in the issues choice appear to be attributable to cultural differences. For instance, in the kibbutz research it seemed predictable that kibbutz adolescents, who are raised communally, would be more likely than Middle Eastern youth, who are raised in patriarchal families, to question parental authority and to consider the father's request to be unfair. Thus, the issue choice contained within each dilemma seems to allow for cultural variation in the stress placed on particular issues while still searching for universals in the way people reason about the issues.

The most radical form of adjustment that has been attempted is to create completely new dilemmas in which both the content and issues are derived from the population under study. As admirable as this approach appears, the results of such nonstandardized interviews have not been reported to be significantly different from those of culturally adapted standardized dilemmas. To examine the possible cultural bias of the dilemmas, for instance, White created "a moral dilemma based upon the experiences directly relevant to the outislanders . . . and administered [it] to a portion of the sample" (White, Bushnell, & Regnemer, 1978, p. 63). He concluded that "it was apparent upon inspection of the participants' responses that there were no stage differences in their responses to that Bahamian dilemma and their responses to

the standard Kohlberg dilemmas" (1978, p. 63). Although Kohlberg's interview cannot be culture free, it does appear to be reasonably culture fair when the content is creatively adapted and the subject is interviewed in the native language. Testing bias is still possible, however, and future researchers should pay closer attention to this general issue.

Invariant Sequence

This proposition requires that stage development be upwardly invariant in sequence, with stage regressions and skipping no greater than what can be accounted for by measurement error. Table 2 also summarizes the relation of age with the modal stage and stage range for all 45 studies.

Examining the cross-sectional stage distributions, the increase in modal stage, and in the upper limits of the stage range, with a parallel increase in the age of the subjects is usually clear and sometimes dramatic. In the 20 cultural areas in which only cross-sectional studies have been completed, 85% of the cases indicated an increase in modal stage, and an increase in the upper extreme of the stage range, with increases in age. The remaining 15% of the cases (India, Guatemala, Kenya) showed a regression in either the modal stage or the stage range, but never in both. Further, all three of these cross-sectional cases of apparent regression involved adult subjects in which one could expect to find greater variation, because development has slowed and individuals with different terminal points in development accumulate in the same adult-age cohorts. Regarding the issue of stage skipping, 100% of the cross-sectional studies found all major stages present between the lowest and highest stage in their distribution.

Despite the supportive nature of these cross-sectional findings, they are not adequate to test the hypothesis of invariant sequence. The hypothesis of invariant sequence can only be tested adequately by longitudinal research because it involves testing the same persons over time. The seven longitudinal studies reported strikingly similar findings. No regressions were reported in the three 1-to-2 year longitudinal studies (Bahamas, Canada, Indonesia). The three 9-to-20 year longitudinal studies (Israel, United States, Turkey) and the one 2-year longitudinal study (India) reported some regressions, and each is now examined.

In the Israeli kibbutz longitudinal study, which included both kibbutz-born and Middle-Eastern Israeli youths and adults, regressions occurred in 6.3% (6) of 96 longitudinal changes, using the customary 9-point scale, and in 7.3% (7) of the 96 cases using the most differentiated 13-point scale. In the United States study, which included both middle-class and working-class subjects, longitudinal regressions occurred in 5.2% (11) of the 209 longitudinal interviews using the 9-point scale and in 7.2% (14) using the 13-point scale. Saraswathi and Sundaresan's (1982) 2-year longitudinal study of boys in India reported that 12.7% (7) of the 55 longitudinal cases regressed in moral stage. Of these 7 cases, only 1 subject regressed a full stage, whereas the other 6 had half-stage or smaller regressions. Are these regressions significant? Colby, Kohlberg, Gibbs, and Lieberman (1983) reported test–retest error to be 19%, using the 9-point scale. Because test–retest reversals are always much higher than each case of longitudinal reversals, one could attribute the violations of longitudinal sequence to measurement error. Of course, some of the nonreversals might also be due to measurement error, but measurement error would not account for the overwhelming evidence of nonreversal.

This conclusion is also supported by three additional findings. First, in nearly every individual case of regression in all four studies, the downward change was only at one interview time and was only a half-stage or one-third-stage regression. Second, in no case did a longitudinal subject skip a stage (i.e., each subject reached his or her highest stage at the last interview time by going through each of the preceding intermediate stages between their first and last interview stage scores). Third, it is difficult to accept the argument that the invariant sequence evidence is due simply to differing moral norms that adults hold for children of differing ages in the process of socialization (e.g., Denny & Duffy, 1974), given that cultures are so different from each other, and that there has been a consistent failure to find empirical evidence

supporting the socialization-learning interpretation of moral stage structures (cf. Gorsuch & Barnes, 1973; Pacheco-Maldonado, 1972).

Despite the lack of empirical support for a simple socialization-learning explanation of developmental stages, future research may well demonstrate that culturally defined variations in the socialization process provide a partial and complementary explanation of cultural variations in the developmental rate and cognitive style of moral reasoning. Cultural groups do accommodate themselves to the process of individual development by socializing their members through a series of age-graded periods. These age-graded periods, I have previously argued, are correlated with modal stage changes in development in a manner that clearly builds on and probably facilitates development (Rogoff, Sellers, Pirrotta, Fox, & White, 1975; Snarey et al., 1983). In the area of cognitive development, for instance, the academic subject of algebra in North American public schools is generally synchronized with the early adolescent years when the students are first able to make use of formal operational thought. In the area of moral development, the results of the kibbutz longitudinal research indicated that gains in a group's mean level of moral development were loosely parallel to shifts in the culturally defined age periods of socialization in the kibbutz life cycle (Snarey, 1982). Of course, this phenomenon is not inconsistent with Kohlberg's theory. Although he did not link moral development to changes in the content of socialization, he did link it to the equilibration of new social role-taking experiences and to general cognitive development (e.g., the construction of reciprocity in both social and nonsocial senses).

Full Stage Range

The fourth proposition requires that the full range of stages—including the preconventional (1, 1/2, 2), conventional 2/3, 3, 3/4, 4), and postconventional (4/5, 5)—be present in all types of cultures. It is often assumed that Stage 5, for instance, is common among middle-class men in the United States but absent among non-Westerners, the lower classes, and women. The following findings indicate that this belief is not fully correct.

A survey of Table 2 indicates that in 67% of the 27 cross-cultural sample areas, some subjects were found reasoning at Stage 1; in 89% of the cultural samples, some subjects were found reasoning at Stage 2; in 100% of the cases, subjects were reported at Stage 2/3 or 3; in 89% of the cases, subjects were reported at Stage 3/4 or 4; and in 67% of the cases, some subjects were reported at Stage 4/5 or 5. Stages 2 to 4 are thus virtually universal but Stages 1 and 5 are represented in only 67% of the samples. Before drawing any conclusions, however, it is necessary to control for the age range of the sample, and for the types of samples, to combine the studies meaningfully (cf. Light & Pillemer, 1982; Light & Smith, 1971).

Table 4 reports the presence or absence of Stage 1 or 1/2 in those studies that included children aged 10 or younger and the presence or absence of Stage 4/5 or 5 in those samples

that included subjects aged 18 or older. The studies are further stratified according to a variant of Robert Redfield's fold-urban continuum (1955, 1956), an approach similar to one previously applied to Kohlberg's work by Carolyn Edwards (1975). The continuum, as I have modified it, includes: 1. complex urban societies that are also Western European; 2. complex urban societies that are non-European but Westernized to some degree; 3. tribal or village folk societies of Western European origin; and 4. tribal or village folk societies that are non-Western.

When one controls for age, Stage 1 is present in 100% of the Western urban samples, in 86% of the Westernized non-European urban societies, and in 86% of the folk societies. Presumably, if younger Iranian and Hutterite children were interviewed, Stage 1 would also be found in these two exceptions. Thus, Stage 1 or 1/2, along with Stages 2 to

Table 4

Association Between Folk-Urban Societies and Stage 1 or 5, Controlling for Age

Type of society	Is Stage 1 or 1/2 reported as present among subjects aged 10 or younger?		Is Stage 4/5 or 5 reported as present among subjects aged 18 or older?	
	No	Yes	No	Yes
Urban complex societies (Western European)		Canada (English) England New Zealand USA (middle class) USA (lower class)		Canada (French) Canada (English) Finland Germany USA (middle class) USA (lower class)
Urban complex societies (Westernized, non-European)	Iran	Honduras India Mexico (city) Puerto Rico Taiwan Turkey (city)	Indonesia	Hong Kong India Iran Israel Japan Kenya (urban) Puerto Rico Taiwan Thailand Turkey (city)
Folk tribal or village societies (Western European)	Hutterite		Hutterite	
Folk tribal or village societies (non-Western, non-European)		Alaskan Eskimos Bahamas Guatemala Turkey (village) Yucatan (village) Zambia	Alaskan Eskimos Bahamas Guatemala India (Ladakh) Kenya (rural) New Guinea Turkey (village)	

4, seems to be represented in a wide range of cultural groups. Stage 4/5 or 5 is also more commonly present when one controls for age, but the distribution is significantly and strongly associated with the type of society under study and the frequency within any particular sample is seldom high. On the other hand, Stage 4/5 or 5 was present to some degree in 100% of the urban Western samples and in 91% of the urban non-Western societies. It was quite common, although the actual number of individuals within any particular sample was often low, ranging from 1 out of 20 Turkish city residents (5%) to 10 out of 12 subject in a selective sample of senior kibbutz members (83%). On the other hand, Stage 4/5 or 5 was absent in 100% of the 8 traditional tribal or village folk societies, both non-Western and Western. The available data thus suggest that the significant difference lies between folk versus urban societies rather than between Western versus non-Western societies (cf. Edwards, 1975; Redfield, 1956, 1962).

Another approach to the question of the full range of stages is to examine subcultures within the various societies studied and ask if the subgroups differ significantly. Data were available from a number of studies on social class and sex. Table 5 summarizes those studies that include both middle-class and non-middle-class populations or included both males and females.

Thirteen cross-cultural studies in 11 countries included both middle class and lower or working-class subjects. In nine cases statistically significant social-class differences were reported. Only one case reported finding no class effects (Taiwan); and in one case two studies reported class differences, whereas a third study did not (England). Because one of the English studies that reported differences had used a superior scoring system, it is possible to conclude that samples from 10 of the 11 countries showed significant class differences in moral development. Of the 10 cases in which class differences were reported, 100% found that upper middle- or middle-class subjects scored higher than lower class or working-class subjects. These findings are similar to the results of other research in the United States; class differences were common and virtually always favored the middle class (DeVos, 1983).

Seventeen cross-cultural studies in 15 countries included both male and female subjects. In 14 studies there were no significant sex differences. In the remaining 3 studies, a clear sex difference favoring males was found in only one case (England). The German study (Gielen, 1982) did not find any significant overall difference, but it was reported that females were more likely than males to score at Stage 3. In India, two studies did not find any significant sex differences and one did; because the latter study used a less reliable scoring system than the first two studies, it seems appropriate to conclude that the evidence against sex differences in moral judgment in India is stronger.

Table 5

Distribution of Social Class and Sex Differences in Moral Development

Social class differences?	Sex differences?
Countries for Which Studies Did Not Report Statistically Significant Differences	
England (Weinreich)[a]	Bahamas[b]
Taiwan[b]	Canada, Hutterite[a]
	Finland[c]
	Guatemala[a]
	Hong Kong[d]
	India (Gielen)[b]
	India (Vasudev)[b]
	Iran[a]
	Israel, kibbutz[b]
	Japan[d]
	Kenya[b,d]
	Puerto Rico[a]
	Taiwan[b]
	Zambia[d]
Countries for Which Studies Reported Significant Differences	
England (Simpson)[a]	England (Simpson)[a]
England (Grimley)[d]	Germany (Gielen)[d]
Hong Kong[d]	India (Parikh)[d]
India (Saraswathi)[d]	
Israel[b]	
Japan[d]	
Mexico[a]	
Thailand[a]	
Turkey[b]	
United States[b]	
Zambia[d]	

[a] A cautionary scoring manual was used (Kohlberg, 1958, 1968).
[b] The more acceptable standardized scoring manual was used (Colby et al., 1978).
[c] The scoring system was not reported.
[d] The borderline scoring manuual was used (Kohlberg, 1972).

Thus, to summarize, 3 of the 17 studies reported significant sex differences, only 1 of these 3 studies reported a clear sex difference, and no study that used the most reliable scoring system reported any significant sex differences. These cross-cultural findings are also similar to the results of other research in the United States. Walker (1984) reviewed 54 North American studies that had used Kohlberg's moral judgment interview and found that only eight cases of significant sex differences were reported. Walker concluded that sex differences in moral reasoning are found only in a minority of studies, and in each of these cases sex differences are confounded with differences in levels of education and occupation (i.e., indexes of social class). Sex differences were also less frequent when the current standardized scoring manual was used. However, in those few studies where sex differences were reported, they virtually always favored men. The most impressive argument for women's voices being incompletely represented in Kohlberg's scheme has been made by Carol Gilligan (1982). She cautioned, however, against generalizing her perspective to other cultures.

To clarify these associations between moral development and social setting or social class, it is important to examine more closely only those studies that used the standardized scoring manual. It is also important to compare the actual age-by-stage distributions for each study to determine the cultural variation in the age of onset of each stage in the range. This approach allows one to control for scoring reliability and to consider individual subjects as the unit of analysis, because these more recent studies, unlike most of the earlier studies, also reported the actual number of individuals at each stage. Taken together, research in 8 cultures (12 subcultures) makes use of the 1978 standardized scoring manual. These include the Bahamas, India (Tibetan and upper middle class), Israel (kibbutz and city), Kenya, New Guinea, Taiwan, Turkey (city and village), and the United States (working class and upper middle class). Table 6 presents the age-by-stage distribution for each of these 12 populations; within each age range, the populations are ranked in order of their moral maturity scores, a continuous rather than categorical measure of moral development.

Overall, the full range of stages is represented—from 100% of the 10-to-11-year-old Tibetan children at Stage 1 to 83% of a selected sample of senior kibbutzniks at Stage 4/5 or 5. One can also note that, as the age ranges increase, the stage scores also consistently increase. Stages 1/2 to 3/4 are quite common. Stage 4 first appears among 4 Taiwanese high-school students and becomes common in most populations in the 19-to-28 age range. Stage 4/5 is first seen in an 18-year-old Taiwanese high-school student, but it is represented in 7 of the 8 populations in the 19-to-28 age range and by 6 of the 10 populations in the 28-to-60+ age range. No subjects were scored as fully Stage 5 until after age 30; these included only 2 subjects in India and 8 kibbutz founders or adult members. Interestingly, no subjects in the United States were scored as fully Stage 5 on the Form A interview, although six interviews from upper middle class subjects and two interviews from working-class subjects were scored at Stage 4/5, which indicates that Stage 5 was represented in 25% or more of their moral judgments. Although a competitive comparison of the samples would be extremely inappropriate, it is interesting that the United States sample did not rank first in even one of the five age divisions. Taiwanese, kibbutzniks, and Indians all ranked higher in one or more age divisions than even upper middle class Americans, and Turkish urban subjects also often ranked higher than working-class subjects in the United States. In contrast, the cultural distribution of the stages within each age range continued to confirm that subjects in urban societies have a faster rate and higher terminal point of development than do subjects from traditional folk societies. The data also confirm a social-class difference: Upper middle and middle-class subjects always have a faster rate of development than working- or lower class subjects within the same society, although their terminal points of development can be the same.

Why is Stage 5 a rare empirical phenomenon, and why is its distribution skewed toward particular types of societies and classes? Part of the answer may lie with the size of the adult samples; 6 of the 11 populations in the 28-60+ age range included fewer than 20 subjects each. It might be

Table 6

Cross-Cultural Samples in Rank Order by Mean Moral Maturity Score, Controlling for Age

Sample[a]/age range (years)	N					Global moral stage score					M
		1	1/2	2	2/3	3	3/4	4	4/5	5	
Kibbutz, selected seniors/45–56	12					8.3	8.3	66.7	16.7		458
Kibbutz, founders/51–54	39				5.0	31.7	33.3	25.0	5.0		396
USA, upper middle class/28–36	24				8.3	25.0	41.7	25.0			391
Taiwan, graduate students/adult	10					30.0	20.0	50.0			370
India, upper middle class/30–50	48				29.2	31.3	27.1	8.3	4.2		363
USA, working class/28–36	16					6.2	68.8	18.8	6.2		363
India, Tibetan adults/adult	10		30.0		10.0	60.0					265[b]
Kenya, rural/28–74	12			8.3	33.3	25.0	33.3				238[b]
Papua New Guinea/40–70	22		4.5	13.6	68.2	13.6					238[b]
India, Tibetan monks/adult	10	40.0		30.0		30.0					190[b]
Bahamas, lower class/57–95	19	NR		NR	NR	NR					153[b]
Kibbutz, selected adults/20–30	12						16.7	25.0	33.3	25.0	433
Kibbutz, kibbutz born/18–26	24					66.7	29.2	4.2			366
Taiwan, college/23	43				9.3	55.8	27.9	6.9			365
USA, upper middle class/20–26	51			3.9	15.7	47.1	23.5	9.8			361
India, upper middle class/21–28	32				23.2	46.2	20.6	9.9			355
Kibbutz, Middle Eastern/18–26	35			2.9	14.3	68.6	8.6	5.7			349
USA, working class/20–26	32			9.4	31.3	53.1	3.1	3.1			332
Turkey, city/19–28	20				20.0	35.0	40.0		5.0		313
Turkey, village/19–28	16				31.3	56.3	12.5				279
Taiwan, high school/18	29					17.2	65.5	13.7	3.4		348
Kibbutz, kibbutz born/15–17	16				6.2	50.0	43.8				322
Israel, upper-middle city/15–17	9				11.1	66.7	22.2				312
USA, upper middle class/16–18	25				20.0	36.0	44.0				312
India, upper middle class/15–17	16				6.2	75.0	18.8				309
Kibbutz, Middle Eastern/15–17	18				16.6	61.1	22.2				306
Israel, lower class city/15–17	10				40.0	50.0	10.0				286
USA, working class/16–18	22		4.5	9.0	27.3	31.8	27.3				284
Turkey, city/16–18	6				66.7	16.7	16.7				275
Turkey, village/16–18	16		12.5	12.5	75.0						229
Bahamas, lower class/15–16	8		NR	NR	NR						194[b]
Kibbutz, kibbutz born/13–14	12				8.3	50.0	41.7				316
Taiwan, junior high/14	40		2.5		7.5	60.3	30.0				308
Kibbutz, Middle Eastern/13–14	23			8.6	56.5	34.7					264
USA, upper middle class/13–14	21		4.8	4.8	66.7	19.0	4.8				259
Turkey, city/13–15	9		11.1		88.9						243
USA, working class/13–14	17		17.6	11.8	52.9	17.6					237
Turkey, village/13–15	14		35.7	21.4	42.9						203
Bahamas, lower class/13–14	44		NR	NR	NR						176[b]
India, Tibetan children/14–16	10	70.0		20.0	10.0						135[b]
Taiwan, elementary school/12	30				10.0	73.0	17.0				301
Kibbutz, kibbutz born/12	8				37.5	62.5					281
India, upper middle class/11–13	16		6.2		68.8	25.0					258
USA, upper middle class/10	11		9.1	54.5	18.2	18.2					229
Turkey, city/10–12	11		36.4	18.2	36.4	9.1					207
USA, working class/10	10	10.0	50.0	30.0	10.0						176
Turkey, village/10–12	17	5.9	70.6	17.6	5.9						167
Bahamas, lower class/11–12	170		NR	NR	NR						140[b]
India, Tibetan children/10–11	8	100.0									112[b]

Note. NR = exact figures not reported.
[a] Samples include all studies that used a more reliable standardized scoring manual. [b] Mean moral maturity score has been estimated or recalculated.

unreasonable to expect such small samples of adult moral reasoning to represent the population of moral reasoning instances. However, 6 of the 11 populations in the oldest age range were selected because they were thought to have a higher probability of including some subjects at the higher stages. Of these six, three did in fact include a substantial number of subjects at Stage 4/5 or 5 (India, kibbutz, Taiwan), but the other three selected populations did not go beyond Stage 3 or 3/4 (Kenyan village leaders, Tibetan monks, New Guinea village leaders). It is important to note that all three of the samples that included subjects scoring at the postconventional level were modern societies and two of them were urban, and all three of the selected samples that failed to score beyond the conventional level were traditional folk societies. Village leaders in Kenya and New Guinea did score significantly higher than nonleaders, suggesting that their fellow villagers recognized them as more morally mature; Tibetan monks, however, usually scored lower than lay Tibetans. However, the failure of all members of traditional folk societies, including leaders, to use Stage 4/5 or 5 reasoning suggests the additional possibility of a bias in the scoring system. Specific possible scoring biases are considered under Assumption 5 in the next section.

General Applicability

This final proposition suggests that all instances of moral reasoning, regardless of culture, will correspond to one of the finite modes of moral reasoning described by Kohlberg. It is important to note that Kohlberg's stages rely on the notion of structure or internal cognitive operations and on the distinction between structure and content. The process of matching interview responses to examples in the scoring manual, therefore, does not consist of finding elements that are literally identical. The reasoning by which different people arrive at a moral conclusion can be structurally the same even though the specific issues attended to, the circumstances modifying the problem, and the concrete details may be different.

The following responses were given by five different individuals to the classic dilemma in which a husband has a choice between letting his wife die or stealing something to save her life.

Example 1:
Q. Should the husband have stolen the food?
A. Yes. Because his wife was hungry . . . otherwise she will die.
Q. Suppose it wasn't his wife who was starving but his best friend. Should he steal the food for his friend?
A. Yes, because one day when he is hungry his friend would help. . . .
Q. What if he doesn't love his friend?
A. No, [then he should not steal] because when he doesn't love him it means that his friend will not help him later.

Example 2:
Q. Should the husband have stolen the food?
A. Yes. Because his wife is starving. Because they need food, they never eat.
Q. If the husband doesn't love his wife, should he still steal the food?
A. Yes. Because [otherwise] nobody will cut fish for him.

Example 3:
Q. If the husband doesn't love his wife, should he steal the drug for her?
A. No. Because he could get caught and put in jail and he can get married again and he could collect money from her death from the insurance company and get away on top.
Q. Suppose it was a stranger?
A. . . . What did the stranger ever do for him?

Example 4:
Q. Should the husband steal the drug?
A. Yes, because he should save the life of his wife. . . . Because he should protect the life of his wife so he doesn't have to stay alone in life.
Q. Should you steal the drug to save your wife's life?
A. Yes, because she is the only one that I have. The law says that one can't have more than one wife, so I have to save her life because she is the only one.

Example 5:
Q. Should the husband steal the food?
A. He should steal the food for his wife because if she dies he'll have to pay for the furneral, and that costs a lot.

The five subjects who gave these responses are all from different cultural groups (1. Turkey, 2. Kalskagamuit Eskimos in Alaska, 3. United States, 4. Puerto Rico, and 5. Chinese in Taiwan). They made different choices, and their responses were sensitive to different elements of the situation: the advantages of having a wife; the importance of jail; or the cost of funerals. Some of these sensitivities may be the result of specific social conditions, cultural values, or the individual's personal history, and as such they constitute appropriate objects of study. Despite the differences, however, the five responses seem to be constructed by the same structures of moral reasoning: Action is motivated by a self-interested conception of relations, an appreciation of the instrumental value that stealing may have for the husband in terms of a *quid pro quo* exchange, punishment is similarly seen as something to be instrumentally avoided, and love is contingent upon and relative to the husband's wishes rather than being a shared normative value. All of the responses can thus be scored as primarily Stage 2 modes of reasoning, the stage of individual instrumental purpose and exchange, because their deeper meaning or underlying structure is similar.

Although examples of data that could be easily scored were common, Mordechai Nisan suggested, "It is possible that, in other cultures, principles are held which are distinct from ours, and moral reasoning is used that does not fit the structures defined by Kohlberg" (Nisan & Kohlberg, 1982, p. 874). Being in agreement with Nisan, I reviewed all studies for empirical observations and specific examples of moral judgments that were difficult to score, because the presence of such material could call this final assumption into question. It was rare for authors to report difficult-to-score material or to document empirically a specific problem area that they observed, even though Kohlberg's open-ended testing method allows one to gather such material. This rarity may have been due to the fact that few authors seem to have systematically examined judgments that were not scorable. Recently, however, samples have been successively reported from research in the Israeli kibbutz (Snarey, 1982), India (Vasudev, 1983), Taiwan (Lei & Cheng, 1984), Papua New Guinea (Tietjen & Walker, 1984), and Kenya (Edwards, in press).

Kibbutz. In the longitudinal study of moral development among kibbutz-born kibbutz members in Israel, I reported a postconventional communal equality and collective happiness principle which was missing from Kohlberg's theoretical model and scoring manual. My findings indicated that all Kohlberg's stages, including the postconventional, were present among kibbutz members, but that Kohlberg's scoring manual failed to capture some elements of kibbutz postconventional reasoning. To identify what might be missing from the model and manual, I ex-

amined clinically all interview judgments on which the blinded scorers had given a "guess" score, indicating that the material was a genuine moral judgment but not easily scored according to the standardized manual. I found that the lower stage statements were usually difficult to score because of the incompleteness of that particular judgment by the subject. I also found that the higher stage judgments that were difficult to score were usually complete, but that they reflected the cooperative working-class values of the kibbutz. Some judgments scored as guess Stage 4 or guess Stage 4/5 could be understood as full postconventional Stage 5 judgments if one took a socialist kibbutz rather than a middle-class capitalist perspective to the data. The following brief excerpts from two kibbutz-born subjects' interviews illustrate some of these elements of kibbutz principled reasoning:

Excerpt 1 (kibbutz female):
Q. It is against the law for Moshe to steal the drug. Does that make it morally wrong?
A. It will be illegal or against the formal law, but not against the law which is the moral law. Again, if we were in a utopian society, my hierarchy of values, and the hierarchy of others, through consensus, would be realized.
Q. What are those values?
A. Socialism. But (laughter) don't ask me to explain it.
Q. What is wrong with a nonsocialistic society that makes it unjust?
A. In a utopia . . . everyone will be equal. . . . It is our dream, our ideal. In one way it is ridiculous since this utopia will never be achieved, of course. . . .
Q. Should people still do everything they can to obey the law in an imperfect world?
A. Yes, unless it will endanger or hurt another important value. . . . But generally speaking, people should obey the law. The law was created in order to protect . . . from killing, robbery, and other unjust uses of power. . . . I believe everyone has the right to self-growth and the right to reach *happiness.* . . . People are not born equally genetically and it is not fair that one who is stronger physically should reach his *happiness* by whatever means at the expense of one who is weaker because *the right to happiness* is a basic human right of everyone, equal to all. A nonkibbutz society that is based on power negates the right and possibility of those who are weaker to get their *happiness.* . . .
Excerpt 2 (kibbutz male):
Q. Should Moshe steal the drug? Why or why not?
A. Yes. . . . I think that the community should be responsible for controlling this kind of situation. The medicine should be made available to all in need; the druggist should not have the right to decide on his own . . . the whole community or society should have the control of the drug.
Q. Is it important for people to do everything they can to save another's life? Why or why not?

A. If I want to create a better community, a nice and beautiful one, an ideal world, the only way we can do it is by cooperation between people. . . . We need this cooperation among ourselves in order to achieve this better world. . . . The *happiness . . . principle* underlies this cooperation—the greatest *happiness* for the greatest number of people in the society.

Q. Should people try to do everything they can to obey the law?

A. In principle, yes. It is impossible to have any kind of state, country, society without laws. [Otherwise,] it will be complete anarchy and those who have the power will dominate the weaker.

Q. Why is that wrong?

A. I am [not] strong. (Laughter.) But really, you can see in the totalitarian countries today in contrast to, for example, the kibbutz. You damage the principle of democracy and, most importantly, you destroy the principle of equality. Which is why I [have chosen to] live on a kibbutz. (Snarey, 1982, pp. 295–298)

There is a sense in which the collective equality and happiness principle common to these interviews is more mature than Kohlberg's definition of Stage 4 but is missing from Kohlberg's definition of Stage 5. The kibbutz functions for some subjects as an imperfect embodiment of a more utopian ideal. In raising the kibbutz as a moral argument, they are making a Stage 5 rather than a Stage 4 judgment to the extent that they view kibbutz membership as based on a commitment to cooperative equality and the equal right to happiness by all persons. Allusions in some interviews to the system falling apart or becoming dysfunctional are also not necessarily conventional system-maintenance judgments when the reason they are protecting the social system is to protect the principle of collective equality and happiness. Although Poland's Lech Walesa would perhaps recognize this, Kohlberg's scoring manual does not.

India. Jyotsna Vasudev found that all of Kohlberg's modes of moral reasoning were present in India, but that all Indian modes of moral reasoning were not reflected in Kohlberg's scheme. In the West, as one of Vasudev's subjects points out, "An ethical problem usually involves another conscious human being," but in some traditions in India it is reasoned that "any action that involves any form of life, any creature which cannot react towards your own action as would a human being, should still be considered a valued life. . . . Moral situations are not limited to relations between humans alone

but are extended to other forms of life" (1983, p. 7). Vasudev offered the following excerpt from an interview with a 50-year-old Indian to illustrate how Indians may use a different conception of the moral sphere and a different postconventional principle to resolve moral conflicts:

Q. What if Heinz was stealing to save the life of his pet animal [instead of his wife's life]?

A. If Heinz saves an animal's life his action will be commendable. The right use of the drug is to administer it to the needy. There is some difference, of course—human life is more evolved and hence of greater importance in the scheme of nature—but an animal's life is not altogether bereft of importance. . . . Life is known, understood and felt by everyone. It is [just] a matter of fact whether it is manifest in man or animal. The basic unity of life and its importance cannot be denied. . . . All of life, human or nonhuman, is divine, sacred, and a manifestation of the Supreme reality. . . . We in India are vegetarians; the principle of vegetarianism is that life should not be destroyed. If it must be destroyed then the lower forms of life such as plants may be destroyed to preserve the higher forms. One makes choices between many forms of life but the overall guiding or spiritual principle should be that all forms of life are of value. In the spiritual tradition, for example, carelessly or needlessly breaking a leaf on a flower is also construed as an act of violence. Whenever possible, minimize violence. Man as a realized being should appreciate and defend not only his life and that of other human beings but should be responsible for other forms of life. Power, physical or mental, should not be a reason for destruction. Spiritual consciousness is for enlightenment. It should propel one towards recognising *the unity of all life* [italics added] rather than selecting victims that are powerless. It is only in very special conditions that life survives and evolves to the standards known to us. (Vasudev, 1983, pp. 7–8)

This interview illustrates how the moral principle of the unity of all life informs some Indian subjects' decision making. Yet it only became fully evident in the interview when the subject was asked about a domain that does not commonly concern Westerners (i.e., non-human animal life). Vasudev concluded that Indian moral reasoning, in addition to illustrating all modes of moral reasoning in Kohlberg's scheme, also reflects other moral values at the postconventional or Stage 5 level. She further concluded, on the basis of her own Indian background, that these principles have emerged from the characteristics of Indian philosophical, spiritual, and religious traditions.

Vasudev's conclusions are supported by Uwe Gielen's (1983) study of Buddhist monks from Ladakh, a Tibetan culture in India.

"Surprisingly," stated Gielen, "monks received lower moral reasoning scores than laymen" (p. 1). He concluded that, although Kohlberg's scheme was sufficient to score the preconventional and conventional elements of Buddhist reasoning, it was not sufficient for an understanding of their cooperative and nonviolent principles. His data also suggested that it is possible to do mature moral reasoning about animal life, the gods, respect for the caste system, and the issues of purity, sanctity, and chastity. Such reasoning may be so antithetical to North American moral values, however, that it is not scorable using Kohlberg's model.

Other Indian research in progress by Richard Shweder also lends support to this contention (personal communication, February, 1984). Because Kohlberg's measure is open ended or semiclinical in nature, subjects occasionally respond in a narrative style (i.e., by telling a parable or story). Shweder found this type of response to be more common in India because, as he noted, a major mode of moral discourse in traditional Hindu society is narrative. When his informants responded to a Kohlbergian probe question by saying "Let me tell you a story" and proceeded to tell a moral tale from which the listener was expected to draw a lesson, Shweder indicated that highly trained Kohlbergian scorers were unable to score the interview material. This may be due in part to the fact that the storyteller had shifted from the role of respondent explaining personal reasoning to the role of teacher trying to stimulate the interviewer's reasoning. It may also be due in part, however, to a possible overlap between the moral principles addressed by their narrative material and the moral principles not addressed by Kohlberg's scoring system. As Kohlberg himself acknowledged to Shweder, "This material fits our scoring manual much less easily than other cross-cultural interviews on which I have personally worked" (personal communication, February, 1984).

Taiwan. Ting Lei and Shall-way Cheng (1984) studied Chinese children and adults living in Taiwan. Their research findings are generally quite supportive of the assumptions underlying Kohlberg's theory, and their Taiwanese sample did include subjects reasoning at each one of Kohlberg's stages up to Stage 4/5. Yet the infrequency with which interviews were scored as using postconventional reasoning prompted Lei to question if Taiwanese were usually missing the higher levels of moral maturity or if Kohlberg's scoring manual was missing Taiwanese expressions of principled reasoning. To answer this question, Lei examined the frequency with which Taiwanese subjects used the different criterion judgments in the scoring manual. (Criterion judgments are basically different types of examples of reasoning at a particular stage and are used as the criterion by which to match interview judgments in the scoring process.) Lei found that the use of the various criterion judgments was far from equally distributed; some of the criterion examples were matched to Taiwanese judgments unusually frequently, whereas many others were rarely or never illustrated in the interviews. As he stated, "Though many of the Chinese subjects' interview judgments can be scored by matching with the criterion judgments in the *Standard Form Scoring Manual,* a considerable number of subjects' moral concerns were hard to give scores to due to the lack of appropriate criterion judgments to match with" (1984, p. 3). More interestingly, Lei found that the most frequently matched criterion judgments were those related to the Chinese traditional values of filial piety and collective utility. He concluded that this selection of scorable interview judgments "tended to centralize subjects' responses into conventional levels" (p. 11) because examples of these values were absent in the criterion judgments given for the higher stages. Filial piety, for instance, is represented in criterion judgments given for Stage 3—affiliation—but no examples are given under Stage 5. Lei had not yet systematically analyzed those moral judgments that were unscorable, however, and thus felt it premature to make specific claims about the cultural patterning of the unscorable responses. He did, however, offer the following example from the father–son dilemma:

Q. Should Joe refuse to give his father the money? Why or why not?
A. No. In terms of parent–child relations, he has the role as father, and the son should fulfill whatever his father wants. This is because the father has reared Joe for such a long time and given him affection and protection. So Joe should give his father the money to show how much he appreciates his father's caring.

Q. The father promised Joe he could go to camp if he earned the money. Is the fact that the father promised the most important thing in the situation? Why or why not?

A. Yes, though Joe is just a kid, he has his own rights and should be respected. The father should not treat his son as a means to fulfill his own wishes.

Q. What do you think is the most important thing a son should be concerned about in his relationship to his father? Why?

A. Understanding his parents' intent. Parents' expectations for their child are derived out of their own experiences, and with the purpose for the child's own good. Though the child need not do everything his parents demand, considering their intention and affection, the child should eliminate conflict with parents to as few as possible by standing up on his own position [only] if he truly believes he is right. But later on he should compensate his parents' loss in other respects. . . . Camping is not an important thing. [What] I am talking about [is that] one should not sacrifice one's basic principles for other people's happiness. (Lei & Chung, 1984, pp.12–13)

Lei pointed out that the judgments changed over the course of the three questions. In response to the first question the subject took the role of the son and gave a filial pious answer that Kohlberg's manual would score at Stage 3. By taking the role of the father, the subject answered the second question with a more principled, but also more Western-sounding, response. In the third question, when the two ideas confronted each other, the subject solved the dilemma by maintaining both values within a hierarchy. Lei noted that "this type of judgment which resolves the dilemma between the fulfillment of filial piety and the commitment of personal principles has not appeared in the scoring manual" (Lei & Chung, 1984, p. 13). Note that this interview ends with the word *happiness,* but on a sad note. Lei suggested that, under influence of a Western education, this subject is losing the collective perspective of Chinese cultural values. As we saw in the kibbutz data, the equal right to happiness is itself a principle, but one that can only be reasonably achieved within a communitarian setting. The Chinese collectivist perspective has been presented more fully in Dien's (1982) non-empirical critique of Kohlberg's work. Her comparison of Judeo-Christian and Confucian moral thought also concluded that Kohlberg's description misses some elements of collectivist moral principles and modes of conflict resolution. In particular, Dien suggested that there may be different but equally principled

end points to moral development in these two different cultural systems.

New Guinea. Most recently, Tietjen and Walker (1984) applied my method of reanalyzing guess-scored material for cultural patterns in their study of Maisin village leaders in Papua New Guinea. They found that the difficult-to-score material was not random, but rather reflected particular cultural concepts. In particular, their examination of the interviews and related ethnographic material indicated "that the issue of the relationship of the individual to the community is a moral issue of central importance to the collectivistic [and egalitarian] oriented Maisin" (Tietjen & Walker, 1984, p. 1). Some village leaders, for instance, placed blame for the dilemma on the community: "If nobody helped him [save his dying wife] and so he [stole to save her], I would say *we* had caused that problem" (p. 21). Tietjen and Walker concluded that "there is nothing in the scoring manual that deals with maintaining human relationships between the level of individual interpersonal and the level of society in general" (1984, pp. 1, 24).

Kenya. Although culturally patterned difficult-to-score material usually occurs at the Stage 4/5 transition, Carolyn Edwards' reanalysis of her Kenyan interviews found examples at the Stage 3/4 transition among the adult community moral leaders in her sample. Edwards offered the following example from an interview with a 55-year-old unschooled Kipsigis villager; the excerpt is from an adapted version of Dilemma I:

Q. Should the father always direct the son?

A. For the son to refuse to take his father's advice shows that he is not well cared for. . . . But when you [a father] convince him [your son] by telling him, "Do this sort of thing because this will earn us our living. You didn't do it this time, but do it next time," then the child will comply since you did not command [shout at] him . . . and so both of you will be in good unity and understanding of each other.

Q. Which is worse, for a father to break his promise or for a son?

A. [If a father breaks his word] it will cause hatred because the son will be angry, saying, "I wanted to follow my own intentions, but my father cheated: he permitted me and then refused me. Now I don't want to hear more of his words. He can't love me and is unable to protect me." So it is bad. [However,] the one for the son is worse. Imagine a child disobeying my own words, is he really normal? . . . Rules are mine and I want him to follow, [e.g.,] "Do this thing to earn you a living," as I did follow my father's rules also. . . . Father's bad deeds are revealed when he does not care for his children . . . that man is like a drunkard whose children do not sleep at home because he drives them away when not sober. The man does not have rules which work and so it is bad. But if he has good functioning rules, he is able to keep his family. The maize will be growing because of his good work. Then it is clear that his family is well looked after. (Edwards, in press, pp. 12–13).

Edwards suggested that this excerpt raises questions about Kohlberg's requirement that Stage 4 include "a full-blown understanding of organizational aspects of a social structure and the operation of a legal system" (p. 11). Perhaps, she argued, Stage 4 should properly require only "a rough appreciation of society's need for institutionalized roles." From this perspective, the Kenyan leaders would qualify in that they have a "clear and elaborated vision of fair and reasonable rules for running a prosperous extended family based on [the values of] unity, respect, and understanding" (in press, p. 11).

In sum, the evidence from the Israeli kibbutz, India, Taiwan, New Guinea, and Kenya suggests that some culturally unique moral judgments do not appear in the theory or scoring manual. Collective or communalistic principled reasoning, in particular, is missing or misunderstood.

Conclusion

Forty-five studies of moral development (38 cross sectional and 7 longitudinal) have been carried out in 27 countries. The range of cultural diversity was considered sufficient to evaluate with acceptable confidence the validity of Kohlberg's claim for the cross-cultural universality of his model and method. The evidence suggests that Kohlberg's interview is reasonably culture fair when the content is creatively adapted and the subject is interviewed in his or her native language. The invariant sequence proposition was also found to be well supported, because stage skipping and stage regressions were rare and always below the level that could be attributed to measurement error.

The combined cross-sectional and longitudinal data indicated that Stage 1 to Stage 3/4 or 4 were in evidence virtually universally when one took into consideration the age range and sample size of the population under study. Although the presence of Stage 4/5 or 5 was extremely rare in all populations, it was evident to some degree in approximately two thirds of the subcultures sampled that included subjects in the 18-to-60+ age range. An examination of the presence or absence of the higher stages in different types of cultural groups and social classes, however, indicated that nearly all samples from urban cultural groups or middle-class populations exhibited some principled reasoning but that all folk cultural groups failed to exhibit any postconventional reasoning. This near perfect association was further supported by the data on the general applicability of the stages. Although strongly supportive of the stage structures currently identified, these findings also indicated that other values, such as collective solidarity, that are commonly stressed in either traditional folk cultures or in working-class communities are missing from the theory's explication and the scoring manual's examples of reasoning at the higher stages.

Because the only clearly problematic area of the data, in terms of its empirical support for Kohlberg's universality claim, involves the relative absence of postconventional reasoning in many populations, I now wish to consider some of the more general possible conclusions that one might draw. One possible interpretation is that the present definitions of the higher stages are completely culture bound and ethnocentric. Such radical cultural relativism could even be extended to challenge the possibility of valid cross-cultural comparisons. However, this perspective is difficult to accept in view of the research that has been reviewed. Although postconventional reasoning is not found in all studies, it is found in many, including several non-Western societies. People in diverse cultures have come to maintain structurally similar principles of human dignity, equality, and the value of life. To draw a conclusion of complete ethnocentrism would seem to require that one confuse cultural relativity with ethical relativity (cf. Brandt, 1961; Mayers, 1974). As Kohlberg suggested, the accurate understanding that "moral principles are culturally variable in a fundamental way" (i.e., cultural relativism) is fundamentally distinct from the conclusion "that there are no rational principles . . .

that could reconcile observed divergencies of moral beliefs" (i.e., ethical relativity; 1981, p. 106). The former can be accepted without the latter.

Another possible interpretation is that the data support a doctrine of social evolution with so-called primitive societies at the bottom of the hierarchy and the United States at the top. Such radical cultural ethnocentrism is not seriously presented in the literature, but Kohlberg sometimes seemed to present a mild version of this position:

Not only are the moral stages culturally universal, but they also correspond to a progression in cultural history. Principled moral thinking appeared first in human history in the period 600–400 B.C., when universal human ideas and rational criticism of customary morality developed in Greece, Palestine, India, and China. . . . My findings that the two highest stages are absent in preliterate or semiliterate village culture also suggests a mild doctrine of *social evolutionism,* such as was elaborated in the classic work by Hobhouse in 1906. (Kohlberg, 1981, pp. 128, 378, 383)

Kohlberg qualified these remarks by stating that "although cultures differ in most frequent or modal stages, a culture cannot be located at a single stage, and the individual's moral stage cannot be derived directly from his or her culture's [modal] stage" (1981, p. 129). Kohlberg's qualifier and his remarks elsewhere (1981, pp. 107ff) make it clear that he did not wish to endorse a doctrine of extreme social evolutionism, and that he did not believe that one can rank an entire culture on a moral hierarchy. Yet, his essential argument is still that individuals in some societies should not be expected to develop Stage 5 reasoning because they do not possess or experience the cognitive and social prerequisites for such mature reasoning. On a cognitive level, according to Kohlberg, individuals need to have achieved formal operations to develop postconventional reasoning. Socially, individuals need to be aware of conflict between two societies to generate a need for universal principles that transcend the conflict.

I believe that Kohlberg's postulate of even a mild doctrine of social evolutionism is misguided on three grounds. First, the research of Claude Levi-Strauss has persuasively demonstrated that preliterate peoples of the world possess the ability to use formal struc-

tures to make sense of their world (1962, 1963). As Levi-Strauss stated:

This thirst for knowledge is one of the most neglected aspects of the thought of people we call "primitive." Even if it is rarely directed towards facts of the same level as those with which modern science is concerned, it implies comparable intellectual application and methods of observation. In both cases the universe is an object of thought at least as much as it is a means of satisfying needs. (1962, p. 3)

Although the question of cognitive development in preliterate folk societies has not been fully settled (cf. Sharp, Cole, & Lave, 1979), individuals in folk societies often do possess the cognitive abilities that Kohlberg defined as prerequisites for mature moral reasoning (cf. Feldman, Lee, McLean, Pillemer, & Murray, 1974). Their thinking is so complexly differentiated that Western psychologists are often not equal to the task of comprehending its complexity. Further, as Malinowski demonstrated in his pioneering field research, individuals in traditional societies clearly use these intellectual abilities to reason about their customs and norms rather than blindly conforming to them (1926a, 1926b, 1944). Second, it is not at all clear why the social prerequisites of postconventional moral reasoning are not experienced by the members of tribal or village folk societies. They experience conflict, for instance, between neighboring villages or tribal groups, and the leaders of their communities must be able to resolve these conflicts in a manner that recognizes the needs and rights of both groups. Kohlberg also argued that the experience of dealing with ultimate or religious issues, such as life and death, are a necessary condition for, and an integral part of, Stage 6 reasoning (1981). Here again, however, villagers certainly have to make meaning of such issues and may do so more frequently and directly than individuals in Western urban communities. Whereas recent research does support the understanding that there are both cognitive and social prerequisites for the development of mature moral reasoning (Snarey, 1982, in press), many individual members of folk communities achieve or experience these prerequisites and, thus, one would expect that at least a few of them would also achieve the higher stages of moral judgment. Third, this present review of the empirical studies does not support a supremacist view of North America. The United States sample did not rank first in mean moral maturity scores in any one of the five age divisions in Table 6; Taiwanese, kibbutzniks, Indians, and Turkish subjects all ranked higher than parallel groups from the United States at one or more points in the life cycle.

Claims that Kohlberg's theory is completely ethnocentric and universal are not consistent with the empirical research. So, why do subjects from traditional folk societies never score at Stage 5? I would suggest a third perspective that avoids the extremes of the two previous positions, but also assimilates important aspects of these arguments. In brief, sociocultural systems should be expected to vary in modal stage of usage and should also be understood as fully equal. A key to this position is to distinguish between society and culture and to bring a developmental perspective to both. This classic distinction (Linton, 1945) has implicitly underlied the strongest previous critiques of Kohlberg's universality claim: Susan Buck-Morss' socioeconomic critique (1975) and Carolyn Edwards' social complexity critique (1975). The social features of sociocultural systems (e.g., demographics, sociotechnical complexity) vary tremendously, not only when comparisons are made between societies, but also within one society over time. As the distribution of age groups varies, for instance, one would expect the modal stage to vary accordingly. Further, even if some individuals in a society espouse principled morality, the social structure may hinder its acceptance or operationalization. For example, the social structure of most prisons is so inadequate that it makes it dangerous to reason beyond Stage 2, just as the social structure of the United States made it dangerous for Martin Luther King to reason beyond Stage 4 (cf. Kohlberg, 1981). Thus, social systems should be expected to differ in their modal stage or level of moral reasoning.

In contrast, a society's culture or world view provides each member with a rich pool of cultural values to digest cognitively. Cultural world views can, in fact, be reasoned about on any stage level. This phenomenon is visible, for instance, with regard to religious world views. The pool of cultural content is sufficiently rich in Judaism, Christianity, Hinduism, and other traditions that varying levels of sophistication within any particular tradition are possible despite important differences between it and other religions. Thus, one finds children making sense of God as a concrete person and theologians who make meaning within the same religious tradition by referring to a transcendent reality or the Ground of Being. An appealing counterargument to the position that cultural world views cannot be placed at a particular stage is to point to Nazi Germany as a clearly morally inferior culture. However, this misses the point. One can reason about one's nation on a Stage 4 or 5 level, as many citizens of modern Germany apparently do (Gielen, 1982) and as some German citizens did during Hitler's reign of terror (cf. Bonhoeffer, 1953; London, 1970), or one can reason about it on a Stage 2 level, as many Nazis obviously did (cf. Garbarino & Bronfenbrenner, 1976). Thus, although every society may not have a significant proportion of its population reasoning at the higher stages, every culture is capable of supporting higher stage reasoning.

When this third perspective is brought to bear on the previously reviewed research, one of the methodological problems is highlighted—the stage definitions and scoring manual are incomplete, especially for Stage 5. Although Kohlberg's preconventional and conventional stages are well based on empirical operative judgments rather than on philosophical ethical systems, this is only weakly true of the postconventional stages. Descriptions of higher stage reasoning are primarily based upon Kant, Rawls, and other Western philosophers. Of course, a system of philosophy common to the entire world does not exist, and the integration of all existing systems is not feasible. Thus, it is not surprising that Kohlberg's postconventional stage descriptions are incomplete. The stage model and scoring manual, nevertheless, should draw examples of reasoning at the higher stages from a wider range of cultural world views. As Elizabeth Simpson (1974) suggested regarding the value of life in Hindu philosophy, for instance, "It is not that life is not valued . . . but that it is valued situationally in highly culturally specific ways" (p. 97). The cultural specificity of principled moral reasoning has not been adequately explored, and thus Kohlberg's stage schema and scoring system appear to misinterpret the presence of higher stage reasoning in some types of cultural groups. In sum, there is a need for a more pluralistic stage theory and for a scoring manual that is elaborated with culturally specific examples of formal principles from diverse cultures.

The cross-cultural elaboration of postconventional principles could, I believe, reveal Stage 5 to be a more common empirical phenomenon. Future researchers should seek to find negative results and alternative structures; future research needs to be maximally open to the possibility of discovering additional modes of moral reasoning, especially at the postconventional level (cf. Price-Williams, 1975). Such a constructive approach to future cross-cultural moral development research will result in a more adequate and pluralistic understanding of universality and variation in social–moral development. The current problems and future research strategies suggested by this review, of course, simply highlight the natural limitations of any scheme, including Kohlberg's. The significant shortcomings of Kohlberg's work should not overshadow its remarkable achievements.

References

Ashton, P. (1975). Cross-cultural research: An experimental perspective. *Harvard Educational Review, 45*(4), 475–505.

Awa, N. (1979). Ethnocentric bias in development research. In M. Asante, E. Newmark, & C. Blake (Eds.), *Handbook of intercultural communication* (pp. 263–282). London: Sage.

Bar-Yam, M., & Abrahami, A. (1982). *Sex and age differences in moral reasoning of kibbutz adults.* Unpublished manuscript, School of Education, Boston University.

Batt, H. W. (1974). *Obligation and decision in Thai administration: From patrimonial to rational-legal bureaucracy.* Unpublished doctoral dissertation, State University of New York at Albany.

Batt, H. W. (1975). *Thai conceptions of justice on Kohlberg's moral development scale.* Unpublished manuscript, State University of New York at Albany.

Berry, J., & Dasen, P. (1974). *Culture and cognition.* London: Methuen.

Bloom, A. H. (1977). Two dimensions of moral reasoning: Social principledness and social humanism in cross-cultural perspective. *Journal of Social Psychology, 101*(1), 29–44.

Bonhoeffer, D. (1953). *Letters and papers from prison.* New York: Macmillan.

Brandt, R. B. (1961). *Value and obligation: Systematic readings in ethics.* New York: Harcourt, Brace & World.

Bredemeier, H. (1955). The methodology of functionalism. *American Sociological Review, 20,* 173–180.

Broughton, J. (1978). The cognitive-developmental approach to morality: A reply to Kurtines and Grief. *Journal of Moral Education, 7*(2), 81–96.

Buck-Morss, S. (1975). Socioeconomic bias in Piaget's theory and its implications for the cross-cultural controversy. *Human Development, 18,* 35–49.

Chern, Y. H. (1978). *Moral judgment development in Chinese adolescents.* Unpublished manuscript, Ku-ashung Normal College, Taiwan.

Colby, A. (1978). Evolution of a moral-development theory. *New Directions for Child Development. 2,* 89–104.

Colby, A., Kohlberg, L., Gibbs, J., Candee, D., Speicher-Dubin, B., Hewer, A., & Power, C. (1978). *Measuring moral judgment: Standardized scoring manual.* Cambridge, MA: Harvard University, Moral Education Research Foundation.

Colby, A., Kohlberg, L., Gibbs, J., & Lieberman, M. (1983). A longitudinal study of moral judgment. *Monographs of the Society for Research in Child Development, 48*(1–2), 1–124.

Cole, M., & Scribner, M. (1974). *Culture and thought.* New York: Wiley.

Dasen, P. R. (1972). Cross-cultural Piagetian research: A summary. *Journal of Cross-Cultural Psychology, 3,* 23–39.

Denny, N., & Duffy, D. (1974). Possible environmental causes of stages in moral reasoning. *Journal of Genetic Psychology, 125,* 277–283.

DeVos, E. (1983). *Socioeconomic influences on moral reasoning: A structural developmental perspective.* Unpublished doctoral dissertation, Harvard University, Cambridge, MA.

Dien, D. S. (1982). A Chinese perspective on Kohlberg's theory of moral development. *Developmental Review, 2,* 331–341.

Eckensberger, L. (1983). *Research on moral development in Germany.* Unpublished manuscript, University of the Saarland, Germany.

Edwards, C. (1974). *The effect of experience on moral development: Results from Kenya.* Unpublished doctoral dissertation, Harvard University, Cambridge, MA.

Edwards, C. (1975). Societal complexity and moral development. *Ethos, 3,* 505–527.

Edwards, C. (1978). Social experience and moral judgment in East African young adults. *Journal of Genetic Psychology, 133,* 19–29.

Edwards, C. (1981). The comparative study of the development of moral judgment and reasoning. In R. Munroe, R. Munroe, & B. Whiting (Eds.), *Handbook of cross-cultural human development* (pp. 501–527). New York: Garland.

Edwards, C. (1982). Moral development in comparative cultural perspective. In D. Wagner & H. Stevenson (Eds.), *Cultural perspectives on child development* (pp. 248–278). San Francisco: Freeman.

Edwards, C. (in press). Cross-cultural research on Kohlberg's stages: The basis for consensus. In S. Modgil & C. Modgil (Eds.), *Lawrence Kohlberg: Consensus and controversy.* Sussex, England: Falmer.

Feldman, C., Lee, B., McLean, J., Pillemer, D., & Murray, J. (1974). *The development of adaptive intelligence: A cross-cultural study.* San Francisco: Jossey-Bass.

Garbarino, J., & Bronfenbrenner, U. (1976). The socialization of moral judgment and behavior in cross-cultural perspective. In T. Lickona (Ed.), *Moral development and behavior* (pp. 70–83). New York: Holt, Rinehart & Winston.

Gibbs, J. (1977). Kohlberg's stages of moral development: A critique. *Harvard Educational Review, 47*(1), 43–61.

Gielen, U. (1982). *Moral reasoning in radical and nonradical German students.* Unpublished manuscript, St. Francis University, Brooklyn, NY.

Gielen, U., & Kelly, D. (1983, February). *Buddhist Ladakh: Psychological portrait of a non-violent culture.* Paper presented at the annual conference of the Society for Cross-Cultural Research, Washington, DC.

Gilligan, C. (1982). *In a different voice.* Cambridge, MA: Harvard University Press.

Gorsuch, R., & Barnes, M. (1973). Stages of ethical reasoning and moral norms of Carib youths. *Journal of Cross-Cultural Psychology, 4,* 183–301.

Grimley, L. (1973). *A cross-cultural study of moral development.* Unpublished doctoral dissertation, Kent State University, Kent, OH.

Grimley, L. (1974). Moral development in different nations. *School Psychology Digest, 3*(2), 43–51.

Guidon, A. (1978). Moral development: A critique of Kohlberg's sequence. *University of Ottawa Quarterly, 48*(3), 232–263.

Harkness, S., Edwards, C., & Super, C. (1981). Social roles and moral reasoning: A case study in a rural African community. *Developmental Psychology, 17,* 595–603.

Helkama, K. (1981). *Toward a cognitive-developmental theory of attribution of responsibility.* Unpublished doctoral dissertation, Helsinki University.

Kohlberg, L. (1958). *The development of modes of thinking and choice in the years 10 to 16.* Unpublished doctoral dissertation, University of Chicago.

Kohlberg, L. (1968). *Global rating guide: Preliminary moral judgment scoring manual.* Cambridge, MA: Harvard University, Moral Education Research Foundation.

Kohlberg, L. (1969). Stage and sequence: The cognitive-developmental approach to socialization. In D. A. Goslin (Ed.), *Handbook of socialization theory and research* (pp. 347–480). Chicago: Rand McNally.

Kohlberg, L. (1971). From is to ought: How to commit the naturalistic fallacy and get away with it in the study of moral development. In L. Mischel (Ed.), *Cognitive development and epistemology* (pp. 151–284). New York: Academic Press.

Kohlberg, L. (1972). *Structural issue scoring manual.* Cambridge, MA: Harvard University, Moral Education Research Foundation.

Kohlberg, L. (1981). *The philosophy of moral development: Moral stages and the idea of justice: Vol. 1. Essays on moral development.* San Francisco: Harper & Row.

Kohlberg, L., & Bar-Yam, M. (1971). Cognitive-developmental theory and the practice of collective moral education. In M. Wolins & M. Gottesman (Eds.), *Group care: An Israeli approach* (pp. 342–371). New York: Gordon & Breach.

Kohlberg, L., & Kramer, R. (1969). Continuities and discontinuities in childhood and adult moral development. *Human Development, 12,* 93–120.

Kuhn, D., & Angeleu, J. (1976). An experimental study of the development of formal operational thought. *Child Development, 47,* 697–706.

Kurtines, W., & Grief, E. C. (1974). The development of moral thought: Review and evaluation of Kohlberg's approach. *Psychological Bulletin, 81,* 453–470.

Lei, T. (1980). *An empirical study of Kohlberg's theory and scoring system of moral judgment development in Chinese society.* Unpublished bachelor's thesis, National Taiwan University.

Lei, T. (1981). *The development of moral, political, and legal reasoning in Chinese societies.* Unpublished master's thesis, University of Minnesota, Minneapolis.

Lei, T., & Cheng, S. W. (1984). *An empirical study of Kohlberg's theory and scoring system of moral judgment in Chinese society.* Unpublished manuscript, Harvard University, Center for Moral Education, Cambridge, MA.

Levi-Strauss, C. (1962). *The savage mind.* Chicago: University of Chicago Press.

Levi-Strauss, C. (1963). *Structural anthropology.* New York: Basic Books.

Lickona, T. (1969). Piaget misunderstood: A critique of the criticisms of his theory of moral development. *Merrill-Palmer Quarterly of Behavior and Development, 16,* 337–350.

Lickona, T. (Ed.). (1976). *Moral development and behavior: Theory, research, and social issues.* New York: Holt, Rinehart & Winston.

Light, R., & Pillemer, D. (1982). Numbers and narrative: Combining their strengths in research reviews. *Harvard Educational Review, 52,* 1–26.

Light, R., & Smith, P. (1971). Accumulating evidence: Procedures for resolving contradictions among different research studies. *Harvard Educational Review, 41,* 429–471.

Linton, R. (1945). *The cultural background of personality.* New York: Appleton-Century-Crofts.

London, P. (1970). The rescuers: Motivational hypotheses about Christians who saved Jews from the Nazis. In J. Macaulay & L. Berkowitz (Eds.), *Altruism and helping behavior* (pp. 240–248). New York: Academic Press.

Malinowski, B. (1926a). *Crime and custom in savage society.* New York: International Library of Psychology, Philosophy and Scientific Method.

Malinowski, B. (1926b). Primitive law and order. *Nature, 117,* 9–16.

Malinowski, B. (1944). *A scientific theory of culture.* Chapel Hill, NC: University of North Carolina.

Marchand-Jodoin, L., & Samson, L. (1982). Kohlberg's theory applied to the moral and sexual development of adults. *Journal of Moral Education, 11,* 247–258.

Maqsud, M. (1976). *The effects of different educational environments on the moral development of Nigerian children.* Unpublished doctoral dissertation, University of London.

Maqsud, M. (1977a). The influence of social heterogeneity and sentimental credibility of moral judgments of Nigerian Muslim adolescents. *Journal of Cross-Cultural Psychology, 8,* 113–122.

Maqsud, M. (1977b). Moral reasoning of Nigerian and Pakistani Muslim adolescents. *Journal of Moral Education, 7,* 40–49.

Maqsud, M. (1979). Cultural influences on transition in the development of moral reasoning in Nigerian boys. *The Journal of Social Psychology, 108,* 151–159.

Mayers, M. K. (1974). *Christianity confronts culture.* Grand Rapids, MI: Zondervan.

Moir, J. (1974). Egocentrism and the emergence of conventional morality in preadolescent girls. *Child Development, 45,* 299–304.

Naroll, R., & D'Andrade, R. (1963). Two solutions to Galton's problem. *American Anthropologist, 65,* 1053–1067.

Nisan, M., & Kohlberg, L. (1982). Universality and variation in moral judgement: A longitudinal and cross-sectional study in Turkey. *Child Development, 53,* 865–876.

Okonkuo, R. (1983). *Moral development research in Nigeria: Preliminary report of a pilot study in progress.* Unpublished manuscript, Harvard University, Cambridge, MA.

Pacheco-Maldonado, A. (1972). *A cognitive-developmental study of moral judgments in Puerto Rican children.* Unpublished doctoral dissertation, State University of New York at Albany.

Parikh, B. (1975). *Moral judgment development and its relation to family environmental factors in Indian and American urban upper middle class families.* Unpublished doctoral dissertation, Boston University, Boston, MA.

Parikh, B. (1980). Development of moral judgment and its relation to family environmental factors in Indian and American families. *Child Development, 51,* 1030–1039.

Price-Williams, D. R. (1975). *Explorations in cross-cultural psychology.* San Francisco: Chandler & Sharp.

Redfield, R. (1955). *The little community.* Chicago: University of Chicago Press.

Redfield, R. (1956). *Peasant society and culture.* Chicago: University of Chicago Press.

Redfield, R. (1962). *Human nature and the study of society: The collected papers of Robert Redfield.* Chicago: University of Chicago Press.

Reimer, J. (1977). *A study in the moral development of kibbutz adolescents.* Unpublished doctoral dissertation, Harvard University, Cambridge, MA.

Rest, J. (1983). Morality. In J. Flavell & E. Markman (Eds.), *Manual of child psychology: Vol. 3. Cognitive development* (pp. 556–629) New York: Wiley.

Rogoff, B., Sellers, M. J., Pirrotta, S., Fox, N., & White, S. H. (1975). Age of assignment of roles and responsibilities to children: A cross-cultural survey. *Human Development, 18,* 353–369.

Saadatmand, B. (1972). *Cross-cultural investigation of the influences of parents, culture, and age on the moral reasoning of children.* Unpublished doctoral dissertation, Brigham Young University, Provo, Utah.

Samson, J. (1983, February). *General moral and sexual moral judgments among French-Canadian adolescents.*

Paper presented at the annual conference of the Society for Cross-Cultural Research, Washington, DC.

Saraswathi, T. S. (1977). *The development of moral judgment of Indian children.* Unpublished research report, University of Baroda, Gujarat, India.

Saraswathi, T. S., & Sundaresan, J. (1982). *A short-term longitudinal study of the development of moral judgment in Indian Boys.* Unpublished manuscript, University of Baroda, Gujarat, India.

Saxe, G. (1970). *The development of moral judgment: A cross-cultural study of Kalskagagmuit Eskimos.* Unpublished manuscript, University of California, Berkeley.

Setiono, T. (1982). *The development of social cognition in university students: Some effects of Padjadjaran University's study-service on social-perspective coordination and moral reasoning.* Unpublished manuscript, Padjadjaran University, Bandung, Indonesia.

Sharp, D., Cole, M., & Lave, C. (1979). Education and cognitive development: The evidence from experimental research. *Monographs of the Society for Research in Child Development, 44* (1–2, Serial No. 178).

Shweder, R. (1982a). Beyond self-constructed knowledge: The study of culture and morality. *Merrill-Palmer Quarterly, 28,* 41–69.

Shweder, R. (1982b). Liberalism as destiny. *Contemporary Psychology, 27,* 421–424.

Simpson, A., & Graham, D. (1971). *The development of moral judgment, emotion, and behavior in British adolescents.* Unpublished manuscript, University of Durham, England.

Simpson, E. L. (1974). Moral development research: A case study of scientific cultural bias. *Human Development, 17,* 81–106.

Snarey, J. (1982). The social and moral development of kibbutz founders and sabras: A longitudinal and cross-sectional cross-cultural study. (Doctoral dissertation, Harvard University, 1982). *Dissertation Abstracts International, 43*(10), 3416b. (University Microfilms No. 83-02, 435)

Snarey, J. (in press). The relationship of social-moral development with cognitive and ego development: A cross-cultural study. *Behavior Science Research.*

Snarey, J., & Blasi, J. (1980). Ego development among adult kibbutzniks: A cross-cultural application of Loevinger's theory. *Genetic Psychology Monographs, 102,* 117–157.

Snarey, J., Kohlberg, L., & Noam, G. (1983). Ego development in perspective: Structural stage, functional phase, and cultural age-period models. *Developmental Review, 3,* 303–338.

Snarey, J., Reimer, J., & Kohlberg, L. (in press). The development of social–moral reasoning among kibbutz adolescents: A longitudinal study. *Developmental Psychology.*

Sullivan, E. (1977). A study of Kohlberg's structural theory of moral development: A critique. *Human Development, 20,* 352–376.

Sullivan, E., & Beck, C. (1975). Moral education in a Canadian setting. *Phi Delta Kappan,* 697–700.

Sullivan, E., Beck, C., Joy, M., & Pagliuso, S. (1975). *Moral learning: Some findings, issues and questions.* New York: Paulist.

Sullivan, E., McCullough, G., & Stager, M. (1970). A developmental study of the relationship between conceptual, ego, and moral development. *Child Development, 41,* 399–411.

Sullivan, E., & Quarter, J. (1972). Psychological correlates of certain post-conventional moral types: A perspective on hybrid types. *Journal of Personality, 40,* 149–161.

Tietjen, A., & Walker, L. (1984). *Moral reasoning and leadership among men in a Papua New Guinea village.* Unpublished manuscript, University of British Columbia, Vancouver, Canada.

Turiel, E., Edwards, C., & Kohlberg, L. (1978). Moral development in Turkish children, adolescents, and young adults. *Journal of Cross-Cultural Psychology, 9,* 75–85.

Vasudev, J. (1981, December). *The morality of care and responsibility in Indian women and men: An application of Gilligan's scheme.* Paper presented at the International Conference on Morality and Moral Development, Miami Beach, FL.

Vasudev, J. (1983). *A study of moral reasoning at different life stages in India.* Unpublished manuscript, University of Pittsburgh, PA.

Villenave-Cremer, S., & Eckensberger, L. (1983, August). *On the role of affective processes in moral judgment performances.* Paper presented at the International Symposium on Moral Education, Fribourg, Switzerland.

Walker, L. J. (1984). Sex differences in the development of moral reasoning: A critical review of the literature. *Child Development, 55,* 677–691.

Weinreich-Haste, H. (1977). Some consequences of replicating Kohlberg's original moral development study on a British sample. *Journal of Moral Education, 7,* 32–39.

White, C. (1975). Moral development in Bahamian school children: A cross-cultural examination of Kohlberg's stages of moral reasoning. *Developmental Psychology, 11,* 535–536.

White, C. (1977). *Moral reasoning in Bahamian and United States elders: Cross-national comparison of Kohlberg's theory of moral development.* Unpublished manuscript, University of Texas Health Science Center, Dallas.

White, C. (1983, February). *Moral reasoning in Bahamian and United States adults and children.* Paper presented at the annual meeting of the Society for Cross-Cultural Research, Washington, DC.

White, C. B., Bushnell, N., & Regnemer, J. L. (1978). Moral development in Bahamian school children: A 3-year examination of Kohlberg's stages of moral development. *Developmental Psychology, 14,* 58–65.

Whiting, J. W. M. (1968). Methods and problems in cross-cultural research. In G. Lindzey & E. Aronson (Eds.), *The handbook of social psychology* (pp. 693–728). Reading, MA: Addison-Wesley.

Received August 3, 1984
Revision received October 10, 1984 ∎

The Effects of Situational Factors on Moral Judgments

William E. Sobesky

University of Denver

SOBESKY, WILLIAM E. *The Effects of Situational Factors on Moral Judgments.* CHILD DEVEL-
OPMENT, 1983, **54**, 575–584. Little empirical investigation has focused on how specific situational
variables, such as negative consequences, interact with cognitive developmental variables, such
as moral judgment stage, to influence moral decisions and moral thinking. In this study, 223 high
school and college students completed 2 questionnaires. In the first, students answered the
short form of the Defining Issues Test, which provided a measure of their predisposition to use
principled-level rationales in solving moral dilemmas. In the second, students made moral judgments about what they should and would do, and they indicated their use of principled-level
thinking in resolving 4 versions of the Heinz dilemma. Each version presented a different
combination of negative consequences for the actor (Heinz) and for another (Heinz's wife). Results indicated that, when the negative consequences for the actor were severe, students were
less certain that they should and would act to help another person; they also displayed less
principled thinking. When the consequences for another were severe, individuals who had displayed a greater predisposition to make use of principled thinking were more certain of acting to
help.

In the typical moral dilemma used by Kohlberg, the needs of two or more individuals are in conflict (Kohlberg, 1971). In the Heinz story, for example, Heinz considers stealing a drug that might save his wife's life. If Heinz steals the drug, he might be caught and sent to prison. If Heinz does nothing, his wife might die. The dilemma lies in the likelihood that either action or inaction will result in negative outcomes for one or both of the parties involved.

In research using the Kohlberg style of dilemmas, the consequences of action and inaction have been left ambiguous, often to the point, as Rest (1976, p. 202) has noted, that readers must "imagine the consequences." This vagueness makes it difficult to determine the impact of situational factors upon moral decisions (i.e., What should Heinz do?) and moral thinking (i.e., Why should he do that?).

Such ambiguity was by design. Kohlberg's work has focused on defining qualitatively distinct stages of moral reasoning, a cognitive developmental factor. Kohlberg (1976) views these stages as structured wholes that are consistently employed across different content areas. Re-

cently, however, a number of authors have questioned this "simple-stage" approach. Fischer (1980), for example, has proposed that the cognitive structure one uses to solve a problem is a function of both the range of cognitive structures available to the individual and the particular content of the specific problem.

The purpose of this study was to explore situational and cognitive developmental factors that affect moral thinking and moral decision making about a hypothetical dilemma, the Heinz story, adapted from Kohlberg (Note 1) and Rest (Note 2). The situational factor was negative conse-quences. Two types of consequences were manipulated: those for the actor (Heinz) and those for another (Heinz's wife). The cognitive developmental factor was principled moral thinking as defined by Kohlberg (1969). Principled thinking was selected be-cause of its theoretical relevance for both types of negative consequences. In part be-cause the Kohlberg system yields so few principled individuals (Kohlberg, 1976), moral reasoning was measured using the method developed by Rest, Cooper, Coder, Masanz, and Anderson (1974). Two types of moral decisions were studied. One was a

The author wishes to express his appreciation to Dr. Kurt Fischer and to Drs. G. N. Braucht,
S. Harter, J. Phillips, and B. Rossman, as well as to several anonymous reviewers, for their helpful
comments. Portions of this article were presented at the biennial meeting of the Society for
Research in Child Development, San Francisco, March 1979. Requests for reprints should be sent
to William E. Sobesky, Department of Psychology, University of Colorado, Campus Box 345,
Boulder, Colorado 80309.

[*Child Development*, 1983, **54**, 575–584. © 1983 by the Society for Research in Child Development, Inc.
All rights reserved. 0009-3920/83/5403-0021$01.00]

judgment of obligation: What *should* be done? The other was a judgment of prediction: What *would* be done? Both types were made for a hypothetical "other" and for oneself. Finally, moral thinking, as a variable influenced by specific sets of consequences, was measured using an individual's preference for principled thinking in particular situations.

Work by Piaget (1932) and others (e.g., Breznitz & Kugelmass, 1967) has indicated that, as the severity of negative consequences caused by an actor increases, evaluative judgments about that actor became increasingly negative. Such findings suggest that individuals perceive a moral obligation to avoid causing negative consequences for others. Within the attribution-theory tradition, investigators (Miller & Ross, 1975; Shrauger, 1975) have suggested that the amount of effort individuals put into performing a task is in part determined by their estimates of the likelihood of success. One indication of success in a particular situation is the degree of need another has (see Hoffman, 1977); the greater another person's need, the more likely it is that helpful behavior will be of substantive assistance. Hence, in this study, it was expected that individuals would be more likely to act to help another person when the consequences for that person were very severe than when the consequences were less severe.

Kohlberg's (1969, 1971) descriptions of moral development depict an increasing ability to balance the needs of others with one's own needs in an equitable manner. As an individual becomes more morally mature, this ability, according to Kohlberg (1971, p. 216), leads to the growing importance of a particular moral value "with each stage obligation to preserve human life becomes more categorical." Thus, more principled individuals should be more likely than less principled individuals would be to act to help another when the consequences for that person are severe (and especially life-threatening).

In studying the impact of situational factors on moral thinking, both Gerson and Damon (1978) and Leming (1978) have speculated that, as the negative consequences for oneself become clearer, these consequences are more likely to exert a downward effect on moral thinking. Gerson and Damon (1978) argued that this occurs because it is easier to rationalize self-interest at lower stages of moral thinking. Kohlberg's (1976) suggestion that individuals at lower

levels of moral reasoning are more responsive to self-interest factors than are principled-level individuals offers support for this argument. Thus, I expected that, when the negative consequences for action were more severe, individuals would indicate less of a preference for principled-level moral thinking than they would when the consequences were less severe.

Negative consequences for action were expected to influence moral decisions as well. Krebs and Kohlberg (Note 3) have speculated that individuals may be dissuaded from acting on the dictates of their moral reasoning if the personal "sacrifice" involved is great. In support of this speculation, Gerson and Damon (1978) found that young children were less fair in apportioning candy bars when "fairness" involved the loss of real, as opposed to "pretend," candy. In the present study, it was expected that severe negative consequences for acting would lead individuals to be less certain in their decisions about performing a helpful action.

The differential influence of negative consequences for acting on different types of judgments and different judgment targets was also investigated. Baumrind (1978) and Krebs and Kohlberg (Note 3) have speculated that judgments of obligation and prediction might conflict with one another. They suggested that individuals' decisions about what they will do may reflect a greater tendency toward self-protection than decisions about what they believe they should do. In the present study, I expected that all individuals would demonstrate a significant discrepancy between what they thought *should* be done and what they predicted *would* be done when the negative consequences for acting were more severe, as opposed to little difference between the two when the consequences were less severe.

Finally, Baumrind (1978) has theorized that judgments about self or "I" may differ from judgments about others in that pragmatic concerns may exert a greater influence on personal judgments. In the present study, I predicted that subjects' judgments about themselves would be more affected by potential negative consequences for acting than would their judgments about others.

In summary, greater negative consequences for another were expected to (1) increase the likelihood that individuals would decide to help, and that (2) such an increase would be more marked in individuals who demonstrated a greater-than-average preference for principled-level moral thinking. An increase in the severity of negative consequences for acting was expected to (1) decrease an individual's consideration of principled-level moral issues in solving dilemmas, (2) decrease the likelihood of deciding to act, (3) increase the disparity between should and would judgments, and (4) increase differences between self and other judgments.

Method

Subjects

There were 344 high school and college students who volunteered to participate in the study; 199 students were from the ninth through twelfth grades of four high schools (113 females, 86 males) in a large metropolitan area, and 145 college students were recruited (96 females, 49 males). The preponderance of females in the college group appeared to reflect accurately the ratio of females to males in the psychology classes from which they were drawn. Subjects were predominantly Caucasian and middle- to upper-middle-class.

A final sample was created by means of a consistency check. This procedure, adapted from Rest (Note 2), was designed to eliminate from the sample students who might not have been responding to the moral dilemmas in a thoughtful and veridical manner. Consistency was measured by determining the extent of congruence between a student's ratings of issues and rank ordering of those issues, as well as by determining if sufficient variability existed in a student's ratings. Of the 344 students, 233 (65%) passed the consistency check; 144 were female, and 83 were male. The mean age of college students was 19.6 years (SD = 1.1); the mean age of high school students was 16.1 years (SD = 1.3).

The number of dropped subjects may appear to be somewhat large. It is my impression that in many cases inconsistency did not indicate a student's failure to take the test seriously so much as difficulty in understanding that ratings and rankings were to be congruent. Students learned to be more consistent: the average amount of inconsistency progressively decreased across each of the four dilemmas that all students read in an invariant, consecutive sequence. Also, the results of analyses based on a subsample (N = 301, or 88% of the sample) from which only the most inconsistent subjects were removed were identical to those reported in this paper.

Procedure

Students were tested in groups. Each group participated in two sessions of approximately 1 hour each. In the first session, they completed the short form of the Defining Issues Test (Rest, Note 2), which provided a measure of their principled-level thinking, and a number of instruments related to another study. Approximately 1 week later, students completed the questionnaire that contained five versions of the Heinz dilemma. Four of these dilemmas represented the factorial combination of two levels (high and low severity) of consequences for Heinz and the same two levels for Heinz's wife. In response to each dilemma, students rated the importance of various stage-related moral issues in resolving the dilemma. They also made judgments about what they thought Heinz should do and what most people would do in the situation, as well as judgments about what they thought they should and would do if they were Heinz in each situation.

Measures

P level.—Individuals' predisposition to prefer principled-level thinking in solving moral dilemmas was measured by the short form of Rest's (Note 2) Defining Issues Test. This test consists of three dilemmas (student takeover, escaped prisoner, and newspaper) of the Kohlberg type. After reading a dilemma, the subject decides what a character in the dilemma should do. Then the subject rates the importance of 12 issues in making his or her decision and ranks the four most important issues. On the basis of these rankings, an index, P, is calculated that reflects the "relative importance a subject gives to principled moral considerations" (Rest, Note 2, p. 4-3). Because there are only three statements reflecting principled-level issues for two of the stories, the actual range of P is 0–93. The obtained range for this sample was 0–83, with a mean and median of 38.00 (SD = 18).

A student's score on this measure was labeled P level. It was utilized as an indicator of an individual's cognitive developmental moral ability. It should be distinguished from P score, the individual's response to a specific version of the Heinz dilemma, which is discussed below. Students were blocked into high and low P level groups on the basis of a sample median split. The mean for the low P level group was 23 (SD = 10) and for the high P level group was 53 (SD = 10). Of the high P level group, 48% obtained a score greater than 50, which indicated that a preponderance of their thinking reflected principled-level concerns.

Negative consequences.—The impact of

negative consequences on decisions and moral thinking was measured through the administration of four versions of the Heinz dilemma adapted from Kohlberg (Note 1) and Rest (Note 2).

The relationship between moral stage and moral decision may be unclear because at any one of several stages an individual can justify a decision of either action or inaction (Kohlberg, 1971, Note 1; Rest, Note 4). To clarify the relationship between P level and moral decisions in this study, the content of the Heinz dilemma was modified slightly. Using the Kohlberg (Note 1) *Moral Judgment Scoring Manual* as a guide, facts important at Stages 1–4 were deleted or added to the dilemma so that individuals favoring nonprincipled stages of moral thinking (Stages 1–4) would have difficulty in constructing an adequate rationale for deciding that Heinz should steal the drug.[1] Hence, I expected that individuals relatively low in P level would tend to choose not to act (i.e., steal the drug). The modified version of the Heinz dilemma reads as follows:

In Europe, a woman was near death from a special kind of cancer. There was one drug that the doctors thought might save her. It was a form of radium that a druggist in the same town had recently discovered. The drug was expensive to make and had taken many years to develop. The druggist, a leading businessman in the town, paid $200 for the radium and charged $2,000 for a dose of the drug.
The sick woman's husband, Heinz, did not love her very much. He was afraid that, if his wife died, some people might think it was his fault. Heinz went to everyone he knew to borrow the money; but he could only get together $1,000, which was half of what the drug cost. He told the druggist that his wife was dying and asked him to sell it cheaper. But the druggist said, "No, I discovered the drug and I'm going to make money from it."
The friends of Heinz and his wife told Heinz that he had done all he could. But Heinz began to think about breaking into the man's store to steal the drug. As he was thinking, he remembered that there had been a lot of robberies in his town over the last few months. Because of those robberies, the town council had passed a new law that would punish thieves severely.

To alert students to the main details of this modified Heinz story and to avoid a primacy effect, all students first read the Heinz dilemma, as seen above, without any specified consequences. In order to avoid unnecessary repetitiveness, for each of the four versions of the dilemma with consequences, students read only the new conse-

quence combinations (see Table 1). The order of presentation of the pairs of consequences was randomly distributed throughout the subject population.

To determine if subjects did indeed perceive the high and low levels of negative consequences as intended, after reading each story students rated the severity of consequences for Heinz if he stole the drug and for his wife if he did not. A four-point scale was used which ranged from 1 (not severe at all) to 4 (very severe).

P scores.—After reading each of the five dilemmas, students rated the importance of various moral issues and ranked them according to their importance in a manner identical to that of Rest (Note 2). A P score for each story was calculated in the manner already described for P level. Because there were only three principled-level issues, the possible range of each P score was 0–90.

To allow room for downward movement in P scores, three issues reflecting preconventional-level thinking were added to the issues list, while the nonmoral filler items and a third issue were removed. The specific modifications were as follows. *Items removed:* (a) Isn't it only natural for a loving husband to care so much for his wife that he'd steal? (Stage 3); (b) Whether Heinz is a professional wrestler or has considerable influence with professional wrestlers (filler); and (c) Whether the essence of living is more encompassing than the termination of dying, socially and individually (filler). *Items added·* (a) Whether stealing such an expensive drug from such an important man would get Heinz in a lot of trouble (Stage 1); (b) Whether there is a good chance that the drug

TABLE 1

Consequences for Heinz and His Wife

Level of Severity	Consequences
Heinz:	
High	Heinz will be caught for sure and sent to prison because everyone in town knows about his troubles.
Low	Heinz can take the drug and the druggist will never miss it.
Heinz's wife:	
High	The drug will cure Heinz's wife completely and save her life.
Low	The drug will give Heinz's wife a slim chance of living for a few more months.

[1] A complete description of these modifications is available from the author on request.

will work and save his wife's life (Stage 2); and (c) Whether Heinz will be caught and punished (Stage 1).

The result of these modifications was a more equal representation of the various moral stages among the issues, which, in Rest's (Note 2) original test, were biased in frequency toward the conventional and principled levels (as has also been noted by Martin, Shafto, & VanDeinse, 1977).

To determine if the P scores obtained displayed some concurrent validity, Pearson correlation coefficients were calculated between P level, derived from the unmodified Defining Issues Test, and the P scores obtained from each story. Correlations ranged from .28 to .37, all significant at $p < .001$. The magnitude of these correlations is consistent with the perspective of this study: content affects responses to the stories. Thus it was not expected that the size of the correlations would be large.

Moral decisions.—For each dilemma, students made two types of judgments (i.e., should and would) for others and for self. Prior to rating and ranking the moral issues, students decided "Should Heinz steal the drug?" The other three decisions were made after rating and ranking the issues.

During piloting, it became clear that many individuals balked at making a "would" decision for Heinz. They protested that they could not predict what he would do. To overcome this difficulty, the following question was asked, "Without thinking about what a person should do, what do you think most people would be most likely to do if they were Heinz?"

For the self decisions, students were asked to place themselves in Heinz's position and to decide what they should and would do. A judgment of obligation was made in response to the question, "If you were Heinz in this situation, from a moral point of view, what would you believe *you should do?*" A judgment of prediction was made in response to "Taking all factors into consideration, what do you think *you would be most likely to do* if you were Heinz in this situation?"

In a manner after Rettig and Rawson (1963), all decisions were made on a six-point scale that reflected an individual's definiteness or certainty about his or her decision. The scale ranged from 1 (definitely should not/would not steal) to 6 (definitely should/would steal).

Results

Manipulation Check

To determine if the two levels of severity of consequences were perceived as differing in the expected manner, students were asked to rate the severity of consequences for Heinz and for his wife for each dilemma. Analysis of students' ratings of severity was made by means of a three-factor repeated-measures analysis of variance. The three factors were Heinz severity level (high or low), wife severity level (high or low), and individual (Heinz or wife).

There were significant main effects for Heinz severity level, $F(1,222) = 624.90, p < .001$, and for wife severity level, $F(1,222) = 49.16, p < .001$. As expected, when the consequence for Heinz was "jail," that consequence was rated as more severe ($M = 3.7$) than when the consequence was that he would be "free" ($M = 1.7$). Likewise, when the consequence for Heinz's wife was that she could be "saved" if Heinz acted, the severity for her if he did not act was rated as higher ($M = 3.6$) than the severity when there was only a "slim" chance of saving her life ($M = 3.0$).

Effects of Situational and Cognitive Developmental Variables on Should and Would Judgments

The hypotheses of this study were tested by means of a seven-factor and a five-factor analysis of variance, resulting in 158 tests of significance. Twenty-eight tests were significant at the .05 level or less; all six tests of the hypotheses and five additional tests were significant at the .005 level or less. While the .005 level seems a reasonably stringent level of significance, the Bonferroni procedure (Meyers, 1979) required a significance level of .0003 for each individual test to insure that the probability of making a single Type I error was less than .05 for the entire set of 158 tests. Four of the six hypotheses and two other effects were statistically significant by this somewhat conservative estimate. All effects, predicted or not, that were significant by the Bonferroni procedure are reported below. Other results pertaining to the hypotheses are also described but will not be labeled as statistically significant.[2]

The effects of the negative consequences on judgments were examined by means of a seven-factor repeated-measures analysis of variance. The factors were age

---

[2] Complete analysis of variance tables are available from the author on request.

(high school or college), sex, P level (high or low), Heinz consequences (high or low), wife consequences (high or low), target (self or other), and judgment type (should or would). To assess significant interaction mean differences, post hoc pair-wise comparisons were conducted using the Scheffé procedure set at the .05 significance level.

As expected, there was a significant main effect for the Heinz consequences, $F(1,215) = 246.40$, $p < .0001$. Students were less certain about stealing the drug when the consequence for Heinz was jail (M judgment $= 3.1$) than they were when he would go free (M judgment $= 4.2$). An unpredicted significant interaction between judgment type and age, $F(1,215) = 15.82$, $p < .0001$, indicated that college students were more certain (M judgment $= 4.0$) than high school students (M judgment $= 3.4$) that they should steal the drug. The two groups did not differ in their certainty about whether they would steal.

It was predicted that when the consequences for Heinz were high there would be a discrepancy between should and would judgments, such that students would be more certain that they should steal than that they would steal. An interaction between Heinz consequences and judgment type, $F(1,215) = 11.31$, $p = .0009$, suggested an effect opposite to the one predicted. When the consequences for Heinz were high, there was no difference between the two types of judgments. When the consequences for Heinz were low, students were slightly more certain that they would steal ($M = 4.24$) than that they should steal ($M = 4.10$).

This unexpected finding appeared to be due to a sex-related effect. An interaction among Heinz consequences, judgment type, and sex was obtained, $F(1,215) = 3.89$, $p = .05$. Post hoc comparisons indicated that, when the Heinz consequences were low, females were more certain that they would steal than that they should steal. When the Heinz consequences were high, there was not a difference between should and would. For males, there were no significant differences between should and would for either level of severity.

It was also expected that, when consequences for the wife were high, students would be more certain about stealing the drug than they would be when the consequences were low. There was a significant main effect for wife consequences, $F(1,215) = 376.60$, $p < .0001$. Across the entire sample, students were more certain about stealing the drug when there was a good possibility the wife could be saved (M judgment $= 4.3$) than when there was only a slim chance that she could be helped ($M = 3.0$).

Additionally, the prediction that high P level students, those whose P level indicated a predisposition to use principled thinking to solve dilemmas, would be more certain than low P level students about stealing the drug when the consequences for the wife were high, was supported, $F(1,215) = 8.03$, $p < .005$. When the consequences for the wife were very severe, high P level students were more certain about stealing the drug ($M = 4.6$) than were low P level individuals ($M = 4.1$). When the consequences for the wife were low, there was little difference between high ($M = 3.0$) and low ($M = 3.1$) P level students.

Another issue of interest was whether there would be a difference in students' judgments about others and about themselves. A main effect for target was statistically significant, $F(1,215) = 16.34$, $p < .0001$. Students were more certain about stealing when asked to decide about others ($M = 3.8$) than when deciding about themselves ($M = 3.5$).

It was expected that when the consequences for the actor (Heinz) were high there would be a greater discrepancy between self and other judgments than when the consequences for Heinz were low. A significant interaction between Heinz consequences and target was obtained, $F(1,215) = 94.88$, $p < .0001$. Unexpectedly, there was little difference between self ($M = 3.2$) and other ($M = 3.1$) judgments when the consequences for Heinz were high. When the consequences for Heinz were low, students were more certain in their judgments about others ($M = 4.4$) than in their judgments about themselves ($M = 3.9$). Thus the findings were opposite to those predicted.

Effects of Situational Variables on Principled Thinking

The hypothesis that the magnitude of principled thinking displayed for individual stories, P score, would differ in the two Heinz consequence conditions was tested by a five-way analysis of variance. The factors were age, sex, P level, Heinz consequences, and wife consequences.

A significant main effect was found for P level, $F(1,215) = 26.11$, $p < .0001$. Across the four stories, high P level students obtained a higher average P score ($M = 31.31$) than low

P level students (M = 17.46). The predicted difference between Heinz consequence levels was significant, $F(1,215) = 23.17, p < .0001$. When the consequences for Heinz were low, the average P score (M = 27.65) was significantly higher than when the consequences for Heinz were high (M = 20.73).

There was an effect for wife consequences as well, $F(1,215) = 5.71, p < .02$. The average P score when the wife consequences were high (M = 22.94) was lower than the average P score when the wife consequences were low (M = 25.43). Thus, when faced with more severe consequences for either Heinz or his wife, students gave less consideration to principled-level moral issues in resolving dilemmas than they gave when the consequences were less severe.

Discussion

The results suggest that both types of consequences, those for the actor, Heinz, and those for another, Heinz's wife, influence moral judgments and moral thought. Such influences point to the sensitivity of moral decisions and the organization of moral thought to the context in which they are made. In effect, variations in the consequences for Heinz and his wife produced different moral problems, which called for different action choices and different ways of thinking.

The effects of severe consequences for Heinz on moral decisions demonstrates that situational factors such as negative consequences may influence moral choices. Whether the wife's need was great or not, when the consequences for acting were severe, students were less certain about acting to save her life. Importantly, this pattern was found regardless of an individual's predisposition to prefer principled thinking to resolve moral dilemmas.

The variation of should judgments in a pattern similar to would judgments, across the Heinz conditions, implies that decisions about moral obligation may be influenced by consequences as much as judgments of prediction. An exception to this pattern was found when the consequences for Heinz were low. In that situation, females were more certain that stealing would be done than they were that stealing should be done. Such a finding indicates that individuals may, on occasion, feel compelled to act in ways they are not sure are morally correct.

Differences in judgments about self and

other appear primarily to be due to a significant difference when the consequences for the actor, Heinz, were low. Students' judgments that others would be more certain about acting in such a situation than they themselves would be suggests that less severe consequences may be viewed as a more potent influence on the behavior of others than on one's own behavior.

The interaction between wife consequences and P level is consistent with Kohlberg's (1969, 1971) position that the behavior of principled individuals is more predictable than that of individuals at other levels of moral development. The interaction also suggests that principled thinking may influence behavior only under certain circumstances. While all the dilemmas in the present study can be considered "moral" in the sense that they involved the conflicting rights of individuals, principled thinking was predictive of decision making only when the wife consequences were high. In that situation, the greater likelihood that stealing would save the wife's life may have imposed a more compelling moral obligation on principled individuals than it did on others. Such a greater obligation would be consistent with the theoretical position of Kohlberg (1971), that the value of human life supercedes all other values for more principled individuals.

Not only was moral decision making affected by consequences, but moral thinking was affected as well. The P scores of individuals decreased when both the Heinz and the wife consequences were high as compared with when they were low. The reason for the unexpected decrease in P scores when the wife consequences were high is unclear. One possibility, however, is that the greater obligation to act, posed by the consequences that would befall the wife if action were not taken, made students more concerned about nonprincipled issues (e.g., Will the drug work?).

It was expected that a decrease in principled thinking would occur when the Heinz consequences were high because individuals would give consideration to self-interest issues usually associated with lower stages. To examine this possibility, "Q" scores were calculated in a manner identical to that of P scores. The Q score for a particular story indicated the preference of a student for preconventional moral issues, just as the P score indicated the degree of preference for principled issues. As expected, a significant main effect for Heinz severity level, $F(1,215) =$

32.70, $p < .0001$, was obtained. When the consequences for Heinz were high, students displayed a significantly greater preference for preconventional issues in solving the moral dilemmas than they did when the consequences for Heinz were low. Such results are consistent with the findings of Gerson and Damon (1978) and Leming (1978).

It could be argued that individuals characterized as principled by Rest's method may not be as stable in their thinking as those so characterized by Kohlberg's. The classification of principled thinking using the Defining Issues Test is based on a recognition, comprehension, and preference task, a somewhat less demanding test than the spontaneous production task of Kohlberg. Research cited by Rest (1979) indicates that subjects score at higher stages on the Defining Issues Test than on Kohlberg's production task.

Generally, moral maturity as measured by the Defining Issues Test has been found to correlate in the low $+.70$s with scores from Kohlberg's test (Rest, 1979). But Davison and Robbins (1978) found that for two homogeneous age groups the correlations dropped to .17 and .35 (see also Froming & McColgan, 1979). Davison and Robbins (1978) argued that the two tests could not "be considered measures of the same construct" (p. 379). Reviewing such correlational data, however, Kohlberg (1979, p. xiv) concluded that the "two different tests of cognitive moral development tap the same general domain." And Rest has suggested that the Defining Issues Test taps "the earlier and more tacit understanding" of individuals while Kohlberg's test reflects the "more consolidated understanding . . . which the subject can put into words" (p. 159). Thus, it is not certain that principled thinking as measured by Kohlberg's procedures would show the same responsiveness to situational factors as has principled thinking measured by Rest's test.

How likely is it that results found with Rest's measure would generalize to principled thinkers as measured by Kohlberg?

Within the cognitive-developmental approach that underlies Kohlberg's research (1969, 1976) there is currently little evidence that a particular stage of thought is consistently applied across different content domains (Fischer, 1980; Flavell, 1982). Kohlberg's (1976) own problems in accurately measuring moral judgment in part stem from subjects' tendency to give different stage responses to different dilemmas or even to different questions about the same dilemma. His solution has been to characterize individuals in terms of their most frequently used, or modal, responses. Hence, he ignores variability rather than focusing on it as a legitimate phenomenon (Rest, 1979).

Empirical support also exists for the possibility that the results of the present study might also be obtained using Kohlberg's methodology. Leming (1978), employing Kohlberg's (1972) scoring system, found that adolescents reasoned about moral dilemmas at a higher moral maturity level when the dilemmas were abstract and hypothetical than when they reasoned about dilemmas set in a practical, familiar context. He suggested that such differences might result from negative consequences being clearer in his "practical" dilemmas than they were in the hypothetical stories. The present findings based on the Defining Issues Test offer support for Leming's (1978) speculation, based on data from Kohlberg's interview, that negative consequences exert a downward effect on moral thinking.[3]

The results suggest that a person does not display moral thinking in the same invariant way that he or she might have blue eyes or blond hair. The hierarchical nature of moral judgment (i.e., higher stages subsume lower stages) indicates that higher-stage individuals are able, theoretically, to consider more factors relevant to a moral situation than individuals at lower levels (Kohlberg, 1971). While stage designations reflect a modal manner of solving moral problems, they suggest something about an individual's range of potential kinds of reasoning as well. For example, a Stage 1 per-

---

[3] Data based on the latest revision of the Kohlberg scoring system, standard form scoring, present remarkable evidence (correlations of .82–.95) for stage stability across different dilemmas (Colby, Kohlberg, Gibbs, & Lieberman, 1983). Kohlberg (1981) has suggested that these results support his position that moral stages are "structured wholes." These findings, however, have not been replicated by other researchers, and Rest (1979) has criticized the new scoring criteria, arguing that high levels of stage consistency are created by restricting stage variability. Finally, Colby et al. (1983) report that the three different forms of the Kohlberg moral interview "pull" for different stages of moral thinking; hence, moral maturity scores from the different forms must be equalized by means of a conversion formula. Thus, even in Kohlberg's new system, evidence remains for situational effects on moral thinking.

son may have a narrower range of stage usage than a Stage 5 person. The kinds of moral thinking an individual uses in a particular dilemma will vary according to certain contextual features of the specific moral situation itself, interacting with an individual's range of stages (Fischer, 1980; Rest, 1979).

Because contextual factors influence moral thinking, traditional ways of measuring moral cognitive level might be re-evaluated. For example, the typical moral dilemmas employed by Rest, Kohlberg, and others do not specify consequences for behavior. Thus, differences in stage scores based on responses to these dilemmas might reflect individual differences in the anticipation of consequences as well as differences in the available range of moral stages. Also, failure to use similar content domains to measure moral behavior and moral reasoning may result in spuriously low relationships between the two. Hence, devices used to measure moral thinking should reflect the specific issues, circumstances, and task demands relevant to the particular moral behaviors to be examined.

In light of the present finding that content affected moral reasoning and decision making, care must be taken in generalizing results from the Heinz dilemma to other moral situations. Evidence suggests, for example, that there are several broad categories of helping behaviors (Bryan, 1975). Additionally, the various stages of moral thinking may differ in their relevance to decision making according to different contextual factors (see Rest, 1979). For example, it might be that, in friendship situations, conventional-level moral thinking would exert a more salient impact on moral decisions than principled thinking. Further research is needed to determine whether the effects of negative consequences found with the Heinz dilemma are true for other types of moral situations, other levels of moral reasoning, and different methods of measuring moral thinking.

Reference Notes

1. Kohlberg, L. *Test of moral development and scoring manual.* Mimeographed paper, Harvard University, 1973.
2. Rest, J. R. *Manual for the Defining Issues Test.* Unpublished manuscript, University of Minnesota, 1974.
3. Krebs, R., & Kohlberg, L. *Moral judgment*

and ego controls as determinants of resistance to cheating. Unpublished manuscript, Harvard University, 1973.
4. Rest, J. R. *Major concepts in moral judgment development.* Unpublished manuscript, University of Minnesota, 1974.

References

Baumrind, D. A dialectical materialist's perspective on knowing social reality. In W. Damon (Ed.), *New directions for child development.* (Vol. 2): *Moral development.* San Francisco: Jossey-Bass, 1978.

Breznitz, S., & Kugelmass, S. Intentionality in moral judgment: Developmental stages. *Child Development,* 1967, **38,** 469–479.

Bryan, J. H. Children's cooperation and helping behaviors. In E. M. Hetherington (Ed.), *Review of child development research* (Vol. **5**). Chicago: University of Chicago Press, 1975.

Colby, A., Kohlberg, L., Gibbs, J., & Lieberman, M. A longitudinal study of moral judgment. *Monographs of the Society for Research in Child Development,* 1983, **48**(1, Serial No. 200).

Davison, M. L., & Robbins, S. The reliability and validity of objective indices of moral development. *Applied Psychological Measurement,* 1978, **2**, 389–401.

Fischer, K. W. A theory of cognitive development: The control and construction of hierarchies of skills. *Psychological Review,* 1980, **87**, 477–531.

Flavell, J. H. Structures, stages, and sequences in cognitive development. In A. Collins (Ed.), *Minnesota symposia on child psychology* (Vol. **15**). Hillsdale, N.J.: Erlbaum, 1982.

Froming, W. J., & McColgan, E. B. Comparing the Defining Issues Test and the Moral Dilemma Interview. *Developmental Psychology,* 1979, **15**, 658–659.

Gerson, R., & Damon, W. Moral understanding and children's conduct. In W. Damon (Ed.), *New directions for child development.* (Vol. **2**): *Moral development.* San Francisco: Jossey-Bass, 1978.

Hoffman, M. L. Empathy, its development and prosocial implications. In C. B. Keasey (Ed.), *Nebraska Symposium on Motivation* (Vol. **25**). Lincoln: University of Nebraska Press, 1977.

Kohlberg, L. Stage and sequence: The cognitive-developmental approach to socialization. In D. Goslin (Ed.), *Handbook of socialization theory and research.* Chicago: Rand McNally, 1969.

Kohlberg, L. From is to ought: How to commit the naturalistic fallacy and get away with it. In T. Mischel (Ed.), *Cognitive development and epistemology.* New York: Academic Press, 1971.

Kohlberg, L. *Issue scoring guide.* Cambridge, Mass.: Laboratory of Human Development, 1972.

Kohlberg, L. Moral stages and moralization: The cognitive-developmental approach. In T. Lickona (Ed.), *Moral development and behavior.* New York: Holt, Rinehart & Winston, 1976.

Kohlberg, L. Foreword. In J. R. Rest, *Development in judging moral issues.* Minneapolis: University of Minnesota Press, 1979.

Kohlberg, L. *The meaning and measurement of moral development.* Worcester, Mass.: Clark University Press, 1981.

Leming, J. Intrapersonal variations in stage of moral reasoning among adolescents as a function of situational context. *Journal of Youth and Adolescence,* 1978, **7**, 405–416.

Martin, R. M., Shafto, M., & VanDeinse, W. The reliability, validity, and design of the Defining Issues Test. *Developmental Psychology,* 1977, **13**, 460–463.

Meyers, J. *Fundamentals of experimental design* (3d ed.). Boston: Allyn & Bacon, 1979.

Miller, D. T., & Ross, M. Self-serving biases in attribution of causality: Fact or fiction? *Psychological Bulletin,* 1975, **82**, 213–225.

Piaget, J. *The moral judgment of the child.* New York: Harcourt, Brace, 1932.

Rest, J. R. New approaches in the assessment of moral development. In T. Lickona (Ed.), *Moral development and behavior.* New York: Holt, Rinehart & Winston, 1976.

Rest, J. R. *Development in judging moral issues.* Minneapolis: University of Minnesota Press, 1979.

Rest, J., Cooper, D., Coder, R., Masanz, J., & Anderson, D. Judging the important issues in moral dilemmas—an objective measure of development. *Developmental Psychology,* 1974, **10**, 491–501.

Rettig, S., & Rawson, H. The risk hypothesis in predictive judgments of unethical behavior. *Journal of Abnormal and Social Psychology,* 1963, **3**, 243–248.

Shrauger, J. S. Responses to evaluation as a function of initial self-perceptions. *Psychological Bulletin,* 1975, **82**, 581–596.

Developmental Psychology
1987, Vol. 23, No. 4, 577–582

Korean Children's Conceptions of Moral and Conventional Transgressions

Myung-Ja Song and Judith G. Smetana
University of Rochester

Sang Yoon Kim
Dong-A University, Busan, Korea

The purpose of this study was to examine whether children in a non-Western cultural context make conceptual distinctions between morality and social convention. Fifty children from Busan, Korea, 10 each in kindergarten, third, sixth, ninth, and twelfth grades, were presented with prototypical moral and conventional transgressions. They made judgments of rule contingency, generalizability, and permissibility. At all ages, children treated moral transgressions as more generalizably wrong and independent of rules than conventional transgressions. All transgressions were seen as not permissible, but moral transgressions were judged as less permissible than conventional transgressions. Younger children (kindergarten and Grade 3) judged conventional transgressions as less permissible than older children. Further, all children justified moral transgressions on the basis of obligation, fairness, and welfare, whereas they justified conventional transgressions on the basis of authority, social nonconformity, social coordination, prudential reasons, and (among young children) sanctions and pragmatic reasons. The results indicated that, like American children, Korean children develop moral and social conventional orientations to their social world.

This article presents the results of a study of Korean children's social judgments. The purpose of the research was to examine whether moral judgments and concepts of social convention coexist in children's judgments in a non-Western (specifically, middle-class Confucian) cultural context. Previous research on American children has indicated that they differentiate the two domains along a number of dimensions (referred to here as criterion judgments). Moral issues are evaluated as generalizable, universal, unalterable, and independent of rules and authority sanctions, whereas conventional issues are evaluated as contextually relative, alterable, and subordinated to rules and authority dictates. Furthermore, children reason about moral issues in term of others' welfare and justice, whereas they reason about social conventions in terms of social order, customs, authority, and sanctions (Davidson, Turiel, & Black, 1983; Nucci, 1981; Smetana, 1981, 1985; Smetana, Bridgeman, & Turiel, 1983; Turiel, 1978; Weston & Turiel, 1980).

American children of varying social classes consistently have been found to distinguish between morality and social convention from early childhood on, but there have been few studies that examine these forms of social knowledge cross-culturally. Two such studies, one of rural, isolated children from the island of St. Croix in the U.S. Virgin Islands (Nucci, Turiel, & Encarnacion-Gawrych, 1983), and another of children and adolescents from the Ijo communities in Nigeria (Hollos, Leis, & Tu-

riel, 1986) yielded results comparable to American children. However, research in different types of non-Western settings would extend our understanding of the development of social knowledge. Most research in non-Western settings has been conducted in isolated, rural cultures, thus entailing a confound between differences in cultural traditions and differences between rural and isolated settings and more urbanized settings. Therefore, research examining non-Western, nonrural settings is needed.

Korean society is guided by the traditional maxims of Confucian ethics. Loyalty to the ruling class, respect for elders, obedience to one's parents, courtesy in human relationships, and duty to community over individual rights are all Confucian maxims that are thought to regulate the individual's behavior in Korean society. The Buddhist influence is not necessarily seen as coercive, but rather reflects a genuine concern and love for others (Dien, 1982). Thus, Korean society has been characterized as more traditional, conforming, authoritarian, and status-oriented than Western culture (Park & Johnson, 1984). Furthermore, the importance of authority, conformity, and duty are commonly found public justifications for adhering to all rules.

Since the 1960s, Korea has also shown a trend of rapid urbanization, which is reflected by the presence of one-fourth of the Korean population in the capital city, Seoul. Nearly 40% of Korean school-age children live in the four largest cities in Korea (Korean Ministry of Education, 1985), and another 53% live in urbanized small cities and towns. Only 6% of the population live in isolated rural islands and communities. Korea is well known for its uniformity in race, language, and cultural background, features that are promoted by both the Korean educational system and the mass media. The Korean Ministry of Education imposes a strict control over school curricula, and television and other media reach the isolated regions, promoting uniformity in cultural patterns.

The authors gratefully acknowledge the teachers and students at the participating schools in Busan, Korea, for their cooperation with this project and Elliot Turiel for his comments on an earlier draft of this article.

Correspondence concerning this article should be addressed to Judith Smetana, Graduate School of Education and Human Development, University of Rochester, Rochester, New York, 14627.

Although individuals at all levels of Korean society have had exposure to Western culture in the 40 years since World War II, the population still retains the unique cultural patterns of its 5,000 year history (Nakamura, 1964). Confucian maxims, and particularly the role of authority, are still emphasized (Rohner & Pettengill, 1985), and Koreans take pride in their unique cultural heritage and history. Although they have had contact with the West, they cannot be said to have assimilated Western values. Some exposure to Westerners should not be simply taken to mean that the indigenous society is transformed by it (see Discussion section).

The stereotypical view is that the cultural orientation is homogeneous with respect to transgressions, rules, and authority. Thus, moral and conventional issues alike might be treated as issues of custom and convention (e.g., Benedict, 1934), or conventions may be "moralized" (Smetana, 1983; Turiel & Smetana, 1984) and therefore not differentiated from moral issues (e.g. Rest, 1983). A third possibility is that the Korean cultural orientation systematically affects the way particular issues are viewed, so that issues that are seen as moral in Western society are treated as conventions in Korea, or vice versa. Thus, convention and morality might be distinguished on different bases than in Western culture (Shweder, Mahaptra, & Miller, in press).

A final hypothesis is that different social orientations coexist, much as they do in Western society. According to this view, moral judgments would entail similar concerns (welfare and justice) in Western and non-Western cultures, but because conventions may differ under varying social arrangements, the content of the conventional domain might be expected to differ (but be evaluated along the same criteria as in Western society). Thus, Korea provides an interesting society in which to test domain distinctions in children's social judgments. Consistent with the final alternative, we predicted that children's judgments would vary according to the type of act under consideration and that different social orientations would coexist in children's judgments. Moreover, we predicted that morality would be evaluated on the basis of generalizability and independence from rules and that conventions, although perhaps differing in content from Western conventions, would be evaluated on the basis of relativity and contingency on rules. Further, we hypothesized that the Korean focus on cultural traditions and social status might promote an earlier understanding of conventionality and a sharper differentiation between the domains among Korean than among American children.

In this study, judgments and justifications regarding familiar moral and conventional transgressions were examined in a sample of kindergarten through twelfth-grade Korean children from Busan, Korea. The selection of moral and conventional stimuli was based on the conceptual definitions of the domains (Nucci, 1981; Smetana, 1981, 1985; Turiel, 1983) and the events' salience for the Korean children studied. The items chosen for the moral domain, although similar to those used in previous research on American children, were culturally significant for Korean children. Conventional items were chosen by Myung-Ja Song and Sang Yoon Kim, who are native Koreans residing in Korea, to sample four aspects that were thought to best represent the conventional domain (manners, status, dress, and conformity to school regulations). On the basis of current knowledge of Korean schools and culture-specific information

about the events as important, socially determined regulations, we chose the stimuli as the most important and representative examplars of each type of convention.

Method

Subjects

Subjects in this study were 50 middle- to upper middle-class children attending a kindergarten, primary school (third and sixth grades), junior high, and secondary (high) school in Busan, Korea. There were 10 children each, 5 boys and 5 girls, in the kindergarten, third, sixth, ninth, and twelfth grades (the mean ages were 5.37, 9.43, 12.40, 15.10, and 18.13 years, respectively). Busan, the second largest city in Korea, is a commercial center located on the south end of the Korean pennisula.

Stimuli

Stimuli for this study were chosen on the basis of research on the definition of the domains (Smetana, 1983; Turiel, 1983) and on knowledge of Korean middle-class culture provided by Myung-Ja Song and Sang Yoon Kim. Children were presented with short vignettes describing moral and conventional acts. In each vignette, the actor was described as the same age as the subject, and the sex of the depicted child was counterbalanced. The moral items included hitting, stealing, not paying back borrowed money, and giving up a seat to an old man on a bus. For example, the children were presented with this vignette for stealing: "Hwaja wanted to have a doll, but she had no money to buy it. Yesterday, she stole a doll at the department store."

The social-conventional items included eating food with fingers, not greeting elders cordially, not putting shoes in the shoe rack before entering the classroom, and a girl wearing earrings and nail polish. For example, the children were presented with this vignette for not greeting elders cordially: "Kyungsook does not greet her elders cordially. Yesterday she came across an old man who was her neighbor on the road, and she passed him without greeting him."

In Korean society, not greeting elders cordially is considered a very serious transgression, because showing respect for elders reflects a very highly valued cultural tradition. Children are taught correct table manners early, and issues of etiquette are strictly enforced; thus, all children would be expected to treat eating food with their fingers as a serious breach. Furthermore, putting shoes in a shoe rack before entering the classroom is a school regulation that is uniformly enforced. Finally, although an issue of personal choice in the United States, wearing earrings and nail polish is considered a serious breach of social status in Korea, and a girl who violates this social convention is seen to be displaying indecent behavior.

Procedures

Each subject was individually interviewed by Sang Yoon Kim, a Korean developmental psychologist, who was skilled in interviewing children. The interviewer presented the subject with the descriptions of moral and conventional acts. For each act, subjects were then asked the following questions in fixed order: (a) "Would it be wrong to . . ." (indicating the *permissibility* of the act), (b) "Why?" (indicating subjects' *justifications* for the act's rightness or wrongness), (c) "Would it be OK to . . . in another country?" (indicating the *generalizability* of the act's wrongness), and (d) "Would it be wrong to . . . if there were no rules about it here?" (indicating the *contingency* of the act on the presence of rules).

Scoring

For each of the three criterion judgments (Questions a, c, and d), affirmative responses were assigned a score of zero, and negative re-

Table 1
Justification Categories

Category	Description
Others' welfare	Appeal to the interests of persons other than the actor
Obligation	References to feelings of obligation, including personal conscience and duty
Appeal to fairness	References to maintaining a balance of rights between persons
Psychological	Appeal to the actor's psychological state, dispositions, or specific virtues
Appeal to authority	Appeal to the approval of specific authority figures or to the existence of rules
Social nonconformity	References to the negative personal–social consequences of acting contrary to group norms
Social coordination	Appeal to the need for social organization or for maintaining a system of shared expectations between persons
Custom or norm	Appeal to personal and family customs as well as to social customs and traditions
Personal choice	Appeal to individual preferences, prerogatives, the general permissibility of the act
Prudential	Appeal to the nonsocial negative consequences to the actor, such as personal comfort or health
Sanctions	References to the reactions of persons toward the actor, including social condemnation and explicit punishment, as well as praise
Pragmatic	References to practical needs and consequences

sponses were assigned a score of one. Subjects' justifications were translated by a Korean native-speaker (Myung-Ja Song). A content analysis of responses indicated that Korean children's responses could be categorized in justification categories similar to those used reliably in previous research (Davidson et al. 1983; Nucci, 1981; Smetana, 1985). These categories are described in Table 1. Two coders scored all justifications, and interrater reliability was 84%.

Results

Criterion Judgments

Sex differences were examined in a preliminary analysis. As in previous research (Davidson et al. 1983; Smetana, 1981), no sex differences were found; therefore, sex was not included in further analyses.

Responses for the four items within each domain were summed for each judgment; summed scores were used in subsequent analyses. Repeated measures analyses of variance (ANOVAs) for Domain × Grade (2 × 5), with domain as the repeated measure, were performed separately on the three criterion judgments. Where significant results were obtained, group comparisons were performed using Duncan multiple-range tests for between-subjects effects or Bonferroni t-tests for within-subjects effects.

All children judged moral transgressions to be more generalizably wrong, $F(1, 45) = 96.91$, $p < .0001$, and more wrong independent of rules, $F(1, 45) = 584.89$, $p < .0001$, than conventional transgressions. Whereas virtually all children treated moral events as generalizably wrong and wrong independent of rules (93% and 94%, respectively), 49% and 79% of the sample judged conventional transgressions to be contextually relative and contingent on the presence of rules, respectively. There were no significant main effects for grade or Grade × Domain interactions for these two judgments. (Means are presented in Table 2.)

The findings for permissibility were expected to differ somewhat from the findings for the two criterion judgments. That is, although a distinction between the domains was expected, neither moral nor conventional transgressions were expected to be treated as permissible. Consistent with this prediction, moral and conventional transgressions were judged as not permissible by 97% and 86% of the sample, respectively, a difference that was statistically significant, $F(1, 45) = 20.09$, $p < .0001$.

Children's judgments of permissibility also showed a highly significant main effect for grade, $F(4, 45) = 7.55$, $p < .0001$. Post hoc tests revealed that kindergartners and third graders judged all transgressions to be less permissible than did older subjects ($p < .0001$). There was a significant Domain × Grade interaction, $F(4, 45) = 3.19$, $p < .05$, which was due to differences by grade in children's responses regarding social-conventional items. Kindergartners and third graders judged conventional events to be less permissible than did all older subjects ($p < .001$).

Table 2 indicates that, although there was strong consistency in responses to the four moral items, there was variation in responses to conventional items for judgments of generalizability and rule contingency. In particular, judgments regarding not greeting elders cordially appeared to differ from judgments regarding the other three conventional items (as well as from the moral items). Such a difference would have been obscured by summing responses within domains, as was done in the previous analyses. In order to determine whether these hypothesized conventional items were treated differently at statistically significant levels, 5 × 4 (Grade × Conventional Items) repeated measures ANOVAs were performed on judgments of generalizability and rule contingency.

The analyses indicated main effects for stimulus item for judgments of generalizability, $F(3, 135) = 3.36$, $p < .01$, and rule contingency, $F(3, 135) = 18.95$, $p < .0001$. Bonferroni t-tests indicated that the wrongness of not greeting elders cordially was seen as more independent of rules than the other

311

Table 2

Proportion of Subjects at Each Grade Level Affirming Nonpermissibility, Generalizability, and Independence From Rules

Domain/Item	Nonpermissibility					Generalizability					Independence from rules				
	K	3	6	9	12	K	3	6	9	12	K	3	6	9	12
Moral															
Hitting	100	100	90	90	100	100	100	90	100	100	100	90	80	100	100
Stealing	100	100	100	100	100	90	90	100	100	100	100	100	90	100	100
Not paying back money	100	100	70	90	100	100	100	80	100	90	100	100	70	90	80
Not giving up seat	100	100	100	100	90	70	90	100	70	100	80	90	100	100	100
M	100	100	90	95	98	90	95	93	93	95	95	95	85	98	95
Social Conventional															
Eating with fingers	100	100	50	50	50	50	40	10	50	50	00	10	00	10	00
Not greeting elders	100	100	90	90	100	50	40	90	70	80	60	40	70	90	60
Wearing earrings and nail polish	100	90	90	100	60	80	50	50	50	10	00	10	20	00	00
Leaving shoes in corridor	100	100	70	80	80	50	50	30	70	50	10	10	00	10	10
M	100	98	75	80	78	58	45	45	60	48	18	18	23	28	18

three conventional items ($p < .001$), and that not greeting elders cordially was seen as more generalizably wrong than not eating with fingers ($p < .001$).

There were also significant Grade $\times$ Item interactions for judgments of generalizability, $F(12, 135) = 2.53$, $p < .01$, and rule contingency, $F(12, 135) = 1.89$, $p < .05$. Post hoc analyses indicated that these were due to grade differences in judgments of the generalizability, $F(4, 40) = 2.79$, $p < .05$, and rule contingency, $F(4, 49) = 1.89$, $p < .05$, of wearing earrings and nail polish. Kindergartners viewed this transgression as more generalizably wrong than did twelfth graders, and ninth graders viewed it as more contingent on rules than did third graders.

Justifications

Table 3 provides subjects' proportionate use of justifications for (combined) moral and conventional items. Moral items were justified primarily in terms of others' welfare, obligation, and fairness. Conventional items were justified in terms of authority, sanctions, social nonconformity, social coordination, customs and traditions, and prudential, pragmatic, and personal reasons. Thus, despite the differences in childrens' judgments regarding not greeting elders cordially (discussed above), children's reasoning was entirely conventional (and not moral) about this item.

Multivariate analyses of variance (MANOVAs) by grade and sex were performed separately on the proportionate use of the justifications associated with each domain. Arc sin transformations were performed to normalize the distributions (Winer, 1971). Psychological statements were not included in either analysis, because they were used with nearly equal frequency to justify moral and conventional transgressions. Sex was not significant in either analysis, nor were the Sex $\times$ Grade interactions. However, both MANOVAs yielded highly significant effects for grade ($p < .0001$). Therefore, separate ANOVAs were performed by grade on the justifications associated with each domain. Post hoc comparisons were performed using Duncan multiple-range tests.

The analyses for moral transgressions revealed significant effects for grade in children's reasoning regarding others' wel-

fare, $F(4, 45) = 10.37$, $p < .0001$, and obligation, $F(4, 45) = 5.58$, $p < .001$. Kindergartners were significantly more likely to reason about welfare than subjects at all other grades, and third graders were more likely to reason about welfare than twelfth graders. Twelfth graders were more likely to reason about obligation than subjects at all other grades with the exception of ninth graders, and ninth graders were more likely to reason about obligation than kindergartners. There were no differences according to grade in children's reasoning regarding fairness.

The analyses for conventional transgressions revealed significant effects for grade in children's reasoning about sanctions, $F(4, 45) = 4.07$, $p < .01$, social coordination, $F(4, 45) = 5.10$, $p < .01$, customs and traditions, $F(4, 45) = 5.19$, $p < .01$, pragmatic reasons, $F(4, 45) = 7.98$, $p < .0001$, and prudential reasons, $F(4, 45) = 11.70$, $p < .0001$. Post hoc analyses indicated that kindergarten children were more pragmatic in justifying the wrongness of conventional transgressions than subjects at all other grades. They also reasoned more about sanctions than children in the sixth, ninth, and twelfth grades and engaged in more prudential reasoning than ninth or twelfth graders. Third graders were more likely to reason prudentially than all other subjects. In contrast, twelfth graders were more likely to reason about customs and traditions than subjects in other grades, whereas ninth graders were more likely than all other subjects to reason about the function of social conventions in coordinating social interactions.

Discussion

The results of this study indicate that across a broad age range, middle-class Korean children from a Confucian culture distinguish between morality and social convention. Distinctions between the domains were found in both criterion judgments and justifications. As in research with American children, all children, regardless of grade, treated moral transgressions as more generalizably wrong and less contingent on the presence of rules than conventional transgressions. Moral transgressions were also treated as less permissible than conventional transgressions, and younger children treated conventional transgressions as less permissible than did older children.

Table 3

Proportionate Use of Justifications For Moral and Conventional Transgressions

Justification category	Moral items					Conventional items				
	K	3	6	9	12	K	3	6	9	12
Others' welfare	62$_a$	37$_b$	23$_{bc}$	23$_{bc}$	20$_c$	0	0	0	0	3
Obligation	3$_{ab}$	0$_a$	10$_{ab}$	17$_{bc}$	30$_c$	0	0	3	3	3
Fairness	23	22	27	30	23	0	0	3	0	0
Sanctions	8	8	6	0	0	17$_a$	7$_b$	3$_b$	0$_b$	3$_b$
Appeal to authority	0	3	5	0	0	7	17	25	20	13
Social nonconformity	0	0	5	7	5	10	6	13	3	10
Social coordination	0	3	7	10	5	17$_a$	27$_a$	27$_a$	55$_b$	23$_a$
Customs or traditions	0	0	0	0	3	0$_a$	0$_a$	5$_a$	7$_a$	20$_b$
Psychological	0	5	5	5	7	3	3	5	0	5
Personal choice	0	0	0	0	0	0	0	5	5	7
Prudential	0	0	0	0	0	12$_b$	23$_a$	9$_{bc}$	0$_c$	0$_c$
Pragmatic	3	18	8	3	3	35$_a$	12$_b$	3$_b$	5$_b$	7$_b$
Unscorable	3	5	5	5	5	0	3	3	3	7

Note. Different subscripts indicate statistically significant differences between means. Percentages may not equal 100 due to rounding.

These findings are very similar to the findings for American children of varying social classes using similar tasks (Davidson et al., 1983; Nucci, 1981; Smetana, 1981, 1985; Smetana et al., 1983; Smetana, Kelly, & Twentyman, 1984).

Furthermore, Korean children provided different justifications for the wrongness of acts in the two domains. Like American children (Davidson et al., 1983; Nucci, 1981; Smetana, 1985; Smetana et al., 1983), and consistent with the definition of morality, Korean children justified the wrongness of moral transgressions primarily on the basis of others' welfare, obligation, and fairness. Reasoning about obligation was found to increase with age, whereas reasoning about others' welfare was found to decline with age. These age trends also parallel findings observed among American children.

Children appealed to authority, sanctions, social nonconformity, social coordination, customs and traditions, and to prudential, pragmatic, and personal considerations in order to justify the wrongness of conventional transgressions. Children's pragmatic understanding and reliance on external sanctions to justify the wrongness of conventional transgressions declined with age, whereas their understanding of social conventions as customary or as means of coordinating social interactions increased. These findings are consistent with those for American children (Davidson et al., 1983; Nucci, 1981; Smetana, 1985; Smetana et al., 1983), although the categorization scheme used here may have obscured some cultural differences. First, whereas American children have been found to focus on punishment avoidance or negative sanctions to justify the wrongness of conventional transgressions, Korean children reasoned both about positive and negative sanctions. That is, children reasoned about the praise they would receive for appropriate behavior as well as the punishment they would receive for inappropriate behavior. Children also explicitly focused on social status, social roles, appropriate role behavior, and courtesy, which they related clearly to social coordination and conventional concerns; these concerns are not commonly observed in American children's reasoning.

In addition, Korean children's reasoning about courtesy was often coordinated with conceptions of cultural traditions and national pride (e.g., "It is our traditional courtesy to respect adults."; "Our country is one that respects courtesy."). Thus, some cross-cultural differences were observed in children's justifications for conventional but not moral transgressions. This is consistent with the notion that conventions are variable within different social systems and may be justified according to these different arrangements. These findings also provide some support for the hypothesis that the greater emphasis in Korean society on cultural traditions, social status, and appropriate role behavior results in a greater understanding of conventionality among Korean than among American children.

Variation was also observed in subjects' judgments regarding the different conventional items. In particular, grade differences were found in children's judgments regarding wearing earrings and nail polish, with younger children treating this item as more generalizably wrong than older children. Informal examination of justifications for this item suggests that even kindergarten children reasoned about it in terms of social status and the inappropriateness of this behavior for children. Subjects were also significantly more likely to treat not greeting elders cordially as more wrong independent of rules than the other conventional items and as more generalizably wrong than eating with fingers, although judgments regarding this item also appeared to differ from judgments regarding moral items. Children reasoned about not greeting elders cordially primarily in terms of the importance of maintaining social status differences for social order and cultural expectations regarding politeness and courtesy. Thus, the pattern of judgments suggested that children might have treated this item as an issue of domain overlap—that is, as an issue entailing both conventional and moral components (Turiel & Smetana, 1984). Indeed, cultural differences may be most likely to occur in the ways that domains are coordinated or in the relative emphasis on one domain or the other in cases of domain overlap. However, children's justifications regarding not greeting elders cordially were entirely conventional. The cultural meaning ascribed to courtesy and social status further suggests that norms regarding respect for the elderly are functional in maintaining respect for the culture and social system, which is valued highly. Thus, Korean children appear to de-

313

velop a clearer understanding of the function of conventions in structuring social interactions within social systems than do American children.

Finally, we wish to stress the validity and value of research with samples of the type used in this study. Often, it is assumed that research with non-Western cultures must be conducted with what is referred to as "non-Westernized" subjects. This is taken to mean that the samples must be rural, uneducated, and have had no contact at all with Western culture or values. There are, however, several problems and pitfalls with this assumption. Most important, contact with Western culture does not necessarily mean assimilation of Western values. (Indeed, this assumption can be seen to reflect an implicit ethnocentric bias, on the part of American researchers, that the influence is unidirectional from Westerners to non-Westerners.) Thus, the middle-class, homogeneous, urbanized Confucian children in our study provided an appropriate cross-cultural comparison of domain distinctions in social judgments, although the sample studied here can be seen to differ from the less educated and urbanized populations examined in other cross-cultural studies of domain differences (Hollos et al., 1986; Nucci et al., 1983; Shweder et al., in press). Further, the items sampled here were carefully chosen to represent important middle-class cultural social conventions, unlike in other cross-cultural studies, in which notions of cosmology, natural law, and convention have been confused (e.g., Shweder et al., in press; see Turiel, Killen, & Helwig, in press, for further elaboration of this argument). In addition, the more rural, isolated populations, which have been favored by researchers of moral development, may actually provide unrepresentative samples of their cultures. For instance, in studying individuals from a religious temple town in India, Shweder and colleagues (in press) appear to have selected an unusual sample that is not characteristic of the wider Indian culture.

The results of this study also suggest that attempts to characterize cultures (our own, as well as others) in terms of uniform orientations (such as individualistic or collectivistic; Turiel et al., in press) may be inaccurate and seriously misinform our understanding of individuals' social judgments. Our findings stand in contrast to the commonly held assumption that children from non-Western cultures treat all types of social acts alike—either as conventions (Benedict, 1934) or as moral issues (Rest, 1983)—or that there is little continuity between our own and other cultures in the way in which conventional and moral acts are evaluated (Edwards, in press; Shweder et al., in press). Korean culture has been described as traditional, authoritarian, and conforming, yet Korean children's social judgments were found to be heterogeneous from early childhood through late adolescence. Acts that were seen to affect others' rights and welfare (moral issues) were seen as independent of rules and the cultural context, whereas social conventions were not. Like children in Western cultures, Korean children were not found to exhibit a unitary orientation to their social world.

References

Benedict, R. (1934). *Patterns of culture*. Boston: Houghton Mifflin.

Davidson, P., Turiel, E., & Black, A. (1983). The effect of stimulus familiarity on the use of criteria and justifications in children's social reasoning. *British Journal of Developmental Psychology, 1*, 49–65.

Dien, D. S. (1982). A Chinese perspective on Kohlberg's theory of moral development. *Developmental Review, 2*, 331–341.

Edwards, C. P. (in press). Culture and the construction of moral values: A comparative ethnography of moral encounters in two cultural settings. In J. Kagan & S. Lamb (Eds.), *The emergence of morality in young children*. Chicago: University of Chicago Press.

Hollos, M., Leis, P., & Turiel, E. (1986). Social reasoning in Nigerian children and adolescents. *Journal of Cross-Cultural Psychology, 17*, 352–374.

Korean Ministry of Education (1985). *Statistical yearbook of education*. Seoul: Author.

Nakamura, H. (1964). *Ways of thinking of Eastern people*. Honolulu, HI: East–West Center Press.

Nucci, L. P. (1981). The development of personal concepts: A domain distinct from moral or societal concepts. *Child Development, 52*, 114–121.

Nucci, L., Turiel, E., & Encarnacion-Gawrych, G. E. (1983). Children's social interactions and social concepts: Analyses of morality and convention in the Virgin Islands. *Journal of Cross-Cultural Psychology, 14*, 469–487.

Park, J. Y., & Johnson, R. C. (1984). Moral development in rural and urban Korean children. *Journal of Cross-cultural Psychology, 15*, 35–40.

Rest, J. (1983). Morality. In P. H. Mussen (Series Ed.) & J. H. Flavell & E. M. Markman (Vol. Eds.) *Handbook of child psychology: Vol. 3. Cognitive development* (4th ed., pp. 556–629). New York: Wiley.

Rohner, R. P., & Pettengill, S. M. (1985). Perceived parental acceptance–rejection and parental control among Korean adolescents. *Child Development, 56*, 524–528.

Shweder, R. A., Mahaptra, M., & Miller, J. G. (in press). Culture and moral development. In J. Kagan & S. Lamb (Eds.), *The emergence of morality in young children*. Chicago: University of Chicago Press.

Smetana, J. (1981). Preschool children's conceptions of moral and social rules. *Child Development, 52*, 1333–1336.

Smetana, J. (1983). Social–cognitive development: Domain distinctions and coordinations. *Developmental Review, 3*, 131–147.

Smetana, J. (1985). Preschool children's conceptions of transgressions: The effects of varying moral and conventional domain-related attributes. *Developmental Psychology, 21*, 18–29.

Smetana, J., Bridgeman, D., & Turiel, E. (1983). Differentiation of domains and prosocial behavior. In D. Bridgeman (Ed.), *The nature of prosocial development.* (pp. 163–183). New York: Academic Press.

Smetana, J., Kelly, M., & Twentyman, C. T. (1984). Abused, neglected, and nonmaltreated children's conceptions of moral and conventional transgressions. *Child Development, 55*, 277–287.

Turiel, E. (1978). Social regulations and domains of social concepts. In W. Damon (Ed.), *New directions for child development: Vol. 1. Social cognition* (pp. 45–74). San Francisco: Jossey-Bass.

Turiel, E. (1983). *The development of social knowledge: Morality and convention*. Cambridge: Cambridge University Press.

Turiel, E., Killen, M., & Helwig, C. C. (in press). Morality: Its structure, function, and vagaries. In J. Kagan & S. Lamb (Eds.), *The emergence of morality in young children*. Chicago: University of Chicago Press.

Turiel, E., & Smetana, J. (1984). Social knowledge and action: The coordination of domains. In W. M. Kurtines & J. L. Gewirtz (Eds.), *Morality, moral behavior, and moral development* (pp. 261–282). New York: Wiley.

Weston, D., & Turiel, E. (1980). Act-rule relations: Children's concepts of social rules. *Developmental Psychology, 16*, 417–424.

Winer, B. T. (1971). *Statistical principles in experimental design*. New York: McGraw-Hill.

Received January 27, 1986
Revision received October 3, 1986
Accepted October 24, 1986 ■

DEVELOPMENTAL REVIEW 2, 331–341 (1982)

A Chinese Perspective on Kohlberg's Theory of Moral Development

DORA SHU-FANG DIEN

California State University, Hayward

This essay uses the Chinese culture as an example to underline the culturally specific contextual problems regarding Kohlberg's theory of moral development and to point to a new direction for cross-cultural research in this area. The Western view of man as an autonomous being who makes free and rational choices as a moral agent is clearly reflected in Kohlberg's stages of moral development as well as his methodology. The Confucian view of man as an integral part of an orderly universe with an innate moral sense to maintain harmony is quite different. Further, the preferred mode of resolving human conflict in China is reconciliation and collective decision making rather than individual choice, commitment, and responsibility as in the West. In the light of these fundamental differences in the two cultural traditions, an alternative to Kohlberg's theory is suggested.

Historian John Fairbank (1980), one of the West's leading authorities on China, recently observed that the Chinese "seem to be law-abiding without law" because the doctrine of Confucianism serving as a system of ethics "had the effect of producing a socialized people who had a sense of individual duties and limits. . . . China did not develop a doctrine of civil liberties and individual rights in the same way as the modern West," but they have a "profound moral sense of justice and proper conduct inherited from Confucianism" (12). Such a fundamental difference between China and the West must have far reaching implications for Kohlberg's theory of moral development when "the dilemmas presented to the subjects are designed to place obedience to authority and law in opposition to individual rights and human welfare" (Rosen, 1980: 66).

Based upon Piaget's (1965) conception of the moral judgment of the child, Kohlberg (1969) elaborated six stages of moral reasoning, from an obedience and punishment orientation to self-accepted moral principles, which are held to be developmentally fixed, invariant, and universal. This hierarchy of moral reasoning has been to a certain extent substantiated cross-nationally. However, "the rate and terminus of moral development is highly variable from one cultural setting to another. Individuals in highly industrialized settings seem to move through the lower stages at a more rapid rate and to achieve higher stages than do individuals in less

Reprint requests should be sent to the author, Department of Human Development, California State University, Hayward, CA 94542.

315

industrialized and less urban settings'' (White, Bushnell, & Regnemer, 1978: 59). Even within the United States, children of high socioeconomic background develop more rapidly along the sequence and are more likely to attain higher levels of moral judgment'' (Hetherington & Parke, 1979: 613). As a matter of fact, Stage 4 (authority and social-order maintaining orientation) seems to be the dominant mode of moral reasoning among urban middle-class American adults (Rosen, 1980: 67). Kohlberg acknowledges that Stage 6 (conscience or principle orientation) is a rare occurrence; probably only 5% of American adults ever achieve this level (Rosen, 1980: 93). Nevertheless, he continues to assert that the ''principled morality'' based upon our conception of justice is a ''culturally universal'' stage of moral judgment (Kohlberg, 1980: 74) and that ''justice is a naturalistic virtue, emerging in children (at differing rates and with differing points of final equilibration) in all cultures as a result of their interaction with other persons and with social institutions'' (Fowler, 1980: 130).

This assertion of the universality of the stage sequence has been severely criticized by Simpson (1974) as well as Kurtines and Grief (1974). The latter even recommended the wholesale abandonment of Kohlberg's theory. Nevertheless, most researchers have accepted the validity of at least the earlier stages while finding the upper half or third of the stages problematic (Murphy and Gilligan, 1980). What has been overlooked is that even though the stage progression at the lower levels has been found cross-culturally, there may still be qualitative differences in the responses classified within the same stage. Gorsuch and Barnes (1973), for example, found in their study of the Black Caribs of British Honduras, that the respondents ''seemed to express a real concern with helping others, a concern seldom found in stage 2s in the United States. They were concerned not because of a moral norm within the culture, but because they could reasonably expect to have the favor returned to them. Another element that made these 2s distinctive was that the possible violations of norms were not perceived as a live option because group pressure would be immediately applied'' (297). The authors further pointed out that because of a strong collectivistic orientation in their culture, some respondents could not relate to the dilemmas at all. They therefore suggested that ''these moral dilemmas were insufficient to catch the nuances of this culture's thinking, and might also imply that a different set of 'stages' or typologies of moral reasoning might be developed in collectivistically oriented cultures'' (298). The present author believes that even among the so-called ''collectivistic'' societies, there may be enough diversity to warrant closer scrutiny into the culturally specific contextual differences. We will use the Chinese culture as an example to highlight this point and to suggest a new approach to this area of research.

TWO CONCEPTIONS OF MORALITY

The Judeo-Christian religious tradition holds that God is the creator of all things and that the act of creation is not something that God had to do but rather it was a completely free act. Futhermore, man is said to be made in the image of God, therefore, he "somehow possesses a freedom which resembles the freedom by which God creates." Thus the idea that man has freedom of self-determination is inherent in this tradition, though "the Bible always assumes that the fulfillment of divine commands will work for man's Good" (Grisez & Shaw, 1974: xi).

Greek philosophers, on the other hand, developed conceptions for judgments of moral good and moral evil, of right and wrong, based upon reasoning in accordance with the requirement of human nature. Rationality became the key to the definition of morality in Western philosophy. Thus when animals act instinctively to save human lives, they are not seen as acting morally. By the same token, the undesirable behaviors of the insane, senile, or brain damaged are not considered immoral because they lack the moral reasoning faculty (Sapontzis, 1980).

Deriving from these two traditions is the idea that man is an autonomous being, free to make his own choices and to determine his own destiny. As a moral agent, he has to take the responsibility for his actions. Existential philosophers in the West believe that while freedom characterizes the human condition, it brings with it the anguish of taking the responsibility for making individual choices (Sartre, 1966) and the feeling of overwhelming loneliness while doing so (Moustakas, 1961). We admire indomitable individuals who fulfill their human condition by exercising their responsibility for making decisions according to their beliefs and principles.

Despite his claim for universality, Kohlberg's six-stage hierarchy that progresses from an obedience and punishment orientation to a conscience or principle orientation clearly reflects this cultural ideal. Simpson (1974) believes that "Kohlberg's stage 6s are not functioning independently of their socialization; they have been very thoroughly socialized into the company of intellectual elites who value and practice analytic, abstract, and logical reasoning" (95). In a study of forms of intellectual and ethical development during the college years at Harvard, Perry (1968) also identified a developmental progression from reliance on authority to individual choice, commitment, and responsibility, and he attributed this to the impact of our liberal arts education. Thus, the conclusions drawn by Perry may suggest a cultural bias in the formulation of Kohlberg's scheme.

In China, the Confucian conception of morality has been the cultural ideal held by the educated elite but it permeates through the lower classes "because of a constant 'trickling down' and a constant, centuries-long process of indoctrination of the lower classes by the elite" (Eberhard, 1971: ix). This is most effective through public education as we can see in Taiwan. Although Socialist China has rejected Confucianism as archaic and feudalistic, there are strong similarities between Maoist and Confucian conception of man, in particular, the importance of character molding and the minimizing of any distinction between a private and a public domain (Munro, 1977). Thus in reality, we find close resemblance between the observed behaviors of school children in Taiwan (Wilson, 1970) and those on mainland China (Kessen, 1975).

The Confucians believe that there is a "common principle of order running through heaven, earth, and human society" (Munro, 1969: 39). They see the universe as moral, with a design exhibiting justice and goodness. It is man's responsibility to interpret the signals of nature's way and act accordingly. Rules of conduct are integrally parallel to the ways of nature; therefore, morality is absolute and universal. This view has dominated the Chinese value system for such a long time that the belief that "society cannot function unless the individual relinquishes some of his freedoms" has become one of the three major organizing principles of the Chinese society (Eberhard, 1971: 1). The individual is expected to subordinate his own identity to the interest of the group.

As part of the scheme of things, human beings are believed to be born with certain innate moral tendencies whose preservation and cultivation insure a harmonious social order. Ignoring the proper rules of conduct results in chaos. The most important of these moral tendencies is *jen*. The character *jen* combines the symbol for man and the symbol for two, and is pronounced exactly like the word for man. It has been variously translated as "love," "benevolence," "human-heartedness," "man-to-manness," "sympathy," and "perfect virtue." It is basically the deep affection for kin rooted in filial piety and extended through the family circle to all men. Confucius said, "The man of *jen* is one who, desiring to develop himself, develops others, and in desiring to sustain himself, sustains others. To be able from one's own self to draw a parallel for the treatment of others; that may be called the way to practice *jen*" (Welty, 1973: 143 – 144). This tendency is innate and instinctual. It is illustrated in *Mencius,* a Confucian classic, by "an adult who 'all of a sudden' sees a child about to fall into a well and immediately experiences alarm and distress." He would spontaneously reach out to rescue the child. Acting morally is therefore a natural inclination and is judged by the "ease" with which the action occurs and the "joy" one derives from such an action (Munro, 1969: 68).

The Confucian ideal is a sage, a man who, through long study and self-discipline, has "developed humanness or love (*jen*); it gave a man an almost mystical empathy for his fellow men, and an acute sensitivity to all the delicately balanced forces at work in the universe'' (Wright, 1964: vii—viii). He is one who has attained the highest wisdom and understanding of justice to judge human affairs, taking into consideration all the aspects of a given situation. This ideal terminus for moral development which emphasizes spontaneous feelings, intuition, and synthesis, certainly contrasts with Kohlberg's stage 6 which strives for analytical thinking, individual choice, and responsibility. The process of development is also seen as a gradual accumulation of knowledge and wisdom rather than progressing along a sequence of qualitatively different stages.

These two differing views of man and morality are closely related to the preferred mode of resolving human conflict in the respective cultures. A comparison of these two modes will bring to light the cultural embeddedness of Kohlberg's moral dilemmas.

MODES OF RESOLVING CONFLICTS

In the West, social order and the rights of individuals are under the protection of an elaborate set of laws. However, laws cannot fully take into account all the complexity of human situations. Sometimes one has to violate a law in order to fulfill a higher moral principle, but justice must be done no matter how noble the deed may be. Thus we have the story of John Brown who violated the law in his attempt to liberate the slaves in the American South and was executed. He knowingly made his choice and accepted the consequence. We can only admire his lofty spirit and self-sacrifice. In the story of Billy Budd, the Captain had to execute a perfectly good man who was provoked into killing an evil superior. We know how painful the Captain must have felt in making that decision, yet we understand his commitment to uphold the law. This mode of making individual choices and taking individual responsibilities is part of the individual orientation that characterizes the Americans in contrast to the group orientation of the Chinese (Hsu, 1970).

The Chinese emphasize harmonious interdependent social existence. Therefore, the preferred mode of resolving conflict is reconciliation rather than choice and commitment as in the West. The concept of justice in this context is based upon the proper weighing of *ch'ing* (human sentiments or feelings), *li* (reason), and *fa* (law). The Confucians have always argued against control by penal law on three grounds. First, universally applied laws would undermine the natural distinctions between the noble and mean, leading to chaos. Second, laws cannot cover all possible circumstances. It is therefore better to have good officials decide each case, taking into consideration any unique circumstances. Third, law controls through fear of punishment and this may result in people becoming contentious in their attempt to evade the law rather than changing their attitudes and behaviors (Munro, 1969: 111).

Although China today, in its new efforts at Westernization, is working toward developing a more comprehensive legal system, the traditional mode of conciliatory resolution has persisted. This is evidenced by a recent trial conducted in Shanghai, which was tellingly described as a "busybody" divorce trial by a Western observer (Beecher, 1979).

This case involves a 35-year-old woman who filed a divorce suit against her 39-year-old husband because of a domestic dispute which stemmed from her desire to separate her household from that of her in-laws. Her purpose was to gain more personal freedom and exclusive attention from her husband, but the husband could not go along, undoubtedly because of his filial feelings. A court hearing was held after numerous investigations and attempts at conciliation had failed. At the trial there were no lawyers. Instead, representatives of the couple's Neighborhood Committee and of their respective workplaces were called upon to report on their efforts at reconciliation and their evaluations of the case. The hearing was held before a judge and two assistants called "people's assessors." There was heavy pressure against the breakup because the couple had a child. The general consensus was that as both parties had a college education, began their marriage with romantic love, and, above all, loved their child deeply, they therefore could have a good marriage if they tried harder. A compromise was reached and the judge concluded, "In our society we should have unity in the family. After mediation today, both agreed to try reconciliation. And both offered some self-criticism. You have also agreed on some family matters. I should like to point out that in our Socialist country men and women enjoy equality. This is stipulated in the First Article in the Marriage Law. When anything goes wrong you should discuss it together. Take her temperament as an example. When you fly into a rage, you're very bad tempered. And he's very obstinate. . . . If you quarrel with each other very often your work will suffer" (7).

In this instance we not only see the importance of reconciliation, but also the primacy of the collective over the individual. This approach was carried to the extreme during the Cultural Revolution, as Ruth Sidel (1973) reported: "When there are quarrels within or between families, the leaders gather everyone together and study how Mao's thought applies to the problem. Everyone participates—aged people, "little Red Guards" (children), and workers. An entire building might participate" (29).

THE CULTURAL EMBEDDEDNESS OF KOHLBERG'S MORAL DILEMMAS

In order to identify the developmental process of moral judgment, Kohlberg devised a series of moral dilemmas suitable for children 10 to 16 years of age, in which the protagonist must choose between alternative actions either in conformity with rules and authority or in accordance with the needs and welfare of others contrary to the requirements of the former. The subject is questioned as to whether the protagonist should have taken such an action and why. Based upon the form of reasoning behind his/her responses, he/she is placed at one of the six stages of moral development from "obedience and punishment" orientation to "conscience or principle" orientation (the description of the stages can be found in numerous textbooks on child or human development). The following is one of the dilemmas:

> Joe is a 14-year-old boy who wanted to go to camp very much. His father promised him he could go if he saved up the money for it himself. So Joe worked hard at his paper route and saved up the $40 it cost to go to camp and a little more besides. But just before camp was going to start, his father changed his mind. Some of his friends decided to go on a special fishing trip, and Joe's father was short of the money it would cost. So he told Joe to give him the money he had saved from the paper route. Joe didn't want to give up going to camp, so he thought of refusing to give his father the money.
>
> Should Joe refuse to give his father the money or should he give it to him? Why? (Duska & Whelan, 1975: 121)

If this story were to be used in China, one would of course question whether Chinese subjects could really understand the meaning of going to camp or going on a fishing trip in the lives of these individuals. But more importantly, one must examine the significance of the father–son relationship in the context of the subject's culture. Under the Confucian precept regarding filial piety, the son is expected to obey parental orders and to make sacrifices for the happiness of his parents. What choice does the child in the story have?

In conducting cross-cultural research, Kohlberg and others do make an effort to revise some of the stories to be appropriate for the culture in question. For example, the Heinz dilemma involving a druggist was changed in the following way to be used in a village in Taiwan:

> A man and his wife had just migrated from the high mountains. They started to farm but there was no rain and no crops grew. No one had enough food. The wife got sick from having little food and could only sleep. Finally she was close to dying from having no food. The husband could not get any work and the wife could not move to another town. There was only one grocery store in the village, and the storekeeper charged a very high price for the food because there was no other store and people had no place else to go to buy food. The husband asked the storekeeper for some food for his wife, and said he would pay for it later. The storekeeper said, "No, I won't give you food unless you pay first." The husband went to all the people in the village to ask for food but no one had food to spare. So he got desperate and broke into the store to steal food for his wife.
>
> Should the husband have done that? Why? (Kohlberg, 1980: 29–30)

Although the setting and the characters are appropriate enough for the village, the situation still seems highly contrived. When one compares this with a real-life situation described by Margery Wolf (1968), one wonders if such a heartless village storekeeper could actually exist. Wolf witnessed the owner of a village store, Mr. Ng, trying to collect a bad debt from a neighbor in the presence of Mr. Ng's wife who tends the store most of the time.

>Mr. Ng was saying angrily to his wife, "You think that everyone is of good heart and just give things to them."
>
>Mrs. Ng, looking anxiously at her husband's rising color, answered, "Well, they said they would give me the money after they sold the pig. How could I know that they wouldn't give it to me?"
>
>Mr. Ng gave his wife a look of utter scorn and, turning his attention to the hapless debtor, a Mrs. Lim, he continued, "You all come here and get things and don't give me any money, but when I go buy all these things I have to give money. How can I go along like this? I have to go and borrow money so that I can buy things for the store!"
>
>Some of the on-lookers exchanged skeptical glances over this statement. Mr. Ng did not seem to notice and warmed to his subject. "How can I borrow money and then lend it to other people? That's what it amounts to. And that is no way to do business."
>
>Mrs. Lim answered, soothingly, "Now, Ng, your temper is thin, but my son is not a bad person. It is just that we have no money. The money we got from the pig had to go to people we borrowed money from and we still owe them more money. My poor son is the only one earning money in our family and he has to feed us all. We have to borrow a little each month just to have enough to eat. He only makes NT$700 a month and you can't feed six people on that."
>
>Several of the loungers began at this point to calculate just how much money would be needed to feed a family the size of Mrs. Lim's, and the consensus of opinion was that her son's income was indeed not up to the job. Mr. Ng did not join in these interesting calculations but continued to rub his head and make frustrated comments about the store, debtors, fate, etc. He finally growled at the group in general, "Oh, this store! This store just can't give people food if they don't give it money!"
>
>Mrs. Lim smiled at him sympathetically, and said, "Well, if you had a store in the city, you could do things that way, but not in the country. In the country you have to let people have things whether they have money or not. I know it is hard on you, but you just have to do it that way."
>
>Several members of the group agreed with Mrs. Lim and informed Mr. Ng of it (20–21).[1]

In this story we see how a village storekeeper needs to let poor villagers shop on credit with no specified terms. As Mrs. Lim said, "In the country you have to let people have things whether they have money or not. I know it is hard on you, but you just have to do it that way." In such a village the storekeeper in Kohlberg's dilemma would appear to be quite a villain. One wonders if he is really comparable to the druggist in Heinz' dilemma. The situation described by Wolf also brought out the use of public opinion for arbitration. A dilemma for a single individual in the West may be perceived as a problem to be discussed openly in the social setting in China. In Kohlberg's methodology, the subject is asked to make

---

[1] Reprinted, with permission of the publisher, from Wolf (1968).

an either—or choice between two major alternatives; he/she is not given the option of proposing a solution. Rest (1979) carried it even further by constructing a multiple-choice instrument and thereby forcing the respondent to select one of a set of given choices. Such a method precludes the culturally characteristic approach of reconciliation through public discussion in China.

A NEW DIRECTION

In short, built into Kohlberg's methodology as well as the scheme of his developmental theory is the prevailing Western conception of man as an autonomous being, free to make choices and determine his destiny. Conflicting claims need to be adjudicated by law, yet obedience to such man-made laws may compete with other principles governing individual rights and human welfare. The choice of action is ultimately left to the individual who must take the responsibility for his action. One is ideally socialized to develop fully one's rational faculty so that one may arrive at well-reasoned decisions. Applying this theory to a culture which emphasizes harmony, reconciliation, collective decision making, and cultivation of sensitivity to the balancing forces in human affairs does not help us see and trace the development of that society's most important characteristic features.

The Chinese commonly use the phrase *pu-tung-shih* to refer to a child, meaning the child does not understand human affairs. What we need to look at is the process by which the child acquires this understanding. Anthropologist Harumi Befu (1977) has pointed out that norms of reciprocity and rules of exchange govern social interaction in every society, but these rules may be more salient in some societies than others. He has studied the ubiquitous gift-giving custom in Japan and related it to the concepts of *on* and *giri* which imply a strong moral compulsion to return a favor (Befu, 1967, 1974). One does not, of course, wish to maintain that there are not very important differences between Japanese and Chinese social systems, but in this regard, at least, there are interesting similarities. Although the present author knows of no comparable analysis of the Chinese society, the importance of establishing "connections" in China is a well-known fact. The rules of exchange are complex and unspecified. Furthermore, as objects of exchange, there are instrumental resources as well as expressive ones. Moral maturity in such a society may well mean an ability to make a judgment based upon an insight into the intricate system of cultural norms of reciprocity, rules of exchange, various available resources, and the complex network of relationships in a given situation. The learning process involved cannot be easily conceptualized by existing learning theories. Youniss' (1978) new interpretation of Piaget's notion of social knowledge offers some promise.

According to this interpretation, the child is motivated to seek regularity in his interaction with others. He eventually finds it in two general methods of interpersonal relations. One is the relations of constraint, that is, "one person's imposition of rules or ideas on another without equal reciprocity," and the other is the relations of cooperation that involves reciprocity and collaboration. The former leads to heteronomous knowledge whereas the latter leads to the development of rational and autonomous thought. This interpretation can account for the general finding of a basically two-stage distinction in cross-cultural studies. However, the mature stage is one that is subject to cultural variation in meaning. In addition, Youniss seems to think that rational and autonomous thought develops through the cognitive process of mathematical–logical abstraction. This may well be true in the West. If White's (1972) characterization of Western mode of thinking as being "lineal/sequential/either-or" and the Eastern mode as being "multi-level/integrated/simultaneous" has any validity, a different process of abstraction would need to be considered in the case of the Chinese.

In conclusion, the present analysis casts strong doubt as to the applicability of Kohlberg's theory of moral development cross-culturally even within the lower levels. A two-stage theory based upon Youniss' (1978) interpretation of Piaget's conception of moral development with attention paid to cultural variation in the definition of moral maturity as well as to the developmental process offers an alternative for future exploration.

REFERENCES

Beecher, W. A "busybody" divorce trial in China. *The San Francisco Sunday Examiner and Chronicle,* Aug. 26, 1979, 2.

Befu, H. Gift-giving and social reciprocity in Japan, an exploratory statement. *France-Asia/Asia,* 1967, **188,** 161–177.

Befu, H. Power in exchange: Strategy of control and patterns of compliance in Japan. *Asian Profile,* 1974, **2,** 601–622.

Befu, H. Social exchange. *Annual Review of Anthropology,* 1977, 6, 255–281.

Duska, R., & Whelan, M. *Moral development: A guide to Piaget and Kohlberg.* New York: Paulist Press, 1975.

Eberhard, W. *Moral and social values of the Chinese: Collected essays.* Chinese Materials and Research Aids Service Center, 1971.

Fairbank, J. K. China: The center of the world. *China: Advertising Supplement to the San Francisco Examiner,* Sept. 7, 1980, 12–14.

Fowler, J. Moral stages and the development of faith. In B. Munsey (Ed.), *Moral development, moral education, and Kohlberg: Basic issues in philosophy, psychology, religion, and education.* Birmingham, Ala.: Religious Education Press, 1980. Pp. 130–160.

Gorsuch, R. L., & Barnes, M. L. Stages of ethical reasoning and moral norms of Carib youths. *Journal of Cross-Cultural Psychology,* 1973, 4, 283–301.

Grisez, G., & Shaw, R. *Beyond the new morality: The responsibility of freedom.* Indiana: University of Notre Dame Press, 1974.

Hetherington, E. M., & Parke, R. D. *Child psychology: A contemporary viewpoint.* New York: McGraw–Hill, 1979.

Hsu, F. L. K. *Americans and Chinese: Reflections on two cultures and their people.* New York: Doubleday, 1970.

Kessen, W. (Ed.) *Childhood in China.* New Haven: Yale University Press, 1975.

Kohlberg, L. Stage and sequence: The cognitive-developmental approach to socialization. In D. A. Goslin (Ed.), *Handbook of socialization theory and research.* Chicago: Rand McNally, 1969. Pp. 347–480.

Kohlberg, L. Stages of moral development as a basis for moral education. In B. Munsey (Ed.), *Moral development, moral education, and Kohlberg: Basic issues in philosophy, psychology, religion, and education.* Birmingham, Ala.: Religious Education Press, 1980. Pp. 15–98.

Kurtines, W., & Grief, E. The development of moral thought: Review and evaluation of Kohlberg's approach. *Psychological Bulletin,* 1974, **81**, 453–470.

Moustakas, C. E. *Loneliness.* New York: Prentice-Hall, 1961.

Munro, D. J. *The concept of man in early China.* Stanford: Stanford University Press, 1969.

Munro, D. J. *The concept of man in contemporary China.* Ann Arbor: The University of Michigan Press, 1977.

Murphy, J. M., & Gilligan, C. Moral development in late adolescence and adulthood: A critique and reconstruction of Kohlberg's theory. *Human Development,* 1980, **23**, 77–104.

Perry, W. G., Jr. *Forms of intellectual and ethical development in the college years: A scheme.* New York: Holt, Rinehart & Winston, 1968.

Piaget, J. *The moral judgment of the child.* (M. Gabain, trans.) New York: The Free Press, 1965 (originally published, 1932).

Rest, J. R. *Development in judging moral issues.* Minneapolis: The University of Minnesota Press, 1979.

Rosen, H. *The development of sociomoral knowledge: A cognitive-structural approach.* New York: Columbia University Press, 1980.

Sapontzis, S. F. Are animals moral beings? *American Philosophical Quarterly,* 1980, **17**, 45–52.

Sartre, J. *Of human freedom* (W. Baskin, Ed.), New York: Philosophical Library, 1966.

Sidel, R. *Women and child care in China.* Baltimore, Md: Penguin Books, 1973.

Simpson, E. L. Moral development research: A case study of scientific cultural bias. *Human Development,* 1974, **17**, 81–106.

Welty, P. T. *The Asians: Their heritage and their destiny.* Philadelphia: Lippincott, 1973.

White, C. B., Bushnell, N., & Regnemer, J. L. Moral development in Bahamian school children: A 3 year examination of Kohlberg's stages of moral development. *Developmental Psychology,* 1978, **14**, 58–65.

White, J. *The highest state of consciousness.* Garden City, N.Y.: Doubleday, 1972.

Wilson, R. W. *Learning to be Chinese: The political socialization of children in Taiwan.* Cambridge, Mass.: MIT Press, 1970.

Wolf, M. *The house of Lim.* Englewood Cliffs, N.J.: Prentice-Hall, 1968.

Wright, A. F. *Confucianism and Chinese civilization.* New York: Atheneum, 1964.

Youniss, J. Dialectical theory and Piaget on social knowledge. *Human Development,* 1978, **21**, 234–247.

RECEIVED: October 5, 1981; REVISED: February 5, 1982

Social Cognition, Vol. 5, No. 4, 1987, pp. 383–402

MORAL DISOBEDIENCE DURING THE LEBANON WAR: WHAT CAN THE COGNITIVE-DEVELOPMENTAL APPROACH LEARN FROM THE EXPERIENCE OF THE ISRAELI SOLDIERS?

RUTH LINN
Haifa University, Israel

This paper focuses on the interplay of hypothetical and actual moral reasoning, as well as attitudes, in the construction of a real-life action of disobedience. The sample consisted of 36 Israeli reserve soldiers who refused to serve in Lebanon within the first year of Israel's war with Lebanon (June 1982–June 1985), claiming that this service would go against their moral conscience. According to Kohlberg's (1984) measure of moral development, 44% of the subjects were "postconventionals" and 36% manifested postconventional thinking in justifying their action (when transitional Stage 4–5 was included). Disobedience was guided primarily by Stage 4 moral logic. The correlation between hypothetical and actual moral reasoning (derived from interviews) was highly significant ($r = .89$, $p < .001$). The higher soldiers were on the hierarchy of moral stages, the more their disobedience was found to be motivated by political rather than by moral factors, and the more it was perceived by the soldiers as implying a protest against the law rather than a personal statement of belief. Postconventional moral thinking was associated with the experience of the self as having active control over the action of disobedience. Multivariate analysis indicated that disobedience depended on education and active self-involvement.

I would like to thank Sybil and Stephen Stone for their important comments and dedication to this project, and Yaakov Khoushy for his care and help throughout my stay in the United States. This paper was written when I was Associate in Education at Harvard Graduate School of Education (1985–1986). Requests for reprints should be sent to Ruth Linn, University of Haifa, School of Education, Haifa, Israel 31999.

INTRODUCTION

Only 248 of the 3421 years of recorded history have been without war (Durant & Durant, 1968). Yet the attention given by psychologists to combatants' decision-making processes is relatively minimal. This is particularly surprising for researchers who adopt the cognitive-developmental approach to morality (Kohlberg, 1976, 1984), given its genuine concern with the individual's resistance to authority. The military setting, with discipline as a fundamental cornerstone, could have served as a fertile ground for expanding our understanding of the ways in which obedience and disobedience to authority are decided upon.

In spite of its being the only social institution in which individuals are not only permitted but expected to kill, war has not attracted cognitive-developmental research, even though traditionally such research questions the ways in which individuals define their actions within conflicting, ambiguous situations revolving around the issues of life and law, conscience and punishment (Kohlberg, 1976). When one takes into account the growing interest in the relationship between moral judgment and moral action (Blasi, 1980, 1983; Candee, 1976; Kohlberg, 1980, 1984; Kohlberg & Candee, 1983; Locke, 1983a, 1983b), and particularly the contextual meaning of this relationship (Weinrich-Haste & Locke, 1983), it seems that substantial attention to individuals' behavior in relation to their military obligations might expand our knowledge about the cognition–conduct connection.

The complexity of judgment–action relationships has often been studied with trivial examples, such as returning questionnaires (Krebs & Rosenwald, 1977), cheating on tests (Krebs & Kohlberg, 1973), or individual behavior in a simulated distress situation (McNamee, 1978). The nature of real-life irreversible actions (Gilligan, 1982; Gilligan & Murphy, 1979; Murphy & Gilligan, 1980), within social settings with significant ideological attributes (Haan, 1975; Milgram, 1974), has not been a major focus of inquiry. Exceptions are the analysis of Michael Bernhardt's refusal to take part in the My Lai massacre (Kohlberg, 1984) and of Adolf Eichmann's reasoning for compliance to his superiors' orders.

The present paper utilizes Kohlberg's theoretical framework as the basis for analyzing a specific real-life action in time of war: the refusal of soldiers to fulfill one of their most serious obligations as citizens—that is, to fight for their own state (Walzer, 1968, 1970, 1977). Within the Israeli context, this obligation is quite different from that in other democratic countries. Israel's security is maintained largely by civilians in uniform. Upon the completion of 3 years of compulsory military service (starting at age 18), each male citizen is obliged to perform annually 1–2 months of reserve service wherever his unit is called, until he reaches his mid-50s. Naturally, in time of emergency, the frequency, length, and seriousness of the service increase. Israel often has had to defend her physical survival when attacked; however, in spite of frequent wars and the lengthy military service that results for the individual male citizen, only few have chosen to avoid service on moral grounds, and these cases have usually not been widely publicized (Blatt, Davis, & Klinbaum, 1975).

During the recent war with Lebanon (June 1982–June 1985), this scenario was dramatically changed. Following continuous terrorist attacks on Israeli civilians by the Palestine Liberation Organization (PLO), Israel started 48- to 72-hour limited military operations in the neighboring country of Lebanon; these were attempts to destroy the PLO's infrastructure, which is often located within a Lebanese civilian setting. The operation expanded, however, into 3 years of war with guerillas in the area. For the first time in the country's history, a number of reserve soldiers (a total of 143) disobeyed the command to join their units in Lebanon, claiming that this military mission was inconsistent with their moral convictions. The Israeli army treated these soldiers as having committed a disciplinary offense, and they were court-martialed and sentenced to 14–35 days in military prison. Some were jailed two and three times as a result of repeated refusal to obey additional orders for service in Lebanon.

It must be emphasized that in spite of public controversy over the necessity and the morality of the war (Linn, 1986a; Shiff & Yaari, 1984; Shiffer, 1984), this disobedience was widely condemned. Those who chose this mode of action were regarded as extreme leftists, delinquents, or lawbreakers who were undermining democracy (Linn, 1985b). Most of the soldiers who objected to the war chose to fulfill their duty and protested in front of the government offices upon their return from the reserve service (Linn, 1987). Because the disobedient soldiers protested on behalf of their moral convictions, I felt that it would be appropriate to examine their moral reasoning.

Based on a study with adolescent boys (Kohlberg, 1958), which was followed by substantial empirical evidence (Mosher, 1980), Kohlberg has argued that when faced with hypothetical moral dilemmas (situations revolving around conflicting rights and duties), individuals tend to construct their moral choices and to ascribe meaning to their actions in one of a hierarchy of six distinct stages (modes of prescriptive valuing of the socially good and right). The stages represent three possible approaches to moral dilemmas with respect to society's moral norms: "preconventional," "conventional," and "postconventional" perspectives. Each of these broad perspectives is divided into two stages for a total of six stages.

The "preconventional" perspective emerges from an egocentric point of view and is mostly characteristic of children's moral logic. Stage 1 represents an unreflective acceptance of rules and labels; the law itself is never challenged. Stage 2 represents those judgments that recognize a possible conflict between a rule and individual needs. The "conventional" perspective, used by most adults, encompasses the understanding of the origin and the function of rules as social utilities. Stage 3 judgments reflect awareness of mutual interpersonal expectations, relationships, and interpersonal conformity. In Stage 4, the individual reaches the abstract: He or she realizes the role of the rules in the preservation of the society at large, yet realizes that under specific circumstances disobeying the law fosters maintenance of the social system. The "postconventional" perspective is used by a minority of individuals and represents an objective, impartial point of view. Stage 5 embodies a social contract view of the relationship between individuals and society, based on utilitarian considerations. Stage 6 is based on respect for the dignity of individuals and for morality as justice. Postconventional or principled thinking entails the premise that when there is a conflict between the legal and moral domains, the moral should almost always take precedence, because it represents the more objective and impartial solution within and across societies.

Particular stages of moral reasoning contribute to the performance of moral action in two ways. First, they determine actions by concretely defining rights and duties in the situation. Second, each new stage brings sensitivity to new aspects of moral conflict (Kohlberg, 1984). Eventually, the individual's moral stage provides no information as to whether a particular person will "live up to his stage of moral reasoning in a particular situation" (Kohlberg, 1976, p. 32). Yet Kohlberg views the stage as the most powerful and meaningful predictor of moral action, since "it gives rise to the distinctive ways of defining concrete situational rights and duties in socially ambiguous situations" (1969, p. 397). Assuming that freedom from situational and personality constraints are essential for mature moral thinking, Kohlberg has hypothesized "greater consistency between moral judgment and moral action with advancing stages of moral development" (Kohlberg, 1984, p. 571).

Given the nature of the actions examined in this study—that is, a deliberate and rational breaking of the law—it was reasonable to expect that conscientious refusers would justify their actions on the basis of concerns for universal justice (Cohen, 1971; Walzer, 1970;

Zashin, 1972). Accordingly, from this ideal mode of moral disobedience, it was first hypothesized that there would be a significant number of postconventional subjects among the group of disobedient men. Second, it was hypothesized that the refusers would exemplify judgment–action consistency, since "one cannot follow moral principles ([Stages] 5 and 6) if one does not understand and believe in them" (Kohlberg, 1976, p. 32).

Methodologically, the connection between cognition and moral conduct can best be assessed if hypothetical and actual moral reasoning are recorded in the same type of moral situation (Damon, 1980), starting from the concrete behavioral choice (Blasi, 1983). The present study began with the soldiers' concrete behavioral choice (to refuse). Their justification for the action of disobedience was compared with their moral reasoning on Kohlberg's Standard Moral Judgment Interview (Cobly et al., 1983). However, moral reasoning is not the only factor that affects refusal to serve in an army. This kind of nonviolent and overt breaking of the law is also a deviant behavior that might entail some long-term emotional consequences as well as legal punishment. As noted by Cohen (1971), this kind of action exposes individuals to attacks upon their characters and damage to their reputations. Therefore, the study needed to clarify how various attitudes, values, and motives affected the intended meaning of the action and the experience of self in this action's choice.

The two major categories of motives for refusing to serve are "political" and "moral" (Cohen, 1971). Ultimately, there is no clear distinction between them, since political acts have moral consequences. Yet, as clearly explained by Cohen (1971), although politics and morality cannot be separated, they can be distinguished:

> Some acts and decisions take place within an essentially political framework, being addressed primarily to the whole community in view of its common concern. Other acts and decisions are more specifically personal, being undertaken by man for himself, out of chief regard for principles and values that he accepts as governing his conduct. These later often have political import—import for the whole community—just as the former have moral import. But in being differently conceived and differently aimed, the two kinds of acts may reasonably be distinguished from one another, the first called political, the second moral. (p. 58)

Given the nature of Kohlberg's theory of moral development, it might be expected that the higher soldiers were on the hierarchy of moral stages, the more likely it would be that they would be morally rather than politically motivated (in line with Cohen's categories).

In addition to the categories that focus on the actor's motivation (political–moral), there are categories that focus on the act. According to Cohen (1971), disobedience may be direct (an act in which the law, deliberately broken, is itself the object of protest) or indirect (the law broken is other than, although more or less closely related to, the object of protest). Whereas most of the soldiers who were jailed because of their refusal to serve in Lebanon performed a direct act of disobedience, they might have perceived its implications in different ways. In line with Cohen's categorization, the present study focused on the action's performance as well: The refusers might have perceived their action's consequences as holding either "protest" or "personal" implications. In line with Kohlberg's theory, it was further hypothesized that the higher soldiers were on the hierarchy of moral stages, the more they might view their action as implying a personal statement of belief rather than an act of protest against the law.

Finally, taking an action such as this within a hostile milieu may entail different modes of emotional involvement in the dilemma and in the initiation of the action. While Kohlberg does not ignore behavioral and emotional components of experience, he considers them as mediated through moral channeling mechanisms. Thus, an individual may follow moral principles in a situation because he or she feels that "they correctly define the situation, not because of an abstract affective identification with these principles as verbal abstractions" (Kohlberg, 1969, p. 231). The extent to which the acting self is involved in the dilemma and controls and initiates the resolution of the conflict has not been thoroughly investigated by Kohlberg, mainly because of the limited scope of studies. Most judgment–action research has been conducted in situations of "resistance to temptation," where the actor is required to break normative expectations for the sake of his or her self-interest. Thus, in such a situation, the expected moral action is eventually that of "nonaction," when the ideal moral self is detached from the other people in the situation and watches the status quo as an outside objective observer. Bernhardt's case may serve as a dramatic example for this "passive" mode of involvement: "When I thought of shooting people, I figured: Well, I am going to be doing my own war, let them do their own war" (quoted in Kohlberg, 1984, p. 549). Less is known about situations where the individual is called to break normative expectations on behalf of others—when the self should initiate an altruistic action and when the moral resolution needs to be found and constructed *in* the dilemma situation. This mode of "active" self-involvement is represented by the case of

Hugh Thompson, an American soldier who accidently came to My Lai after the massacre, and rescued nine Vietnamese by telling Lieutenant William Calley not to interrupt him from pursuing a rescue mission (Hersh, 1970).

Obviously, both types of self-involvement and action are needed in different (and sometimes in the same) real-life conflicts. Moreover, they may be manifested on different occasions by the same person. Here, the action of disobedience, as performed by the Israeli soldiers, might have been perceived by the actors as a response to a conflicting situation of "resistance to temptation" (not to join the crowd of fighters) or as a form of "altruistic action" (to prevent others from going by committing an act of self-sacrifice). The present study examined one dimension of the action's emotional component—that of "passive" or "active" involvement. In line with Kohlberg's theory, it was hypothesized that the higher soldiers were on the hierarchy of moral stages, the more likely it was that their emotional involvement would be active rather than passive.

METHOD

SUBJECTS

The study, begun in September 1983, was based upon interviews with 36 subjects after their release from prison. The subjects were randomly selected from a list of 86 reserve soldiers who had been in jail up to this date as a consequence of their refusal to serve in Lebanon. Their ages ranged between 23 and 46 years (mean 31.1, mode 28), and they came from the three main cities in Israel and five kibbutzim. Of the 36 subjects, 16 were married (11 with children), 5 were divorced (4 with children), and 15 were single. A majority (23) had academic degrees (mean 14.9 years of study); of these, 4 had Ph.D.'s and another 3 were doctoral candidates. The group included 7 officers up to the rank of captain, and 22 of the 36 had had military experience in war prior to this conflict. Circumstances regarding refusal to serve were as follows: 26 subjects decided to refuse *after* serving in Lebanon; 30 subjects were the only refusers in their units; 28 subjects did not make any attempt to convince others; and 30 subjects asked to return to their units upon their release from prison. In terms of political orientation, 3 defined themselves as Communists, 18 as Zionist leftists, and 15 as close to the orientation of the Labor party.

MEASURES AND PROCEDURES

Each subject was interviewed individually in his home by me. The interviews lasted 2–4 hours and were tape-recorded with the subjects' consent. The subjects' stages of moral development were measured with the use of Form B of the standard Moral Judgment Interview (MJI) (Colby et al., 1983). Actual Moral Reasoning (AMR) was assessed from the subjects' justification of their action during a semiclinical open-ended interview in which they were asked to justify and reflect upon their actions. The order of administration of the MJI and AMR measures was counterbalanced.

SCORING

All the interviews were transcribed and typed. The protocols were scored blindly by an independent rater who had not done the initial interviewing. Following Kohlberg's revised manual (Colby et al., 1983), the scoring procedure for the MJI involved the classifying of responses to a dilemma into two broad-issue categories and then assigning a stage score for each match between a manual-criterion judgment and a moral judgment in the interview. The scores were given in the form of Moral Maturity scores for the MJI and global scores for the AMR interview for each subject. The Moral Maturity score represents a weighted average of the issue scores and ranges from 100 (pure Stage 1) to 500 (pure Stage 5). Stage 6 does not appear in the revised scoring manual, since in practice there is no difference between Stages 5 and 6 (Gibbs, Widaman, & Colby, 1982). The AMR interview was scored clinically and blindly with regard to the MJI by the same scorer, who was notamiliar with the identity of the subjects.

The AMR interview was further analyzed for attitudinal factors, such as the motivation of the action ("political" or "moral"), its intended implications ("protest" or "personal"), and the role of the self ("active" or "passive"). The assessment of "political" versus "moral" motivation was conducted in line with Cohen's (1971) criteria, as presented in Table 1. When no clear motivation could be identified, a score of "unidentified" was assigned and when the two motives were equally presented, a score of "both" was assigned. The subjects' perceptions of the implications of their actions were categorized as "protest" when the action was perceived by the actor as holding social significance and as "personal" when perceived as holding a solution for the individual actor. "Active" versus "passive" self-involvement was assessed in line with the criteria presented in Table 2. When the

TABLE 1

Cohen's (1971) Criteria for the Identification of "Political" versus "Moral" Motivation of Disobedience

POLITICAL	MORAL
1. The individual wishes the action to be public.	1. The action may or may not be performed in public.
2. The individual refers to the action as essentially a tactic.	2. Ethical convictions have priority; tactical functions are secondary.
3. The individual is worried about the appeal of the action to the members of the community.	3. The scope of the action is less ambitious than political action.
4. The action has as an external goal the changing of policy.	4. The action is more limited in object and more specific in intent than political action.
5. The action's effectiveness is emphasized.	5. The principles rather than the result are emphasized.
6. There is a focus on the act.	6. There is a focus on the actor.

Note. Adapted from *Civil Disobedience: Conscience, Tactics, and the Law* by C. Cohen, 1971, New York: Columbia University Press.

TABLE 2

Criteria for the Identification of "Active" versus "Passive"

ACTIVE	PASSIVE
1. Emphasis on the self as the initiator of the action.	1. Emphasis on the self as detached from the action.
2. Experience of competence in controlling the situation; the self is part of the dilemma.	2. Indirect control over the situation; the self is not part of the dilemma.
3. Identification of action strategy and planned consequences (the individuals did not surprise themselves by acting the way they did).	3. No action strategy or planned consequences (the individuals surprised themselves by acting the way they did).
4. Emphasis on the action as a choice.	4. Emphasis on the "no-choice" nature of the action.
5. Feeling in control of performing a deviant behavior.	5. Defending the self for being part of a deviant behavior.

actor reported himself as "passive," though following the criteria for "active," he was categorized as "active."

STATISTICAL ANALYSIS

The three hypotheses were examined via statistical analysis in the following ways:

1. *The percentage of MJI and AMR postconventional subjects in the sample*: The distributions of MJI postconventionals and conventionals, and of AMR postconventionals and conventionals, were examined by chi-square tests (transitional Stage 4-5 was included as postconventional). Similar analyses with Stage 4 as a cutoff point were performed as well.

2. *Consistency between judgment and action*: Stage consistency was measured by Pearson correlation between MJI and AMR scores. The sign test was then used to compare individuals' AMR and MJI scores.

3. *Association between attitudinal factors and AMR distribution*: AMR scores were analyzed for the categories of "political" versus "moral," "protest" versus "personal," and "active" versus "passive." Chi-square tests (with Yates's correction) were used to examine these variables in relation to conventional–postconventional AMR scores.

4. Finally, multiple linear regression procedures were used to examine the independent contribution of the following potential predictors of AMR and MJI to the score level: age, military role, profession, marital status, fighting experience, timing of disobedience (i.e., before or after service in Lebanon), "political" versus "moral" motivation, "protest" versus "personal" implications, and "active" versus "passive" attitude.

RESULTS

Table 3 presents the distributions of MJI and AMR stage scores of the sample. Table 3 shows that the subjects' stage scores ranged between transitional Stage 2-3 and Stage 5, with the modal stages being transitional Stage 3-4 for the MJI and Stage 4 for the AMR. The hypothesis that a majority of subjects would be postconventional was not supported. However, when Stage 4 was used as a cutoff point, 69.4% of AMR subjects could support their action using Stage 4 or higher moral reasoning; this was a statistically significant majority ($\chi^2 = 5.44$, $p < .025$).

The subjects' moral consistency, as measured by the correlation between MJI and AMR stage scores, was found to be highly signifi-

TABLE 3
Subjects' MJI and AMR Global Stage Distributions

| | STAGE | | | | | |
INSTRUMENT	2-3	3	3-4	4	4-5	5
MJI	3 (8.3)	1 (2.8)	10 (27.8)	6 (16.7)	8 (22.2)	8 (22.2)
AMR	3 (8.3)	2 (5.6)	6 (16.7)	12 (33.3)	3 (8.3)	10 (27.8)

Note. The numbers in parentheses indicate percentages.
$n = 36$.

cant ($r = .89$, $p < .001$). When MJI and AMR scores for each individual were compared, it was found that 19 subjects had similar scores on the two interviews. Nine had AMR scores that were at least half a stage lower than their MJI scores, and eight had AMR scores at least half a stage higher than their MJI scores. The sign test allowing for ties was not statistically significant; this indicated consistent achievements on the MJI and AMR.

Of the attitudinal variables ("political" vs. "moral," "protest" vs. "personal," and "active" vs. "passive"), only the variable of "active" versus "passive" involvement was statistically significantly associated with postconventional versus conventional AMR scores. Of the 36 subjects, 12 were identified as having a "political" motivation (4 of these were postconventional); 15 had a "moral" motivation (3 of these were postconventional); 6 had both motivations (all were postconventional); and 3 could not be classified (all were preconventional). The chi-square test, after those with both attitudes or unclassified attitudes (total of 27 subjects) were excluded, was not significant ($\chi^2 = 0.12$, $p = .731$). The subjects' perceptions of their action's implications were evenly split: 18 were classified as "protest" (4 of them were postconventional) and 18 as "personal" (9 of them were postconventional) ($\chi^2 = 1.93$, $p = .165$). In regard to emotional involvement, 21 subjects were classified as "passive" and 15 as "active." Of the "active" subjects, 9 (60%) had postconventional AMR scores, whereas of the "passive" subjects, only 4 (23.5%) were postconventionals. This proportion indicates a statistically significant association between being "active" and justifying one's own action with postconventional logic ($\chi^2 = 4.71$, $p = .02$).

Separate stepwise multiple linear regression analyses, with MJI scores as dependent variables, that included the demographic and attitudinal variables suggested that number of years of education was the only statistically significant predictor of MJI scores ($p < .00001$).

337

When AMR scores were examined as the dependent variables, both education and "active" versus "passive" involvement were statistically significantly associated with AMR scores. A change from "passive" to "active" involvement was found to contribute almost half a stage (42 points) to the AMR score, while each year of studies contributed 15 points. Thus, these findings presented the action of disobedience as depending upon education and "active" involvement in the following way: $AMR = 165 + [15 \times n \text{ (years of study)}] + [42 \times 1 \text{ (if "active") or } 0 \text{ (if "passive")}]$. The following variables did not have statistically significant beta coefficients: age ($\beta = -.11$), military role ($\beta = -.11$), profession ($\beta = .20$), marital status ($\beta = .143$), "political" versus "moral" motivation ($\beta = -.19$), "protest" versus "personal" implications ($\beta = .05$), fighting experience ($\beta = .0008$), and timing of disobedience ($\beta = .18$).

DISCUSSION

The demographic data of this study suggest that the Israeli soldiers refusing to serve in Lebanon can be portrayed as an experienced reserve soldier in his 30s (and, when over 30, typically married with children) and a college graduate. In 83% of the cases, the soldier was the only one in his unit to disobey the command to serve in Lebanon (in 72% of the cases, after serving there). His moral concerns revolved around the objectives of this war and/or its moral handling, but 78% made no attempt to convince others to do the same.

In line with Kohlberg's (1976, 1984) theory, it was first hypothesized that conscientious refusers would be postconventional moral thinkers. Second, since the refusers often claimed that this was the only action by which they were able to preserve their moral integrity (Walzer, 1970), stage consistency was hypothesized. Third, given the behavioral and emotional components of this action, it was hypothesized that there would be a relationship between the AMR stages and the action's motivation ("political" vs. "moral"), its perceived implications ("protest"vs."personal"), and the subject's mode of involvement ("active"vs."passive").

The findings of the study do not confirm the first hypothesis. On the MJI, 22% were fully postconventional with an additional 22% falling into transitional Stage 4-5. On the AMR, 36% fell into Stages 4-5 and 5. These data fail to confirm the hypothesis that objection to serving in the Lebanon war was due to postconventional moral thinking. On the other hand, although precise data on levels of postconventional moral reasoning among comparable groups of Israeli males are not readily available, the percentage of such people in the present study was higher than would normally be expected (Colby *et al.*, 1983).

The refusers' major argument revolved around the idea that though it is usually wrong to disobey in the Israeli defense forces whose values they endorsed, it was justified in the specific circumstances of the Lebanon war, which deviated from their beliefs regarding the objectives of a just war (*jus ad bello*) and the way it should be handled (*jus in bello*) (Walzer, 1977). The following is a sample statement of this attitude (from a soldier who for a long time could have obtained a release from the army because of kidney disease):

> Israel has enormous problems of survival, and we have more wars waiting for us. We cannot allow ourselves to make wars in vain. A condition of going to war is that our lives are severely threatened. The second requirement is that we have done all we can to remove the threat. Only then I feel that the war is just and that I am obliged to do all I can to take part in it.

When Stage 4 was used as a cutoff point, a significant group of refusers was identified (69.4%). The construction of the action of refusal from the minimum understanding of Stage 4 moral logic may further point toward the soldiers' deep concern for the collective security (Emler, 1983; Emler, Renwick, & Bernadette, 1983) and their belief that the validity of one's moral claims emerges from membership in the unit (recall that most of the refusers asked to return to their units after release from prison):

> I am close to 40 years old, and I took part in every war since I was 18 years old. I could easily be transferred to a unit where I could serve in an office and not on the battlefield. I am not going to do so, since I feel it would be an escape to close my eyes and say to myself, "I am O.K., I got out." This is not right because although I solve *my* problem, I let my friends in the unit do the work. I want to return to my unit upon release from prison, since by the fact that I continue to serve and remain part of the unit, I buy myself the right to criticize and the right to shout.

Kohlberg's measure with its "middle-class American perspective," does not provide "culturally sensitive scoring," as he himself has only recently acknowledged (Snarey, Reimer, & Kohlberg, 1985). Thus, justifications in the support of "collective" moral resolutions can hardly rise above Stage 4 moral logic as defined by the measure. Also, the Kohlberg scale is not sensitive to "nonmoral" factors, such as the inclination to be included within the social system while criticizing it. His model praises the moral actor who can be "aware of values and rights prior to the social attachment and contracts" (Kohlberg, 1976, p.

35). When this formula is examined within the Israeli context, where loyalty is critical to one's own survival, it may be argued that rigid adherence to moral logic, which reflects an impartial, outside-the-society moral view, is to a certain extent a luxurious mode of moral perception:

> The worst parts of the refusal were going to the commander [and] facing the unit. The commander is really my friend. We went through the same experience throughout the Yom Kippur war and other campaigns, and suddenly I found myself on the other side. And what happens after prison? You come back to serve with the same people, and you still believe that if Syria attacks us tomorrow, you should go with them to fight, to protect your country without hesitation. How would they accept you?

The case of these Israeli reserve soldiers seems to delineate Kohlberg's neglect of an essential moral vector in real-life action—the morality of loyalty (Linn, 1986b). Thus, at the same time that the soldiers constructed the action of refusal (i.e., detachment from the unit) out of justice logic, a majority (78%) insisted on returning to their units after prison. This tendency may perhaps explain why refusal did not emerge exclusively from postconventional, "prior to society" moral thinking (Kohlberg, 1976, p. 32).

The second hypothesis, regarding consistency between individuals' MJI and AMR stage scores, was dramatically confirmed: The correlation between the subjects' MJI and AMR stage scores was highly significant and suggests an impressive manifestation of coherence in reasoning across stages. Though Kohlberg's model entails the premise that postconventional moral thinkers are more likely to experience stage correspondence across hypothetical and actual social contexts (Kohlberg, 1984), the findings of this study suggest that in the case of the Israeli soldiers, the correspondence in reasoning (as measured by MJI and AMR scores) was not exclusive to postconventional refusers, but was manifested in the case of the conventional refusers as well. Perhaps the choice of this specific action was more closely connected with the subjects' isolation tendencies (Linn, 1985a, 1985b) or with their courage to stand alone (Fromm, 1982) than with their moral reasoning. Indeed, the decision to refuse was individually reached: 83% of the subjects were the only refusers in their units. It might be argued that the ability to act at the same level of one's moral competence is not necessarily the sole function of the more elaborate form of moral reasoning or the ability to reach an impartial moral view, but also the function of the ability to coordinate moral criticism of society as an individual with efforts to remain a member of society. Thus, in line with Piaget's (1932/1965) ideas that thoughts reveal themselves in action, these findings seem to suggest that Kohlberg's justice structures reveal themselves in "individualistic" actions.

The third hypothesis, regarding the behavioral and emotional components of refusal, was partially confirmed. The original expectations that higher positions on the hierarchy of moral stages would be linked with more "moral" motivations and the perception of more "personal" implications were not confirmed. The findings suggest that with higher positions on the hierarchy, "political" motivations and "protest" implications prevailed. To a certain extent, these findings are not surprising, since Kohlberg's highest stages are biased in favor of those political actions that aim at breaking normative political orientations (Emler *et al.*, 1983). Yet there is growing awareness that this prediction (of certain "political" versus "moral" actions) is partly context-specific (Weinrich-Haste & Locke, 1983). Obviously, further inquiry into these behavioral tendencies is needed.

The subjects' perception of themselves as having "active" or "passive" control over their performed actions was the only statistically significant independent attitudinal factor that was linked to AMR stages. Moreover, when the sample was divided into conventionals and postconventionals (including those at transitional Stage 4/5), it was found that whereas the conventional moral actors seemed to conceptualize themselves as passively involved in the action, the postconventionals seemed to experience active control over the action. Examples of the "active" attitude were as follows:

It started with a feeling of restlessness. For years I used the conventional modes in expressing my disapproval of government policy, but at the same time I continued to pay taxes, to go to the reserves, and to continue to discuss the situation. By being a conscientious objector I moved toward another phase of involvement—that of personal involvement, a feeling that I am in control of my actions.

The apathy existed for me before the refusal. For me, refusal was a deviation from this state of mind. I felt that I could change the situation and be responsible for my actions—I could even decide to go to prison.

I felt good that I could give my own personal response to the situation—to prick the balloon myself.

I tried to work in different ways, to convince my buddies to demonstrate, to write letters—they were all depressed. I knew I'd have to choose the most effective action, since nothing was being done. I had to choose the most effective action and the one that I could act on.

> I am proud to be a conscientious objector. I don't care what the others think of me. It is much easier for me to defend this behavior than to explain to myself why I am going to Lebanon.

Examples of the "passive" attitude were as follows:

> The one who took the stand was not me. I was passive throughout the whole action. Now, after performing the action of disobedience, we are all named by the public as conscientious objectors, as if we have taken the initiative. The truth of the matter is that the one who had taken initiative was the other side—those who started the war and those who punished us and those who are fighting against us now. We just didn't want to fight against anybody.

> I just could not wait for the trial to be over. I was waiting to be jailed.

> I didn't believe that I had the strength to say no. I guess a person does not know his strength until he acts.

> I am just simply a soldier. I do not have many choices—to go or not to go. I can't even say to myself: "As an officer I have to go since my soldiers are going." [It] all comes down to my own personal stand—I have no choice.

> I could never seem myself as a conscientious objector in the Israeli defense forces—but when I became one, I saw that I could be in this situation.

According to Kohlberg's theory, the attainment of postconventional moral thinking does not necessarily imply action. That is to say, the ability of a given individual to reason at a high moral stage does not imply translation into action. In fact, it is almost the reverse: "[T]he more sophisticated our moral understanding, the more difficult it may be to resolve conflicting moral claims" (Locke, 1981, p. 177).

It is important to note that the subjects in this sample were only those individuals who *succeeded* in translating their more resolution of refusal into action. Many other potential refusers were either granted permission by sympathetic commanders not to serve in Lebanon or simply could not translate their decision to disobey into action (Linn, 1987). Perhaps, as noted by Blasi (1983, 1985), the judgment–action gap for the refusers was eliminated by their moral identity. In the present formulation of Kohlberg's theory, little attention is given to the acting self *vis-à-vis* the principled self. One refuser explained why this distinction is imperative:

> If I had to follow my principles all the time, I would find myself a prisoner of principles, and in this situation you cannot act. I am not only motivated by moral principles but also by practical considerations. Could I pursue the action? What is its effectiveness? How could I contribute to the whole goal of the country's security?

However, in spite of the interesting association between the subjects' "active" attitude and postconventional AMR scores, a comprehensive understanding of the action also requires contextual analysis (Brown & Herrnstein, 1975). When judged within the Israeli context, where the army serves many social functions (Gal, 1986), an action such as disobedience demands a "passive" than an "active" moral stand. The refusers were not the only soldiers who morally objected to the war, but rather the only soldiers who chose to manifest their objection by disobeying. Many more Israeli reserve soldiers who objected to the war on moral grounds chose to do extra effort to preserve their principles in the battlefield, rather than stepping outside the army; upon their return from duty, they changed from their uniforms into civilian clothing and voiced their objection in demonstrations in front of the government offices. They also knew that in Israeli society there is a special moral weight accorded to criticism from a reservist who has stood up to his duties, and who brings his military experience to his civilian life (Linn, 1987). Thus, at least within the Israeli context, it might be argued thathe action of disobedience is primarily the decision *not to act* (i.e., not to fulfil the obligation of reserve service, and thus to refrain from participation in a more complex mode of protest).

By analogy, it might be argued that Kohlberg's context-free evaluation of Bernhardt's disobedience is not a comprehensive evaluation of the moral dilemma. After all, Bernhardt's nonaction (in Bernhardt's words, an attitude of "let them do their own war") did not prevent the My Lai disaster from happening. Thompson, however, who took an active stand and tried not only to save wounded Vietnamese, but also to prevent further wrongdoing, can be regarded as "active." It seems that the action of disobedience need not be viewed as identical within each context: A disobedient individual's decision not to leave protesting friends, as in the case of the Free Speech Movement arrestees (Haan, Smith, & Block, 1968), is not identical to the Israeli refusers' decision to leave their group of fighting comrades. Kohlberg does not relate disobedience to the content of the action, nor to its contextual moral weight and to the different risks to the self. The refusers, however, indicated these differences when asked to reason on Kohlberg's hypothetical dilemmas:

In the case of Dr. Cohen [Kohlberg's first dilemma on Form B of the MJI], the law does not instruct him what to *do*, but rather what *not* to do [not to perform a mercy killing]. And this is a big difference. In our case, the law instructs us to *do* something that is against our conscience. Here, the active part is the law that enforces the doing, and we say "no."

Moreover, Kohlberg does not specify the extent to which his theory and model can explain the behavior of "doers" and "nondoers" and whether the psychological stress of saying "yes" is equal to that of saying "no." Further analysis of the moral reasoning and attitude of those soldiers who objected to the Lebanon war, yet decided to take part in it and made extra efforts in order to preserve their principles, is required efforts in order to preserve their principles, is required (Linn, 1987). Though the findings suggest that refusers higher on the hierarchy of moral stages experienced more "active" control of their actions, it must also be remembered that this "active" mode was measured while "passive" action was the target of inquiry. It is questionable whether the refusers would hold the same level of moral reasoning and degree of stage consistency if they were called to act in more "active" missions, such as rescuing a friend or an enemy woman from a mine field.

In summing up this paper, it might be helpful to recall Gandhi's statement that "God never occurs to you in person but always in action" (quoted by Erikson, 1970, p. 93). The findings of this study seem to suggest that for these disobedient Israeli soldiers, Kohlberg's morality of justice revealed itself by their exercising of an individualistic, "active" action.

REFERENCES

Blatt, M., Davis, U., & Klinbaum, P. (1975). *Dissent and ideology in Israel: Resistance to the draft (1948/1973)*. London: Ithaca Press.

Blasi, A. (1980). Bridging moral cognition and moral action: A critical review of the literature. *Psychological Bulletin, 88*, 1–45.

Blasi, A. (1983). Moral cognition and moral action: A theoretical perspective. *Developmental Review, 3*, 178–210.

Blasi, A. (1985). The moral personality: Reflection for social science and education. In M. Berkowitz and F. Oser (Eds.), *Moral education: Theory and application* (pp. 433–444). Hillsdale, NJ: Erlbaum.

Brown, R. & Herrnstein, R. J. (1975). *Psychology*. Boston: Little, Brown.

Candee, D. (1976). Structure and choice in moral reasoning. *Journal of Personality and Social Psychology, 34*, 1293–1301.

Cohen, C. (1971). *Civil disobedience: Conscience, tactics, and the law*. New York: Columbia University Press.

Colby, A., Gibbs, J., Kohlberg, L., Speicher Dubin, B., Candee, D., Hewer, A., &

Power, C. (1983). *The measurement of moral judgment: Standard issue scoring manual*. New York: Cambridge University Press.

Damon, W. (1980). Structural developmental theory and the study of moral development. In M. Windmiller, N. Lambert, & E. Turiel (Eds.), *Moral development and socialization*. Boston: Allyn & Bacon.

Durant, W., & Durant, A. (1968). *The lessons of history*. New York: Simon & Schuster.

Emler, N. (1983). Morality and politics: The ideological dimension in the theory of moral development. In H. Weinrich-Haste & Locke (Eds.), *Morality in the making: Thoughts, action, and social context* (pp. 47-70). Chichester, England: Wiley.

Emler, N., Renwick, S., & Bernadette, M. (1983). The relationship between moral reasoning and political orientation. *Journal of Personality and Social Psychology, 45*, 1073-1080.

Erikson, E. H. (1970). *Gandhi's truth: On the origins of militant nonviolence*. London: Faber & Faber.

Gal, R. (1986). *A portrait of the Israeli soldier*. Westport, CT: Greenwood Press.

Fromm, E. (1982). *On disobedience and other essays*. New York: Seabury Press.

Gibbs, J. C., Widaman, K. F., & Colby, A. (1982). Construction and validation of a simplified group administerable equivalent to the moral judgment interview. *Child Development, 53*, 895-910.

Gilligan, C. (1982). *In a different voice*. Cambridge, MA: Harvard University Press.

Gilligan, C., & Murphy, J. M. (1979). Development from adolescent to adulthood: The philosopher and the "dilemma of the fact." In D. Kuhn (Ed.), *Intellectual development beyond childhood: New directions for child development* (pp. 35-99). San Francisco: Jossey-Bass.

Haan, N. (1975). Hypothetical and actual moral reasoning in a situation of civil disobedience. *Journal of Personality and Social Psychology, 32*, 255-269.

Haan, N., Smith, B., & Block, J. (1968). The moral reasoning of young adults. *Journal of Personality and Social Psychology, 10*, 183-201.

Hersh, S. M. (1970). *My Lai 4: A report on the massacre and its aftermath*. New York: Random House.

Kohlberg, L. (1969). Stages and sequence: The cognitive-developmental approach to socialization. In D. A. Goslin (Ed.), *Handbook of socialization theory and research* (pp. 347-480). Chicago: Rand McNally.

Kohlberg, L. (1958). *The development of modes of moral thinking and choice in the years of ten to sixteen*. Unpublished doctoral dissertation, University of Chicago.

Kohlberg, L. (1976). Moral stages and moralization. In T. Lickona (Ed.), *Moral development and behavior: Theory, research, and social issues* (pp. 31-53). New York: Holt, Rinehart & Winston.

Kohlberg, L. (1980). *The meaning and measurement of moral development* (Heinz Werner Lecture). Worcester, MA: Clark University Press.

Kohlberg, L. (1984). *The psychology of moral development*. New York: Harper & Row.

Kohlberg, L., & Candee, D. (1983). The relationship of moral judgment to moral action. In W. Kurtine & J. Gewirtz (Eds.), *Moral behavior and moral development* (pp. 52-73). New York: Wiley.

Krebs, R. & Kohlberg, L. (1973). Moral judgment and ego controls as determinants of resistance to cheating. Cambridge, MA: Center for Moral Education, Harvard University. Mimeo.

Krebs, D., & Rosenwald, A. (1977). Moral reasoning and moral behavior in conventional adults. *Merrill-Palmer Quarterly, 23*, 79-84.

Linn, R. (1985a, November). The moral judgment of the Lebanon war refusers. *Studies in Education*, pp. 19-32. (In Hebrew.)

345

Linn, R. (1985b). Morality in action: The relationship between moral judgment and moral action of Israeli reserve soldiers who refused to serve in Lebanon. *Research in Education*, ED 262367.

Linn, R. (1986a). Conscientious objection in Israel during the war in Lebanon. *Armed Forces and Society, 12*, 489–511.

Linn, R. (1986b). *One action, two moral orientations: Justice and care voices among conscientious objectors*. Unpublished manuscript, Harvard University.

Linn, R. (1987). *The power to act morally: Refusers and Peace Now activists discuss their moral integrity*. Manuscript in preparation.

Locke, D. (1981). Cognitive stage or developmental phases? A critique of Kohlberg's stage structural theory of moral reasoning. *Journal of Moral Education, 8*, 168–181.

Locke, D. (1983a). Doing what comes morally. *Human Development, 26*, 11–25.

Locke, D. (1983b). Theory and practice in thought and action. In H. Weinrich-Haste & D. Locke (Eds.), *Morality in the making: Thoughts, action, and social context* (pp. 157–170). Chichester, England: Wiley.

McNamee, S. (1978). Moral behavior, moral development and motivation. *Journal of Moral Education, 7*, 27–31.

Milgram, S. (1974). *Obedience to authority*. New York: Harper & Row.

Murphy, J. M., & Gilligan, C. (1980). Moral development in late adolescence and adulthood: A criticism and reconstruction of Kohlberg's theory. *Human Development, 23*, 77–104.

Mosher, R. (1980). *Moral education: A first generation of research and development*. New York: Praeger.

Piaget, J. (1965). *The moral judgment of the child*. New York: New Press. (Original work published 1932)

Shiff, Z., & Yaari, E. (1984). *Israel's Lebanon war* (I. Friedman, Ed. and Trans.). New York: Simon & Schuster.

Shiffer, S. (1984). *Snowball: The story behind the Lebanon War*. Tel Aviv: Edanim/Yediot Acharonot Books. (In Hebrew.)

Snarey, J. R., Reimer, J., & Kohlberg, L. (1985). Development of social–moral reasoning among Kibbutz adolescents: A longitudinal cross cultural study. *Development Psychology, 21*, 3–17.

Walzer, M. (1968, January–February). Civil disobedience and "resistance." *Dissent*, pp. 13–15.

Walzer, M. (1970). *Obligations: Essays on disobedience, war and citizenship*. Cambridge, MA: Harvard University Press.

Walzer, M. (1977). *Just and unjust wars*. New York: Basic Books.

Weinrich-Haste, H., & Locke, D. (Eds.). (1983). *Morality in the making: Thoughts, action, and social context*. Chichester, England: Wiley.

Zashin, E. M. (1972). *Civil disobedience and democracy*. New York: Free Press.

Polish Psychological Bulletin
1988, Vol. 19 (1), 43–53.

ADAM NIEMCZYŃSKI
DOROTA CZYŻOWSKA
MARIOS POURKOS
ANDRZEJ MIRSKI

Jagiellonian University
Cracow

THE CRACOW STUDY WITH KOLBERG'S MORAL JUDGMENT INTERVIEW: DATA PERTAINING TO THE ASSUMPTION OF CROSS-CULTURAL VALIDITY

The paper contributes to the body of Kohlbergian cross-cultural research on universality of social-moral development. At the same time, the validity of Kohlberg's measure is examined on a Polish sample. The study follows Snarey's (1985) formulation of empirical assumptions underlying Kohlberg's claim for cross-cultural universality, i.e., culturally diverse sampling, universal moral questions, invariant stage sequence, full range of stages, and general applicability of the stages. The data against which these assumptions are evaluated are cross-selectional and were gathered in 1985-1987. The sample comprises 291 men and women at ages 15 to 80. Although the sample is limited in a number of ways from the perspective of cross-cultural study, it is a reasonably sufficient basis to conclude that the data from Poland generally support each of the assumptions. Some difficulties were identified regarding the range and general application of stages. It is hypothesized that traditional Polish values of individual autonomy and affiliative concern for social ideal and harmony are not adequately representad by the criterion judgments in the present manual (Colby and Kohlberg, in press).

In a critical review of Kohlbergian cross-cultural research Snarey (1985) examined 45 studies from 27 cultural areas. „If this research were begun from scratch, one might have selected 27·somewhat different countries to obtain a larger representation of non-Western traditional folk societies, including hunter-gatherer groups, and of non-capitalist societies, including Eastern European countries" (Snarey, 1985, p. 207). The Cracow study with Kohlberg's *Moral Judgment Interview* provides data from Poland and may partially fill the gap, as far as Poland falls under the second category in Snarey's passage. However, this study was not originally intended to contribute to the cross-cultural universality issue. The primary focus was on post-adolescent cognitive change with social-moral judgment as one of the domains of cognitive development in adulthood.

English language supervision — B. Jankowski. Please send requests for reprints to the first author at Instytut Psychologii, Uniwersytet Jagielloński, ul. Gołębia 13, 31-007 Kraków, Poland.

There are at least two ways in which the social-moral cognitive measure might enter studies of adult intellectual development. One of them is related to Kohlberg's proposal to consider the post-conventional stages in his system to be the adult stages, which are not available in adolescence. There is, thus, room left for adults to continue their development along the Kohlberg scale. The other way of looking at Kohlbergian measures in adults is to acknowledge a suggestion which seems to be warranted both theoretically and partially empirically, that the nature of intelligence changes with age (Labouvie-Vief, 1982; Kramer, 1983; Pascual-Leone, 1983; Baltes, Dittman-Kohli, and Dixon, 1984; Dittman-Kohli and Baltes, 1984; Cavanaugh, Kramer, Sinnott, Camp, and Markley, 1985; Sternberg and Berg, 1986). And the social-moral reasoning ability might be viewed as one of the life-relevant abilities in adulthood, in contrast to other aspects of intelligence which are more life-relevant in adolescence, e.g., Piagetian formal operational intelligence.

The studies we performed with our data make use of social-moral cognitive measures to search the social-moral domain for changes with age and to compare the possibly different patterns of age-differences in the social-moral aspect, on the one hand, and the formal operational aspect of intellectual functioning in adulthood, on the other hand. It is only natural to precede the two studies, which will be reported on elsewhere, with analyses of the validity of Kohlberg's measures in our Polish sample. This is made in this paper, which at the same time contributes to the body of research on cross-cultural universality of social-moral development.

ASSUMPTIONS AND HYPOTHESES

Snarey (1985) derived five empirical assumptions from Kohlberg's claim for the cross-cultural universality of moral development. Kohlberg stated his claim as follows: „All individuals in all cultures use the same thirty basic moral categories, concepts, or principles, and all individuals in all cultures go through the same order or sequence of gross stage development, though they vary in rate and terminal point of development" (Kohlberg, 1971, p. 175). Table 1 contains a brief description of Kohlberg's stages.

All of the five empirical assumptions were discussed by Snarey (1985) as testable hypotheses. These are, (1) a sufficiently wide range of cultural diversity of the samples studied with Kohlberg's method, (2) universality of Kohlberg's moral issues and dilemmas, (3) the same stage-sequence followed in a step-wise order, (4) demonstration of all levels of moral reasoning, and (5) correspondence of all instances of moral reasoning to one of the modes of reasoning described by Kohlberg. Since it is possible to test and empirically support each of the five assumptions in a number of ways depending on the types of data one has, e.g., cross-sectional or longitudinal, it was decided to place both the detailed specification of and predictions from the hypotheses together with the findings in the *Results* section of the paper.

METHOD

Subjects

291 persons participated in the study, 161 females and 130 males. Their age ranged from 15 to 80 years. 15-year-old subjects were students of the eighth grade;

TABLE 1

STAGES OF MORAL DEVELOPMENT ACCORDING TO KOHLBERG (1981)

Stage	What is considered to be right
Stage 1: Obedience and punishment orientation	To avoid breaking rules backed by punishment, obedience for its own sake, avoiding physical damage to persons and property
Stage 2: Instrumental purpose and exchange	Following rules only when it is to someone's immediate interest; acting to meet one's own interests and letting others do the same; right is equal exchange, a good deal
Stage 3: Interpersonal accord and conformity	Living up to what is expected by people close to you or what people generally expect of people in your role; being good is important
Stage 4: Social accord and system maintenance	Fulfilling the actual duties to which you have agreed; laws are always to be upheld except in extreme cases where they conflict with other fixed social duties; right is also contributing to society, a group, or institution
Stage 5: Social contract, utility, individual rights	Being aware that people hold a variety of values and opinions, that most values and rules are relative to your group but should usually be upheld because they are the social contract; some nonrelative values and rights like life and liberty, however, must be upheld in any society regardless of majority opinion
Stage 6: Universal ethical principles	Following self-chosen ethical principles; particular laws or social agreements are usually valid because they rest on such principles; one acts in accordance with the principles; when laws violate these principles, one acts in accordance with the principles; principles are universal principles of justice, equality of human rights and respect to the dignity of human beings as individual persons; the reason for doing right is the belief, as a rational person, in the validity of universal moral principles and a sense of personal commitment

Note: Stage 5 and 6 not distinguished for research purposes; there is also a transition stage (e.g., 2/3) between each two stages.

the older subjects were recruited with the minimal education criterion, which was high school graduation. The method of recruitment consisted of looking for persons meeting the educational, age, and gender criteria in two ways, either by examining the lists of employees of an institution, e.g., a school, a university, a social security agency, etc., or by asking friends, family, and colleagues for help in finding the appropriate persons. After a person was identified to meet the criteria he or she was individually approached and invited to participate. All subjects participated on a volunteer basis.

Interview and scoring

Our research method was Form A of the *Standard Issue Moral Judgment Interview and Scoring System* (Colby and Kohlberg, in press). We have been using

a typescript of the manual obtained from the Harvard Graduate School Center of
Moral Education and Development in July, 1984.

The interview was administered orally in each case, taperecorded, and full
transcription of the material was scored by four scorers. They had quite extensive
experience in scoring before this study was started. The training in scoring was
made in the form group discussions on both scoring procedure and practice cases,
independently scored and jointly discussed. In addition to the training itself, each
of the four scorers had scored, as a part of other studies, at least 15 protocols, up
to 48 protocols in case of one of them.

Inter-rater reliability of scoring was examined about half-way during the
study; 40 pair comparisons resulted in complete agreement in 60% of the cases,
while the agreement within half-stage was 97.5%. One case (2.5%) was scored one
stage apart. Complete agreement is lower than that reported by Colby and
Kohlberg (in press). They have reported 75-88% for Form A with the 9 categories
classification, which is also used in our study. They did not report on the percent
of agreement within half-stage on the 9 point scale, which is 97.5% in our study.
However, they did report on agreement within 1/3 stage on the 13 point scale,
which ranges from 88 to 100%. One may conclude that inter-rater reliability is
generally lower in our study than in the original study. If a simple lack of training
and experience is to be excluded as an explanation, the lower inter-rater
reliability might be taken as a warning that a cultural bias is present in the scoring
system. On the other hand, the actual inter-rater agreement, i.e., 60% of complete
agreement and 97.5% of agreement within half-stage on the 9 point scale, is
sufficiently pronounced to make further data analyses reasonably warranted.

RESULTS AND DISCUSSION

Cultural diversity

Our sample comes from a culture type that is not represented among the 45
samples reviewed by Snarey (1985). Data from Poland evidently enlarge the range
of cultural variety, since only England, Finland, and West Germany represent
Europe in Snarey's cross-cultural review.

The internal diversity of our sample rests on differences in age, gender,
education, living area, and cohort. The cohort differences confound the age
differences, since the data are cross-sectional. As mentioned before, the study was
not originally intended to validate Kohlberg's system for the Polish population.
Thus, the sample is limited in a number of ways from the perspective of
cross-cultural validation study. It does not include children: the youngest
subjects are 15 year old. In addition to adolescents, however, the sample
comprises adults greatly varying in age: 20 through 80 years. It does not include
lower educational groups; the minimum education criterion is relatively high
i.e., high school completed. There are, however, two levels of education
represented by our subjects; one is high school, the other is university level. Both
males and females are included. There are three categories of the living area
variable; i.e., capital of an administrative district or big town, small town, and
village. Broadly speaking, the village might be taken as the culturally most
traditional of the three and the big town as the most modern, with the small town
falling in between. The latter differences, however, are attenuated by having at
least high-school graduates in our sample. And finally, although the cohort
variable is confounded with the age variable, both cohort range, 1905-1970, and
age range, 15-80, are wide enough to represent a vast variety of cultural and

sectional findings cannot be conclusive. Cross-sectional evidence against inva-historical experience. Without losing sight of the above mentioned limitations of the sample from the perspective of cross-cultural validation study, it seems reasonable to conclude that the sample is sufficiently diverse internally to evaluate the next four assumptions of the universality claim and to reach conclusions that would be warranted within the limits of the data.

Universality of moral issues

Kohlberg argued that the dilemmas which serve to elicit moral judgment and reasoning focus on universal issues, e.g., life, property, trust, authority, etc., and represent moral conflict to anyone anywhere. Are Kohlberg's dilemmas culture-bound? Snarey has summarized his discussion of the cross-cultural data which are relevant to this assumption in favor of universality. „Although Kohlberg's interview cannot be culture-free, it does appear to be reasonably culture-fair when the content is creatively adapted and the subject is interviewed in the native language." (Snarey, 1985, p. 215). Our subjects were interviewed in Polish, and a direct translation of Form A dilemmas and the accompanying questions into Polish was the only adaptation. The decision that no content adaptation was necessary has been confirmed during the interviewing. The issues on which the dilemmas are based seem to be truly salient issues in Polish society. It should be remembered that the choice of issue, e.g., life versus law or contract versus authority, does not determine the stage score of a subject. It is the mode of thinking a subject uses to justify his or her choice that counts in stage classification. Thus, even if the issue choice elicited by each dilemma may reflect cultural variation in the stress placed on particular issues, it is still valid to look for universals in the way people reason about the issue. Our subjects more often made the choice of life against law, leniency against punishment, and contract against authority.

In summary, the interview with a direct translation of Kohlberg's Form A dilemmas seems to arouse effectively conflict of values in our subjects, who respond to the dilemma as to real ones, although presented in a hypothetical mode. A cultural testing bias is, nevertheless, still possible in the Polish population even if it seems to be absent in the forms which have been attended to in cross-cultural Kohlbergian research so far. For example, one of the possible ways of cultural bias entering in testing our sample with Kohlberg's interview could emerge with a difference of approach to the dilemmas. If Polish subjects differ from American subjects in construing the moral problem, the way they are asked to answer the standard questions might rather interfere with their lines of thinking than go along with them. This possibility resembles one of the ways Gilligan (1982) presents argument for a bias against women in Kohlberg's system. We shall return to his issue in the section on applicability of stages to our material.

Sequence of stages

It is only in longitudinal research that one can adequately test the hypothesis of invariant sequence, i.e., upward stage development with no stage regression and skipping greater than measurement error, because it involves measurement with the same persons over time. Since our data are cross-sectional so far, the second measurement is planned for 1990, testing with them can also provide evidence in support of the invariant sequence hypothesis, although the cross-

ADAM NIEMCZYŃSKI ET AL.

riant sequence would show absence of a stage between the lowest and highest stages present in the sample as well as irregular and nonsequential relations between stage and age.

TABLE 2

MORAL STAGE FREQUENCY (AND PERCENT) BY AGE

Stage Age	2.5	3	3.5	4	4.5	N
15	3(14)	10(48)	7(33)	1(5)	0(0)	21
20	1(5)	11(50)	10(45)	0(0)	0(0)	22
25	0(0)	5(23)	15(68)	1(5)	1(5)	23
30	0(0)	4(19)	14(67)	3(14)	0(0)	21
35	1(5)	6(30)	12(60)	1(5)	0(0)	20
40	2(10)	6(32)	10(53)	1(5)	0(0)	19
45	0(0)	8(40)	11(55)	1(5)	0(0)	20
50	1(4)	18(69)	5(19)	2(8)	0(0)	26
55	0(0)	10(50)	10(50)	0(0)	0(0)	20
60	0(0)	9(47)	9(47)	1(0)	0(0)	19
65	1(5)	7(35)	12(60)	0(0)	0(0)	20
70	1(5)	15(68)	6(27)	0(0)	0(0)	22
75	0(0)	11(55)	9(45)	0(0)	0(0)	20
80	1(5)	13(68)	5(26)	0(0)	0(0)	19
	11(3.8)	133(45.7)	135(46.4)	11(3.8)	1(.3)	291

Chi-square (52 df) = 69.1063 ($p < .0564$)

The highest stage in our sample, as Table 2 shows, is Stage 4/5, while the lowest one is Stage 2/3. All three stages between these two extreme ones are present, which provides some support of the invariant sequence hypothesis. As to the relation between stage and age, one can notice an upward change in modal stage, i.e., from Stage 3 to Stage 3/4, over the age span of 15 years through 45 years with a stability on Stage 3/4. In turn, looking at modal stage from the age level 55 years till 80 years, one can see the two-modal distributions first, i.e., at age 55 through 65, which are followed by regression to Stage 3 as the modal stage in the groups of 70 through 80; 50-year-old subjects and 65-year-old subjects are the two age groups in the sample which deviate from a regular shape of relation of stage and age in the sample. This is a relation of growth, stabilization, and decline in modal stage with age. The 50-years group, showing a clear downward shift in comparison to both the preceding and the following age groups, includes a slightly greater proportion of women and both men and women with only high school education than the respective proportion in other age groups, the adjacent ones included. These two subgroups demonstrate a tendency to Stage 3 rather than a higher stage in our sample. In contrast to age group 50, the group 65 years includes slightly more men, and men and women at a higher level of education. The imbalance of group composition as to both gender and education is, probably, the source of the downward shift at 50 years and upward shift at 65. The group composition imbalance is attenuated when we collapse the rows of Table 2 into the rows of Table 3, which reports quite regular growth, stability, and decline of modal stage over age.

TABLE 3

MORAL STAGE FREQUENCY (AND PERCENT) BY AGE (14 ROWS OF TABLE 2 COLLAPSED INTO 5 ROWS)

Stage Age	2.5	3	3.5	4	4.5	N
15–20	4(9)	21(49)	17(40)	1(2)	0(0)	43
25–30	1(1.5)	15(24)	41(65)	5(8)	1(1.5)	63
35–45	2(5)	14(36)	21(54)	2(5)	0(0)	39
50–65	2(2)	44(52)	36(42)	3(4)	0(0)	85
70–80	2(3)	39(64)	20(33)	0(0)	0(0)	61
	11(3.8)	133(45.7)	135(46.4)	11(3.8)	1(.3)	291

Chi-square (16 df) = 35.2205 ($p < .0037$)

The regression after age 70 cannot be automatically taken as evidence against an invariant sequence, since (1) Kohlberg's claim was not referred by him to old age, and (2) our cross-sectional data confound age differences with cohort differences. There is no idea in Kohlbergian literature as to how to treat old-age structural regression, if there really is any such regression. The issue parallels the debates over Piagetian formal intelligence changes with age (Hooper, Hooper & Colbert, 1982). On the other hand, even if cohort differences could not explain the cross-sectional decline in our sample, the regular relation of stage and age would still hold, although in the form of growth, stability, and decline. Anyhow, the data seem not to speak against the hypothesis of an invariant sequence of stages but rather support it both by the presence of all stages between the highest and the lowest stages which occur in the sample and by the regular relation between stage and age. If there is documented a stage regression after 70, it would not of necessity contradict the invariant sequence hypothesis; it rather presents an issue to be considered for its own sake.

Stage range

This assumption implies that the full range of moral judgment levels be present in all types of cultures. Snarey's review (1985) reports that Stages 2 to 4 are virtually universal but Stages 1 and 5 are represented in only 67% of the samples. While controlling for age, Snarey (1985) found the cross-cultural data to suggest Stage 1 and 1/2 to be represented in a wide range of cultural groups. However, the distribution of Stages 4/5 and 5 was found to be associated with the type of society, i.e., folk versus urban societies, and the frequency was seldom high in any sample.

There is no Stage 1 through 2 and no full Stage 5 cases and there is only one postconventional Stage 4/5 case in our sample. While full Stage 4 is very low in frequency (3.8% of all cases, see Table 2 or 3), if it is taken together with Stage 3/5 — one can see cases of part or full social system perspective to be almost equally high in frequency as the cases of full (Stage 3) and part (Stage 2/3) interpersonal perspective (see again Table 2 or 3).

Finding no pure preconventional cases, i.e., Stages 1 to 2, is not surprising at all, since the youngest group in our sample is at age 15. That most of the adolescents and adults are at conventional level is a common finding in all other samples reviewed by Snarey (1985). However, one cannot overlook the rarity of full Stage 4 and high frequency of the transient stage, i.e., Stage 3/4, which equals in frequency the full Stage 3 in our sample. It follows that while the two most popular perspectives, which include 93% of the Ss, represent the interpersonal accord and conformity perspective and the social system perspective, the latter one, however, consequently appears in a not-fully-developed form in our data. Before accepting the suggestion that Stage 3/4 really might be the most popular social system perspective among adults in Poland, it seems reasonable to examine a possible cultural bias in the scoring system. We shall focus on this in the next section.

One cannot use the almost complete absence of postconventional cases in our sample, i.e., only one Stage 4/5 case and no full Stage 5 case, to argue against the universality of postconventional stages. In order to make a convincing argument against the presence in a particular culture or society of postonventional cases as they are defined by Kohlberg's system, one would have to interview subjects selected by other members of this population as the most morally mature persons and fail to find postconventional cases among them. No attempt in this direction was made while recruiting Ss for our sample (see again *Method* section). That some postconventional reasoning as well as preconventional thinking is present even in our material, might be shown by the issue scores (see Table 4) which are stage ascriptions of reasoning supporting particular issues of the dilemmas. Nevertheless the relative frequencies of both preconventional and postconventional issue scores remain very low.

TABLE 4

FREQUENCY (AND PERCENT) OF MORAL STAGES: ISSUE SCORES

				Stage				
1	1.5	2	2.5	3	3.5	4	4.5	5
5(.3)	2(.1)	32(1.9)	119(7)	723(42)	600(35)	186(11)	15(.9)	20(1.5)

Note: 291 cases × 6 issues = 1746 issue scores; 39 issue scores are not present in the table because of „no material" in the respective interviews

To examine subgroup differences within a culture or society is another way of approaching the question of the full range of stages. We have found no significant differences between inhabitants of village, small town, and big town while matching 26 subjects from each of these three groups for age, gender, and education level.

As to the gender and education level differences, Table 5 presents the age by stage distribution for each of the four subgroups (male/female x high school/university). We note, as Table 5 shows, a consistently higher level of development within both gender subgroups at the university level in comparison to the respective subgroups at high school level of education. This pattern repeats itself in early, middle, and late adulthood.

Gender differences are not so clear and they seem to depend on education level. The only difference between males and females pertains to age over 70 years in subgroups of high school graduates where men score higher than women. At university level only young females do not differ from young males, while both middle age and later age reveal gender differences in favor of men (see Table 5). The gender differences are more clearly visible when one pays attention to the declines between early and later age within the gender subgroups. Regardless of education level, the decrease in women is somewhat greater, as Table 5 shows, than the decrease in men. It encompasses 24 to 28 AWS points in women, while only 4 to 10 AWS points in men. One can also see that it is the subgroup of men

TABLE 5

EDUCATION LEVEL[a] AND GENDER[b] SUBGROUPS IN RANK ORDER BY AVERAGE WEIGHTED SCORE (AWS)[c],
CONTROLLING FOR AGE

Subgroup/age range	N	Moral stage score (%)[d]		AWS
		3	4	
Level 2, F/20−35	23	26	74	349
Level 2, M/20−35	31	19	81	346
Level 1, F/20−35	19	42	58	329
Level 1, M/20−35	12	42	58	328
Level 2, M/40−65	32	31	69	338
Level 2, F/40−65	28	43	57	323
Level 1, F/40−65	42	64	36	316
Level 1, M/40−65	22	59	41	315
Level 2, M/70−80	9	33	67	342
Level 2, F/70−80	15	67	33	321
Level 1, M/70−80	13	69	31	318
Level 1, F/70−80	24	87.5	12.5	305

a − Two levels: level 1 − high school graduation, and level 2 − university level

b − Gender: F − female, M − male

c − Average Weighted Score (AWS) -a continuous rather than categorical measure of moral development

d − Part (Stage 2/3) and full (Stage 3) interpersonal accord perspective are taken together under Stage 3, while part and full social system maintenance perspective (Stages 3/4 and 4) are grouped under the Stage 4 heading

with university education which is the only one with practically no decline throughout the span of life from 20 to 80 years.

Although our data are classified almost exclusively to conventional stages, the patterns of differences between subgroups might be viewed as strongly suggesting that the lower the level of education the more carefully one should control for a possible scoring and interviewing bias against lower-educated people. The same seems to be true with reference to women, whose moral voice (Gilligan, 1982) might be incompletely reflected by the standard manual (Colby and Kohlberg, in press). The women voice does not seem to be underestimated in young adulthood in comparison to men's reasoning, but at middle and later age it deserves a closer examination to exclude a possible bias against women at these ages. On the other hand, it is still possible that the quality of experience which might be associated with social position determined by both education and sex role, can explain away the observed differences in performance.

It seems plausible to conclude the discussion of the fourth empirical aspect of the cross-cultural validity of Kohlberg's system with an open question. While our data cannot be taken to contradict Kohlberg's universality claim, they strongly suggest a possibility of incompleteness either in the stage definitions or in the scoring manual, which might be insufficient in representing both the Stage 4 perspective and the perspective of postconventional stages as they are elaborated in Poland. We shall consider this possibility in the next section, which is focused on the last of the assumptions of the universality claim.

General applicability of stages

That all instances of moral reasoning will correspond to one of the modes of reasoning described by Kohlberg, is what the last assumption is all about. One should remember that the process of matching interview responses to examples in the scoring manual does not consist of finding elements that are literally identical. Kohlberg's stages rely on the distinction between structure and content. The reasoning may be the same even though the issues attended to may be different as well as the circumstances and details may widely differ and modify the problem in many ways.

Snarey (1985) reviewed all cross-cultural studies for empirical observations and specific examples of moral judgments that were difficult to score, since the presence of such material could call this final assumption into question. The researchers have reported such materials from Israeli kibbutz, India, Taiwan, Papua New Guinea, and Kenya. The evidence of this difficult material suggests to Snarey "that some culturally unique moral judgments do not appear in the theory or scoring system. Collective or communalistic principled reasoning, in particular, is missing or misunderstood." (Snarey, 1985, p. 226).

As to our data, they are generally supportive of the assumptions underlying Kohlberg's theory and we can find at least some reasoning at each of the stages. Yet the infrequency with which interviews were scored as using either full Stage 4 or postconventional reasoning, induced us to wonder whether Poles are usually missing the higher levels of moral judgment or whether Kohlberg's scoring manual does not include Polish expressions of the higher level reasoning. One way of looking for an answer to this question was to examine the frequency with which the different criterion judgments, i.e., examples in the scoring manual of reasoning at a particular stage, were used in the scoring process to match interview judgments. We found that some of the criterion examples were matched to our Polish subjects' judgments very frequently. We also found that the most frequently matched criterion judgments seem to be related to the Polish traditional values of human individual autonomy and affiliative concern for social ideal and harmony. It is our hypothesis, to be tested in a further study, that this selection of scorable interview judgments brought about a tendency to centralize subjects' responses into conventional Stages 3 and 3/4 because examples of these values are either absent or differently elaborated in the criterion judgments given in the manual (Colby and Kohlberg, in press) for Stage 4 and postconventional stages.

REFERENCES

Baltes, P. B., Dittmann-Kohli, F., & Dixon, R. (1984). New perspectives on the development of intelligence in adulthood: Toward a dual-process conception and a model of selective optimization with compensation. In P. Baltes & D. Brim (Eds.). *Life-span development and behavior* (Vol. 6, pp. 33–76). New York: Academic Press.

Cavanaugh, J., Kramer, D., Sinnott, J. D., Camp, C., & Markley, R. P. (1985). On missing links and such: Interfaces between cognitive research and everyday problem solving. *Human Development,* 26, 146–168.

Colby, A., & Kohlberg, L. (in press). *The measurement of moral judgment.* New York: Cambridge University Press.

Dittmann-Kohli, F., & Baltes, P. B. (1984). Towards an action-theoretical and pragmatic conception of intelligence during adulthood and old age. In C. N. Alexander & E. Landerg (Eds.). *Beyond formal operations: Alternative end-points to human development.*

Gilligan, C. (1982). *In a different voice: Psychological theory and women development.* Cambridge: Harvard University Press.

Hooper, F. H., Hooper, J. O., & Colbert, K. K. (1982). *Personality and memory correlates of intellectual functioning: Young adulthood and old age.* Final research project report. Spencer Foundation.

Kohlberg, L. (1971). From is to ought: How to commit the naturalistic fallacy and get away with it in the study of moral development. In L. Mischel (Ed.). *Cognitive development and epistemology* (pp. 151–284). New York: Academic Press.

Kohlberg, L. (1981). *The philosophy of moral development: Moral stages and the idea of justice. Vol. I: Essays on moral development.* San Francisco: Harper and Row.

Kramer, D. A. (1983). Post formal operations? A need for further conceptualization. *Human Development, 26,* 91–105.

Labouvie-Vief, G. (1982). Dynamic development and mature autonomy: A theoretical prologue. *Human Development, 25,* 161–191.

Pascual-Leone, J. (1983). Growing into maturity: Toward a metasubjective theory of adulthood stages. In P. B. Baltes & O. Brim (Eds.). *Life-span development and behavior* (Vol. 5, pp. 118–156). New York: Academic Press.

Snarey, J. R. (1985). Cross-cultural universality of social-moral development: A critical review of Kohlbergian research. *Psychological Bulletin, 97,* 202–232.

Sternberg, R. J., & Berg, C. A. (1986). *What are theories of intellectual development theories about?* Manuscript submitted for publication.

(Received July, 1987)

Hum. Dev. *30:* 105–118 (1987)

Moral Stage Sequence and Principled Reasoning in an Indian Sample[1]

Jyotsna Vasudev, Raymond C. Hummel

University of Pittsburgh, Pittsburgh, Pa., USA

Key Words. Cross-cultural differences · India · Kohlberg · Moral development · Postconventional reasoning

Abstract. This study investigated the cross-cultural generality of Kohlberg's stages of moral development in India. A sample of 112 males and females between 11 and 50-plus years was drawn from an urban middle- and upper-middle-class population and interviewed individually on Kohlberg's dilemmas. A two-way analysis of variance performed on the moral maturity scores indicates a significant effect of age ($p < 0.001$) but a nonsignificant effect of sex. A qualitative analysis of postconventional reasoning among Indian adults revealed two themes: (a) the adaptation of principles to real-life dilemmas; and (b) the integration of indigenous moral and philosophical values in principled thought. These findings support the cross-cultural generality of Kohlberg's model of moral development; they also raise cross-cultural issues in morality which cannot be assimilated in an overly formalized theory of moral reasoning.

Kohlberg's theory of moral development charts a universal course along which each individual is seen actively to construct increasingly complex, hierarchical, and more adequate systems of moral thought. This construction represents an invariant sequence of definable, qualitatively different stages of moral reasoning. Following a Piagetian model of equilibration, Kohlberg emphasizes that movement through this sequence involves not simply a reactive internalization of cultural norms, values, and beliefs, but also a proactive transformation of structures of moral thought.

A most controversial feature of Kohlberg's theory is his assumption that the developmental sequence he discerns is culturally universal. Research in various cultures tends to support his claim of universal sequence through preconventional and conventional stages [Snarey, 1985]. The infre-

[1] This paper is based on the first author's doctoral dissertation. We would like to thank Clark Powers and Anne Higgins for scoring the interviews, and our anonymous reviewers for their critical suggestions.

quent appearance of postconventional reasoning in cross-cultural studies, however,
has produced counterclaims that this stage
may be specific to Western cultures. Some
critics have objected to Kohlberg's reliance
on Western philosophies and have described
his 'universal' scheme as ethnocentric, elitist, and overly abstract [Buck-Morss, 1975;
Simpson, 1974; Sullivan, 1977].

Critics of Kohlberg's claims of universality have tended to take either a relativistic or
a constructivist stance [Kohlberg et al.,
1983]. The relativists deem it inappropriate
to theorize about universal aspects of morality. In a radical critique, Shweder [1982], for
example, denies the similarity across cultures of forms of moral reasoning and of a
developmental stage sequence; he declares
that the 'orthodox Piagetian paradigm' is on
the wane, and ridicules Kohlberg's 'quest for
a rationally dictated objective morality.'

The constructivists share Kohlberg's am-
bition to describe higher, more adequate
stages of morality, but some differ in their
definitions of principled thought. Gibbs
[1977] proposes a distinction between structural and existential phases of development.
He views postconventional thought as a
philosophical, existential phase of adult development. The Piagetian structural stage
model which Kohlberg applies to childhood
and adolescent reasoning, according to
Gibbs, is insufficient to describe postconventional thought. Murphy and Gilligan
[1980] propose that postconventional
thought is not purely formal and abstract, as
Kohlberg believes, but primarily contextual.
Gilligan [1982] describes morality in terms
of an ethic of care, responsibility, and nonviolence; she distinguishes her framework
from Kohlberg's deontological conception of
rights, duties, and justice.

In responding to his critics, Kohlberg
[Kohlberg et al., 1983] asserts his metaethical assumption of universalism. As a 'methodological non-relativist,' he continues to
believe that there are universally applicable
values and rational, analytical, formal methods for describing these values. Justice,
Kohlberg maintains, is at the heart of rational morality. At the highest stage, principles of justice are rational, reversible, universalizable, comprehensive, and prescriptive. His emphasis on universality, as both a
philosophical and an empirical claim, implies a search 'for some minimal value conceptions on which all persons could agree
regardless of differences in detailed aims or
goals' [Kohlberg et al., 1983, p. 93]. Kohlberg argues that postconventional reasoning
has been evidenced in a sufficient variety of
cultures to encourage the search [Snarey,
1985].

Rationale for the Study

The debate over the universality of higher
stages is complicated not only by a paucity of
data on the moral reasoning of adults from
different cultures but also by differing conceptions of principled morality. This research was designed to study moral reasoning in the context of Indian culture. Its objectives were twofold: First, to test the generality of Kohlberg's stage sequence for different
ages and sexes in another culture; second, to
examine adult thought and principled reasoning in a non-Western context.

The cultures of the East, such as India,
provide an optimal setting for testing the generality of higher stages. India contains sociocultural settings that are as structurally complex as those in Western societies, and it is

home to a class of adults who have had adequate educational and sociocultural opportunities to progress to higher stages of reasoning. Despite the wide influence of Western ideas, Indian indigenous traditions, religions, and philosophies, with their unique conceptions of morality, also have evolved and prevailed. To assess the validity of Kohlberg's scheme, one may thus seek in an Indian sample an evident representation of his stages, including a postconventional stage.

In an open inquiry, one may also expect to find culturally-shaped forms of moral thought which are not described or anticipated in Kohlberg's framework. Nisan and Kohlberg [1982] recognize this possibility. They observe that a claim to universality does not imply that Kohlberg's scheme encompasses 'the whole domain' of morality in every culture: 'It is possible that in other cultures, principles are held which are distinct from ours, and moral reasoning is used that does not fit the structure described by Kohlberg' [Nisan and Kohlberg, 1982, p. 874].

Method of the Study

Moral reasoning interviews were conducted with 112 males and females in seven different age groups between 11 and 50-plus years. The sample was drawn from an urban middle- and upper-middle-class population. This was done to maximize the recruitment of persons who might evidence higher stages of reasoning. Movement to higher stages, according to Kohlberg and other investigators, is associated with formal education and participation in complex social institutions. The sample was controlled to exclude Indians who had lived much of their lives abroad, or were Muslims, Christians, or Parsees. Its religious representation was Hindus, Jains, and Sikhs. The latter groups share a common religious heritage and can be considered as a homogeneous group.

Individuals in the 11–13 and 15–17 age groups were drawn from two English medium schools in Jaipur for girls and boys, respectively. All these individuals were recommended by their teachers. The adults were contacted and interviewed in three cities: Jaipur, Calcutta, and Delhi. The adult women and men represented a wide variety of professions, such as teachers, lawyers, doctors, engineers, and civil servants.

Each person was interviewed on three standard hypothetical dilemmas from Form A (Heinz, Officer Brown, and Joe). Given the multitude of languages and dialects in India, all interviews were conducted in English, which is a common language among most educated Indians. The taped interviews were transcribed and scored by an expert scorer using the revised scoring manual [Colby et al., 1983]. The moral maturity scores (MMS) were based on four rather than six issues.[2] To establish the interrater reliability, all interviews were sorted into five groups according to the following global stages: 2/3, 3, 3/4, 4, and 4/5 and 5. Three protocols, a total of 15, were randomly selected from each group and rescored by another expert scorer. There was 60% exact agreement, 93% agreement within half a stage, and a 0.93 correlation between the two scorers.

Analysis of Stage Sequence by Age and Sex

To test for effects of age, sex, and age × sex interaction, a two-way analysis of variance was performed on the MMS. The results indicate an effect of age, $F_{(6, 98)} = 13.00$, significant at the 0.001 level. Post hoc Scheffé analysis reveals that only the mean of the youngest age group, 11–13 years, is significantly lower than the means of the other age groups. The lack of significant separation among the other groups is understandable because conventional stages are common to both adolescents and adults [Reimer et al., 1983].

[2] Scores on 4 versus 6 issues in form A were compared using Kohlberg's longitudinal sample between 10 and 30 years. This sample had ben used to establish the reliability and validity for his scoring manual [Colby et al., 1983]. Results show an agreement between 63 and 79% on global stage scores and correlations from 0.94 to 0.95.

Table I. Percentage of subjects at each stage by age

Age years	Stage							
	1	1/2	2	2/3	3	3/4	4	4/5 and 5
11–12		6.2		56.2	31.2	6.2		
15–17				6.2	75.0	12.5	6.2	
21–23					25.0	43.8	25.0	6.2
24–28					18.8	56.2	12.5	12.5
30–35					43.8	18.8	18.8	18.8
40–45					21.4	42.9	21.4	14.3
50+					22.2	33.3	38.8	5.5

Table I presents the percentages of individuals at different stages by age. The subjects with a mixed score, i.e., with 20% of their reasoning at another stage, were included in the mixed-stage category. For example, subjects with mixed stages 3(4), 3/4, and 4(3) were all included in the mixed category 3/4. The data in table I show a shift in percentages with increasing age. Although derived from a cross-sectional sample, the data agree with those on moral development obtained from longitudinal samples in the United States, Turkey, and Israel [Snarey, 1985]. The mean MMSs increase steadily from ages 11 to 28 years, when the level of moral reasoning stabilizes.

In the 11–13 age group, as table I shows, 56% of the preadolescents are in the mixed stage 2/3, reflecting a transition from preconventional to conventional forms of reasoning; 31% already are consolidated at stage 3. Other research on middle-class preadolescents has reported a slower rate of development; in those findings, stage 2 remains predominant and stage 3 only begins to emerge [Reimer et al., 1983].

In the Indian 15–17 age group, 75% of the adolescents are at stage 3 compared with 31% of the 11–13 year olds. In the 21–23 year age group, 25% are at stage 3, 44% are in transition between stages 3 and 4, and 25% are at stage 4. Beyond the 21–23 age group, no significant shift is evident in the percentages across the various stages; the majority of the adults are at stages 3/4 or 4, with some in every age group at 4/5 and 5, and none at preconventional stages.

An analysis of variance reveals no significant difference between the reasoning of males and females,

$F(1, 98) = 2.37$, $p > 0.13$, and no age $\times$ sex interaction, $F(6, 98) = 1.30$, $p > 0.26$. Combining these results shows no sex differences in the reasoning of males and females in any of the age groups. Walker's [1984] extensive review indicates that when sex differences in moral reasoning appear, usually favoring the males, these differences are likely to be associated with limited opportunities for females in personal decision-making, of education, and occupation. Since such opportunities are available to both the male and female subjects in this study, the finding of no sex differences is expected.

Postconventional Reasoning

The moral reasoning of about 11% of the Indian adults age 21 and over was scored as postconventional. This finding is consistent with the implications of Kohlberg's revised theory and scoring system [Colby et al., 1983]. In the revised scoring system, only adults attain fully principled reasoning. In this study as well, no person under age 21 was scored as postconventional.

From a cross-cultural perspective, the comparable percentage of postconventional subjects gives support to Kohlberg's claim that principled thinking is not simply a Western phenomenon. Higher stages of reasoning do appear, as Kohlberg suggests, in a complex society among persons who have had adequate social, educational, and role-taking opportunities. In his review of cross-cultural studies, Snarey [1985], commenting on the absence of stages 4/5 and 5 reasoning in tribal or village folk societies, observes that principled reasoning actually may be associated more with urbanization than with Westernization per se.

It may be protested, given India's long colonization by the British and her openness to the West, that postconventional Indian reasoning is not representative, but a reflection of substantial Western education and socialization. Without denying the Western influence, one must give significant credit to India's own cultural, philosophic, and spiritual heritage. Principles of justice, nonviolence, freedom, and human dignity, independent of and predating Western philosophers, can readily be discerned in Indian traditions [Vasudev, 1986].

In the context of this study, the reasoning over moral dilemmas by some Indian persons provides a resource for inquiring into the nature of postconventional morality, into how principles may be adapted to real-life dilemmas, and how indigenous moral values may inform principled thinking.

Adaptation of Principles to Action in Real-Life Dilemmas

Among the criticisms of Kohlberg's theory for its emphasis on abstraction and formalism is the claim that it has failed to take sufficient account of the dialectics of development. In the simplest dialectical formula-tion, moral reasoning informs action, and action in turn restructures thought. In adults especially, postconventional reasoning involves more than a formal application of principles; it entails an equilibration between logical principles and the contextual particulars of a conflict. In this dialectical process, thought is restructured and a synthesis achieved which supersedes the formal implications of the principles themselves [Labouvie-Vief, 1980; Murphy and Gilligan, 1980; Perry, 1970].

In his rejoinder to critics, Kohlberg [Kohlberg et al., 1983] concedes the need for further explication of the relation between reasoning and action, but he argues that the focus on reasoning itself is justified. He does not construe principles to be immutable rules, impervious to the demands of real life. In application, moral principles do not presuppose actual solutions but perforce are adapted to real-life conditions. This adaptive application, however, does not render the principles arbitrary or invalid.

In a standard Kohlberg interview, Heinz's situation is posed as a 'hypothetical' dilemma. Many of the Indian subjects, however, saw this as an immediate and 'real' dilemma. Heinz's predicament signified the mass deprivations, poverty, and social injustice observable across the Indian scene. By viewing Heinz as real rather than as a hypothetical person faced with a terrible choice, these subjects in fact addressed moral choices, actions, and consequences as they might in real situations. Given this fact, the reasoning of these Indians reflects the tension between the ideal and real, a tension familiar to adults who commonly face moral choices.

In the following excerpts, 2 respondents describe the alarming parallel between the dilemmas of Heinz and of every poor Indian. 'What should Heinz do?' becomes a real rather than a hypothetical question, one they have faced frequently. Heinz's problem is viewed not as an independent case to be solved within its own terms, but as a symptom of larger socioeconomic failures that require some resolution at a 'macro level.'

Interview No. 1, Woman, Age 40

[What should Heinz do?] The problems that Heinz is up against are not individual problems that are afflicting 1 or 2 Heinzes of the world. These are social problems. Forget Heinz in Europe, just come to India and you are speaking of the same thing with 60% of the people living below the poverty line. In fact, Heinz's story is being repeated all around us all the time with wives dying, with children dying, and there is no money to save them.... So Heinz in his individual capacity – yes, okay, steal the drug, but it's not going to make any difference on a larger scale; and if his wife dies it is not going to make any difference on a larger scale. I don't think in the final analysis a solution can be worked out on an individual basis.... It will probably have to be tackled at a macro level.

This person's views are not confined to conventional rules: She accepts stealing to save lives; she weighs the importance, moreover, of a single theft in relation to a complex situation.

I am not against stealing under conditions like these.... If a poor man steals so he can feed his children or because his wife is dying, that is not even theft. I feel it is the society which has driven him to that.... So if I could help Heinz, I would go along with him but I would try to tell him, sweetheart, this is not going to solve anything in the end. It might solve a particular problem.... There is a much larger problem Heinz will have to appreciate at some stage or another if he really wants to do something.

Throughout her interview, she construes these protagonists in the hypothetical stories as real people facing endless problems of survival. At every opportunity, she stresses the responsibility of each actor in the Heinz drama to remain aware of the social ramifications of Heinz's situation. When asked what the judge should do with the guilty Heinz, she says:

(As a judge,) I have been through this case; this is the first theft in Heinz's life. I have seen the extenuating circumstances under which he has done it.... I would lecture the jury on the social evils in society and about private property which makes men like Heinz resort to a step like this. The social implications of this case are very important. I would highlight those to the press and in the court to the best of my ability. Heinz is a victim of the society.... It is the failure of the state to provide any relief and to discourage monopoly of such drugs.... I would insist that the state treat Mrs. Heinz. I don't think I would like Heinz to think I am encouraging him to go around stealing. But I think I would try to get him to realize that this is not a solution. The solution is a more collective, social one.

In the second example, a man uses the Heinz dilemma to reconstruct a real-life situation in which he was confronted with a moral choice. He conveys the conflict between one's ideals and the reality in which one struggles to realize those ideals. From experience he explains why duties and rights cannot be exactly correlative. He is undoubtedly postconventional: He values principles encompassed in Kohlberg's conception of morality, but he also questions the impact of single solutions on a larger problem.

Interview No. 2, Man, Age 28

If Heinz does not love his wife, it is more complicated. My feeling still would be that one is talking within a code of ethics and he should steal the drug. (Why?) Because if one has to make a choice between stealing of a civic kind and letting a person die, if one has the power to prevent that death, it would be a moral crime not to. I think a civic crime is easier to bear than moral crime. (Why?) If you do not act, it is belittling yourself as a moral human being. I would tend to react against the person who deprives me of my basic rights of humanity.

[Would you steal for a stranger?] Although one values human rights and dignity, it becomes difficult to prescribe what Heinz should do for a stranger, because once again it is not an individual problem. If there were a few strangers dying of cancer or hunger or whatever, it would be easy to say, yes, one ought to steal. But when one is faced with innumerable people dying for different reasons, it is not possible to say one ought to steal even if one values life ideally.

Let me describe an actual similar situation. I was in a village with friends, one of whom was a doctor who had been doing educational programs for the last 5 years. A villager came, said his wife was dying and that he needed 400 rupees to transport his wife to the hospital. There was no surety of his wife surviving. After he made his appeal, we discussed this as a group. The choices were first to take a human stand, give him the money, and try to save the life. As a social choice, however, it becomes more complicated: the group understood that even if the woman was saved, her ability to survive would depend on the conditions of the village – whether she would be able to get a job, whether the villagers would take care of her or not, since the group was in no position to undertake her care. More important, the group did not feel responsible to get into this relief act, because they were there to understand the social situation and if possible to change it. The other major point that came out was that if they made one such choice for the person, they would have to do the same thing for any other person, which is kind of a logical expectation. In spite of much heart-rending, they decided they would not help. Coming back to the Heinz situation, if there is no specific personal bond, and if your understanding is that a lot of people are going to continue to die because of the particular social situation, than I don't see how Heinz or anyone is bound to save the life of a specific stranger. It is not only an issue of violating civic laws but really an issue of how one understands the issue of charity.

[Would you explain?] The notion of charity is based on the understanding that the individual makes an attempt to intervene in a social situation to change something. Having accepted the situation based on principles, they do whatever is in their ability to take care of the distressed or poor or disadvantaged people. Now as a personal act, a personal choice, I have no major complaint against it. But as a strategy of social action, it leads to total nonquestioning of existing structures. In that sense, I think it is an etiology of nonaction. If Heinz thinks clearly [about the stranger], within any society there will be a large number of underprivileged people who will die not only because they are hungry or poor. And if Heinz extends the same kind of argument to every case, he would go mad trying to take care of it. It is better to reach some objective conclusions about why such situations recur in the social order. Then it is important for Heinz to act as per this analysis. It is more important to see how change can be brought about and to put effort into that process.

In both these examples, the respondents, construing Heinz's status as real rather than hypothetical, are reluctant to prescribe that Heinz should steal to save a life. This position does not indicate a lack of postconventional reasoning but ensues from their experience and knowledge of a social reality in which principles are acted upon and tested to their limits. Their regard for collective social resolutions is not an endorsement of conventional social standards but a principle in favor of socially and morally responsible solutions which cannot, should not, under their conceptions of justice, be the burden of a single individual.

The distinctions in these protocols between individual and 'macro level' solutions, between personal charity and collective social actions, are not recognized in Kohlberg's scoring criteria. In his review of 45 studies across 27 countries, Snarey [1985] found similar incompleteness in Kohlberg's theoretical model and scoring manual. Among Israeli kibbutz members, for example, Snarey cites instances of a principle of 'cooperative equality and equal right ot happiness' which is 'more mature than Kohlberg's definition of stage 4 but missing from Kohlberg's definition of stage 5' [Snarey, 1985, p. 223]. The principles underlying the social collective solutions advanced by these Indian interviewees appear to be counterpart to those of Snarey's kibbutz members, and similarly postconventional.

It is possible to explain the reasoning of these respondents alternatively using Kohlberg's concept of principled reasoning and the point of view of his critics who emphasize contextually relevant reasoning. Riegel [1973], a critic of the structural models of development and of universalistic orientations, might have viewed these instances of reasoning as codetermined by factors of history, practical social significance, intent, and motivation. Sullivan [1977], from his 'critical social' viewpoint, might note that these respondents do not treat Heinz as an isolated, independent entity; nor do they bifurcate reasoning from action. Employing arguments from Perry [1970], Labouvie-Vief [1980], and Murphy and Gilligan [1980], one might interpret these excerpts as examples of contextual thinking by persons striving to balance formal conceptions of morality with the exigencies of real-life conflicts. Stealing to save a single life may not be universalizable, for example, where a multitude of lives are in jeopardy.

Kohlberg might rejoin with his metaethical assumptions, in particular, that principles are not absolute rules to be implemented blindly in real life. These excerpts might exemplify for him '...the difficulties encountered in getting clarity or consensus on their application to concrete situations' [Kohlberg et al., 1983, p. 147]. The principles advanced in these interviews might also be interpreted as congruent with Kohlberg's concept of postconventional morality. In

Kohlberg's scheme, their reasoning was scored at stage 4/5. They deferred from prescribing that Heinz should steal to save a life, but their regard for human life is neither conventional nor relative, and their application of principles to real-life situations is neither simplistic nor arbitrary.

Both Kohlberg and his critics provide cogent arguments for their respective points of view; one would not wish to trivialize the differences between them. But it seems instructive that these Indian respondents express mature moral positions which embody contextual, dialectical, and principled elements. If such elements were essentially polar or incompatible, would they be so intertwined in the reasoning of these obviously sophisticated thinkers? May principled and contextual reasoning be understood better as complementary than as exclusive? These questions imply the need for an integrated theory that would recognize the interlock between moral principles and actions which are predicated on those principles. When one freezes reasoning in either direction one tends to limit and compromise the meaning of morality.

The complementarity between principles and action has been discussed by other writers as well. According to Edelstein and Noam [1982], the contradiction between 'rationally focussed problem-solving' and 'actual decision-making' requires a redefinition of formal principles. This is done

...not by restricting its universality through reparticularization of the formal norm, but by establishing meta-rules that permit transcending the restrictions of the principle in view of the case.... By demonstrating the principle's inadequacy in handling the practical problem, the problematic case reveals limits to the principle's applicability and thus to its universality. At the same time, the meta-rule, by attending to the particular, ascertains the universalizability of the principle. This is done by appeal to an adequacy judgment guided both by principle and the particular situation that elicits its use [p. 415].

Principles of Justice and of Nonviolence

Kohlberg's assumption of universality has made his theory notably different from theories which are premised on the concept of cultural relativism. Kohlberg [Kohlberg et al., 1983] has been searching for some 'minimal value' concepts which will be universally relevant regardless of other differences among cultures. At the heart of Kohlberg's theory is justice; at the highest level, principles of justice, as noted earlier, are autonomous, universal, prescriptive, and reversible; they affirm as universal the values of human dignity, equality, and freedom.

Kohlberg maintains that one may begin with different philosophies and still arrive at universalizable principles. The philosophies Kohlberg relies on, however, are all Western and mainly in the formalistic tradition (Kant, Hare, Dewey, and Rawls). Critics thus have identified a possible contradiction in Kohlberg's thesis and his assumption of universalism. Sullivan [1977] notes that by attributing universality to his scheme, Kohlberg makes stage 6, which is morally and structurally most adequate and equilibrated, 'the' rather than 'a' model of a moral person. Simpson [1974] also objects to the assumption of universality because Kohlberg, in her view, has not examined the meaning of morality in the non-Western world.

One can agree, generally, that the moral values central to Kohlberg's thesis have roots in Western systems of thought. This does not preclude Kohlberg's framework, however, from embodying core moral values and

models of moral persons from non-Western philosophies. In the absence of data on the diversity of moral principles and philosophies across cultures, however, both Kohlberg's philosophical stance and the admonitions of his critics do not lead to any sustained discussion of their differences. This inquiry is in part an effort to expedite such discussion.

In this study, some interviewees spontaneously reflected on the differences between Western and Indian philosophies. Their responses suggest at least two related moral values, rooted in the Indian tradition, that are not a part of Western philosophy or of Kohlberg's conception of morality. These are the principles of nonviolence and the related value of all life. These moral concepts can be traced to pre-Christian philosophies in India and are central in the views of major Indian thinkers and mystics, as well as the respondents in this study. These values thus have originated and developed independently of Western systems of thought. Nonviolence and the value of all life are analogous to Kohlberg's view of justice where the latter embodies respect for human life, personality, and dignity, and is nonrelativistic, universal in scope. This complementarity between meanings of justice and nonviolence suggests their universal relevance and prevalence.

Ahimsa (nonviolence) in the Hindu tradition is identified as a cardinal virtue. In essence an axiomatic principle, it prescribes a fundamental obligation based on the sanctity of life. Ahimsa is to Indian thought as justice is to Kohlberg's theory. From the ancient scriptures to the modern philosophies, this concept occupies a central position. The Mahabharata states that 'nonviolence is the highest religion, the highest penance, the highest truth from which all other virtues proceed.' Although the notion takes some form in every Indian tradition, in Jainism it became an absolute law of life and an influence over every aspect of life and behavior. In the Jain scriptures this principle was generalized to animal and plant life as well.

In Jainism, ahimsa is based on the simple recognition that 'for all sorts of living things pain is unpleasant, disagreeable, and greatly feared'; knowing one's own pain and observing it in others, a true Jain ought not to augment pain in any form. The Jain scriptures introduce a hierarchical order of life in terms of the number of senses living organisms possess; the rule of life is to partake of that which has the minimum number of senses, such as plants, fruits, and nuts.

Respect for all forms of life in the Indian tradition is related to a salient characteristic of Indian thought, one which construes reality as an integral whole. This principle minimizes duality and emphasizes connectedness and harmony. This monistic view of reality leads to a view of nature in which life is classified in terms of degrees of consciousness. 'The difference between a person and an animal or tree is the degree of consciousness each exhibits. Man exhibits a much higher degree than a tree; however, they have a sentiency as a common characteristic' [Bishop, 1975a, b, p. 372].

Hinduism has always maintained a philosophic basis for respecting nature. Crawford [1982] contrasts the Hindu view of man in nature, which is biocentric, with the Western view of man and nature, which is rather anthropocentric. The Hindu view leads to an environmental ethic. It allows one to comprehend the world as a dynamic equilibrium of interrelated systems 'within which man must play his part as a responsible spectator

and participant. In the balance of ecology, the responsibility or irresponsibility of an act is defined by its ability to preserve or to destroy the integrity of the biotic community' [Crawford, 1982, p. 150].

In this study, several people discussed the value of life and nonviolence from their comprehensive perspectives on life. The moral views of these subjects are personal statements guided by their philosophical and spiritual reflections. In the first excerpt, an interviewee differentiates between the Western and Indian traditions and defines the centrality of nonviolence as a moral goal.

Interview No. 3, Man, Age 35

In any moral situation you have to have some end values. I would say that to save life or not to take it away, as far as possible, would be a goal. Human life being the best expression of life that we know of, one should try to save it rather than let it end.... An ethical problem usually involves another conscious human being who has a sense of responsibility, of morality, similar to yours, and where you know that doing something against him can cause him pain or degradation. I think that in the Western tradition any action involving another person can have moral overtones. But in some traditions, the Indian, for example, it has been thought that any action that involves any form of life, any creature which cannot react towards your action as would a human being, should still be considered a valued life.... Moral situations are not limited to relations between men alone but are extended to other forms of life.

[Should one do everything possible to save any life?] I am not a pacifist to that extent. That would amount to being a Jain Sadhu [a monk] who does everything possible as a human being not to kill, to save the life of any creature. This involves an extremist view, in which one value is the sole value to follow. In a reasonably well-lived human life, some kinds of creatures have to be killed. In the Mahabharat, there are two kinds of moral ends in terms of 'Ahimsa' [nonviolence]. One is nonviolence of the saint who has given up all social living and who does not, on principle, kill even if someone comes to kill him. The path suggested for ordinary human beings is 'Aanrishan', that is, not to be cruel, to avoid unnecessary killing. Since I believe other ends are also worthwhile, I would vote for the second idea.

Interview No. 4, Man, Age 50

In the next interview, another respondent applies the Indian philosophical notions to the Heinz dilemma. His interview reflects the primacy of Indian ethical and spiritual ideals in his moral conception. His reasoning is not simply an iteration of conventional values; he presents a moral point of view in which received values are interpreted at a postconventional level. In accord with Kohlberg's view of principled morality, he distinguishes between laws of conscience and legal rules. His reference to 'conscience' as a source of superior laws appears to emanate from the ancient Vedas. In the Vedanta, conscience is identified as the highest source of knowledge about righteousness and is placed above every other source of authority. Conscience is described as 'what is agreeable to one's heart and born of careful thought,' that 'which gives satisfaction to one's antaratma [inner self].' When asked what Officer Brown should do with Heinz, whom he caught stealing, this man said:

By letting Heinz go, Officer Brown will be doing a greater duty towards man, because to serve humanity is the ultimate end of all existence. This may not be right according to principles of social behavior or strict morality, but one's conscience is higher than social or legal laws. Spiritual laws are superior to legal laws and these laws are known to the conscience. When one acts according to the conscience one may be punishable under the legal system but not under the spiritual system. To me morality means giving more importance to life than non-life. Moral principles are more than a matter of personal opinion, but they have to be followed by personal judgment, which means that judgment will be personal and the reality objective.

When asked if Heinz should save the life of his pet, this interviewee evoked the principles of unity of all life and of nonviolence. His application of the former follows, as described, from Jainism, which implores one to destroy only life which has the least degree of consciousness. In his application of the latter, he derives rules for moral conduct; man as a 'realized' being ought to behave in a responsible and protective manner towards all forms of life. Bishop [1975] also noted that 'the classical Indian view is that the higher one is endowed the greater his responsibilities towards others' (p. 375). The same interviewee continues:

If Heinz saves an animal's life his action will be commendable. The right use of the drug is to administer it to the needy. There is some difference, of course – Man's life is more evolved and hence of greater importance in the scheme of nature – but an animal's life is not altogether bereft of importance.... Life is known, understood, and felt by everyone. It is a matter of fact whether it is manifest in man or animal. The basic unity of life and its importance cannot be denied.... [In my opinion] all life, man or animal, is divine, sacred, and a manifestation of the Supreme reality.... We in India are vegetarians; the principle of vegetarianism is that life should not be destroyed. If it must be destroyed, then the lower forms of life such as plants may be destroyed to preserve the higher forms. One makes choices between many forms of life but the overall guiding or spiritual principle should be that all forms of life are of value. In the spiritual tradition, for example, carelessly or needlessly breaking a leaf or a flower is also construed as an act of violence. Whenever possible, minimize violence. Man as a realized being should appreciate and defend not only his life and that of other human beings but should be responsible for other forms of life. Power, physical or mental, should not be a reason for destruction. Spiritual consciousness is for enlightenment. It should propel one towards recognizing the unity of all life rather than selecting victims that are powerless. It is only in very special conditions that life survives and evolves to the standards known to us.

The concept of nonviolence in Indian thought is not simply restricted to valuing the tangible life of living organisms; one is enjoined not to injure 'by mind, word, or deed.' Furthermore, ahimsa is not simply an absence of violence; it includes universalizable values of love, compassion, impartiality, and sympathy.

In the 20th century, ahimsa acquired a political significance when it became a guiding principle in Mahatma Gandhi's mission to liberate India from British rule. The concept of nonviolence is not, therefore, a rigid, religious dogma, nor is it simply an abstract metaphysical supposition. It is a principle that can be applied to all forms of life and can regulate interactions among people in keeping with compassion, justice, and truth. Similar to Kohlberg's view of justice at stage 6, nonviolence also may be viewed as a comprehensive, universalizable, reversible, and prescriptive principle. Although Kohlberg has not considered this concept in his theory, it is not surprising that Kohlberg regards Gandhi, an admitted votary of ahimsa, to be at stage 6. Nonviolence can be posed either as a parallel to justice or as inclusive of justice.

This study has offered some empirical support for Kohlberg's claim to the universality of his scheme. There are, however, important issues to be discussed and accounted for. A comprehensive valuing of all life, which is central to the Indian tradition and was also integrated in the moral reasoning of some respondents, is a case in point. How might Kohlberg's conception assimilate this non-Western value? Interview No. 4, quoted here, contains a principled statement regarding the unity and sanctity of life from an Indian perspective. An expert Kohlberg scorer assigned this interview to stage 4; he observed that its spiritual content was unscorable in Kohlberg's system. Indeed, this principle seems to be an example of those 'other' moral principles that are not represented in the particular structures of Kohlberg's stages. To increase the generality of Kohlberg's theory, both the scoring scheme of moral judgments and Kohlberg's conception of morality will need to assimilate and accommodate more readily to moral principles that operate in other cultures.

In his writings, Kohlberg presents both a global and a relatively more restricted view of morality. In the global view, morality represents ideals of human life, dignity, personality, and autonomy. In the restricted view, stages of moral reasoning represent 'a rational reconstruction of the ontogenesis of the justice principle' [Kohlberg et al., 1983]. The global view is congruent with the Indian principles of nonviolence and comprehensive value for life. One may begin, as Kohlberg might suggest, with at least two diverse philosophies, the Indian and the Western, and arrive at 'some minimal value conceptions' which could be shared despite other cultural differences. Given Kohlberg's restrictive concern with a rational and formally derived view of justice, however, it is difficult to assess its congruence with other value orientations.

Kohlberg [July 1984, personal commun.] is uncertain how 'spiritual' and 'metaphysical' notions, such as unity of all life and nonviolence, square with his formal view of morality. Kohlberg's response to writers who have taken other moral perspectives intimates what his argument might be. These indigenous values probably would be relegated to a 'soft' status and would be seen to compare unfavorably. Kohlberg's concept of hard stages and his adherence to metaethical assumptions in judging the adequacy of principles other than justice are thus problematic for testing the universality of his scheme.

Blasi [1986] suggests that cognitive developmentalists should reconsider their 'mixed' use of philosophical and psychological principles. By becoming overly preoccupied with the moral adequacy of judgments, one might exclude morally relevant phenomena and subjective constructions which are intrinsic to psychological research. The formalistic perspective which does philosophical justice may compromise the rich moral meanings the Indian respondents have integrated in their reasoning.

Summary and Conclusion

The findings reported above support Kohlberg's model of moral reasoning in important ways. First, preconventional, conventional, and postconventional stages can be found in a complex non-Western culture. Second, the attainment of stage is significantly related to age. Third, there is no significant difference in stage attainment between women and men when both are afforded similar educational and socioeconomic opportunities.

Although postconventional reasoning has been shown among Indian adults, how adults adapt principles to the exigencies of real life and how they integrate culture-specific moral values in their reasoning require further study. To discover the unique expression and interpretation of 'minimal values,' a study of moral reasoning in another culture should involve a deep study of that culture's philosophical systems. At present, there is a paucity of research that goes beyond finding Kohlberg's specific stages across cultures.

The Kohlbergian methodology is sufficiently flexible to allow such exploration.

The outcome envisioned from such research is an expanded view of moral reasoning which would encompass principles from a plurality of cultures. The search for universally relevant 'minimal value conceptions' remains an important one, and Kohlberg's contributions are imaginative landmarks. From a cross-cultural perspective, the argument of universality, paradoxically, should discern not only commonalities but diversity as well in principled thought.

References

Bishop, D.H.: Prologue; in Bishop, Indian thought (Wiley, New York 1975a).

Bishop, D.H.: Epilogue; in Bishop, Indian thought (Wiley, New York 1975b).

Blasi, A.: How should psychologists define morality? Or, the negative side effects of philosophy on psychology; in Edelstein, Nunner-Winkler, Zur Bestimmung der philosophischen und sozialwissenschaftlichen Beiträge zur Moralforschung (Suhrkamp, Frankfurt/Main 1986).

Buck-Morss, S.: Socio-economic bias in Piaget's theory and its implications for cross-cultural studies. Hum. Dev. 18: 35–49 (1975).

Colby, A.; Kohlberg, L.; Gibbs, J.; Lieberman, M.: A longitudinal study of moral development. Monogr. Soc. Res. Child Dev. 48: (1–2, Serial No. 200) (1983).

Crawford, S.C.: Concepts of Indian ethical ideals (University Press of Hawaii, Honolulu 1982).

Edelstein, W.; Noam, G.: Regulatory structures of the self and 'postformal' stages in adulthood. Hum. Dev. 25: 407–422 (1982).

Gibbs, J.C.: Kohlberg's stages of moral development: a constructive critique. Harvard Educ. Rev. 47: 43–61 (1977).

Gilligan, C.: In a different voice. Psychological theory and women's development (Harvard University Press, Cambridge 1982).

Kohlberg, L.: Essays on moral development. The philosophy of moral development, vol. 1 (Harper & Row, London 1981).

Kohlberg, L.; Levine, C.; Hewer, A.: Moral stages: a current reformulation and a response to critics (Karger, New York 1983).

Labouvie-Vief, G.: Beyond formal operations. Uses and limits of pure logic in life span development. Hum. Dev. 23: 141–161 (1980).

Murphy, J.M.; Gilligan, C.: Moral development in late adolescence and adulthood. A critique and reconstruction of Kohlberg's theory. Hum. Dev. 23: 77–104 (1980).

Nisan, M.; Kohlberg, L.: Universality and variation in moral judgment. A longitudinal and cross-sectional study in Turkey. Child Dev. 53: 865–876 (1982).

Perry, W.G.: Forms of intellectual and ethical development in the college years (Holt, Rinehart & Winston, New York 1970).

Reimer, J.; Paolitto, D.P.; Hersh, R.H.: Promoting moral growth (Longman, New York 1983).

Riegel, K.: Dialectical operations. The final period of cognitive development. Hum. Dev. 16: 345–376 (1973).

Shweder, R.: Review of the philosophy of Lawrence Kohlberg's essays on moral development: vol. 1, the philosophy of moral development. Contemp. Psychol. 27: 421–424 (1982).

Simpson, E.L.: Moral development research. A case of scientific cultural bias. Hum. Dev. 17: 81–106 (1974).

Snarey, J.R.: Cross-cultural universality of social-moral development. A critical review of Kohlbergian research. Psychol. Bull. 97: 202–232 (1985).

Sullivan, E.: A study of Kohlberg's structural theory of moral development. A critique of liberal social science ideology. Hum. Dev. 20: 325–376 (1977).

Vasudev, J.: A study of moral reasoning at different life stages in India; unpubl. diss. University of Pittsburgh (1985).

Vasudev, J.: Kohlberg's claims to universality: an Indian perspective; in Edelstein, Nunner-Winkler, Zur Bestimmung der philosophischen und sozialwissenschaftlichen Beiträge zur Moralforschung (Suhrkamp, Frankfurt/Main 1986).

Walker, L.J.: Sex differences in the development of moral reasoning. A critical review. Child Dev. 55: 677–691 (1984).

Jyotsna Vasudev,
Department of Psychology,
Wayne State University,
71 West Warren,
Detroit, MI 48202 (USA)

Part XIV: Cross-Cultural Morality

26. Cross-Cultural Research on Kohlberg's Stages: The Basis for Consensus

CAROLYN POPE EDWARDS

When Lawrence Kohlberg (1969, 1971a) claimed that his moral stages were culturally universal, he ensured that a storm of controversy would greet his theory. He then intensified the controversy by further claiming that preliterate or semiliterate village peoples would generally fall behind other cultural groups in their rate and terminal point of development due to a relative lack of 'role-taking opportunities' in their daily lives.

Moral values are known to vary so greatly from culture to culture that a universal, invariant sequence in development or moral judgment is a provocative claim. Furthermore, to characterize the difference between the moral judgment of people in traditional face-to-face societies versus modern, complex, national states as a difference in 'adequacy' of moral judging (Kohlberg, 1971a) seems to violate norms of inter-cultural respect and ethical relativism.

Kohlberg's statements have been met by many theoretical statements attempting to refute aspects of his conclusions or assumptions about cultural universality (see, for example, Bloom, 1977; Buck-Morss, 1975; Edwards, 1975, 1982; Shweder, 1982a; Simpson, 1974; Sullivan, 1977). Equally of importance, the theoretical controversy has stimulated much empirical research intended, at least in part, to test the cross-cultural claims. Cross-cultural research is the only empirical strategy that can actually establish or discount the universalizability of the theory, and for that reason it has been actively pursued. This paper will review the status and current progress of comparative studies of moral judgment. I will attempt to show why the work as a whole can be considered productive, tending toward increased rather than diminished understanding of the moral reasoning of humankind. I will answer each of the following, pivotal questions below with a 'Yes, but . . .' argument. Finally, I will try to show how, as comparative research has proceeded to become increasingly elaborated in theoretical intent and sophisticated in design and methods of analysis, it has quietly established its position as a viable field of research. Controversy remains, of course, but it is a fruitful one, and there is a solid core of issues upon which we can reach reasonable consensus.

Questions Central to Establishing the Universality of Kohlberg Moral Stages

1 Is the dilemma interview method a valid way of eliciting the moral judgments of people in other cultures?
2 Is the standard scoring system appropriate and valid for cross-cultural use?
3 Is cognitive-developmental theory useful for understanding psychological development in comparative cultural perspective?

THE VALIDITY OF THE INTERVIEW METHOD

For the moral dilemma methodology to be considered valid for either a particular research study or comparative research in general requires three things. First, the specific dilemmas used in research must be 'real' to the particular people involved, that is, they must raise issues and pit values important to the respondents. This criterion requires either development of new dilemmas appropriate to particular cultural contexts or adequate adaptation of Kohlberg's Standard Interview. Secondly, dilemmas and probing questions must be well translated into respondents' native language, and respondents' answers must be translated without distortion back into the language of scoring. Thirdly, the interview methodology itself must be adequate to the sensitive task of eliciting respondents' 'best', 'highest', and most 'reflective' reasoning about morality (Edwards, 1981). The third criterion is the most subtle and difficult to determine, but it is absolutely critical to the success of the cross-cultural endeavour.

Research to date is uneven in quality according to the first criterion, but recent research can surely be judged generally more satisfactory. Most researchers have opted to adapt Kohlberg's standard stories rather than to create entirely new dilemmas, in order to take advantage of standard scoring systems. This practice assumes that standard stories (if adequately modified in details to fit the local setting) present real and relevant dilemmas to people everywhere because they share certain universal moral concerns, such as affectional, property and authority issues. Such an assumption seems to me a fair one, with a notable exception. True hunter-gatherer societies do not contain headmen or chiefs; nor do they contain formal courts or governing institutions. People in these societies would not be expected to make sense of problems pitting 'law' and 'life', or 'authority' and 'conscience'.

Regarding the first criterion, we can feel most confident about research conducted by investigators who are thoroughly familiar with the cultures studied. We can expect such researchers to have the best sense that the dilemmas used are relevant and adequately adapted. The early research studies (especially Grimley, 1973; Kohlberg, 1969; Saadatmand, 1972) are flawed by serious weakness in terms of trying to cover too much ground (four or five cultural settings each) with little or no ethnographic description provided for each sample and its moral values. In contrast, many of the recent researchers have focused in depth on their own society or cultural group (e.g., Lutz Eckensberger, Germany; Jean-Marc Samson, French-speaking Canada; Y. H. Chern, S. W. Cheng and T. Lei, Taiwan; Muhammed Maqsud, Nigeria; Bindu Parikh, India). In other cases, researchers have gained thorough familiarity of the cultures they studied. For example, Sara Harkness lived as an anthropologist for three years in Western Kenya, and John Snarey provides detailed ethnographic description of the Israeli kibbutz where he based his work. Although these researchers have not generally commented on how well dilemmas have seemed to 'work' in their studies, when they do, their comments have been generally positive. For example, Harkness, Edwards and Super (1981) say, 'All of the men readily accepted this task and became quite involved in giving their judgments' (p. 598).

Only a few researchers have experimented with creating entirely new dilemmas. I found (Edwards, 1975, 1978) that Kenyans were intensely interested and provoked by a new dilemma, called Daniel and the School Fees. However, I did not systematically compare subjects' level of responses to the new versus standard stories. Charles White and colleagues (1978) found in pilot work in the Bahamas that there were no stage differences in response to their new versus the standard dilemmas, so they did not pursue its use. By far the most original approach has been taken by Benjamin Lee (1973, 1976). Lee, an American of Chinese descent, departed completely from the standard stories and developed a series of 'filiality' stories to study moral reasoning in Taiwan. Filiality is a core Chinese value, of course, and Lee reports (personal communication) that subjects, especially those of the older generation, scored higher on filiality than standard stories, because 'fairness' was not an important issue for them. Lee's research illustrates how broadening the interview base to issues outside the core concerns of Westerners can enrich, not undermine, the structural approach to moral development. Further work, in my opinion, should involve quantitative and qualitative comparison of people's responses to original versus standard dilemmas. Such an approach would fully and adequately meet criterion one and lead to an improvement or elaboration of the theory.

Criterion two concerns adequacy of translation. Only one set of German researchers has taken the notable step of translating not only dilemmas but also the scoring manual into another language (Eckensberger, Eckensberger and Reinshagen, 1975–6). Most other researchers have translated the dilemmas into subjects' native language, then translated answers back into English for scoring. Their procedures have probably met at least minimal standards, especially when investigators, such as Jean-Marc Samson, are bilingual, with their first language the target non-English language. They have considered carefully problems of translating ethical terminology. For example, Parikh (1980) states, 'The first 10 translations were checked by a professor of English and a native of Gujarat. A list was made of those words for which it was difficult to get equivalents in English and this list was then discussed with a professor of Gujarati and another of English' (p. 1033).

However, translation is a fascinating subject in its own right that deserves closer inspection and analysis. No researcher, for example, has yet compared responses to a dilemma as translated by several different people, or compared moral maturity scores given to the same interview as translated into English by several different translators. Past researchers, quite rightly perhaps, have been more interested in simply taking the initial step of seeing whether moral judgment scores distribute themselves in a predictable or reasonable way over a target sample of people.

Criterion three concerns whether the interview method is able to elicit the very best and most mature reasoning about moral problems in cultures other than our own. This is an extremely difficult question, and common to research on cognition and social cognition in general, not just Kohlbergian research. The crux of the problem revolves around those groups who seem to show least high-stage reasoning. Findings from a large number of studies (reviewed in Edwards, 1981, 1982) have indicated that moral judgment Stage 5, and perhaps even full-Stage 4, are not found in interviews with preliterate or semiliterate adults who live in relatively 'traditional', small-scale societies, such as isolated peasant or tribal communities. Are these stages really missing, or are the results an artifact of testing bias? There are, in my opinion, good theoretical grounds for thinking that Stage 3 may be the stage at which the judgment of village adults stabilizes. The underlying structure of Stage 3 corresponds well to the social and moral order of a society based on face-to-face relations and a relatively high level of normative consensus (Edwards, 1975, 1981, 1982; Nisan and Kohlberg, 1982). However, it is still important to consider carefully the fundamental problems that exist with eliciting moral reasoning by asking people to reflect upon moral dilemmas.

The moral dilemma interview is best seen as a way to elicit a particular part of people's moral thinking, their 'conscious reflections' rather than intuitive or implicit knowledge about morality (cf. Pool, Shweder and Much, 1983). The interview stimulates people to explain their justifications and to self-reflectively volunteer criteria for decision-making. Do adults in all types of societies have this capacity? 'Yes', we can answer, considering the fact that adults in a wide range of cultural groups studied so far seem to enjoy dilemma discussions. They find it congenial to play the role of what Kenyans called the 'moral elder' and formulate their wisest, most considered opinion about posed, hypothetical problems.

Richard Brandt, a philosopher who many years ago studied Hopi ethical systems, similarly concluded that ethical principles are probably culturally universal. He inferred that 'wrong' had a true ethical meaning to the Hopi: 'If I were normal, impartial, and fully informed, I should feel obligated not to perform X' (Brandt, 1954, p. 109). Although Brandt had to piece together his picture of the Hopi's implicit principles from rather brief answers to formal dilemmas supplemented by many related remarks in other conversations, he believed that his results make 'a highly unfavorable beginning for any person who thinks the "moral" concepts of primitive peoples are quite different from, and vastly more simple and less elevated than our own' (p. 98).

Nevertheless, Kohlberg's highest stages are consistently missing in the interviews from certain groups, and this may relate to the level of formal discourse required for them. John Gibbs (1977, 1979; Gibbs and Widaman, 1982) has put forward the case that Stages 5 and 6 of Kohlberg's system are different from Stages 1 to 4. While Stages 1 to 4 are genuine developmental stages, Gibbs feels that Stages 5 and 6 are something else—namely, 'second-order' thinking about morality, 'meta-ethical reflections' on the decision-criteria constructed at an earlier stage—a kind of thinking made possible primarily by higher education. Gibbs, a close collaborator of Kohlberg, proposes to constructively revise the system by re-labelling Stages 1 and 2 as 'immature', Stages 3 and 4 as fully 'mature', and Stages 5 and 6 as a 'theory-defining level of discourse'. In a somewhat similar vein, Eckensberger and Reinshagen of Germany (1977, 1981), on the basis of theoretical analysis and their reading of the comparative literature, have suggested that Stages

1 to 3 are the basic developmental structures. Stages 4, 4/5 and 5, they speculate, represent horizontal *decalages* of the first three structures into less obvious content areas (social systems rather than concrete others).

Both of these sets of suggestions are very important from a comparative perspective. Although many adults in all societies seem able to step into the 'moral elder' role (Stage 3 or 4) in reflecting upon moral problems, they are not equally able to assume the 'moral theorist' role, as required for Stages 5 and 6. As anthropologist Richard Shweder (1982b) has said, 'Children and most adults in most cultures are not very good at spontaneously articulating the distinctions, ideas, and concepts underlying their sense of morality. Most people do not know how to talk like a moral philosopher' (pp. 58–9). While every cultural environment is indeed 'packed with implicit messages about what is of importance, what is of value, who counts as a person' (Shweder, 1982b, p. 56; also see Read, 1955), nevertheless most people in traditional societies may not be able to discourse at the 'theory-defining level' about what they know and think (Horton, 1968). Still, if critics are correct that the first 3 or 4 stages are the core developmental ones, then we can comfortably conclude that the moral dilemma method has shown itself surprisingly congenial to a wide variety of cultural groups with social systems at very different levels of political and economic complexity.

THE VALIDITY OF THE SCORING SYSTEM

The standard scoring system depends upon the theoretical notion that basic, universal moral judgment structures can be differentiated from highly variable, culturally-specific contents. Cross-cultural data, therefore, should 'fit' the scoring system. Problems can arise from two types of data: (1) data which seem to match most closely the criterion statements of one stage (e.g., Stage 2), but which really seem to flow from the social perspective or underlying structure of another stage (e.g., Stage 3); and (2) data which are 'unscorable', i.e., do not match any of the standard scoring categories. Insofar as empirical data present a serious challenge to either of these two varieties, they suggest that the scoring system is invalid or at least in need of revision.

Finding *any* anomalies, however, is not necessarily bad news for the theory. The scoring system is regarded by cognitive-developmental researchers as a living being, and new data that suggest ways to improve the scoring system can represent good news. The task of constructing and revising scoring categories that adequately distinguish form from content has been a continual one. Hard-to-score data are actually helpful if they suggest concrete ways to improve the scoring system.

Past researchers have reported that their cross-cultural data are generally readily scorable. Inter-rater reliabilities, where determined, have achieved acceptable standards of agreement. Researchers have commonly presented illustrative material to show how the reasoning of their target group had culturally-typical contents yet revealed an easily recognizable underlying structure. Most data labelled as 'unscorable', especially from child subjects, consisted merely of brief 'yes' or 'no' statements, or responses that were too incomplete to reveal their underlying stage (but for an exception, see Tomlinson, 1983).

Recently, however, researchers have begun to report upon and critically examine hard-to-score data from adult subjects and to suggest that these data are problematical. All of these scoring problems refer to ambiguities in Stages 3, 4 and 5. For example, Snarey (1982) and Snarey, Reimer and Kohlberg (1984) analyze difficult-to-score reasoning by Israeli kibbutz respondents. They describe how some subjects blind-scored as Stage 4 or 4/5 were determined by a 'culturally sensitive' scorer to be Stage 5. They conclude that the scoring manual needs to be 'fleshed out with culturally indigenous examples', especially at the higher stages (Snarey, 1982, p. 317). Cheng and Lei (1981) provide examples of Taiwanese reasoning that they thought difficult-to-score: some of the material seemed to be either transitional between 3 and 4, or between 4 and 5, but the categories and distinctions provided in the scoring manual did not allow accurate determination. They concluded, 'More clear delineation of the structure of the stages and better designed probing questions seem to be in need' (p. 16).

In research in Kenya, I too found several examples of hard-to-score interviews. While most of the interviews were readily scored, the most difficult ones were long and complete but arguably either Stage 3 or 4. These were interviews with mature adults who had not attended formal schooling beyond the primary grades. The men were 'community moral leaders', that is, respected elders often called to advise at hearings between local disputants.

To illustrate the way that interviews reflecting a non-Western frame of values and perspective upon society can be difficult to score—and to add to the growing literature seeking to elaborate constructively the scoring system—let me present two examples. The excerpts raise the fundamental question of whether Stage 4 merely requires a rough appreciation of society's need for institutionalized roles, or whether it requires a full-blown understanding of the organizational aspects of a social structure and the operation of a legal system (paraphrase of Cheng and Lei, 1981, p. 16). What the Kenyan elders have is a clear and elaborated vision of fair and reasonable rules for running a prosperous extended family, based on 'unity', 'respect', and 'understanding', key Kenyan traditional values.

From an interview with a Kikuyu man, age 53, with three years of schooling (Edwards, 1975; dilemma is Daniel and the School Fees):

Question: In general, should a grown-up son obey all of his parents' wishes? Why, or why not?

Answer: The parents should not authorize Daniel to educate his brother's son. They should only advise him. Daniel has a home to look after since he left his parents, and it's a complete house with one person as head, not two. So he should not obey his parents but should consider their advices.

Question: Is it more important for Daniel to maintain harmonious relations with his wife, or with his brother and parents? Why?

Answer: Once one is married, we say in Kikuyu society that, 'He is out of his parents' hands....' The husband will be the Chairman and the wife the Treasurer, and as such she will control the resources. That is why Daniel's wife wants [to use the family money] to put her son in school.

Question: Would you condemn Daniel if he just moved away to the city and did not help his brother's son?

Answer: We cannot condemn Daniel ... because it's right. He can only carry with him one home, not two. He can offer help if he can in other ways. If we draw a picture like this, we see that there are different generations being founded. Daniel is now very far from Kamau [his older brother who put Daniel himself through school]....

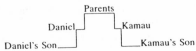

From an interview with a Kipsigis man, age 55, unschooled (Harkness, Edwards and Super, 1981; dilemma is adaptation of Joe story).

Question: Should James refuse to give his father the money?

Answer: If his father is a squanderer, then he shouldn't be given. But if he keeps it well, the father is like a bank, and he should keep it.

Question: Should the father always direct the son?

Answer: For the son to refuse to take his father's advice shows that he is not well cared for ... But when you [a father] convince him [your son] by telling him, 'Do this sort of thing because this will earn us our living. You didn't do it this time, but do it next time,' then the child will comply since you did not command (shout at) him ... and so both of you will be in good unity and understanding of each other.

Question: Which is worse, for a father to break his promise or for a son?

Answer: [If the father breaks his word] it will cause hatred because the son will be angry, saying, 'I wanted to follow my own intentions, but my father cheated: he permitted me and then refused me. Now I don't want to hear more of his words. He can't love me and is unable to protect me.' So it is bad. [However], the one for the son is worse. Imagine a child disobeying my own words, is he really normal? ... Rules are mine and I want him to follow, e.g. 'Do this thing to earn you a living', as I did follow my father's rules also ... Father's bad deeds are revealed when he does not care for his children ... That man is like a drunkard whose children do not sleep at home because he drives them away when not sober. The man does not have rules which work and so it is bad. But if he has good functioning rules, he is able to keep his family. The maize will be growing because of his good work. Then it is clear that his family is well looked after....

In conclusion, there seems a clear consensus that the scoring system has provided a useful tool for analyzing cross-cultural data. However, subtle distinctions between the higher stages need to be further clarified, and form and content need to be further differentiated to broaden definitions of stages or levels beyond Stage 3.

THE USEFULNESS OF THE THEORY FOR EXPLAINING HUMAN DEVELOPMENT

As explained in the earlier sections of this paper, recent years have seen the accumulation of many studies focused on groups other than the dominant majority culture of the USA. These studies allow us to consider our final question, whether cognitive-developmental theory has proven useful for understanding individual development within or between cultural groups.

The *within* question is surely less controversial and includes two parts. First, do the central claims of the theory about development (especially invariance of sequence) hold up in cross-cultural studies? Second, do specific examinations of moral judgment in relationship to experiential or background variables lead to increased understanding of the processes facilitating development? We cannot examine each of these questions in detail, but we can indicate the general shape of an answer.

In my recent survey, I found the following studies focused on groups from outside the mainstream US culture (also see review in Snarey, 1982):

The Americas
    USA   Alaskan Eskimo (Saxe, 1970)
                Puerto Rican (Pacheco-Maldonado, 1972)

      Canada   Germanic Hutterite (Saadatmand, 1972)
              French (Marchand-Jodoin and Samson, 1982; Samson, 1983)
              English (Sullivan, 1975; Sullivan and Beck, 1975; Sullivan,
              McCullough and Stager, 1979; Sullivan and Quarter, 1972)
     Bahamas (White, 1975, 1977; White, Bushnell and Regnemer, 1978)
     Guatemala (Saadatmand, 1972)
     Honduras (Gorsuch and Barnes, 1973)
     Mexico (Kohlberg, 1969)

   Asia
     India (Parikh, 1975, 1980; Saraswathi, Saxena and Sundaresan, 1977)
     Iran (Saadatmand, 1972)
     Israel Kohlberg, with Bar Yam, 1971b; Snarey, 1982; Snarey, Reimer
        and Kohlberg, 1984)
     Hong Kong (Grimley, 1973, 1974)
     Japan (Grimley, 1973, 1974)
     Taiwan (Cheng and Lei, 1981; Chern, 1978; Kohlberg, 1969; Lee, 1973,
        1976)
     Thailand (Batt, 1974, 1975)
     Turkey (Nisan and Kohlberg, 1982; Turiel, Edwards and Kohlberg,
        1978)

   Africa
     Kenya (Edwards, 1974, 1975, 1978; Harkness, Edwards and Super,
        1981)
     Nigeria (Maqsud, 1976, 1977a, 1977b, 1979, 1982)
     Zambia (Grimley, 1973, 1974)

   Europe
     France (O'Connor, 1974, 1980)
     Finland (Helkama, 1981)
     Germany (Eckensberger, 1983; Gielen, 1982; Villenave and Eckensber-
        ger, 1982)
     Great Britain (Grimley, 1973, 1974; O'Connor, 1974, 1980; Simon and
        Ward, 1973; Simpson and Graham, 1971; Tomlinson,
        1983; Weinreich, 1977)

   Australia and Oceania
     New Zealand (Moir, 1974)

Two types of societies still represent critical missing cases: (1) foraging (hunter-gatherer) societies, which lack social classes or hierarchy and also formal political and legal institutions; and (2) societies such as those of Eastern Europe, USSR, and Peoples' Republic of China, which are complex nation-states but based on non-capitalist economies. A further serious weakness of the literature is that the only longitudinal cases in the above list are from the Bahamas, French Canada, Israel, Great Britain and Turkey. The great majority of studies are cross-sectional, due to the enormous expense and difficulty of conducting longitudinal work.

    The proposition of invariant sequence requires that stage development be stepwise and progressive, with stage regressions and stage skippings no greater than expected by chance (measurement error). All of the cross-sectional studies have found average moral maturity and/or upper-stage-range to increase with age during the childhood and adolescent years (with the exception of the Hutterite sample). No studies have found any 'missing' stages between the lowest and highest stages present in a sample. Furthermore, the longitudinal studies (with the probable exception of Tomlinson's, 1983, British sample) have supported these conclusions by indicating no significant amounts of stage regression over time. Thus, while the available data cannot positively demonstrate invariant sequence, taken together they strongly suggest that development change is generally gradual and positive throughout the childhood and adolescent years, in a wide variety of cultural groups.

Most investigators, naturally, conducted their research with broader questions in mind than merely invariant sequence. Taking advantage of the natural range of variation in social life worldwide, they have been able to gain increased leverage on understanding experiential influences. For example, a number of researchers from the list above have been able to show that the following experiential factors relate positively to moral judgment. (*Note:* the dates of the studies are provided only when necessary for the reader):

> *socioeconomic status* (Grimley; Kohlberg with Bar Yam; Nisan and Kohlberg; Simpson and Graham; Turiel *et al.*);
>
> *residential factors*, e.g., living in city or village, or city versus kibbutz (Gorsuch and Barnes; Nisan and Kohlberg; Snarey; Turiel *et al.*);
>
> *educational level* (Batt; Edwards, 1975);
>
> *school experiences* (Edwards, 1978; Maqsud, all studies; Marchand-Jodoin and Samson; Sullivan, 1975; Sullivan and Beck);
>
> *parental discipline, warmth or identification* (Parikh; Saadatmand; Simpson and Graham).

These studies taken together converge to suggest that moral judgment level is stimulated by at least three general types of experiences, that increase: (1) an individual's contact with a *diversity of personal or cultural values*; (2) an individual's ability to *reason in formal or school-like ways* about moral issues; and (3) an individual's tendency to *take as one's reference group a complex society*. The research allows a general consensus that conditions that lead to development in one group are comparable to conditions that lead to development in other groups.

Finally, we return to the issue with which this paper opened: how valid is Kohlberg's theory for comparing moral development (and moral adequacy) *between* people of different cultural groups?

Even on this controversial issue a certain consensus may be achievable. It is noteworthy that in response to criticism, Kohlberg has revised his own earlier position. He now states (in Kohlberg, Levine and Hewer, 1983):

> We do not believe that the comparison of one culture to another in terms of moral development is a theoretically useful strategy for the growth of scientific knowledge.... It is difficult to understand what a valid concept of 'comparative moral worth of culture' might be, but in any case such a concept could not be established on the basis of a comparison of means on our moral judgment assessment scale. There is no direct way in which group averages can be translated into statements of the relative moral worth of groups (p. 113).

In other words, cross-cultural differences have nothing to do after all with the relative moral worth or adequacy of moral judging. Moral judgment stages, from a cross-cultural point of view, are simply not achievements for which higher is necessarily better. Rather, Kohlberg's theory and methods offer just one useful way to study developmental growth in wisdom or 'conscious reflectiveness' in moral decision-making. Certainly they do not begin to encompass all that we would like to know in terms of understanding how human beings across the spectrum of world cultures develop in the capacity to make moral choices. Nevertheless, Kohlberg's theory and methods have surely generated a productive line of comparative research that has become more sophisticated, multidimensional and theoretically lively over time.

REFERENCES

Batt, H. W. (1974) 'Obligation and decision in Thai administration: From patrimonial to rational-legal bureaucracy'. Unpublished doctoral dissertation, State University of New York at Albany.

Batt, H. W. (1975) 'Thai conceptions of justice on Kohlberg's moral development scale'. Unpublished manuscript, Department of Political Science, State University of New York at Albany.

Bloom, A. H (1977) 'Two dimensions of moral reasoning: Social principledness and social humanism in cross-cultural perspective', *The Journal of Social Psychology*, 101, pp. 29–44.

Brandt, R. B. (1954) *Hopi Ethics*, Chicago, Ill., University of Chicago Press, [Midway Reprint, 1974].

Buck-Morss, S. (1975) 'Socio-economic bias in Piaget's theory and its implications for cross-cultural studies', *Human Development*, 18, pp. 35–49.

Cheng, S. W. and Lei, T. (1981) 'Performance of Taiwanese students on Kohlberg's moral judgment inventory'. Unpublished manuscript, National Taiwan University.

Chern, Y. H. (1978) 'Moral judgment development in Chinese [Taiwanese] adolescents', *Journal of Education*, Kuashung Normal College Press.

Colby, A., Kohlberg, L., Gibbs, J. and Lieberman, M. (1983) 'A longitudinal study of moral judgment', *Monographs of the Society for Research in Child Development*, 48, Serial No. 200.

Eckensberger, L. H. (1981) 'On a structural model of the development of stages of moral development', in L. Oppenheimer (Ed.), *Action Theoretical Approaches to (Developmental) Psychology*, Proceedings of the Symposium: Action Theory and Developmental Psychology, Amsterdam.

Eckensberger, L. H. (1983) 'Research on moral development', *German Journal of Psychology*, 7, pp. 195–244.

Eckensberger, L. H. and Reinshagen, H. (1977) 'Cross-cultural research as a touchstone for Kohlberg's stage theory of moral development', Paper presented to the biennial conference of the ISSBD, Pavia, Italy.

Eckensberger, L. H., Eckensberger, U.S. and Reinshagen, H. (1975–6) 'Kohlberg's Interview zum moralischen Urteil Teil I–Teil IV', *Arbeiten der Fachrichtung Psychologie*, 31–34, Universitaet des Saarlandes.

Edwards, C. P. (1974) 'The effect of experience on moral development: Results from Kenya', Doctoral dissertation, Harvard Graduate School of Education, Ann Arbor, Mich., University Microfilms, 1975, 75–16860.

Edwards, C. P. (1975) 'Societal complexity and moral development: A Kenyan study', *Ethos*, 3, pp. 505–27.

Edwards, C. P. (1978) 'Social experience and moral judgment in Kenyan young adults', *Journal of Genetic Psychology*, 133, pp. 19–29.

Edwards, C. P. (1981) 'The comparative study of the development of moral judgment and reasoning', in R. H. Munroe, R. L. Munroe and B. B. Whiting, *Handbook of Cross-Cultural Human Development*, New York, Garland Press.

Edwards, C. P. (1982) 'Moral development in comparative cultural perspective', in D. Wagner and H. Stevenson (Eds.), *Cultural Perspectives on Child Development*, San Francisco, W. H. Freeman.

Gibbs, J. C. (1977) 'Kohlberg's stages of moral judgment: A constructive critique', *Harvard Educational Review*, 47, pp. 43–61.

Gibbs, J. C. (1979) 'Kohlberg's moral stage theory: A Piagetian revision', *Human Development*, 22, pp. 89–112.

Gibbs, J. C. and Widaman, K. F., with A. Colby (1982) *Social Intelligence: Measuring the Development of Sociomoral Reflection*, Englewood Cliffs, N.J., Prentice-Hall.

Gielen, U. P. (1985) 'Moral reasoning in radical and non-radical German students', *Behavior Science Research*, (in press).

Gorsuch, R. L. and Barnes, M. L. (1973) 'Stages of ethical reasoning and moral norms of Carib youths', *Journal of Cross-Cultural Psychology*, 4, pp. 283–301.

Grimley, L. (1973) 'A cross-cultural study of moral development', Unpublished doctoral dissertation, Kent State University.

Grimley, L. (1974) 'Moral development in different nations', *School Psychology Digest*, 3, pp. 43–51.

Harkness, S., Edwards, C. P. and Super, C. M. (1981) 'Social roles and moral reasoning: A case study in a rural African community', *Developmental Psychology*, 17, pp. 595–603.

Helkama, K. (1981) 'Toward a cognitive-developmental theory of attribution of responsibility', Unpublished doctoral dissertation, Helsinki University.

Horton, R. (1968) 'Neo-Tylorianism: Sound sense or sinister prejudice?' *Man*, 3, pp. 625–34.

Kohlberg, L. (1969) 'Stage and sequence: The cognitive-developmental approach to socialization', in D. Goslin (Ed.), *Handbook of Socialization*, New York, Rand McNally, pp. 347–480.

Kohlberg, L. (1971a) 'From is to ought: How to commit the naturalistic fallacy and get away with it in the study of moral development', in T. Mischel (Ed.), *Cognitive Development and Epistemology*, New York, Academic Press, pp. 23–92.

Kohlberg, L., with Bar-Yam, M. (1971b) 'Cognitive-developmental theory and the practice of collective education', in M. Wolins and M. Gottesman (Eds.), *Group Care: An Israeli Approach*, New York, Gordon and Breach, pp. 342–79.

Kohlberg, L., Levine, C. and Hewer, A. (1983) *Moral Stages: A Current Formulation and a Response to Critics*, New York, Karger, Contributions to Human Development, Vol. 10.

Lee, B. (1973) 'A cognitive-developmental approach to filiality development', Unpublished master's dissertation, Committee on Human Development, University of Chicago.

Lee, B. (1976) 'Fairness and filiality: A cross-cultural cultural account', Paper presented at the annual meeting of the American Anthropological Association, Washington, D. C., November.

Maqsud, M. (1976) 'The effects of different educational environments on moral development of Nigerian children belonging to various tribes', Unpublished doctoral dissertation, University of London.

Maqsud, M. (1977a) 'The influence of social heterogeneity and sentimental credibility on moral judgments of Nigerian Muslim adolescents', *Journal of Cross-Cultural Psychology*, 8, pp. 113–22.

Maqsud, M. (1977b) 'Moral reasoning of Nigerian and Pakistani Muslim adolescents', *Journal of Moral Education*, 7, pp. 40–9.

Maqsud, M. (1979) 'Cultural influences on transition in the development of moral reasoning in Nigerian boys', *The Journal of Social Psychology*, 108, pp. 151–9.

Maqsud, M. (1982) 'Effects of Nigerian children's group discussion on their moral progression', *Journal of Moral Education*, 11, 3.

Marchand-Jodoin, L. and Samson, J. M. (1982) 'Kohlberg's theory applied to the moral and sexual development of adults', *Journal of Moral Education*, 11, pp. 247–58.

Moir, D. J. (1974) 'Egocentrism and the emergence of conventional morality in preadolescent girls', *Child Development*, 45, pp. 299–304.

Nisan, M. and Kohlberg, L. (1982) 'Universality and variation in moral judgment: A longitudinal and cross-sectional study in Turkey', *Child Development*, 53, pp. 865–76.

O'Connor, R. E. (1974) 'Political activism and moral reasoning: Political and apolitical students in Great Britain and France', *British Journal of Political Science*, 4, pp. 53–78.

O'Connor, R. E. (1980) 'Parental sources and political consequences of levels of moral reasoning among European university students', in R. W. Wilson and G. J. Schochet (Eds.), *Moral Development and Politics*, New York, Praeger.

Pacheco-Maldonado, A. (1972) 'A cognitive-developmental study of moral judgments in Puerto Rican children', Unpublished doctoral dissertation, University of New York at Albany.

Parikh, B. (1975) 'Moral judgment development and its relation to family environmental factors in Indian and American urban upper-middle class families', Unpublished doctoral dissertation, Department of Special Education, Boston University.

Parikh, B. (1980) 'Development of moral judgment and its relation to family environmental factors in Indian and American families', *Child Development*, 51, pp. 1030–9.

Pool, D. L., Shweder, R. A. and Much, N. C. (1983) 'Culture as a cognitive system: Differentiated rule understandings in children and other savages', in E. T. Higgins, D. N. Ruble and W. W. Hartup, *Social Cognition and Social Development: A Sociocultural Perspective*, New York, Cambridge University Press.

Read, K. E. (1955) 'Morality and the concept of the person among the Gahuku-Gama', *Oceania*, 25, pp. 233–82.

Saadatmand, B. (1972) 'Cross-cultural investigation of the influences of parents, culture, and age on the moral reasoning of children', Unpublished dictoral dissertation, Brigham Young University.

Samson, J. M. (1983) 'Sexual and general moral reasoning of French Canadian adolescents', Paper presented at the annual meeting of the society for Cross-Cultural Research, Washington, D.C., February.

Saraswathi, T. S., Saxena, K. and Sundaresan, J. (1977) 'Development of moral judgment in Indian children between ages eight to twelve years', in Y. H. Poortinga (Ed.), *Basic Problems in Cross-Cultural Psychology*, Amsterdam, Sweets and Zeitlinger, pp. 168–77.

Saxe, G. (1970) 'The development of moral judgment: A cross-cultural study of Kalskagagmuit Eskimos', Unpublished manuscript, University of California, Berkeley.

Shweder, R. A. (1982a) 'Liberalism as destiny', *Contemporary Psychology*, 27, pp. 421–4.

Shweder, R. A. (1982b) 'Beyond self-constructed knowledge: The study of culture and morality', *Merrill-Palmer Quarterly*, 28, pp. 41–69.

Simon, A. and Ward, L. O. (1973) 'Variables influencing pupils' responses on the Kohlberg schema of moral development', *Journal of Moral Education*, 2, pp. 283–6.

Simpson, A. L. and Graham, D. (1971) 'The development of moral judgment, emotion, and behavior in British adolescents', Unpublished manuscript, University of Durham.

Simpson, E. L. (1974) 'Moral development research: A case study of scientific cultural bias', *Human Development*, 17, pp. 81–106.

Snarey, J. R. (1982) 'The social and moral development of kibbutz founders and sabras: A cross-sectional and longitudinal cross-cultural study', Unpublished doctoral dissertation, Graduate School of Education, Harvard University.

Snarey, J. R., Reimer, J. and Kohlberg, L. (1985) 'The development of social-moral reasoning among kibbutz adolescents: A longitudinal cross-cultural study', *Developmental Psychology*, 21 (1), pp. 3–17.

Sullivan, E. V. (1977) 'A study of Kohlberg's structural theory of moral development. A critique of liberal social science ideology', *Human Development*, 20, pp. 352–76.

Sullivan, E. V., with Beck, C., Joy, M. and Pagliuso, S. (1975) *Moral Learning: Some Findings, Issues, and Questions*, New York, Paulist Press.

Sullivan, E. V. and Beck, C. M. (1975) 'Moral education in a Canadian setting', *Phi Delta Kappan*, 56, pp. 697–701.

Sullivan, E. V. and Quarter, J. (1972) 'Psychological correlates of certain postconventional moral types: A perspective on hybrid types', *Journal of Personality*, 40, pp. 149–61.

Sullivan, E. V., McCullough, G. and Stager, M. A. (1970) 'A developmental study of the relationship between conceptual, ego, and moral development', *Child Development*, 41, pp. 399–411.

Tomlinson, P. (1983) 'Six years in the moral lives of some British adolescents', Paper presented to the psychology section of the Annual Meeting of the British Association for the Advancement of Science, University of Sussex, August.

Turiel, E., Edwards, C. P. and Kohlberg, L. (1978) 'Moral development in Turkish children, adolescents, and young adults', *Journal of Cross-cultural Psychology*, 9, pp. 75–86.

Villenave-Cremer, S. and Eckensberger, L. H. (1982) 'On the role of affective processes in moral judgment performances', Paper presented to the International Symposium on Moral Education, Fribourg, Switzerland, August-September.

Weinreich, H. (1977) 'Some consequences of replicating Kohlberg's original moral development study on a British sample', *Journal of Moral Education*, 7, pp. 32–9.

White, C. B. (1975) 'Moral development in Bahamian school children: A cross-cultural examination of Kohlberg's stages of moral reasoning', *Developmental Psychology*, 11, pp. 535–6.

White, C. B. (1977) 'Moral reasoning in Bahamian and United States elders: Cross-national comparison of Kohlberg's theory of moral development', Unpublished manuscript, University of Texas at Dallas.

White, C. B., Bushnell, N. and Regnemer, J. L. (1978) 'Moral development in Bahamian school children: A three-year examination of Kohlberg's stages of moral development', *Developmental Psychology*, 14, pp. 58–65.

Journal of Personality and Social Psychology
1988, Vol. 55, No. 6, 1009–1015

Finding Universal Dimensions of Individual Variation in Multicultural Studies of Values: The Rokeach and Chinese Value Surveys

Michael Harris Bond
Chinese University of Hong Kong
Shatin, New Territories, Hong Kong

Both cross-cultural psychology and theories of value would benefit from the empirical identification of value dimensions that are pancultural and comprehensive. Accordingly, in this article, I report the results of a 21-culture study of the Chinese Value Survey (CVS) and a 9-culture study of the Rokeach Value Survey (RVS). The analysis began with a "deculturing" of the data to remove the cultural positioning effect, then proceeded with a pooled factor analysis to discover pancultural patterns of association among the values. Two factors emerged from the CVS, four from the RVS. The individuals in each survey were then given factor scores, which were analyzed for sex and culture effects. Average scores for individuals from the cultures common to both surveys suggest that the CVS contained a dimension of valuing not found in the RVS. The discussion focuses on the factors' validity, their use in cross-cultural research, and the potential of different cultural traditions for extending psychology's conceptual net.

From 1983 through 1985, a number of colleagues in universities around the world collected responses from a representative group of their students to a 40-item Chinese value survey. These data were then subjected to an ecological factor analysis, a procedure that uses culture means for each value as its input (see, e.g., Hofstede, 1980, Ch. 2). This type of data processing yields groupings or dimensions of values, which can then be used to assign scores to cultures (see, e.g., Chinese Culture Connection, 1987). The resulting "culture maps" can then be used to explain a variety of cultural differences, both a priori and *ex post facto.*

The concern of this article is that this ecological or culture-level approach does not yield individual-level dimensions of values. By analyzing culture scores, one can find only dimensions of *cultural* variation (Scheuch, 1970). These culture-level relations have no necessary parallels with individual level relations, as Shweder (1973) and Hofstede (1980, Ch. 1) have taken pains to emphasize. Indeed, culture-level groupings of psychological phenomena such as values often appear puzzling and are subject to considerable interpretive debate (see, e.g., Triandis's 1982 review of Hofstede, 1980).

Psychologists are much more comfortable at the individual level of analysis, in part because they can use their own phenomenology to make sense of the factor groupings and generate hypotheses. Within a given culture this procedure is relatively straightforward (see, e.g., Braithwaite & Law, 1985), subject

The author wishes to express his gratitude to the Centre for Contemporary Asian Studies of Chinese University of Hong Kong for its financial assistance in running this study. Kwok Leung and Shalom Schwartz provided constant support and wise counsel on all aspects of this research.

Correspondence concerning this article should be addressed to Michael Harris Bond, Department of Psychology, Chinese University of Hong Kong, Shatin, New Territories, Hong Kong.

only to the inevitable debates about the merit of the input, the method of analysis used, the number of dimensions extracted, the labeling of the identified constructs, and so forth.

When one ventures to sample responses across a number of cultures, however, the Furies are unleashed. The main conceptual challenge is that of establishing equivalence, that is, the basis by which the cultures may be compared. Psychologists using theory-driven approaches may analyze their data culture by culture, establishing equivalence by interpreting resulting patterns with the assistance of their theoretical constructs and cultural informants (see, e.g., Schwartz & Bilsky, 1987). Psychologists using data-driven approaches, however, must establish equivalence metrically by showing similarities in factor composition within *each* of the cultures from which the individual respondents have been drawn (Buss & Royce, 1975).

Elsewhere (Leung & Bond, in press), it has been argued that this requirement is too restrictive, for it is unlikely that the coefficients of factorial congruence for all possible pairings from *m* cultures across *n* factors could all attain a common, high level. This restriction is rarely applied by psychologists working within a particular culture to see if all individuals (or indeed subgroups, such as men and women) subscribe to the same factor groupings descriptive of the whole sample of individuals from that culture. Rather, the result of the analysis across all individuals is instead taken as a best fit to the data, and the usefulness of the yield is then explored by searching for relations between these dimensions and other behaviors of interest.

The same best-fit approach may be taken to data derived from a large number of cultures. That is, each respondent from the *n* cultures sampled may be taken as a representative of the human race and the data then analyzed to reveal the dimensions necessary to describe the human respondents in the sample. The obvious advantage of this approach is that any resultant dimensions are robust across cultures, because culturally idiosyncratic patterns of relations (emics) filter out in the overall analysis. The relations that survive this pancultural sifting then have a strong claim to the status of a universal (etic) dimension. The strength of this claim depends, of course, on the number and the differentness of the cultural groups sampled. The usefulness of the yield is determined by the cash value of the dimensions in the scientific marketplace, namely, their ability to be integrated into a nomological network that is persuasive.

With this intent it may be especially instructive to explore universal dimensions of values derived from a *Chinese* survey of values. Much concern has been expressed recently about the limitations imposed on psychological knowledge by doing social science exclusively from a Western cultural background (e.g., Sampson, 1985). One way to address this issue empirically is to use the constructs available in a different cultural tradition as one's starting point. The Chinese heritage certainly meets this requirement of difference: philosophically, artistically, socially, and historically (see, e.g., Fung, 1948; Hookham, 1969; King & Bond, 1985).

One aspect of values that may be relatively more salient from the Chinese tradition is, of course, the value of tradition itself. Four thousand years of relatively successful adaptation to historical vicissitudes might well be hypothesized to confer a respect for aspects of received wisdom that is unlikely to be found in the comparatively short-lived cultures of the West. Other possible lacunae in such Western instruments as Rokeach's (1973) Value Survey might concern the benefits deriving from concentrations of individual power (see Pye, 1968), from a collective orientation (Hsu, 1953), and from a philosophy of self-restraint (Wu & Tseng, 1985).

Unfortunately, there is little Western research against which to compare the results of this study. Very few multicultural studies of values have been done (Zavalloni, 1980). Of those available, most are theory-driven (e.g., the work of Kluckhohn & Strodtbeck, 1961), and hence impose a priori groupings on the results. Of the few remaining (e.g., Ng et al., 1982), none has partialed out the ecological or cross-cultural confound prior to analyzing the data (see Method section). However, it is possible to reanalyze the data from the Ng et al. study with due methodological rigor. As those investigators used the Rokeach Value Survey, it is possible to compare the yield from that Western instrument with that from the Chinese Value Survey, an Eastern instrument.

Recently, Braithwaite and Law (1985) expressed the concern that the Rokeach Value Survey may not sample the whole range of important human values. If true, the oversights may in part be culturally based, given that the Western origin of the Rokeach Value Survey may have blinded its creator to values more salient from other cultural perspectives. One way to assess this claim is to examine the empirical convergence produced by applying the two different instruments to the same populations (e.g., Hofstede & Bond, 1984). In this research, one can calculate the average score for people from each country on the individual-level dimensions of value. If these average levels of response to Rokeach Value Survey and Chinese Value Survey factors correlate across common countries, one may conclude that the factors are functionally equivalent; if not, the two instruments may be used to complement one another, suggesting where each is inadequate. This procedure is applied for the

overlapping cultures in this study and in the earlier study by Ng et al. (1982).

This approach is, of course, atheoretical and deliberately so. If a universal psychology is to be developed, psychologists must "consult all that is human," to use Murphy's (1969, p. 528) memorable phrase, and in so doing, scrupulously avoid premature foreclosure on our conceptual options. An informed culling of alternative cultural prescriptions is one antidote to the putative egocentrism of Western social science. Even if these alternative approaches merely confirm mainstream theorizing, the discipline will be on surer footing and less vulnerable to sniping from defenders of other cultural traditions.

Method

Subjects

In the original study (Chinese Culture Connection, 1987), colleagues in 22 cultures each administered the Chinese Value Survey (CVS) to 50 male and 50 female undergraduates. Every effort was made to include the full range of undergraduate majors and to ensure that the universities in the sample enjoyed a similar high status in all participating countries.

The choice of university students as a subject population was motivated partly by considerations of easy access for colleagues and partly by a desire to maximize the equivalence of the respondents across so many cultures. Although university students around the world are similar in many important respects (intelligence, social status, etc.), they are hardly representative of their cultures. The resulting averages for subjects from a given culture must therefore be interpreted with some flexibility.

Instrument

The CVS consists of 40 items whose degree of perceived importance is rated by each respondent on a 9-point scale. The stem items (with synonyms in brackets) are values deemed to be of fundamental importance in Chinese culture by a group of Chinese scholars consulted before the instrument was put together. These include such fundamental components of the Chinese tradition as moderation (following the middle way), ordering relationships by status, benevolent authority, being conservative, and having a sense of shame (Bond & Hwang, 1986). The scale's construction mimicked the process by which it was supposed that value surveys are typically produced, namely, that researchers mine their own cultural traditions without any regard for the traditions of other distinct groups.

The scale has already been analyzed at the level of culture means, using what Hofstede (1980) termed an *ecological factor analysis*. The resulting four factors ordered countries in ways that showed high correlations with the economic indexes of wealth and growth (Chinese Culture Connection, 1987). Further validity studies are in progress, focusing on country-level measures of health.

Procedure

If Chinese or English was not the language of classroom instruction, colleagues translated the CVS into the appropriate language, using the original Chinese version as the basis for a translation if possible. The CVS was administered in class and required about 5 min to complete.

Results

It is important that each cultural group be equally represented in the pooled factor analysis (described later). Otherwise,

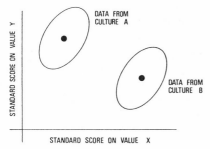

Figure 1. A reversal of X–Y correlation when data is pooled across cultures without correction.

the numerically superior cultures will have a greater impact on the final factor structure. In one culture, the collaborator responsible found only 33 women, so that all cultural samples were subsequently reduced by random selection to 33 men and 33 women. Furthermore, another collaborator did not provide individual data, so that the final results represent 21 rather than 22 cultures.

Standardizing Subject Responses

Both individually and culturally based response sets (acquiescence, negativism, variability) were eliminated by first standardizing each subject's 40 responses. This procedure retained the ordering of value importance and a measure of their relative strength one to another.

Deculturing the Data

Although standardized, the data contain average differences across the 21 cultures for each variable. These differences distort the factor pattern of the variables at *the individual level* if they are not first eliminated before pooling (see Leung & Bond, in press, for elaboration of this argument).

These standardized data do, of course, show average differences across the 21 cultural groups for each of the 40 values. These differences among cultures shift the distribution of scores for a given value up or down the scale. If the data from many different cultures are pooled at this point, the universal pattern of correlation among the variables will be distorted by this cultural positioning effect (Leung & Bond, in press). That is, the pattern of relations between Value X and Value Y found across all subjects from all cultures may be artifactually increased, decreased, or reversed depending on the size of the cultural positioning effect. Figure 1 illustrates this phenomenon with a simplified example.

As can be seen in Figure 1, the pattern of X–Y correlation for people in Culture A and people in Culture B is positive. If one pools the data at this point, however, the overall correlation between Variables X and Y will be negative as a result of the cultural positioning effect (Leung & Bond, in press, provide other examples). If one's interest is in the universal pattern of

value relations *at the individual level,* this positioning effect of culture must first be eliminated.

One may easily "deculture" data in this way by standardizing responses to *each* variable within *each* culture separately. The correlation between any two variables within a given culture is thereby not affected, but the cultural confound (i.e., the cross-cultural or ecological correlation) is removed because the average score for the two variables in each of the pooled cultural samples is zero. Following this procedure, a factor analysis will reveal the average pattern of relation between any two variables across all individuals regardless of culture (Leung & Bond, in press).

Pooled Factor Analysis

I then submitted the decultured ratings of 1,386 individuals (66 people × 21 cultures) to a principal-components factor analysis. A scree test (Cattell, 1966) of the resulting eigenvalues indicated the presence of two reliable factors accounting for 13.8% of the matrix variance. Although this figure may at first blush seem small, one must recall that the sample itself is heterogeneous to an extreme degree, so that common variance is bound to be small. A high level of unexplainable variance is part of the price paid in the search for universality.

The two factors were then subjected to a varimax rotation.

Social Integration versus Cultural Inwardness. The items at the positive end of this bipolar factor all involve prosocial virtues that enhance cohesiveness with others in general. Those virtues on the negative pole concern loyalty to more narrowly defined groups (family, culture) along with their defining habits and customs. The composition of this factor bears a striking

Table 1

Factor Structure and Loadings of Individual-Level Responses to the Chinese Value Survey in 21 Cultures

Item	Loading
Factor 1: Social Integration vs. Cultural Inwardness	
Tolerance of others	.58
Patience	.53
Harmony with others	.50
Noncompetitiveness	.43
Trustworthiness	.37
Persistence	.36
Filial piety	−.49
Respect for tradition	−.42
Chastity in women	−.40
A sense of cultural superiority	−.39
Observation of rites and social rituals	−.36
Factor 2: Reputation vs. Social Morality	
Protecting your "face"	.47
Wealth	.46
Reciprocation of greetings, favors, and gifts	.39
Keeping oneself disinterested and pure	−.54
Chastity in women	−.40
Sense of righteousness	−.37

Note. The percentage of matrix variance subsumed by Factor 1 was 8.1, and by Factor 2, 5.7.

resemblance to the first factor identified in the culture-level analysis of the CVS (Chinese Culture Connection, 1987). Indeed, the coefficient of congruence between the two factor patterns was .80, suggesting considerable overlap. Elsewhere, Leung & Bond (in press) have suggested that this convergence between the cultural and individual levels of analysis indicates the presence of a strong universal.

It is worth noting the similarity of the positive pole with Schwartz and Bilsky's (1987) prosocial and maturity domains of values. The negative pole overlaps conceptually with Schwartz's (1987) domains of tradition maintenance and restrictive conformity.

Reputation versus Social Morality. The values defining the positive pole of this factor are all related to establishing or maintaining one's standing in society. They seem to be related to Schwartz and Bilsky's (1987) domain of social power.

The negative pole is anchored with values reflecting a correct and principled approach to life. This constellation taps into Schwartz's (1987) domains of maturity and possibly restrictive conformity.

Analyses of Variance

The preceding factors represent the shared groupings of the CVS values across individuals from 21 countries. These factors afford dimensions along which the respondents may be statistically compared with respect to their cultural backgrounds and gender. Such comparisons are, of course, impossible when data are analyzed at the level of culture scores (e.g., in Hofstede's 1980 work) because in that case cultures, not individuals, constitute the level of analysis.

At this point in the data analysis, the cultural positioning effect is of fundamental interest. Consequently, it is the original data standardized within individuals that must be grouped according to the patterns discovered in the pooled factor analysis. Accordingly, each respondent's original standardized scores were recalled, so that each could be given two factor scores: one for Social Integration versus Cultural Inwardness, the other for Reputation versus Personal Morality. The score on each factor was obtained by summing the original standardized scores for each of the salients listed in Table 1. A more conservative alpha level of .01 was adopted.

Social Integration versus Cultural Inwardness. There was a main effect for culture, $F(20, 1290) = 50.6$, $p < .001$, and an interaction between culture and sex of subjects, $F(20, 1290) = 2.79$, $p < .001$. The average score of respondents from the 21 cultures can be found in Table 2. The significance of the differences between any two cultural groups is, of course, dependent on the sample size and alpha level chosen. In the interest of space, these differences are not presented in this article.

Reputation versus Social Morality. As before, there was a main effect for culture, $F(20, 1290) = 33.7$, $p < .001$, and an interaction between culture and sex of subjects, $F(20, 1290) = 2.29$, $p < .001$. Again, average scores are presented in Table 2.

Analysis of the Rokeach Value Survey

Ng et al. (1982) used the same response format, sample size, and populations in collecting their data, using an expanded ver-

Table 2

Mean Individual Scores by Country on Chinese Value Survey Factors

Social Integration (+) vs. Cultural Inwardness (−)		Reputation (+) vs. Social Morality (−)	
Country	M	Country	M
The Netherlands	8.57	England	2.62
West Germany	8.30	Brazil	2.00
New Zealand	5.55	New Zealand	1.81
Brazil	5.35	Australia	1.35
Australia	5.26	Zimbabwe	1.24
Japan	4.97	United States	1.20
England	4.65	Canada	0.65
Sweden	3.81	Sweden	0.63
Canada	3.80	West Germany	0.13
Singapore	3.09	Nigeria	0.07
Poland	2.91	Pakistan	−0.29
United States	2.84	The Netherlands	−0.32
Hong Kong	2.53	Taiwan	−0.80
South Korea	2.43	Japan	−1.50
Zimbabwe	2.37	Singapore	−1.68
Nigeria	1.79	Bangladesh	−1.91
Thailand	1.29	Poland	−2.37
Taiwan	1.13	Hong Kong	−2.47
Pakistan	−1.61	Thailand	−2.53
India	−1.83	India	−2.73
Bangladesh	−2.80	South Korea	−3.42

Note. Plus and minus signs denote positive and negative poles.

sion of the Rokeach Value Survey (RVS). Their data set may be treated and analyzed in the same way as that from the CVS. As seven cultures are common to both samples, results may then be checked for convergence empirically by assessing how the two factor solutions locate the typical person from the seven common cultures (see, e.g., Hofstede & Bond, 1984).

Factor analysis. Too few female subjects were available in the original sample from Papua-New Guinea to include its respondents in the factor analysis. The final sample consisted of 29 men and 29 women from nine different cultures, giving a total of 522 respondents. A factor analysis of this decultured data set yielded four factors by the scree test, together accounting for 25.2% of the total matrix variance. I then applied a varimax rotation to these four factors. (See Table 3 for factor loadings.)

Competence versus Security. This first factor contrasts personal intellectual skills against safety concerns. These domains correspond to the self-direction–security contrast theoretically posited and empirically confirmed by Schwartz (1987) and Schwartz and Bilsky (1987).

Personal Morality versus Success. This second factor presents the telling contrast between characteristics of individual rectitude and aspects of the "good life." The positive pole is one component of Schwartz and Bilsky's (1987) prosocial morality; the latter overlaps with their social power and achievement domains.

Social Reliability versus Beauty. The positive pole is a well-defined reflection of socialized virtues, tapping the domain Schwartz and Bilsky (1987) called *restrictive conformity.* The negative pole is less well defined, perhaps because the RVS contains so few values in this area. It would seem to correspond to

Table 3
*Factor Structure and Loadings of Individual-Level Responses
to the Expanded Rokeach Value Survey in Nine Cultures*

Item	Loading	Item	Loading
Factors 1: Competence vs. Security		Factor 3: Social Reliability vs. Beauty	
Intellectual	.61	Responsible	.63
Independent	.52	Polite	.60
Capable	.51	Self-controlled	.56
Logical	.50	Obedient	.56
Imaginative	.36	World of beauty	−.35
Family security	−.51		
World of peace	−.41		
Factor 2: Personal Morality vs. Success		Factor 4: Political Harmony vs. Personal Sociability	
Forgiving	.55	Equality	.51
Helpful	.55	World of peace	.45
Honest	.48	Social justice	.44
Courageous	.38	Cheerful	−.47
Social recognition	−.53	Clean	−.45
Power	−.51	Loving	−.44
Comfortable life	−.41		

Note. The percentage of matrix variance subsumed by Factor 1 was 7.9; by Factor 2, 7.0; by Factor 3, 5.7; and by Factor 4, 4.7.

the aesthetic dimension of Schwartz and Bilsky, which is positioned in opposition to restrictive conformity in both their theory and empirical findings.

Political Harmony versus Personal Sociability. The positive pole of this factor reflects a happy vision of social and international concord. It is the more universal, less personal aspect of what Schwartz (1987) defined as *prosocial morality.* The negative pole taps personal characteristics conducing toward interpersonal attractiveness, the narrowness of this goal perhaps contrasting with the wider concerns about political harmony. It appears to have no counterpart in the Schwartz typology.

Analyses of Variance

As before, the preceding factors may be used to generate factor scores for each individual in the sample. The original standardized scores of each value loading >.35 on a given factor were algebraically summed for each individual to produce four factor scores, one for each of the factors. These scores were then tested using a two-way analysis of variance (ANOVA) with nine levels of the culture variable and two levels of the sex variable. Means for all factors are listed in Table 4.

Competence versus Security. There was a main effect for culture, $F(8, 503) = 4.40, p < .001$. There was also an effect for sex, $F(1, 503) = 21.8, p < .001$, with men scoring higher than women ($Ms = -.16$ vs. -1.42, respectively).

Personal Morality versus Success. Again, there was a main effect for culture, $F(8, 503) = 4.55, p < .001$. There was also an effect for sex, $F(1, 503) = 10.6, p < .005$, with women scoring higher than men ($Ms = 2.84$ vs. 1.87, respectively).

Social Reliability versus Beauty. The only effect for this analysis was a main effect for culture, $F(8, 504) = 10.3, p < .001$.

Political Harmony versus Personal Sociability. There was a main effect for culture, $F(8, 504) = 2.72, p < .01$.

Convergence of Profiles From the Two Value Samples

The average score of an individual respondent in the seven cultures common to both samples can be calculated for each of the six factors (two CVS, four RVS). Scores from the RVS and the CVS may then be intercorrelated across these seven "average citizens" to assess whether there is any suggestion of overlap in the value domains they tap. Although the sample size was small, this empirical method of identifying overlap sidesteps the judgment calls typically made by researchers who "eyeball" the factor groupings to establish conceptual equivalence.

The correlation between the second CVS factor, Reputation versus Social Morality, and the third RVS factor, Social Reliability versus Beauty, was a strikingly high −.99 ($p < .001$). The morality of the CVS would thus seem to overlap closely with the reliability of the RVS, showing more underlying similarity than the content of the values may initially have suggested. Both clearly involve virtues of restraint and discipline, which Schwartz (1987) called *restrictive morality,* and are opposed by more self-indulgent pursuits.

The first CVS factor did not correlate significantly with any of the four RVS factors.

Discussion

The yield from this research is five etic dimensions of values, one unique to the Chinese Value Survey, three unique to the

Table 4
*Mean Individual Scores by Country on Rokeach
Value Survey Factors*

Country	M	Country	M
Competence (+) vs. Security (−)		Social Reliability (+) vs. Beauty (−)	
Taiwan	0.90	Malaysia (Malays)	2.02
Malaysia (Malays)	−0.38	Malaysia (Chinese)	0.89
Australia	−0.39	Indian	0.87
New Zealand	−0.70	Hong Kong	0.67
India	−0.75	Bangladesh	0.55
Hong Kong	−0.93	Japan	0.24
Malaysia (Chinese)	−1.09	Taiwan	−0.18
Bangladesh	−1.83	Australia	−0.89
Japan	−1.95	New Zealand	−1.43
Personal Morality (+) vs. Success (−)		Political Harmony (+) vs. Personal Sociability (−)	
New Zealand	3.82	Bangladesh	0.79
Hong Kong	3.28	Hong Kong	0.00
Australia	3.15	Australia	−0.09
Malaysia (Malays)	2.55	New Zealand	−0.32
Malaysia (Chinese)	2.43	Malaysia (Chinese)	−0.51
Taiwan	1.93	India	−0.51
Japan	1.65	Japan	−0.61
Bangladesh	1.47	Malaysia (Malays)	−0.86
India	0.90	Taiwan	−1.22

Note. Plus and minus signs denote positive and negative poles.

Rokeach Value Survey, and one common to both. These five dimensions are defined as etic because they are derived from factor analyses of the responses to the value surveys by respondents from a number of heterogeneous cultures. The pooling procedure used weeds out associations unique to particular cultures (emics), leaving a residue of relations common across all. This shared structure constitutes a universal grid of values instrumental in making empirically grounded statements about cultural differences *at the level of individuals.*

It is, of course, true that the factor structure common across all cultural samples in a pooled analysis is only an approximation of the structure to be found in any one sample taken by itself. This consequence is the price paid for attempting to generalize across such diversity, and occurs in less dramatic ways whenever scientists pool across potentially distinctive groupings within a culture. The categories of sex, age, wealth, education, ideology, and so forth are often ignored in the search for common structure. In any case, there is at present no way of determining statistically which degree of departure from the common factor structure should constitute grounds for discarding any particular sample.

Ultimately, the crucible of merit for these pancultural dimensions of value is their *scientific cash value,* as James termed it. Can they be knit into a theoretical framework and can they be related to empirical phenomena of interest? Concerning empirical validities, the sex differences found in the ratings of the competence–security and personal morality–success dimensions of the RVS are persuasive. Any sex effects that generalize across so many different cultures must be robust indeed, and probably reflect universal differences in socialization practices distinguishing the sexes (see, e.g., Block, 1973; Munroe & Munroe, 1975, Ch. 7). Furthermore, the higher endorsement by women of values related to security and to personal morality is consistent with the socialized emphasis on communion as opposed to agency in the female role across cultures (Bakan, 1966), and parallels results found by Feather (1975) and Schwartz (personal communication).

The use of cultural main effects as a source of validation for the value dimensions is much more problematic. The ideal situation would be to sample individual behavior of interest from a number of cultures and compute the score of average individuals from each culture. These typical scores could then be related to the value profiles for average individuals from the same cultures. Unfortunately, there have been very few multicultural studies of behavior (e.g., Whiting & Whiting, 1975), and those that exist do not overlap in sufficient number with this study. Perhaps more importantly, there is too little theory on the linkages between *specific* value dimensions and behavior to guide the search for connections in any case.

Another approach to validating the use of these factors is to relate the typical citizen scores on the value dimensions to culture-level data, such as suicide rates, economic indexes, measures of civil disorder, and so forth. Obviously some theoretical guidance is required to relate individual-level to cultural-level phenomena, as they are conceptually distinct (Scheuch, 1970). Promising attempts have, however, already been made (Berry, 1979; Triandis, 1984).

The results of the CVS survey are appropriate in this regard, as 21 scores lend considerable confidence to any empirical

finding. Correlations between country wealth (GNP per capita in 1984) and typical citizen scores on the first CVS factor (Social Integration vs. Cultural Inwardness) yield $r(19) = .63, p < .005$. Likewise, correlations between economic growth over the past 20 years and scores on the second CVS factor (Reputation vs. Personal Morality) yield $r(19) = -.50$, $p < .025$. To date, only these two indexes of economic performance have been examined for relations with CVS factor scores. There are undoubtedly other phenomena to which these value data may be linked. The present results, however, serve to illustrate the potential of the CVS constructs as scientific tools.

Such value constructs have an important and growing role to play. It is clear that cross-cultural psychology is in dire need of more theory-driven, multicultural studies. Expectancy-value theories (Feather, 1979) have already demonstrated their usefulness in cross-cultural research (e.g., Leung, 1988); work on the values construct is increasing (e.g., Braithwaite & Law, 1985; Schwartz & Bilsky, 1987); and multicultural projects are now more feasible (e.g., Triandis et al., 1986). This research has provided value "maps" for typical university students from 21 cultures on two dimensions and from 9 cultures on four dimensions. These maps can be used to plan a priori selections of cultural groups (and to ground *post hoc* explanations of resulting differences when no a priori selection is made).

So, for example, values loading on the first CVS factor (Social Integration versus Cultural Inwardness) may well relate to the making of weak versus strong discriminations between ingroup and out-groups. Likewise, endorsements of the competence versus security dimension may relate to risk-taking behavior. On the other hand, ratings along the Personal Morality versus Success factor may relate to altruism. Cross-cultural comparisons of these and other behaviors could be preceded by a judicious selection of cultural samples so as to be maximally informative about the theory being tested. Any theory so confirmed would have demonstrated universality in its application, an outcome that would strongly support its validity.

The question remains as to whether the five independent dimensions identified in this study are exhaustive or not. Recent criticism of the RVS and other instruments in this regard (e.g., Braithwaite & Law, 1985) reflects concerns that have in part encouraged Schwartz's (1987) recent development of a more comprehensive instrument to measure values. With the exception of his stimulation, hedonism, and perhaps spiritual clusters, however, all of Schwartz's putative value domains appear to have been tapped by the factors identified in the present research.

The *Chinese* values appear to contribute a dimension that complements those identified by the RVS. One pole, that of cultural inwardness, involves the sense of valued tradition itself. It is precisely these sorts of values that critics such as Sampson (1981) would argue are invisible to Westerners, constrained as they are by their individualistic cultural agendas. The other pole of this factor, social integration, involves values that can be broadly construed as prosocial, but that capture a decidedly Chinese focus on harmony in interpersonal relations (Bond & Hwang, 1986). Comparable values do not appear on the RVS.

The present research thus demonstrates the potential of alternative cultural realities to broaden and extend our conceptual resources in psychology. It is one response to Sampson's (1985) plea for "a body of empirical research that has been cast from a different mold." (p. 1210) Other responses are forthcoming (Yang & Bond, 1988). In sufficient number, such work will contribute to a universalizing of psychology.

References

Bakan, D. (1966). *The duality of human existence.* Chicago: Rand McNally.

Berry, J. W. (1979). A cultural ecology of social behavior. In L. Berkowitz (Ed.), *Advances in experimental social psychology* (Vol. 12, pp. 177–206). New York: Academic Press.

Block, J. H. (1973). Conceptions of sex role: Some cross-cultural and longitudinal perspectives. *American Psychologist, 28,* 512–526.

Bond, M. H., & Hwang, K. K. (1986). The social psychology of Chinese people. In M. H. Bond (Ed.), *The psychology of the Chinese people* (pp. 213–266). Hong Kong: Oxford University Press.

Braithwaite, V. A., & Law, H. G. (1985). Structure of human values: Testing the adequacy of the Rokeach Value Survey. *Journal of Personality and Social Psychology, 49,* 250–263.

Buss, A., & Royce, J. B. (1975). Detecting cross-cultural commonalities and differences: Intergroup factor analyses. *Psychological Bulletin, 82,* 128–136.

Cattell, R. B. (1966). The scree test for the number of factors. *Multivariate Behavioral Research, 1,* 245–276.

Chinese Culture Connection (1987). Chinese values and the search for culture-free dimensions of culture. *Journal of Cross-Cultural Psychology, 18,* 143–164.

Feather, N. T. (1975). *Values in education and society.* New York: Free Press.

Feather, N. T. (1979). Values, expectancy, and action. *American Psychologist, 14,* 243–260.

Fung, Y. L. (1948). *A short history of Chinese philosophy.* New York: Macmillan.

Hofstede, G. (1980). *Culture's consequences: International differences in work-related values.* Beverly Hills, CA: Sage.

Hofstede, G., & Bond, M. H. (1984). Hofstede's culture dimensions: An independent validation using Rokeach's value survey. *Journal of Cross-Cultural Psychology, 15,* 417–433.

Hookham, H. (1969). *A short history of China.* New York: New American Library.

Hsu, F. L. K. (1953). *Americans and Chinese: Two ways of life.* New York: Abelard-Schuman.

King, A. Y. C., & Bond, M. H. (1985). The Confucian paradigm of man: A sociological view. In W. S. Tseng & D. Y. H. Wu (Eds.), *Chinese culture and mental health* (pp. 29–45). Orlando, FL: Academic Press.

Kluckhohn, F., & Strodtbeck, F. (1961). *Variations in value orientations.* Evanston, IL: Row, Peterson.

Leung, K. (1988). Theoretical advances in justice behavior: Some cross-cultural inputs. In M. H. Bond (Ed.), *The cross-cultural challenge to social psychology* (pp. 218–229). Beverly Hills, CA: Sage.

Leung, K., & Bond, M. K. (in press). On the empirical identification of dimensions for cross-cultural comparison. *Journal of Cross-Cultural Psychology.*

Munroe, R. L., & Munroe, R. H. (1975). *Cross-cultural human development.* Belmont, CA: Brooks-Cole.

Murphy, G. (1969). Psychology in the year 2000. *American Psychologist, 24,* 523–530.

Ng, S. H., Akhtar-Hossain, A. B. M., Ball, P., Bond, M. H., Hayashi, K., Lim, S. P., O'Driscoll, M. P., Sinha, D., & Yang, K. S. (1982). Values in nine countries. In R. Rath, H. S. Asthana, & J. B. H. Sinha (Eds.), *Diversity and unity in cross-cultural psychology* (pp. 196–205). Lisse, The Netherlands: Swets & Zeitlinger.

Pye, L. W. (1968). *The spirit of Chinese politics: A psychocultural study of the authority crisis in political development.* Cambridge, MA: M.I.T. Press.

Rokeach, M. (1973). *The nature of human values.* New York: Free Press.

Sampson, E. E. (1981). Cognitive psychology as ideology. *American Psychologist, 36,* 730–743.

Sampson, E. E. (1985). The decentralization of identity: Toward a revised concept of personal and social order. *American Psychologist, 40,* 1203–1211.

Scheuch, E. K. (1970). Cross-national comparisons using aggregate data. In A. Etzioni & F. L. Dubow (Eds.), *Comparative perspectives: Theories and methods* (pp. 365–386). Boston: Little, Brown.

Schwartz, S. H. (1987). *Invitation to collaborate in cross-cultural research on values.* Unpublished manuscript, Hebrew University of Jerusalem, Jerusalem, Israel.

Schwartz, S. H., & Bilsky, W. (1987). Toward a universal psychological structure of human values. *Journal of Personality and Social Psychology, 53,* 550–562.

Shweder, R. A. (1973). The between and within of cross-cultural research. *Ethos, 1,* 521–545.

Triandis, H. C. (1982). [Review of *Culture's consequences*]. *Human Organization, 41,* 86–90.

Triandis, H. C. (1984). Toward a psychological theory of economic growth. *International Journal of Psychology, 19,* 79–95.

Triandis, H. C., Bontempo, R., Betancourt, H., Bond, M. H., Leung, K., Brenes, A., Georgas, J., Hui, H. C., Marin, G., Setiadi, B., Sinha, J. B. P., Verma, J., Spangenberg, J., Touzard, H., & de Montmollin, G. (1986). The measurement of the etic aspects of individualism and collectivism across cultures. *Australian Journal of Psychology, 38,* 257–267.

Whiting, B. B., & Whiting, J. W. M. (1975). *Children of six cultures: A psycho-cultural analysis.* Cambridge, MA: Harvard University Press.

Wu, D. Y. H., & Tseng, W. S. (1985). Introduction: The characteristics of Chinese culture. In D. Y. H. Wu & W. S. Tseng (Eds.), *Chinese culture and mental health* (pp. 3–13). Orlando, FL: Academic Press.

Yang, K. S., & Bond, M. H. (1988). *Exploring implicit personality theories with indigenous or imported constructs: The Chinese case.* Manuscript submitted for publication.

Zavalloni, M. (1980). Values. In H. C. Triandis & R. W. Brislin (Eds.), *Handbook of cross-cultural psychology: Vol. 5, Social* (pp. 73–120). Boston: Allyn & Bacon.

Received November 9, 1987
Revision received April 26, 1988
Accepted May 10, 1988 ■

Hum. Dev. *30:* 268–281 (1987)

The Development of Political Reasoning

Evan Simpson

McMaster University, Hamilton, Ont., Canada

Key Words. Cognitive development · Developmental stages · Group discussion · Moral development · Political attitudes · Social interaction

Abstract. This discussion explores a striking correspondence between conservative, liberal, and egalitarian political attitudes and the three upper stages in Kohlberg's schema of moral development. In the context of cognitive-developmental theory, the correspondence entails that political ideologies can be ranked in order of cognitive adequacy, but analysis of the evidence uncovers only 'soft' political stages. The success of Habermas's alternative attempt to derive the moral stages from stages of interactive competence depends upon viewing competence in terms of the evolution of communicative practices rather than genuine structural development. His reconciliation of broadly Piagetan and broadly Marxist forms of structuralism leaves the former able to account for prepolitical reasoning but ties political argument to a set of alternative institutional forms rather than to a hierarchy of historical stages.

The ordinary practical disagreements which arise among friends and associates can usually be resolved through discussion. Political questions, by comparison, tend to resist consensus, and many political issues remain permanently unresolved. These facts are too familiar to be surprising, but the absence of a good explanation for the limitations of political communication is a matter of interest and concern. There are technical explanations – ranging from the costs of information to the nature of the media through which modern political discussion is conducted – and they undoubtedly state some of the truth, but there also seem to be developmental reasons. One of the most interesting possibilities arises from recent work in moral psychology.

The most intractable political questions are those whose answers express competing ideologies. A number of studies of moral development have suggested that the main political ideologies can be ranked in order of cognitive adequacy. The idea that philosophical differences can be treated as developmental pervades genetic epistemology [Broughton and Freeman-Moir, 1982], but Kohlberg's work expresses this theme particularly clearly. It implies that different individuals have markedly different capacities for political reasoning and that valid positions may seem inferior or irrational to persons whose reasoning is less advanced.

Let us assume that Kohlberg's [1971] account of moral growth is descriptively adequate. As Henry [1983] suggests, it succeeds in providing 'an empirical ordering' of moral orientations. The thinness of political argument in democratic societies can then be understood as follows: many people whose consent must be won lack the mature political understanding required for adequate discussion and debate. The data show that arguments representing superior orientations are easily misinterpreted. A principled advocate of equality, for example, may be convincingly caricatured as simply envious to an audience unable to appreciate the reasons for egalitarian claims. Kohlberg has shown, in effect, that such attacks may be honest misrepresentations rather than deliberate distortions. His remedy is moral education.

This explanatory sketch is usefully contrasted and compared with a sociological perspective on the same empirical ordering. Marxists, among others, stress the effects of social structures on political argument. In traditional and hierarchical forms of social organization, the ideological perception of conventional norms as natural standards rigidly constrains practical discussion. In a system of cooperation which endorses the free competition of individual interests, the ideology of freedom makes it impossible to take egalitarian alternatives seriously and limits discussion to finding compromises rather than permitting it to generate consensus about public objectives. In both systems forms of self-deception reflect structural barriers to adequate political reasoning. On this view, political maturity presupposes further social development.

Developmental psychologists agree upon a structuralist account of practical reasoning, but the structures they identify are basically cognitive. If they are right, and problems of communication can be traced to inflexible patterns of individual development, then the obstacles to rational agreement are not simply artifacts of the system of organization. Parts of this view are too well confirmed to be displaced by sociological accounts, but the available evidence makes the developmental view more compelling for the moral reasoning of children than for political thought. There is also evidence that neither of the familiar structuralist accounts by itself sheds much useful light on specifically political reasoning. Recent attempts by Habermas [1979] to describe interactive competencies which bring the opposing viewpoints together suggest a fruitful synthesis, but the result is an account which ties political reasoning to contingently changing communicative practices. It does not (as Habermas once thought) conform to a Piagetan logic of development defined by a series of irreversible stages none of which can be passed over and each of which constitutes a more successful mode of problem-solving than the one before. The following analysis supports these theses by (1) describing the political dimension of Kohlberg's view in sharper detail; (2) elaborating the alternative models of political development, and (3) using Habermas's writings to fashion an understanding of political reasoning as neither strictly developmental nor merely fortuitous.

The Moral Dimension of Political Reasoning

Political argument is largely moral, for it aims at determining right action. As noted in Simpson [1980], any political decision is incorrect if it violates the requirement of community that no member suffer unjustified domination, which is always an injustice or wrong. There is *Realpolitik,* of course, but deliberations about the use of force without right are surrogates for political discussion, not instances of it. Like de Waal's [1982] chimpanzee communities, political systems can be described without employing moral concepts; but conceptions of right and justice form an inescapable part of the context of political reasoning because they are integral to the participants' standpoint and to discussions amongst political agents. It is thus Kohlberg's conception of morality as justice which makes his studies of moral development particularly important for understanding political ideologies.

Lest this point be misunderstood, let me note in the spirit of Youniss [1983] rather than of Buck-Morss [1975], Reid and Yanarella [1977], and others that it is no part of my claim that Kohlberg's explanatory scheme is itself ideological. Even if the latter account should be correct, the case I want to make here leaves this issue aside. The argument does not depend upon supposing that Kohlberg's preference for certain ideologies is presupposed in his theoretical framework. Likewise, I employ the word 'ideology' simply in order to refer summarily to familiar bodies of political belief. The disputes surrounding this sometimes controversial term lie outside the focus of the present discussion.

Kohlberg groups 6 stages of moral development into three levels - preconventional, conventional, autonomous – but his original depiction of the stages makes a dual division

– prepolitical and political – equally appropriate. The evaluative conceptions in the former group may be labeled (1) physical, (2) pragmatic, and (3) interpersonal. They are prepolitical in lacking the systematic vision which is necessary for understanding the complex interdependencies of social organizations in which questions of property and justice are central. They cause practical matters to be viewed primarily in terms of what is good rather than in terms of what is right. The following representations make it clear that considerations of justice arise significantly only with the political morality of stage 4.

The prepolitical focus on relatively naive conceptions of the good is evident in Kohlberg's well-known characterizations. In stage 1 'the physical consequences of action determine its goodness or badness' [Kohlberg, 1971, p. 164]. In the stage 2 'instrumental-relativist' orientation, the best action 'consists of that which instrumentally satisfies one's own needs and occasionally the needs of others' [p. 164]. The orientation is identical to the viewpoint expressed by Hobbes [1651] in saying that 'No man giveth but with intention of Good to himselfe; ... and of all Voluntary Acts, the Object is to every man his own Good' [p. 116]. Finally, and in contrast to Hobbes's unduly restricted conception of altruistic judgment, from the stage 3 viewpoint 'good behavior is that which pleases or helps others and is approved by them' [Kohlberg, 1971, p. 164]. One here exhibits the patterns of social relationship and motivation which involve the ascription of intrinsic value to other people and their opinions.

Although such interpersonal judgments are social, this perspective is not yet a political one. The conception of value typical of intimate communities is as distinct from later perspectives as from the pragmatic form of reasoning. In being based upon concrete, personal relationships, its typical issues concern how to be 'good girls and boys'. These are not the questions of formal right and wrong which arise within a social order defined by laws. Genuine political discussion requires the comprehension of social systems, including the concepts of law and formal authority characteristic of states. While political thinking is inherently systematic, however, it differs according to one's conception of right. Kohlberg's descriptions of these conceptions make clear the appropriateness of labeling the ostensible stages of political reasoning (4) conservative, (5) liberal, and (6) egalitarian.

An impersonal '"law and order" orientation ... towards authority, fixed rules, and the maintenance of the social order' characterizes stage 4 and corresponds to a sense of justice as the performance of duty, respect for authority, and preservation of the basic rules and structure of society [Kohlberg 1971, p. 164]. The defining features of the stage 5 prior-to-society or social-contract orientation are 'awareness of the relativism of personal values' [p. 165] and the recognition of individual rights. An element of 'rule-utilitarianism' – the mode of assessing social norms according to their tendency to promote social welfare – also enters into this perspective. That welfarism should become a possible part of the content of liberalism in this way is not surprising, since the norms justified by utilitarian considerations have the backing of social agreement. Where agreement is lacking, however, it would seem to follow that welfare policies may lack justification. If so, stage 5 thinking can be expressed either in the ideals of fraternal liberalism or in the laissez-faire ideals of libertarianism.

This stage 5 orientation assumes a democratic social order in which people coordinate their actions to ensure that all may seek their own good in their own way. It does not, however, seem to accommodate the importance of respect for personality, at least as this is understood at stage 6. The liberal conception of justice stresses 'equality of opportunity, that is, equality of formal liberty to attain substantive equality' [p. 202]. Respect for personality, by contrast, embodies a sense of justice which focuses on 'the rights of humanity'. It implies that 'equality of opportunity means a fundamental treatment of all persons as of basic human worth'. Moral judgment, from this perspective, 'requires substantive moral principles' which say of all people that 'they are to be treated equally' [p. 212].

A number of emphases mark this 'universal ethical principle orientation' as an egalitarian rather than liberal outlook: the superiority of human to merely civil rights, the appeal to substantive principles of justice which limit the relativity of valid individual interests, and, of course, the strong sense of equality which characterizes it. Egalitarian conceptions of property, in particular, find support in stage 6 thinking. Whereas 'private property is conceived as the core of our society' at stage 4, and as 'an institutional arrangement for maximizing the welfare of the individuals composing society' at stage 5, the 'claim to life at the expense of property rights ... is a valid claim' at stage 6 [pp. 201, 213]. This highest stage expresses the 'radical and substantive ... principle of justice as equity in the distribution of income and respect' [Kohlberg, 1980, p. 457].

Against this background of changing moral conceptions many of our impressions of political argument become more substantial. On one hand, the fact that most people are motivated by moral beliefs rather than simply by hedonistic considerations explains why politicians in constitutional regimes generally avoid intimidation and bribery. Since such appeals are usually perceived as inferior and unsatisfactory, they would tend to offend most participants in a democratic system. On the other hand, given the difficulty or impossibility of understanding claims representing developmentally later stages, the fact that stage 4 is the commonest adult morality in any modern society should seriously limit the appeal of liberal and egalitarian arguments.

According to Kohlberg, fewer than a quarter, and perhaps only a tenth, of people deliberate at stage 5 or 6. Politicians who hope to succeed may therefore have to make their claims largely in conservative and interpersonal terms. Egalitarians must be continually wary of the dangers involved in suggesting disrespect for established authority and seeming to defend greed and envy. Liberals must appeal to the conventional majority without suggesting an unprincipled cynicism that could undermine their main base of active support. These problems of political communication are moderated to some extent by evidence [Kohlberg, 1971; Rest, 1979] that people may have an intuitive preference for somewhat higher-stage claims than those they can justify; and, contrary to Burke [1982], their solution will not include a tendency for political rhetoric 'to fall to the lowest common denominator of the community'. Rather, political utterances and manifestos need to include a rich concoction of claims

crafted so as to appeal from both lower and higher perspectives. Kohlberg's observations thus provide interesting insights into both the primitiveness and the complexity of much political discussion.

Theoretical Alternatives

We should be cautious about understanding ideological differences as reflections of cognitive capacities. The idea must be attractive to liberals and egalitarians who can claim logical superiority for their political positions, but there are theoretical explanations of these moral differences which diverge from the model of cognitive development and lack its appeal.

The argument is persuasive that cognitive-moral maturation continues through stage 4: the developmental steps in that process are marked by a series of clear and sharp conceptual differentiations – instrumental value from threat of punishment, the inherent value of other persons from their instrumental value, impersonal standards of evaluation from the inherent value of associates. An inability to make any of these discriminations leaves the later ones opaque. It has been suggested, however, that stages 4, 5, and 6 are not distinguishable in terms of cognitive structures [Gibbs, 1979; Simpson, 1983], so that the several later orientations can be viewed as alternative interpretations of a single Piagetan stage. The political characterization of Kohlberg's account adds support to this thesis. No sharp differentiations mark the conservative, liberal, and egalitarian viewpoints. Any political orientation may be intelligible to those of contrary persuasion.

Consider Burke's [1790] famous views on the social contract. He clearly seems to comprehend the 'stage 5' orientation in saying, 'Society is indeed a contract ... but the state ought not to be considered as nothing better than a partnership agreement in a trade of pepper and coffee ... Each contract of each particular state is but a clause in the great primaeval contract of eternal society ... This law is not subject to the will of those, who by an obligation above them, and infinitely superior, are bound to submit their will to that law' [pp. 194–195]. In the absence of contrary evidence, this conservative rendering of a liberal concept should be regarded as a disagreement, not a misunderstanding. Similar recent treatments of the same matters, such as Oakeshott's [1974] and Scruton's [1980], further strengthen the point. Once real disputes among philosophers are taken seriously, it becomes very difficult to maintain convincingly that cognitive structures are the most significant barriers to mature political reasoning. Puka [1982] has indicated that Kohlberg now regards conservative content as an ideological accompaniment rather than a defining feature of stage 4, and it seems possible to say the same of other ideologies. All of them can then be regarded as expressions of the stage 4 capacity for systematic thinking.

To propose that stage 4 is consistent with several different political orientations is not to say that everyone who reaches it has political beliefs. Full-fledged political reasoning becomes possible at stage 4, but not all systematic thinkers are likely to formulate a consistent political philosophy. In this respect stage 4, like those preceding it, is nonpolitical, and the contrary characterization only reflects Kohlberg's original descriptions. The newly recognized independence of the cognitive structure from particular political positions is borne out by a distinction [Kohlberg et al., 1983; Kohlberg, 1984] between A and B substages. This conception is too complex and problematical to be discussed here, but it can be noted that because stage 4A is authority-centered, whereas stage 4B has the liberal content of 'stage 5', the current formulation of the theory cannot easily represent this political difference as a matter of developmental maturity.

That differences in adult moral reasoning reflect political positions rather than developmental stages is corroborated by recent empirical work [Ember et al., 1983]. On empirical grounds Kohlberg has himself been more ambivalent about the existence of postconventional stages than the original theory implies [Kohlberg and Kramer, 1969; Kohlberg, 1973], and he now [Kohlberg et al., 1983] finds that stage 6 reasoning cannot be adequately documented. Even in his latest work, however, he rejects an early perception that stages 4, 5 and 6 might be viewed as 'alternative types of mature response rather than as a sequence' [Kohlberg, 1969, p. 385]. Instead, he tries to retain stage 5 as a 'hard', or Piagetan, stage by characterizing it as a particular set of formal rationales, procedures, and operations for dealing with problems of justice. It could be said, pursuing Kohlberg's thinking about conservative content beyond his own reflections, that the alternatives between welfare liberalism and libertarianism which occur within the prior-to-society orientation constitute differences of moral and political content accompanying the principled form of thinking. Liberalism might then be regarded as a family of ideologies associated with, but distinct from, a new social-perspective level and the justice operations peculiar to it.

There are several difficulties with such an attempt to save stage 5. Firstly, it further undermines the assumption that developmental theory is relevant to political philosophy and thereby negates the primary point of trying to sustain the superiority of the prior-to-society perspective. An 'association' is not a necessary connection. If there is only an association between liberal thinking and justice operations, there is no ruling out the possibility of contrary political associations. A preference for liberal society is not then justifiable on cognitive-developmental grounds.

Secondly, even if this perspective is neutral between various forms of liberalism, it is not after all neutral between generic liberal ideas and other families of political belief. In all its forms the prior-to-society perspective understands individuals as having natural rights and freedoms whose protection requires recognizing the operation of reversibility as the ultimate criterion of justice. This reestablishes the political relevance of 'stage 5' thinking by contradicting the conservative idea that social norms are authoritative and that rights flow from established institutions and customary expectations. Unfortunately, this conflict of ideologies cannot by itself establish the liberal philosophy as tied to a logically discrete stage. We know only that one of the contradictory positions must be mistaken. We do not thereby know that one is cognitively superior to the other.

Thirdly, there is no other way to show the general commitments of 'stage 5' to be superior to conservative views. They remain open to doubt because the political disagreement can be regarded as a contest of customs. The contractarian perspective can be seen as an expression of traditions of freedom and independence, but of traditions

nonetheless and no more or less defensible than any other system of social practices or values. So seen, reasoning according to justice operations need only express expectations about acceptable argument in a liberal culture rather than the achievement of a more adequate vision. The point is strengthened in so far as the values of freedom and independence can be represented, as by MacIntyre [1981], not as an advance but as a result of the decay of community. In sum, the status of stage 5 is debatable, and because conservatives are full partners in the debate there is no identifiable failure of understanding as there is in disagreements prompted by operating at genuinely different cognitive stages. To suggest that a social-contract perspective is superior to acceptance of a system of antecedently existing customs may only express an ethnocentric preference for one set of political values over another. The point now seems to have been conceded by Rawls [1980], Kohlberg's primary philosophical authority and the leading advocate of a liberal theory of justice.

A significant logical consideration underlies this last problem. It is important in discussions of development to distinguish this key concept from evolution. 'Development' implies progress and logical direction, whereas 'evolution' (after Darwin at any rate) implies logically random adaptation to environmental contingencies. Kohlberg interprets his entire empirical ordering as requiring a developmental rather than an evolutionary explanation, but his data for the latter part of the sequence are consistent with both accounts. There is more in developmental theory than the evidence demands, which means that the changes of political philosophies expressed as stages 4–6 do not have a demonstrated logical order.

In order to be quite clear about this, let us give a further hearing to the view that moral philosophies and political ideologies are shaped by social rather than cognitive structures. The Marxist alternative is well known and can be quickly summarized. The generation of an economic surplus and the development of states involve people in dealings with strangers and stimulate the spread of the law-and-order thinking which is needed for the settlement of disputes arising beyond the circle of kinship. Persons with whom one forms secondary relationships are then ascribed rights which identify them as fellow participants in a social system, and individuals are considered in their role of subjects whose disputes must be resolved by a higher authority. It is not consistent with political domination, however, to tolerate critical attitudes towards laws or to encourage the transfer of legislative thinking to the population at large. Myths of natural law may serve to prevent development of standards which encourage popular government and to reinforce the need to observe the authority of existing rules.

Just as the growth of states stimulates the spread of law-and-order thinking, evolution of the market mode of organization seems largely responsible for the spread of autonomous moral thought and the social-contract orientation. The value of commodities is determined by the fact that people want them, and unless these wants can express themselves the market cannot respond. Freedom of choice as the standard of right is the appropriate ideology for such a society, and it provides the intelligible grounds for assessing and criticizing legal arrangements and for requiring the legitimacy of law to be defined by consent. At the same time, the doctrine of freedom serves to suppress the idea that there might be collective efforts made to define social purposes in the same sort of way that rational individuals define their own.

Kohlberg's finding that stage 6 reasoning cannot be documented is easily explained by such an account of social structures. In a still-capitalist society the conditions which would encourage egalitarian reasoning are not generally available. The social circumstances do not exist in which persons might be treated simply as persons, that is, as without relevant distinctions of the sorts which define familiars, subjects, and citizens. The discontents of privatism which are often observed in market society prevent seeing oneself as an inseparable member of the human community and thus retard the growth of a standard of political justification which requires rule by consensus rather than by electoral processes and market transactions.

Only a small further step is needed in order to account for the paucity of stage 5 as well as of stage 6 reasoning. A majority of individuals may maintain a stage 4 outlook even in a capitalistic system of organization because they have little occasion to progress beyond conservative reasoning. In spite of inhabiting a market society, most people do not act significantly in the market, engaging only in simple exchanges rather than capitalist acts. Most of us, therefore, are only shallowly imbued with the ethos of liberty, and because the rule of the market disturbs traditional ways of life we may be ready to accept authoritarian guarantees of social order. This helps to explain the finding that a society's constitutional principles can be morally in advance of a majority of its citizens. 'A sociopolitical system based on Stage 5 premises can move in a direction of moral progress even though the bulk of the members of the system and even sometimes its leaders may be Stage 4, or conventional' [Kohlberg, 1981, p. 239]. At each point in this pattern of explanation social structures serve as well as novel cognitive capacities.

While the available data seem as consistent with this sociological account of political philosophies as with the psychological one, they again fall short of sustaining a form of developmental theory. Orthodox historical materialism represents social stages as 'hard'. Each social stage has its distinctive ideology, its characteristic criterion of acceptable argument which presupposes the previous viewpoint and prevents appreciation of those still to come. It is difficult to reconcile this claim with the fact that in all civilizations there have been partisans of every political philosophy. Individual capacities for such thinking are not strongly determined by forms of social organization. A social 'stage' may define a predominant public philosophy, but the appeal of certain standards only shows that they have a functional role in a society's survival, not that they reflect Piaget's criteria for stage development. The pattern of succession is logically loose and suggests evolutionary adaptation rather than structural change.

To sum up, there are reasonable psychological grounds for maintaining the existence of prepolitical stages of moral development, while features of socioeconomic evolution are largely adequate to explain the dominance of particular political convictions during particular historical periods. Seen in this way, the accounts provide complementary and consistent explanations of changing patterns of moral thinking. Moreover, although neither shows that the changing political viewpoints of individuals and cultures follow the Piagetan logic of development, they

agree in holding that each type of moral reasoning has its own standards of rational argument. This leaves open the possibility of connecting prepolitical and political reasoning in an account of the acceptability of standards which is more potent than either explanation by itself – not quite developmental, but not merely evolutionary. Habermas's [1979] attempt to unite processes of cognitive and social change within the single framework of communicative competencies is a promising beginning.

Between Development and Evolution

Communicative competence may be defined as the ability to reach agreements according to justifiable standards of rationality. Since such standards define particular political philosophies, it should be possible to derive an ordered series of philosophical positions from an ordered series of such competencies. It should also be possible to envisage an advanced form of communication in which open discussion leads to social consensus in the manner of debate in small associations. This possibility lies outside those perceived by Kohlberg in limiting the use of 'moral' to 'judgments involving deontological concepts such as right and wrong' as opposed to 'conceptions of the good, the good life, intrinsic value or purpose' [Boyd and Kohlberg, 1973, p. 360]. On this restricted view of morality, moral and political reasoning serve solely to resolve conflicting claims. Any agreement on common purposes is a fortunate accident. Habermas [1979, p. 90] seeks to go beyond this stage 6 position and its 'monologically applicable principle of generalizability' to a 'communally followed procedure of redeeming normative validity claims discursively'. This represents the derivation of a seventh stage – the universal ethic of speech – from mature communicative competence.

Reflected in social practice, such a derivation would move humanity beyond politics in Kohlberg's sense. Politics and criteria of right and justice are necessary as long as irresolvable conflicts of interest are normal, but when such conflicts can be settled through agreements on objectives a postpolitical form of human organization is in view. Habermas's distinction between stage 6 and 7 could be designed to reflect this movement beyond politics, since it describes two stages of egalitarianism distinguished by Marx [1875]: the first is marked by an equality enforced through political authority, the second by equality preserved through the will of persons collectively deliberating without the intervention of the state.

Unfortunately, these possibilities and designs are weakened by the difficulty which afflicts all structuralist accounts of changing political viewpoints. In attempting to demonstrate that Kohlberg's sequence of moral stages can be derived from stages of 'interactive competence', Habermas becomes vulnerable to the problem that the developmental sequence may actually terminate at stage 4. If what appear to be genuine stages can be viewed as merely an empirical ordering of political philosophies, then the kinds of interactive competence from which they are derived also lack a demonstrated logical order. Liberal and egalitarian ethics cannot be said to be inherently superior to the concrete morality of social groups without further reasons, and lacking these reasons we cannot identify the directional changes which distinguish genuine devel-

opment from evolution in society or personality.

The problem persists only as long as the sequence of interactive competencies is required to conform to the model of 'hard' stages. As Piaget always recognized [Chapman, 1986], and as Habermas [1982, 1983] now realizes, this is an unwarranted condition. It is also unnecessary. By understanding interactive competencies in terms of social practices rather than hierarchical structures we can define a pattern of change in political discourse which reflects the changing needs of intricate human organizations rather than imposing a logic upon a succession of dominant philosophies. Even if stage 4 is the most comprehensive cognitive structure, we can then identify the series of political interpretations of this structure in a way which permits saying that it constitutes development, albeit in an extended sense.

Habermas [1973] points out that the practice of rational argument is commonly thought to have begun with the separation of philosophy from myth and the emergence of the polis from associations based on kinship. New rules of discourse developed and created the expectation that the conclusions of discussion should conform to criteria of open dialogue and deductive validity. The differentiation of experimental science from philosophical cosmologies marked another important transition, and expectations about empirical evidence became central to the appraisal of many arguments. Practices of empirical inquiry were supplemented in turn by the institutionalization of discourse in which practical questions and political decisions were supposed to be democratically questioned and tested.

Each of these communicative practices constitutes the growth of an ability which is important to a certain level of social complexity. The appearance of philosophy marks a new social capacity for arriving at acceptable conclusions by using logical rules, a prerequisite for any legal-political form of organization. The scientific revolution reflects the appearance of a further capacity to reach agreements by using the rules of empirical inquiry. Its occurrence can hardly be separated from the freedom of action and investigation essential for the rule of the market. Principled political discussion coincides with a capacity for mass democracy, and the rules of the universal ethic of speech represent a further capacity for reaching practical agreement beyond the reach of now established practices of communication. This last capacity may not become institutionalized unless further social complexity demands it, but it clearly illustrates the connection between a mode of social organization and accepted standards for the validity of arguments and decisions.

This series of practices indicates how a theory of communicative competence can be described independently of structuralist suppositions. For a communicative practice to become established, the cognitive capacity for it must already exist. The problem facing any such practice is not that of gaining intelligibility but that of gaining and maintaining currency. This is a matter of entrenching rules of argument and the expectations they generate, of institutionalization rather than structural development. Hence, to represent extensions of practical reasoning as tied to social practices in this way is to detach them from stages in the standard sense. We are dealing rather with a variety of ways of employing the cognitive capacity for systematic thinking.

The process of interpreting cognitive capacities does not logically justify preference for any particular political orientation but only reflects the fact that one set of argumentative practices has prevailed over others. However, the way in which this happens is important and may justify a preference in a weaker sense. If Habermas is right, the historically changing capacity for communicative practices is explained by the functional needs of social organizations, and the forms of communicative competence required by more complex types of organization are desirable in reflecting and protecting existing ways of life. This is not to show that liberal and egalitarian institutions are inherently superior to other communicative possibilities, since, as far as is known today, all postmythopoeic practices operate on the same cognitive level. It does, however, place them within a framework of change which is not merely evolutionary, assuming that they do have the direction suggested by increasing social complexity.

This direction is not guided by a compelling logic of development. Where a new communicative practice arises no unimpeachable criteria of success require a preference for it. The gain is always achieved at an expense, which may persuade some to challenge the way of life it makes possible. The differentiation of philosophical from mythopoeic thinking created enhanced capacities for logical argument, but it also meant a loss of unity and intimacy with gods and nature. The differentiation of empirical inquiry from philosophy meant a tremendous gain in capacity for experimental reasoning, but at the expense of revealed religion and the 'natural ties' which bound inferiors to their superiors. Democratic political thinking creates the possibility of a self-determining society, but it requires forms of public participation which threaten some powerful interests and impinge upon the pleasures of privatism. It is because this loss may seem to outweigh any gain that conservative political thinkers do not believe that making decisions through critical and open public discussion is a desirable or even possible mode of problem solving. Too many people will take part in practices of discourse which are governed by other standards. This voluntaristic aspect of social practices entails that patterns of communicative competence are not irreversible, being subject to decay from nonconformity.

Structural and institutional matters are not sufficiently distinguished in Kohlberg's latest writings, where he returns Habermas's earlier compliment of appropriating the other's work. When Habermas suggested that Kohlberg's 6 stage schema could be supplemented by distinguishing between 'monological generalization' and public standards of discourse, Kohlberg replied by insisting that the use of justice operations like ideal reversible role-taking is perfectly consistent with the notion of actually engaging in dialogue. It obviously is, but the process of imaginatively putting oneself in another's position and the process of having a discussion governed by social expectations are strikingly different – so much so that it is a puzzling further claim that the 'Stage 6 reasoning procedure logically requires dialogue in actual, real-life moral conflicts' [Kohlberg et al., 1983, p. 164]. To say that dialogue is logically compatible with a mode of thinking is one thing; to say that it is logically required is quite another. The one is subject to empirical confirmation, the other is a priori speculation which runs up against contrary speculations.

Discussion of the literature on relationships between communication and moral development is beyond the scope of this assay, but the matter is addressed in Simpson [1986]. See the references there to Freire [1970], McCarthy [1981], and Broughton [1982]. The last of these provides access to contributions by Damon and Killen, Berkowitz and Gibbs, Blatt and Kohlberg.

Kohlberg's assimilation of Habermas's seventh stage of communicative competence resembles interpretations of Piaget which emphasize the importance Piaget placed on peer interaction for cognitive development. Youniss [1978], for example, suggests that 'social or moral knowledge is constructed by the subject in collaboration with other subjects' [p. 235]. The point to stress about such interpretations is the respective roles of social and cognitive factors in the process of construction. This relationship is best understood in terms of the difference between the abstract conceptual capacities which define each true developmental stage and the concrete interpretations placed upon them amidst changing social practices and the expectations they generate. Such developments are 'soft'.

As a form of interaction, discussion plays a most important role in interpreting the cognitive structures which arise, at least in part, from other causes. Discussion influences what a stage 3 reasoner considers to be worthwhile, but it does so by shaping one's standards of behavior towards persons whose interests are seen as valuable in themselves. Such interpretations can differ widely, since discussions which arise under different circumstances will lead to different conceptions of what should be tolerated; but this point can be articulated only when cognitive capacities are distinguished from the effects of social contingencies upon them. Discussion affects our understanding of the conceptual content of stage 3 judgments; it is not logically necessary for the existence of the capacity. So, too, for the role of discussion in shaping the political content of systematic reasoning. Political discussion presupposes the existence of this cognitive structure but is compatible with its conservative, liberal, or egalitarian interpretation.

Conclusion

As represented here, Habermas's conjoining of the Piagetan and Marxist understandings of human development demonstrates that political reasoning, and Kohlberg's ordering of stages 4–6, should not be understood in terms of cognitive or social structures alone but also in terms of communicative practices which embody public standards of judgment. Since the possibility of new practices of political reasoning clearly exists, it makes sense to seek 'to loosen up the existing form of social integration by embodying in new institutions the rationality structures already developed in world views' [Habermas, 1979, p. 122]. This is a prescription, however, not a requirement upon those who find the existing form of social organization agreeable. Within any set of institutions, including those of political discourse, there are competing interpretations. In the absence of structural foundations for these interpretations, they represent equally intelligible political preferences. What governs these preferences is a central question in the study of human development. As complete an answer as is possible will bring together the results of developmental inquiry in all of the human sciences.

References

Boyd, D.; Kohlberg, L.: The is-ought problem: a developmental perspective. Zygon 8: 358–372 (1973).

Broughton, J.M.: Cognitive interaction and the development of sociality: a commentary on Damon and Killen. Merrill-Palmer Q. 28: 369–378 (1982).

Broughton, J.N.; Freeman-Moir, D.J.: The cognitive-developmental theory of James Mark Baldwin: current theory and research in genetic epistemology (Ablex, Norwood 1982).

Buck-Morss, S.: Socio-economic bias in Piaget's theory and its implications for cross-culture studies. Hum. Dev. 18: 35–49 (1975).

Burke, E.: Reflections on the revolution in France (1790) (Penguin, Harmondsworth 1978).

Burke, R.J.: Politics as rhetoric. Ethics 93: 45–55 (1982).

Chapman, M.: The structure of exchange: Piaget's sociological theory. Hum. Dev. 29: 181–194 (1986).

Ember, N.; Renwick, S.; Malone, B.: The relationship between moral reasoning and political orientation. J. Personality soc. Psychol. 34: 1073–1080 (1983).

Freire, P.: Pedagogy of the oppressed (Seabury, New York 1970).

Gibbs, J.C.: Kohlberg's moral stage theory. A Piagetian revision. Hum. Dev. 22: 89–112 (1979).

Habermas, J.: Theory and practice (Beacon, Boston 1973).

Habermas, J.: Communication and the evolution of society (Beacon, Boston 1979).

Habermas, J.: A reply to my critics; in Thompson, Held, Habermas: critical debates (MIT, Cambridge, Mass. 1982).

Habermas, J.: Moralbewusstsein und kommunikatives Handeln (Suhrkamp, Frankfurt 1983).

Henry, R.M.: The psychodynamic foundations of morality (Karger, Basel 1983).

Hobbes, T.: Leviathan (1691) (Clarendon Press, Oxford 1965).

Kohlberg, L.: Stage and sequence: the cognitive-developmental approach to socialization; in Goslin, Handbook of socialization theory and research (Rand McNally, Chicago 1969).

Kohlberg, L.: From is to ought: how to commit the naturalistic fallacy and get away with it in the study of moral development; in Mischel, Cognitive development and epistemology (Academic Press, New York 1971).

Kohlberg, L.: Continuities in childhood and adult moral development revisited; in Baltes, Schaie, Life-span developmental psychology: research and theory (Academic Press, New York 1973).

Kohlberg, L.: Educating for a just society: an updated and revised statement; in Munsey, Moral development, moral education and Kohlberg (Religious Education Press, Birmingham, Ala., 1980).

Kohlberg, L.: The philosophy of moral development. Essays on moral development, vol. I (Harper & Row, San Francisco 1981).

Kohlberg, L.: The psychology of moral development. Essays on moral development, vol. II (Harper & Row, San Francisco 1984).

Kohlberg, L.; Kramer, R.: Continuities and discontinuities in childhood and adult moral development. Hum. Dev. 12: 93–120 (1969).

Kohlberg, L.; Levine, C.; Hewer, A.: Moral stages: a current formulation and a response to critics (Karger, Basel 1983).

MacIntyre, A.: After virtue (Notre Dame University Press, Notre Dame, Ind. 1981).

Marx, K.: Critique of the Gotha program (1875); in Tucker, The Marx-Engels reader; 2nd ed. (Norton, New York 1978).

McCarthy, T.: The critical theory of Jürgen Habermas (MIT, Cambridge, Mass. 1981).

Oakeshott, M.: Rationalism in politics and other essays (Methuen, London 1974).

Puka, B.: An interdisciplinary treatment of Kohlberg. Ethics 92: 468–490 (1982).

Rawls, J.: Kantian constructivism in moral theory: the Dewey lectures 1980. J. Phil. 77: 515–572 (1980).

Reid, H.; Yanarella, E.J.: Critical political theory and moral development. On Kohlberg, Hampden-Turner, and Habermas. Theory Society 4: 505–541 (1977).

Rest, J.R.: Development in judging moral issues (University of Minnesota Press, Minneapolis 1979).

Scruton, R.: The meaning of conservatism (Penguin, Harmondsworth 1980).

Simpson, E.: The subjects of justice. Ethics 90: 490–501 (1980).

Simpson, E.: Emile's moral development. A Rousseauan perspective on Kohlberg. Hum. Dev. 26: 198–212 (1983).

Simpson, E.: A values-clarification retrospective. Educ. Theory 36: 271–287 (1986).

Waal, F. de: Chimpanzee politics: power and sex among apes (Cape, London 1982).

Youniss, J.: Dialectical theory and Piaget on social knowledge. Hum. Dev. 21: 234–247 (1978).

Youniss, J.: Beyond ideology to the universals of development; in Kuhn, Meacham, On the development of developmental psychology (Karger, Basel 1983).

Evan Simpson
Department of Philosophy
McMaster University
Hamilton, Ont. L8S 4K1 (Canada)

12 Social Construction In Piaget's Theory

James Youniss
The Catholic University of America

William Damon
Brown University

Piaget's views on the role of social relations in the individual construction
of knowledge are less known than his position on the child's construction of
logical thought. This may be due to the timing of Piaget's reintroduction
into American psychology. In the late 1950s, psychologists were seeking a
new model of the human subject who would be an active agent and bring
reflective powers to the task of controlling the external environment
(Bruner, Goodnow, & Austin, 1956). Piaget's emphases on construction
and the development of logical thinking provided some first steps toward
this desired model; as a consequence, his theory and findings spread quickly
through the American psychological scene (Flavell, 1962).

At this time in Piaget's own theory building, however, his efforts were
focused on elaborating the structures of logical thought (Inhelder & Piaget,
1958). His moral judgment work was almost three decades behind him, and
his other "sociological" studies — finally collected as a group in the mid-
1960's — would never be published in English (Chapman, 1986). In America,
Piaget would forever be seen as an investigator of "cold cognition," a
theorist who viewed the child as a scientist discovering intellectual insights
in splendid isolation.

After a burst of interest lasting almost two decades (admittedly a long life
by the faddish standards of contemporary American social science),
Piaget's approach has been largely discarded as too cognitive, too structural, and too universalist in its claims. It has been replaced by more
process-oriented, more affective, and more contextualist approaches. The
theory's connotative imprint was stamped at the time of its second entry
into American psychology, and the theory is still read primarily as a

statement about the individual's ability to control physical reality through logical means. To this day, it retains the indelible trademark of the apocryphal child who discovers formal properties of things, such as number, while playing alone with pebbles on the beach.

We do not deny that there are grounds for such a depiction. Sources for it can be found in Piaget's extensive writings. Yet there is an equally clear, though less frequently articulated side that we believe deserves serious attention. In our view, Piaget's ideas about social construction are integral to his general epistemology and have important implications not just for social and moral knowledge, but for his theory in general (Dean & Youniss, 1991; Youniss, 1983). We do not consider his ideas on social construction to be a minor theme or afterthought. Rather, they provide a serious account of the knowledge process that entails co-constructive exchanges between children and other persons as much as between children and physical objects.

In the present chapter, we elaborate on a particular theme that is central to the theory but has not been adequately noted by Piagetian scholars. We refer to the concept of the *culture-acquiring child,* which denotes children's identification with and desire to be part of the culture they know through interacting with other children and adults. Damon (1983) proposes that psychologists must address two issues in explaining social development. One is how children become individuals with unique personalities and senses of self. The second is how children become members of society who think, like, and share knowledge with other members. Most developmental theories have been directed to the former issue in the sense of accounting for individual differences among children.

The aim of this chapter is to describe Piaget's account of how children adopt cultural patterns of interacting and, in the process, identify with these patterns and the culture they represent. We shall describe Piaget's position, show its roots in Piaget's distinctive epistemological stance, note some points of resistance to this position among contemporary psychologists, and link the position to other social constructivist work on culture and development.

PIAGET'S EARLY WRITINGS

We begin by reviewing an essay that Piaget wrote as a speech for the New Education Fellowship (Piaget, 1932a). The NEF was an association of European scholars who were devoted to reforming post-World War I European politics through educational reform. They viewed the war as a product of reactionary forces that were based in financial self-interest and cultural nationalism. Rather than attacking political structures directly, these scholars chose to reform politics through the education of a new kind of citizen. They sought to create citizens who were committed to cooperation and open to cultural diversity. Persons' views would necessarily be based on particular experience, but each person would try to coordinate his or her views with those of other individuals. Piaget introduced the problem as follows:

> Contemporary society is an extremely recent phenomenon when compared to the history of mankind. Social occurrences take place today on a new scale, a new plane. All important events in the modern world are international. What happens at one point on our planet has an immediate repercussion all over the world. This interdependence has gradually established itself in every sphere of life. The economics of isolation, purely internal politics, intellectual and moral reactions limited to one group, no longer exist. (p. 4)

It is clear that Piaget's interest was shared by other intellectuals of his day. According to Heilbroner (1970), the post-World War I period witnessed a renewal of the liberal perspective. Mid-19th-century surges of democracy were met with late-century reaction and ultimately with the fractionation that led to nationalistic confrontation in a devastating war. The new liberalism called for a perspective that acknowledged interdependence of nations and engendered a spirit of respect for cultural diversity. Throughout his essay, Piaget was as concerned about adults' adaptation to the problem as he was about children's adaptation. Piaget said that even informed scholars were uncertain of how to proceed beyond traditional boundaries of national, ethnic, and religious truths. In his words, "We are like children faced by the grown-up world" (p. 6).

Piaget's solution is interesting because it expresses for the first time what was to became a lifelong concern in his work. He suggested that educators should try to instill in children, not information, but a "tool" or "intellectual instrument" by which they could begin to develop coordinated knowledge. For this task he chose the model of science that he thought possessed this instrument and was responsible for its monumental successes. Piaget was contrasting 19th-century progress in science to 19th-century chaotic fluctuations in political affairs. Since he understood this instrument to be simultaneously intellectual and moral, the analogy between science and politics fit his argument neatly.

Piaget outlined three explicit benefits of the scientific attitude:

1. It would help diminish egocentric thinking by helping children to see their own intellectual and moral positions in coordination with other positions.
2. It would free children from the social coercion of tradition that imposes beliefs without regard to others' possible beliefs. The

scientific attitude would encourage serious consideration of diverse beliefs and coordination among them.

3. It would bring children into reciprocal relations with other positions.

Piaget elaborated on this point as follows: "Each of us must come to see that his own individual, group, or national world is only one among many other possible worlds. It is this method of confronting points of view which appears to be . . . analogous to the scientific method of coordination" (pp. 12–13).

Piaget then proceeded to consider education as the means by which this instrument might be developed. He proposed that it be formed not "by the old-fashioned school . . . of master and pupil, that is the relation of an inferior who passively obeys to a superior . . ." (p. 24). Rather, the new education would stress: "Group work, common study, self government, etc." This is because "Only a type of education founded upon a social relationship which is of a kind to succeed in uniting adults, will allow of the development of sane moral and international attitudes, and make of our children a finer generation than ourselves" (p. 25).

This essay emphasizes five critical aspects of Piaget's thinking, many of which are usually covert in his writings (Piaget, 1932 a and b). First, it reveals his political stance, which was liberal in the classic sense of that term. Second, it shows him to be a product of his intellectual times in that he shared with other NEF members a stance against the late-19th-century reactionary attempt to replace democracy with enlightened state-regulated capitalism (Heilbroner, 1970). Third, and more to the point of developmental psychology, the essay embodies an early form of Piaget's interest in peer socialization insofar as he argued for its advantages over master–pupil teaching. Fourth, it shows that, at this early date, Piaget understood science to be a social and not an individual enterprise. The operations of science were precisely those that countered the narrowness that came from individualistic thinking. And fifth, it provides a rough draft of his elaborated argument that social communication, reciprocity, and cooperation are the basic means for achieving balanced — later called equilibrated — intellectual and moral knowledge.

It is important to note that this essay does not stand as an isolated piece in the Piagetian corpus. The basic ideas can be found elsewhere, such as in the better-known work on "moral judgment" also published in English in 1932 (Piaget, 1932b). One sees in his conceptualization of moral development an even sharper argument regarding the importance of cooperative relationships. Beginning with young children's commitment to understand the interactions in which they are partners, Piaget builds a systematic case for two streams of development, one emerging from relations of unilateral authority and the other emanating from cooperation among peers. We have covered this argument in detail in previous work (Damon, 1983; Youniss, 1980).

In describing the autonomous moral agent that would ensue from cooperative relations, Piaget (1932b) took explicit care to deny the position that, today, is often attributed to him. He consciously took issue with Kant, who based autonomy on rational calculation so that when pressed for justification, an individual would take recourse in the logical derivation of a principle. Piaget countered that view by arguing for a morality based on mutual respect in which each person would feel both responsible to *justify* his or her position to another person and would, reciprocally, *listen* to the other person's views.

SOCIALIZATION IN PIAGET'S THEORY

In this section we review aspects of Piaget's writings that form a sketch of his theory of socialization. Our main sources for this section are Piaget's (1932b) study of moral judgment and his (1970) review of his general theory. We suggest that it helps for the moment to set aside the usual view that social experience is a means to promote individual development. While Piaget argues for this, he also describes social experience as a means for the child's introduction into and identification with an existing social order. It is the latter that we want to emphasize.

Basic Elements.   Socialization occurs through normal, everyday inter-actions, wherein the child's actions meet resistance and need to be adjusted to the actions of other persons, as other persons adjust their actions in relation to the child. This point is found throughout Piaget's (1932b) monograph and is emphasized to combat the view that children develop in cognitive isolation from other persons. When the point is coupled with the fact that knowledge is a construction, one sees the broader implications of the theory. First, the main premise of traditional approaches to socialization becomes radically altered. Adults cannot directly transmit ideas to children because their ideas must be reconstructed by the child. Reconstruction fundamentally changes whatever the adult brings to the interaction and transforms it into an understandable scheme in the child's cognitive reality. Second, because ideas are presented in an interactive format, the child's schemes necessarily take account of the adult's position. In this manner, children's schemes are socialized at the point of communicative contact through a normal process of the child's actions meeting resistance when the objects they affect, react, and provide reciprocal effects.

A basic element in Piaget's theory is that children seek order in the realm of the action by abstracting formal invariances from real actions. The process of constructing order necessarily requires that children deal with interactions and not just their own actions. The invariant properties that children abstract would be properties of interactions. Piaget (1932b, p. 360) proposes that the psychological individual cannot exist in isolation from other individuals.

We realize that this point stands in opposition to those commentaries that stress that children are naturally egocentric and must work their way toward the realization that there are other views of reality. Piaget, however, is unambiguous in his argument. If the central task is to construct order from actions, then children must at a very early age realize that other views exist. This is because their actions necessarily run into the actions and intentions of their interactive partners. According to Piaget (1932b), children already at 2 years of age recognize intentions. His argument is that children would concretely experience numerous occasions when their intentions were thwarted by the intervention of intentions from other persons. Hence, they would be maladaptive in believing that their own intentions and actions could alone create results in social situations (Dean & Youniss, 1991).

Role of Relationships.   In his writings during the 1930s, Piaget was adamant about the distinct roles played by different interpersonal relationships in the knowledge acquisition process (Piaget, 1932a, 1932b). He proposed that relationships of unilateral authority generated respect for the views espoused by the authoritative figure. However, such respect lacked a grounding in communicative understanding, because it was not open to development in the classic Piagetian meaning of that concept. This is because construction is one-sided with the result that the child cannot accommodate adequately to the authority figure's initiatives. While children understand that adults bring points of views to interactions, and while children try to grasp adults' views, they end up failing to comprehend adults' perspectives and distort the views toward their own schemes (Piaget, 1932b, p. 36). Piaget subsequently came to call this "sociocentrism" (Piaget, 1970, p. 724).

Piaget contrasted relationships of unilateral authority sharply to relationships of cooperation. In the latter, children act as partners with other persons to co-construct knowledge. Cooperation begins in symmetrical reciprocity, whereby any person can contribute to an interaction with the same act the other person has or will initiate. This elemental fact ultimately leads to exchanges of ideas in processes by which children jointly construct reality. In contrast to unilateral authority, cooperation implies that neither person would hold to a view without attending to the view offered by the other. Hence, the tendency is for each person to build on the other's ideas while explaining his or own ideas to the other. As will be shown later, cooperation thus leads to mutual understanding and contrasts to the alienation of views that tends to result from unilateral authority.

Peers.   Damon (1983) has outlined Piaget's position with respect to the role of peers in the knowledge process and in socialization. In his 1932 writings, Piaget depicted children's relationships with peers as the ideal context for cooperation. His reasoning was that peers would, on the average, have to cooperate to get along since their relationship was based on symmetrical reciprocity. This means that any initiative from one child could be matched by a different initiative from another peer. Hence, peers would tend to be at loggerheads if they were to operate solely according to the principle of symmetry. It is precisely in trying to overcome stalemate that peers would need to develop procedures of cooperation so that each would express points of view that would be heard, and so that each would learn to respect the points of view expressed by others.

In his 1932 monograph, Piaget (1932b) argued strongly that in the process of discovering and practicing procedures that mediate peer cooperation, children form a common sense of social solidarity. This is based on two specific components. The first is reliance on processes that require the cooperation of others. An illustrative process would be arbitrating disputes over rules of games. In order to cultivate democratic procedures, such as debate, discussion, and majority rule, children have to cooperate. Piaget's argument is that continued practice of such procedures would engender a sense of solidarity as a by-product. The second is based in mutual understanding that results from children's communicative exchanges of ideas. As children rely on each other for feedback about ideas, they would come to know one another's views because they were parties to a mutual construction. Thus mutual understanding would produce solidarity in the very ways children came to interpret reality. Not only would experience be shared, but the meaning of the experience would be the product of joint construction.

Morality.   Piaget (1932b) proposed that morality was based on respect for persons rather than respect for tradition or rules. One can see this proposal as the consequence of his broader theory of socialization. Respect for persons is grounded in the processes of human interaction by which knowledge is co-constructed. In keeping with his theory of relationship, Piaget distinguishes between kinds of respect. Unilateral relationships engender respect of authority, but it is precarious because it lacks the ultimate grounding in mutuality. Should competing views between author-ities arise, children would lack the procedural calculations by which these views could be analyzed and reassessed. Respect based on cooperation, however, allows views to be submitted to procedures that must follow the norms of reciprocity and discussion.

Throughout the socialization process, children believe that the interaction patterns they find as orderly, are in fact necessary patterns that all other persons share. Piaget illustrated the point by reporting children's beliefs about the origin of rules for games. To paraphrase the typical child: Rules are learned from older children who learned rules from their fathers who, in turn, learned rules from their fathers. Piaget proposed that children want to learn these rules because they believe that in doing so, they themselves become like adults and get closer to seeing reality as adults see it. In this regard, Piaget's socialization process leads to acquiring culture and identification with what children believe to be the root of culture—adults' views of it.

The final point in our analysis is that for Piaget, culture is not a static entity but consists in ways of interacting by which persons co-construct knowledge. Piaget makes this point quite powerfully when he describes the characteristics of the autonomous moral individual. We are aware that this hypothetical individual has already been depicted in the literature as the person who can think logically and, in moments of dispute, can turn to reason to justify his or her position. This depiction does not accurately reflect Piaget's own view on the matter. To show what that view is, we allow Piaget (1932b) to speak for himself: The autonomous self "takes up its stand on the norms of reciprocity and objective discussion, and knows how to submit to these in order to make itself respected" (pp. 95-96). Autonomy entails learning how "to understand the other person and be understood by him" (p. 95) and is based on "the norm of reciprocity in sympathy" (p. 107).

POINTS OF RESISTANCE

Reaction—and resistance—to Piaget's moral theory has been replete with ironies of distortion and misapprehension. The strangest of these ironies is that many of those who have considered themselves Piagetians—most notably Kohlberg and his followers—have approached moral development in a diametrically opposite manner from Piaget. A more aggravating irony is that other work, springing from a more empiricist tradition, has been so misdirected as actually to discredit Piaget's moral theory without accurately representing it in the first place. This is because many of the experimental research programs intended to test Piaget's moral judgment theory were directed at phenomena that were largely peripheral to Piaget's major claims, or in some cases even directed at claims that Piaget never really made.

To his credit, Kohlberg did more than any other individual to resuscitate

Piaget's moral judgment work from the obscurity to which it had fallen by the late 1950s. In fact, in many ways Kohlberg's bold and seminal work recaptured the entire area of moral development for the field of psychology. Once Kohlberg published his ground-breaking dissertation, the empirical study of people's moral beliefs and the growth thereof again became a legitimate topic for scientific researchers. It has remained so ever since. Kohlberg (1963, 1969) considered himself a Piagetian and placed his own studies squarely within the Genevan tradition. The immediate popularity of Kohlberg's work gave new life both to Piaget's theory and to the topic of moral development.

In this context, however, it must be noted that Kohlberg presented his dissertation—as well as the 1963 *Vita Humana* (now *Human Development*) article that reported it—as a repudiation of Piaget's central thesis in *The Moral Judgment of the Child*. Piaget had based his developmental position on the notion that children live within two moral worlds, the one arising from their relations with adults and the other arising from their relations with peers. Kohlberg rejected this notion entirely and set out to disprove it.

On the surface, Kohlberg's argument with Piaget may seem like a minor dispute within the coherent "cognitive–development approach" (Kohlberg's [1969] term, significantly, not Piaget's). Yet in actuality the difference is not a minor one at all. It represents radically separate views about what moral judgment is, where it comes from, how it changes during ontogenesis, and how it is linked to social action.

Simultaneous but Separate Spheres.   For Piaget, the child's values are functionally tied to the social contexts in which the child is embedded. Children operate in two main spheres, with adults and with peers. These two spheres engender—and demand—different sorts of values. To live within the adult world, children need to acquire respect for authority, social tradition, and the established order of things. To live within the peer world, children need to acquire mutual respect for one another, an ability to cooperate with equals, and a sense that rules and other social standards may be negotiated and modified through agreed-upon procedures of fairness. *Both* sets of values are required for adaptation to the childhood social universe. They can, and do, coexist during the main part of childhood; and the child's gradual shift to the peer-oriented values is more a result of changing life circumstances than stage-like cognitive transformations.

Like other American social scientists of the late 1950s, Kohlberg no doubt read Piaget's moral judgment work in light of Piaget's structuralist writings on logical reasoning—the most formalistic of which, the book on formal operations, had just been published in English (Inhelder & Piaget, 1958). (The book had been translated, to complete the ironies, by the renowned chronicler-to-be of postchildhood heteronomous morality, Stanley Milgram). To Kohlberg, Piaget's insistence on two simultaneous sets of moral values in one child must have seemed like a simple early-career error by the Swiss structuralist-to-be. How could a child juggle such conflicting ideas without quickly trying to resolve them? Kohlberg believed that a mind could not be divided against itself for long.

Kohlberg's own resolution was that there was only one dominant childhood structure of morality, a structure that resembled Piaget's heteronomy: Adult-centered, blindly obedient to authority, rigidly loyal to those in charge. All other forms of morality, Kohlberg believed, bore a strictly developmental relation to this original authoritarian view. Later in life, other forms arose from this primitive one and went beyond it both structurally and functionally. The forms of mutual respect and peer fairness that Piaget described, therefore, showed up in Kohlberg's stage descriptions only after childhood had passed.

Empirically, Kohlberg's position proved problematical, as work by Damon (1977), Eisenberg (1982), and Youniss (1980) showed. Even at a very early age, children express – and act on – rich and robust notions of kindness, sharing, fairness, reciprocity, and other peer-oriented moral standards. They hold these notions at the same time that they avow deep respect for authority and traditional rules (Damon, 1980). It is not at all uncommon to hear a child say in one breath that he would always do whatever Mom tells him, and then in the next breath that he would share his bike with his friend even if Mom said not to, because his friend had always been generous with him (Damon, 1983).

Practical and Theoretical Modes.   But even more problematical than the empirical anomalies of Kohlberg's position were its theoretical vulnerabilities. Because of its extreme holism and cognitivism, Kohlberg's approach lost much of the explanatory power of Piaget's original formulation. At the same time, ironically, these very choices that Kohlberg made as a departure from Piaget's original treatise cast doubt on Piaget's own approach. Once Kohlberg had appropriated the "cognitive–developmental" position for his own particular view of things, implausible claims and assumptions about moral behavior forever became associated with Piagetianism in the public mind.

An illustration of this can be found in how the two theorists handled the judgment–conduct relation. The relation between judgment and conduct is of course at the center of most psychologists' concern with moral judgment. Generally, statements of moral belief are seen as interesting only insofar as they reveal propensities toward actual social conduct. Piaget did not wrestle with this problem *per se,* but his account of children's rule following in a marbles game makes clear that he approached judgment and conduct as inseparable systems of action. Rather, Piaget distinguished between practical and theoretical modes of behavior: The practical occurs on the plane of direct action, the theoretical on the plane of consciousness. Piaget proposed a developmental relation between the two. First the child works out the conception of rules in the course of actual play with peers, then later the child grasps in consciousness a symbolic representation of this once-practical conception. For Piaget, therefore, the origins of both judgment and conduct are to be found in the child's behavior within social relations. The child's theoretical and hypothetical reasoning about morality comes later, a developmental product of the earlier practical activity.

Kohlberg drew the distinction differently and turned Piaget's proposed developmental relation on its head. Rather than contrasting practical to theoretical moral activity, Kohlberg (1971) contrasted judgment to action. Although closer to our commonsense way of viewing morality, the judgment/action split is impossible to conceptualize with any clarity. Does a verbal statement (say, Patrick Henry's "Give me liberty or give me death!") represent judgment or conduct? Are the two ever really separated in reality? Even in the throes of embattled action, is there not judgment? Even in the solitude of reflection, is there not action? Piaget avoided this problem by focusing on modes of action (practical versus theoretical) that are closely attached to distinct contexts of behavior (real-life vs. hypothetical).

Kohlberg's view of the relation between the two (which he generally conceptualized as "reasoning" vs. "action") presented even more difficulties. His methods of interrogation and analysis, of course, were entirely dedicated toward identifying a subject's stage of reasoning about hypothetical moral issues. The problem for Kohlberg then became determining how well this reasoning stage would predict how the subject behaved in "real life" (that is, outside the interview situation). Inevitably this led Kohlberg to a model of prediction that gave priority to reasoning as the primary agent in the construction of moral behavior.

The original Kohlbergian assumption was that people acquire moral beliefs as part of their intellectual development. Moral reasoning was closely linked to other intellectual achievements — particularly logic and role taking, both of which were seen as necessary though not sufficient for higher stages of moral judgment. The process of moral growth in Kohlberg's eyes was a process of "figuring out" the right thing to do. The problem of "real-life" moral behavior, then, became simply a problem in application: Would subjects apply the moral principles that they had "figured out" to their own conduct in various life circumstances? In his early writings, Kohlberg assumed that, in the long run, they would; because it is a human tendency (à la cognitive dissonance theory) for people to resolve internal contradictions among their own beliefs and acts. There may be momentary gaps between reasoning and action (as when fear prevents persons from "living up to" their moral principles). But eventually there will be coherence, either through adoption of more noble behavior or through distortion and forced regression in one's moral reasoning.

Too many inconclusive experimental results, plus an extended foray into the real-world cauldron of educational reform, led Kohlberg to rethink his views on reasoning and action. Clearly the children and adults he had observed were not behaving in a manner that could be directly predicted from their moral stages. In a somewhat patchwork fashion, Kohlberg added Durkheimian notions such as societal perspective and moral atmosphere to his explanatory model. But he never retreated from his belief in the priority of an individual's reasoning. He saw this as the best entry point for intervention as well as the true causal agent in an individual's moral conduct. Parameters of the social context remain situational factors that could facilitate or hinder the application of the individual's moral beliefs about what is right.

It is not, of course, possible to know exactly how Piaget would have addressed the whole complex of issues surrounding moral conduct. His treatment of these issues was limited to the developmental account that he sketched in his one book on the matter. But Piaget's own approach, however limited, avoided many of the pitfalls created by Kohlberg's revised "cognitive–developmentalism."

For one thing, Piaget's theory assumes no fundamental split between reasoning and action: Thought is a form of action, derivative of praxis-based forms, but with a capacity to operate on the plane of mental representation. Thus it is meaningless to split moral reasoning and moral conduct in order to discuss their "relation." Instead, it becomes possible to speak of the reasoning elements — such as intention, evaluation, choice — that are an essential part of any moral act.

For another thing, Piaget's theory places absolutely no priority on reasoning over any other component of moral behavior. If anything, at least developmentally, Kohlberg's priority on reasoning reverses Piaget's. Practical activity, writes Piaget, precedes and shapes the intellectualized consciousness that grows out of it.

Individuals in Society.   But most importantly, Piaget's moral work sets moral development and moral behavior firmly in the social relations that engender morality. For Piaget, individual moral judgment is always adaptive to social situations. As the child's primary social situation moves from the family to the peer group, the child develops a new form of morality in response. There are key cognitive processes that are implicated in this development; but these cognitive processes always go hand in hand with the child's shifting social circumstances, *because their function is to adapt to these circumstances.* Piaget's view of intelligence-as-adaptation prevented him from disconnecting the moral reasoner from the moral actor, or the individual moral agent from the social context. In this regard, he was far closer to Durkheim than to Kohlberg; although of course Piaget argued vehemently against Durkheim's singular focus on the constraining and authoritative elements of morality. For Piaget, unlike Durkheim, morality grew out of not one but two social relations in childhood; and the child played an active role in constructing moral meaning out of this bifurcated social experience. Piaget's "moral child," therefore was less socially isolated than Kohlberg's and more mentally active than Durkheim's.

Misdirected Research. Piaget's social-relational position was lost not only on Kohlberg but on most of the psychological research community. The most dramatic examples of this were the host of experiments on moral intentionality carried out after the publication of Piaget's moral judgment book in English. By far the most famous experimental finding in the book was the intentions/consequences sequence suggested by Piaget's "15 broken cups" dilemma. Children's judgments that were based on considerations of intentions ("he did worse because he was trying to steal jam") represented what Piaget called "subjective responsibility." Piaget reported that these subjective judgments usually appeared later in a child's life than "objective" judgments that are based on consequences ("he did worse because he broke more cups"). Piaget's report of children's actual judgments, however, clearly revealed that even young children understood both intention and consequences as potentially operative factors in judgment (Dean & Youniss, 1991).

Moral intentionality became the "conservation" of the moral development field. It provided psychologists with a means of testing (and criticizing) Piaget's theory by seeing whether they could get a higher-level response from children who were supposedly too young to provide such according to Piaget. As in the conservation literature, the experiments were carried out in hundreds of different ways, some quite foreign to anything that Piaget had in mind when he described the phenomena. And, as in the conservation literature, an uninterpretable *mélange* of findings were produced over a decade or so of intense experimentation. Some researchers replicated Piaget's reported findings. Others, by altering situational variables in the dilemma, managed to get very young children to make judgments based on considerations of intentions.

The problem for this whole literature was that Piaget never intended to locate the shift from objective to subjective responsibility solely in the child's intellectual abilities. Rather, commensurate with Piaget's entire position, he located this shift in the gradual transformation taking place within the child's social world.

Demands of Social Construction.   As the child spends more and more time in peer interaction, different sorts of social necessities come to the fore. Unlike the child's relations with adults—where adults need to be obeyed, no matter what—the peer relation requires negotiation, compromise, a continual "meeting of the minds." In this kind of setting, the child becomes forced to take others' intentions into account. Enough experience in such settings does indeed facilitate the development of a new cognitive perspective, more attuned to the inner mental life; but Piaget did not make the claim that such insights about others' thinking could not appear at an earlier time. In Piaget's moral book—unlike in his earlier work on language or his later work on space—it is social, rather than mental, decentration that is portrayed as the main mover of judgmental change during the childhood years. So it is not surprising—and not at all a critical test of Piaget's theory—that, by altering key situational variables, contemporary researchers could get children to make intentional moral judgments. Piaget was interested in moral intentionality not as a milestone of mental progress but as a feature of social relationships, a feature that, in the peer world at least, children must mutually coordinate for optimal adaptation.

In the course of managing features of social interaction such as the intentions of others, children construct their social and moral intelligence. This is the heart of Piaget's position on social construction and for us the most profound distinguishing mark of Piaget's approach.

Again, the contrast to Kohlberg could not be more dramatic. For Kohlberg, intellectual development was a relatively self-contained process. Just as he gave priority to the relation between "judgment" and "action," so too he gave priority to intellectual reasoning in the process of developmental change. Moral judgment, he believed, derived developmentally from insights about role taking, which in turn derived from logical skills—all of which stood in a kind of nesting relation with one another, with logic being necessary but not sufficient for role taking and role taking being necessary but not sufficient for moral judgment. Kohlberg, of course, also saw some role for social influence. He wrote of social dimensions such as the complexity of social systems, as well as social experiences such as education and work, as spurs to moral growth (Kohlberg & Higgins, 1987). But the primary driving force in Kohlberg's developmental scheme was the individual's reasoning, a process of "figuring out" what is right.

In Piaget's position, we have found a more promising way of looking at social influence and developmental change. Piaget begins with the relationship, determines its qualities, identifies the opportunities that these qualities offer its participants as well as the constraints that they place upon them, and from there draws conclusions about the relationship's developmental impact. Of course, Piaget was by no means a social determinist, and he never lost sight of the individual's construction of meaning within the relationship. But, at least in his moral judgment book (as well as in his untranslated essays on sociology), he gives the social relationship a prior and operative role in the individual's development (Chapman, 1986; see also Chapman, this volume).

It is this relational perspective that we have emphasized in this chapter, partly because this is a part of Piaget that is little known and partly because we both have drawn heavily on Piaget's fertile position in our own work (Damon, 1977, 1983; Damon & Colby, 1987; Youniss, 1980, 1981, 1987). For us, Piaget's account of social construction is all the more valuable because he did manage to balance it with an account of the individual's role in the meaning-making process.

There are not many developmental theorists who have been able to navigate between the opposing hazards of extreme individualism and extreme social determinism. Vygotsky is certainly another and the virtues of his approach are well appreciated at present (Vygotsky, 1978; Wertsch, 1987). Perhaps because Vygotsky wrote so much less than Piaget, his theory has not met with the resistance that Piaget's has. Ironically, Piaget's theory has met with quite contradictory points of resistance. There are those, such as the social learning theorists and the radical social constructivists, who have found the theory hopelessly cognitive and universalistic; and there are those, such as Kohlberg, who have found it not enough oriented toward global structures of individual thought. We, however, have taken a different message from Piaget's moral judgment work, and have found in this message a good starting point for understanding the role of social construction in development.

A CONTEMPORARY VIEW ON PEER CULTURE

In his writings during the 1930s, Piaget addressed the neglected importance of peer interaction and the sense of solidarity that resulted from the practice of cooperation. He did not use the term peer culture, but his description is similar to that found in contemporary writers. For present purposes, we review the work of Corsaro (1985), who has conceptualized peer culture in an insightful way. It is interesting that Corsaro (Corsaro & Eder, 1990; Corsaro & Rizzo, 1988) views his work as perhaps at odds with Piaget's major emphasis. We obviously, differ with regard to this aspect of his thinking because we see agreement on fundamental issues. In particular, Corsaro believes that Piaget proposed that the primary function of inter-personal experience was to promote "individual development." Whatever truth this view contains, we believe that Piaget was also concerned with the function of interpersonal experience in promoting cultural identity. This possible difference aside, we propose to describe the points on which

Corsaro's contemporary thinking extends ideas that Piaget proposed in his early work.

First, Corsaro, emphasized the importance of peer experience in children's social development. Peer experience is not viewed as an "apprenticeship for adult society" but is seen as the means for establishing peer culture in its own right. In this regard, Corsaro, like Piaget, stands apart from the mainstream of socialization theorists who view peer experiences either as teaching the rudiments of adult society or as a potential source of deviance from adult society's norms.

Second, Corsaro proposed that children's socialization is a collective process that occurs in public rather than an individual process that takes place in private reflection. A chief task of childhood is to construct knowledge, not primarily for oneself, but for a community of persons who share the same sense of culture (Corsaro & Eder, 1990, p. 199). Knowledge is not constructed for its own or the individual's sake but is directed to mutual understanding with other persons (Cook–Gumperz & Corsaro, 1977).

Third, Corsaro proposed that "By interacting and negotiating with others [children] establish understanding that become fundamental social knowledge on which they continually build" (Corsaro & Eder, 1990, p. 200). In this regard, children create a culture in which they co-construct the procedures by which meaning can be socially created and re-created. And fourth, children do not become socialized by internalizing adult culture. Rather, they "become part of adult culture and contribute to its reproduction through their negotiations with adults and their creative reproduction of a series of peer cultures with other children" (p. 201).

We propose that Corsaro's analysis agrees with Piaget's on three fundamental points and carries them a step further than Piaget toward a more complete view of negotiation.

Knowledge is co-constructed through interactions and is negotiated in the interactive process. It can be argued that Piaget's writings on social development were ignored in part because his view of the knowledge process clashed so sharply with those of standard socialization theories, which emphasized transmission of items and their internalization. In a constructivist approach, items are reconstituted in the process of interaction so that they become negotiated into new items apropos the schemes of the persons involved.

Corsaro and Piaget would agree that meaning is constructed by the procedures being used and, Piaget would add, by the structure of the relationship between the persons. In a sense, the content of the items recedes in importance relative to the mutuality of meaning that is established. While content remains important, the key to identification is more the procedures that allow the persons to continue to produce meaning while remaining within a common framework. This fact takes account of the close connection between the generative character of social knowledge and the social means by which it is reproduced. "The structural properties of social systems are both medium and outcome of the practices they recursively organize" (Giddens, as cited by Corsaro & Eder, 1990, p. 200).

Peer experience is not incidental to "primary" socialization but is part of the child's overall socialization.   Corsaro, as Piaget, proposes that peer socialization is primary and constitutes an important domain that contributes uniquely to children's social development. Corsaro focuses on the fact that peer interaction has patterns that pertain to it and may not be evident in interactions with adults. Rather than stressing their differences from adult patterns, however, Corsaro emphasizes that in adopting these patterns, children learn how to co-construct reliably with other persons in a shared social system. For instance, children learn about the procedures that mediate sharing, participation, dealing with concerns publicly, and resisting adult authority.

There is little doubt that the peer aspects of Piaget's writings were a deterrent to their being recognized as relevant to concerns of major socialization theorists. In many theories, peer experience was construed as a source of deviance from adult, normative socialization. Corsaro, as Piaget, has tried to demonstrate that recurrent patterns of peer interaction are not "deviant" but replicate norms that adults would want to convey. As Piaget, Corsaro recognizes that peers, compared with adults, may be better able to produce these norms because they are in a reciprocal relationship. An example is seen in pretend play during which children cooperatively co-construct story lines, being individually creative while they also take account of the other person's contribution to their evolving construction (Garvey, 1977; Cook–Gumperz & Corsaro, 1977).

Peer and adult cultures are not separated by a barrier that needs special remedial work for reconciliation.   Corsaro has proposed that peer culture is a separate construction from the culture that is constructed through adult–child interactions. However, there is not a single peer culture that is created once and retained thereafter. Rather, children are pictured as continuously involved in reconstructing peer cultures in a time series running from the preschool through the adolescent years. The practical consequence is that the patterns one finds, let us say, in very young children, are not fixed for life but are themselves open to reconstruction in a developmental fashion. Piaget recognizes this point in arguing that children develop procedures in a progressive manner in order to help them sustain cooperative relationships. Tit-for-tat exchanges may be adequate for a peer relationship between 5-year-old children, but that form must be transformed to allow for compromise and negotiation when disputes arise between adolescent friends (Youniss & Smollar, 1985).

Corsaro also recognizes the presence of two worlds and addresses their relation by showing how peer culture is bridged with adult culture. Corsaro (1985) recognizes that children experience peer interactions at the same time they experience interactions with adults. It would be unimaginable that children keep the respective experiences totally apart. Corsaro suggests that many properties of one culture are brought into the other. For instance, children may transport notions of age, size, and intelligence into the peer culture, when they otherwise would not consider them important for peer interactions. Since coexistence with peers and adults persists through time, the crossing between them must be continuous. It is noted, however, that crossing entails reconstruction as data from one domain are adapted to the other domain. The long-range effect is that the original separation becomes permeable and content from the two relations may interact over the course of development.

CONCLUSION

In this chapter, we have made the case that Piaget's approach to social construction was both more farsighted and more revolutionary than many have realized. It took seriously the origins of thought in social interaction while not veering as far toward social determinism as Durkheim had done previously, or as the American social learning theorists and social constructivists were to do subsequently. Although Piaget's theory had been misrepresented by its followers such as Kohlberg as well as by its legion of detractors, it offers an unusually plausible account of how persons construct meaning in the course of their social transactions. With the single exception of Vygotskian theory, it stands alone among developmental approaches in its capacity to explain how the quality of particular social experience influences the nature of the ideas and values that arise from that experience. For this reason, Piaget's theory remains valuable for those, such as ourselves, who are interested in the social construction of knowledge, as well as for those, such as Corsaro, who are interested in the social construction of culture. Our hope is that, when properly understood, Piaget's theory can be exploited to its full potential.

REFERENCES

Bruner, J. S., Goodnow, J. J., & Austin, G. A. (1956). *A study of thinking*. New York: Wiley.
Chapman, M. (1986). The structure of exchange: Piaget's sociological theory. *Human Developmental*, 29, 181–194.

Cook–Gumperz, J., & Corsaro, W. A. (1977). Social ecological constraints on children's communicative strategies. *Sociology, 11,* 411–434.

Corsaro, W. A. (1985). *Friendship and peer culture in the early years.* Norwood, NJ: Ablex.

Corsaro, W. A., & Eder, D. (1990). Children's peer cultures. *Annual Review of Sociology, 16,* 197–220.

Corsaro, W. A., & Rizzo, T. A. (1988). *Discussione* and friendship: Socialization processes in the peer culture of Italian nursery school children. *American Sociological Review, 53,* 879–894.

Damon, W. (1977). *The social world of the child.* San Francisco: Jossey-Bass.

Damon, W. (1980). Patterns of change in children's social reasoning. *Child Development, 51,* 1010–1017.

Damon, W. (1983). *Social and personality development.* New York: Norton.

Damon, W. (1988). *The moral child: Nurturing children's natural moral growth.* New York: Free Press.

Damon, W., & Colby, A. (1987). Social influence and moral change. In W. M. Kurtines & J. L. Gewirtz (Eds.), *Social interaction and sociomoral development.* New York: Wiley.

Dean, A. L., & Youniss, J. (1991). The transformation of Piagetian theory by American psychology: The early competence issue. In M. Chapman & M. Chandler (Eds.), *Criteria for competence.* Hillsdale, NJ: Lawrence, Erlbaum Associates.

Eisenberg, N. (Ed.). (1982). *The development of prosocial behavior.* New York: Academic Press.

Flavell, J. H. (1962). Historical and bibliographic note. In W. Kessen & C. Kuhlman (Eds.), *Thought in the young child. Monographs of the Society for Research in Child Development,* V *27* (Serial No. 83).

Garvey, C. (1977). *Play.* Cambridge, MA: Harvard University Press.

Heilbroner, R. L. (1970). *Between capitalism and socialism.* New York: Vintage Books.

Inhelder, B., & Piaget, J. (1958). *The growth of logical thinking from childhood to adolescence.* New York: Basic Books.

Kohlberg, L. (1963). The development of children's orientations toward a moral order: I. Sequence in the development of moral thought. *Vita Humana, 6,* 11–33.

Kohlberg, L. (1969). Stage and sequence: The cognitive-developmental approach to socialization. In D. A. Goslin (Ed.), *Handbook of socialization theory and research.* Chicago: Rand McNally.

Kohlberg, L. (1971). From is to ought: How to commit the naturalistic fallacy and get away with it in the study of moral development. In T. Mishel (Ed.), *Cognitive development and epistemology.* New York: Academic Press.

Kohlberg, L., & Higgins, A. (1987). School democracy and social interaction. In W. M. Kurtines, & J. L. Gewirtz (Eds.), *Social interaction and sociomoral development.* New York: Wiley.

Piaget, J. (1932a). Social evolution and the new education. *Education Tomorrow,* No. 4. London: New Education Fellowship.

Piaget, J. (1932b). *The moral judgment of the child.* London: Routledge & Kegan Paul.

Piaget, J. (1970). Piaget's theory. In P. H. Mussen (Ed.), *Carmichael's manual of child psychology.* New York: Wiley.

Vygotsky, L. (1978). *Mind in society: The development of higher psychological processes.* Cambridge, MA: Harvard University Press.

Wertsch, J. V. (1987). *Vygotsky and the social formation of mind.* Cambridge, MA: Harvard University Press.

Youniss, J. (1980). *Parents and peers in social development.* Chicago: University of Chicago Press.

Youniss, J. (1981). An analysis of moral development through a theory of social construction. *Merrill-Palmer Quarterly, 27,* 384–403.

Youniss, J. (1983). Piaget and the self constituted through relations. In W. F. Overton (Ed.), *The relationship between social and cognitive development*. Hillsdale, NJ: Lawrence Erlbaum Associates.

Youniss, J. (1987). Social construction and moral development: Update and expansion. In W. M. Kurtines & J. L. Gewirtz (Eds.), *Social interaction and sociomoral development*. New York: Wiley.

Youniss, J., & Smollar, J. (1985). *Adolescent relations with mothers, fathers, and friends* Chicago: University of Chicago Press.

ACKNOWLEDGMENTS

Colby, Anne, Lawrence Kohlberg, John Gibbs, and Marcus Lieberman. "A Longitudinal Study of Moral Judgment." *Society for Research in Child Development, Monographs of the* 48 (1983):1–124. Reprinted with the permission of the Society for Research in Child Development. Courtesy of Yale University Medical Library.

Kohlberg, Lawrence, Charles Levine, and Alexandra Hewer. "Moral Stages: A Current Formulation and a Response to Critics: 3. Synopses of Criticisms and a Reply; 4. Summary and Conclusion." *Contributions to Human Development* 10 (1983): 104–66. Reprinted with the permission of S. Karger AG. Courtesy of Yale University Medical Library.

Higgins, Ann, Clark Power, and Lawrence Kohlberg. "The Relationship of Moral Atmosphere to Judgments of Responsibility." In William M. Kurtines and Jacob L. Gewirtz, eds., *Morality, Moral Behavior, and Moral Development* (New York: John J. Wiley & Sons, Inc., 1984): 74–106. Reprinted by permission of John Wiley & Sons, Inc. Courtesy of Yale University Cross Campus Library.

Kohlberg, Lawrence, Peter Scharf, and Joseph Hickey. "The Justice Structure of the Prison—A Theory and an Intervention." *Prison Journal* 51 (1971): 3–14. Reprinted with the permission of the Pennsylvania Prison Society. Courtesy of Yale University Law Library.

Gibbs, John C. and Steven V. Schnell. "Moral Development 'Versus' Socialization: A Critique." *American Psychologist* 40 (1985): 1071–80. Copyright 1985 by the American Psychological Association. Reprinted by permission. Courtesy of Yale University Sterling Memorial Library.

Nisan, Mordecai and Lawrence Kohlberg. "Universality and Variation in Moral Judgment: A Longitudinal and Cross-sectional Study in Turkey." *Child Development* 53 (1982): 865–76. Reprinted with the permission of the Society for Research in Child

Development. Courtesy of Yale University Sterling Memorial Library.

Parikh, Bindu. "Development of Moral Judgment and Its Relation to Family Environmental Factors in Indian and American Families." *Child Development* 51 (1980): 1030–39. Reprinted with the permission of the Society for Research in Child Development. Courtesy of Yale University Sterling Memorial Library.

Snarey, John R. "Cross-Cultural Universality of Social-Moral Development: A Critical Review of Kohlbergian Research." *Psychological Bulletin* 97 (1985): 202–32. Copyright 1985 by the American Psychological Association. Reprinted by permission. Courtesy of Yale University Medical Library.

Sobesky, William E. "The Effects of Situational Factors on Moral Judgments." *Child Development* 54 (1983): 575–84. Reprinted with the permission of the Society for Research in Child Development. Courtesy of Yale University Sterling Memorial Library.

Song, Myung-Ja, Judith G. Smetana, and Sang Yoon Kim. "Korean Children's Conceptions of Moral and Conventional Transgressions." *Developmental Psychology* 23 (1987): 577–82. Copyright 1987 by the American Psychological Association. Reprinted by permission. Courtesy of Yale University Sterling Memorial Library.

Dien, Dora Shu-Fang. "A Chinese Perspective on Kohlberg's Theory of Moral Development." *Developmental Review* 2 (1982): 331–41. Reprinted with the permission of Academic Press, Inc. Courtesy of Yale University Sterling Memorial Library.

Linn, Ruth. "Moral Disobedience during the Lebanon War: What Can the Cognitive-Developmental Approach Learn from the Experience of the Israeli Soldiers?" *Social Cognition* 5 (1987): 383–402. Reprinted with the permission of Guilford Publications, Inc. Courtesy of Yale University Sterling Memorial Library.

Niemczynski, Adam, Dorota Czyzowska, Marios Pourkos, and Andrzej Mirski. "The Cracow Study with Kohlberg's Moral Judgment Interview: Data Pertaining to the Assumption of Cross-Cultural Validity." *Polish Psychological Bulletin* 19 (1988): 43–53. Reprinted with the permission of the Polish Scientific Publishers. Courtesy of Yale University Sterling Memorial Library.

Vasudev, Jyotsna and Raymond C. Hummel. "Moral Stage Sequence and Principled Reasoning in an Indian Sample." *Human Development* 30 (1987): 105–18. Reprinted with the permission of S. Karger, AG. Courtesy of Yale University Sterling Memorial Library.

Edwards, Carolyn Pope. "Cross-Cultural Research on Kohlberg's Stages: The Basis for Consensus." In Sohan Mogdil and Celia Mogdil, eds., *Lawrence Kohlberg: Consensus and Controversy* (Philadelphia, PA: Falmer Press, 1985): 419–30. Reprinted with the permission of The Falmer Press. Courtesy of Yale University Sterling Memorial Library.

Bond, Michael Harris. "Finding Universal Dimensions of Individual Variation in Multicultural Studies of Values: The Rokeach and Chinese Value Surveys." *Journal of Personality and Social Psychology* 55 (1988): 1009–15. Copyright 1988 by the American Psychological Association, Inc. Reprinted by permission. Courtesy of Yale University Sterling Memorial Library.

Simpson, Evan. "The Development of Political Reasoning." *Human Development* 30 (1987): 268–81. Reprinted with the permission of S. Karger, AG. Courtesy of Yale University Sterling Memorial Library.

Youniss, James and William Damon. "Social Construction in Piaget's Theory." In Harry Beilin and Peter Pufall, eds., *Piaget's Theory: Prospects and Possibilities* (Hillsdale: NJ: Lawrence Erlbaum Associates, Publishers, 1992): 267–86. Reprinted with the permission of Lawrence Erlbaum Associates, Inc. Courtesy of Yale University Sterling Memorial Library.